Medical Sociology

Duane A. Matcha
Siena College

Allyn and Bacon

Boston ∎ London ∎ Toronto ∎ Sydney ∎ Tokyo ∎ Singapore

Series Editor: *Sarah L. Kelbaugh*
Editor-in-Chief, Social Sciences: *Karen Hanson*
Editorial Assistant: *Jennifer DiDomenico*
Marketing Manager: *Brooke Stoner*
Composition Buyer: *Linda Cox*
Manufacturing Buyer: *Julie McNeill*
Cover Administrator: *Linda Knowles*
Production Administrator: *Rosalie Briand*
Editorial-Production Service: *Spectrum Publisher Services*
Electronic Composition: *Bi-Comp, Inc.*

Library of Congress Cataloging-in-Publication Data

Matcha, Duane A.
    Medical sociology : a comparative perspective / Duane A. Matcha.
      p. cm.
    Includes bibliographical references.
    ISBN 0-205-26309-7
    1. Social medicine Cross-cultural studies.   I. Title.
  RA418.M327 1999   99-13142
  306.4961—dc21   CIP

Printed in the United States of America

10 9 8 7 6 5 4 3 2 1   02 01 00 99

Portions of Chapter 2 are reprinted by permission from Erwin H. Ackerknecht. (1982).
A Short History of Medicine, revised edition. The Johns Hopkins University Press, Baltimore, MD.

CONTENTS

10 **Traditional and Alternative Medicines/Practitioners   281**

PART FOUR The Organization of Health Care in Society   305

11 **Hospitals   307**

12 **Financing the Health-Care System   337**

PREFACE

The academic environment too often shelters faculty and students from the larger world community. Although the intellectual climate of most colleges and universities is generally stimulating, all too often it is culturally limited. For instance, some courses broadly address issues of multiculturalism in the United States whereas others provide students with a cross-cultural exploration of the world community. Although these courses serve as an overview of the multiplicity of cultural experiences that exist in our world, they do not address, in depth, academic content areas. The purpose of this text is to take us one step further. In other words, providing the reader with a cross-cultural exposure to a specific content area: in this case, medical sociology. Thus, each chapter in this book acquaints the reader not only with American research and outcomes, but also research findings from other industrialized nations. In addition, each chapter includes some reference to appropriate research in developing nations. The purpose of this approach is to provide the reader with a cross-cultural or comparative knowledge base of medical sociology. As we approach the 21st century, it is imperative to understand the health-care community on a global as well as national level. For example, all member nations of the industrialized community (except for the United States) provide health care as a right. At the same time, relative to most of the industrialized community, the United States has a significantly higher proportion of its population without access to the health-care community. Finally, the United States spends more per capita on health care than any other country in the world. Thus, to adequately comprehend the issue of access to health care, this book transcends traditional national explanations and examines the global context within which access is defined and implemented. Through such a process, the reader will more accurately understand the impact of economic and political decision making on the health-care community.

In addition to a cross-cultural emphasis, a fundamental component of any learning process is continuity. That is, an integration of knowledge that transcends individual chapter boundaries. Such an approach incorporates the necessary information relevant to any particular topic with the broader knowledge base associated with the discipline itself. In this case, knowing not only the topical areas associated with medical sociology, but also understanding how and why they are interrelated. For example, the reader will notice that many of the chapters are built around the four basic sociological variables of age, sex, race and ethnicity, and social class.

Organizationally, each chapter begins with a quote. The purpose of the quote is to provide, in broad strokes, an overview of the chapter. The basic framework of each chapter is outlined in the introduction. At the end of each chapter, the summary reiterates the major points covered while the review questions elicit reader responses to recent as well as earlier material. Finally, each chapter ends with a glossary of significant concepts and suggestions for further reading. Throughout this process, the emphasis is on continuity of information. That is, attempting to engage the reader to not only extract particular knowledge from each chapter, but also to integrate such information into the broader context of what constitutes medical sociology.

First, however, what is medical sociology? According to the definition located in Chapter 1, "medical sociology is the study of health care as it is institutionalized in a society, and of health, or illness, and its relationship to social factors" (Ruderman, 1981, p. 927). Although this is one of many definitions available, Ruderman captures the dynamic qualities associated with medical sociology as well as the interrelationships inherent among the various factors involved. Organizationally, medical sociology is the third largest specialty area within sociology. Academically, medical sociologists are located primarily in departments of sociology at the college and university level. They are also found in medical schools, schools of public health, research centers, and schools of pharmacy. Research interests among medical sociologists, ranges from studying the dynamics of communication between physicians and nurses to understanding the social factors that influence health and illness to the construction of health-care systems. As an example of the breadth of intellectual inquiry available within medical sociology, consider the following facts and their potential for sociological explanation.

- The number of students applying for medical school continues to increase, despite predictions of decreasing opportunity for future medical practitioners.
- The United States is the only industrialized nation without universal health care.
- Sweden and Great Britain continue to experience continued financial strain on their health-care systems. As a result, they are experimenting with increased "free market" efforts to alleviate the problem.
- Health maintenance organizations (HMOs) continue to increase their percentage of the population covered for care.
- Because of the increasing cost of entitlement programs, such as Medicare and Medicaid, government (at all levels) has resorted to "managed care" arrangements (HMOs) to control the cost of care to recipients.
- The creation of life-saving drug therapies, medical intervention methods, and diagnostic tools continues to fuel the increasing cost of medical care in the United States.
- The availability of life-saving drug therapies, medical intervention techniques, and diagnostic tools creates ethical dilemmas for medical personnel charged with saving lives yet left questioning the quality of that life.

All of these "facts" are examined within various chapters of this book as they are in other medical sociology texts. However, this book expands on these facts by incorporating a cross-cultural, or what is referred to throughout the book as a comparative explanation. Utilizing a comparative explanation, I then address many of the standard topical areas associated with a medical sociology text. Thus, the reason for a comparative explanation is grounded in the realization that the study and application of medical sociology exists within a global context rather than the more limited American framework readers are generally provided. A comparative approach to medical sociology also distinguishes this book from other available texts.

This book is arranged into four basic sections. The first section examines the structure of medical sociology. Here, Chapter 1 offers an introduction to medical sociology, as well as appropriate theoretical frameworks and research methodologies. In addition, the chapter addresses the concept of culture as it relates to issues of health. The chapter concludes with an explanation of the cross-cultural or comparative perspective utilized throughout the book. Chapter 2 examines the historical development of medicine within a Western context. More specifically, the emergence of medicine within the United States is chronicled. The development of medicine within non-western nations is also explored. Finally, the future of medicine is questioned within the framework of technology, demographic changes, and the influence of political will. Chapter 3 outlines the history and significance of epidemiology. Indicators of social and medical outcomes such as morbidity, mortality, and life expectancy are explained, as well as the basic sociological variables of age, sex, race and ethnicity, and social class.

The second section of the book addresses health and illness behavior. Chapter 4 on health behavior examines models of health behavior. Employing the four sociological variables identified earlier, the chapter examines the influence of lifestyle and culture on issues such as health status. The chapter also examines the growing area of health promotion and life style. Chapter 5 (Illness Behavior—Part I) also addresses theoretical explanations of illness as well as predictors of illness (age, sex, race and ethnicity, and social class), whereas Chapter 6 (Illness Behavior—Part II) explains one of the best known concepts in medical sociology—the sick role. Criticism of the sick role and an alternative explanation are offered. The chapter concludes with an examination of the medicalization of society. Chapter 7 explores the various theoretical frameworks associated with mental illness, as well as the relationship between mental illness and the sociological variables of age, sex, race and ethnicity, and social class.

The third section of the book moves from a focus on the behavior of those identified as healthy or with an illness, to an examination of those providing services to patients. Chapter 8 examines the role of physicians within a historical context in the United States. The chapter also addresses the emergence of women as physicians and the changing role and future of physicians. In much the same format, Chapter 9 covers the historical emergence of nursing, current problems, and future concerns. In addition to "mainstream" health care providers, a number of alternative/traditional medicines and practitioners are discussed in Chapter 10.

The final section of the book is devoted to macrolevel issues that address the organization of health care in society. Chapter 11 begins with a historical accounting of the hospital. Relative to the United States, emphasis is given to the changing nature and structure of hospitals in terms of size, ownership, and type. Finally, the future of hospitals is addressed as is the role of medical technology. Chapter 12 offers a view into the cost of care, payment methods, and questions of how much is enough. Here, issues such as allocation and rationing of health care are examined. Chapter 13 begins with a comparison of health-care models. The focus of the chapter is a comparison of health systems. Beginning with the United States, we travel to a number of industrialized nations as well as to former Eastern European nations and, finally, a number of developing nations. Finally, Chapter 14 offers a glimpse into the future of medical sociology. Examining changes in the health-care community relative to demographics, economics, and politics worldwide, it is argued that medical sociology offers not only a unique insight, but is an invaluable asset to an increasingly global health-care community.

Acknowledgments

As with any book, there are many people who should be recognized for their efforts. Karen Hanson as Editor-in-Chief, Sarah Kelbaugh, Series Editor, and the entire staff of Allyn and Bacon have been most kind and supportive of this work. The library staff at Siena College, who have endured my constant demands for material, must also be recognized for their dedication to the pursuit of information, no matter how difficult it may be to locate. Finally, thank you to all of my students in medical sociology. This is my effort to enrich their lives as they have mine.

I would also like to thank the following reviewers for their instructive and insightful comments: Fred Hafferty, University of Minnesota, Duluth; Jerome R. Koch, Texas Tech University; Elizabeth Jacobs-Jenner, University of Illinois at Urbana-Champaign; Edward Morse, Tulane University; Marilyn Schmit, Cardinal Stricht University; Pamela Elkind, Eastern Washington University; and James Huber, Bloomsburg University.

This book is dedicated to my spouse, Bonnie, who has always been my greatest supporter and most ardent critic.

I welcome comments from students and faculty. My e-mail address is matcha@siena.edu.

References

Ruderman, F. A. (1981). What is medical sociology? *Journal of the American Medical Association, 245,* 9 (March 6), 927–929.

PART ONE

The Structure of Medical Sociology

1

Introduction
A Comparative Approach

The medical sociologist is concerned with the ways in which social groups influence and are influenced by illness and medical care. The sociological perspective focuses on the social aspects of medicine with particular emphasis on the position of medicine in the structure of society. Given a specific social structure, the sociologist is interested in the social processes that define relationships between groups within that structure. The study of medical care and the treatment of illness in a society is a concern of the sociologist because the practice of medicine affects every aspect of complex societies. In fact, health appears consistently as a primary positive social value that permeates the fabric of most societies.

—Albrecht, 1979, p. 5

The Importance of Cultural Norms and Values in Health-Care Communities

In what can only be described as a fortuitous set of events, the author began this book at the same time that he became a participant–observer of the health-care system. In other words, the book contract arrived the day of my splenectomy. After surgery, the author (as patient) had an opportunity to observe and analyze the organizational structure of the hospital as well as the multiplicity of relationships that exist among its participants. This organizational structure and its attendant relationships exist as they do within the context of the broader sociocultural norms and values of a particular society. These cultural norms and values help define health, health care, illness, and the institutional structures within which such definitions are constructed and applied. As Pingitore (1993, p. 168) points out, "[A]merican medicine also reflects key values and practices found in the larger society." Thus, when one patient questioned a nurse regarding her instructions, the nurse replied, "It's not me, it's the rules." Here, the nurse is identifying her position vis-à-vis the hospital and is deferring authority to the organizational structure within which she works. Although not specifically stated in this example, one explanation for such deference is the historically established gender-specific and occupationally stereotypic relationships between nurses (primarily women) and doctors (primarily men). Or, as Cockerham (1995, p. 208) suggests, "the physician as father figure and the nurse as mother figure."

An example of cultural values is the strong American belief in individualism. Mechanic (1993, p. 97) argues that "[T]he individualistic ethic, pervasive in so much of American life, also affects how broad health issues are seen. Much of the focus in public health is on seeking solutions to major health risks by urging individual responsibility and personal health action." Another example of the relationship between cultural values and health care is the generally negative value associated with age and the aging in America, even by those within the medical profession (Butler, 1996). Given that the American population is getting older, interest in geriatric medicine should be increasing, but that is apparently not occurring.

As a result of these values, health-care issues can be very divisive. Consider, for example, the variation in response to the question "Do we (as citizens) have a 'right' to health care?" From the cultural value of individualism, the answer would be no. Health and health care would be considered the responsibility of each person within society. However, others would argue that as a society we also value community. This would suggest a greater sense of social responsibility within the broader context of the common good (see, for example, Beauchamp, 1988; Aday, 1994). Regardless of the interpretation, the norms and values of the culture significantly impact the medical care system. For example, why is the cost of health care in the United States far greater than any other country? Part of the answer lies in American values associated with individual expectations of immediate care. In addition, a capitalist economic system encourages people to invest money in the development of medical technology. In return, these investors expect to earn a profit on their investment. As a result, the technology is readily available, but at an increasing expense to all involved.

The purpose of this overview is to illustrate the importance of cultural values to the American health-care community. At the same time, the cultural values that are characteristic of the United States are not unique, but are shared with multiples of other cultures. For example, individualism is not a uniquely American value. Cultural differences, however, lie in the interpretation of the value. Thus, the impact of culture on various aspects of the health-care community are continually addressed. The purpose of this approach is to remove the implication that medical sociology is confined to the study of "American" or "Western" health-care communities. Instead, findings from cultures in developed as well as developing nations serve as examples of the multiplicity of possible interpretations available within the various topical areas associated with medical sociology.

The preceding illustrates one component of the health-care community. Throughout the following chapters, however, this author examines, in depth, various actors and social structural characteristics of the health-care community within their specific cultural context.

Sociology and Sickness Defined

This section begins with a brief review of basic sociology. Although this material is intended to reacquaint the reader with fundamental concepts, it is assumed that the reader has had an introductory course in general sociology, thus negating the necessity of a review of sociology itself.

Numerous definitions of sociology abound. Although all are quite similar, there are subtle distinctions. Consider three definitions drawn from introductory texts. Perhaps the most succinct definition is that **sociology** is, "The scientific study of human society" (Macionis, 1995, p. 26). Other definitions attempt to expand on this definition. For example, Henslin (1995, p. 6) states that "Sociology (is) the scientific study of society and human behavior." Doob (1991, p. 4) takes the definition one step further and states that "Sociology is the scientific study of human behavior in groups and of the social forces that influence that behavior." This definition is most appropriate, because it identifies the significance of social forces and establishes a connection between social forces and behavior. The importance of that connection is reiterated throughout this book.

In addition to defining sociology, there are a myriad of associated concepts. Following is a brief review of the concepts that readers will encounter continually throughout the book. A **role** is a set of rights and obligations associated with a particular status. For example, one of the classic components of medical sociology is the identification of the "sick role" by Parsons (1951). Although the sick role is examined in considerable detail later, the concept basically refers to the rights and obligations associated with being sick in American society. Relative to the definition of a role is the next concept: **status.** A status is a position that locates an individual in society. Again, applying the concept to medical sociology, a physician, nurse, and patient are all statuses. Whenever a role relationship develops, it is influenced by the status of the players. This becomes particularly evident in Chapter 8 and the discussion of patient–physician relationships. A **group** refers to two or more persons who interact with one another on a regular basis and over a period of time. In the process, group members establish patterns of interaction. Groups can be primary (i.e., family) or secondary (i.e., work location). A **social institution** consists of a cluster of groups with specific norms and values related to a unique social need (i.e., the provision of health care). Finally, **deviant behavior** is defined as a violation of social norms. Although accurate, this definition does not adequately address the evaluation of behavior by the social audience. In other words, it is the reaction of others to behavior that is defined as relative to a variety of circumstances and conditions that determine whether a behavior is deviant. Returning to the "sick role" as an example, Parsons (1951) argued that if being healthy is normal, then being sick represents deviant behavior.

Medical Sociology Defined

A historical exploration of the origins of medical sociology also requires definitions of basic concepts. As with sociology in general, definitions of **medical sociology** are often reconstructed by individual authors, thus making a single definition difficult (Petersdorf & Feinstein, 1981). Ruderman (1981, p. 927) however, offers the following definition:

> medical sociology is the study of health care as it is institutionalized in a society, and of health, or illness, and its relationship to social factors.

According to Weiss and Lonquist (1997, p.1), the American Sociological Association Committee on Certification in Medical Sociology (1986) states that:

> Medical sociology is the subfield which applies the perspectives, conceptualizations, theories, and methodologies of sociology to phenomena having to do with human health and disease. As a specialization, medical sociology encompasses a body of knowledge that places health and disease in a social, cultural, and behavioral context. Included within its subject matter are descriptions and explanations of theories relating to the distribution of diseases among various population groups; the behaviors or actions taken by individuals to maintain, enhance, or restore health or cope with disease, disability and medical care providers and organizations; medical occupations or professions and the organization, financing, and delivery of medical care services; medicine as a social institution and its relationship to other social institutions; cultural values and societal responses with respect to health, illness, and disability; and the role of social factors in the etiology of disease, especially functional and emotion-related disorders and what are now being called stress-related diseases.

This description provides a framework regarding the field of medical sociology today. As you reread the statement, note that topics such as epidemiology, health and illness behavior, medical professions, financing, and delivery of services all represent specific chapters in this book. Finally, note that the description of medical sociology considers the relationship between cultural values and health and illness an important component. The question, however, is what was the evolutionary process that brought medical sociology to its present form? The following sections outline its historical emergence as a specialty area within its parent discipline of sociology.

The Rise of "Social Medicine"

Historically, we know that medical sociology does not have a defining moment. It is, however, inextricably tied to the historical development of social medicine. Although the terms have been used synonymously, they are not interchangeable. Although the preceding material has established the meaning of medical sociology, **social medicine** has historically "been associated with public health and politics" (Henderson et al., 1997, p. ix). Rosen (1979, p. 23) provides an example of the interconnection between health, social position, and environment.

> By the early eighteenth century some of the basic elements of a concept of social medicine had been assembled: the need to study the relation between the health of a given population and the living conditions determined by its social position; the noxious factors that act in a particular way or with special intensity on those in a given social position; and the elements that deleteriously affect health and impede improvement of general well-being.

Historically, these criteria provided a framework for investigation of health-related concerns within increasingly industrialized and urbanized centers of Europe. These criteria remain as important today as they did almost 200 years ago, and they also provide the basis for the emergence of epidemiology (see Chapter 3 for a detailed explanation).

Rosen (1979) offers an excellent historical accounting of social medicine. He begins with its inception in Germany (where Johann Peter Frank referred to it as *medical police*), then to France, and eventually to Great Britain and the United States. It was not until 1848, however, that the term *social medicine* was used by Jules Guerin (Rosen, 1979). At the same time, others were also exploring the relationship between medicine and the social sciences. For example, in 1848, Virchow noted that: "Medicine is a social science, and politics nothing but medicine on a grand scale" (Rosen, 1979, p. 29). This argument is founded on three principles.

> The *first* of these is that the health of the people is a matter of direct social concern. Society has an obligation to protect and ensure the health of its members. The *second* principle is that social and economic conditions have an important effect on health and disease, and that these relations must be subjected to scientific investigation . . . it follows logically that steps must be taken to promote health and to combat disease, and that the measures involved in such action must be social as well as medical. This is the *third* principle involved in the idea of medicine as a social science . . . . (Rosen, 1978, pp. 7–8)

These early efforts to legitimize the relationship between the social environment and medicine provides a conceptual framework that is still relevant. For example, the concept of social medicine in the United States evolved from areas such as public health and social welfare, a concept that remained well into the twentieth century. As a result, there is an overlapping of social medicine with the emergence and development of medical sociology. For example, in a 1951 paper, Bernhard J. Stern (1991, p. 40) argues that "the concept of social medicine remains vague and ill-defined." In the same 1951 paper, Stern (1991, p. 40) presents a case "for the emergence of a sociology of medicine." Stern continues by identifying a number of significant developments in medicine and public health and then examines their relevance to the sociology of medicine. These developments range from demographic changes within the population to changes within the profession and practice of medicine.

A History of Medical Sociology

Historically, the term *medical sociology* was first used in an 1894 article by Charles McIntire (1991, p.31). In the article, McIntire stated that:

> Medical sociology then has a two-fold aspect. It is the science of the social phenomena of the physicians themselves . . . and the science which investigates the laws regulating the relations between the medical profession and human society as a whole . . . and indeed, everything relating to the subject.

Although medical sociologists today may be more specific in their description of the discipline, this statement expresses the intellectual breadth that was initially accorded medical sociology.

In the early twentieth century, however, sociologists were not particularly interested in studying issues of health and illness. Instead, sociology was concerned with issues associated with the rapidly changing social landscape (i.e., urbanization and industrialization). As a result, others, such as Elizabeth Blackwell (1902), the first woman doctor in the United States, appropriated the term *medical sociology* "as a title for a collection of her essays on social work and public health" (Hollingshead, 1973, p. 532). Professional organizations (for example, the American Public Health Association) even attempted to include sociology, but few sociologists were interested (Hollingshead, 1973). Throughout this period (until the 1930s), medical sociology "was a synonym for 'social medicine'" (Aiken & Freeman, 1980, p. 528). It was not until the 1930s that sociologists began to investigate and report on the relationship between social factors and health outcomes. Identifying an even broader time frame, Bloom and Zambrana (1983) argue that the time period between World War I and World War II provided an impressive intellectual basis for medical sociology. They suggest that "much of the early work anticipated the major trends which were to develop later" (p. 75). They categorized this early work into four broad areas: (1) social histories of medicine; (2) the social psychology of interpersonal relations in therapeutic institutions; (3) social epidemiology; and (4) the sociology of the professions (Bloom & Zambrana, 1983). World War II offered sociologists and others an opportunity to develop interdisciplinary activities (Hollingshead, 1973). Also, beginning in the latter 1940s and continuing into the 1950s, a number of philanthropic foundations (for example, the Russell Sage Foundation and the Milbank Memorial Fund) provided a source of funding for sociologists and other social scientists (Hawkins, 1958; Hollingshead, 1973; Mauksch & Day, 1978). For example, the Russell Sage Foundation "devoted a significant proportion of its funds to the establishment of social science units within schools of medicine, public health, and nursing, almost all of which included sociologists" (Freeman & Levine, 1989, p. 3). During this same period, the National Institute of Mental Health (NIMH) was established, thus providing additional opportunities for sociologists interested in health-related research issues.

The Formalization and Institutional Advancement of Medical Sociology

Medical sociology became formalized during the 1950s. For example, training of medical sociologists during this time period (1940s and 1950s) generally occurred at those universities with already well-known sociology departments. These institutions included Yale, Harvard, Columbia, and the University of Chicago (Olesen, 1975). The theoretical formalization of medical sociology began with the introduction of *The Social System* by Talcott Parsons (1951). Here, Parsons' (1951) description of the "sick role" has become perhaps the most significant conceptualization within the history of medical sociology.

Organizationally, Wardwell (1982, p. 565) offers a historical accounting of the emergence of medical sociology in the United States. In 1950, during a meeting of the Society for Applied Anthropology at Vasser College, a number of individuals "interested in applying social science knowledge to the broad field of medicine" met to discuss where such an interest should be organizationally located. As Wardwell (1982) explains, because the majority of interested participants were sociologists, it was believed that the then American Sociological Society (ASS) would be the most logical location. In 1955, an informal Committee on Medical Sociology was created (Straus, 1957). In 1959, the American Sociological Society was renamed the American Sociological Association (ASA), and medical sociology "became the first formally constituted section" (Wardwell, 1982, p. 565).

Another benchmark in the formalization of medical sociology was the work of Strauss (1957), who differentiated between the sociology *of* medicine and the sociology *in* medicine. According to Straus (1957, p. 203)

> the sociology of medicine is concerned with studying such factors as the organizational structure, role relationships, value systems, rituals, and functions of medicine as a system of behavior. . . . Sociology in medicine consists of collaborative research or teaching often involving the integration of concepts, techniques, and personnel from many disciplines.

Explaining these "two streams" within the context of specific occupational areas, Mechanic (1990, p. 87) points out that sociology *in* medicine is an applied approach in which the medical sociologist addresses issues of interest to those outside of sociology (e.g., government or medical schools). However, the sociology *of* medicine involves the study of medicine within a sociological context.

Rather than attempting to differentiate the relationship even further, Petersdorf and Feinstein (1981) suggest that it is perhaps best to "stop worrying over whether a medical sociologist's work is the sociology of medicine or the sociology in medicine" (Wardwell, 1982, p. 571). Wardwell (1982) offers two reasons why medical sociologists should stop worrying. First is that the majority of research (as well as textbook focus) addresses the sociology of medicine. Second is that medical sociology has been held to a different standard than other subfields. In other words, debate within the sociological profession is not centered on such issues as the sociology *of* and the sociology *in* other subdisciples, such as religion (Wardwell, 1982).

The next step in the formalization process was the establishment of a medical sociology journal published by the ASA. This was accomplished in 1966 with the acquisition of *The Journal of Health and Human Behavior* by the ASA, who renamed it *The Journal of Health and Social Behavior.*

With the formalization of medical sociology under the broader umbrella of the ASA, the section has continued to grow numerically and has become one of the most active sections. Research efforts continue to expand and the number of books examining various aspects of medical sociology continues to grow.

The institutional advancement of medical sociology within the medical community began with the first Department of Behavioral Sciences in the newly established University of Kentucky Medical School in 1960. Straus (1959, 1963) offers a first-hand description of how the Department of Behavioral Sciences was constructed, as well as the larger medical center. Earlier (1949), Odin W. Anderson had been hired as "the first full-time sociologist by a college of medicine" (the Department of Psychiatry and Preventive Medicine at the University of Western Ontario; Olesen, 1975, p. 421).

With the establishment of its institutional and organizational base, medical sociology began to flourish. Relative to the work begun in the 1950s and 1960s, however, the more recent history of medical sociology has not had any significant defining moments. This is not meant to imply that medical sociology has not contributed research outcomes or theoretical insights since the 1950s. Rather, by the 1980s, medical sociology was "at a 'crossroads' because the major socio-medical conditions under which medical sociology grew up were changing radically" (Pescosolido & Kronenfeld, 1995, p. 7). For example, Pescosolido and Kronenfeld (1995, p. 8) point to the work of Oleson (1975) and Gold (1977) as challenging "assumptions of much work in medical sociology . . . and that there seemed to be a change in the larger societal support for medical sociology." Pescosolido and Kronenfeld (1995, p. 8) also state that, according to Gold (1977), "medical sociologists tended to start their research with physicians' diagnoses—in today's terminology, already socially constructed phenomena." Furthermore, many employed as medical sociologists utilize a variety of occupational labels such as behavioral scientists or health service researchers. It is often thought that such titles more accurately describe their work efforts rather than the narrowly interpreted "medical sociologist" (Pescosolido & Kronenfeld, 1995).

The Future of Medical Sociology

Not only has medical sociology experienced change, but, according to Aiken and Freeman (1980, p. 531) "the general health scene itself has changed; it is now generally more hospitable to social research." The question, then, is: What is the future for medical sociology? Although somewhat dated, Aiken and Freeman (1980, pp. 533–537) identify a number of emerging trends in medical sociology. These include:

1. *Epidemiological investigation.* The continued need to investigate social factors as they relate to disease is important.

2. *Orientations and values in health.* Research continues to investigate the changing attitudes within the larger society toward health and health care issues such as mental health and the increasing cultural diversity among patients.

3. *Health behavior.* Continued investigation of patient decision-making behaviors regarding health care.

4. *Selection and socialization of health providers.* Recognizing the contributions of earlier efforts to examine the socialization of medical practitioners, research efforts continue to explore the impact of educational experiences on the medical profession. Because the location of providing care continues to change, research efforts are addressing changing organizational structures as well.

5. *Practitioner–patient relations.* Research efforts continue to explore questions such as service delivery and treatment regimens.

6. *Organization of medical care.* As the transition from solo practice to large Health Maintenance Organizations (HMOs) continues, questions such as quality, cost, and efficiency must be addressed.

7. *Delivery of health services.* The concern is with the broader issues surrounding how care is provided, methods of payment, and the allocation of health resources.

8. *Program evaluation.* Considering that delivery of services and the organization of health care are becoming increasingly complex, methods of ensuring program effectiveness will continue to emerge.

More recent examples of what the future may offer medical sociology are offered by Elinson (1985), Mechanic (1993), and by Gray and Phillips (1995). For instance, Elinson (1985, pp. 269–273) identifies a number of areas in which medical sociology will be challenged. These include (1) the area of "unmet needs for health care," (2) "social change and the health professions," (3) "the relation between medical care and the quality of life," and (4) "the relation between social networks and health status." Furthermore, as the United States contemplates fundamental policy changes in its health-care system, the role of the medical sociologist could become increasingly important. Unfortunately, as Mechanic (1993) points out, medical sociologists have been relegated to the periphery of social policy analysis. Nonetheless, medical sociology will continue to offer research and analysis to the ever-increasing debate over the implementation of change within the current health-care system. Mechanic (1993, p. 99) argues that medical sociology should focus on "scholarship that examines the direction and performance of health care institutions, and professional practices, in relation to our values, aspirations, and ethical standards." The question posed by Gray and Phillips (1995), however, is whether medical sociologists are interested in policy issues, and if persons already involved from other disciplines value the input of medical sociologists. At present, only a small percentage of medical sociologists appear to be involved in the health-policy field. However, as Gray and Phillips (1995, p. 180) point out: "Policy-oriented research seems likely to become more important in medical sociology in the future." For instance, as the interrelationship between government (at all levels) and health-policy organizations becomes increasingly complex, the investigation of health-related issues will require increased sophistication of societal-level analysis. An example of this interrelationship is offered by Temkin (1977, pp. 97–98), who discusses the relevance of medical sociology (and economics) to medicine by suggesting that "they [medical sociology and economics] are assumed to further the aims of medicine by unveiling the social conditions that breed disease, and the ways and means that bring medical care to the widest possible stratum of society."

Finally, Elinson (1985, p. 273) offers what is perhaps the most succinct and optimistic assessment of medical sociology's future: "Medicine and medical sociology are alive and well." At the same time, Pescosolido and Kronenfeld (1995, p. 19) argue that:

> In these times of social reconfiguration, the sociological imagination that sees the inevitable link between social history and personal biography is paramount. We need basic understanding of the new social and socio-medical landscape, including the stratification system, social institutions or their substitutes, and the nature of communities—understanding which sociology has traditionally provided. The key challenge for medical sociology is whether our generation comes to understand the larger task at hand or is doomed to a myopia that results in continual tinkering with outdated intellectual and social systems and that reifies stale and destructive debates about the "right" way to do sociology. The key challenge from medical sociology is aimed at policymakers and asks that they place their own concerns and shape their agendas for action in larger perspective.

The future of medical sociology is also met through its continued attraction of new members. For those interested readers, Elling and Sokolowska (1978) humanize the profession through the use of personal accounts of generally first-generation medical sociologists in the United States and other countries. An example of the introspection that is offered in this book is in the introduction, in which the authors quote Hans Mauksch (one of the contributors).

> As I look back I might have become a sociologist committed to functioning in any of several areas of social concern. One thing I know for sure: I never could have been satisfied to remain confined to the community of my own discipline. Maybe it is my need to discover new questions in real situations; maybe it is my not-so-hidden missionary streak. Maybe it is my, as yet unfulfilled, search for a laboratory in which theoretical knowledge can be tested, and in which sociological experimentation can be undertaken. Maybe—a peculiar personal characteristic—medical sociology offered me a career where I could always be "one of the few," where I could have all of the titillation of ritualized marginality. (Elling & Sokolowska, 1978, pp. 20–21)

Such insight provides a unique view of the pioneers of medical sociology in the United States. Medical sociology, however, is not confined to the United States. The following section examines the development of medical sociology in Europe.

Medical Sociology in Europe

Medical sociology has also established a historical presence outside the United States. Most notably, medical sociology emerged in Great Britain after World War II. The enactment of the National Health System in Great Britain "provoked sociological interest in medicine and health" (Palosuo & Rahkonen, 1989, p. 264). Medical sociology also became established throughout the European continent during the 1960s and 1970s. European medical sociology (or *sociologies,* as Claus, 1983, suggests) does not have the same cohesive organizational and developmental structure typical of American medical sociology. The most influential work detailing the development of European medical sociologies is that of Claus (1982a,b; 1983). In addition to providing a historical accounting of medical sociology within the broader European community, Claus (1982a,b) offers case studies of five European nations within which medical sociology has developed. Claus (1983) also provides an analysis of American and European medical sociology. Here, in addition to the identification of enabling and disabling factors relative to the emergence of medical sociology in Europe, Claus (1983, p. 1593) argues that there are:

> Three major and interrelated characteristics of European medical sociologies . . . (1) The boundaries of the discipline are ill-defined and broad; (2) European medical sociologies have an applied character; and (3) European medical sociologies are "policy" analysis oriented.

In addition, others have addressed the development of medical sociology within specific European nations [Stacey & Homans, 1978 (Great Britain); Herzlich, 1985 (France); Horobin, 1985 (Great Britain); Lehelma & Riska, 1988 (Finland); Palosuo & Rahkonen, 1989 (Finland)]. The lack of common ground between medical sociologists in Europe is the result of "ethnocentrism, which precludes genuine professional communication and contact" (Claus, 1983, p. 1596). Finally, the relationship between medical sociology and medicine is best summarized in the following statement made by Freidson (1983, p. 212). Although addressed to an audience in Great Britain, it is appropriate regardless of continent or country:

> Sociology . . . has the technical and conceptual resources to greatly deepen and widen understanding of the grounds for formulating policies of change. Medicine . . . needs sociology in order to be able to preserve what is valuable in its present institutions while participating creatively and effectively in adapting them to the inescapable forces confronting them.

Theoretical Orientations in Medical Sociology

Today, the theoretical arguments put forth by medical sociology mirror the broader field of sociology. According to Lupton (1994), these theoretical models include functionalism, political economy, and social constructionism. Gerhardt (1989) identifies four theoretical paradigms that include structural functionalism, interactionism, phenomenological, and conflict. Because of an overlapping of some theories, the discussion will be limited to three broad theoretical frameworks: functionalism, conflict (with political economy and social constructionism), and interactionism. A brief explanation of these theoretical orientations and their relationship to medicine is presented below.

Functionalism

As a theoretical orientation, *structural functionalism,* or simply **functionalism,** attempts to explain social behavior as an effort to establish and maintain structural consensus through institutional equilibrium. What does that mean? As sociology developed throughout the nineteenth century in Europe, functionalism emerged as the dominant theoretical framework among the leading proponents of sociology. During this period of time, society was conceptualized as a biological organism. Within this analogy, "we could study the specialized functions of its organs (the heart, the lungs, etc.). In the case of society however, the organs are its social institutions, such as the family, the church, and the state" (Etzkowitz & Glassman, 1991, p. 6). Also, as with a biological organism, the whole (organism) was conceived as larger than its individual components. Expanding on this analogy, Durkheim "focused . . . on the institutions and norms which make up the organic whole of society" (Etzkowitz & Glassman, 1991, p. 8). Furthermore, Durkheim argued that "the basic institutions of each society must be studied, and the function of each institution identified as it relates to the whole society" (Etzhowitz & Glassman, 1991, p. 8). Thus, functionalist theory offers a view of society in which equilibrium is expected to exist between its component parts (institutions). Following is a summary made by Turner (1978, p. 37) of the key points associated with functionalism.

1. The social world was viewed in systemic terms. For the most part, such systems were considered to have needs and requisites that had to be met to assure survival.
2. Despite their concern with evolution, thinkers tended to view systems with needs and requisites as having "normal" and "pathological" states—thus connoting system equilibrium and homeostasis.
3. When viewed as a system, the social world was seen as composed of mutually interrelated parts; the analysis of these interrelated parts focused on how they fulfilled requisites of systemic wholes and, hence, maintained system normality or equilibrium.
4. By typically viewing interrelated parts in relation to the maintenance of a systemic whole, causal analysis frequently became vague, lapsing into tautologies and illegitimate teleologies.

An example of a functionalist approach to a health-care issue would be efforts to limit access to medical procedures such as dialysis on the basis of age. Given the cost of health care in the United States, some argue that health outcomes among elderly persons are not justified in comparison to the cost of treatment. According to Evans (1991, p. 52) "on virtually all indicators of social worth, elderly persons, regardless of their health status, tend to be judged less worthy than younger persons." If one's social "value" declines with age and their social "cost" increases, do the elderly have a "duty to die," as some suggest? What is the impact of such a decision on role performances at the occupational or institutional levels? In other words, will hospital personnel employ less strenuous efforts (i.e., limit access to medical services) to save the life of a 70-year old compared with that of a 20-year old?

At the beginning of this chapter, this author referred to his observation of a nurse–patient interaction. Consider the hospital as a social structure within which participants (doctors, nurses, patients, and so forth) all have specific functions to perform (Jones & Jones, 1975). Depending on their status (position), the relationship and resultant expectations between participants vary. For example, consider the following statement by Lupton (1994, p. 7), who points out that "the role of the doctor is seen as socially beneficent, and the doctor–patient relationship as inherently harmonious and consensual even though it is characterized by an unequal power relationship." Another example is the sick role. Here, Parsons (1951) argues that if health is the expected state of humans, then sickness is a deviant health state with access gained primarily through the physician. Once the sick role is conferred upon an individual, the person is provided certain rights. At the same time, the person assumes specific responsibilities necessary to end the sick role (Lupton, 1994) and return to their normal social roles. Cross-culturally, an example of medical sociology employing a functionalist approach is "the conceptions of sick-role held by female members of the Sick Fund . . . in Israel" (Honig-Parnass, 1981, p. 615).

Conflict Theory and Social Constructionism

Following in the tradition of Marxist thought, **conflict theory** (as it relates to medical sociology) attempts to address inequities (structural and interpersonal) that are inherent within the medical community. In other words, a Marxist perspective believes that "people produce their ideas and conceptions of the world in light of the social structures in which they are born, are raised, and live" (Turner, 1991, p. 185). More specifically, conflict theory understands human arrangements as the result of a process referred to as dialectics. The dialectic process involves the following:

> (1) Conflict is assumed to be an inexorable process arising out of opposing forces within social/structural arrangements; (2) such conflict is accelerated or retarded by a series of intervening structural conditions or variables; (3) conflict resolution at one point in time creates a structural situation that, under specifiable conditions, inevitably leads to further conflict among opposed forces. (Turner, 1991, p. 205)

As a result, the dialectic as a creation of its past and current circumstances continues to evolve. In addition to the concept of the dialectic, conflict theory offers a number of basic assumptions regarding the social condition. These assumptions provide a framework for explanation of the conflict perspective.

1. While social relationships display systemic features, these relationships are rife with conflicting interests.
2. This fact reveals that social systems systematically generate conflict.
3. Conflict is therefore an inevitable and pervasive feature of social systems.
4. Such conflict tends to be manifested in the bipolar opposition of interests.
5. Conflict most frequently occurs over the distribution of scarce resources, most notably power.
6. Conflict is the major source of change in social systems. (Turner, 1978, p. 127)

Again, relative to the medical community, conflict theory offers medical sociology a unique perspective of the social system. For example, the literature generally identifies elderly persons (those aged 65 and older) as consuming a disproportionate share of the health-care dollars spent in the United States. As a result, elderly persons have been accused of taking monies that could be better spent on more effective outcomes for other age populations. Thus, some have suggested limiting life-saving measures among the elderly. Others (Binstock & Post, 1991) offer a counterargument. Although similar to the functionalist example applied earlier, conflict theorists would disagree with the "reality" that elderly persons utilize a disproportionate share of available health-care dollars. Rather, medical sociologists utilizing a conflict perspective would examine rising health-care expenditures within the broader context of the medical institution: for example, the growth of medical technologies, accompanying technological support, and increasing administrative costs associated with institutional control (bureaucratization) of medical services. Waitzkin and Waterman (1974) provide another example of the conflict perspective. In addition to the social structural (institutional) inequalities that exist within the American health care system, Waitzkin and Waterman also address the impact of sociodemographic characteristics on health access. Similarly, this author is interested in the ethical arguments associated with health-care rationing, social control, and the aging of the American population. That is, as the population of elderly persons continues to increase in number and as a percentage of the population, what methodologies will be employed to limit their access to necessary medical intervention, and why? The fact that a segment of the population is singled out and controlled on the basis of age for differential health-care treatment is an example of the interests of the political economy perspective and illustrates the influence of sociopolitical forces in matters related to health. In addition, the political economy perspective is interested in the distribution of power and power resources (such as money) as they relate to health and control. For example, there has been an increase in the **medicalization** of society in the recent past. This refers to the granting of power to the medical community to control an increasing array of human behaviors such as pregnancy, childbirth, dying, and so forth. A number of authors (for example, McKinlay, 1994; Zola, 1972; Conrad & Schneider, 1992) offer excellent discussions of the topic. According to Gerhardt (1989, p. 273), there are

> Two arguments [that] characterize the relationship between politics and medicine as seen by the conflict-theory approach. First, medicalisation of much of everyday life is diagnosed. This renders medicine one of the most potent agencies of social control. It calls for the demystification by sociology of the claim to value-free scientific rigour of modern clinical practice. Second, politicisation of medicine is demanded which implies that medicine is a social science.

In other words, medicine is more than a biological interpretation of symptoms. For instance, medicine involves the values of the health-care provider and the patient, as well as the resultant consequences associated with the similarities or differences of these values (i.e., noncompliance, difficulty in communication).

Another interpretation of the conflict perspective is offered through social constructionism. Although more popular among Europeans than Americans, social constructionism "argues therefore that all knowledges are inevitably the products of social relations, and are subject to change rather than fixed. Knowledge is seen not as a universal, independent reality but as a participant in the construction of reality" (Lupton, 1994, p. 11). As a result, "the application of this perspective (postconstructionism) in sociology and history is generally termed 'social constructionism' " (Lupton, 1994, p. 11). Perhaps the best explanation of the relationship between social constructionism and medicine is offered by Lupton (1994, p. 11):

> The social constructionist approach does not necessarily call into question the reality of disease or illness states or bodily experiences, it merely emphasizes that these states and experiences are known and interpreted via social activity and therefore should be examined using cultural and social analysis.

This argument is integrated throughout the book as the influence of culture on health behaviors and outcomes is examined.

Cross-culturally, an example of medical sociologists employing a conflict approach is the work of de Miguel, Porta, and Rodriguez (1990). The authors address the on-going political struggle between the socialist central government and the more conservative and often privately owned components of the health-care system in Spain.

Symbolic Interactionism

Symbolic interactionism, or simply **interactionism,** is quite distinct from the first two theoretical perspectives discussed. Functionalism and conflict theory are referred to as macro-level theories, whereas interactionism focuses on micro-level analysis of behavior. That is, although the first two theoretical perspectives examined behavior at the societal level, interactionism is more interested in behavior at the individual level. Historically, interactionism grew out of American pragmatism (Martindale, 1988). As Rothman (1991, p. 151) points out, interactionism "is a perspective on the social world which focuses on interaction as the unit of study, and can and should be used to study and to understand the larger social structure as well as the nature of individual interactions." There are three basic premises of interactionism:

1. Human beings act toward things on the basis of the meanings that the things have for them.
2. The meaning of such things is derived from, or arises out of, the social interaction that one has with one's fellows.
3. These meanings are handled in, and modified through, an interpretive process used by the person in dealing with the things he encounters. (Blumer, 1968, p. 2)

As the name implies, interactionism focuses on the ability of humans to communicate via the use of symbols. Also, the ability to communicate emerges out of the social interaction process that occurs between human beings. Thus, through the use of a language system or objects that have shared meaning, humans are able to communicate with one another. Furthermore, humans engage in *reflexivity,* or the interpretation of how others will respond to them within a given set of circumstances. A number of basic principles associated with symbolic interactionism include the following:

1. Human beings, unlike lower animals, are endowed with a capacity for thought.
2. The capacity for thought is shaped by social interaction.
3. In social interaction, people learn the meanings and the symbols that allow them to exercise their distinctively human capacity for thought.
4. Meanings and symbols allow people to carry on distinctively human action and interaction.
5. People are able to modify or alter the meanings and symbols that they use in action and interaction on the basis of their interpretation of the situation.
6. People are able to make these modifications and alterations because, in part, of their ability to interact with themselves, which allows them to examine possible courses of action, assess their relative advantages and disadvantages, and then choose one.
7. The intertwined patterns of action and interaction make up groups and societies. (Ritzer, 1988, p. 320)

These principles provide a framework within which medical sociology can address the intricacies of human interaction and meaning within the health-care community. For example, the physician–patient relationship offers opportunities for the misinterpretation of words or gestures by either actor.

Finally, interactionism is related to health care in that "illness is what given societies define and treat as such" (Gerhardt, 1989, p. 85). For example, Kleinman (1994) examines the differences in meaning attached to the problem of neurasthenia in the United States and China. Although symptomology is the same, the interpretation of the condition is dependent on the specific culture. Similarly, the interpretation of a situation may differ depending on the position of the actor. Consider the following example by Rothman (1991, pp. 162–163):

> A woman comes to the maternity floor of a large hospital. She is upset, almost crying, holding her huge belly and leaning against her husband, who seems nearly as upset as she is. "My wife is in labor," he states, and hands over a scrap of paper with times marked off—the seven to eight minute intervals they have timed between contractions. The woman is ushered into a cubicle and examined. "No," the doctor tells her, "you're not in labor yet. You have not yet begun to dilate. This is just a false alarm, false labor. You can go home and come back when you really are in labor."

In this situation, the expectant parents believe that the woman is in labor because of the sensations being experienced. However, the physician is applying a different criteria to the meaning of labor: the extent of dilation. Depending on whose definition is accepted (in this case, the physician's) determines the behavioral expectations of the actors. In this situation, the expectant parents return home and the physician returns to his or her duties.

Cross-culturally, an example of medical sociologists employing a symbolic interactionist approach is that of Field (1996), who interviewed nursing staff in England regarding their experiences and attitudes toward dying patients in their care.

All three theories offer explanations of health and illness-related behavior at distinct levels of analysis. Turner (1995) connects these levels (individual, social, and societal) to specific topics and theoretical perspectives.

In addition to an understanding of, and appreciation for, the basic theoretical frameworks associated with medical sociology, three research techniques utilized within medical sociology are examined. A brief overview illustrates the various research designs and their general application to medical sociology.

Research Techniques in Medical Sociology

The research process involves a number of stages that begin with the identification of the topic and conclude with a presentation of findings. Given the extent of information available within this area, this section focuses on three research techniques generally applied in medical sociology: survey research, participant observation, and secondary data analysis.

Survey Research

Perhaps the most common form of research within sociology, **survey research** offers the user a number of advantages. The survey involves the standardization of questions and available responses. Advantages of the survey method include ease of application and the number of cases that can be included. Because of standardization, quantitative analysis of data offers statistical basis for interpretation.

Survey research can be conducted in a number of ways. Questionnaires can be completed by mail, asked face-to-face, or over the telephone. Respondents are provided anonymity by the aggregation of data. Surveys are also relatively inexpensive and, with the aid of computer packages, are able to generate statistical outcomes allowing for immediate analysis of a particular problem. A quick glance at the *Journal of Health and Social Behavior* offers examples of survey research. For instance, the work of Miller and colleagues (1998) examines the relationship between athletic participation and sexual activity among adolescent boys and girls. In order to obtain the data, the researchers utilized face-to-face interviews with teenagers and their parents. The researchers also allowed "questions about sensitive issues such as sexual behavior . . . [to be] reported through a self-administered portion of the survey" (p. 113). Survey research offers the medical sociologist the opportunity to gain access to considerable information regarding specific health-related behaviors and/or attitudes from relatively large populations. As with any form of research, there are disadvantages associated with surveys. For example, there are always questions regarding the truthfulness of respondents. Also, the wording of questions and available responses may bias the outcome of the survey.

Participant Observation

Medical sociology also has an extensive body of knowledge developed through the use of **participant observation.** An example is the classic work by Becker and colleagues (1961) entitled *Boys in White: Student Culture in Medical School.* Here, rather than relying on standardized questions and answers from anonymous respondents, the researcher observes the subjects within their own environment. In this case, the researchers observed students and their progression through medical school. Whether the subjects are aware of the researcher is dependent on the role assumed by the researcher. This role can range from being an unknown observer to being a total participant in the activities of the group being investigated. The obvious advantage of this research design is the opportunity for the researcher to evaluate the broader range of behaviors, interactions, and the impact of organizational structures that emerge and have an impact on the everyday social world of the subjects. One disadvantage of this design is the potential for the author to "go native"—that is, the researcher loses objectivity by identifying too closely with the group under investigation.

The following is an example of participant observation (Becker et al., 1961, p. 301). In this observation, two medical students are discussing the allocation of new patients admitted to the hospital.

Dearborn and Martin were talking about who would take the two new patients who were coming in and about who would do the blood counts on them. Martin said, "Well, I'll tell you, Harry, seeing that I have two new patients coming in, I'll let you do the blood counts." Harry said, "Now wait a minute Jack, how many patients do you have now? After all, we've been here getting patients for over a week while you were over at Psychiatry." Jack said, "I only have two patients now." Harry said, "Well, I have three." Martin agreed that this being the case he should do the work. (*Junior Pediatrics,* November, 1955)

In this situation, the observer is not an active participant in the conversation. However, there are situations within which the observer may participate with those being observed. Whether those being observed realize the intent of the observer is also important.

Secondary Data Analysis

Although not a research methodology, the analysis of **secondary data** offers the researcher another opportunity through which the social world of medicine may be studied. Here, the researcher examines data previously gathered by others. Existing data can range from large survey data sets compiled by governmental agencies to obituary notices in the local newspaper. An obvious advantage of this research method is the cost and relative ease of conducting research. The researcher easily manipulates the data in an effort to glean what is believed to be of significance. A disadvantage of existing data is the inability of the researcher to make changes in the questions or to ask follow-up questions. The researcher is at the mercy of the original design. An example of existing data sources in medical sociology would be the National Survey of Institutionalized Persons (SIP). The Inter-University Consortium for Political and Social Research (ICPSR) is an excellent source of existing data addressing health-related issues. For example, this author has been using the World Values Survey, acquired through ICPSR, to examine value similarities and dissimilarities between nations regarding the justification of euthanasia and suicide.

The Influence of the State on Medical Sociology

The study and application of medical sociology is not confined to the United States or Western Europe. Medical sociologists are engaged in research efforts throughout the world; in developed as well as developing nations (see, for example, Gallagher, 1989). The following chapters explore the growing, yet limited, cross-cultural knowledge base that medical sociology continues to develop. To understand the cross-cultural or comparative perspective that is employed, the chapters not only examine the meaning and significance of culture relative to medical sociology, but also the role of the **state** in defining health and illness behavior. For example, the impact of the political and economic institutions and the development of health care (Waitzkin & Waterman, 1974; Najman, 1989). This influence includes areas such as which services will be provided, who will provide them, how they will be paid for, and who will pay for them. Consider, for example, the United States. Economically, the United States represents a corporate capitalist system, within which access to goods and services are dependent on one's ability to pay for them. As a result, the United States provides an extensive array of health services to persons able to pay for them. At the same time, many of these same services are not as available to persons less able to afford the cost. Attempts to reform the American health-care system have failed because the present health-care system reflects the cultural values of those with political and economic power (see the work of Navarro, 1994, for an example of the historical relationship between the state and health policy). Deppe (1989, p. 1160) points to the relationship between the economic system and the health of its workers and argues that "Capital's interest is not only for enough workers in the labour market, but that they are healthy and qualified." Another example of the relationship between the state and health is offered by Lena and London (1993, p. 599), who argue that as the former Eastern Bloc nations are transformed economically and politically, "it would be appropriate for scholars interested in the relationships between political systems and health outcomes to pay special attention to trends in mortality, life expectancy, and general basic needs provision in those nations that have recently experienced abrupt political transformation." The reason for such interest is to understand the changing role of government relative to the health needs of its citizens. For example, this author is currently examining the relationship between end-of-life decisions, cultural values, and aging in the Russian Republic and former Eastern European nations. It is these relationships and their influence and outcome that are continually addressed throughout the book.

A Comparative Approach to the Influence of Culture on Health-Related Behavior

All health-related behaviors occur within a cultural context. Furthermore, the definition and interpretation of what constitutes health, health care, illness, and so forth are influenced by the socioeconomic forces that exist within each culture (Kleinman, 1986). Consider, for example, the following analysis of work by Waitzkin and Waterman (1974) as reported by Bloom and Zambrana (1983, p. 99):

> They [Waitzkin & Waterman] argue that in American society medicine is organized essentially for profit, reflecting the normative principles of capitalism. . . . One group exploits the other. Only in this way can the persistent maldistribution of health services favoring wealthy patients be explained. They document the structure of the growing industries which provide health services and produce medical products, together with the increasingly concentrated distribution of profits among certain small groups of physicians.

Although reflective of American medicine, this statement does not explain economic or political influence on medicine within other cultures. Thus it is imperative that the myriad of concepts associated with medical sociology [see, for example, the work of Jones and Jones (1975), or Kurtz and Chalfant (1991)] are understood within a comparative framework.

This section begins with a definition of culture. Next, the relationship between culture and health is explored, followed by a brief examination of the increasingly important (and complementary) role of medical anthropology.

Culture Defined

Although a variety of definitions of **culture** exist, Helman (1994, p. 2) offers perhaps the most inclusive by suggesting that

> Culture is a set of guidelines (both explicit and implicit) which individuals inherit as members of a particular society, and which tells them how to view the world, how to experience it emotionally, and how to behave in it in relation to other people, to supernatural forces or gods, and to the natural environment.

It is understood that those who have economic and political power often establish the cultural guidelines. For example, the concept of **cultural hegemony** "refers to the precise ideas which are used, at a particular time and place, by the ruling economic class, to win the hearts and minds of the people over to an acceptance of the existing *status quo*" (Krause, 1977, p. 258).

The Relationship between Culture and Health

In an effort to establish continuity of material, a perspective that addresses the ever-changing relationship between health and culture has been incorporated; in other words, a comparative perspective of health. The purpose of the comparative approach is to connect the social institution of medicine to the larger framework understood as culture and examine the results relative to other societies. The comparative approach to medical sociology provides the reader insight into how culture, within the context of political and economic institutions, influences the structure, delivery, and organization of health care within society. Thus, behaviors associated with health and illness can be understood not only within the confines of the medical model (as understood within Western medicine), but from varied sources, all grounded in a cultural explanation (see, for example, Gallagher & Subedi, 1995; Subedi & Gallagher, 1996). Although the term *comparative approach* to health care is being employed, others have utilized the term *transcultural health care,* which is defined as

> an evolving body of knowledge and practices regarding health–illness care patterns from a comparative perspective of at least two or more designated cultures in order to determine the major care features and the health services of cultures (Leininger, 1976, p. 3).

Leininger (1976) even offers a transcultural health model, complete with levels of analysis ranging from social structural features to the roles of health providers.

Such efforts to broaden medical sociology beyond the medical model are valuable, but have had limited success. One reason may be that most medical sociologists are located in the United States and Great Britain, and when they engage in research, they generally concentrate their efforts within their own borders. As Conrad and Gallagher (1993, p. xiii) point out, "medical sociologists have neglected the study of developing societies." One explanation is that medicine has been defined by those in the social sciences not as a "product or part of culture, but as an objective body of scientific knowledge external to culture" (Lupton, 1994, p. 17). Furthermore, Gallagher and Subedi (1992) suggest that the lack of social science research in developing countries is the result of several factors, including the potential for research within one's own country is greater, research tools do not adequately transfer to the study of developing nations, and the potential irrelevance of current paradigms to developing nations. As a result, the separation of medicine and health from culture has created an ethnocentric image of medicine generally structured around a Western value system. For example, Payer (1988, p. 26) states that "while medicine benefits from a certain amount of scientific input, culture intervenes at every step of the way."

More specifically, our concepts of what constitutes health, health care, and relationships with health-care providers are all influenced by the particular culture within which we live (Specter, 1985; Kleinman, 1986; Albrecht & Tang, 1990). Referring to the United States, Stein (1990, p. 21) argues that "cultural beliefs, values, attitudes, roles, images, and the like govern the definition, experience, expectations of treatment, and outcome of illness episodes for practitioner and patient alike." In a similar fashion, Qureshi (1989) offers an excellent accounting of various cultural interpretations that address similar health-related circumstances. A consequence of differing cultural interpretations is an increase in the potential for disagreement and noncompliance of health behavior between provider and patient. Although *cultural relativism* might reduce tensions between provider and patient, Kavanagh and Kennedy (1992, p. 23) point out that "many health care practitioners find it unsettling." Practitioners are concerned because "of a lack of absolute values and of criteria" (Kavanagh & Kennedy, 1992, p. 23). Outcomes such as this provide the medical sociologist with the evidence necessary for a comparative analysis of the cultural and health beliefs of the participants as well as the larger social system. Although most medical sociologists have not been attracted to a comparative analysis of their discipline, others, such as medical anthropologists, have, and this chapter concludes with a brief examination of their role.

A Comparison of Medical Anthropology and Medical Sociology

The incorporation of a comparative approach to medical sociology necessitates the acknowledgement of medical anthropological research and analysis (see, for example, the work of Read, 1966; Lynch, 1969). Although the distinction between medical sociology and medical anthropology is clear, there are also areas of similarity.

Medical sociology and medical anthropology enjoy similar training and socialization, theories, and research methodologies. Occupationally, medical sociologists and medical anthropologists find similar employment opportunities in facilities such as medical schools, hospitals, and so forth. Finally, their areas of research, such as health and illness, epidemiology, and mental health, are also similar (Foster, 1975). However, there are also significant differences between medical sociologists and medical anthropologists. Medical anthropologists identify with those they study (i.e., the patient), whereas medical sociologists identify with the establishment (physicians). Methodologically, medical anthropologists are more likely to utilize participant observation, whereas medical sociologists generally employ survey research. Medical sociologists are also more interested in Western health care systems, whereas medical anthropologists are more likely to investigate non-Western systems (Foster, 1975). Further differentiation includes the fact that medical anthropology addresses the historical intersection between human biology and its behavior within a cultural framework, and the effect of that intersection on health and illness (Helman, 1994). For example, Inhorn (1995, p. 286) points out that "medical anthropologists have provided rather convincing evidence that disease itself is a cultural construction." However, medical sociology is interested in the intersection of health, illness, and social factors within a society. Finally, Helman (1994) offers a brief but valuable insight into the role medical anthropologists play relative to our understanding of the medical community. For example, individuals respond differently to events such as death or illness depending on their cultural belief system (Helman, 1994). These insights enrich the comparative analysis offered throughout this book.

Summary

Although medical sociology has had a relatively short history, its intellectual presence has been felt for a much longer period of time. Historically, medical sociology emerged from the social medicine movement that began in the mid-1800s. Initially, American sociologists did not view social medicine as an area worth pursuing. It was not until the 1930s that a handful of sociologists began research efforts involving the medical field. Beginning in the 1940s, sociology became increasingly involved in health-related research, and by 1959, medical sociology became a specialty area within sociology. Since that time, medical sociology has enjoyed continued growth in membership as well as importance within the discipline. The future of medical sociology is one of optimism. Medical sociology has a significant role to perform as changes ranging from physician–patient interaction to system-level analysis continue to emerge and shape the health care community.

Medical sociology utilizes a number of theoretical frameworks and research methodologies found within the broader discipline of sociology. At the present time, medical sociology is not dominated by any one theoretical framework or research methodology. This intellectual eclecticism is necessary considering the range of areas addressed by those in the field.

Although intellectually expansive, medical sociology has been somewhat remiss at addressing the significance of health-related issues within other countries, particularly among the developing nations. Furthermore, cross-cultural or comparative research that has been conducted has not been systematically presented within the context of a standard medical sociology text. It is also understood that medical sociology does not occur in a political and economic vacuum. Regardless of the country, the state has some level of interest in the health-care community and its participants. Finally, a cross-cultural examination of the health-care community requires a distinction between medical sociology and medical anthropology. Although similar in terms of their academic training, theoretical frameworks, and research methodologies, there are differences. Perhaps the most important distinction involves their interpretation of who is studied. According to some, medical sociologists are more likely to focus on the profession of medicine, whereas medical anthropologists are more likely to examine the effect of the health-care community on the patient.

CHAPTER REVIEW

The purpose of the chapter review is to challenge the readers' knowledge of material covered. The following questions are intended to elicit a critical analysis of the information presented. Future chapter reviews provide a venue within which material from previous chapters can be integrated into current information, thus creating continuity throughout the book.

1. Construct a time line that traces the development of medical sociology. Are there any historical events that might have influenced the emergence of medical sociology? If so, what are they and how did they influence development?

2. Based on your reading of the material in this chapter, what is the future of medical sociology?

3. Identify a health-related research project that would utilize the survey method. Do the same thing for participant observation.

4. Using the research projects identified in question 3, which theoretical framework would you employ for analysis of data? Why?

5. Locate a medical sociology research article that utilizes a comparative perspective. Compare this article to others that do not employ such an approach. Other than the obvious difference of perspective, how else do they differ?

6. Discuss the relationship between health and culture. Do you agree that health behaviors are related to the culture? Why or why not?

GLOSSARY

conflict theory   Based on the writings of Karl Marx, this theoretical perspective argues that social relationships represent inherent inequalities within society.

cultural hegemony   Ideas influenced by temporal and spatial quantities and constructed by those in power that are intended to placate the larger society.

culture   The process by which an individual learns the rules and regulations associated with all interpersonal contact within society.

deviant behavior   Behavior that is considered in violation of social norms by its social audience.

functionalism   A theoretical perspective emphasizing equilibrium and consensus between structural components.

group   Two or more persons who interact on a regular basis. Groups are either primary (family) or secondary (work).

interactionism   A theoretical explanation concerning the meanings attached to individual level behavior.

medical sociology   The study of health and health care as a social institution.

participant observation   A method of conducting research in which subjects are studied in their own environment. The researcher can utilize a variety of techniques, ranging from complete participant to complete observer.

role   The rights and obligations associated with a specific status (for example, the sick role).

secondary data   A method of conducting research that generally involves the use of data that has already been collected. Usually such data sets represent large-scale efforts by governmental agencies such as the Census Bureau.

social institution   The arrangement of a particular set of norms and values associated with a specific group structure (for example, health care as a social institution).

sociology   The scientific study of the impact of societal forces on behavior within social groups.

state   A unique arrangement of the political and economic institutions within a society that identify and justify arrangements of equity and power.

status   The position a person occupies within the social system.

survey research   A method of conducting research that involves the use of questionnaires to gather data.

SUGGESTED READINGS

Conrad, P., & Gallagher, E. B. (Eds.). (1993). *Health and health care in developing countries: Sociological perspectives.* Philadelphia: Temple University Press.
    As the title states, the editors incorporate original works authored primarily by sociologists. This book offers a rare glimpse into the research efforts of sociologists interested in health-related issues in developing countries.

Elling, R. H., & Sokolowska, M. (Eds.). (1978). *Medical sociologists at work.* New Brunswick, NJ: Transaction Books.
    Here is an opportunity for the reader to understand how and why some of the finest medical sociologists in the world decided upon their career path.

Gallagher, E. B., & Subedi, J. (Eds.). (1995). *Global perspectives on health care.* Englewood Cliffs, NJ: Prentice-Hall.
    A most welcome cross-cultural reader. As the title indicates, this book addresses health care; that is, what those (including Western as well as non-Western providers) who deliver health care do.

Gerhardt, U. (1989). *Ideas about illness: An intellectual and political history of medical sociology.*
Washington Square, NY: New York University Press.
One of the few books that provides an in-depth analysis of the major theoretical paradigms
in medical sociology.

Lupton, D. (1994). *Medicine as culture: Illness, disease and the body in Western societies.* London:
SAGE.
The book addresses the relationship between Western culture and its practice of medicine.
The author utilizes a variety of theoretical and empirical evidence throughout.

Qureshi, B. (1989). *Transcultural medicine: Dealing with patients from different cultures.* Dordrecht,
The Netherlands: Kluwer Academic Publishers.
This is a fascinating book that addresses language and meanings associated with health care
provision. Although intended for practitioners, all readers of medical sociology will gain insight into the significance of culture.

Subedi, J., & Gallagher, E. B. (Eds.). (1996). *Society, health, and disease: Transcultural perspectives.*
Englewood Cliffs, NJ: Prentice-Hall.
The companion piece to the Gallagher & Subedi (1995) book listed above. Here, the authors
have compiled articles addressing health behavior.

In addition, there are a number of journals within which you will find articles addressing issues associated with medical sociology. Check with your reference librarian for the location of the following:

Health Affairs
Health Care Financing Review
Journal of the American Medical Association
Journal of Health and Social Behavior
Journal of Health Politics, Policy and Law
Journal of Medical Ethics
Journal of Public Health Policy
Lancet
Milbank Quarterly
New England Journal of Medicine
Research in the Sociology of Health Care
Social History of Medicine
Social Science and Medicine
Sociology of Health and Illness

REFERENCES

Aday, L. A. (1994). Equity, accessibility, and ethical issues: Is the U.S. health care reform debate
asking the right questions? In P. V. Bosenau (Ed.). *Health care reform in the nineties*
(pp. 83–103). Thousand Oaks, California: SAGE.

Aiken, L. H., & Freeman, H. E. (1980). Medical sociology and science and technology in medicine.
In P. T. Durbin (Ed.). *The culture of science, technology, and medicine* (pp. 527–580). New
York: The Free Press.

Albrecht, G. L. (1979). Social aspects of medical care: Conceptual approaches to the field. In G. L.
Albrecht & P. C. Higgins (Eds.). *Health, illness, and medicine: A reader in medical sociology*
(pp. 1–14). Chicago: Rand McNally.

Albrecht, G. L., & Tang, X. (1990). Rehabilitation in the People's Republic of China: A reflection
of social structure and culture. *Advances in Medical Sociology, 1*, 253–267.

American Sociological Association Committee on Certification in Sociology. (1986). *Guidelines for the certification process in medical sociology.* Washington, DC: American Sociological Association.

Beauchamp, D. E. (1988). *The health of the republic: Epidemics, medicine, and moralism as challenges to democracy.* Philadelphia: Temple University Press.

Becker, H. S., Geer, B., Hughes, E. C., & Strauss, A. L. (1961). *Boys in white: Student culture in medical school.* Chicago: University of Chicago Press.

Binstock, R. H., & Post, S. G. (1991). Old age and the rationing of health care. In R. H. Binstock & S. G. Post (Eds.). *Too old for health care? Controversies in medicine, law, economics, and ethics* (pp. 1–12). Baltimore: The Johns Hopkins University Press.

Blackwell, E. (1902). *Essays in medical sociology.* London: Ernest Bell.

Bloom, S. W., & Zambrana, R. E. (1983). Trends and developments in the sociology of medicine. In J. L. Ruffini (Ed.). *Advances in medical social science, Vol. 1* (pp. 73–122). New York: Gordon and Breach Science Publishers.

Bloom, S. W. (1990). Episodes in the institutionalization of medical sociology: A personal view. *Journal of Health and Social Behavior, 31,* 1–10.

Blumer, H. (1969). *Symbolic interactionism.* Englewood Cliffs, NJ: Prentice-Hall.

Butler, R. N. (1996). Dispelling ageism: The cross-cutting intervention. In J. Quadagno & D. Street (Eds.). *Aging for the twenty-first century: Readings in social gerontology* (pp. 131–140). New York: St. Martin's Press.

Claus, L. M. (1982a). *The growth of a sociological discipline: On the development of medical sociology in Europe, Vol. 1: The general study.* Leuven: Katholieke Universiteit Leuven, Sociological Research Institute.

Claus, L. M. (1982b). *The growth of a sociological discipline: On the development of medical sociology in Europe, Vol. 2: Case studies.* Leuven: Katholieke Universiteit Leuven, Sociological Research Institute.

Claus, L. M. (1983) The development of medical sociology in Europe. *Social Science and Medicine, 17,* (21), 1591–1597.

Cockerham, W. C. (1995). *Medical sociology,* (6th Ed.). Englewood Cliffs, NJ: Prentice Hall, Inc.

Conrad, P., & Schneider, J. W. (1992). *Deviance and medicalization: From badness to sickness.* Expanded Edition. Philadelphia: Temple University Press.

Conrad, P., & Gallagher, E. B. (1993). Introduction. In P. Conrad & E. B. Gallagher (Eds.). *Health and health care in developing countries: Sociological perspectives* (pp. ix–xxi). Philadelphia: Temple University Press.

De Miguel, J. M., Porta, M., & Rodreguez, J. A. (1990). Socialist health policies and politics in Spain. *Advances in Medical Sociology, 1,* 269–295.

Deppe, H.-U. (1989). State and health. *Social Science and Medicine, 28,* (11), 1159–1164.

Doob, C. B. (1991). *Sociology: An introduction* (3rd Ed.). Fort Worth: Holt, Rinehart and Winston, Inc.

Elinson, J. (1985). The end of medicine and the end of medical sociology? *Journal of Health and Social Behavior, 26,* 268–275.

Elling, R. H., & Sokolowska, M. (Eds.). (1978). *Medical sociologists at work.* New Brunswick, NJ: Transaction Books.

Etzkowitz, H., & Glassman, R. M. (1991). Introduction: The renascence of sociological theory. In H. Etzkowitz & R. M. Glassman (Eds.). *The renascence of sociological theory.* (pp. 1–64). Itasca, IL: F.E. Peacock Pub., Inc.

Evans, R. W. (1991). Advanced medical technology and elderly people. In R. H. Binstock & S. G. Post (Eds.). *Too old for health care? Controversies in medicine, law, economics, and ethics* (pp. 44–74). Baltimore: The Johns Hopkins University Press.

Field, D. (1996). "We didn't want him to die on his own"—Nurses' accounts of nursing dying patients. In B. Davey, A. Gray, & C. Seale (Eds.). *Health and disease: A reader.* (pp. 320–326). Buckingham, England: Open University Press.

Foster, G. M. (1975). Medical anthropology: Some contrasts with medical sociology. *Social Science and Medicine, 9,* 427–432.

Freeman, H. E., & Levine, S. (1989). The present status of medical sociology. In H. E. Freeman & S. Levine (Eds.), *Handbook of Medical Sociology* (4th Ed.) (pp. 1–13). Englewood Cliffs, NJ: Prentice-Hall.

Freidson, E. (1983). Viewpoint: Sociology and medicine: A polemic. *Sociology of Health and Illness, 5,* 208–219.

Gallagher, E. B. (1989). Sociological studies of third world health and health care: Introduction. *Journal of Health and Social Behavior, 30,* 345–352.

Gallagher, E. B., & Subedi, J. (1992). Studying health in developing societies: A conceptually-informed research agenda. *Central Issues in Anthropology, 10,* 127–133.

Gallagher, E. B., & Subedi, J. (Eds.). (1995). *Global perspectives on health care.* Englewood Cliffs, NJ: Prentice-Hall.

Gerhardt, U. (1989). *Ideas about illness: An intellectual and political history of medical sociology.* Washington Square, New York: New York University Press.

Gold, M. (1977). A crisis of identity: The case of medical sociology. *Journal of Health and Social Behavior, 8,* 16–28.

Gray, B. H., & Phillips, S. R. (1995). Medical sociology and health policy: Where are the connections? *Journal of Health and Social Behavior* (extra issue), 170–181.

Hawkins, N. B. (1958). *Medical sociology: Theory, scope and method.* Springfield, IL: Charles C. Thomas.

Helman, C. G. (1994). *Culture, health and illness: An introduction for health professionals* (3rd Ed). Oxford: Butterworth-Heinemann, Ltd.

Henderson, G. E., King, N. M. P., Strauss, R. P., Estroff, S. E., & Churchill L. E. (Eds.). (1997). *The social medicine reader.* Durham, NC: Duke University Press.

Henshin, J. E. (1995). *Sociology: A down to earth approach.* (2nd Ed.). Boston: Allyn & Bacon.

Herzlich, C. (1985). Sociology of health and illness in France, retrospectively and prospectively. *Social Science and Medicine, 20,* (2), 121–122.

Hollingshead, A. B. (1973). Medical sociology: A brief review. *Milbank Memorial Fund Quarterly, 51,* 531–542.

Honig-Parnass, T. (1981). Lay concepts of the sick role: An examination of the professionalist bias in Parsons' model. *Social Science and Medicine, 15A,* 615–623.

Horobin, G. (1985). Review essay: Medical sociology in Britain: True confessions of an empiricist. *Sociology of Health and Illness, 7,* 94–107.

Inhorn, M. C. (1995). Medical anthropology and epidemiology: Divergences or convergences? *Social Science and Medicine, 40* (3), 285–290.

Jones, R. K., & Jones, P. A. (1975). *Sociology in medicine.* New York: John Wiley & Sons.

Kavanagh, K. H., & Kennedy, P. H. (1992). *Promoting cultural diversity: Strategies for health care professionals.* Newbury Park, CA: SAGE.

Kleinman, A. (1986). Concepts and a model for the comparison of medical systems as cultural systems. In C. Currer & M. Stacey (Eds.), *Concepts of health, illness and disease: A comparative perspective* (pp. 29–47). Leamington Spa, UK: Berg.

Kleinman, A. (1994) Neurasthenia: Weakness and exhaustion in the United States and China. In H. D. Schwartz (Ed.), *Dominant issues in medical sociology* (3rd Ed.) (pp. 178–189). New York: McGraw Hill.

Krause, E. A. (1977). *Power and illness: The political sociology of health and medical care.* New York: Elsevier.

Kurtz, R. A., & Chalfant, H. P. (1991). *The sociology of medicine and illness* (2nd Ed.). Boston: Allyn & Bacon.

Lahelma, E., & Riska, E. (1988). The development of medical sociology in Finland. *Social Science and Medicine, 27* (3), 223–229.

Leininger, M. (1976). Towards conceptualization of transcultural health care systems: Concepts and a model. In M. Leininger (Ed.). *Transcultural health care issues and conditions* (pp. 3–22). Philadelphia: F. A. Davis Co.

Lena, H. F., & London, B. (1993). The political and economic determinants of health outcomes: A cross-national analysis. *International Journal of Health Services, 23*(3), 585–602.

Lupton, D. (1994). *Medicine as culture: Illness, disease and the body in Western societies.* London: SAGE.

Lynch, L. R. (Ed). (1969). *The cross-cultural approach to health behavior.* Rutherford, NJ: Associated University Presses, Inc.

Macionis, J. J. (1995). *Sociology* (5th Ed.). Englewood Cliffs, NJ: Prentice Hall.

Martindale, D. (1988). *The nature and type of sociological theory* (2nd Ed.). Prospect Heights, IL: Waveland Press.

Mauksch, H. O., & Day, R. A. (1978). The current status of medical sociology training in the U.S.A. In Y. Nuyens & J. Vansteenkiste (Eds). *Teaching medical sociology: Retrospection and prospection* (pp. 73–85). Boston: H.E. Stenfert Kroese B.V.

McIntire, C. (1991). The importance of the study of medical sociology. *Sociological Practice, 9,* 30–37. (Originally published in the *Bulletin of American Academy of Medicine, 1,* 1894.)

McKinlay, J. B. (1994). A case for refocusing upstream: The political economy of illness. In P. Conrad & R. Kerns (Eds.). *The sociology of health and illness: Critical perspectives* (4th Ed.) (pp. 509–523). New York: St. Martin's Press.

Mechanic, D. (1990). The role of sociology in health affairs. *Health Affairs, 9,* 85–97.

Mechanic, D. (1993). Social research in health and the American sociopolitical context: The changing fortunes of medical sociology. *Social Science and Medicine, 36,* (2), 95–102.

Miller, K. E., Sabo, D. F., Farrell, M. P., Barnes, G. M., & Melnick, M. J. (1998). Athletic participation and sexual behavior in adolescents: The different worlds of boys and girls. *Journal of Health and Social Behavior, 39, 2,* 108–123.

Najman, J. M. (1989). Health care in developing countries. In H. E. Freeman & S. Levine (Eds.). *Handbook of Medical Sociology* (4th Ed.) (pp. 332–346). Englewood Cliffs, NJ: Prentice-Hall.

Navarro, V. (1994). *The politics of health policy: The U.S. reforms, 1980–1994.* Cambridge, MA: Blackwell.

Olesen, V. (1975). Convergences and divergences: Anthropology and sociology in health care. *Social Science and Medicine, 9,* 421–425.

Palosuo, H., & Rahkonen, O. (1989). Sociology of health in Finland: Fighting an uphill battle? *Acta Sociologica, 32,* (3), 261–274.

Parsons, T. (1951). *The social system.* New York: Free Press.

Payer, L. (1988). *Medicine and culture: Varieties of treatment in the United States, England, West Germany, and France.* New York: Henry Holt and Company.

Pescosolido, B. A., & Kronenfeld, J. J. (1995). Health, illness, and healing in an uncertain era: Challenges from and for medical sociology. *Journal of Health and Social Behavior* (extra issue), 5–33.

Petersdorf, R. G., & Feinstein, A. R. (1981). An informal appraisal of the current status of "medical sociology." *Journal of the American Medical Association, 245,* (9), (March 6), 943–956.

Pingitore, D. (1993). American culture in American medicine. *Science as Culture, 4,* (2), 167–211.

Qureshi, B. (1989). *Transcultural medicine: Dealing with patients from different cultures.* Dordrecht, The Netherlands: Kluwer Academic Publishers Group.

Read, M. (1966). *Culture, health, and disease: Social and cultural influences on health programmes in developing countries.* Philadelphia: JB Lippincott.

Ritzer, G. (1988). *Social Theory* (2nd Ed.). New York: Alfred A. Knopf.

Rosen, G. (1948). Approaches to a concept of social medicine: A historical survey. In *Backgrounds of social medicine* (pp. 9–23). New York: Milbank Memorial Fund.

Rosen, G. (1979). The evolution of social medicine. In H. E. Freeman, S. Levine, & L. G. Reeder (Eds.), *Handbook of medical sociology* (2nd Ed.) (pp. 23–50). Englewood Cliffs, NJ: Prentice-Hall.

Rothman, B. K. (1991). Symbolic interaction. In H. Etzkowitz & R. M. Glassman (Eds.). *The renaissance of sociological theory* (pp. 151–165). Itasca, IL: F. E. Peacock Publishers.

Ruderman, F. A. (1981). What is medical sociology? *Journal of the American Medical Association, 245,* (9), (March 6), 927–929.

Spector, R. E. (1985). *Cultural diversity in health and illness* (2nd Ed.). Norwalk, CT: Appleton-Century-Crofts.

Stacey, M., & Homans, H. (1978). The sociology of health and illness: Its present state, future prospects and potential for health research. *Sociology, 12,* 281–307.

Stein, H. F. (1990). *American medicine as culture.* Boulder, CO: Westview Press.

Stern, B. J. (1991). Toward a sociology of medicine. *Sociological Practice. 9,* 38–42. (Originally published in 1959 in *Historical sociology: The selected papers of Bernhard J. Stern* (pp. 419–424) by the Citadel Press).

Straus, R. (1957). The nature and status of medical sociology. *American Sociological Review, 22,* 200–204.

Straus, R. (1959). A department of behavioral science. *The Journal of Medical Education, 34,* 662–666.

Straus, R. (1963). A role for behavioral science in a university medical center. *The Annals of the American Academy of Political and Social Sciences, 346,* 99–108.

Subedi, J., & Gallagher, E. B. (Eds.). (1996). *Society, health, and disease: Transcultural perspectives.* Englewood Cliffs, NJ: Prentice-Hall.

Temkin, O. (1977). *The double face of Janus and other essays in the history of medicine.* Baltimore: The Johns Hopkins University Press.

Turner, B., & Samson, C. (1995). *Medical power and social knowledge* (2nd Ed.). London: SAGE.

Virshow, R. (1851). Die epidemien von 1848, essen in der Jahressitzung der Gesellschaft fur wissenschaftliche Medzin am 27 (November 1848). *Archiv für pathologische Anatomie und Physiologie und für Klinische Medcin 3,* 3–12.

Waitzkin, H. B., & Waterman, B. (1974). *The exploitation of illness in capitalist society.* Indianapolis: Bobbs-Merrill.

Wardwell, W. I. (1982). The state of medical sociology-A review essay. *The Sociological Quarterly, 23* (autumn), 563–571.

Weiss, G., & Lonnquist, L. E. (1997). *The sociology of health, healing, and illness* (2nd Ed.). Upper Saddle River, NJ: Prentice-Hall.

Zola, I. K. (1972). Medicine as an institution of social control. *Sociological Review, 20,* 487–504.

CHAPTER

2

The History of Medicine

. . . disease is more than the physiological and psychological breakdown of an individual. Powerful social factors determine whether people fall sick or not, and how and with what results they are treated. A doctor cannot appreciate too early the fact that his profession is a part and product of society and that it is always closely connected with religion, philosophy, economics, politics, and the whole of human culture. His education, social status, and remuneration—and unfortunately, his specialization as well—depend in the last instance on the tastes and decisions of society. Medical history is forced to deal with this nonscientific social background of medicine and thus serves, as no other medical discipline can, to open the eyes to those social factors without which the problems of health and disease cannot be properly understood.

—Ackerknecht, 1982, p. xviii

Social History and Sociology

The application of a historical context is essential within medical sociology. The evolutionary progression of knowledge being transformed throughout the ages connects the medical to the social environment. It is this appreciation of the past that allows us to create expectations for the future.

Most medical sociology texts today offer a limited historical analysis. This chapter attempts to rectify some of that by returning to the belief that a historical accounting is essential to an understanding of, and appreciation for, medical sociology today (see Mills, 1959, for his argument regarding the importance of history to sociology). The relationship between social history and sociology has been firmly established by the extensive writings of Henry E. Sigerist. Roemer (1960, p. xii), acknowledging the influence of Sigerist, states that "all his historical writings are certainly sociological in that they view developments against the social background at different times and places." Consider the following assessment by Sigerist of the social character of medicine.

> In consulting the past of medicine, we are interested not only in the history of health and disease, of the physician's actions and thoughts, but also in the social history of the patient, of the physician, and of their relationship. What was the position of the sick man in the various societies? What did disease mean to the individual, how did it affect his life? (Sigerist, 1951, p. 15)

This statement is as important today as it was then. Many of the questions raised by Sigerist are addressed in subsequent chapters.

Furthermore, McKeown (1970, p. 342) argues that "the social history of medicine . . . is essentially an operational approach which takes its terms of reference from difficulties confronting medicine in the present day." It is the interpretation of these events within the context of political and economic forces that is of significance to medical sociology. For example, a Marxist interpretation would portray American medicine as a social institution influenced by continual class conflict (Navarro, 1984).

Unfortunately, this chapter does not specifically integrate the four sociological variables of age, sex, race and ethnicity, and social class into this historical sequencing of events. However, as you read the chapter, note the exclusion of women throughout the historical development of medicine. Also, consider the impact of race and social class as variables that define inclusion or exclusion from medicine, regardless of the historical period.

This journey begins at its historical inception. The following pages traverse some nine millennia through the emergence, decline, and eventual rebirth of medicine.

The History of Medicine in Western Civilization

Modern medicine owes much of its knowledge base to the advances put forth by previous generations of individuals who practiced "medicine," as they knew it. Their efforts, curiosity, and determination established the foundation on which modern medicine is built. This statement is meant as one of inclusiveness, thus not limiting advances to that of Western medicine. The rationale for segmenting the rise of medicine is that by isolating the development of medicine by region of the world, we can better understand its historical progression. The investigation of Western medical history begins during what is generally referred to as the *Dawn of Civilization.*

The Dawn of Civilization to Egyptian Medicine

The earliest known recordings of medicine date back some 17,000 years to the discovery in 1914 of wall paintings in Les Trois Freres, a cave in France. These paintings depict what "may well be the oldest known representation of a medicine man: An Ice-Age witch doctor wearing an animal mask" (Venzmer, 1972, p. 16). Moving forward, the Neolithic period (7,000–10,000 years ago) represents a significant historical change from "a food-gathering to a food-producing economy" (Sigerist, 1951, p. 107). With the increasing domestication of life, medicine became increasingly important. Of particular interest during this period was the practice of **trepanning,** a surgical procedure that involved the drilling of holes through the skull. Although most patients probably died during the operation, evidence suggests that some actually survived (Venzmer, 1972). Although the purpose of the trepanation is unknown, a number of theories exist. The most common reason suggests that it was performed to allow evil spirits to escape (perhaps because of behavior displayed by the patient, such as seizures or madness); as a ritual; or as a method of relieving pressure due to blows to the head from fighting (Sigerist, 1951; Walker, 1955; Venzmer, 1972; Ackerknecht, 1982). Whereas evidence of this procedure has been found primarily on the European continent, Sigerist (1951) also reports evidence of trepanning in areas of North America, Mexico, and Peru.

Moving forward in time, the next historical period is some 5,000 years ago. Here, with the advent of the written word, is the cradle of civilization. Located in the area between the Tigris and Euphrates rivers was Babylonia, also referred to as Mesopotamia (Ackerknecht, 1982). To the west was Egypt, and in between, in the area known as the Fertile Crescent, were the Hebrews (Atkinson, 1956). Although Babylonian writings on medicine are more numerous and better preserved (they were written on clay tablets compared with the use of papyrus in Egypt), they are not as extensive as the writings of the Egyptians (Ackerknecht, 1982). It was here that the Code of Hammurabi was written that detailed penalties for errors made by a physician (such as having his hands cut off if a patient died during surgery) as well as his fees (Venzmer, 1972). Among the Babylonians, disease was closely linked to religion. For example, illness was identified as the result of some sin committed by the afflicted. Ackerknecht (1982, p. 27) states that "disease, sin, punishment of sin, and uncleanliness—were so close in meaning that they could sometimes be expressed by the same term." Examples of their concern with cleanliness are the elaborate sewage systems and water closets they constructed (Ackerknecht, 1982). Babylonians were also obsessed with the liver as "the dwelling-place of life and soul" (Venzmer, 1972, p. 26) as well as number magic (the number 7 was of particular importance) (Stubbs & Bligh, 1931).

In Hebrew medicine, "disease was considered a result of the wrath of the Devine Being" (Atkinson, 1956, p. 30). Thus, as with other early cultures, there was a strong connection between religion and medicine. Perhaps the most important points of ancient Jewish medicine are that extensive rules for hygiene were developed and the Jewish doctor was accorded little prestige (Castiglioni, 1947; Walker, 1954; Venzmer, 1972).

A particularly important era in the development of medicine is the influence of early Egyptian medicine. As Atkinson (1956, p. 22) states, "Egypt is, no doubt, the birthplace of medical science." The first known man of medicine is **Imhotep,** an Egyptian considered "the God of Healing" (Leff & Leff, 1958, p. 38). Imhotep lived some 5,000 years ago and has been widely identified as influencing Greek medicine and, in particular, Hippocrates (Pickett, 1992). Expanding the time period of influence, Hurry (1928, p. 182) suggests that the influence of "Imhotep extended far into the Roman period, certainly as late as the sixth century of our era." It is of little surprise that Western medicine has taken from Imhotep the title of "father of medicine" (Newsome, 1979). An excerpt from an oath to Imhotep states that:

> I shall recognize the impact that a changing society has on my medical practice and when faced with an ethical dilemma, arrive at a solution through the acknowledgement of the truth and the use of reason. (Pickett, 1992, p. 637)

Among Egyptians, the role of physician was not limited to Imhotep. Castiglioni (1947, p. 59) points out that, "among all the peoples of antiquity the Egyptians enjoyed the reputation of being excellent physicians." Like medicine in other cultures, the supernatural was a component of Egyptian medicine. However, it is here that the transition of medicine to an empirical science begins (Ackerknecht, 1982). Here, as well, "the first written accounts of medical experience are found in the Egyptian Papyri" that date to 1600 BC (Clendening, 1960, p. 1). An example of the transition of medicine to a more empirical format is found in the Edwin Smith Papyrus and in the Eber Papyrus.

> In both papyri the case approach is as follows: (1) the provisory diagnosis; (2) instructions on how to examine the patient and the diagnostic signs to be looked for; (3) the diagnosis and prognosis of the case; and (4) an indication of the necessary therapeutic measures, such as manipulation, drugs, and magic formulas or prayers. (Ackerknecht, 1982, pp. 22–23)

Progressing forward to the Greek and Roman period, it is instructive to realize the extent to which Egyptian medicine was advanced relative to other cultures. An example of their level of advancement is offered by Atkinson (1956, p. 24) who points out that Egyptian medicine "realized the importance of dividing the practice of medicine and surgery into specialties." For those interested in further study, an extensive historical accounting of Egyptian medicine is found in Sigerist (1951).

The Influence of Greek and Roman Medicine

Greek medicine spanned a period of 800 years, from the sixth century BC to the end of the second century AD (Walker, 1954). It is because of the influence of the Greek civilization that Western medicine is said to have flowered. One of the reasons why Greek medicine is considered so important is because it represents the transition era from medicine and the supernatural to medicine as an empirical science (Ackerknecht, 1982).

Undoubtedly the most important figure in Greek medicine is **Hippocrates.** According to Sigerist (1961), Hippocrates is to Western medicine what Charaka is to India. Born in 460 BC on the island of Cos, Hippocrates reportedly died in 377 BC. In addition to the disassociation of medicine from the supernatural and philosophy, Hippocrates is also known for a variety of other works including " 'Airs, Waters, and Places,' 'Epidemics,' 'Regimen,' 'Prognostics,' 'The Sacred Disease' (refutation of the idea that disease was sent by a god), 'Aphorisms,' [and] 'Ancient Medicine' " (Clendening, 1960, p. 13). Beyond his writings, Hippocrates' contributions were in the development of medical ethics (DeBaz, 1975). It is here, with the Hippocratic Oath, that physicians affirmed their role relative to the patient. Ackerknecht (1982, p. 61–62) illustrates the context of that relationship

> It was the treatment of an individual not of a disease, and the treatment of a whole body, not of any part of it. Treatment was based on the fundamental assumption that nature, physis, had a strong healing force and tendency of its own, and that the main role of the physician was to assist nature in this healing process, rather than to direct it arbitrarily. Health was a state of harmonic mixture of the humors (eucrasia), and disease was a state of faulty mixture (dyscrasia).

Another important development during this period was the theory of the "humours." Empedocles of Croton, who developed this theory, believed that:

> the world consisted of four elements: earth, air, fire, and water. In the body the elements were yellow bile (chole) which was dry; phlegm (pituita) which was cold; blood (sanguis) which was hot; and black bile (melanchole) which was moist. Imbalance affected health and character. (Hastings, 1974, p. 18)

Through the theory of the humours it was believed that a person would "show a balance towards one humour. They are sanguine, phlegmatic, choleric, or melancholy" (Clendening, 1960, p. 39). Utilizing the observational methods detailed by Hippocrates, physicians not only were able to provide a diagnosis, but more importantly, they could also offer a prognosis and therapy (Venzmer, 1972).

After the death of Hippocrates, Greek medicine survived through the works of such notables as Aristotle, as well as Herphilus and Erasistratus, who served in Alexandria (Venzmer, 1972). Unfortunately, the downfall of Greek civilization also led to the demise of Hippocratic medicine (Castiglioni, 1947).

At the same time, Greek medicine was being transposed into the emerging Roman civilization. For example, the Roman Empire had been home to Greek physicians for some two centuries. However, it was not until 46 BC, when they were granted citizenship by Caesar, that Greek physicians were accorded any status. Although Roman civilization excelled in many areas, medicine was not one of them. The two exceptions were in the areas of military medicine and public health (Hastings, 1974). Although influenced by the Greeks, medicine in the early Roman Empire was built on the use of magic. For instance, Roman gods were identified with virtually every disease as well as the ability to heal (Castiglioni, 1947). Although Roman physicians incorporated methodological skills such as observation and the use of prognosis, their medicine suffered from a serious lack of clinical knowledge and skill (Leff & Leff, 1958).

Nonetheless, numerous Romans have been identified as contributing to the advancement of medicine, and the two who had the greatest impact are Celsius and **Galen.** Celsius was not a physician. He was a compiler or, as Castiglioni (1947, p. 204) suggests, an "encyclopaedist who proposed to gather together everything that was known in their time about a given subject." His writing addressed a number of issues such as agriculture, philosophy, and medicine and was compiled into a volume entitled *De Artibus,* which was published in 1478. The book on medicine ranged from the translation of Greek medical terms into Latin, to what is considered "the first attempt that we know of at an organic history of medicine" (Castiglioni, 1947, p. 205).

The most important figure from the Roman period was the Greek physician, Claudius Galen. Venzmer (1972, p. 92) characterizes the impact of Galen by stating that "with him the creative period of classical Greek medicine came to an end." A follower of Hippocrates, Galen did not, however, accept many of his teachings. For example, Galen was a believer in clinical observations, but did not accept the relationship between the physician and patient, as presented by Hippocrates. Instead, "it was to be a philosophic system with theory of at least equal importance to observation" (Stubbs & Bligh, 1931, p. 78). Galen was an experimenter who made assumptions of the human body based on dissections of pigs and monkeys (Ackerknecht, 1982). Nonetheless, his work on human anatomy and physiology, the circulation of blood, and the categorization of disease provided the basis for significant medical advancement. He was also a prolific writer, with some 400 works to his credit (Castiglioni, 1947). However, the problem, as stated by Castiglioni (1947, p. 225–226), was that

> his disciples followed the letter of his work rather than the spirit; they did not follow the ideas of the observer, whose work was excellent, but of the philosopher, who was mediocre, and of the dogmatist, who gave to his personal observations the semblance of infallibility and to his hypotheses the appearance of immutable precepts.

The result was that for more than 1,000 years, medical research essentially came to an end. Adherence to Galen's teachings suppressed any further debate of medical knowledge. In fact, "it was nothing short of sacrilege to question Galen's teachings in any way" (Venzmer, 1972, p. 99).

Historically, the pinnacle of early medicine was the Greco-Roman era. This was followed by the medieval period, or more appropriately, the "Dark Ages." Here, the advancement of medicine had been literally stopped.

Medicine and the Medieval Period

The Medieval period (also referred to as the Middle Ages) ranges from the sixth to the fourteenth centuries AD. Others (such as Venzmer, 1972, p. 122) use medical and social catastrophes such as "the Justian plague, which raged in the sixth century [to] the Black Death, which swept away a quarter of the population of Europe during the fourteenth century" to define this period. Although some (Ackerknecht, 1982) subdivide this period, the following material addresses in very broad strokes the changing medical beliefs and practices that occurred throughout the era.

With the fall of the Roman Empire, the role of medicine in Western civilization became increasingly less important. In its place, the Christian Church defined the meaning and methodology of medicine (Hastings, 1974). Beginning in the sixth century with the Dark Ages (or *monastic medicine*, according to Ackernecht, 1982), medicine was transformed from a science built on experimentation, observation, and knowledge to a blend of mysticism, magic, and religion. For instance, Coe (1978, p. 180) points out that, "disease and illness were considered punishment for sin," whereas Marti-Ibanez (1960) explains that during the Middle Ages, impotence was believed to be caused by witchcraft.

Essentially, monastic medicine "conceived medicine as a mystic form of assistance given to the soul rather than the body" (Castiglioni, 1947, p. 293). As the period implies, the study of medicine took place within monasteries. Unfortunately, the study of medicine was not for an understanding of disease, but rather to engage in a scholastic exercise that involved reading and commenting on the works of the great physicians of the past (Major, 1954). Nevertheless, given the limited knowledge base of those involved, the quality of care was considered quite adequate (Coe, 1978). Monastic medicine ended in 1130, when the Council of Clermont forbade monks to practice medicine. It was believed that, occupationally, medicine was too disruptive, given the solitary lifestyle expected of monks (Ackerknecht, 1982). The church was, however, instrumental in the establishment of a hospital system.

The second broad area within the medieval period is referred to as *scholastic medicine*. It is during this historical era that institutions of learning were created (for example, Salerno, Toledo, Paris, & Oxford). First, however, the Arabian influence on the development of scholastic medicine must be explained. Castiglioni (1947) divides this era into three periods. The first period began in the seventh century AD, when Arabs began conquering foreign territory. Within a single century, the Arabian empire stretched "from the Pyrenees to the Indus River" (Marti-Ibanez, 1960, p. 121). The impact of the Arabian Empire on Western medicine was, for the most part, positive. Whereas monastic medicine limited the advancement of medicine, Arabs absorbed Greek medicine, expanding on its base. The second Arabian period involved not only the ability to read, but also to comment on, Greek medicine. As a result, Arabic medicine began to publish their own works (Walker, 1954). An indication of the Arabian interest in Greek medicine is the fact that within two centuries, virtually all of the scientific literature of Greece was translated into Arabic (Dols, 1984). The Arabian Empire also established medical centers in Rhazes and in the conquered area of Spain. Also, as an example of Moslem tolerance toward those they conquered, Jews reportedly lead the medical center located in Spain (Ackerknecht, 1982). By the tenth century, however, Arabic medicine had reached its peak. For example, hospitals were more than almshouses. Instead, "they were places where sick people were treated, where physicians gathered experience and instructed students" (Marti-Ibanez, 1960, p. 126). Beginning with the twelfth century and ending in the seventeenth century, Arabic medicine entered its third, or decadent, period. Throughout this era, Arabic medicine, along with the Arabian Empire, entered a period of decline. The Arabian Empire began to deteriorate because of internal differences between Arab dynasties. Externally, the increasing presence, and power, of Christianity also influenced the eventual decline of the Arabian Empire (Castiglioni, 1947).

Scholastic medicine, beginning in the twelfth century, offered a reintroduction of Greek methodologies. It was during this period that universities began to develop (Bullough, 1961) with Bologna the oldest in Europe (Major, 1954). The influence of the Arabian Empire on the emergence of this period is understood by the geographic proximity of these universities to the Empire. An example is that of Salerno. DeBaz (1975, p. 32) states that "the curriculum required three years of pre-medical studies and five years to get the degree of Doctor." DeBaz (1975) also points out that medical schools were not confined to men. Salerno admitted women students as early as the mid-eleventh century (Walker, 1954). Interestingly, during this period one area that did not develop was that of surgery (Ackerknecht, 1982). Surgeons were relegated to a lower social status because they engaged in manual labor. Bullough (1961, p. 206) argues that "all manual performances connected with treatment of the sick came to be looked upon as unworthy of the physician." With all of the problems associated with the medieval period, medical science began moving forward and progressing during the renaissance, toward a more egalitarian attitude of care for the masses of people.

Medicine and the Renaissance

The renaissance is a particularly difficult period to date. For example, DeBaz (1975) places the renaissance between the fourteenth and sixteenth centuries. Major (1954) locates the beginning of the renaissance in the mid-fifteenth century and ending in the early sixteenth century, whereas Castiglioni (1947) sketches the period as falling between the fifteenth and sixteenth centuries. The renaissance offered a revival of such classical cultures as Greece and Rome (Hastings, 1974). More specifically, this cultural renewal included "a revival of the Greek spirit of research" (Marti-Ibanez, 1960, p. 158) with a return to "objectivity of observation and experiment" (Castiglioni, 1947, p. 500). As DeBaz (1975, p. 33) points out, this "was one of the most stimulating steps in the history of mankind." It was during the renaissance, for example, that the work of Galen was proved inaccurate (Walker, 1955). It was also during this period that public health boards were established (Cipolla, 1976).

It was also during the renaissance that significant improvements were made in correcting many of the past mistakes of human medicine. For example, one of the leading figures during this period was that of Leonardo da Vinci, who is considered one of the greatest anatomists who ever lived, even though his efforts were not immediately recognized. It is through his writings and drawings that the human body came to be understood in a more detailed manner (Castiglioni, 1947). In addition to da Vinci, there are a number of other significant figures associated with medicine during the renaissance.

Vesalius (1514–1546), one of the founders of modern medical science, challenged the work of Galen. As a surgeon at Padua, Italy, Vesalius began work on his most important work, *De Fabrica Humani Corporis,* which means an effort to "make anatomy a science" (Atkinson, 1956, p. 153). For example, he correctly identified the construction of the heart. Because his work required the use of cadavers, he occasionally engaged in grave robbing, which resulted in considerable conflict with his peers. He eventually left Padua because of the animosity of others toward his work.

Another major contributor to the advancement of medicine was Aureolus Theophrastus Bombastus von Hoenheim (who was given the nickname Paracelsus by his father). Paracelsus was born in 1493 and died in 1541 (Atkinson, 1956). An unabashed critic of Galen (he publicly burned his work), Paracelsus "was a scientist in search of a philosophy of medicine . . . He wanted to understand the world in which he was living and man's part in it in health and disease" (Marti-Ibanez, 1960, p. 176). As a physician, Paracelsus was perhaps the first to connect one's occupation and a specific disease (Major, 1954). His research established the relationship between a specific problem (chronic arsenic and mercury poisoning) and an occupation (mining) (Pagel, 1958). Such reasoning provided the basis for the emergence of social epidemiology that is discussed in Chapter 3.

In addition to the more significant figures presented, countless others also contributed to the reawakening of medicine during the renaissance. Two excellent historical explanations of this period include Castiglioni (1947) and Major (1954).

The renaissance marked the beginning of significant medical events that provided the foundation for modern scientific medicine. However, the following century (seventeenth) offered even greater scientific substance. From philosophers (Descartes & Bacon) to astronomer–mathematician (Galileo), to medicine (Harvey), the seventeenth century brought fundamental change to the world of science (Walker, 1955). Although the extent of scientific investigation during this period was immense, "the greatest discovery of the 17th century was the discovery of the circulation of the blood by William Harvey" (DeBaz, 1975, p. 35).

Medical science continued its advancement into the eighteenth century with "a logical evolution of facts and ideas in their most ample and complex manifestations" (Castiglioni, 1947, p. 578). This was the period of "Enlightenment" that "shifted the center of interest from preoccupation with the fate of the soul in another world toward improvement of conditions in this world" (Ackerknecht, 1982, pp. 137–138). Because of the improved status accorded physicians during this period, the enlightenment has been referred to as the "golden age" for physicians (Ackerknecht, 1982).

Another historic benchmark during this period was the development of a vaccination against smallpox by Englishman Edward Jenner. The work of Jenner is considered by many to have had the most significant impact on the world not only during the latter years of the eighteenth century, but also well into the twentieth century. Although Jenner is credited with the discovery that an inoculation of cowpox provided protection against the more virulent smallpox, others provided him with the basis for its pursuit. For example, a variation of his method, referred to as *variolation,* had been in practice in Eastern medicine well before Jenner's discovery.

Another outcome of this time period was the emergence of public health as a new area within medicine. This development was fostered by "the State's accepting responsibility for dealing with ill-health" (Leff & Leff, 1958, p. 148). Expanding on this point, Johann Peter Frank suggested that the state "should be responsible for the public health at all times" (Castiglioni, 1947, p. 645).

Although any number of others could be singled out for their accomplishments, Major (1954b, p. 565) enumerates in broad strokes what had been accomplished during the eighteenth century.

> Before the century had passed, pathology had been founded as a science, physical diagnosis had been placed on a firm basis by the discovery of percussion, chemistry had witnessed one of its greatest triumphs in the discovery of oxygen, and medical science had learned how to prevent one of the worst scourges of the human race—smallpox. Clinical medicine also did not lag behind but developed an imposing array of clinicians whose careful observation of disease and study of various methods of treatment mark an epoch in the history of the healing art. It was a great century in the history of medicine and the harbinger of greater triumphs yet to come.

Given the achievements associated with the eighteenth century, it is little wonder that modern medicine continued its advance throughout subsequent centuries. It is at this temporal juncture that the United States is not only emerging as a fledgling nation, but that its medical community is beginning to define itself.

Medicine in an Industrial Society

Beginning with the initial colonization in the early 1600s and ending in the 1950s, the Industrial period covers some 350 years. During this period of time, significant changes occurred not only in the medical community, but within the larger society as well. It is impossible to identify and address all of the events or individuals that contributed to the development and advancement of medicine in the United States.

This section is an overview, with special focus on some of the more significant contributions within medicine. Also, remember that this history of medicine is couched within the larger historical experience of the nation.

Medicine in the United States: 1620–1950

European colonists brought with them not only the governmental and religious institutions of their countries, but also associated medical beliefs and practices. These beliefs and practices were not only varied, but were generally more representative of traditional rural England than the emerging urban communities. However, because of its physical isolation, medicine in the United States was non-European in its construction (Stevens, 1971). Because most colonial settlements did not have their own physician (or access to one), the local clergy became a logical substitute. The reason for the inclusion of the clergy is that they knew perhaps better than anyone else not only the members of their community, but also those medical events that marked everything from birth to death (Cassedy, 1991).

While the new settlers struggled to remain alive following their months long voyage and subsequent adaptation to a new life, they also transmitted diseases heretofore unknown to Native Americans. Duffy (1993, pp. 2–3) points out that smallpox "was the chief factor in the virtual elimination of the Native Americans in the East during the colonial period." The reason why Native Americans were more susceptible to the disease is not altogether known, and has resulted in conflicting historical explanations.

The economic and political growth of the American colonies in the eighteenth century provided the basis for the development of American medicine. During the eighteenth century efforts to professionalize medicine as a legitimate area of study included the founding of medical societies, establishing hospitals, and defining the training necessary to practice medicine. There were also attempts to organize the profession through the enactment of state licensure laws. Although passed in a number of states, the laws were later overturned or not enforced (Kett, 1968). Nevertheless, the professionalization of medicine began in the second half of the century. Relative to the medical profession, "the first medical school was chartered in Philadelphia in 1765 [by John Morgan]; the first provincial medical society was organized in New Jersey in 1766; and the first licensure law calling for prospective examination of doctors was passed in New York City in 1760" (Starr, 1982, p. 40). Within 100 years there were more than 40 medical schools in the United States (Starr, 1982), and the number continued to increase throughout the nineteenth century. However, many of those who practiced medicine continued to subject patients to treatments that generally "consisted of bleeding, blistering, purging, vomiting, and sweating—all designed to restore the proper balance of body humors or to rid the body of putrid or peccant humors" (Duffy, 1993, p. 14).

Perhaps the most significant physician of this time was **Benjamin Rush.** Educated at Edinburgh, Rush returned to the United States to practice medicine and teach at the Medical College of Philadelphia. Because of his earlier political involvement (he was one of the signers of the Declaration of Independence) as well as his contributions to medicine, Rush was highly respected by his contemporaries. Unfortunately, Rush was also a firm believer in bloodletting and daily purging. Long after his death in 1813, supporters of Rush continued to apply his techniques. Over time, however, Rush's system declined in usage as less invasive therapies arrived from the continent and disease time lines became apparent (Bordley & Harvey, 1976).

Throughout this period of time, there was considerable diversity of educational experiences associated with medical training. When the United States entered the Revolutionary War, only one-tenth of the physicians (some 4,000) had any formal training in medicine. Among those with training, only half had received their medical degree (Starr, 1982). Almost one century later, mortality rates among soldiers fighting in "the Civil War made painfully clear the deficiencies of mid-nineteenth century American medical education" (Lundmerer, 1985, p. 10). At the time, medical education generally consisted of two 4-month semesters (with the second semester a repeat of the first). All material was presented via lecture with little, if any, clinical experience available. Written exams were not required because many of the students "had completed elementary school only, and many were illiterate" (Ludmerer, 1985, p. 13). Although some medical schools attempted to ameliorate the dismal quality of the program by increasing their level of expectation, they would soon retract their position because of decreased student attendance (see, for example, the work of Bordely & Harvey, 1976).

During this period of American history, women had been relegated to the provision of home health, particularly childbirth. The following description by Bogdan (1992, pp. 101–102) illustrates the role of women in an area of medicine that today is dominated by those in the medical profession:

> Around age twenty-one, then, the cycle of conception, pregnancy, birth, nursing, weaning, and conception began that would occupy most months for the next twenty to twenty-five years of their lives.

In seventeenth century America, midwives and other female members of the family were responsible for assisting with childbirth. Because educational opportunities for midwifery did not exist in the United States during the eighteenth and early nineteenth centuries, women were forced to travel to Europe for training (Lopata, 1968). At the same time, the occupation of midwife began to change. For example, formal training required students to pay for the opportunity to attend. Because women were less able to afford the fees, an increasing number of men (who were also going into medicine) became midwives. In addition to an economic barrier, cultural attitudes and increasing social class distinctions regarding the role of midwives at childbirth reduced opportunities for women (Wertz & Wertz, 1994).

Although women were removed from many opportunities to participate in the development of medicine in the United States, it is important to realize the extent to which women were historically involved in the broader medical care system (see, for example, Lynaugh, 1992). Others have identified the significant role of women in various health-related occupational settings such as nursing (Baer, 1992; Reverby, 1994), pharmacy (Higby & Gallagher, 1992) and physicians (Lopata, 1968; Morantz-Sanchez, 1992). (Many of these areas are covered in greater detail in later chapters.)

As medicine progressed throughout the nineteenth and into the twentieth centuries, provider services became increasingly consolidated and professionalized. In addition to the increasing level of professionalization associated with the physician in the twentieth century, the contemporary hospital was also undergoing fundamental change. As hospitals institutionalized the process of medical care, they provided a location for saving lives rather than taking them (see Chapter 11 for more information on hospitals).

The early twentieth century was also the beginning of the reform movement not only in the American political system, but within the health care system as well. Perhaps the most significant event of the early twentieth century was the work of Abraham Flexner. A survey of the nation's medical schools by Flexner culminated in the publication of the Flexner Report in 1910. In the report, Flexner was quite critical of most medical education programs. Although many medical schools closed down following the report, Starr (1982) suggests that the decline in numbers of medical schools had begun before the report was released. The Flexner Report is examined in greater detail in Chapter 8.

The early twentieth century also brought forth interest in how the health care system can better provide for its members. An example is the interest in "sick clubs." Allen (1914, pp. 526–527) explains how miners in Carbonado, Washington, were provided health care:

> In return for his $1 each employee of the company is given all necessary surgical, medical, and hospital care in case of sickness or accidental injury, and the members of his family are provided with all necessary medical care and medicines.

Allen (1914) points out that family members did not receive the same unlimited services as the worker. This type of arrangement between the medical community and worker was not atypical in the state of Washington at the time.

On a much larger scale, in 1927 the Committee on the Costs of Medical Care (CCMC) began to investigate how the American health-care system could better serve society. One of the recommendations put forth by the CCMC (1932, p. 120) states the following (boldface original):

> **Recommendation 3.—The Committee recommends that the costs of medical care be placed on a group payment basis, through the use of insurance, through the use of taxation, or through the use of both these methods. This is not meant to preclude the continuation of medical service provided on an individual fee basis for those who prefer the present method. Cash benefits, i.e., compensation for wage-loss due to illness, if and when provided, should be separate and distinct from medical services.**

Some 70 years later, efforts to reform the American health-care system continue. Although some changes in the health-care system have taken place [for example, passage of Medicare and Medicaid, and the emergence of health maintenance organizations (HMOs)], the American health-care system has retained its primary feature—that health care is a commodity not a right.

There are a number of reasons why the American health-care system came under such scrutiny in the twentieth century. To begin, life expectancy improved considerably throughout the century. However, after examining available data,

McKinlay and McKinlay (1977, p. 425) conclude "that at most 3.5 percent of the total decline in mortality since 1900 could be ascribed to medical measures introduced for the diseases considered here." Thus, in reality, improved public health measures have had a more profound impact on the lowering of death rates than many advances in medicine. For instance, Starr (1982) points to the increased use of health exams and the increased likelihood of further medical treatment because of findings associated with those exams. Table 2.1 offers evidence of the change in life expectancy. Note, however, that as the century progressed, the gap in life expectancy at birth between males and females in the aggregate and for whites continues to widen. Only recently has the gap between white males and females begun to shrink. However, the life expectancy gap between black males and females has continued to increase (National Center for Health Statistics, 1995).

The twentieth century has also witnessed an explosion of medical technology. Throughout the first half of the century, significant technological achievements include breakthroughs in drugs such as sulphonamides and antibiotics (Leavitt & Numbers, 1985), the emergence of anesthesiology as an area of specialization and the ability to provide blood transfusions (Duffy, 1993). These achievements are identified because they represent broad-based medical implications for the general public. Concomitantly, physicians enjoyed an increasing status during the first half of the twentieth century. This improved status was, to some extent, the result of their increased use of the newly discovered medical technologies. At the same time, however, physicians were being faulted for not maintaining the image and behaviors previously associated with doctoring. Thus, the one area left for the public to assess the physician was in terms of their "responsiveness to the patient" (Burnham, 1985, p. 252); in other words, the physician–patient relationship.

The medical care system began to experience even greater changes in the second half of the twentieth century. With the increasing sophistication of technology, physicians became increasingly dependent on the skill of others to assess client needs.

Medicine in a Postindustrial Society

Because there is no specific date that clearly distinguishes the early industrial from the postindustrial period, the mid-twentieth century will be utilized as the historical marker. Before we proceed, however, it is important to distinguish between these two periods. Essentially, the industrial period refers to the production of goods, whereas the postindustrial period refers to the production of services (particularly knowledge). What is it about medicine in the postindustrial United States that distinguishes it from earlier historical eras? Consider the following quote from the Office of Technology Assessment (1994, p. 12) as a broad overview of health care prior to 1950.

> Until the 1950s, the structure of the Nation's health care system was relatively easy to understand. The system was highly fragmented, highly individualistic, and free of anything but self-regulation by professional societies like the American Medical Association (AMA).

TABLE 2.1 Life Expectancy at Birth by Race and Sex: Selected Years, 1900–1993

		Remaining Life Expectancy in Years							
	All Races			White			Black		
Selected Years	Both sexes	Male	Female	Both sexes	Male	Female	Both sexes	Male	Female
1900[1,2]	47.3	46.3	48.3	47.6	46.6	48.7	33.0[3]	32.5[3]	33.5[3]
1950[2]	68.2	65.6	71.1	69.1	66.5	72.2	60.7	58.9	62.7
1960[2]	69.7	66.6	73.1	70.6	67.4	74.1	63.2	60.7	65.9
1970	70.8	67.1	74.7	71.7	68.0	75.6	64.1	60.0	68.3
1980	73.7	70.0	77.4	74.4	70.7	78.1	68.1	63.8	72.5
1990	75.4	71.8	78.8	76.1	72.7	79.4	69.1	64.5	73.6
Provisional data:									
1992	75.7	72.3	79.0	76.5	73.2	79.7	69.8	65.5	73.9
1993	75.5	72.1	78.9	76.3	73.0	79.5	69.3	64.7	73.7

[1] Death registration area only. The death registration area increased from 10 states and the District of Columbia in 1900 to the coterminous United States in 1933.

[2] Includes deaths of nonresidents of the United States.

[3] Figure is for the all other population.

Notes: Final data for the 1980s are based on intercensal population estimates. Provisional data for 1992–1993 were calculated using 1990s-based postcensal population estimates. See Appendix 1, National Center for Health Statistics and Department of Commerce.

Sources: Data compiled from the U.S. Bureau of the Census: U.S. Life Tables 1890, 1901, 1910, and 1901–1910, by J.W. Glover, Washington. U.S. Government Printing Office, 1921; Centers for Disease Control and Prevention, National Center for Health Statistics; Vita Statistics Rates in the United States, 1940–1960, by R. D. Grove and A. M. Hetzel, DHEW Pub. No. (PHS) 1677. Public Health Service. Washington: U.S. Government Printing Office, 1968; K. D. Kochanek and B. L. Hudson, Advance report of final mortality statistics, 1992. *Monthly Vital Statistics Report, 43,* No 6, suppl. Hyattsville, MD: 1994; Annual summary of births, marriages, divorces, and deaths: United States, 1992 and 1993. *Monthly Vital Statistics Report, 41–42,* No 13. Hyattsville, MD: Public Health Service, 1993 and 1994; Unpublished data from the Division of Vital Statistics; Data for 1960 and earlier years for the black population were computed by the Office of Research and Methodology from data compiled by the Division of Vital Statistics; National Center for Health Statistics. *Health, United States, 1994.* Table 30. Hyattsville, MD: Public Health Service, 1995.

Utilizing the same broad overview of the American health care system since 1950 would include increased external control of the health care system through corporatization and bureaucratization (Conrad & Schneider, 1994). It is this change (and others) that is examined in this final section on the history of medicine in Western societies.

Medicine in the United States: 1950 and Beyond

By the mid-twentieth century, the health-related problems that plagued the United States earlier had begun to fade. In their place, a new set of problems began to emerge. Many of these newer problems reflected the changing demographic structure of society. For instance, at the turn of the twentieth century, the cause of death was generally the result of infectious diseases (pneumonia, influenza, tuberculosis). By mid-century, cardiovascular–renal diseases accounted for more than half of all deaths (U.S. Department of Health, Education, and Welfare, 1968).

In addition to changes in the cause of death, medicine as a social institution experienced a number of changes. These changes, which are all interrelated, are the result of factors that are internal as well as external to the institution of medicine. One change is the level of governmental involvement in the medical community (Cassedy, 1991). Increased regulation of physicians and the practice of medicine have developed in the recent past because of the escalating costs associated with health care (Frenk & Duran-Arenas, 1993; Light, 1993). For example, the institutionalization of diagnostic related groups (DRGs) for Medicare patients offered a control mechanism over the length of time a patient might spend in the hospital (McKinlay & Stoeckle, 1994).

An associated change was the legislative enactment of Medicare and Medicaid in 1965. Intended to provide medical coverage to the elderly (Medicare) and the poor (Medicaid), the programs continue to expand in terms of numbers covered and overall costs. These programs have been successful in that the aging population continues to enjoy increased life expectancy and the poor have received increased (albeit second-class) contact with the health-care community. Unfortunately, concerted efforts by the 106th Congress to reduce federal spending on these programs may potentially result in decreasing health status for these population categories. Another example of how health care has become politicized was the Health Security Act proposed by President Clinton in 1993. Although never voted on by the 103rd Congress, the Act engendered negative television and print responses from organizations with vested interests in the current health-care system (Navarro, 1996). The overall negative publicity lead to the eventual withdrawal of the proposal by the president. For example, the negative media campaign portrayed the Clinton proposal as intrusive on cultural values such as individual patient decision-making regarding the choice of physician.

The delivery of medicine has also changed considerably since the late 1940s. Anderson and Mullner (1989, pp. 146–147) present a "more-or-less" timetable demonstrating changes in patient care organizations. They identify the mid-1960s as the end of the solo practitioner era and the emergence of large-scale organizations (i.e., HMOs) for patient care. Although prepaid plans have existed throughout this century (Allan, 1914), the creation of Kaiser Permanente in California, HIP in New York City, and the Group Health Cooperative of Puget Sound in the 1940s marked the beginning of their increasing presence within the medical community (Starr, 1982). As physicians move from private (and solo) practice into increasingly larger group practices, research has begun to examine what has been called the *proletarianization of physicians* (McKinlay & Stoeckle, 1989). (This issue is addressed in greater detail in Chapter 8.)

Still another factor that has influenced the social institution of medicine in the latter half of the twentieth century is the increasing levels of medical technology. America's belief in the ability of technology is evident in the following quote from Bernstein (1994, p. 344):

> The early 1960s constituted an era of euphoria in which federal funds seemed plentiful, social problems soluble, and scientific triumphs imminent. Money, technology, and prowess, it appeared, would speedily produce any number of medical miracles.

Today, technology continues to offer life-saving opportunities. As the cost of creating and implementing medical technology increases and concomitant questions regarding the quality of life experienced by the recipient patient continue to frame the debate, the role of medical technology is not so easily defined. Ludmerer (1985, p. 280) suggests that "the misuse of technology can, and does, result in depersonalized and exorbitantly expensive care." Again, cultural expectations and the life-affirming role performed by physicians force them to provide extensive life-support technology even against the wishes of the patient.

Finally, the ability of medical technology to solve "problems" has led to the increased medicalization of society. This is reflected in greater social control of segments of the population (particularly women) by the medical community (see, for example, Conrad, 1992).

The last factor associated with mid-century changes in medicine as a social institution is the cost of medical care. Perhaps the most widely used measure of medical care costs is the percentage of gross domestic product (GDP) spent on health care. In 1960, the United States spent 5.3% of GDP on health care. Increasing to 7.4% in 1970, the percentage continued its upward trend. By 1980, the United States spent 9.3% of GDP on health care and 12.6% by 1990. In 1992, the United States was spending almost one-seventh of its GDP on health care (National Center for Health Statistics, 1995). For comparative purposes, the United States spends a greater proportion of its GDP on health care than any other nation. The issue of cost of care has become interrelated with virtually every other issue surrounding the medical community. The inextricable consequences associated with cost, particularly in a system in which health is considered a commodity cannot be ignored. All of these issues are addressed in greater detail in later chapters.

Understanding the evolution of medicine in Western cultures offers one perspective in the development of medicine. The following section examines, in very broad strokes, the historical growth of medicine in Africa and Asia.

Medicine and the Developing World

An examination of conditions in many non-Western or "developing" nations to-day reveals the continued existence of many health-related problems. For example, examining the "health" of developing nations on the basis of crude indicators such as life expectancy and infant mortality rates, it is not surprising that many of the developing countries continue to lag behind developed nations (Perry, 1988). However, there is also considerable discrepancy between nations. Table 2.2 identifies the differences in infant mortality and life expectancy between selected nonwestern nations. A number of Western nations are added for comparative purposes.

Therefore, to assume that all developing nations have inferior health care is misleading. It is evident that within many of these nations "health" and its delivery is interrelated with the political and economic institutions of the society (Najman, 1989). Furthermore, within many developing or non-Western nations there are currently two forms of medicine: traditional medicine and modern (Western) medicine. Rather than creating problems, the application of a pluralistic health-care system

TABLE 2.2   Life Expectancy and Infant Mortality Rates in Selected Countries: 1992

	1992 (Est.)	
Country	*Life Expectancy (at birth)*	*Infant Mortality Rate*
Sweden	77.9	5.3
Canada	77.8	6.8
United States	76.6	8.6
United Kingdom	76.2	7.0
Sri Lanka	71.6	17.6
Thailand	69.3	26.0
China	69.1	31.0
Algeria	67.3	55.0
India	61.1	79.0
Pakistan	59.0	95.0
Kenya	58.9	66.0
Cameroon	56.1	61.0
Ghana	56.0	81.0
Bangladesh	55.5	91.0
Nepal	53.5	99.0
Ethiopia	48.6	122.0
Chad	47.5	122.0
Mozambique	44.0	162.1

Source: The World Tables, 1994. Baltimore, MD: The Johns Hopkins University Press. Reprinted with permission of the World Bank.

can have positive outcomes within society (Hyma & Ramesh, 1994). In the following sections, medicine within two geographic regions of the world, Asia and Africa, are examined.

Health Care in Asia

As a geographic region, Asia encompasses a significant proportion of the world's population and landmass. Geographically, Asia includes (but is not limited to) countries such as China, Japan, India, Korea, Vietnam, and Thailand. Rather than attempt to discuss health care within each individual country, this section focuses on a brief explanation of two. Health care in China can be traced to the Shang Dynasty, which existed between the eighteenth and sixteenth centuries BC (Unschuld, 1985). According to Haifeng (1984), health-care concerns date to the Xia Dynasty (twenty-first century BC). More specifically, Haifeng (1984, p. 14) suggests that "some form of medical and health service appeared in the thirteenth century BC." Although Chinese medicine has become increasingly pluralistic, there are many features that remain culturally unique. Haifeng (1984, p. 49) argues that:

> Traditional Chinese medicine is the summation of the experience of the Chinese people in their centuries of struggles against diseases. It is a great treasure house, which has played an important part in the development of the Chinese nation and had a great bearing on the development of medicine in the world.

Any effort to chronicle the history of Chinese medicine would require much more space than can be devoted here. The work of Bridgman (1974) offers perhaps the clearest and most concise historical accounting of Chinese medicine. Essentially, traditional Chinese medicine was built on the belief that "the universe is composed of five basic elements: water, fire, wood, earth, and metal" (p. 11). In the second century BC, Tung Chung-shu synthesized these elements into a systematic framework of Chinese medicine. In this synthesis is the development of the interrelated forces yin and yang (Bridgman, 1974). For an example of the five phases and associated categories as well as the interrelationship of yin and yang, see the work of Ergil (1996). Although traditional Chinese medicine was never a monolithic system (Unschuld, 1985), contemporary Chinese medicine represents an accommodation of the past and an acknowledgment of present-day needs.

Western medicine entered China during the seventeenth century (Albrecht & Tang, 1990) with the arrival of merchants and missionaries. With the construction of hospitals run by missionaries, Western medicine became established. Before the end of the nineteenth century, 61 missionary hospitals were in existence (Unschuld, 1985). The twentieth century brought with it conflict and change for China. Political unrest, culminating in a civil war and the eventual founding of the People's Republic of China in 1949 also brought forth changes in Chinese medicine. Confucianism was being replaced by science (Unschuld, 1985) and the implementation of health services in the 1950s was couched in the ideology of the revolution. Consider the following statements that serve as an ideological basis for health services.

1. Medicine must serve the working people—in the Chinese idiom, *gong-nong-bing,* "workers, peasants, and soldiers";
2. Preventive medicine must be given priority over curative medicine;
3. Practitioners of Chinese traditional medicine (*zhongyi*) must be "united" with practitioners of Western medicine (*xiyi*);
4. Health work must be integrated with mass movements. (Sidel, 1974, p. 106).

Even after the revolution, health services were not evenly distributed. Urban areas continued to receive greater funding for health services and traditional medicine was losing its importance. It was only after the Cultural Revolution and the training of **barefoot doctors** that health services in rural China improved (Roemer, 1991). Efforts to integrate traditional and Western medicine have remained a constant political imperative (see, for example, the comments of Sidel & Sidel, 1973). In 1980, a conference to integrate Western and traditional medicines for the explicit purpose of evolving "a new branch of medicine with Chinese Characteristics" was called (Haifeng, 1984, p. 50). As a result of recent improvements in the health status of its population, China is considered a model for other developing nations (Ru-Kang, 1994). In that light, the reader is encouraged to peruse the work of Schneider (1993), who studied the role of a hospital patients' family vis-à-vis the institutional structure. Schneider (1993) illuminates the influence of culture and the political structure on the provision of health care.

The second Asian health-care system outlined is that of India. Traditional health care in India evolved into its present state beginning in the fifth and sixth centuries BC (Basham, 1976). Whereas Ackerknecht (1982) partitioned Indian medicine into two eras, the Vedic and the Brahmanic, Zysk (1996, p. 233) identifies four phases in the historical development of Indian medicine. The first phase occurred between 1200 to 800 BC and is known as the *Vedic phase.* Next was the *classic phase,* which is identified as occurring between the introduction "of the Sanskrit medical treatises, the Caraka and Sushruta Samhitas . . . [and] dating from before the Muslim invasions of India at the beginning of the eleventh century." Traditional Ayurveda [defined as "the science of [living to a ripe] age" (Basham, 1976, p. 20)] developed during this phase. The *third phase* ranges from the invasion of the Muslims to the present day. Finally, the fourth phase is referred to as *New Age Ayurveda.* Here, "the classical paradigm is being adapted to the world of modern science and technology, including quantum physics, mind–body science, and advanced biomedical science" (Zysk, 1996, p. 233). Regardless of the historical classification utilized, Indian medicine today has becoming increasingly pluralistic (Leslie, 1976).

Efforts by the government to provide health care to its citizens has proved difficult. Because most Indians live in rural villages, efforts have been made to establish local health centers (Roemer, 1991). However, gender-based cultural differences continue to hinder the development of health practice for women in rural India. For example, because women are responsible for activities such as water collection, childcare, housecleaning, and, among the poor, additional labor, there is little time for health maintenance. Furthermore, women are expected to gain the husband's approval to visit a physician. If she sees a physician, particularly for gynecological problems, she invariably will have difficulty because the physician is generally male (Kumar, 1995). In addition to gender-based differences, the socioeconomic status of the individual influences their access to the delivery of health services. The very poor rely primarily on Ayurvedic medicine, whereas the very wealthy rely on a private health-care system. Those in between these economic extremes rely on a large supply of urban-based allopathic and homeopathic physicians (Roemer, 1991).

Although crude health indicators suggest an improving national health, the Indian population remains divided. Although increased levels of education may help explain some of the increase in health, other social forces such as political ideology have also influenced these outcomes. For instance, the state of Kerala is more economically disadvantaged than the country as a whole. At the same time, the health status of residents in Kerala is generally higher than the rest of the country. The reason for the improved health status is attributed to the election of the Communist Party to head the Kerala government when the state was initially developed in 1956. Because of the level of economic poverty, governmental emphasis was on the development of education and health care for its citizens (Roemer, 1991). The relationship between one's political, economic, and health opportunities is not limited to India. The interactive effects of these variables are observed throughout this book.

Another area of developing nations is located on the continent of Africa. In essence, we are returning to the birth of medicine embodied in the Egyptian, Imhotep.

Health Care in Africa

As with any geographic region, the development of health care in Africa is dependent on the particular country under investigation. A brief examination of health and health-care outcomes reveals considerable variation between nations and present-day health outcomes of their populations. Table 2.2 illustrates that even today, many African nations continue to experience high infant mortality rates and relatively low life expectancies. Also, as Airhihenbuwa (1995) points out, gender-based health differences are persistent throughout Africa. Women not only experience gender inequality, but also exploitation, based on social class and the effects of colonialism.

As in China and India, many African nations have a pluralistic health-care system. That is, culturally defined traditional health systems exist in conjunction with Western medical practices (see, for example, Kirby, 1993), and, as in other developing nations (and developed as well) access to health delivery in many African nations is dependent on one's social status (Iyun, 1994). According to Airhihenbuwa and Harrison (1993, p. 124):

> African traditional medicine seeks to secure and maintain a balance between the individual, elements of nature, and the heavenly bodies. Within the individual, a bal-

ance is maintained between organic disorders, physiological disorders, and social conflicts. This balanced state is, in turn, balanced with elements of nature—earth, fire, water, air, and metal. Finally, balance is sought with the heavenly bodies—the sun, moon, and stars.

Historically, traditional medicine had considerable influence over individual and public behavior. However, following colonization by European powers, the practice of traditional medicine was banned and a variant of Western medicine installed (Ulin, 1980). Efforts by the colonial powers to eliminate traditional medicine were ineffective. Traditional medicine in Africa has survived and has become part of a pluralistic approach to health care (see, for example, Bellakhdar, 1989). Chavunduka (1986) reports that for many, illness is categorized as either normal or abnormal. Normal illnesses, such as colds, occur as a consequence of daily living. These illnesses are treated by modern medicine. Abnormal illnesses, such as a persistent headache, are considered to be the result of spirits and can only be treated through traditional medicine. For example, in addition to traditional and modern medicine, Ethiopia also has a transitional health-care system that involves the sale and distribution of illegal pharmaceuticals primarily to rural populations (Slikkerveer, 1982). Although these broad generalizations provide an overview of the types of health care in Africa, it is understood that national political and economic institutions are highly influential in the formulation of characteristics unique to each health-care system. These differences are addressed in a brief examination of health care in two African nations. The West African country of Ghana gained independence from Britain in 1957. Although the population remains primarily rural, the distribution of physicians and medical services is urban. Because the rural populations are generally poorer, they cannot afford the cost of Western medicine. Thus, as in other African nations, traditional healers serve primarily rural populations. These healers are referred to as *ethnomedical practitioners* and have been identified as fitting the following categories: traditional birth attendants, faith healers, herbalists, and spiritualists (Senah, 1995).

Economically, the modern health-care system in Ghana is entrepreneurial, with the majority of funding coming from private sources (Roemer, 1991). Because of the extremely low per capita GDP, any fluctuation in the economy can have a tremendous impact on the ability of the modern health-care system to function. As a result, modern medical doctors are becoming increasingly concentrated in urban areas, providing services to the middle and upper classes. Understanding the disparity between Western and traditional medicine, Ghana has been recognized for its efforts to incorporate biomedicine and traditional medical practitioner (TMP) (Good, 1987). Outcomes, as measured by such crude indicators as infant mortality rate, suggest that life has improved, but only slightly. In 1970, the infant mortality rate was 111 per 1,000 live births. In 1991, it was 83 per 1,000 live births (World Development Report, 1993).

Although Ghana represents a significant effort to integrate TMPs with a free-enterprise system of modern health care, population health outcomes continue to represent geographic and economic disparity. Roemer (1991, p. 491) offers a cogent reminder of these outcomes when he states that:

> The handful of upper-class merchants, landowners, high public officials, and military personnel in Accra can doubtless obtain an adequate amount and good quality of medical care, but most of the population in the rural areas and periurban slums accept either very deficient health service or none at all.

Differentiation in health outcomes based on economic position and geographic location are not specific to Ghana. Rather, such outcomes are increasingly common in many developing nations.

Compared to Ghana, a country with a free-enterprise type of modern health-care system, Zimbabwe has a welfare-oriented health-care system. Historically, Zimbabwe is a recent addition to African national independence. As a former British colony, Zimbabwe (formerly Southern Rhodesia) had a highly centralized (and unequal) health-care system (Roemer, 1991). Since gaining independence in 1980, the government has attempted to create an affordable health-care system that would be available to the general population. In addition to establishing access, the government, through the Minister of Health (MOH), reorganized the delivery of health services. Health-care delivery consisting of a "pyramidal structure of MOH health services—from village to health center to district to province to capital— integration of the former vertically directed health programs would be the guiding policy in Zimbabwe" (Roemer, 1991, p. 543). In addition to the development of modern medicine, multiple types of traditional healers provide patients with a secondary source of health treatment (Chavunduka, 1986). Thus, how disease is treated is dependent on how it is defined by the affected individual or their social grouping (Good, 1987). As a nation, Zimbabwe has experienced increased health status since the late 1970s. For example, the infant mortality rate has been reduced from 96 per 100,000 live births in 1970 to 48 per 100,000 live births in 1990, a 50-percent reduction in a 20-year period of time (World Development Report, 1993). Unfortunately, research also indicates that socioeconomic factors such as level of maternal education are directly related to reduced infant mortality rates (Gray, 1993). Thus, as the health-care system in Zimbabwe attempts to progress (see Hyma and Ramesh, 1994, for an example of the developing alliance between the modern health-care system and traditional healers), the persistence of economic differences is a reminder of the continued inequalities associated with health outcomes.

The Future of Medicine

The final section of this chapter addresses three variables that have an impact (directly, indirectly, and perceptually) on the health-care system in the United States. This section explores the relationship of each variable on medicine as the United States enters the twenty-first century.

The Impact of Technology on Medicine

Historically, one of the driving forces in the development of medicine has been the continued development of technology. Although much of the health-related technology has resulted in positive outcomes for many members of society, there have also been other, less desirable, social and economic ramifications.

There has also been considerable controversy surrounding some of the supposed effects of health technology. For example, life expectancy has continued to expand throughout the twentieth century. Whereas health-related technology has generally been acknowledged as the reason for the decreasing mortality rates, other researchers (McKinlay & McKinlay, 1977) point to the significant impact of more basic public health measures. In a more positive application, health-care technology is generally cited as one of the key reasons for the increased percentage of elderly persons who are surviving into old-old age. Although technology may help some people live longer, questions regarding their quality of life and the expense of the procedures continue to be raised (Levine, 1987). For example, one of the most fundamental questions associated with organ transplantation is whether limited health-care funds should be allocated for a procedure that may not produce a positive outcome. That is, should society spend thousands of dollars to help one person when those same funds could be used to assist perhaps hundreds of other individuals instead (Kutner, 1987)? Other bioethical concerns range from when does life begin to when does it end. These concerns often involve not only the ethicist, but the patient as well. Throughout many of these concerns, Gray and Osterweis (1995, p. 393) point out the inherent conflict between the parties involved: "many ethical dilemmas in medicine occur in situations in which the actions judged to be in the patient's best interests may not be the actions that the patient would choose." A sociological explanation, however, would address more fundamental questions, such as which cultural values are associated with defining when life begins or ends. Many societies also experience cultural lag because the norms and values of society are unable to maintain the same pace as the technology.

As suggested earlier, the underlying issue surrounding the future of health-care technology is how much a society can afford and whom it will benefit. Consider the following statement by Fuchs (1993, p. 181): "over the long run, technology, more than anything else, drives the cost of care." For example, health-care expenditures in the United States are now reaching some $1 trillion (one-seventh of GDP). Furthermore, it is estimated that in the recent past, approximately one-half of the increased cost of health care is the result of technology (Schwartz, 1994). One example of the efforts to control the cost of health care includes the use of technology assessment, which is "designed to [determine] the value of technologies, making it possible to adopt and abandon medical interventions selectively" (Garber, 1994).

The distribution of medical technology is very unequal. One solution, offered by Bell (1992, p. 192) suggests that, from a Marxist perspective, "the solution to control of medical technology development lies in the curtailment of private profit." The viability of such an option in America today is, at best, minimal. The medical technology market is extremely lucrative, and given the propensity of recent government initiatives to remove government "interference" in the marketplace, does not bode well for solutions suggesting a redistribution of economic resources. At the same time, questions regarding the fairness of health technology are also important (see, for example, Ratcliff, 1989).

Aging Populations and Health Care

All developed nations are experiencing a maturing of their populations. In the United States today, the percentage of the population aged 65 and older is approximately 13 percent. As the United States progresses into the twenty-first century, the percentage of the population aged 65 and older will reach some 24.5 percent by the year 2080. More specifically, the percentage of the population aged 85 and over will increase from 1.3 percent in 1990 to 5.8 percent in 2080 (U.S. Bureau of the Census, 1989). It is also understood that as a society ages (demographically), the health needs of its members change. The likelihood of limited activity and diminished health status also increases with age (National Center for Health Statistics, 1994).

The consequences of these demographic changes on the health-care system will depend on its structure and the value society places on growing older. If the present health-care system categorizes recipients on criteria such as income level or age, then the relationship between an increasingly aging population and the health-care system will remain fragmented.

Political Will and Health-Care Costs

The political will (in other words, the willingness of those in positions of political power to affect broad-based change in the medical community) and the cost of health care are interconnected with technology and the aging of society. It is political will that will develop the regulations necessary to control (or not) the amount of health technology, the cost of health care, and the type of system that will provide services to an increasingly aged population. Ultimately then, the state and its cultural values represent the final authority regarding the future of health care.

Unfortunately, if the 106th Congress is representative of the prevailing political will, the future of health care in America is in peril. Current political wisdom regarding health care believes that "market forces" will provide needed regulation of, and access to, the system (Chapman, 1994). It is believed by many in Congress that increased competition between health-care providers will maintain quality and reduce cost. Although such outcomes are possible (in a perfect economic world), the United States already has the most competitive (and the most expensive) system in the world. Thus, there is little reason to believe that health-care costs will experience any appreciable decline in the near future.

In summary, the future of health care in the United States can be characterized as being in a state of flux. That is, the need for health care will certainly continue, but how health care is provided, to whom, and at what price has yet to be understood (Navarro, 1994). Questions concerning the future of health care are not confined to the United States, nor is the American health-care system representative of other industrialized nations. For further examination of health care systems, see Chapter 13.

Summary

This chapter begins with the rather formidable task of presenting a historical development of medicine in Western civilization. Beginning with the earliest known inferences to medicine, the chapter progresses through a number of historical periods. In particular, primitive medicine, the Greco-Roman era, the medieval period, and the renaissance are examined. These historical periods illustrate the importance of medicine within ever-changing social systems. Special emphasis has been placed on the emergence of American medicine from the colonial period to the present. Here, the evolution of American medicine from an occupation with little status to one of the most prestigious occupations in the country is examined. Furthermore, the industrial and postindustrial periods are differentiated, thus addressing those changes that have had an impact on the medical community.

Although the emphasis has been on the history of medicine within a Western framework, a comparative perspective allowing for an analysis of various developing nations in Asia and Africa is also examined. The chapter concludes with a brief look at the future of medicine in the United States. Although medicine will survive into the twenty-first century, its role is increasingly dependent on the economic and political institutions within society.

CHAPTER REVIEW

The chronological order utilized in the historical presentation of Western medicine provides a convenient framework for learning and discussion. Some of the following questions address specific information found throughout this chapter. Other questions force the reader to extrapolate from available information and develop responses based on the on-going relationship between medicine, history, and the state.

1. The era of "primitive medicine" identified the emergence of medicine within a number of cultures. Identify these cultures and the role of medicine within each culture.

2. Compare and contrast the development of medicine during the Greek and Roman periods.

3. Hippocrates is often cited as the father of medicine. Yet it is apparent that Imhotep (an Egyptian) is the real father of medicine. Why do we continue to validate this inaccurate portrayal?

4. Explain the differences in the development of medicine between the medieval and renaissance periods.

5. Chronicle the development of medicine in the United States.

6. Discuss the influence of cultural values in the development of medicine in the United States.

7. Many developing nations have a "pluralistic" medical system. Generally speaking, how has this system influenced the health of these nations?

8. The future of medicine is interconnected to governmental decision making. Address the impact of political ideology on health-care policy. What are the consequences regarding the future of medicine?

GLOSSARY

barefoot doctor   A significant component of the Chinese health-care system. They are rural peasants trained to provide basic health services at the local level.

cultural lag   A situation in which the norms and values of a society do not keep pace with concomitant technological advances.

Imhotep   An Egyptian physician who predates Hippocrates and is considered by many to be the real "father of medicine."

Galen   A Roman physician whose medical writings were considered the ultimate authority throughout the Middle Ages.

Hippocrates   A Greek physician who, in Western medicine, is considered to be the father of medicine.

Rush, Benjamin   A leading American physician during the latter eighteenth and early nineteenth centuries. Because of his reputation, his use of purging and bloodletting was maintained long after his death.

trepanning   A surgical procedure from primitive medicine in which a hole was bored in the skull, presumably for the purpose of allowing evil spirits to escape.

SUGGESTED READINGS

Ackerknecht, E. H. (1982). *A short history of medicine* (rev. ed.). Baltimore: The Johns Hopkins University Press.
A highly respected contemporary examination of the history of medicine. This is a concise book, covering primarily the rise of medicine in the Western world, but also devotes a chapter to ancient India and China.

Sigerist, H. E. (1951). *A history of medicine. Vol. 1: Primitive and archaic medicine.* New York: Oxford University Press.
The reader is provided with an in-depth examination of the social history of Egyptian as well as primitive medicine.

Sigerist, H. E. (1961). *A history of medicine. Vol. II: Early Greek, Hindu, and Persian medicine.* New York: Oxford University Press.
A continuation of the first volume in which the author provides a comprehensive examination of the development of early medicine.

Starr, P. (1982). *The social transformation of American medicine.* New York: Basic Books.
An excellent analysis of the development of medicine in the United States. This is must reading for anyone seriously interested in medical sociology.

Roemer, M. I. (ed.). (1960). *Henry E. Sigerist on the sociology of medicine.* New York: MD
Publications, Inc.
In particular, the forward is recommended reading. Additional essays address various topical areas of medicine (Europe, the United States, and other countries, as well as specific topics). Although dated, Sigerist offers a sociological analysis to social history that is worth the
effort.

REFERENCES

Ackerknecht, E. H. (1982). *A short history of medicine* (rev. ed.). Baltimore: The Johns Hopkins
University Press.
Airhihenbuwa, C. O., & Harrison, I. E. (1993). Traditional medicine in Africa: Past, present, and fu-
ture. In P. Conrad & E. B. Gallagher (Eds.). *Health and health care in developing countries:
Sociological perspectives* (pp. 122–134). Philadelphia: Temple University Press.
Airhihenbuwa, C. O. (1995). *Health and culture: Beyond the western paradigm.* Thousand Oaks, CA:
SAGE.
Albrecht, G. L., & Tang, X. (1990) Rehabilitation in the People's Republic of China: A reflection
of social structure and culture. *Advances in Medical Sociology, 1,* 235–267.
Allen, R. A. (1914). "Sick clubs": Co-operative medical service. *The Survey,* August 22, 526–527.
Anderson, R. M., & Mullner, R. M. (1989). Trends in the organization of health services. In H. E.
Freeman & S. Levine (Eds.). *Handbook of medical sociology* (4th Ed.) (pp. 144–165).
Englewood Cliffs, NJ: Prentice-Hall.
Atkinson, D. T. (1956). *Magic, myth and medicine.* Cleveland: The World Publishing Company.
Baer, E. D. (1992). Nurses. In R. D. Apple (Ed.). *Women, health, and medicine in America*
(pp. 451–467). New Brunswick, NJ: Rutgers University Press.
Basham, A. L. (1976). The practice of medicine in ancient and medieval India. In C. Leslie (Ed.).
Asian medical systems: A comparative study (pp. 18–43). Berkeley, CA: University of
California Press.
Bell, S. E. (1989). Technology in medicine: Development, diffusion, and health policy. In H. E.
Freeman & S. Levine (Eds.). *Handbook of medical sociology* (4th Ed.) (pp. 185–204).
Englewood Cliffs, NJ: Prentice-Hall.
Bellakhdar, J. (1989). Pharmacopoeia and traditional medicine in Morocco. *Curare, 12,* 1:23–40.
Bernstein, B. J. (1994). The misguided quest for the artificial heart. In P. Conrad & R. Kern (Eds.).
The sociology of health and illness: Critical perspectives (4th Ed.) (pp. 344–350). New York:
St. Martin's Press.
Bogdan, J. C. (1992). Childbirth in America, 1650 to 1990. In R. D. Apple (Ed.). *Women, health, and
medicine in America* (pp. 101–120). New Brunswick, NJ: Rutgers University Press.
Bordley, J., & Harvey, A. M. (1976). *Two centuries of American medicine: 1776–1976.* Philadelphia:
WB Saunders Co.
Bridgman, R. F. (1974). Traditional Chinese medicine. In J. Z. Bowers & E. F. Purcell (Eds.).
Medicine and society in China (pp. 1–21). New York: Josiah Macy, Jr. Foundation.
Bullough, V. L. (1961). Status and medieval medicine. *Journal of Health and Human Behavior, 1,*
204–210.
Burnham, J. C. (1985). American medicine's golden age: What happened to it? In J. W. Leavitt &
R. L. Numbers (Eds.). *Sickness and health in America: Readings in the history of medicine
and public health* (pp. 248–258). Madison, WI: University of Wisconsin Press.
Cassedy, J. H. (1991). *Medicine in America: A short history.* Baltimore: The Johns Hopkins
University Press.
Castiglioni, A. (1947). *A history of medicine* (2nd Ed.) (revised and enlarged). Translated and
edited by E. B. Krumbhaar. New York: Alfred A. Knopf.
Chapman, A. R. (1994). Introduction. In A. R. Chapman (Ed.). *Health care reform: A human rights
approach* (pp. 1–32). Washington, DC: Georgetown University Press.

Chavunduka, G. L. (1986). Zinatha: The organisation of traditional medicine in Zimbabwe. In M. Last & G. L. Chavunduka (Eds.). *The professionalisation of African medicine* (pp. 29–49). Manchester, UK: Manchester University Press.

Cipolla, C. M. (1976). *Public health and the medical profession in the renaissance.* Cambridge: Cambridge University Press.

Clendening, L. (1960). *Source book of medical history.* New York: Dover Publications, Inc.

Coe, R. M. (1978). *Sociology of medicine* (2nd Ed.). New York: McGraw-Hill.

Committee on the Costs of Medical Care. (1932). *Medical care for the American people: The final report. Number 28.* Chicago: The University of Chicago Press.

Conrad, P., & Schneider, J. W. (1994). Professionalization, monopoly, and the structure of medical practice. In P. Conrad & R. Kern (Eds.). *The sociology of health and illness: Critical perspectives* (4th Ed.) (pp. 167–173). New York: St. Martin's Press.

Conrad, P. (1992). Medicalization and social control. *Annual Review of Sociology, 18,* 209–232.

DeBaz, P. (1975). *The story of medicine.* New York: Philosophical Library.

Dols, M. W. (1984). *Medieval Islamic medicine.* Berkeley, CA: University of California Press.

Duffy, J. (1993). *From humors to medical science: A history of American medicine* (2nd Ed.). Urbana, IL: University of Illinois Press.

Ergil, K. V. (1996). China's traditional medicine. In M. S. Micozzi (Ed.). *Fundamentals of complementary and alternative medicine* (pp. 185–223). New York: Churchill Livingstone.

Frenk, J., & Duran-Arenas, L. (1993). The medical profession and the state. In F. W. Hafferty & J. B. McKinlay (Eds.). *The changing medical profession: An international perspective* (pp. 25–42). New York: Oxford University Press.

Fuchs, V. R. (1993) *The future of health policy.* Cambridge, MA: Harvard University Press.

Garber, A. M. (1994). Can technology assessment control health spending? *Health Affairs, 13,* (1–3), 115–126.

Good, C. M. (1987). *Ethnomedical systems in Africa: Patterns of traditional medicine in rural and urban Kenya.* New York: The Guilford Press.

Gray, A. (Ed). (1993). *World health and disease.* Buckingham, UK: Open University Press.

Gray, B. H., & Osterweis, M. (1995). Ethical issues in a social context. In W. G. Rothstein (Ed.). *Readings in American health care: Current issues in socio-historical perspective* (pp. 392–406). Madison, WI: University of Wisconsin Press.

Haifeng, C. (1984). Brief history of public health in China. In C. Haifeng & Z. Chao (Eds.). *Modern Chinese medicine: Vol. 3—Chinese health care* (pp. 13–58). Lancaster: MTP Press Limited.

Hastings, P. (1974). *Medicine: An international history.* New York: Praeger.

Higby, G. J., & Gallagher, T. C. (1992). Pharmacists. In R. D. Apple (Ed.). *Women, health, and medicine in America: A historical handbook* (pp. 489–508). New Brunswick, NJ: Rutgers University Press.

Hurry, J. B. (1928). *IMHOTEP: The vizier and physician of King Zoser and afterwards the Egyptian god of medicine* (2nd and revised Ed.). Humphrey Milford: Oxford University Press.

Hyma, B., & Ramesh, A. (1994). Traditional medicine: Its extent and potential for incorporation into modern health systems. In D. R. Phillips & Y. Verhasselt (Eds.). *Health and development* (pp. 65–82). London: Routledge.

Iyun, B. (1994). Health care in the third world: Africa. In D. R. Phillips & Y. Verhasselt (Eds.). *Health and development* (pp. 249–258). London: Routledge.

Kett, J. F. (1968). *The formation of the American medical profession: The role of institutions, 1780–1860.* New Haven, CT: Yale University Press.

Kirby, J. P. (1993). The Islamic dialogue with African traditional religion: Divination and health care. *Social Science and Medicine, 36,* 3, 237–247.

Kumar, A. (1995). Gender and health: Theoretical versus practical accessibility of health care for women in north India. In E. B. Gallagher & J. Subedi (Eds.). *Global perspectives on health care* (pp. 16–31). Englewood Cliffs, NJ: Prentice-Hall.

Kutner, N. G. (1987). Issues in the application of high cost medical technology: The case of organ transplantation. *Journal of Health and Social Behavior, 28,* 23–36.

Leavitt, J. W., & Numbers, R. L. (1985). Sickness and health in America: An overview. In J. W. Leavitt & R. L. Numbers (Eds.). *Sickness and health in America: Readings in the history of medicine and public health* (2nd Ed.) (Revised) (pp. 3–10). Madison, WI: University of Wisconsin Press.

Leff, S., & Leff, V. (1958). *From witchcraft to world health.* New York: Macmillan.

Leslie, C. (1976). The ambiguities of medical revivalism in modern India. In C. Leslie (Ed.). *Asian medical systems: A comparative study* (pp. 356–367). Berkeley, CA: University of California Press.

Levine, S. (1987). The changing terrains in medical sociology: Emergent concern with quality of life. *Journal of Health and Social Behavior, 28,* 1, 1–6.

Light, D. W. (1993). Countervailing power: The changing character of the medical profession in the United States. In F. W. Hafferty & J. B. McKinlay (Eds.). *The changing medical profession: An international perspective* (pp. 69–79). New York: Oxford University Press.

Lopata, C. (1968). *Women in medicine.* Baltimore: The Johns Hopkins University Press.

Lundmerer, K. M. (1985). *Learning to heal: The development of American medical education.* Baltimore: The Johns Hopkins University Press.

Lynaugh, J. E. (1992). Institutionalizing women's health care in nineteenth- and twentieth-century America. In R. D. Apple (Ed.). *Women, health, and medicine in America: A historical handbook* (pp. 247–269). New Brunswick, NJ: Rutgers University Press.

Major, R. H. (1954a). *A history of medicine. Vol. 1.* Springfield, IL: Charles C. Thomas.

Major, R. H. (1954b). *A history of medicine. Vol. 2.* Springfield, IL: Charles C. Thomas.

Marti-Ibanez, F. (1960). *Henry E. Sigerist on the history of medicine.* New York: MD Publications, Inc.

McKeown, T. (1970). A sociological approach to the history of medicine. *Medical History, 14,* 342–351.

McKinlay, J. B., & McKinlay, S. M. (1977). The questionable contribution of medical measures to the decline of mortality in the United States in the twentieth century. *Milbank Memorial Fund Quarterly, 55,* 405–428.

McKinlay, J. B., and Stoeckle, J. D. (1994). Corporatization and the social transformation of doctoring. In P. Conrad & R. Kern (Eds.). *The sociology of health and illness: Critical perspectives* (4th Ed.) (pp. 186–197). New York: St. Martin's Press.

Mills, C. W. (1959). *The sociological imagination.* New York: Oxford.

Morantz–Sanchez, R. (1992). Physicians. In R. D. Apple (Ed.). *Women, health, and medicine in America: A historical handbook* (pp. 469–487). New Brunswick, NJ: Rutgers University Press.

Najman, J. M. (1989). Health care in developing countries. In H. E. Freeman & S. Levine (Eds.). *Handbook of medical sociology* (4th Ed.) (pp. 332–346). Englewood Cliffs, NJ: Prentice-Hall.

National Center for Health Statistics. (1994). *Health, United States, 1993.* Hyattsville, MD: Public Health Service.

National Center for Health Statistics. (1995). *Health, United States, 1994.* Hyattsville, MD: Public Health Service.

Navarro, V. (1984). Medical history as justification rather than explanation: A critique of Starr's The Social Transformation of American medicine. *International Journal of Health Services, 14* (4), 511–528.

Navarro, V. (1994). *The politics of health policy: The U.S. reforms, 1980–1994.* Cambridge, MA: Blackwell Publishers.

Navarro, V. (1996). Why Congress did not enact health care reform. In P. Brown (Ed). *Perspectives in medical sociology (*2nd Ed.*)* (pp. 582–589). Prospect Heights, IL: Waveland Press, Inc.

Newsome, F. (1979). Black contributions to the early history of Western medicine: Lack of recognition as a cause of black under-representation in US medical schools. *Journal of the National Medical Association, 71,* 2, 189–193.

Office of Technology Assessment. (1994). The changing health care system. In P. Conrad & R. Kern (Eds.). *The sociology of health and illness: Critical perspectives* (4th Ed.) (pp. 202–210). New York: St. Martin's Press.

Pagel, W. (1958). *Paracelsus: An introduction to philosophical medicine in the era of the renaissance.* Basel: S. Karger.

Perry, H. B. III. (1988). Health in the developing world: An overview of obstacles and opportunities. In C. I. Zeichner (Ed.). *Modern and traditional health care in developing societies: Conflict and co-operation* (pp. 3–19). Lanham, MD: University Press of America.

Pickett, A. C. (1992). The oath of Imhotep: In recognition of African contributions to western medicine. *Journal of the National Medical Association, 84* (7), 636–637.

Ratcliff, K. S. (1989). Health technologies for women: Whose health? Whose technology? In K. S. Ratcliff, M. M. Ferree, G. O. Mellow, B. D. Wright, G. D. Price, K. Yanoshik, & M. S. Freston (Eds.). *Healing technology: Feminist perspectives* (pp. 173–198). Ann Arbor: University of Michigan Press.

Reverby, S. (1994). A caring dilemma: Womanhood and nursing in historical perspective. In P. Conrad & R. Kern (Eds.). *The sociology of health and illness: Critical perspectives* (4th Ed.) (pp. 210–221). New York: St. Martin's Press.

Roemer, M. I. (Ed). (1960). *Henry E. Sigerist on the sociology of medicine.* New York: MD Publications

Roemer, M. I. (1991). *National health systems of the world. Vol. 1: The countries.* New York: Oxford University Press.

Ru-Kang, F. (1994). Health, environment and health care in the People's Republic of China. In D. R. Phillips & Y. Verhasselt (Eds). *Health and development* (pp. 259–275). London: Routledge.

Schneider, J. W. (1993). Family care work and duty in a "modern" Chinese hospital. In P. Conrad & E. B. Gallagher (Eds.). *Health and health care in developing countries* (pp. 154–179). Philadelphia: Temple University Press.

Schwartz, W. B. (1994). In the pipeline: A wave of valuable medical technology. *Health Affairs, 13* (1–3), 70–79.

Senah, K. A. (1995). Ethnomedicine in the context of health care delivery in Ghana. In E. B. Gallagher & J. Subedi (Eds.). *Global perspectives on health care* (pp. 109–120). Englewood Cliffs, NJ: Prentice-Hall.

Sidel, V. W., & Sidel, R. (1973). *Serve the people: Observations on medicine in the People's Republic of China.* New York: Josiah Macy Jr. Foundation.

Sidel, V. W. (1974). Health services in the People's Republic of China. In J. Z. Bowers & E. F. Purcell (Eds.). *Medicine and society in China* (pp. 103–127). New York: Josiah Macy Jr. Foundation.

Sigerist, H. E. (1951). *A history of medicine. Vol. 1: Primitive and archaic medicine.* New York: Oxford University Press.

Sigerist, H. E. (1961). *A history of medicine. Vol. II: Early Greek, Hindu, and Persian medicine.* New York: Oxford University Press.

Slikkerveer, L. J. (1982). Rural health developments in Ethiopia: Problems of utilization of traditional healers. *Social Science and Medicine, 16,* 1859–1972.

Starr, P. (1982). *The social transformation of American medicine.* New York: Basic Books.

Stevens, R. (1971). *American medicine and the public interest.* New Haven, CT: Yale University Press.

Stubbs, S. G. B., & Bligh, E. W. (1931). *Sixty centuries of health and physick: The progress of ideas from primitive magic to modern society.* London: Sampson Low, Marston & Co.

Ulin, P. R. (1980). Introduction: Traditional healers and primary health care in Africa. In P. R. Ulin & M. H. Segall (Eds.). *Traditional health care delivery in contemporary Africa* (pp. 1–11). Syracuse, NY: Maxwell School of Citizenship and Public Affairs.

Unschuld, P. U. (1985). *Medicine in China: A history of ideas.* Berkeley, CA: University of Californian Press.

U.S. Bureau of the Census. (1989). Current Population Reports, Series P-25, No. 1018. *Projections of the Population of the United States, by age, sex, and race: 1988 to 2080,* by Gregory Spencer. Washington, DC: U.S. Government Printing Office.

U.S. Department of Health, Education, and Welfare. (1968). *Vital Statistics of the United States, 1950. Vol. 1.* Table 8.26. New York: Greenwood Press.

Venzmer, G. (1972). *Five thousand years of medicine.* (Translated by M. Koenig). New York: Taplinger Publishing.

Walker, K. (1955). *The story of medicine.* New York: Oxford University Press.

Wertz, R. W., & Wertz, D. C. (1994). Notes on the decline of midwives and the rise of medical obstetricians. In P. Conrad & R. Kern (Eds.). *The sociology of health and illness: Critical perspectives* (4th Ed.) (pp. 174–186). New York: St. Martin's Press.

World Development Report. (1993). *Investing in health.* New York: Oxford University Press.

Zysk, K. G. (1996). Traditional Ayurveda. In M. S. Micozzi (Ed.). *Fundamentals of complementary and alternative medicine* (pp. 233–242). New York: Churchill Livingstone.

3

Epidemiology and Medicine

Modern demographic interests have paralleled some long-standing concerns of a branch of medical investigation, variously labeled public health, preventive medicine, and community medicine. This concern has also been interested in death rates, primarily as an index of the health of population under study. It has also had as a primary focus the study of disease in populations, especially epidemics.

As social patterns have been demonstrated to influence disease and death rate patterns, the measurement of social structures and identities has been incorporated into traditional epidemiology, producing what has come to be known as social epidemiology.

—Twaddle and Hessler, 1987, p. 84

Sociological Explanations of Health Outcomes

Chapters 1 and 2 established the sociological and historical frameworks out of which medical sociology emerged. Beginning with Chapter 3, the importance of sociological explanations relative to health outcomes within and between various population groups in the social environment becomes increasingly evident. It is this application of analytical insights that demonstrates the intellectual value of medical sociology to the health-care community. More specifically, the importance of this chapter lies in its application of group level characteristics to questions of living and dying. Thus, the reader is exposed to differential outcomes regarding life and death that are based on social, rather than biological, determinants. Furthermore, these social determinants are understood as interrelated rather than isolated incidents. This realization will become particularly important as specific aspects of health and illness behavior are examined in subsequent chapters.

A Brief History of Epidemiology

A basic definition of **epidemiology** states that it is "the study of factors related to the distribution of disease in a population" (Coe, 1978, p. 10). This definition provides the historical basis upon which modern-day epidemiology is based. Although epidemiology is primarily associated with areas such as public health and medicine (see Terris, 1987), it is also interconnected with the social sciences. Ashton (1994, p. ix) comments that "it is my view that social science and the epidemiological method are part and parcel of the same culture of inquiry and understanding aimed at improving the human condition." Helman (1994) offers an extensive listing of cultural factors (ranging from economics to contraceptive patterns) that are related to epidemiology. Relative to sociology, Susser (1975, p. 616) states that

> every epidemiological variable is in some sense a sociological variable. But these variables also have social meaning, and their distribution in populations implies a particular configuration of statuses in society; each of these statuses carries its own set of obligations and duties and social relations. The factors affecting the distribution of disease in populations may be biological or environmental, and both have social implications.

As an example of the interrelationship between epidemiology and sociology, Gilbert (1995, p. 122), in an assessment of public health in South Africa, argues that "public health problems are social problems." In other words, Gilbert (1995) argues that the problems of health and the broader social problems are the result of similar social phenomena.

All of this however, does not imply that medical sociology and epidemiology are interchangeable areas of study. Although they both utilize similar variables, their interpretations differ. For instance, epidemiology has historically been connected with the public health movement. As a result, epidemiology has generally examined variables such as age, sex, and marital status within biological terms. Sociology, however, is interested in more than the distribution of these variables within a given population. A sociological interpretation addresses the fact that these variables represent "a particular configuration of statuses in society; [and that] each of these statuses carries its own set of obligations and duties and social relations" (Susser, 1975, p. 617).

A historical assessment of epidemiology draws on the work of many individuals; most notably John Snow, Edwin Chadwick, William Farr, William Budd, John Sutherland, and Ignaz Philipp Semmelweis. Although these individuals are some of the best known historical figures in epidemiology, others in the discipline have made contributions as well. There is, however, little agreement on the origin of epidemiology. For example, Paffenbarger (1977) reminds us that applications of epidemiological methods can be traced to fifteenth century Italy, whereas Schuman (1986) offers a detailed outline of selected historical figures (primarily American) beginning in the early eighteenth century. However, Brockington (1977) traces knowledge of a relationship between a particular disease and behavior back hundreds of years. For example, Brockington (1977, p. 2) states that "the connexion between marshy terrain and malaria had been noted in Roman times and certainly by the eighteenth century drainage had proved itself to be an effective preventive." Similarly, Terris (1987) outlines the public health contributions of the French that predate efforts in England. Terris (1987, p. 318) also states that the first known use of the word "epidemiology" can be traced to a Spanish text published in 1802 by Don Joaquin de Villalba entitled *Epidemiologia Espanola*. Utilizing the work of Lilienfeld and Lilienfeld (1977) and others, only the most significant individuals are located within their appropriate historical time period.

Epidemiology begins with the work of Sir Percival Potts, who was one of the first physicians to recommend a specific treatment for a defined population. An English physician in the latter seventeenth century, Potts observed that men engaged as chimney sweeps had high rates of scrotal cancer. Reasoning that soot was the cause of their increased risk, Potts "prescribed that chimney sweeps bathe after cleaning chimneys to remove the causal agent" (Denton, 1978, p. 53). In the midnineteenth century in Austria, Simmelweis hypothesized that the high rates of maternal **mortality** at the General Hospital in Vienna were related to improper physician hygiene prior to examinations of women in labor. Simmelweis based his argument on observations of two hospitals, one for the training of doctors, the other for the training of midwives. He noted that maternal mortality was considerably lower in the hospital for midwives. Simmelweis also noted that women, who delivered fast, with little opportunity for student doctors to examine them, had lower maternal mortality rates. The problem, according to Simmelweis, was that students and doctors conducting postmortem examinations infected their fingers as they handled the cadaver. Women in the maternity section then seen by the doctor or student became infected with puerperal fever, a form of blood poisoning (Sigerist, 1971). His hypothesis was supported when he "insisted that the students and other medical personnel in his wards scrub their hands in soap and water and then soak them in chlorinated lime before conducting pelvic examinations . . . Within seven months . . . the mortality rate in the wards staffed by medical students dipped below that in the wards of the student midwives" (Rockett, 1994, p. 7). Unfortunately, his findings were rejected for years by many within the medical profession. Resigning his position, Simmelweis moved to another hospital and encountered similar reactions from his colleagues. Eventually placed in an asylum, Simmelweis died as a result of the disease he had attempted to teach others to avoid (Walker, 1955).

A brief historical overview of epidemiology also includes the work of William Budd, who established the contagious nature of tuberculosis 15 years before the tubercle bacillus was identified (Wilner, Walkley, & Goerke, 1973). Others such as Sutherland established a causal connection between an outbreak of cholera and its transmission via the water system (Lilienfeld & Lilienfeld, 1977). Prior to Sutherland was Edwin Chadwick, "a reformist who argued that disease engendered by the physical environment caused poverty" (Susser & Susser, 1996a, p. 669). Chadwick was a lawyer–journalist who, in the mid-1830s was named Secretary of the Poor Law Commission. In this capacity, Chadwick was able to secure approval for the inclusion of cause of death on the Registration of Death Bill. He was also influential in ensuring the hiring of William Farr, a statistician. With an outbreak of typhus fever in London in 1838, Chadwick was able to chart the location of those who died and concluded that death was related to living conditions and that age at death was related to social class (Cartwright, 1977).

The most celebrated example of epidemiology however, is that of John Snow and the 1854 cholera outbreak in London. Earlier, Snow had studied the effects of cholera among coal-miners and in 1849 had written a pamphlet detailing his "opinion that the contagious matter was thrown off from the diseased intestine and might enter the system in polluted water" (Smith, 1941, p. 53). During the 1849 outbreak of cholera in London, Snow calculated death rates by section of the city and by the source of the water supply (Susser, 1973). Another cholera epidemic in 1854 produced the infamous removal of the water pump handle at the Broad Street Pump. Snow arrived at this conclusion following his investigation of some 500 deaths from cholera around the Broad Street Pump of London. His investigation revealed that the vast majority of those who died lived near the pump from which they drew their drinking water. Snow also found that among those who did not live nearby but nevertheless died from cholera, preferred the water from the Broad Street pump. Extending his investigation (what he referred to as the "grand experiment"), Snow examined water pipelines and demonstrated that the likelihood of cholera was related to a specific water pipeline company (Smith, 1941). The outcome of his work, however, "remained for more than a century conceptually separate from the concerns of medicine with its focus on cure" (Lyons, 1993, pp. 303–304).

The significance of Snow to the field of epidemiology was his inclusion of "the physical, chemical, biological, sociological and political processes. All these present as underlying trends, outstanding single cases and other tendencies which in their totality point clearly to a theory of cause and mechanism of infection" (Cameron & Jones, 1983, p. 395). The qualities espoused by Snow are reexamined within the context of modern epidemiology. The movement of epidemiology into the twentieth century has produced an increasingly focused and quantitatively based discipline. At the same time, the epidemiological triangle, which consists of the three elements of agent, host, and environment, has become the basic framework within which current research has progressed. Epidemiological research examines "such things as dietary insufficiencies and excesses, chemical agents, allergens, physical agents, and infectious organisms" as the agent; "attributes of individuals that influence exposure to agents, and susceptibility to disease following exposure" relate to the host;

BOX 3.1

Eleven Blue Men

In the fall of 1944 in New York City, Roueché (1953) chronicles a series of events that represents a truly unique example of epidemiological research. In this example, the three elements of agent, host, and environment (and their interrelationships) are located within a particular set of circumstances.

Unexpectedly, and all within a very short period of time, 11 men were brought to various hospitals, all with the same visible symptom; their skin tone was blue. Carbon monoxide poisoning, the initial diagnosis, was quickly discarded.

All 11 men not only had breakfast at the same cafeteria, they had all had oatmeal. Although health investigators suspected food poisoning, these men did not display symptoms consistent with such a diagnosis. The investigation soon moved to the cafeteria and the personnel employed there. In conversations with the cook, it was discovered that he had inadvertently poured sodium nitrite instead of sodium nitrate into the oatmeal. However, that would not explain why only 11 men became ill with sodium nitrite poisoning, when more than 100 had eaten the oatmeal. On further investigation it was discovered that a busboy had filled one of the salt containers with sodium nitrite instead of salt. Again, the question remained unanswered as to why only these 11 men were stricken with sodium nitrite poisoning. The answer did not emerge until one of the investigators remembered that all of the men were heavy drinkers. Heavy drinkers lack salt in their diet, and as a result, are more likely to substitute salt for sugar in their food. The investigators surmised that these men had eaten at the same table and, using the salt shaker filled with sodium nitrite, gave themselves a double dose of sodium nitrite poisoning.

Roueché, B. (1953). *Eleven Blue Men and Other Narratives of Medical Detection.* Boston: Little, Brown & Company.

---

whereas the environment refers to physical, biological, and socioeconomic factors (Peterson & Thomas, 1978, p. 23). Recently, the role of the agent has been diminishing, with greater emphasis placed on the relationship between the host and the environment (see Cassel, 1976, for an example of the relationship between the social environment and the host). The interrelationship of these three variables is illustrated in the following example. As you read the example (Box 3.1), identify the agent, host, and environment.

Historical Periods in Epidemiology

Historically, the times since the late eighteenth century have been witness to a significant evolution within epidemiology. Throughout most of the nineteenth century (the first era in the development of modern epidemiology), the prevailing theoretical argument regarding the cause of disease was called *miasma,* or "poisoning by foul emanations from the soil, water, and environing air" (Susser & Susser, 1996a, p. 669). This era is in response to the emerging industrial base in the United States and other Western nations. During this era, industrial concerns for human or environmental degradation were minimal.

The second historical period in the development of epidemiology is referred to as "infectious disease epidemiology with its paradigm, the germ theory" (Susser & Susser, 1996a, p. 668). This period began in the latter half of the nineteenth century and ended at the midpoint of the twentieth century. Building on the knowledge base established in the first era, the work of Henle, Pasteur, and Koch isolated single source agents responsible for specific diseases. Although significant advances were made in the eradication of infectious diseases, the role of epidemiology changed from discovery of disease patterns to control of the disease (Susser & Susser, 1996a).

The third historical period is that of "chronic disease epidemiology with its paradigm, the black box" (Susser & Susser, 1996a, pp. 668–669). Beginning at the close of World War II, this historical period faced increased medical and health-related consequences as a result of changing demographics and lifestyles. Within this paradigm, the "black box" refers to relating "exposure to outcome without any necessary obligation to interpolate either intervening factors or even pathogenesis" (Susser & Susser, 1996a, p. 669), or, as Lilienfeld and Lilienfeld (1982, p. 147) point out, "the most dangerous aspect of the state of our discipline today is that there is an unhealthy emphasis on HOW one conducts an epidemiologic study and not WHY and WHAT one does in such a study." Historically, Susser (1985) provides an extensive analysis of American epidemiology since World War II. Although modern epidemiology continues to utilize a black-box approach, others (Pearce, 1996; Susser & Susser, 1996b) have begun to define a new era in the historical development of epidemiology. This latest era is referred to as *eco-epidemiology,* with Chinese boxes as the paradigm. This paradigm refers to the development of tiered structural interrelationships (Susser & Susser, 1996b). An explanation regarding these efforts to redirect the focus of epidemiology can be found in Pearce (1996, p. 682), who points out that:

> Epidemiology has become a set of generic methods for measuring associations of exposure and disease in individuals, rather than functioning as part of a multidisciplinary approach to understanding the causation of disease in populations.

In response, Susser and Susser (1996b, p. 675) argue that "ecologism entails localization and attention to the bounds that limit generalizations about biological, human, and social systems." Although this proposed era expounds the value of a systems level approach, the authors also address the continued need for multiple levels of analysis within epidemiology. The future of this era lies in the ability of those who purport the significance of such a paradigm to demonstrate its relevance to the field of epidemiology.

A further understanding of epidemiology is provided through the epidemiological transition. Here, epidemiology is viewed as a process involving key concepts such as mortality rates and life expectancy within a historical framework.

The Epidemiological Transition

The **epidemiological transition**

> focuses on the complex change in patterns of health and disease *and* on the interactions between these patterns and their demographic, economic, and sociologic determinants and consequences. (Orman, 1971, p. 510)

Orman (1971) identified three stages of change in health and disease. These stages are (1) the Age of Pestilence and Famine, (2) the Age of Receding Pandemics, and (3) the Age of Degenerative and Human-made Disease (see, Orman, 1971, Table 4, for an extensive description of each stage). The characteristics of each stage have been summarized by Olshansky and Ault (1986) and are presented here. Stage 1 is a period of high mortality rates over an extended period of time. Death rates are particularly high among the younger aged members of the population and life expectancy rates for those under age 40 are relatively low. Stage 2 is a period of demographic change. Here, mortality rates begin to decline because of increased awareness in public health outcomes. Because of decreasing infant mortality rates, populations begin to age and experience death from degenerative diseases. In effect, the location of death is shifted to older ages from previously younger ages. Life expectancy increases to about age 50. Kalipeni (1995) identifies Malawi, one of the poorest countries in the world, as an example of a nation caught between the first and second stages. In stage 3, mortality rates stabilize as the limits of mortality decline are reached. Deaths are the result of chronic degenerative diseases and occur primarily among the elderly. Because of decreased infant mortality rates and lower mortality rates among the elderly, life expectancy increases to the seventh decade.

Olshansky and Ault (1986) expand on the epidemiological transition by adding stage 4, which they believe is representative of current disease and mortality patterns. Essentially, they argue that many of the elements that define stage 3 are also characteristic of stage 4. The difference is that the likelihood of death from chronic degenerative diseases continues to be pushed even further into old age. The shifting of disease and death to progressively older ages has an impact on the larger society. Olshansky and Ault (1986, p. 378) state that this shift will "have numerous impacts on two major demographic variables, the size and relative proportions of the population in advanced ages, and the health and vitality of the elderly." The implications associated with this stage have a direct impact on the sociology of health care in the United States and throughout the world.

Throughout the historical framework of epidemiology, a number of specific indicators associated with social and medical outcomes have emerged (e.g., life expectancy, mortality, morbidity). The meaning and significance of these indicators are addressed in the following section.

Epidemiological Indicators of Social and Medical Outcomes

The following pages examine the meaning and importance associated with those basic indicators of health and health status that are utilized in the field of epidemiology. These indicators represent more than numerical rates. They offer a basis for comparison between as well as within nations. For example, the data in the following tables indicate that the mortality rate in the United States is still considerably higher than most other Western industrialized nations. At the same time, overall life expectancy among Americans remains below that of other Western industrialized nations. In addition, these indicators (life expectancy and infant mortality) along with the literacy rate (a nonhealth-related variable) can be calculated into a Physical Quality of Life Index (PQLI) score (Morris, 1976). Because of the variables utilized, the index addresses outcomes within societies, rather than inputs. Thus, nations with relatively low per capita GNP may, depending on the health-care system, experience higher PQLI scores than countries that allocate considerably more per capita GNP on health care.

Before examining the indicators of health and illness, there are two additional concepts that are central to epidemiology: **incidence** and **prevalence.** *Incidence* is the number of new cases associated with a particular condition within a given period of time. *Prevalence* refers to the total number of (living) cases associated with a particular condition. An example of these two concepts is acquired immunodeficiency syndrome (AIDS). According to the National Center for Health Statistics (1995), the number of new cases (incidence) for the year 1993 is 103,463. The estimated prevalence of human immunodeficiency virus (HIV) in North America, Europe, and Australia by mid-1995 is more than 1–2 million. The estimated prevalence of HIV worldwide by 1995 is 14–15 million (d'Cruz-Grote, 1996). Kurtz and Chalfant (1991, pp. 24–26) demonstrate the relationship between incidence and prevalence in a 2 × 2 table and describe four possible patterns. The two most common patterns involve the transition from high incidence and high prevalence rates to low incidence and low prevalence rates—in other words, a condition beginning as an epidemic and eventually leading to low rates not only among new cases, but among the total as well. Polio is an example of a medical condition applicable to this pattern. The other pattern identified as being relatively common is the reverse of the first. Here, incidence and prevalence rates begin at very low rates, with both reaching epidemic proportions. According to Kurtz and Chalfant (1991, p. 25), "AIDS . . . among young adult homosexual males and intravenous drug users" is an example of the second pattern.

Mortality

Perhaps the most fundamental indication of the health of a society is the rate of death experienced by its members. This section demonstrates how to calculate the mortality rate within a given population and compare the most recent rates available between the United States and selected nations. The *mortality rate* is defined as the total number of deaths in a given population in a given period of time divided by the total population. Multiplying the outcome by 1,000 provides a rate useful for comparative purposes. Consider the following statistics from the National Center for Health Statistics, 1996:

$$\frac{\text{Total number of deaths in a given population for a given period of time}}{\text{Total population at a given period in time}} \times 1{,}000 = \text{Mortality rate}$$

Thus, for the 12-month period ending in February, 1996:

$$\frac{2{,}314{,}000 \text{ Deaths}}{263{,}200{,}000 \text{ Total population}} \times 1{,}000 = 8.8 \text{ (Mortality rate)}$$

Compare the mortality rate in the United States with rates in Table 3.1. How would you explain the higher mortality rates in many of the industrialized countries relative to the developing nations? From an epidemiological perspective, when would you expect most deaths to occur—among those who are youngest, middle-aged, or oldest? The answer is obviously among those who are oldest. In fact, almost 75 percent of the deaths in the United States occur among persons aged 65 and older. Examine the data in Table 3.2. Here we have **age-specific death rates.** The data in Table 3.2 illustrate that as one ages the rate of death increases. Because the United States and many of the other industrialized nations have increasingly aged societies, it is not surprising that their death rates are higher than many developing nations that have relatively younger populations.

Infant Mortality

A more specific age-related death is that of infant mortality, which refers to the number of deaths within the first year of life per 1,000 live births. This is "the best available overall indicator of health and development status" (World Health Organization, 1995, p. 5). Although the economic level of development is perhaps the best indicator of infant mortality, there are exceptions. For example, consider the data in Table 3.3. Cuba, with a centrally planned health-care system, is a developing country with a low infant mortality rate. The Philippines, another developing country but with an entrepreneurial health-care system, has a much higher infant mortality rate. It is evident that in addition to level of economic development, variables such as the type of the health-care system can influence the infant mortality rate within a society. In the United States, as in other industrialized nations, infant mortality rates have decreased dramatically throughout the twentieth century. The decline in infant mortality (and concomitant increase in life expectancy) has been the result of im-

TABLE 3.1   Crude Death Rates for Selected Industrialized Countries: 1995

Country	Crude Death Rate[1]
United States	8.8[2]
Australia	7.4
Austria	10.3
Canada	7.4
Burundi	21.5
Chile	5.4
Denmark	11.1
Czech Republic	10.9
France	9.3
Israel	6.4
Japan	7.5
Mexico	4.6
United Kingdom	10.7
Venezuela	4.6

[1] Number of deaths during 1 year per 1,000 persons (based on midyear population)

[2] Midyear 1996 data (National Center for Health Statistics, 1996)

Source: U.S. Bureau of the Census. (1995). *Statistical Abstract of the United States: 1995* (115th ed.). Washington, DC.

TABLE 3.2   Provisional Age-Adjusted Death Rates, United States: 12 Months Ending January 1996

Age	Number of Deaths	Cumulative Percent of Deaths	Rate
Under 1 year	29,000	1.3	753.0[1]
1–4 years	6,540	0.3	41.6
5–14 years	8,300	0.4	21.7
15–24 years	34,480	1.5	95.9
25–34 years	57,920	2.5	141.9
35–44 years	102,750	4.4	241.3
45–54 years	142,310	6.2	455.9
55–64 years	234,010	10.1	1,106.4
65–74 years	477,640	20.7	2,546.5
75–84 years	651,990	28.2	5,834.9
85 years +	562,920	24.4%	15,447.9

[1] Death rates for "under 1 year" (based on population estimates) differ from infant mortality rates (based on live births); see Table 3.3 for infant mortality rates

Source: National Center for Health Statistics. (1996). Births, marriages, divorces, and deaths for February 1996. *Monthly Vital Statistics Report, 45*, 2. Table 5. Hyattsville, MD: Public Health Service.

TABLE 3.3   Infant Mortality Rates, Selected Countries: 1995 and 2000

Country	Infant Mortality Rate[1]	
	1995	*2000*
Afghanistan	152.8	137.5
Austria	6.9	6.2
Belgium	7.0	6.3
Canada	6.8	6.2
Cuba	8.1	7.5
France	6.5	5.9
Haiti	107.5	102.2
India	76.3	65.8
Israel	8.4	7.5
Mexico	26.0	20.7
Philippines	49.6	44.4
Sweden	5.6	5.2
Turkey	45.6	33.3
United Kingdom	7.0	6.3

[1] Number of deaths of children under 1 year of age per 1,000 live births in a calendar year

Source: U.S. Bureau of the Census. (1995). *Statistical Abstract of the United States: 1995* (115th ed.) Washington, DC.

proved public health measures, not improved medical technology (DuBos, 1959; McKinlay & McKinlay, 1977; Armstrong, 1980).

Finally, infant mortality rates are calculated using the same format as with death rates. To determine the infant mortality rate (IMR) for a particular period of time, divide the total number of infant deaths by the total number of live births and multiply by 1,000.

$$\frac{\text{Number of infant deaths}}{\text{Total number of live births}} \times 1,000 = \text{IMR}$$

The following example from Rosenberg et al. (1996) represents preliminary 1995 figures for the United States and shows a mortality rate of 7.5.

$$\frac{29,338}{3,900,089} \times 1,000 = 7.5$$

Alone, the number is meaningless. However, by comparing the rate to that of other countries, the rate for the United States is understood within a broader context.

The data in Table 3.3 indicate that relative to other Western industrialized nations, the United States has a high IMR. There are various interpretations of the rate and the position of the United States in comparison with other industrialized nations. Critics of the American health-care system would argue that because the United States does not have a universal health-care system, many expectant mothers do not receive adequate prenatal care.

After childbirth, children born into poverty are more likely to experience the vicissitudes of the social and physical environment in which they are being raised. Others would argue that the IMR is higher because of the heterogeneity of the American population relative to many of the European nations. A better understanding of this argument occurs by looking more carefully at the IMR and differentiating between deaths that occur between birth and less than 28 days (**neonatal**) and deaths occurring between day 28 and 11 months (**postneonatal**).

In 1995 there were 29,338 infant deaths, with 64 percent of these deaths occurring within the first 28 days of life. More specifically, Table 3.4 presents the neonatal and postneonatal rates by race. The data indicate that neonatal and postneonatal death rates decreased for both African Americans and Caucasians. However, changes in neonatal death rates were greater than postneonatal death rates for both races. Calculating the difference between neonatal and postneonatal death rates by race provides another interpretation of the data. In 1980, the African American neonatal death rate was 0.88 times greater than that for Caucasians. By 1995, the African American neonatal death rate was 1.40 times greater. At the same

TABLE 3.4 Neonatal and Postneonatal Death Rates by Race: 1980 and 1995

Race	Neonatal		Change (%) 1980–1995
	1980	*1995*	
White	7.5	4.0	−46.7
Black	14.1	9.6	−31.9

Race	Postneonatal		Change (%) 1980–1995
	1980	*1995*	
White	3.5	2.2	−37.1
Black	7.3	5.6	−23.3

Source: Data compiled from National Center for Health Statistics. (1985). *Vital Statistics of the United States, 1980. Vol. II. Mortality,* Part A. Table 2-4. DHHS Pub. No. (PHS) 85-1101. Public Health Service, Washington, DC. U.S. Government Printing Office; and Rosenberg, H. M., Ventura, S. J., Maurer, J. D., et al. (1996). Births and deaths: United States, 1995. *Monthly Vital Statistics Report, 45,* 3, suppl. 2, Table 13. Hyattsville, MD: National Center for Health Statistics.

time, postneonatal death rates among African Americans were 1.08 times greater than Caucasians in 1980 and 1.54 times greater in 1995. This observation is important because reductions in neonatal death rates are generally attributed to increased levels of health-related technology, whereas a decline in the postneonatal death rate is related to one's environment (Wolinsky, 1988). The data indicate that between 1980 and 1995, the difference between Caucasian and African American infant neonatal and postneonatal death rates increased although overall rates decreased. These findings suggest continued differences in health-care access and opportunities on the basis of race.

The data in Table 3.3 also identify the IMR for a number of developing nations. There are various reasons why the rate of infant deaths is higher in developing countries. One significant explanation is birthweight. In developing countries, 3 to 4 of every 10 infant deaths is the result of low birthweight (Price, 1994). By comparison, around 10 percent of infant deaths in 1995 in the United States were attributed to "disorders relating to short gestation and unspecified low birthweight" (Rosenberg et al., 1996, p. 27). Furthermore, the "high (infant) mortality rates are due primarily to preventable communicable diseases and malnutrition, reflecting the poverty-stricken environment of (less-developed countries) LDCs" (Kloos, 1994, p. 205). It is also important to remember that the relationship between infant mortality rates and level of health-care resources is weak (Kim & Moody, 1992). As a result, many families in developing countries continue to have a large number of children because of the fear that many will die in early childhood. One of the problems with infant mortality rates in developing countries is the difference in rates between rural and urban populations. Paul (1990) identifies such a difference in the rates between urban and rural Bangladesh. Urban population centers are likely to have lower IMR because of better public health facilities relative to their rural counterparts. However, in a review of the literature, Paul (1990) indicates that IMRs are not consistent, but differ between the rural regions of Bangladesh. Thus, variables such as access to land for farming, the size of the land, and the size of family are all related to differential rates of infant mortality in Bangladesh. As with many of the other indicators of health, the socioeconomic determinants within society are inextricably linked to health status as measured by IMR. Shah and Shah (1990, p. 251) found that "infant mortality . . . varies substantially according to socioeconomic factors such as the education of the mother, the income of the household and place of birth." Furthermore, Campbell (1989) argues that changes in IMR among native Americans in Montana must be understood within a political economy framework. That is, "health is socially defined, not biomechanically defined" (Campbell, 1989, p. 141). In other words, we must consider the impact of historical and economic conditions on the health of a population. Relative to the "American Indians, the core problem is lack of power and control over economic, political, and social institutions" (Campbell, 1989, p. 141). Thus, it should be obvious why the IMR is such a good indicator of the health status of a given population. If the IMR is high, one would expect adult mortality to be high as well (Gray, 1993).

Morbidity

In addition to the rate of death, epidemiologists are also interested in **morbidity,** or the occurrence of disease and/or disability experienced within given populations. Morbidity patterns are a reflection of the basic demographic characteristics of a society, its level of development, and the degree of medical and public health knowledge. For example, at the turn of the twentieth century, the most common causes of death were from infectious diseases. Progressing through the twentieth century, the population of the United States (as well as other industrialized nations) has aged, resulting in death from chronic diseases such as cancer and heart conditions. For example, Uutela and Tuomilehto (1992) point to the relationship between lifestyle (tobacco usage) and chronic health problems.

The data in Table 3.5 reveals a number of interesting relationships. First, the rate of acute conditions generally decreases with age. At the same time, Table 3.6 reveals the opposite relationship; an increasing rate of chronic conditions with increasing age. The second significant relationship in Table 3.5 is the rate of acute conditions between males and females. Not surprisingly, females have slightly higher rates of acute conditions (except for injuries). The higher rates of injuries among males could be attributed to lifestyle, occupational, and risk-taking differences when compared to females. The data reveal that racial differences are mixed, whereas regional differences suggest higher rates of acute illness in the west. Finally, the relationship of family income with acute conditions is dependent on the specific illness (U.S. Bureau of the Census, 1996).

Table 3.6 addresses the prevalence rate of various chronic conditions by age and sex. The data indicate that, depending on condition, a number of relationships with age and sex can be identified.

A comparison of the findings on the basis of age and sex reveals a number of differing outcomes. For example, arthritis increases with age, particularly among females. This relationship is generally true for all identified chronic conditions except heart conditions (U.S. Bureau of the Census, 1996).

Examining how patients cope with chronic illness, de Ridder et al. (1997) employed concept mapping to study coping beliefs regarding illness and the healthcare system among patient organizations in the Netherlands. Concept mapping initially involves the use of free association by the patient to elicit what are referred to as "content" and "priority" dimensions. With the aid of a computer, "the individual arrangements are then calculated into a group map in which the relative importance and the relationships of the association . . . are presented" (de Ridder, et al., 1997, p. 554). The authors also report that in addition to acceptance of the illness, patients prefer maintaining autonomy. This is particularly important, as the patient becomes dependent on the physician. Within a similar context, Bury (1991) argues that chronic illness must be understood within a multidimensional framework.

Within many Third World countries today, "respiratory tract infectious diseases together account for 52 percent of morbidity" (Gray, 1993b, p. 25). In addition, the effects of industrialization (i.e., pollution, unsanitary living and working environments) in many developing nations also lead to increased levels of disease

TABLE 3.5 Acute Conditions by Type: 1970–1994[1]

Year and Characteristic	Infective and Parasitic	Rate per 100 Population		Digestive System	Injuries
		Common Cold	*Influenza*		
1970	24.1	(NA)	(NA)	11.5	29.6
1975	22.8	(NA)	(NA)	10.3	36.4
1980	24.6	(NA)	(NA)	11.4	33.4
1985	20.5	(NA)	(NA)	7.0	27.4
1990	21.0	25.0	43.4	5.3	24.4
1992	22.4	25.7	42.7	7.0	23.7
1993	21.3	26.8	52.2	6.3	24.4
1994, total[2]	20.9	25.4	34.8	6.1	23.8
Under 5 years old	54.7	68.5	37.3	10.5	25.6
5–17 years old	41.9	29.4	46.3	8.3	26.0
18–24 years old	18.5	26.1	38.7	7.4	32.7
25–44 years old	14.6	22.4	37.8	4.7	25.0
45–64 years old	7.7	16.6	25.9	4.1	17.2
65 years old and older	5.2	12.3	18.3	5.6	19.6
Male	18.8	24.0	34.1	5.5	25.8
Female	22.8	26.8	35.5	6.7	22.0
White	21.6	24.3	36.5	5.7	24.8
Black	20.2	29.3	23.2	8.9	20.6
Northeast	24.5	29.4	26.0	5.2	20.2
Midwest	16.6	23.3	42.5	5.2	25.2
South	24.4	19.4	25.0	6.7	23.6
West	17.0	33.3	49.1	7.0	25.8
Family Income					
Under $10,000	16.2	34.4	38.0	10.1	33.9
$10,000–$19,999	18.4	26.0	31.3	8.0	25.1
$20,000–$34,999	20.7	25.1	38.5	5.7	23.0
$35,000 or more	24.6	25.4	38.0	5.1	22.0

NA, not available.

[1] Covers civilian noninstitutional population. Estimates include only acute conditions that were medically attended or caused at least 1 day of restricted activity. Based on National Health Interview Survey; see Appendix III. See headnote, Table 208. For composition of regions, see Table 27.

[2] Includes other races and unknown income not shown separately.

Source: Data compiled from the U.S. National Center for Health Statistics, *Vital and Health Statistics,* series 10, no. 193, and earlier reports; unpublished data; and the U.S. Bureau of the Census. (1996). *Statistical Abstract of the United States: 1996.* Table 218. (116th ed.) Washington, DC.

TABLE 3.6   Prevalence of Selected Chronic Conditions by Age and Sex: 1994[1]

	Rate[2] (age in years)							
	Male				*Female*			
Chronic Condition	*Under 45*	*45–64*	*65–74*	*75+*	*Under 45*	*45–64*	*65–74*	*75+*
Arthritis	27.4	176.8	430.8	429.9	38.2	297.0	513.6	604.4
Dermatitis, including eczema	29.3	21.8	25.3	17.6[2]	43.6	44.6	38.6	40.2
Trouble with								
Dry (itching) skin	17.1	29.6	36.6	46.7	20.5	36.1	30.8	40.5
Ingrown nails	16.0	32.1	40.9	38.8	16.4	29.7	52.9	61.4
Corns and calluses	6.9	25.3	21.0	17.8[2]	12.2	32.5	46.5	58.1
Visual impairments	29.5	52.7	78.4	113.7	12.9	38.0	48.0	110.7
Cataracts	2.5	12.3	79.0	214.7	2.5	21.9	140.0	259.2
Hearing impairments	43.2	191.9	298.8	447.1	30.4	87.5	183.3	307.8
Tinnitus	11.6	60.4	118.1	106.6	9.8	33.2	67.7	79.9
Deformities or orthopedic impairments	93.5	166.7	144.4	169.3	101.3	173.2	161.8	189.9
Ulcer	11.3	27.4	27.1	30.9[3]	13.3	23.3	42.8	22.3
Hernia of abdominal cavity	7.8	31.2	54.7	55.6	5.8	31.3	70.0	72.3
Frequent indigestion	20.5	42.8	44.6	51.5	18.9	39.0	41.0	45.3
Frequent constipation	4.3	6.8	13.8[3]	60.2	15.1	17.3	47.3	102.2
Diabetes	7.3	63.3	102.4	115.6	8.9	63.0	101.0	91.8
Migraine	22.0	24.2	17.1[3]	5.2[3]	67.1	78.9	29.9	26.2
Heart conditions	27.0	162.0	319.3	429.9	33.1	111.0	250.8	361.4
High blood pressure (hypertension)	31.9	220.0	307.7	339.2	32.4	224.5	378.7	417.5
Varicose veins of lower extremities	3.7	17.8	32.5	58.5	23.3	81.0	109.0	83.8

TABLE 3.6   Continued

Chronic Condition	Rate[2] (age in years)							
	Male				Female			
	Under 45	45–64	65–74	75+	Under 45	45–64	65–74	75+
Hemorrhoids	19.1	68.7	51.0	66.6	29.0	55.8	70.2	58.6
Chronic bronchitis	43.6	43.8	41.7	68.0	56.5	82.7	79.0	51.7
Asthma	57.1	32.3	39.3	70.3	60.0	68.0	62.8	34.1
Hay fever, allergic rhinitis without asthma	98.0	107.3	79.6	56.6	99.2	133.4	92.2	78.8
Chronic sinusitis	101.9	147.5	118.2	113.9	135.5	210.2	175.5	176.1

[1] Covers civilian noninstitutional population. Conditions classified according to ninth revision of International Classification of Diseases. Based on National Health Interview Survey; see Appendix III. See headnote, Table 208.

[2] Conditions per 1,000 persons.

[3] Figure does not meet standards of reliability or precision.

Source: U.S. National Center for Health Statistics. (1996). *Vital and Health Statistics,* series 10, No. 193, and earlier reports; unpublished data; and the U.S. Bureau of the Census. (1996). *Statistical Abstract of the United States; 1996.* Table 219. (116th ed.) Washington, DC.

(Mosley & Cowley, 1991). Morbidity can be measured through a variety of methods that include (1) "the use of health services; (2) screening of populations to determine the extent of benefit from treatment; and (3) population or self-assessment surveys" (Gray, 1993a, p. 113). Table 3.7 is an example of days of disability by selected characteristics between 1970 and 1993. In particular, notice that as family income levels increase, days of disability decrease.

Patterns of disease can also be recognized in other nations. A relatively new disease pattern many new developing nations are beginning to experience is referred to as *diseases of affluence* (e.g., heart disease, cancer). This is particularly troublesome because when the poor (whether in the United States or a developing nation) experience these diseases, they are more likely to die (Mosley & Cowley, 1991) because of their lack of access to the medical technology necessary to treat such conditions. Relative to the poor, we also know that illness costs them more in terms of lost wages. For example, "the proportion of normal earnings lost through sickness is over four times greater in Ghana than in the USA" (Gray, 1993, p. 26). From another, and perhaps broader perspective, a relatively new index of mortality and disability is the global burden of disease (GBD). Briefly, the GBD "combines the loss of life from premature death in 1990 with the loss of healthy life from disability" (World Development Report, 1993, p. 213). This burden is then assessed in

TABLE 3.7   Days of Disability, by Type and Selected Characteristics: 1970–1993

Type of Disability Day	Days per Person			
	1970	*1980*	*1990*	*1993*
Restricted-activity days[1]	14.6	19.1	14.9	17.1
Male	13.2	17.1	13.1	14.9
Female	15.8	21.0	16.7	19.2
White[2]	14.4	18.7	14.8	17.0
Black[2]	16.2	22.7	17.7	19.2
Hispanic[3]	(NA)	(NA)	(NA)	(NA)
Younger than 65 years	12.9	16.6	12.6	14.7
65 years and older	30.7	39.2	31.4	33.8
Northeast	14.5	17.9	13.2	15.9
Midwest	12.4	17.2	14.0	15.8
South	15.9	19.8	16.7	18.3
West	15.6	22.0	14.8	17.7
Family income				
Under $10,000	(NA)	(NA)	27.3	30.2
$10,000–$19,999	(NA)	(NA)	19.1	22.3
$20,000–$34,999	(NA)	(NA)	13.5	15.7
$35,000 or more	(NA)	(NA)	10.3	11.2
Bed-disability days[4]	6.1	7.0	6.2	6.7
Male	5.2	5.9	5.2	5.6
Female	6.9	8.0	7.1	7.8
Younger than 65 years	5.3	6.1	5.2	5.8
65 years and older	13.8	13.8	13.6	13.5
Work-loss days[5]	5.4	5.0	5.3	5.6
Male	5.0	4.9	4.7	4.8
Female	5.9	5.1	5.9	6.4
School-loss days[6]	4.9	5.3	4.6	5.3
Male	4.7	4.8	4.3	5.0
Female	5.1	5.7	5.0	5.5

NA, not available.

[1] A day when a person cuts down on his or her activities for more than half a day because of illness or injury. Includes bed-disability, work-loss, and school-loss days. Total includes other races and unknown income, not shown separately.

[2] Beginning 1980, race was determined by asking the household respondent to report his or her race. In earlier days, the racial classification of respondents was determined by interviewer observation.

[3] Persons of Hispanic origin may be of any race.

[4] A day when a person stayed in bed more than half a day because of illness or injury. Includes those work-loss and school-loss days actually spent in bed.

TABLE 3.7   Continued

[5] A day when a person lost more than half a workday because of illness or injury. Computed for persons 17 years of age and over (beginning 1985, 18 years of age and over) in the currently employed population, defined as those who were working or had a job or business from which they were not on layoff during the 2-week period preceding the week of interview.

[6] Child's loss of more than half a school day because of illness or injury. Computed for children 6–16 years of age. Beginning 1985, children 5–17 years old.

Source: Data compiled from the U.S. National Center for Health Statistics. *Vital and Health Statistics*, series 10, No. 190; earlier reports; unpublished data; and the U.S. Bureau of the Census. (1995). *Statistical Abstract of the United States: 1995* (115th ed.) Table 204. Washington, DC. 1995

the form of disability-adjusted life years (DALYs), which are calculated by categorizing diseases and factoring in a discount rate that assumes a progressively lower level of health with increasing age (World Development Report, 1993). Differences between developing and developed nations are considerable. One explanation for the difference is the result of economics and, as a result, a shift from communicable to noncommunicable diseases (World Development Report, 1993). For example, under the major heading of communicable, maternal, and perinatal diseases and injuries, sub-Saharan Africa in 1990 experienced 1,038.7, India 772.9, and China 281.4, whereas the Established Market Economies suffered 48.8 (all in hundreds of thousands of DALYs lost; World Development Report, 1993). Perhaps the disproportionate impact of the GBD on particular geographic and economic areas can best be understood in the following statement by Murray and colleagues (1994, p. 99): "Nearly 90% of the global burden of disease in 1990 therefore occurred because of disease and injury in the developing world."

Although DALYs provide us with regional variations regarding the burden of disease, they do not account for distinct illness patterns that exist within specific geographic locations. For instance, Oths (1996) identifies environmental, nutritional, and political conditions that have an impact on local illness patterns of a highland community of Northern Peru. Thus, the altitude of the community and its relationship with the national government influences the type and rate of particular diseases that afflict its residents. Also, as Oths (1996, p. 122) points out, "these factors are not among the typical morbidity risks considered within a paradigm of international health that emphasizes child survival, infectious and parasitic diseases, and an atomistic view of health behaviors."

Life Expectancy

Life expectancy is the length of time a person born in a particular year is expected to live. Stated differently, life expectancy "is based on the mortality rate of each age level, without respect to the proportions of the total population alive at those age levels" (Roemer, 1991, p. 11). Life expectancy at ages other than birth or age 1 year can also be measured.

TABLE 3.8   Life Expectancy at Birth and at 65 Years of Age, According to Sex: Selected countries, 1986 and 1991

Country[1]	At Birth		At 65 Years	
	1986[2]	1991[3]	1986[2]	1991[3]
Male		Life Expectancy in Years		
Japan	75.5	76.4	16.1	16.6
Israel	73.4	75.1	14.9	15.8
Sweden	74.0	74.9	14.9	15.4
Greece	74.1	74.7	15.4	15.9
Canada	73.1	74.4	15.0	15.7
Switzerland	73.8	74.2	15.1	15.6
Norway	72.9	74.1	14.5	14.9
Netherlands	73.1	74.1	14.1	14.6
Italy	72.7	73.7	14.3	15.1
England and Wales	72.6	73.5	13.9	14.4
France	71.8	73.5	14.7	16.2
Spain	73.4	73.4	15.3	15.5
Cuba	72.7	72.9	15.8	15.9
Federal Republic of Germany	71.9	72.7	13.8	14.3
Denmark	71.9	72.6	14.1	14.4
United States	71.2	72.0	14.6	15.3
Chile	68.9	69.4	13.3	14.0
German Democratic Republic	69.5	69.3	12.4	12.8
Puerto Rico	70.3	68.8	15.4	15.1
Bulgaria	68.6	68.3	12.7	12.9
Czechoslovakia	67.3	67.8	11.7	12.1
Romania	67.1	66.9	12.8	13.0
Poland	66.7	66.1	12.3	12.3
Hungary	65.3	65.1	11.9	12.1
Female				
Japan	81.6	82.8	20.0	21.0
France	80.0	82.0	19.2	20.9
Switzerland	80.6	81.4	19.4	20.1
Canada	79.9	81.0	19.3	20.0
Sweden	80.2	80.6	19.0	19.2
Spain	79.9	80.5	18.7	19.2
Netherlands	79.8	80.4	18.9	19.2
Norway	79.9	80.3	19.0	19.0
Greece	78.9	80.1	17.7	18.4
Israel	77.0	79.8	16.4	17.7
Federal Republic of Germany	78.5	79.2	17.7	18.2
England and Wales	78.3	79.0	17.9	18.1
United States	78.2	78.9	18.6	19.1
Italy	79.2	78.5	18.2	19.1

TABLE 3.8   Continued

Country[1]	At Birth		At 65 Years	
	1986[2]	1991[3]	1986[2]	1991[3]
Denmark	77.8	78.2	18.1	18.1
Puerto Rico	78.0	77.9	18.3	18.3
Ireland	76.4	77.9	16.0	17.1
Cuba	76.1	76.8	17.4	17.8
German Democratic Republic	75.4	76.4	15.3	16.2
Czechoslovakia	74.8	75.7	15.0	15.7
Poland	75.1	75.4	15.9	16.0
Hungary	73.3	74.0	15.1	15.6
Romania	72.7	73.4	14.7	15.1

[1] Refers to countries, territories, cities, or geographical areas.

[2] Data for England and Wales are for 1985. Data for Romania are for 1984.

[3] Data for Australia, Belgium, and Chile are for 1989. Data for Cuba, Federal Republic of Germany, German Democratic Republic, Italy, Israel, Spain, and Sweden are for 1990.

NOTES: Rankings are from highest to lowest life expectancy based on the latest available data for countries or geographic areas with at least 1 million population. This table is based on official mortality data from the country concerned, as submitted to the United Nations Demographic Yearbook of the World Health Statistical Annual.

Source: These data have been compiled from the United Nations *Demographic Yearbook 1992* (United Nations publications, sales No. 92.XII.1, copyright 1992, United Nations, New York) and are reproduced with the permission of the United Nations.

The use of different ages as the starting point offers different interpretations of the health of a country. For example, the purpose of utilizing life expectancy at age 1 year is to remove the impact of infant mortality on the chances of survival for the remaining population. The purpose of examining life expectancy at age 65 is to determine the extent to which medical technology is capable of extending life among the elderly.

The data in Table 3.8 illustrate the range of life expectancy for males and females at birth and at age 65 within selected countries in 1986 and 1991. Notice the 1991 life expectancy rankings for males and females at birth in the United States.

Relative to other industrialized nations, the United States has a moderately low life expectancy, particularly for men. The lower life expectancy rates can be attributed to a number of factors that include lifestyle and environmental and socioeconomic conditions. For example, when compared with other industrialized nations, the United States has the highest murder rate. We also know that life expectancy is inversely related to one's position in the social class structure. Given that the United States continues to experience relatively high rates of poverty, particularly among children, and that economic inequality continues to increase, lower rates of life expectancy would not be unexpected. However, life expectancy at age

65 in the United States is comparable to most other industrialized countries. An explanation for the increased life expectancy at age 65 is the increased sophistication associated with health technology. Examined in later chapters, this argument, although true, comes with a price tag that is increasingly being blamed on the persons kept alive because of the technology.

Together, the infant mortality rate and life expectancy function as a measure of a nation's health status. These indicators convey two significant expectations regarding societal responsibility towards its members. First is the role of the larger society toward the (equal) access of health-care technologies to its youngest and newest members as well as the availability of many preventive measures that may potentially increase the likelihood of healthier babies and mothers at the time of birth. At the opposite end of the life spectrum is the second societal expectation. Here, the question of responsibility is generally framed within the context of societal values. For example, to what extent is it the responsibility of the social institutions to provide basic economic and formal support services to persons within the aging community? Because of technological advances within health-related technology, what is the relationship between the extension of life and quality of life, particularly for persons in the aging community? These questions reflect the influence of a society's political and economic structure on its population's general as well as age-specific health. The next section examines in detail a number of sociological variables as they relate to health outcomes.

Basic Sociological Variables and Health Outcomes

Concepts such as morbidity, mortality, and life expectancy reflect the significance of epidemiology. This section examines four basic sociological variables within the framework of these concepts. Variations in health outcomes that exist within each variable as well as existing cross-cultural research for corresponding outcomes are also analyzed.

Age

The relationship between one's age and mortality and morbidity rates is well known. Data indicate that as one ages, the incidence of morbidity increases, as does the likelihood of death (see, for example, Belgrave, 1993, for the interactive effect of age and sex; and Dressler, 1994, for the interactive effect of age and social status). In Table 3.2, age-adjusted death rates indicate that persons older than age 65 account for almost 75% of all deaths in the United States. Morbidity rates are also higher among the elderly population. Applying age 65 as the transition age, data in Table 3.7 indicate much higher disability days for persons older than age 65 compared to persons younger than age 65. Increased morbidity rates and a disproportionate number of deaths among elderly persons suggest two future scenarios between age and health. The first is that even within the industrial world, the human life span has been (or will soon be) reached. Furthermore, the onset of disease and death are postponed until later in life, thus "compressing" this time period and thereby reducing the cost of health care to the elderly (Fries, 1980). A more negative second scenario suggests that increased life expectancy will result in an increased period of morbidity prior to death. As a result, elderly persons will continue to consume an increasingly disproportionate share of the health-care dollar (House et. al., 1990). House and colleagues (1990) also found that among elderly persons, the relationship between age and health status is influenced by one's socioeconomic status. In other words, lower income elderly persons, particularly elderly persons younger than age of 75, are more likely to experience health problems when compared with higher income elderly persons. Finally, Johannesson and Johansson (1996) report that in Sweden, age was an important variable when determining who should be saved. Meanwhile, Caldwell (1993, p. 127) reports that "differences in attitudes to the relative importance of the old and the young result in contrasting distributions between them of family resources and care." The expanding size of the aging population (numerically and as a percentage of the total population in the United States as well as throughout the world) will force a reexamination of the relationship between age and health-related outcomes.

Sex

Morbidity and mortality rates vary between men and women. A perusal of the statistical source material provides evidence that regardless of age, or if utilizing the point of conception, women are biologically healthier than are men (Woods, 1996). Sex-specific death rates remain biased because males experience higher death rates than do females. Reports of this phenomenon date to the mid-1600s in England (Dennerstein, 1995). In the United States today, differences in mortality rates between younger aged males and females are due to "higher accident rates, and at older ages, to heart disease" (Krieger & Fee, 1994). Sex-based mortality rates have also been attributed to factors such as "(1) biology, (2) technological improvements in health care, (3) stress exposures and stress responses, and (4) lifestyle" (Woods, 1996, pp. 46–51; see also, Waldron, 1994, for an early analysis of these factors).

Data in Table 3.9 also indicate that death rates have decreased significantly among younger age groups of males and females. However, age-specific death rates among persons aged 85 and older have remained relatively constant. Epidemiologically, this shift in age-specific death rates has consequences for the larger society in general and the health-care system in particular. For example, locating an increasingly expensive death and dying process within a highly visible age category can also influence societal attitudes as well as policy toward elderly persons.

Because of higher death rates among males throughout the life cycle, there were 146 females for every 100 males among persons aged 65 and older in 1994. As age increases, the ratio increases to 122, 148, and 259 females for every 100 males in the following age categories: 65–69, 75–79, and 85 and older, respectively (U.S. Bureau of the Census, 1995). Variability in death rates between women and men

TABLE 3.9 Death Rates by 10-Year Age Groups and Sex: United States, 1970 and preliminary 1995[1]

Age	1970[2]		1995[3]	
	Male	*Female*	*Male*	*Female*
All ages	1,090.3[4]	807.8[4]	913.8	847.7
Under 1 year	2,410.0[5]	1,863.7[5]	835.8[6]	685.4[6]
1–4 years	93.2	75.4	44.9	36.4
5–14 years	50.5	31.8	26.7	18.1
15–24 years	188.5	68.1	138.9	48.1
25–34 years	215.3	101.6	204.0	77.1
35–44 years	402.6	231.1	332.2	150.0
45–54 years	958.5	517.2	595.6	326.3
55–64 years	2,282.7	1,098.9	117.5	841.8
65–74 years	4,873.8	2,579.7	3,298.8	1,991.0
75–84 years	10,010.2	6,677.6	7,384.5	4,887.5
85 years and older	17,821.5	15,518.0	17,949.5	14,492.2

[1] Rates per 100,000 population in specified group.

[2] Source: National Center for Health Statistics. (1994). *Vital statistics of the United States, 1990. Vol. II. Mortality, part A.* Table 1-4. Washington, DC: Public Health Service.

[3] Source: Rosenberg, H. M., Ventura, S. J., Maurer J. D., et al. (1996). Births and Deaths: United States, 1995. *Monthly Vital Statistics Report, 45,* 3, suppl. 2. Table 9. Hyattsville, MD: National Center for Health Statistics.

[4] Figures for age not stated included in "total" but not distributed among age groups.

[5] Death rates under 1 year (based on population counts or estimated) differ from infant mortality rates (based on live births): see Technical Appendix.

[6] Death rates for under 1 year are based on population estimates; they differ from infant mortality rates, which are based on live births and are shown separately.

is not confined to the United States. Although dated, Nathanson (1977) examined female–male death rates for a number of Western industrialized nations. Outcomes were consistent with those of the United States.

However, morbidity rates are higher among women. These outcomes are expected, given many of the cultural values and expectations for sex-specific behavior, which continue to permeate American society. Some of these differences include "differences in biology, stress exposures and stress responses, and lifestyle" (Woods, 1996, p. 44). Furthermore, the differential in morbidity rates between males and females continues to reflect the impact of multiple sources such as race and ethnicity as well as social class. According to Krieger and Fee (1994a, p. 272), women "are a mixed lot, our gender roles and options shaped by history, culture, and deep divisions across class and color lines." In addition, there are social structural differences. For example, Bartley et al. (1992) analyze the relationship between work and health for women. They conclude that women with higher status occupations experienced fewer symptoms. Verbrugge (1989, p. 295) argues that increased morbidity among women is related to:

> risks stemming from lesser employment, greater felt stress and unhappiness, stronger feelings of vulnerability to illness, fewer formal time constraints (related to fewer job hours), and less physically strenuous leisure activities.

More recently, Verbrugge (1990, p. 65) suggested that differences in morbidity rates between males and females are influenced by a multiplicity of variables:

> acquired risks rank first; social and recreational activities, stresses, and environmental exposures during life are the prime causes of health problems for each sex, and for differentials between them. Prior health care may rank next, giving a cumulative advantage to women. Biological risks come last.

Thus, the adage that "women get sick and men die" appears to reflect sex differences in American disease and illness (see Gove & Hughes, 1979; Marcus & Seeman, 1981; Cleary, Mechanic, & Greenley, 1982; & Verbrugge, 1989, for explanations of mediating factors).

Addressing cultural but not sex differences, Goodman and colleagues (1995) discuss how disease during various periods in a woman's life in Bangladesh are believed to be the result of evil spirits, food, or physical causes. An example of the interrelationship between culture and sex is that of Japanese males and females who experience *hiesho* (chilling disposition). Although labeled a woman's illness, men also experience the same symptoms but characterize them differently. Thus, rather than refer to the condition (*hiesho*), men are more descriptive of their condition, for example, "My legs and feet get cold easily" (Ohnuki-Tierney, 1984, p. 55).

In Australia, health outcomes differ because women "valued health more highly than men" (Dennerstein, 1995, p. 58), whereas in Norway, the employment of women outside the home has had a positive impact on reported health (Elstad, 1996). Among males and females with a Spanish surname in Texas and California, Rosenwaike and Bradshaw (1989, p. 639) found that "mortality patterns . . . differed significantly from those in the non-Spanish surname white population of Texas and California." Rosenwaike and Bradshaw (1989) also report that relative to non-Spanish whites, males and females with Spanish surnames enjoyed advantages and disadvantages in death rates. Unfortunately, available data on morbidity rates are limited within many countries, and what does exist is suspect because of "limited knowledge on the part of the respondents" (Phillips & Verhasselt, 1994, p. 22). Although internationally women outlive men, Freedman and Maine (1993) argue that many women experience death simply because of being female. In other words, being classified and treated as second-class citizens. Furthermore, they argue that such deaths will continue until women are "valued for their own sake and in their own right" (p. 148). That sentiment is echoed by Turshen (1991, p. 205), who suggests that "there can be no democratic health in Africa until governments take women seriously."

Race and Ethnicity

In addition to outcome differentials on the basis of age and sex, illness and death rates also vary on the basis of race and ethnic heritage. This section examines available data and suggests plausible explanations for the continued racial and ethnic disparity. A note of caution is necessary regarding the concept of race. LaVeist and colleagues (1995 p. 130) point out that within health research, efforts to define race have proved difficult because the variable "suffers from the lack of conceptual clarity and measurement rigor found in other variables" (see also Hahn, 1990). In addition, LaVeist et al. (1995) address the fallacy of racial group homogeneity, which suggests that similar physical characteristics imply similar culture characteristics. Nevertheless, health differences that do exist between Caucasian and African Americans are the result of continued racial segregation that has permeated the social, economic, and political institutions of society (Miller, 1987).

An examination of neonatal and postneonatal death rates by race in Table 3.4 reveals a persistent inequality. That is, African American infants are more than twice as likely to die as are Caucasian infants. One explanation for differences in infant mortality rates is that of poverty (LaVeist, 1993) or, more broadly, the social and economic conditions of life (Council on Ethical and Judicial Affairs, 1990; Greenberg, 1990). Another explanation is that such discrepancies "are merely outward manifestations of underlying race differentials in political and social power" (LaVeist, 1992, p. 1092). Furthermore, African Americans at almost any age are more likely to die than are Caucasian Americans. In particular, the work of McCord and Freeman (1990) illustrates the extent of the problem for African Americans. Examining excess mortality rates in Harlem, the authors conclude that

> For men, the rate of survival beyond the age of 40 is lower in Harlem than Bangladesh. For women, overall survival to the age of 65 is somewhat better in Harlem, but only because the death rate among girls under 5 is very high in Bangladesh. (McCord & Freeman, 1990, p. 174)

A more recent survey concludes that "in Harlem mortality among women relative to that nationwide has not improved since 1980, whereas mortality among men has deteriorated" (Geronimus et al., 1996, p. 1555). Rogers (1992, p. 299), argues that not only could African American life expectancy be improved, but also that the race differential in life expectancy could be reduced "if blacks improve their socioeconomic status (with higher incomes), modify their household status (by increasing their propensity to marry and remain married), and reduce their family size." Williams and Collins (1995, p. 361) suggest instead an examination of "the larger historical context in understanding the health status of population groups." Navarro (1990) argues that the primary focus should be on class rather than race. An example of the effect of social class is offered by Otten et al. (1990, p. 849), who report that "family income or associated factors accounted for 38% of the excess mortality" (of African Americans to Caucasian Americans). However, Blendon, et al. (1989) found that regardless of income level, African Americans were worse off, medically, than were Caucasian Americans (see also Manton, et al., 1987, for an extensive analysis of African American/Caucasian American health differences). It is apparent that the relationship between race, social status (income), and health is not easily explained because the interactive effects of these variables can confound data interpretation. In addition, we can also add the interactive effect of sex. McBarnette (1996) argues that African-American women experience lower health status because they are less likely to have insurance coverage. In addition, African-American women are also the victims of racial discrimination and gender politics.

Health research has also examined the status of Hispanic Americans or Latinos. As with the African-American population, health-care research of Hispanics has been limited and has focused on the aggregate, rather than examining group differences (Giachello, 1996). What is known, however, is that, generally speaking, Hispanics have an infant mortality rate similar to that of Caucasian Americans. However, there is considerable in-group differentiation that is "influenced by varied cultural, social, and economic factors" (Sorlie et al., 1993, p. 2464). For example, infant mortality rates are higher for Puerto Ricans than for other members of the Hispanic community (Williams & Collins, 1995). There are also differences in the Hispanic community regarding expenditures on health care and use of health care (Council on Scientific Affairs, 1991). The relationship between socioeconomic position and health for Hispanics is not particularly clear, but appears connected to migratory patterns. That is, Hispanics born outside the United States appear to be healthier than Hispanics born in the United States. Similar health patterns appear to hold for Japanese and Chinese who have migrated to the United States (Williams & Collins, 1995). In general, Asian and Pacific Islanders (the designation is used as a rubric that includes a number of specific groups such as Japanese, Chinese, Hmong, Vietnamese, and Filipino) have lower infant mortality and mortality rates than other racial categories in the United States (Gardner, 1994).

It is evident that health outcomes are dependent on one's race or ethnic heritage. Historically, the legitimation of racism and the application of institutional racism helped foster the health attitudes and behaviors seen even today. The consequences of this relationship offer little hope to those minorities who also experience economic obstacles as well. This section concludes with an examination of the interrelationship of age, sex, and race/ethnicity to the fourth epidemiological variable, social class.

Social Class

A problematic (and political) feature of health data in the United States is the lack of social class as a variable in virtually all national research. As a result, social class is generally extrapolated from variables such as income, employment, or level of education (Krieger & Fee, 1993). It is generally agreed that our social class position in society influences our point of entry into the health-care system, as well as our likely health status. Consider the impact of social class position relative to other variables, such as the home and work environments (noise and air pollution) and exposure to toxic substances and carcinogens. Thus, social class is more than one's income level. It is a standard of how and where we live and work relative to others within the larger society. Similarly, it is difficult to address the influence of social class without also examining the interactive effects of variables such as race, sex, and age as they influence health status. For example, because African-Americans have experienced centuries of institutionalized discrimination within the United States, their educational, employment, and economic opportunities relative to Caucasian Americas have been limited. As a result, health differences between Caucasian Americans and African Americans is "increasingly attributed to social class or status and less to race" (Livingston, 1996, p. 239). However, as Dutton (1987, p. 32) points out, "the relationship between illness and income . . . involves a two-way effect; being poor often leads to worse health, and, in turn, worse health may also lead to diminished earning capacity and hence reduced income."

Although the impact of social class on health has been understood for some time, the Black Report (Townsend & Davidson, 1982) heightened international awareness. The authors of the report point to continued health inequality in the United Kingdom some 30 years after the implementation of the National Health Service (see Vagero & Illsley, 1995, for a more current examination of the report and an analysis of the work by Barker). In an analysis of current research, Krieger and Fee (1994b, p. 28) state that "the poorest people have the worst health." Although the association between class and health is generally accepted, alternative explanations attempt to clarify the relationship. For example, Syme and Berkman, (1976, p. 6) state that "research should go beyond the superficial description of demographic variables associated with illness and should attempt the identification of specific etiologic factors capable of accounting for the observed morbidity and mortality differences between the social classes."

Adler (1995, p. 9) suggests the relationship between health and social class is the result of "the physical and social environments to which individuals of socioeconomic levels are exposed," whereas Wilkinson (1990, p. 409) broadens the relationship to its eventual limits by arguing that "it appears that health is now a psychosocially mediated function of the structure of inequality in society."

The relationship between health and social class is not limited to the United States. Research outcomes in a number of European nations are consistent with American findings. That is, as the socioeconomic status of the respondent increases, there is a concomitant increase in their level of health. Recent examples include the work of Leeflang and colleagues (1992a,b) in the Netherlands; Najman (1993) in eight European and North American countries; Navarro-Rubio and associates (1995) in Spain; and an editorial by Siegrist (1995), in which Scandinavian countries are identified, and Dahl and Kjaersgaard (1993) for research on Norway. However, it is important to remember that as a concept, social class is composed of a number of indicators that include level of education and occupation as well as one's level of income.

Thus, it is evident that the relationship between social class position and health outcomes is evident throughout much of the Western industrialized world. In addition to indicators of social and medical outcomes, epidemiology is also interested in understanding disease patterns. The next section examines the impact of AIDS within developing as well as developed nations.

Epidemiology and Medical Sociology

This final section integrates, conceptually, medical sociology and epidemiology by examining how and why AIDS has become a worldwide health threat. In the process, many of the epidemiological and sociological concepts discussed throughout this chapter are employed.

A Case Study: AIDS

Acquired immune deficiency syndrome (AIDS) refers to "a cellular deficiency of the human immune system . . . and was acquired from the action of some environmental agent" (Stine, 1993, p. 38). AIDS develops because of the retrovirus human immunodeficiency virus (HIV-1). Although biologically based, AIDS, as a disease, also incorporates a social and cultural context (see, for example, Brandt, 1995). As a result, there has been a proliferation of research and writings on AIDS since the late 1980s. Thus, one could address the study of AIDS from any number of perspectives. The purpose of this section is to better understand the epidemiology and sociology of AIDS not only in the United States, but also within an international perspective.

Without question, the prevalence rate of AIDS has reached epidemic proportions, although it does not fit neatly into past epidemic models. The reason is that, traditionally, epidemics represent an event, followed by a pattern of increased affliction, with an eventual marked decline and an end point (for example, see Rosenberg, 1992). Initially identified in 1981 (the actual date may be much earlier), the number of cases began to grow slowly and then quite rapidly. For example, the number of reported cases in the United States in 1985 was slightly more than 8,000. By 1993, however, the number of reported cases exceeded 103,000. The cumulative number of cases has reached 410,000 as of 1994 (National Center for Health Statistics, 1995). The incidence rate of AIDS in the United States, which had been increasing consistently, has begun to show signs of slowing down. Worldwide, the number of AIDS cases is estimated at 4 million, increasing to 10 million by the end of the twentieth century. At the same time, the estimated worldwide prevalence of HIV is 14–15 million, with some 30–40 million projected by the year 2000 (World Health Organization, 1995). Societal costs include more than just health care. High incidence rates of AIDS also removes workers from the world of employment, and diminishes the consumer market (World Health Organization, 1995).

Sociologically, the spread of AIDS throughout the world is the result of cultural attitudes and social structural impediments such as discrimination in employment opportunities, resulting in increased rates of poverty and crime (Kalichman et al. 1995). For example, Wolffers (1997) discusses the importance of Asian culture relative to those sexual practices and behaviors considered acceptable and valued. Within the context of social structure, Loustaunau and Sobo (1997) point out that in the United States, urban poverty is a major contributor to the higher AIDS rates among African American women. Internationally, Weitz (1996a), in a review of Hunt (1989), concludes that within African nations, many multinational corporations can be implicated in the rapid rise of HIV infection. That is, as corporations increase their purchase of land, they have effectively moved males from rural to urban work environments and away from their families. Similarly, the loss of adequate land for farming has forced women into urban life as prostitutes. According to Weitz (1996a, p. 101), the work of Hunt "suggests that HIV infection first became widespread in African cities and then spread to rural areas as a result of the migratory labor system and the prostitution associated with that system."

Returning to the United States, knowledge of AIDS differs on the basis of race, ethnicity, and socioeconomic status (Sweat & Levin, 1995). Such differences appear to mask the perceived importance of AIDS relative to other social problems encountered by the poor. Thus, it may be less a question of knowledge and more a problem of "perceived threat to individual survival" (Kalichman et al., 1995, p. 305). Others (Chevais & Norman, 1995; Wells et al., 1995) found that even among the well informed, differences exist on the basis of race, income, and marital status. Finally, for those with AIDS, there is a social stigma attached to the disease (Musheno, 1995; Weitz, 1996b). As Alonzo and Reynolds (1995) point out, however, stigma is not static but involves a trajectory that is associated with the illness itself.

AIDS does not discriminate on the basis of geography. Brandt (1995, p. 547) identifies "three epidemiological patterns of HIV transmission, which roughly follow geographical boundaries." These patterns include (1) "North America, Western Europe, Australia, New Zealand, and many urban centers in Latin America . . . (2) countries comprised of sub-Saharan Africa and, increasingly, Latin America . . . (3) countries which include North Africa, the Middle East, Eastern Europe, Asia, and the Pacific." Consistent with the third pattern, Hunt (1993) connects the earlier colonization of Africa and the resultant migratory employment patterns as having a direct impact on the rate of AIDS cases (see also Lear, 1996, for a critical review of AIDS in Africa). Developing countries in Africa and the Far East have experienced rapid increases in incidence and prevalence rates. For example, the prevalence rate in the general public in Zambia is reportedly 6.18% (Campbell & Kelly, 1995). In the latter 1980s, the Caribbean Island nations of Trinidad and Tobago (relative to those countries identified with the Americas) had some of the highest incidence rates of AIDS (Henry & Newton, 1994). One explanation for the differing incidence rates appears to be the method by which the virus is spread. For example, heterosexual contact increases the risk of perinatal contact with the virus, thus adding to the numbers infected (Henry & Newton, 1994). However, countries such as Vietnam (Le & Williams, 1996) and Bangladesh (Folmar & Alam, 1996) have reported very low prevalence rates of HIV infection and reported cases of AIDS. Some of these low rates may be the result of an underreporting of the extent of the problem (Folmar & Alam, 1996).

Finally, increased knowledge of vulnerability does not appear to lessen the behavior of those at risk (Robles et al., 1995). Schoepf et al. (1991), reporting on research in Zaire, point out that even with an increased knowledge base, those most at risk do not change their behavior to lessen the risk of AIDS. In fact, Smith (1996) argues that for some women in developed and developing countries, marriage puts them in an "at risk" category for AIDS. For example, in Thailand, a double standard allows men considerable sexual freedom before and after marriage. As a result, "the greatest societal concern has surrounded infection from prostitutes to their male customers. This mode of infection is generally viewed as having the greatest potential for the widespread transmission of HIV to all strata of society" (Ford, 1994, p. 90). Lyttleton (1995) argues, however, that prostitution does not have widespread public support, particularly within rural areas of Thailand. Nonetheless, women worldwide are increasingly becoming infected with the AIDS virus (McDermott et al., 1993).

Finally, AIDS is a modern-day epidemic that does not discriminate on the basis of age (some 10% of AIDS cases in the United States are among persons aged 50 and older). As life expectancy for those who are HIV positive and who develop AIDS continues to increase because of drug therapies, there will be a slowing of the mortality rate. Concomitantly, an increase in the prevalence rate can be expected even if there is a slowing in the incidence of AIDS.

The AIDS epidemic provides us with an understanding of the importance of medical sociology and epidemiology. As with any epidemic, the biological qualities reveal only one facet of the problem. Utilizing medical sociology and epidemiology, we can better understand the social (structural) and cultural characteristics associated with the pattern of disease and the inherent consequences. In other words, by understanding not only who is infected, but also why they are infected, health policy efforts can better address methods of prevention. The next series of chapters on illness and health behavior continues to build on this knowledge base.

Summary

The intent of this chapter is to familiarize the reader with the epidemiological approach and its relationship to medical sociology. In the process, the historical framework within which epidemiology developed is outlined. Individuals who have had a significant impact on the development of epidemiology are also chronicled.

A number of concepts associated with epidemiology and medical sociology are identified and explained within a cross-cultural perspective. These concepts include mortality, infant mortality, morbidity, and life expectancy. The use of statistical procedures to illustrate these concepts provides the reader with a more thorough grounding in their application. In addition, the impact of the four basic sociological variables of age, sex, race, and social class on health and illness outcomes are examined. The chapter concludes with a case study of AIDS that illustrates not only the epidemiological explanation of disease distribution, but also the sociological significance of social structure and cultural attitudes.

CHAPTER REVIEW

This chapter provides the reader with a grounding in many of the basic conceptual arrangements utilized in medical sociology. In this chapter the reader is introduced to new concepts that examine patterns and rates of disease and death. The following questions are an effort to elicit from the reader an understanding of the information presented.

1. Identify and discuss the historical development of epidemiology. Include all of the individuals identified and explain their importance to the field.

2. Contact your local county health office. Obtain information on the total population of the county and the number of birth and deaths for the most recent year possible. Calculate the birth and death rates for the county.

3. Utilizing the most recent statistical abstract, locate morbidity and mortality rates for the present year and for 1990. What is the rate of change? How would you explain the reduction or increase in the number of illnesses and deaths?

4. Reexamine the four basic variables associated with sociology. Briefly describe the interrelationship of these variables.

5. It could be argued that social class is perhaps the most important of the four basic variables associated with sociology. Would you agree or disagree with this assessment? Explain your answer.

6. Identify a specific disease. Utilizing the latest edition of *Vital Statistics,* examine not only the numbers of people with the disease, but also their age. How would you explain changes in the disease by age?

GLOSSARY

age-specific death rate   The number of deaths at any given age divided by the total population in that age category and multiplied (generally) by 100,000.

crude death rate   The number of deaths in a population divided by the total population and multiplied (generally) by 1,000.

epidemiology   The study of how disease is distributed within populations.

epidemiological transition   The changing nature of diseases and their distribution within society, relative to social and economic conditions.

incidence   The number of new cases associated with a condition within a given period of time.

infant mortality rate   The number of deaths during the first year of life divided by the total number of live births, then multiplied by 1,000.

life expectancy   The expected length of life for persons born in any given year.

morbidity   The occurrence of disease and disability within populations.

mortality rate   The total number of deaths within a given population during a specified period of time. When multiplied by 1,000, a mortality rate can be calculated.

neonatal   Deaths occurring at less than 28 days of life.

postneonatal   Deaths occurring between the 28th day and the 11th month of life.

prevalence   The total number of cases associated with a given condition.

SUGGESTED READINGS

The following is not a comprehensive listing of materials suggested for further study. Rather, this list represents a sample of material from various areas within the chapter. The reader is encouraged to peruse the reference section of this chapter for a more extensive listing of academic sources in epidemiology.

Bayne-Smith, M. (Ed.). (1996). *Race, gender, and health.* Vol. 15. Thousand Oaks, CA: SAGE.
 A good book that covers an all too often neglected area: the health of women of color. This is a recent edition with good coverage of these areas.

Cameron, D., & Jones, I. G. (1983). John Snow, the Broad Street pump and modern epidemiology. *International Journal of Epidemiology, 12,* 4, 393–396.
 A very short article on the work of John Snow and his contribution to the emergence of epidemiology. The authors evaluate a number of current efforts that address the work of Snow and argue that modern epidemiologists approach their craft quite differently than did Snow.

Krieger, N., & Fee, E. (1993). What's class got to do with it? The state of health data in the United States today. *Socialist Review, 23,* 1, 59–82.
 A solid introductory article to an understanding of the relationship between class and health in the United States. The authors not only provide an analysis of the determinants of social class, but also address its connection to the political system.

Livingston, I. L. (Ed) (1994). *Handbook of black American health: The mosaic of conditions, issues, policies, and prospects.* Westport, CT: Greenwood Press.
 As the title implies, this book is a mosaic that addresses physical, legal, mental, and social conditions of health faced by African Americans today.

Phillips, D. R., & Verhasselt, Y. (Eds.). (1994). *Health and development.* New York, NY: Routledge.
 Another excellent book that offers an international view of epidemiological issues occurring primarily within developing nations.

Rockett, R. H. (1994). Population and health: An introduction to epidemiology. *Population Bulletin, 49,* 3, pp. 2–47 (Washington, DC; Population Reference Bureau, Inc.; November).
 As the title suggests, this is an excellent introduction to the history and terminology used in epidemiology. This is a good starting point for anyone interested in the field.

Singh, G. K., Kochanek, K. D., & MacDorman, M. F. (1996). Advance report of final mortality statistics, 1994. *Monthly Vital Statistics Report, 45,* 3, Supp. Hyattsville, MD: National Center for Health Statistics.
 This is only one example of the various governmental publications available. Readers seriously interested should contact the National Center for Health Statistics to receive their material on a regular basis. Internet and e-mail addresses are available.

Susser, M., & Susser, E. (1996). Choosing a future for epidemiology: I. Eras and paradigms. *American Journal of Public Health, 86,* 5, 668–673.
———. (1996). Traditional epidemiology, modern epidemiology, and public health. *American Journal of Public Health, 86,* 5, 678–683.
 The first article examines not only the evolution and current state of epidemiology, but also its future. In the second article, the authors examine the shift in level of analysis as the key issue in this paradigm shift.

Sweat, M. D., & Levin, M. (1995). HIV/AIDS knowledge among the U.S. population. *AIDS Education and Prevention. 7,* 4, 355–372.
 Among the many articles on AIDS/HIV, this one offers a broad overview of the current knowledge base of the American population.

World Health Organization (1995). *The World Health Report 1995: Bridging the Gaps.* Geneva, Switzerland: World Health Organization.
 A brief but concise overview of health around the world. The Table of Basic Indicators is particularly useful for gaining an international perspective.

REFERENCES

Adler, N. E. (1995). Are mind–body variables a central factor linking socioeconomic status and health? *ADVANCES: The Journal of Mind–Body Health, 11,* 3, 6–9.

Alonzo, A. A., & Reynolds, N. R. (1995). Stigma, HIV and AIDS: An exploration and elaboration of a stigma trajectory. *Social Science and Medicine, 41,* 3, 303–315.

Armstrong, D. (1980). *An outline of sociology as applied to medicine.* Bristol, Great Britain: John Wright & Sons Ltd.

Ashton, J. (1994). Preface. In J. Ashton (Ed.). *The epidemiological imagination: A reader* (p. ix). Buckingham: Open University Press.

Bartley, M., Popay, J., & Plewis, I. (1992). Domestic conditions, paid employment and women's experience of ill-health. *Sociology of Health and Illness, 14,* 3, 313–343.

Beckerleg, S., Austin, S., & Weaver, L. (1994). Gender, work and illness: The influence of a research unit on an agricultural community in the Gambia. *Health Policy and Planning, 9,* 4, 419–428.

Belgrave, L. L. (1993). Discrimination against older women in health care. *Journal of Women and Aging, 5,* 3–4, 181–199.

Blendon, R. J., Aiken, L. H., Freeman, H. E., & Corey, C. R. (1989). Access to medical care for black and white Americans. *Journal of the American Medical Association, 261,* 2, 278–281.

Brandt, A. M. (1988). AIDS in historical perspective: Four lessons from the history of sexually transmitted diseases. *American Journal of Public Health, 78,* 367–371.

Brandt, A. M. (1993). Acquired immune deficiency syndrome (AIDS). In K. F. Kiple (Ed.). *The Cambridge world history of human disease* (pp. 547–551). New York, NY: Cambridge University Press.

Brockington, C. F. (1977). The history of public health. In W. Hobson (Ed.). *The theory and practice of public health* (4th Ed). (pp. 1–7). London: Oxford University Press.

Bury, M. (1991). The sociology of chronic illness: A review of research and prospects. *Sociology of Health and Illness, 13,* 4, 451–468.

Caldwell, J. C. (1993). Health transition: The cultural, social and behavioural determinants of health in the third world. *Social Science and Medicine, 36,* 2, 125–135.

Cameron, D., & Jones, I. G. (1983). John Snow, the Broad Street pump and modern epidemiology. *International Journal of Epidemiology, 12* (4), 393–396.

Campbell, G. R. (1989). The political epidemiology of infant mortality: A health crisis among Montana American Indians. *American Indian Culture and Research Journal, 13,* 3 & 4, 105–148.

Campbell, T., & Kelly, M. (1995). Women and AIDS in Zambia: A review of the psychosocial factors implicated in the transmission of HIV. *AIDS Care, 7,* 3, 365–373.

Cartwright, F. F. (1977). *A social history of medicine.* London: Longman.

Cassel, J. (1976). The contribution of the social environment to host resistance. *American Journal of Epidemiology, 104* (2), 107–123.

Chavis, W. M., & Norman, G. S. (1995). A survey of knowledge, attitudes, and beliefs about AIDS in a medical school student population. *Journal of Sex Education and Therapy, 21,* 3, 167–177.

Cleary, P. D., Mechanic, D., & Greenly, J. R. (1982). Sex differences in medical care utilization: An empirical investigation. *Journal of Health and Social Behavior, 23,* 106–119.

Coe, R. M. (1978). *Sociology of medicine* (2nd Ed) New York: McGraw Hill.

Council on Scientific Affairs. (1991). Hispanic health in the United States. *Journal of the American Medical Association, 265,* 248–252.

Council on Ethical and Judicial Affairs. (1990). Black–white disparities in health care. *Journal of the American Medical Association, 263,* 17, 2344–2346.

Dahl, E., & Kjaersgaard, P. (1993). Trends in socioeconomic differentials in post-war Norway: Evidence and interpretations. *Sociology of Health and Illness, 15,* 5, 587–611.

d'Crus-Grote, D. (1996). Prevention of HIV infection in developing countries. *The Lancet, 348,* 1071–1074.

Dennerstein, G. K. (1995). Gender, health, and ill-health. *Women's Health Issues, 5,* 2, 53–59.

Denton, J. A. (1978). *Medical sociology.* Boston: Houghton Mifflin Company.

de Ridder, D., Depla, M., Severens, P., & Malsch, M. (1997). Beliefs on coping with illness: A consumer's perspective. *Social Science and Medicine, 44,* 5, 553–559.

Dressler, W. W. (1994). Social status, age, and blood pressure in an English general practice. *Collegium Antropologicum, 18,* 1, 73–80.

DuBos, R. (1959). *Mirage of health.* New York: Harper.

Dutton, D. B. (1986). Social class, health, and illness. In L. H. Aiken & D. Mechanic (Eds.). *Applications of social science to clinical medicine and health policy* (pp. 31–62). New Brunswick, NJ: Rutgers University Press.

Elstad, J. I. (1996). Inequalities in health related to women's marital, parental, and employment status—A comparison between the early 70s and the late 80s, Norway, *Social Science and Medicine, 42,* 1, 75–89.

Folmar, S., & Nurul Alam, S. M. (1996) Sex, condoms, and risk of AIDS in Bangladesh. In J. Subedi & E. B. Gallagher (Eds.). *Society, health, and disease: Transcultural perspective.* (pp. 262–275). Englewood Cliffs, NJ: Prentice-Hall.

Ford, N. (1994). Cultural and developmental factors underlying the global pattern of the transmission of HIV/AIDS. In D. R. Phillips & Y. Verhasselt (Eds.). *Health and development* (pp. 83–96). New York: Routledge.

Freedman, L. P., & Maine, D. (1991). Women's mortality: A legacy of neglect. In M. Koblinsky, J. Timyan, & J. Gay (Eds.). *The health of women: A global perspective* (pp. 147–170). Boulder, CO: Westview Press.

Fries, J. F. (1980). Aging, natural death, and the compression of morbidity. *New England Journal of Medicine, 330,* 130–135.

Fuchs, V. R. (1975). *Who shall live? Health, economics, and social choice.* New York: Basic Books.

Gardner, R. (1994). Mortality. In N. W. S. Zane, D. T. Takeuchi, & K. N. J. Young (Eds.). *Confronting critical health issues of Asian and Pacific Islander Americans* (pp. 53–104). Thousand Oaks, CA: SAGE.

Geronimus, A. T., Bound, J., Waidmann, T. A., Hillemeier, M. M., & Burns, P. B. (1996). Excess mortality among blacks and whites in the United States. *The New England Journal of Medicine, 335,* 21, 1552–1558.

Giachello, A. L. (1996). Latino women. In M. Bayne-Smith (Ed.). *Race, gender, and health,* Vol. 15 (pp. 121–171). Thousand Oaks, CA: SAGE.

Gilbert, L. (1995). Sociology and the "new public health" in South Africa. *The South African Journal of Sociology, 26,* 4, 115–124.

Goodman, E. A., Gazi, R., & Chowdhury, M. (1995). Beliefs and practices regarding delivery and postpartum maternal morbidity in rural Bangladesh. *Studies in Family Planning, 26,* 1, 22–32.

Gove, W. P., & Hughes, M. (1979). Possible causes of the apparent sex differences in physical health: An empirical investigation. *American Sociological Review, 44,* 126–146.

Gray, A. (Ed). (1993a). *World health and disease.* Buckingham, Great Britain: Open University Press.

Gray, A. (1993b). Mortality and morbidity: Causes and determinants. In A. Gray (Ed). *World health and disease* (pp. 21–37). London: The Open University Press.

Greenberg, D. S. (1990). Black health: Grim statistics. *The Lancet, 335,* 780–781.

Hahn, R. A. (1992). The state of federal health statistics on racial and ethnic groups. *Journal of the American Medical Association, 267,* 2, 268–271.

Helman, C. G. (1994). *Culture, health, and illness* (3rd Ed). Oxford: Butterworth-Heinemann.

Henry, R., & Newton, E. (1994). AIDS costs in Trinidad and Tobago. *Studies in Comparative International Development, 29,* 4, 68–89.

House, J. S., Kessler, R. C., Herzog, A. R., Mero, R. P., Kinney, A. M., & Breslow, M. J. (1990). Age, socioeconomic status, and health. *Milbank Quarterly, 68* (3), 383–411.

Hunt, C. W. (1993). The social epidemiology of AIDS in Africa: Migrant labor and sexually transmitted disease. In P. Conrad & E. B. Gallagher (Eds.). *Health and health care in developing countries: Sociological perspectives* (pp. 1–37). Philadelphia, PA: Temple University Press.

Johannesson, M., & Johansson, P. O. (1996). The economics of aging: On the attitude of Swedish people to the distribution of health care resources between the young and the old. *Health Policy, 37,* 153–161.

Kalichman, S. C., Adair, V., Somlai, A. M., & Weir, S. S. (1995). The perceived social context of AIDS: Study of inner-city sexually transmitted disease clinic patients. *AIDS Education and Prevention, 7,* 4, 298–307.

Kalipeni, E. (1995). Demographic and spatial aspects of the health care delivery system in Malawi. In E. B. Gallagher & J. Subedi (Eds.). *Global perspectives on health care* (pp. 153–172). Englewood Cliffs, NJ: Prentice Hall.

Kim, K., & Moody, P. M. (1992). More resources better health? A cross-national perspective. *Social Science and Medicine 34,* 8, 837–842.

Kloos, H. (1994). The poorer third world. In D. R. Phillips & Y. Verhasselt (Eds.). *Health and development* (pp. 199–215). London: Routledge.

Krieger, N., & Fee, E. (1993). What's class got to do with it? The state of health data in the United States today. *Socialist review, 23,* 1, 59–82.

Krieger, N., & Fee, E. (1994a). Man-made medicine and women's health: The biopolitics of sex/gender and race/ethnicity. *International Journal of Health Services, 24,* 2, 265–283.

Krieger, N., & Fee, E. (1994b). Social class: The missing link in U.S. health data. *International Journal of Health Services, 24,* 1, 25–44.

Kurtz, R. A., & Chalfant, H. P. (1991). *The sociology of medicine and illness* (2nd Ed). Boston: Allyn & Bacon.

LaVeist, T. A. (1992). The political empowerment and health status of African-Americans: Mapping a new territory. *American Journal of Sociology, 97,* 4, 1080–1095.

LaVeist, T. A. (1993). Segregation, poverty, and empowerment: Health consequences for African Americans. *Milbank Quarterly, 71,* 1, 41–64.

LaVeist, T. A., Wallace, J. M., & Howard, D. L. (1995). The color line and the health of African Americans. *Humboldt Journal of Social Relations, 21,* 1, 119–137.

Le, N., & Williams, D. R. (1996). Social factors and knowledge of HIV/AIDS in Vietnam. In J. Subedi & E. B. Gallagher (Eds.). *Society, health, and disease: Transcultural perspectives* (pp. 244–261). Englewood Cliffs, NJ: Prentice-Hall.

Lear, D. (1996). Women and AIDS in Africa: A critical review. In J. Subedi & E. B. Gallagher (Eds.). *Society, health, and disease: Transcultural Perspectives* (pp. 276–301). Englewood Cliffs, NJ: Prentice-Hall.

Leeflang, R. L. I., Klein-Hesselink, D. J., & Spruit, I. P. (1992a). Health effects of unemployment—I. Long-term unemployed men in a rural and an urban setting. *Social Science and Medicine, 34,* 4, 341–350.

Leeflang, R. L. I., Klein-Hesselink, D. J., & Spruit, I. P. (1992b). Health effects of unemployment—II. Men and women. *Social Science and Medicine, 34,* 4, 351–363.

Lilienfeld, D. E., & Lilienfeld, A. M. (1977). Epidemiology: A retrospective study. *American Journal of Epidemiology, 106* (6), 445–459.

Lilienfeld, A. M., & Lilienfeld, D. E. (1982). Epidemiology and the public health movement: A historical perspective. *Journal of Public Health Policy, 3,* 140–149.

Livingston, I. L. (1994). Social status, stress, and health: Black Americans at risk. In I. L. Livingston (Ed.). *Handbook of Black American health: The mosaic of conditions issues, policies, and prospects* (pp. 236–252). Westport, CT: Greenwood Press.

Loustaunau, M. O., & Sobo, E. J. (1997). *The cultural context of health, illness and medicine.* Westport, CT: Bergin & Garvey.

Lyons, M. (1993). Diseases of sub-Saharan Africa since 1860. In K. F. Kiple (Ed.). *The Cambridge world history of human disease* (pp. 298–305). Cambridge, England: Cambridge University Press.

Lyttleton, C. (1995). Storm warnings: Responding to messages of danger in Isan. *The Australian Journal of Anthropology, 6,* 3, 178–196.

Manton, K. G., Patrick, C. H., & Johnson, K. W. (1987). Health differentials between blacks and whites: Recent trends in mortality and morbidity. *Milbank Quarterly, 65,* Suppl 1, 129–199.

Marcus, A. C., & Seeman, T. E. (1981). Sex differences in reports of illness and disability: A preliminary test of the "fixed role obligations" hypothesis. *Journal of Health and Social Behavior, 22,* 174–182.

McBarnette, L. S. (1996). African American women. In M. Bayne-Smith (Ed.). *Race, gender, and health* (pp. 43–67). Thousand Oaks, CA: Sage.

McCord, C., & Freeman, H. P. (1990). Excess mortality in Harlem. *New England Journal of Medicine, 322,* 3, 173–177.

McDermott, J., Bangser, M., Ngugi, E., & Sandvold, I. (1993). Infection: Social and medical realities. In M. Koblinsky, J. Timyan, & J. Gay (Eds.). *The health of women: A global perspective* (pp. 91–103). Boulder, CO: Westview Press.

McKinlay, J. B., & McKinlay, S. J. (1977). The questionable contribution of medical measures to the decline of mortality in the United States in the twentieth century. *Milbank Memorial Fund Quarterly, 55,* 405–428.

Miller, S. M. (1987). Race in the health of America. *Milbank Quarterly, 65,* Suppl 2, 500–531.

Morris, D. M. (1976). *A physical quality of life index (PQLI).* Overseas development council, the United States and world development agenda, pp. 147–171.

Mosley, W. H., & Cowley, P. (1991). The challenge of world health. *Population Bulletin, 46,* 4. Washington DC: Population Reference Bureau.

Murray, C. J. L., Lopez, A. D., & Jamison, D. T. (1994). The global burden of disease in 1990: Summary results, sensitivity analysis and future directions. In C. J. L. Murray & A. D. Lopez (Eds.). *Global comparative assessments in the health sector: Disease burden, expenditures and intervention packages* (pp. 97–138). Geneva: World Health Organization.

Musheno, M. (1995). Legal consciousness on the margins of society: Struggles against stigmatization in the AIDS crisis. *Identities, 2,* 1–2, 101–122.

Najman, J. M. (1993). Health and poverty: Past, present and prospects for the future. *Social Science and Medicine, 36,* 2, 157–166.

Nathanson, C. A. (1977). Sex, illness, and medical care: A review of the data, theory, and method. *Social Science and Medicine, 11,* 13–25.

National Center for Health Statistics. (1995). *Health, United States, 1994.* Hyattsville, MD: Public Health Service.

National Center for Health Statistics. (1996). Births, marriages, divorces, and deaths for February 1996. *Monthly vital statistics report, 45,* 2. Hyattsville, MD: Public Health Service.

Navarro, V. (1990). Race or class versus race and class: Mortality differentials in the United States. *The Lancet, 336,* 1238–1240.

Navarro-Rubio, M. D., Jovell, A. J., & Schor, E. L. (1995). Socioeconomic status and preventive health-care use by children in Spain. *American Journal of Preventive Medicine, 11,* 4, 256–262.

Ohnuki-Tierney, E. (1984). *Illness and culture in contemporary Japan: An anthropological view.* Cambridge: Cambridge University Press.

Olshansky, S. J., & Ault, A. B. (1986). The fourth stage of the epidemiological transition: The age of delayed degenerative diseases. *The Milbank Quarterly, 64* (3), 355–391.

Orman, A. R. (1971). The epidemiological transition. *Milbank Memorial Fund Quarterly, 49,* 509–538.

Oths, K. S. (1996). Ecological and macrolevel influences on illness in northern Peru: Beyond the international health paradigm. In J. Subedi & E. B. Gallagher (Eds.). *Society, health, and disease: Transcultural perspectives* (pp. 107–129). Upper Saddle River, NJ: Prentice Hall.

Otten, M. W., Teutsch, S. M., Williamson, D. F., & Marks, J. S. (1990). The effect of known risk factors on the excess mortality of black adults in the United States. *Journal of the American Medical Association, 263,* 6, 845–850.

Paffenbarger, R. S. (1977). And now Antiquarianism . . . ? Telescoping time with predocumented data. *American Journal of Epidemiology, 106* (6), 460–461.

Paul, B. K. (1990). Factors affecting infant mortality in rural Bangladesh: Results from a retrospective sample survey. *Rural Sociology, 55,* 4, 522–540.

Pearce, N. (1996). Traditional epidemiology, modern epidemiology, and public health. *American Journal of Public Health, 86* (5), 678–683.

Peterson, D. R., & Thomas, D. B. (1978). *Fundamentals of epidemiology.* Lexington, MA: D.C. Heath and Company.

Phillips, D. R., & Verhasselt, Y. (1994). Introduction: Health and development. In D. R. Phillips & Y. Verhasselt (Eds.). *Health and development* (pp. 3–32). London: Routledge.

Price, P. (1994). Maternal and child health care strategies. In D. R. Phillips & Y. Verhasselt (Eds.). *Health and development* (pp. 138–155). London: Routledge.

Robles, R. R., Cancel, L. I., Colon, H. M., Mantos, T. D., Freeman, D. H., & Sahai, H. (1995). Prospective effects of perceived risk of developing HIV/AIDS on risk behaviors among injection drug users in Puerto Rico. *Addiction, 90,* 1105–1111.

Rockett, I. R. H. (1994). Population and health: An introduction to epidemiology. *Population Bulletin, 49,* 3 (Washington, DC: Population Reference Bureau, Inc., November).

Roemer, M. I. (1991). *National health systems of the world: Volume 1: The Countries.* New York: Oxford University Press.

Rogers, R. G. (1992). Living and dying in the U.S.A.: Sociodemographic determinants of death among blacks and whites. *Demography, 29,* 2, 287–303.

Rosenberg, C. E. (1992). *Explaining epidemics and other studies in the history of medicine.* New York: Cambridge University Press.

Rosenberg, H. M., Ventura, S. J., Maurer, J. D., et al. (1996). Births and deaths: United States, 1995. *Monthly vital statistics report, 45,* 3, Suppl. 2. Hyattsville, MD: National Center for Health Statistics.

Rosenwaike, I., & Bradshaw, B. S. (1989). Mortality of the Spanish surname population of the southwest: 1980. *Social Science Quarterly, 70,* 3, 631–641.

Roueche', B. (1953). *Eleven blue men and other narratives of medical detection.* Boston: Little, Brown & Company.

Schoepf, B. G., Engundu, W., Nkera, R. W., Ntsomo, P., & Schoepf, C. (1991). Gender, power, and risk of AIDS in Zaire. In M. Turshen (Ed.). *Women and health in Africa* (pp. 187–203). Trenton, NJ: Africa World Press, Inc.

Schuman, S. H. (1986). *Practice-based epidemiology: An introduction.* New York: Gordon and Breach Science Publishers.

Shah, N. M., & Shah, M. A. (1990). Socioeconomic and health care determinants of child survival in Kuwait. *Journal of Biosocial Science, 22,* 239–253.

Sigerist, H. E. (1971). *The great doctors: A biographical history of medicine.* New York: Dover Publications, Inc.

Sigerist, J. (1995). Social differentials in chronic disease: What can sociological knowledge offer to explain and possibly reduce them? *Social Science and Medicine, 41,* 12, 1603–1605.

Smith, G. (1941). *Plague on us.* New York: The Commonwealth Fund.

Smith, J. M. (1996). *AIDS and society.* Englewood Cliffs, NJ: Prentice-Hall.

Sorlie, P. D., Backlund, E., Johnson, N. J., & Rogot, E. (1993). Mortality by Hispanic status in the United States. *Journal of the American Medical Association, 270,* 20, 2464–2468.

Stine, G. J. (1993). *Acquired immune deficiency syndrome: biological, medical, social, and legal issues.* Englewood Cliffs, NJ: Prentice-Hall.

Susser, M. W. (1973). *Causal thinking in the health sciences: Concepts and strategies of epidemiology.* New York: Oxford University Press.

Susser, M. W. (1975). Social science and public health. In W. Hobson (Ed.). *The theory and practice of public health* (4th Ed) (pp. 616–622). London: Oxford University Press.

Susser, M. (1985). Epidemiology in the United States after World War II: The evolution of technique. *Epidemiological Reviews, 7,* 147–177.

Susser, M. W., & Susser, E. (1996a). Choosing a future for epidemiology: I. Eras and paradigms. *American Journal of Public Health, 86* (5), 668–673.

Susser, M. W., & Susser, E. (1996b). Choosing a future for epidemiology: II. From black box to Chinese boxes and eco-epidemiology. *American Journal of Public Health, 86* (5), 674–677.

Sweat, M. D., & Levin, M. (1995). HIV/AIDS knowledge among the U.S. population. *AIDS education and prevention, 7,* 4, 355–372.

Syme, S. L., & Berkman, L. F. (1976). Social class, susceptibility and sickness. *American Journal of Epidemiology, 104,* 1, 1–8.

Terris, M. (1987). Epidemiology and the public health movement. *Journal of Public Health Policy, 8,* 315–329.

Townsend, P., & Davidson, N. (1992). *The Black report: Inequalities in health.* London: Penguin.

Turshen, M. (1991). Taking women seriously: Toward democratic health care in Africa. In M. Turshen (Ed.). *Women and health in Africa* (pp. 205–220). Trenton, NJ: Africa World Press, Inc.

Twaddle, A. C., & Hessler, R. M. (1987). *A sociology of health* (2nd Ed). New York: Macmillan Publishing Company.

U.S. Bureau of the Census. (1995). *Statistical Abstract of the United States: 1995* (115th ed.), Table 47. Washington, DC.

U.S. Bureau of the Census. (1996). *Statistical Abstract of the United States: 1996.* (116th ed.) Washington, DC.

Uutela, A., & Tuomilehto, J. (1992). Changes in disease patterns and related social trends. *Social Science and Medicine, 35,* 4, 389–399.

Vagero, D., & Illsley, R. (1995). Explaining health inequalities: Beyond Blank and Barker. *European Sociological Review, 11,* 3, 219–241.

Verbrugge, L. M. (1989). The twain meet: Empirical explanations of sex differences in health and mortality. *Journal of Health and Social Behavior, 30,* 282–304.

Verbrugge, L. M. (1990). Pathways of health and death. In R. D. Apple (Ed). *Women, health, and medicine in America: A historical handbook* (pp. 41–79). New Brunswick, NJ: Rutgers University Press.

Waldron, I. (1994). What do we know about causes of sex differences in mortality? A review of the literature. In P. Conrad & R. Kern (Eds.). *The sociology of health and illness: Critical perspectives* (4th Ed) (pp. 42–57). New York: St. Martin's Press.

Walker, K. (1955). *The story of medicine.* New York: Oxford University Press.

Weitz, R. (1996a). *The sociology of health, illness, and health care: A critical approach.* Belmont, CA: Wadsworth.

Weitz, R. (1996b). Life with AIDS. In P. Brown (Ed.). *Perspectives in medical sociology* (2nd Ed) (pp. 727–740). Prospect Heights, IL: Waveland Press, Inc.

Wells, E. A. (1995). Misconceptions about AIDS among children who can identify the major routes of HIV transmission. *Journal of Pediatric Psychology, 20,* 5, 671–686.

Wilkinson, R. G. (1990). Income distribution and mortality: A "natural" experiment. *Sociology of Health and Illness, 12,* 4, 391–412.

Williams, D. R., & Collins, C. (1995). US Socioeconomic and racial differences in health: Patterns and explanations. *Annual Review of Sociology, 21,* 349–386.

Wilner, D. M., Walkley, R. P., & Goerke, L. S. (1973). *Introduction to public health* (6th Ed). New York: Macmillan Publishing Co.

Wolffers, I. (1997). Culture, media, and HIV/AIDS in Asia. *The Lancet, 349,* 52–54.

Wolinsky, F. D. (1988). *The sociology of health: Principles, practitioners, and issues* (2nd Ed). Belmont, CA: Wadsworth.

Woods, N. F. (1996). Women and their health. In P. Brown (Ed.). *Perspectives in medical sociology* (2nd Ed) (pp. 44–76). Prospect Heights, IL: Waveland Press.

World Development Report. (1993). *Investing in health: World development indicators.* New York: Oxford University Press.

World Health Organization. (1995). *The World Health Report 1995: Bridging the Gaps.* Geneva, Switzerland.

PART TWO

Health and Illness Behavior

CHAPTER

4

Health Behavior

In the United States, for example, the structural power of corporate and medical professional interests results in individual responsibility for health being defined in terms of consumer and life-style behavior. The 'responsible' person thus, is one who buys sufficient health insurance, consumes the right diet and avoids consuming the wrong products, purchases health professional care wisely, takes prescribed medications and complies with other 'doctors-orders,' spends stress-reducing vacations, and invests in a good health spa.

—Donahue and McGuire, 1995, p. 48

The Sociology of Health Behavior

At least three times a week, this author can be found at a local fitness center, working out on weights, running on a treadmill, and engaged in what most experts would say is "healthy behavior." To many, the most obvious question is: Why? What is the benefit associated with an hour of trying to strengthen middle-age muscles? Why do we, a culture preoccupied with television and other forms of passive entertainment, not encourage more active involvement by those least physically inclined? Who am I trying to impress—myself? My spouse? Other members of the fitness center? The answer is none of the above. In reality, it is the various social institutions within society (for example, those institutions which define our economic, political, health, and work environments) that have developed guidelines of what constitutes individually based and responsible health behavior as they attempt to impress on me the value of a regular exercise program. Membership in the fitness center also signifies (to some extent) my socioeconomic status, another indicator of health behavior. It is the blending of one's location within the social structure with concomitant cultural expectations that influences individual health behaviors and outcomes (for an interesting analysis of the sociological and economic interpretations of health behavior, see Lindbladh et al., 1996). These health and outcome differences are represented by a variety of health indices. One index that consistently illustrates the consequence of socioeconomic differences is that of health status. Essentially, reported health status improves as a person's income level increases.

Definitions of Health

Numerous definitions of **health** exist. Rather than treat the reader to a multiplicity of similar definitions, it is, perhaps, easiest to begin with a basic definition. First, however, one definition of health that has historical as well as practical importance: In 1946, the World Health Organization (WHO) defined health as "a state of complete physical, mental and social well-being and not merely the absence of disease or infirmity" (WHO, 1966, p. 1). Although this definition may epitomize a commendable goal, the likelihood of achievement may be difficult even within the most affluent of nations. As Ware (1986, p. 205) notes, "health connotes 'completeness' . . . 'proper function' . . . 'well-being' . . . 'soundness' and 'vitality.' " More broadly, Kovacs (1989, pp. 262–263) suggests that "health is that physical or mental state . . . which is capable of adapting to the natural and social–environmental surroundings of the individual with the appropriate advantage/disadvantage ratio for the body and spirit." These definitions identify a number of qualities that provide a framework from which a more specific yet culturally relative definition can be constructed. Mechanic (1992, p. 1345) provides an example of a more definitive and realistic definition of health: "Health is a product of culture and social structure, and derives from the belief systems and patterned activities reinforced by the ways of life of particular cultural communities." The importance of this definition is the integration of cultural patterning and social–structural influences.

Definitions of Health Behavior and Health Status

This chapter provides a broad framework within which health, **health behavior,** and health status are examined. First, however, some definitions and distinctions between key concepts should be addressed. Although *health* incorporates cultural and structural expectations into its definition of the nonexistence of disease, *health behavior* refers to actions that assist individuals in maintaining their health. Utilizing the cultural and structural expectations of health as well as mitigating health behavior, **health status** provides an assessment of one's actual health condition. For example, the wellness movement in the United States is interconnected with cultural values espousing individualism (see Alonzo, 1993) as well as state interests attempting to hold down health-care costs. As Hill (1996, p. 788) argues, however, the state has a responsibility to provide "those means that are beyond the capacity of any one individual to provide if he or she is to have a realistic hope of exercising the right to health." In an effort to achieve that goal, the European Community has taken the lead in an effort to ensure health for all by the year 2000. Within the European Community, Rathwell (1992), addressing Health For All (HFA), criticized the efforts of most nations as not being sufficient to reach the stated goal. The involvement of the state in matters of health can also be deleterious. For example, in Chile, the state (historically) has been directly involved in creating a dual health-care system that offers a private sector for the wealthy and an underfunded public sector for the majority of the population (Trumper & Phillips, 1996). Another example of state involvement and the emergence of unequal health opportunities is the implementation of the North American Free Trade Agreement (NAFTA). Poole (1996) argues that NAFTA has exacerbated health and health-care related problems in the *maquiladora* industry, which refers to " 'offshore' assembly plants owned mostly by U.S. firms" just inside the Mexican border (Poole, 1996, p. 4). Here, American companies build assembly plants and employ Mexican workers at low wages with little if any health benefits. The work is demanding and potentially harmful to the health of the workers. Workers who complain are generally fired.

The Influence of Culture

As mentioned earlier, one's culture influences the definition of health. The following examples illustrate the relationship between cultural expectations and health.

- The Mishing of northeast India consider the following as indicative of good health. They include:
    - (i) no disease,
    - (ii) strong and tall body,
    - (iii) good and white teeth,
    - (iv) ability to carry out day-to-day work happily,
    - (v) ability to laugh loudly,
    - (vi) ability to plough one bigha of land in two days and
    - (vii) ability to walk through a distance of 2 km. at a stretch.
- In the case of a woman, the additional points are to have
    - (i) long and black hair, and
    - (ii) potentiality to give birth to 5–6 children. (Kar, 1993, p. 159)

- Modern (Western) medicine is increasingly available to the Ibo tribe of Nigeria. However, Ezeji and Sarvela (1992, p. 34) point out that traditional medicine and practitioners are more willingly accepted because "modern medicine services is nothing but an antithesis to the people's cultural beliefs."
- Within Guatemala, health among "the Mayan Indians, the Ladino and the Black Carib" is understood and maintained through an intricate relationship between available Western medicines and traditional practitioners (Gonzalez, 1966, p. 122). More specifically, Gonzalez (1966) argues that health is maintained by utilizing Western medicine to determine the symptoms of medical problems while traditional practitioners address the cause.
- On a much broader scale, Prins (1989) addresses the historical context of external (colonial) intervention and its impact on the health of Africans. According to Prins (1989, p. 179):

> Thus Africanists studying medicine and health carry an acute, double responsibility. Their work, by its methodological force, may help rescue the wider spectrum of the African past; but by exposing its medical disasters, explaining their causes and giving prominence to past patterns of indigenous defense of the individual and society against affliction, it may also help change that powerful and persistent image of sick Africa with which I began.

The Interaction of Sex, Race and Ethnicity, Age, and Social Class on Health Behavior

Health and health behavior is also influenced by the interaction of sociological variables such as sex, race and ethnicity, age, and social class. First, however, it is important to distinguish between the central concepts applied in this chapter and in Chapter 3. Although Chapter 3 addresses differences in death and disease between categories of the population, this chapter examines differences in the health-related concepts between similar population categories. Consider, for example, differences in reported health status offered in Table 4.1. Here, for example, women, in comparison with men, consistently report higher levels of fair or poor health status. In addition, the percentage of African Americans reporting fair or poor health status is almost double that of Caucasian Americans. Health status is also directly related to one's income level. That is, as income rises, so does one's health status. As a result of these different health outcomes relative to one's position in society, differing morbidity patterns emerge. In a disturbing assessment of the United States and a number of other Western industrialized nations, Siegrist (1995, p. 1603) points out that "the social inequalities in mortality from chronic disease are widening." These differences will continue to exacerbate the position of women, minorities, and the poor within the larger society. Because of their secondary status, disadvantaged groups are not accorded the same economic opportunities, thus limiting their access to the health-care community. In addition to structural barriers, women, minorities, and those disadvantaged because of social class also face cultural impediments that

TABLE 4.1 Respondent-Assessed Health Status, According to Selected Characteristics: United States, 1987–1993

	Percent with Fair or Poor Health			
Characteristic	*1987*	*1989*	*1991*	*1993*
Total[1,2]	9.5	9.1	9.3	9.7
Age				
Under 15 years	2.4	2.4	2.5	2.8
Under 5 years	2.6	2.6	2.6	3.3
5–14 years	2.3	2.3	2.4	2.6
15–44 years	5.4	5.6	5.8	6.6
45–64 years	17.4	16.1	16.7	17.1
65 years and over	30.8	28.5	29.0	28.0
65–74 years	28.2	26.3	26.0	25.0
75 years and over	34.9	32.0	33.6	32.4
Sex and Age				
Male[1]	9.0	8.6	8.9	9.1
Under 15 years	2.5	2.6	2.5	2.9
15–44 years	4.5	4.6	5.0	5.6
45–64 years	16.6	15.4	16.1	16.0
65–74 years	28.9	27.2	26.7	25.4
75 years and over	36.0	33.0	33.7	31.9
Female[1]	9.9	9.5	9.7	10.4
Under 15 years	2.3	2.3	2.4	2.7
15–44 years	6.3	6.6	6.6	7.6
45–64 years	18.1	16.8	17.2	18.2
65–74 years	27.7	25.6	25.5	24.6
75 years and over	34.2	31.5	33.5	32.7
Race and Age				
White[1]	8.5	8.2	8.6	8.8
Under 15 years	2.0	2.0	2.1	2.4
15–44 years	4.6	4.9	5.2	5.9
45–64 years	15.6	14.5	15.4	15.3
65–74 years	26.8	24.5	24.6	23.4
75 years and over	33.2	30.8	32.4	31.0
Black[1]	16.7	15.9	15.1	16.8
Under 15 years	4.1	4.4	4.5	4.9
15–44 years	10.5	10.2	9.7	11.1
45–64 years	32.9	29.6	27.2	32.0
65–74 years	42.9	44.7	41.2	41.1
75 years and over	52.4	45.2	48.2	48.2
Family Income[1,3]				
Less than $14,000	20.5	19.4	19.9	21.4
$14,000–$24,999	14.1	10.1	10.8	12.1

(*continued*)

111

TABLE 4.1   Continued

Characteristic	Percent with Fair or Poor Health			
	1987	*1989*	*1991*	*1993*
$25,000–$34,999	11.0	6.9	7.1	8.2
$35,000–$49,999	7.1	5.1	5.5	5.7
$50,000 or more	4.7	3.7	3.9	3.9
Geographic Region[1]				
Northeast	7.9	7.2	7.4	8.3
Midwest	8.8	8.3	8.1	8.7
South	11.7	11.2	11.7	11.6
West	8.2	8.5	8.8	9.3
Location of Residence[1]				
Within MSA	9.0	8.6	8.9	9.4
Outside MSA	10.8	10.8	10.7	11.1

[1] Age adjusted.

[2] Includes all other races not shown separately and unknown family income.

[3] Family income categories for 1989–1993. Income categories for 1987 are: less than $10,000; $10,000–$14,999; $15,000–$19,999; $20,000–$34,999; and $35,000 or more. Income categories for 1986 are: less than $13,000; $13,000–$18,999; $19,000–$24,999; $25,000–$44,999; and $45,000 or more.

Source: Data compiled from Centers for Disease Control and Prevention, National Center for Health Statistics, Division of Health Interview Statistics. Data from the National Health Interview Survey; and National Center for Health Statistics. *Health, United States, 1994.* Table 63. Hyattsville, MD: Public Health Services. 1995.

limit their access and continuity to adequate and affordable health care. Again, the consequence is increased levels of morbidity among the less advantaged members of society. As Bayne-Smith (1996, p. 27) points out,

> When gender is considered within race, any analysis of the health status of women must take into account the cultural norms that exist in every group. Racial issues distort these norms and the gendered behaviors that flow from them. These distortions influence the relationship between women of color and society and, as such, have direct impact on the health and mental health of women of color.

Sex

An example of cultural impediments relative to the health of women is offered in the review of the literature on the health status of immigrant women from Southeast Asia (Kulig, 1990). Citing the work of Meleis and Rogers (1987), Kulig

(1990) identifies not only the cultural context of women's health, but also their roles within the family and larger society as intrinsically interconnected to their health status (see also, McElmurry et al., 1993). In other words, cultural expectations associated with sex-specific behaviors, as well as their associated outcomes, have a different impact on women and men.

According to the data in Table 4.1, health status discrepancies persist on the basis of sex. Health behavior experiences also differ between males and females. For example, sex is related to a number of socioeconomic variables such as education, social class, employment (David & Kaplan, 1995), and medication use (Zadoroznyj & Svarstad, 1990). Some explanations for the apparent sex-based differences include biology, gender roles, stress, and technology (Woods, 1995). However, women have higher morbidity rates than do men. Waldron (1988, p. 194), meanwhile, suggests that, viewed more broadly, "differences in health-related behavior vary depending on the type of behavior and the cultural context," whereas Helman (1994) offers sex-specific examples of ill-health located not only in the United States but also in many Western industrialized nations. For example, men are more likely to engage in risky behavior such as smoking, alcohol consumption, and accidents. In an analysis of excess male mortality in European countries, particularly in the 20th century, Hart (1989, p. 133) concludes, "men die before women because of alcohol and cigarettes." This argument (regarding the effect of cigarette smoking) is supported by work in Finland of Koskinen et al. (1985). These differences in sex-related health behaviors are not confined to Western societies. Waldron (1988) points out that cigarette smoking has increased significantly among men in non-Western countries. Sex differences in health and health behavior can also be understood within the context of exclusion. As Kumar (1995) points out, the role of women in the current health-care system of northern India is fragmented at best. Kumar (1995, p. 17) notes that support for such structural disequalibrium is based on the argument that it keeps "women from seeking care (stemming) from cultural roots that are deeply entrenched in the life of the community. Gender ideology and gender-based behavior are some of the cultural beliefs and practices that influence health behavior."

Within many developing countries, health outcomes are directly attributable to one's sex (World Health Organization, 1995). Lewis and Kieffer (1994) and others argue that one's sex influences not only access to medical care, but also the type and level of care. For example, Lear (1996, p. 289) states that it is the lack of social power among women in Africa that "is the cornerstone of their risk for AIDS." Furthermore, one of the difficulties in assessing the health problems of women in developing countries is the lack of adequate research (Raikes, 1989).

Sex differences in health and health behavior are also the result of a multiplicity of factors ranging from the economic productivity of women to culturally defined gender roles. For instance, in Orangi, Pakistan, Mubarak et al. (1990) found that women's health was related to their levels of employment and autonomy. In their study of women in an Egyptian delta hamlet, Lane and Meleis (1991, p. 1206) found "that women's health and the health of their children in Gamileya is influenced by the cultural expectations governing female gender, by women's changing responsibilities as they age, by their work, by their health perceptions and by the health resources available to them." More specifically, Lane and Meleis also found that all women in the hamlet had undergone circumcision or "female genital mutilation." This is a painful and unnecessary removal of the clitoris. In addition to cultural explanations, Lane and Meleis (1991, p. 1201) cite an Egyptian study performed by the High Institute of Nursing in Alexandria, Egypt, in which the authors estimated that 30% of all circumcisions are conducted by physicians, who the authors speculate perform the procedure for economic reasons. This practice occurs throughout the African Continent, Asia, and select populations in Europe, North America, and Australia (WHO, 1995). Although female genital mutilation continues, there have been efforts in Africa and other countries to end the practice. Increasingly, female genital mutilation is viewed as a violation of one's human rights rather than a cultural tradition (Loustaunau & Sobo, 1997).

A comparative analysis of health-related behaviors among residents of Glasgow and Edinburgh, Scotland, and Varna, Bulgaria (Uitenbroek et al., 1996), found that sex differences in health behavior were greater in Varna than in Glasgow and Edinburgh. These differences were attributed to persistent female subjugation within the family. Similarly, Hraba et al. (1996) found little support for sex-based differences in the self-reporting of health in the Czech Republic. However, as in Bulgaria, women in the Czech Republic experienced role overload as they were expected to maintain not only work roles but domestic roles as well. Finally, based on their research of Israeli kibbutzim, Carmel et al. (1991) identified sex differences associated with the impact of life events.

Essentially, "women are more vulnerable than men to the negative effects of life events" (Carmel et al., 1990, p. 1094). In New Zealand, considerable health differences between Maori and non-Maori women led to the development of the Maori Women's Welfare League. Although organized for more politically pragmatic reasons, the League has become involved in attempting to understand and reduce the health gap between the Maori and non-Maori of New Zealand (Armstrong & Armstrong, 1991). Research by Clarke and Lowe (1989, p. 404) in Australia found sex differences in the meaning of health. Males were more likely to associate health with fitness, whereas females believed health to be associated with "feeling well and the ability to cope." Similarly, Kristiansen (1989, p. 187), in a study of British males and females, found differences in the meaning of health. Basically, women "associated 'health' with 'happiness,' 'a comfortable life,' and 'pleasure.' . . . [whereas] . . . males [associated] 'health' with 'family security' and 'national security.' "

Finally, health and health outcomes have been related to sex differences in marital status. For instance, health problems increase with divorce or widowhood. Efforts to explain the relationship between health and marital status have utilized the health selection and the social causation models. The difference between these models is the presumed causal relationship. In the health selection model, health is the independent variable and marital status is the dependent variable, whereas the relationship is reversed in the social causation model. In other words, the health selection model argues that the less healthy are less likely to marry. If the less healthy do marry, their marriages are more likely to end in divorce or separation. Thus, one's health is directly related to the likelihood of finding a marital partner. However, the social causation model identifies four reasons why married people are healthier. They include: greater availability of material resources, the potential for reduced stress, a decrease in risky behaviors such as drinking and smoking, and increased availability of social support (Wyke & Ford, 1992).

Utilizing various explanations in the "health selection" model, research by Wyke and Ford (1992, p. 531) found that among their sample of 55-year olds in Scotland, "marital status is associated with health through higher levels of material resources and lower levels of stress amongst married people." The effect of marital status differs for males and females. For instance, married males and unmarried females experience fewer health problems. Umberson (1992, p. 914) argues that "marriage may benefit the health of men more than women partly because marriage provides more control for men."

Race and Ethnicity

Health and health status are also influenced by race and ethnicity. Research on the relationship between health and race dates to the early 1950s (LaVeist, 1993). As the data in Table 4.2 indicate, in comparison with Caucasian Americans, African Americans are more likely to report their health status as fair or poor. One consequence of this health differential is a continued economic disparity in which African Americans continue to earn less than do Caucasian Americans. Far more seriously, however, is the greater likelihood of death experienced by African Americans relative to Caucasian Americans. In a classic examination of race and health, McCord and Freeman (1990) report that survival rates among young African American males in Harlem is lower than in Bangladesh. On a broader level, King and Williams (1995) outline differences between Caucasian American, African American, and Hispanic American health status. They address health topics ranging from chronic diseases such as cancer and AIDS to infant mortality and the increased risks faced by African Americans and Hispanic Americans. It is at this level that the stark reality of racial inequality in the American health-care system is particularly evident.

Attempting to understand the interrelationship between poverty and health, LaVeist (1993) argues that African American infant mortality rates are related not only to economic hardship, but also to residential segregation and the lack of African American political power. Three basic findings associated with this argument include the following. Although there appears to be a discrepancy between these points, LaVeist argues that in fact, there is not.

1. Black infant mortality is higher in highly segregated cities.
2. Black political power is greater in highly segregated cities.
3. Black infant mortality is lower in cities with greater black political power and higher in cities with higher segregation. (LaVeist, 1993, p. 51).

Stated differently, "the degree to which African-Americans are politically empowered relative to their potential political power is a more potent predictor of mortality than absolute political power" (LaVeist, 1992, p. 1090).

TABLE 4.2   Physician Contacts, According to Respondent-Assessed Health Status, Age, Sex, and Poverty Status: United States, 1987–1989 and 1992–1994[1]

| Age, Sex, and Poverty Status[2] | Respondent-Assessed Health Status; Physician Contacts per Person per Year | | | |
| | Good to Excellent | | Fair to Poor | |
	1987–1989	*1992–1994*	*1987–1989*	*1992–1994*
Total[3]				
Sex				
Male				
Poor	3.4	3.8	11.1	13.6
Near poor	3.7	3.8	13.4	14.7
Nonpoor	4.2	4.7	16.8	17.7
Female				
Poor	4.7	5.4	13.6	15.7
Near poor	4.6	5.0	14.9	17.0
Nonpoor	5.6	5.9	19.4	23.3
Age				
Under 15 years				
Poor	3.6	4.0	10.8	12.5
Near poor	3.8	4.0	15.2	15.4
Nonpoor	5.0	5.0	22.6	23.3
15–44 years				
Male				
Poor	2.8	2.9	9.8	12.9
Near poor	2.9	2.8	11.7	15.4
Nonpoor	3.1	3.3	14.0	16.3
Female				
Poor	5.1	5.4	14.0	15.9
Near poor	4.7	5.0	16.0	16.5
Nonpoor	5.6	5.8	20.4	22.7
45–64 years				
Male				
Poor	3.1	3.8	11.4	15.3
Near poor	3.5	3.9	12.8	14.1
Nonpoor	4.1	5.0	13.8	15.1
Female				
Poor	4.6	6.5	17.3	18.3
Near poor	4.7	5.2	14.5	16.5
Nonpoor	5.7	6.4	16.1	21.0
65 years and over				
Male				
Poor	5.5	6.5	13.2	14.5

TABLE 4.2 Continued

| Age, Sex, and Poverty Status[2] | Respondent-Assessed Health Status; Physician Contacts per Person per Year | | | |
| | Good to Excellent | | Fair to Poor | |
	1987–1989	1992–1994	1987–1989	1992–1994
Near poor	6.5	6.8	12.9	16.6
Nonpoor	6.5	8.1	15.5	19.5
Female				
Poor	6.5	8.0	16.0	20.3
Near poor	6.6	8.0	14.3	19.3
Nonpoor	7.1	8.4	14.9	20.9

[1] Data are based on household interviews of a sample of the civilian noninstitutionalized population. Persons with unknown family income or unknown health status were eliminated from the analysis. Persons who reported their health to be good, very good, or excellent were categorized as good to excellent health. See Appendix II.

[2] Poverty status is based on family income and family size using Bureau of the Census poverty thresholds. Poor persons are defined as below the poverty threshold. Near poor persons have incomes of 100% to less than 200% of poverty threshold. Nonpoor persons have incomes of 200% or greater than the poverty threshold. See Appendix II.

[3] Age adjusted.

Source: Data compiled from Centers for Disease Control and Prevention, National Center for Health Statistics. Data Computed by the Division of Health and Utilization Analysis from data compiled by the Division of Health Interview Statistics and National Center for Health Statistics. *Health, United States, 1995.* Table 76. Hyattsville, MD: Public Health Service. 1996.

In general, the Hispanic American population experiences lower health status than do Caucasian Americans. However, there are considerable differences within the Hispanic American community. In a study of the health of Cuban American, Mexican American, and Puerto Rican children, Angel and Worobey (1991) report meaningful dissimilarities. They found that Cuban American children were the healthiest, with Mexican American children second. Puerto Rican children, however, experienced more health problems. Angel and Worobey (1991) report that this breakdown applies to adult generations of Hispanic Americans as well. An extensive investigation of the health of the Hispanic American community was conducted by the National Center for Health Statistics in the early to mid-1980s. Although problematic, the Hispanic Health and Nutrition Examination Survey provides a wealth of data. Improved health outcomes are dependent on "knowledge of the level of acculturation, social class, and social isolation of the target population [are] needed to determine what type of intervention would be best" (Carter-Pokras, 1994, p. 73). Health outcome differences between ethnic groups occupying similar physical environments are not limited to the United States. Quah (1993) reports different health outcomes between Chinese and Indian inhabitants in Singapore.

Health and health outcomes also vary among Native Americans. Similar to Hispanic Americans, Native Americans also represent a heterogeneous segment of the population. Historically, Native Americans experienced a dramatic decrease in their population throughout the 19th and early 20th centuries. However, that trend has been reversed. The health status of Native Americans, although less than that of Caucasian Americans, has also experienced significant gains in the recent past. In fact, Young (1994) argues that health status differences between Native Americans and the Caucasian American population have been diminishing and, in terms of infant mortality, have become equalized. More specifically, Kunitz (1983) argues that the crude mortality rates between the Navajo and the general population are relatively similar. Williams and Collins (1995) disagree with such an optimistic assessment. They point out that infant mortality rates among Native Americans are higher than the general population. Furthermore, morbidity rates among those age 45 and younger remains considerably higher within the Native American population relative to other groups (Williams & Collins, 1995). There is little disagreement, however, that the economic and social disparities between Native Americans and the general population have diminished.

The influence of culture on the health of population is illustrated in a number of studies. Within the United States, the Amish live in predominantly rural areas of the Midwest and are only tangentially interconnected to any larger community. Research of the Amish in rural Ohio by Fuchs and colleagues (1990) found that Amish men and women were less likely to experience hypertension. Interestingly, life expectancy rates were more similar between Amish men and women than between non-Amish men and women. The researchers suggest that lifestyle and eating habits (particularly among men) may explain this observation.

Research has examined the relationship between ethnicity and health in a number of cultures. A study of 15 countries by the United Nations found that "ethnicity was the only factor other than parental education where large child mortality differentials persisted" (Caldwell, 1993, p. 131). Similarly, Quah (1993) found differences in health outcomes (as measured by the leading causes of death) between the three major ethic groups (Chinese, Malay, & Indian) in Singapore.

An explanation of ethnic group differences lies, to a great extent, in health behaviors that are the result of associated values and beliefs. Finally, Smaje (1995) argues that, in Great Britain, the level of ethnic residential concentration influences health status. That is, as the concentration of an ethnic group in a residential area decreases, so does their reported health.

Age

It is obvious in Table 4.1 that health status is also influenced by age. This is not surprising, considering that as we grow older we encounter increased health problems, particularly chronic diseases. Among elderly persons, this may be manifested by a decreased absence of pain relative to younger age groups (Idler & Angel, 1990). Studying the experience of pain among elderly persons in India, Thomas (1992, p. 504) found that their "world-view did influence both health attitudes and behaviors."

The relationship between age and health interfaces with other variables such as race, residential location, and socioeconomic status. For instance, the health of elderly African Americans is generally poorer than that of elderly Caucasian Americans (Mutchler & Burr, 1991), whereas rural elderly persons experience poorer health than their urban counterparts (Mainous & Kohrs, 1995). One explanation for these differences is the lack of health resources and providers in rural locations, resulting in their limited access to the health-care system. Globally, research of elderly persons in developed as well as developing nations points to not only a population increasing in total numbers and as a percentage of the population, but also to one that is relatively healthy. This statement is less true among the elderly persons of the former Soviet Union and Eastern European nations. In a study of the urban population of the former Soviet Union, Chebotarev et al. (1981, p. 453) state that there has been "an increase of morbidity due to chronic diseases in aging and a sharp decrease of apparently healthy people." However, Laird and Chamberlain (1990) report that although respondents in a New Zealand study experienced some concerns regarding issues such as their workload, children, or sufficient income levels, their overall health was relatively stable. Among the Asian societies of Fiji, the Republic of Korea, Malaysia, and the Philippines, Andrews (1987, p. 26) identifies an impression of "relatively robust health among the subjects in the study." Health differences do exist, however, between developed and developing Asian nations. Even within developing nations there is considerable variation between life expectancy rates (see, for example, Tout, 1989, for an extensive discussion of the emergence of elderly persons in developing nations). Martin (1988) points to respiratory diseases as the major causes of death among elderly persons in developing Asian nations, whereas chronic diseases such as cancer, heart disease, and cerebrovascular disease are the leading causes of death in developed Asian nations. Although the types of chronic diseases as the leading causes of death are consistent with other industrialized nations, their rate of occurrence is different in Japan. Among Western industrialized nations, cardiovascular disease is the leading cause of death, whereas in Japan it is second to malignant neoplasms. The difference between Japan and its industrialized partners is attributed to the eating habits of the Japanese population that includes a well-balanced diet (Maeda et al., 1989). In addition to differences in eating habits in Japan, McConatha et al. (1991, p. 228) identify the promotion of health through the following: "health promotion during a lifetime, a basic format for health promotion, and enlightenment and dissemination of health promotion." Among elderly persons, this includes a healthy lifestyle involving the use of sport throughout one's life.

Social Class

In addition to sex, race and ethnicity, and age, differences in health, health behavior, and health status are also interrelated with one's socioeconomic position. Earlier research (Antonovsky, 1967) chronicled changes in American and European life expectancy by social class. In a pioneering study, Koos (1954) examined the relationship between the health and social class of "Regionville" residents and found social class differences permeating all aspects of community health. More recent research continues to support the conclusion that as one's income, education, or occupational status rises, so does one's health and health status (Berkman & Breslow, 1983). Williams and Collins (1995) point to the continued relationship between socioeconomic status and health outcomes and identify a number of current research efforts supporting their argument.

Relative to differences in health opportunities on the basis of social class, examine the health status differences between the poor, near poor, and nonpoor in Table 4.2. Regardless of age or sex, the percentage of respondents with good to excellent health status increased with level of income. At the same time, respondents with fair or poor health status reported far more physician contacts than did the respondents with good to excellent health status. Physician contacts also increased with level of income.

The relationship between health and social class is true not only within the United States, but in many other countries as well. The following list identifies research addressing the relationship between health and social class: Dahlgren and Diderichsen, 1985 (Sweden); Holstein, 1985 (Denmark); Maseide, 1985 (Norway); Marmot and Theorell, 1988 (England); LePranc, 1989 (Caribbean Islands); Mackenbach, 1992, and Stronks et al., 1996 (Netherlands); Williams et al., 1992 (Guyana); and Dahl, 1994 (Norway).

Perhaps as important as the relationship itself are the attempts to explain its existence. The best-known international research examining the intersection of social class and health is the Black Report (Townsend & Davidson, 1992). Here, the authors report that after some 30 years, health differences between class I (professionals), class II (intermediate), class IIIN (skilled nonmanual), class IIIM (skilled manual), class IV (partly skilled), and class V (unskilled) workers continues to persist in the United Kingdom. The authors address the following four theoretical explanations in an effort to account for the continuing class-based health outcomes.

1. *Artifact explanations.* Briefly, the artifact explanation asserts that the relationship between socioeconomic status and health is artificial and "of little causal significance" (Townsend & Davidson, 1992, p. 105). According to this explanation, continued class-based health inequalities persist because of "the reduction in the proportion of the population in the poorest occupational classes" (Townsend & Davidson, 1992, p. 105). Furthermore, this explanation argues that persons who move up the socioeconomic ladder have better health relative to persons who remain behind. In other words, class differences remain, although the size of the poorest (and less healthy) population has declined.

2. *Theories of natural or social selection.* This explanation is based on the drift hypothesis. That is, those individuals at the bottom of the socioeconomic ladder (classes IV and V) are there because of their health, whereas individuals in class I are the strongest and healthiest.

3. *Materialist or structuralist explanations.* The essential feature of this explanation is that it is rooted in Marxian philosophy. Health inequalities persist because of economic and social–structural differences between the classes. Lowered economic opportunities lead to increasing health problems among persons living in poverty.

4. *Cultural–behavioural explanations.* This explanation is based on the "culture of poverty" philosophy. With the focus on the individual, health differences are explained in terms of personal responsibility. Thus, increased morbidity levels within class V are related to unhealthy behaviors such as smoking, lack of exercise, and so forth.

Although Townsend and Davidson (1992, p. 114) believe that the materialist interpretation offers the best explanation, they also recognize the importance of the other explanations. Research by Stronks et al. (1996, p. 667) suggests that although individual and structural components influence inequalities in health, "the contribution of structural conditions was greater." Others (Marmot et al., 1995) argue that research efforts to establish the relationship between social class and health inequalities have been too narrowly focused and should be expanded to include a wider range of variables, ranging from the distribution of medical care to psychosocial influences. Examining the interrelationship between sex and health inequalities in the United Kingdom, Arber (1989, p. 277) found that "health status is influenced by the class position of the household which is the result of the combination of the roles of both spouses in the labour market."

It is obvious that one's location in the social class structure directly influences access to care (availability of health-related services). However, equality of access will not result in equality of health outcomes (Williams, 1990).

As expected, health outcomes associated with social class differentiation are clear. Middle- and upper-middle class persons are more likely to experience not only better health, but also lower morbidity and mortality rates. Thus, not only do the middle and upper classes live longer, but they also live better. An interesting analysis of middle-class health behavior and beliefs in Edinburgh is offered by Backett (1992, p. 271), who concludes that "health and its relevant behaviours are evaluated and become meaningful contingent on particular social contexts and their associated choices, priorities and constraints."

It is evident that differences in health and health behavior exist not only in the United States, but also in the world. These differences are reflected within group level characteristics ranging from sex to race to socioeconomic status. The next section examines why members of some groups, relative to others, are more likely to engage in particular health behaviors resulting in different health outcomes.

Models of Health Behavior

Health behavior models provide medical sociologists with a tool for assessing utilization of health services and compliance with prescribed treatment regimens. These models offer researchers valuable insight into the nature of health and illness as they are defined within a particular society. More specifically, health behavior is defined as "any activity undertaken by a person believing himself to be healthy, for the purpose of preventing disease or detecting it in an asymptomatic stage" (Kasl and Cobb, 1966, p. 246).

Although a number of models of health behavior have been proposed in the past (Fishbein & Ajzen, 1975; Ajzen & Fishbein, 1980; Green et al., 1980; Flay & Petraitis, 1994), this discussion is limited to the health belief model (Rosenstock, 1974) and the more recent efforts of Ronald Andersen (1995). This limitation is the result of two broad differences between the theories. First, there is little agreement regarding causes associated with health-related behavior. Second is the location of the variables; in other words, the distance of the variable from the health-related behavior (Flay & Petraitis, 1994).

The Health Belief Model

Historically, the **health belief model** (HBM) emerged as a result of public health interest in preventive health issues during the 1950s (Mullen et al., 1987). Developing the model within a Lewinian framework, the researchers constructed a "theory [that] could be expected to focus on the current (ahistorical) dynamics confronting the behaving individual rather than on the historical perspective of his prior experiences" (Rosenstock, 1974, p. 2). More specifically, the Lewinian perspective argues that "behavior depends mainly upon two variables: (1) the value placed by an individual on a particular outcome and (2) the individual's estimate of the likelihood that a given action will result in that outcome" (Maiman & Becker, 1974, p. 9). These points become evident on examination of the components associated with the HBM. One problem with the HBM, however, is its potential to engage in "victim blaming," as it ignores the impact of social forces and the broader health system (Gallagher, 1994). The model is presented in Fig. 4.1.

More recently, Bush and Iannotti (1985, 1988, 1990) developed what they refer to as the children's health belief model (CHBM). Although similar in design, the CHBM incorporates a number of additional factors, such as personality characteristics, and the influence of others. Utilizing the CHBM, Iannotti and Bush (1993, p. 72) suggest that "children's health orientations may develop somewhat independently of their parents' influence."

Returning to the HBM, Rosenstock (1966, 1974) offers a brief explanation of the major components. Beginning with *perceived susceptibility,* individual reactions to the probability of developing a particular condition can range from denial to extreme concern. In other words, what do I consider to be my personal risk relative to any given condition? Perceived seriousness refers to the extent to which the person believes a given condition will potentially lead to death or diminished physical and/or mental capacity. Depending on individual responses, this component may interface with a broad array of social relationships, including family, friends, or the workplace. Not surprisingly, Rosenstock (1974, p. 4) points out that these two components "are at least partly dependent on knowledge."

If a person believes that they are susceptible to a serious condition, they are likely to take some action. Whatever action is taken is the result of the perceived *benefits* associated with an alternative treatment or therapy regimen that reduces

INDIVIDUAL PERCEPTIONS MODIFYING FACTORS LIKELIHOOD OF ACTION

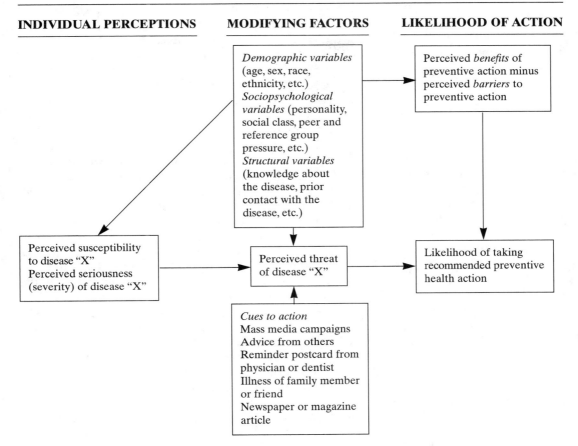

FIGURE 4.1 **Health Belief Model.** The health belief model as predictor of preventive health behavior.

Source: "Historical origins of the health belief model." by I. M. Rosenstock. In M. H. Becker (Ed.). *The Health Belief Model and Personal Health Behavior.* 1974. Thorofare, NJ: Charles B. Slack, Inc. Reprinted with permission.

the threat of the condition. At the same time, the person also experiences perceived *barriers* to the implementation of any action that might reduce the susceptibility and seriousness of the condition. For instance, a person may consider variables such as cost, inconvenience, or increased pain as too much of a price to pay relative to the expected outcome. Within this context, various outcomes are, thus, possible depending on the relationship between perceived benefits and barriers. The most difficult situation is when there are significant benefits as well as barriers associated with a given action. For example, "the person who feels threatened by tuberculosis but fears the potential hazards of x-rays may choose to obtain a tuberculin test for initial screening" (Rosenstock, 1974, p. 5).

But what is the impetus for action? Realizing that susceptibility as well as severity of a given condition were not sufficient to be the pivotal factors in a call for action, proponents of the HBM identified the need for a triggering mechanism to stimulate a response. This cue is related, indirectly, to the degree of susceptibility and severity experienced. That is, the greater the belief of susceptibility and severity of a particular condition, the less intense the cue to action required to stimulate a response. Finally, other factors, such as sociodemographic variables, influence individual attitudes and behavior regarding the efficacy of any preventive action (Rosenstock, 1966, 1974).

There has been extensive research application of the HBM not only in the United States but also in the world. However, as Gallagher (1994, p. 267) points out, "the HBM has not been applied to typical Third World conditions, where adverse environmental factors loom large." For a review of the literature, see Kirscht (1988) for some of the more significant research references, or the work of Suprasert et al. (1995) for a more recent application. Here, it is more advantageous to examine the utility of the model relative to a specific condition.

Research by Arnold and Quine (1994) of helmet use among 30 cyclists aged 11 to 18 in Great Britain illustrates not only the utility of the HBM, but also its predictive power. According to the authors, "the aim of our present study was to try to predict helmet use in a sample of school aged children . . . one month before the dependent measure, actual wearing of a helmet" (1994, p. 103). Research findings indicate that cyclists who considered themselves vulnerable to mishaps were more likely to wear helmets. These cyclists were also more likely to identify the benefits and less likely to perceive the barriers associated with such behavior. Arnold and Quine (1994) also found that a cue to action was a prior cycling accident. Those cyclists that experienced a prior accident were significantly more likely to wear a helmet, compared with cyclists who had not experienced an accident.

Finally, in a correlation between variables, the authors found that "subjects who believe in the benefits of helmet wearing are also those who perceive themselves to be vulnerable to accidents and feel influenced by the advice and actions of powerful others" (Arnold & Quine, 1994, p. 113).

An Emerging Model of Health Behavior

Andersen (1995) has developed a relatively different model of health behavior. Initially devised in the latter 1960s, the model has undergone considerable reformulation since then. Andersen began with a relatively simple explanation of health service usage at the family level of analysis that has evolved into an increasingly complex interpretation of health-service utilization at the individual level (Fig. 4.2). As Andersen (1995, p. 7) points out, the "model portrays the multiple influences on health services' use and, subsequently, on health status." Although not an alternative to the HBM, the model of health services offers an increased number of variables associated with potential outcomes. And, according to Andersen (1995, p. 7) the model "also includes feedback loops showing that outcome, in turn, affects subsequent predisposing factors and perceived need for services as well as health behavior." Only time and continued investigation will determine the value of the model as an explanation of health outcomes.

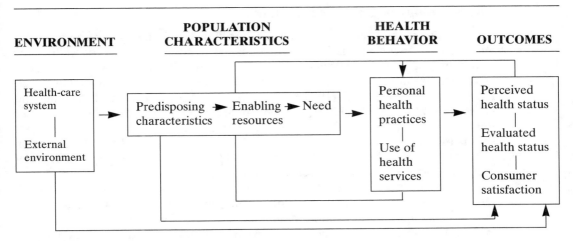

FIGURE 4.2   An Emerging Model—Phase 4.

Source: From "Revisiting the behavioral model and access to medical care: Does it matter?" by R. M. Andersen, *Journal of Health and Social Behavior, 36* 1995, 1–10. Reprinted with permission.

As suggested earlier, models of health behavior provide the medical sociologist with a powerful analytic tool that has cross-cultural relevance. Although deceptively simple, these models allow medical sociologists and others (e.g., health psychologists) to engage in efforts to predict health behaviors. Thus, it is becoming increasingly important for individuals as well as various social institutions to differentiate between those behaviors that are indicative of health versus behaviors resulting in illness or disability. The outcomes associated with such decisions have significant consequences not only for the individual, but for society as well. In the next section some of these outcomes are examined.

The Influence of Health Promotion and Lifestyle on Health Behavior

The life and leisure section of this author's local newspaper recently devoted a major section to the need for proper exercise and diet. In fact, the paper started a regular weekly series on health-related issues. Is this newspaper unusual? Absolutely not. For instance, as a society we are fascinated with devices and diets that will keep us at our optimal weight as well as physically fit while allowing us to remain as physically inactive as possible. Thus, terms such as *couch potato* and *cocooning* apply to an increasingly larger percentage of the total population. The American population is not only overweight, but physically out of shape. Is our fascination with physical fitness necessary given the broader societal movement away from an industrial period to a technology-based information age? Our response to that question is perhaps less important than our realization and understanding of the relationship between our health behavior and our physical and psychosocial condition.

The Sociology of Health Promotion and Lifestyle

The purpose of this section is to integrate our knowledge and application of health and health behavior in relation to issues such as health promotion (or wellness or well-being), self-care, and lifestyle. More specifically, these issues are examined relative to their influence on social-structural variables as well as individual behaviors. For instance, Downie et al. (1996) address not only the practicality of planning and action associated with health promotion, but also its connection to values. Consider the following statement by Burrows et al. (1995, p. 3) as an example of the relationship between sociology and health promotion: "The sociology of health promotion is its concern to analyze the phenomena as a characteristic of the much wider set of socio-economic and cultural processes associated with late modernism."

However, it is necessary to first define the concepts that will be examined. **Health promotion** is "defined as individual and societal actions for the advancement of well-being and the prevention of health risks by achieving and maintaining optimal levels of the behavioral, societal, environmental, and biomedical determinants of health" (Kar, 1989, p. 7). Furthermore, health promotion is based on the twin assumptions of self-determination and "participation in community efforts to control the determinants of health" (Frankish & Green, 1994, p. 215). Stated differently, Berkman (1995, p. 251) argues that, "health promotion rests on the shoulders not only of individuals but also of their families and communities" (see also Mechanic, 1990). There are also questions regarding the lack of a theoretical orientation (Dean & McQueen, 1996) as well as the measurement of quality (Ovretveit, 1996). There have also been criticisms of the health promotion movement. For example, see Downie et al. (1996) for a discussion of various objections. The second major concept, **lifestyle,** has been conceptualized by WHO "as a way of life, a socio-cultural phenomenon arising from interactions between patterns of behaviour and specific life situations rather than individual decisions to avoid or accept certain health risks" (Dean, 1989, p. 137). Even more specifically, Abel (1991, p. 901) defines health lifestyles as "patterns of health-related behavior, values, and attitudes adapted by groups of individuals in response to their social, cultural and economic environment." For a conceptualization of the structure of health promotion as well as lifestyle, see Rutten (1995). Finally, **self-care** involves "the practices of individuals and families through which the forms or symptoms of illness are detected and treated, other diseases are prevented, and positive health behavior is generally promoted" (DeFriese et al., 1989, p. 195). The self-care movement is examined later in this section.

The origins of the health promotion movement can be traced to the very foundation of Western medicine (this section draws heavily on the work of Becker & Rosenstock, 1989). Although dormant for centuries after the demise of Greek civilization, interest in health promotion increased with the advent of technology and the ability to eradicate infectious diseases. Current interest in health promotion is traced to Marc Lalonde, the Canadian Minister of National Health and Welfare. In essence, Lalonde questioned the relationship between one's health and the caliber as well as volume of medical care received (Parish, 1995). In 1974, Lalonde argued that death and disease were the result of: "(1) inadequacies in the health care system, (2) behavioral factors or unhealthy life-styles, (3) environmental hazards, and

(4) human biological factors" (Becker & Rosenstock, 1989, p. 285). Utilizing these factors, American experts then concluded that only a fraction (10%) of the deaths in the United States were the result of deficiencies within the system, whereas one-half could be attributed to behavior associated with lifestyle. Thus, terms such as "risk" and "risk factors," relative to lifestyle behavior, have become commonplace in contemporary American parlance. However, as Cohen (1994, p. 284) points out, whether one participates in health promotion is not the issue. Rather, the issue is "to determine the extent to which health promotion should be pursued and to establish the best balance of activity between various health promotion initiatives."

Another approach to the study of health promotion is the critical social science perspective (CSSP). Beginning with the concept of reflexivity or "the capacity to locate one's research activity in the same social world as the phenomena being studied" (Eakin et al., 1996, p. 158), CSSP examines the basic structures and assumptions of the research process. The CSSP is also interested in "the dialectical relationship between the formal and informal structures of society (institutions, social norms) and individual or collective human action" (Eakin et al., 1996, p. 158). Thus, the level of analysis employed in health promotion research is crucial. For instance, if behavior at the individual level is the primary focus, then problems of health and health behavior are generally blamed on lifestyle behavior or the unwillingness of the individual to participate in those health-related programs that would improve health and health status (see, for example, Taylor, 1989). However, if the problems of health and health behavior are located within the institutional structures of society, then such outcomes can be understood as the result of social inequities grounded in group-level characteristics such as sex, race, age, and social class. Unfortunately, as Eakin et al., (1996, p. 161) note, "health-related problems that are believed to reside in the individual are seen to be easier to address than those residing in such intangible and unwieldy places as the environment, social interaction, economic systems, social class." However, not all group-level characteristics appear to result in health differences. For instance, Weitzel et al., (1994) did not find significant differences regarding health promotion beliefs between Caucasian American, African American, and Hispanic American males. They argue that the paucity of research on health promotion among various minority groups makes it difficult to presume that their health beliefs are, in fact, consistent. More specifically, Weaver and Gary (1996) state that the need for health promotion varied among older African American adults. They report that group-level characteristics such as sex (male), age (young-old), and social involvement (church attendance and social participation) as well as social ties to family and the larger community influenced health behaviors. Furthermore, the Ottawa Charter identified a number of necessary societal level changes such as "public policy, the overall physical and social environment, the more immediate social environment at the community level, personal skills for living, and health services" (Raeburn & Rootman, 1989, p. 386) rather than changes in individual behavior. In an effort to address the integrative nature of health promotion, Rutten (1995) examined a number of elements that previously had been considered in relative isolation from one another. These elements include: (1) the lifestyle approach, (2) the policy approach, (3) the implementation approach, and (4) the transformation approach. Rutten (1995,

p. 1628) argues that taken together, these elements offer a broader and more theoretically viable explanation of health promotion because "it reveals the relationship
among lifestyles, public policy and health promotion implementation."

In the final section, the impact of institutional inequality on health promotion
is examined. In other words, refocusing efforts "toward a range of broader upstream
political and economic forces" (McKinlay, 1994, p. 510) in which the health-care system becomes the focus of empirical analysis (McKinlay, 1993).

Social–Structural Influences on Health and Health Behavior

Theoretically at least, health promotion efforts can occur most anywhere. In reality,
however, there has been a concerted effort, particularly in the United States, to impose health promotion standards within the workplace. In other words, some employers have begun to utilize the concept of health promotion as a means of determining the status of their employees. Conrad (1987), in an assessment of the benefits
and limitations of health promotion or "wellness" in the workplace, found that there
is more to working out than just sweating.

Although the benefits associated with health promotion may include changing
the corporate culture, increasing worker productivity, and providing workers with a
sense of empowerment, there are also a number of potential problems. For instance,
the creation of artificial standards of "health" that workers are expected to maintain. This focuses the emphasis on *individual* health rather than on occupational
health problems within the workplace. The inclusion of workplace health promotion
also increases the power of the employer over the lives of their workers. Finally, and
perhaps the most pernicious problem associated with workplace health promotion,
is the potential that those group-level characteristics related to health (social class,
race, and sex) are "collapsed into handy individual risk factors that can be remedied
by changing personal habits" (Conrad, 1987, p. 265). On an even more fundamental
level, Seedhouse (1995, p. 62) points out that if the relationship between what we believe to be health promotion and well-being "cannot be demonstrated (and without
a workable definition of 'well-being' it obviously cannot) then the pursuit of 'well-
being' by health promoters is nothing more than an act of faith." There is also the
possibility of a "spillover" effect. That is, if workers engage in positive, health-
related activities at work, they will transfer that behavior to their personal life and
healthy lifestyles. Abel et al. (1989, p. 1273) found that those with "occupational self-
direction in their work were not significantly different than those with lesser self-
direction when it came to participating in health lifestyles."

As with any aspect of health, the identification and implementation of health
promotion efforts is not limited to the United States. Examining the relationship between empowerment and health promotion practices in New Zealand, Grace (1991,
p. 332) identifies the "health professionals and health promotion policy advisors and
decision-makers" among those who control decisions regarding health. Rather than
liberating the individual, however, empowerment locates the source of health power
within the "political and economic order" (Grace, 1991, p. 341). The impact of the
state on health promotion efforts is also evident in Singapore (Chern, 1996), where

the government has stated its commitment to a more efficient and less costly health-care system that will rely on a series of health promotion measures. Furthermore, Kumpusalo et al. (1996, p. 112) report on the integration of health promotion efforts in Finland "with the local cultural traditions, values, and norms." Examining health behaviors in Finland, Estonia, and the Republic of Karelia, Puska (1995) reports significant public health differences between the countries. Although health outcomes had been similar in the past, current data indicate lowered outcomes among the peoples of Estonia, and the Republic of Karelia. Also, as Puska (1995) reports, improved health outcomes are dependent on changes in lifestyle and health behaviors that are influenced by health promotion activities. All of these efforts indicate a cross-cultural awareness regarding the importance of health promotion. In addition, it is evident that, regardless of location, the state is intimately involved in the health promotion movement. The concern, as stated earlier, is that the focus of health promotion will be on changing individual behaviors rather than structural-level conditions that have been linked to poor health outcomes. As Grace (1991) reminds us, even societal efforts to empower individuals to control their health may inadvertently (or perhaps purposely) create the conditions that limit such opportunity. In other words, individuals empowered to think as "health consumers" are, in reality, being told by health promoters what their health needs are.

The Self-Care Movement

An example of purported individual empowerment is the self-care "movement" of the 1970s, in which emphasis was placed on self-monitoring of health and illness behavior. The emergence of self-care was not confined to the United States. Researchers have identified its development within a number of European nations during the same period of time. However, differences quickly emerged between the American and European perspectives of self-care. Among many in Europe, self-care was considered "a conservative idea that could strengthen arguments for the dismantling of the welfare state" (Kickbusch, 1989, p. 125). Within the United States the self-care philosophy of patient independence from formal service providers and self-reliance regarding illness and health behavior brought together a curious mix of adherents that included libertarians as well as progressives (DeFriese et al., 1989). Throughout the 1970s the self-care "movement" continued to expand. Today, however, the concept of self-care has generally given way to more palatable terms such as well-being or health promotion. The self-care "movement" has also had a problem with its middle-class bias and lack of interest in issues of health-related inequalities (Kickbusch, 1989). Self-care research has also experienced problems involving its conceptual clarity as well as identifying its correlates. For example, in a survey of the literature, Segall and Goldstein (1989) identify the inconsistency in the research findings relative to a number of demographic variables. In their own research, Segall and Goldstein (1989, p. 158) state that: "no one sociodemographic attribute is systematically related to all of the self-care behaviours investigated, and that no single dimension of self-care is associated with all of these social, cultural and economic characteristics." It is perhaps this lack of conceptual clarity and methodological direction that has reduced the significance of self-care and increased efforts in the direction of health promotion and wellness. Regardless of the reason, self-care has lost favor particularly within the academic community, although it remains relatively popular with the general public.

Returning to the WHO definition of health that argues for "complete physical, mental and social well-being" brings us full circle. Although viable, the process of achieving such a state of health is contingent on that dynamic relationship between individual health-related behaviors and social structural conditions located within a specific cultural context. As a result, "health" remains, as before, an elusive conceptual indicator that we continuously attempt to locate and define.

Summary

This chapter examines not only the concepts of health and health behavior, but also related issues such as health promotion, wellness, and self-care. In addition to the impact of culture, health and health behavior are also influenced by sociodemographic characteristics such as sex, race and ethnicity, age, and social class. For example, health status differs between men and women, African Americans and Caucasian Americans, young and old, and income level. More specifically, sex differences in health behavior were attributed to physiological as well as social explanations.

In developing countries, health outcomes have also been linked to differences in economic opportunities, expected gender role performance, and marital status. Health status differences on the basis of race and ethnicity are the result of economic inequalities, racial segregation, and political power differentials. However, the most significant relationship exists between health status and social class.

Internationally, the most famous research examining the intersection of health and social class is the Black Report. Conducted in Great Britain in the latter 1970s, the researchers found considerable health differences on the basis of social class position. Although the researchers offered various explanations, the conservative government of then Prime Minister Margaret Thatcher attempted to keep the report from being made public.

Health behavior incorporates multiple activities such as compliance with treatment regimens, utilization of services, and performance of the patient role. Perhaps one of the most significant developments in medical sociology was the creation of the health belief model (HBM). The major components of the HBM include perceived susceptibility, seriousness, benefits, and barriers in addition to a triggering mechanism that elicits a response.

Finally, the influence of health promotion (or well-being), self-care, and lifestyle on health behavior in the United States and other countries was addressed. Throughout this section, questions regarding the efficacy of health promotion as an individual behavior and responsibility are raised, thus implicating the influence of "upstream" or institutional-level characteristics relative to health outcomes.

CHAPTER REVIEW

Throughout this chapter, this author has tried to convey not only the significance of health and health behavior, but also the cultural variations associated with these concepts. It is within that context that the following review questions were developed.

1. What is the relationship between the state and health? Give examples and explain the consequences of this relationship.

2. Has the health status of Americans changed in the recent past? Compare and contrast the health status of Americans on the basis of: (a) race; (b) sex; (c) age; (d) income.

3. Discuss health outcomes on the basis of gender in developing countries. Considering the problems that women continue to face today, will their future health outcomes be any better? Explain.

4. What is female genital mutilation? Where is it practiced and why? Who benefits from this practice?

5. What is the Black Report? What were its explanations for the continued health differences between social classes?

6. How would you explain the continued health differential in Great Britain? Is the Black Report satisfactory? What other variables would you include in your analysis? Why?

7. Diagram and explain the HBM. Identify a specific condition and apply it to the model.

8. What is health promotion? Explain the application of health promotion at the individual and institutional level.

GLOSSARY

health   according to the World Health Organization, health exists when disease is not present. Others have defined health by incorporating cultural beliefs and social structural expectations.

health behavior   actions that promote the health of an individual.

health belief model   a model in which the dynamic relationship between a specific health condition and individual behavior can be understood relative to perceived susceptibility, seriousness, benefits, and barriers.

health promotion   actions associated with the maintenance of well-being and the reduction of health risk.

health status   an assessment of one's overall condition of health. Health status responses generally range from excellent to poor.

lifestyle   an arrangement of specific behavioral patterns that are influenced by cultural and structural arrangements.

self-care   an effort by individuals and families to identify and treat illness, promote health, and regulate their health behavior.

stress   a quality located in the environment that produces change and affects one's health.

SUGGESTED READINGS

Bayne-Smith, M. (Ed.). (1996). *Race, gender, and health.* Thousand Oaks, CA: SAGE.
> An excellent examination of the health of minority women in the United States.

Becker, M. H. (Ed.). 1974. *The health belief model and personal health behavior.* Thorofare, NJ: Charles B. Slack, Inc.
> A classic that is required reading for any serious student of medical sociology. The readings offer a rich insight into the development, meaning, and application of the health belief model.

Bunton, Nettleton, R., S., & Burrows, R. (Eds.). (1995). *The sociology of health promotion: Critical analysis of consumption, lifestyle and risk.* London: Routledge.
> As the initial effort into the sociology of health promotion, the book offers the reader a general introduction into the basic literature and parameters of this emerging area of study.

Koos, E. L. (1967). *The health of Regionville.* New York: Hafner Publishing Company.
> A classic study of the relationship between health and a myriad of community-based variables is examined. Must reading for anyone seriously interested in medical sociology.

Phillips, D. R., & Verhasselt, Y. (Eds.). (1991). *Health and development.* London: Routledge.
> As the title indicates, this book is concerned with the health and health problems within the developing world. The readings address topical areas ranging from sex and age to examinations of regional health.

Townsend, P., & Davidson, N. (Eds.). (1992). The Black Report. *Inequalities in health.* London: Penguin.
> Despite apparent equality of access, continued inequality in the health of people in the United Kingdom persists. The authors examine the problem and offer a number of explanations for the continued inequity. However, the authors suggest that ongoing economic and social–structural inequities are interconnected to the problems of health.

Turshen, M. (Ed.). (1991). *Women and health in Africa.* Trenton, NJ: Africa World Press, Inc.
> An excellent interfacing of the contributions of women in Africa to the larger societies in which they live as well as the health problems they continue to experience.

REFERENCES

Abel, T., Cockerham, W. C., Lueschen, G., & Kunz, G. (1989). Health lifestyles and self-direction in employment among American men: A test of the spillover effect. *Social Science and Medicine, 28,* 12, 1269–1274.

Abel, T. (1991). Measuring health lifestyles in a comparative analysis: Theoretical issues and empirical findings. *Social Science and Medicine, 32,* 8, 899–908.

Ajzen, I., & Fishbein, M. (1980). *Understanding attitudes and predicting social behavior.* Englewood Cliffs, NJ: Prentice-Hall.

Alonzo, A. A. (1993). Health behavior: Issues, contradictions and dilemmas. *Social Science and Medicine, 37,* 8, 1019–1034.

Andersen, R. M. (1995). Revisiting the behavioral model and access to medical care: Does it matter? *Journal of Health and Social Behavior, 36,* 1–10.

Andrews, G. R. (1987). Ageing in Asia and the Pacific. *Comprehensive Gerontology,* Section C, Interdisciplinary Topics. *1,* 24–32.

Angel, R. J., & Worobey, J. L. (1991). Intragroup differences in the health of Hispanic children. *Social Science Quarterly, 72,* 2, 361–378.

Antonovsky, A. (1967). Social class, life expectancy and overall mortality. *The Milbank Memorial Fund Quarterly, 45,* 31–73.

Arber, S. (1989). Gender and class inequalities in health: Understanding the differentials. In J. Fox (Ed). *Health inequalities in European countries* (pp. 250–279). Aldershot: Gower Publishing Company Limited.

Armstrong, M. J., & Armstrong, R. W. (1991). New Zealand Maori women's health: Status and self-help action in the 1980s. *Women & Health, 17,* 2, 45–64.

Arnold, L., & Quine, L. (1994). Predicting helmet use among schoolboy cyclists: An application of the health belief model. In D. R. Rutter & L. Quine (Eds.). *Social psychology and health: European perspectives* (pp. 101–130). Aldershot: Avebury.

Backett, K. (1992). Taboos and excesses: Lay health moralities in middle-class families. *Sociology of Health and Illness, 14,* 2, 255–274.

Bayne-Smith, M. (1996). Health and women of color: A cultural overview. In M. Bayne-Smith (Ed.). *Race, gender, and health* (pp. 1–42). Thousand Oaks, CA: SAGE.

Becker, M. H., & Rosenstock, I. M. (1989). Health promotion, disease prevention, and program retention. In H. E. Freeman & S. Levine (Eds.). *Handbook of medical sociology* (4th Ed.) (pp. 284–305). Englewood Cliffs, NJ: Prentice-Hall.

Berkman, L. F. (1995). The role of social relations in health promotion. *Psychosomatic Medicine, 57,* 245–254.

Berkman, L. F., & Breslow, L. (1983). *Health and ways of living: The Alameda County study.* New York: Oxford University Press.

Burrows, R., Nettleton, S., & Bunton, R. (1995). Sociology and health promotion: Health risk and consumption under late modernism. In R. Bunton, S. Nettleton, & R. Burrows (Eds). *The sociology of health promotion: Critical analyses of consumption, lifestyle and risk* (pp. 1–9). London: Routledge.

Bush, P. J., & Iannotti, R. J. (1985). The development of children's health orientations and behaviors: Lessons for substance use prevention. In C. L. Jones & B. J. Battjes (Eds.). *Etiology of drug abuse: Implications for prevention* (pp. 45–74). DHHS Publication No. ADM 85-1335. Washington, DC: U.S. Government Printing Office.

Bush, P. J., & Iannotti, R. J. (1988). Origins and stability of children's health beliefs relative to medicine use. *Social Science and Medicine, 27,* 345–352.

Bush, P. J., & Iannotti, R. J. (1990). A children's health belief model. *Medical Care, 28,* 69–86.

Caldwell, J. C. (1993). Health transition: The cultural, social and behavioural determinants of health in the third world. *Social Science and Medicine, 36,* 2, 125–135.

Carmel, S., Anson, O., Levenson, A., Bonneh, D. Y., & Maoz, B. (1991). Life events, sense of coherence and health: Gender differences on the Kibbutz. *Social Science and Medicine, 32,* 10, 1089–1096.

Carter-Pokras, O. (1994). Health profile. In C. W. Molina & M. Aguirre-Molina (Eds.). *Latino health in the US: A growing challenge* (pp. 45–79). Washington, DC: American Public Health Association.

Chebotarev, D. F., Sachuk, N. N., & Verzhikovskaya, N. V. (1981). Problems of health and position of the elderly in socialist countries of Eastern Europe. *Zeitschrift für Alternsforschung, 36,* 6, 437–472.

Chern, A. (1996). Health promotion policies in Singapore: Meeting the challenges of the 1990s. *Health Promotion International, 11,* 2, 127–136.

Clarke, R., & Lowe, F. (1989). Positive health—some lay perspectives. *Health Promotion, 3,* 4, 401–406.

Cohen, D. (1994). Health promotion and cost-effectiveness. *Health Promotion International, 9,* 4, 281–287.

Conrad, P. (1987). Wellness in the work place: Potentials and pitfalls of work-site health promotion. *The Milbank Quarterly, 65,* 2, 255–275.

Dahl, E. (1994). Social inequalities in ill-health: The significance of occupational status, education and income-results from a Norwegian survey. *Sociology of Health and Illness, 16,* 5, 644–667.

Dahlgren, G., & Diderichsen, F. (1985). Sweden Country Paper: Inequalities in health care—some implications for intersectoral action in Sweden. In L. Kohl & J. Martin (Eds.). *Inequalities in health and health care* (pp. 167–199). Goteborg, Sweden: The Nordic School of Public Health.

David, J. L., & Kaplan, H. B. (1995). Gender, social roles and health care utilization. *Applied Behavioral Science Review, 3,* 1, 39–64.

Dean, K. (1989). Self-care components of lifestyles: The importance of gender, attitudes and the social situation. *Social Science and Medicine, 29,* 2, 137–152.

Dean, K., & McQueen, D. (1996). Theory in health promotion: Introduction. *Health Promotion International, 11,* 1, 7–9.

DeFriese, G. H., Woomert, A., Guild, P. A., Steckler, A. B., & Konrad, T. R. (1989). From activated patient to pacified activist: A study of the self-care movement in the United States. *Social Science and Medicine, 29,* 2, 195–204.

Donahue, J. M., & McGuire, M. B. (1995). The political economy of responsibility in health and illness. *Social Science and Medicine, 40,* 1, 47–53.

Downie, R. S., Tannahill, C., & Tannahill, A. (1996). *Health promotion: Models and values* (2nd Ed.). Oxford: Oxford University Press.

Eakin, J., Robertson, A., Poland, B., Coburn, D., & Edwards, R. (1996). Towards a critical social science perspective on health promotion research. *Health Promotion International, 11,* 2, 157–165.

Ezeji, P. N., & Sarvela, P. D. (1992). Health–care behavior of the Ibo Tribe of Nigeria. *Health Values, 16,* 6, 31–35.

Fishbein, M., & Ajzen, I. (1975). *Belief, attitude, intention, and behavior.* Reading, MA: Addison-Wesley.

Flay, B. R., & Petraitis, J. (1994). The theory of triadic influence: A new theory of health behavior with implications for preventive interventions. *Advances in Medical Sociology, 4,* 19–44.

Frankish, C. J., & Green, L. W. (1994). Organizational and community change as the social scientific basis for disease prevention and health promotion policy. *Advances in Medical Sociology, 4,* 209–233.

Freund, P. E. S., & McGuire, M. B. (1995). *Health, illness, and the social body: A critical sociology* (2nd Ed.). Englewood Cliffs, NJ: Prentice-Hall.

Fuchs, J. A., Levinson, R. M., Stoddard, R. R., Mullet, M. E., & Jones, D. H. (1990). Health risk factors among the Amish: Results of a survey. *Health Education Quarterly, 17,* 2, 197–211.

Gallagher, E. B. (1994). A typology of health rationality applied to third world health. *Advances in Medical Sociology, 4,* 257–280.

Gonzalez, N. S. (1966). Health behavior in cross-cultural perspective: A Guatemalan example. *Human Organization, 25,* 2, 122–125.

Grace, V. M. (1991). The marketing of empowerment and the construction of the health consumer: A critique of health promotion. *International Journal of Health Services, 21,* 2, 329–343.

Green, L. W., Kreuter, M. W., Deeds, S. G., & Partridge, K. B. (1980). *Health education planning: A diagnostic approach.* Palo Alto, CA: Mayfield.

Hart, N. (1989). Sex, gender and survival: Inequalities of life chances between European men and women. In J. Fox (Ed.). *Health inequalities in European countries* (pp. 109–141). Aldershot: Gower Publishing Company Limited.

Helman, C. G. (1994). *Culture, health and illness* (3rd Ed.). Oxford: Butterworth-Heinemann.

Hill, T. P. (1996). Health care: A social contract in transition. *Social Science and Medicine, 43,* 5, 783–789.

Holstein, B. E. (1985). Denmark country paper: Review of recent empirical studies. In L. Kohler and J. Martin (Eds.). *Inequalities in health and health care* (pp. 45–68). Goteborg, Sweden: The Nordic School of Public Health.

Hraba, J., Lorenz, F., Lee, G., & Pechacova, Z. (1996). Gender differences in health: Evidence from the Czech Republic. *Social Science and Medicine, 43,* 10, 1443–1451.

Iannott, R. J. & Bush, P. J. (1993). Toward a developmental theory of compliance. In N. A. Krasnegor, L. Epstein, S. B. Johnson, & S. J. Yaffe (Eds.). *Developmental aspects of health compliance behavior* (pp. 59–76). Hillsdale, NJ: Lawrence Erlbaum Associates, Publishers.

Idler, E. L., & Angel, R. J. (1990). Age, chronic pain, and subjective assessments of health. *Advances in Medical Sociology, 1,* 131–152.

Kar, R. K. (1993). Health behavior among the tribes of North-East India: A profile. *Journal of Indian Anthropological Society, 28,* 157–164.

Kar, S. B. (1989). Introduction: Health promotion action indicators. In S. B. Kar (Ed.). *Health promotion indicators and actions* (pp. 1–22). New York: Springer.

Kasl, S. V., & Cobb, S. (1966). Health behavior, illness behavior, and sick role behavior. *Archives of Environmental Health, 12,* 246–266.

Kickbusch, I. (1989). Self-care in health promotion. *Social Science and Medicine, 29,* 2, 125–130.

King, G., & Williams, D. R. (1995). Race and health: A multidimensional approach to African-American health. In B. C. Amick III., S. Levine, A. R. Tarlov, & D. C. Walsh. (Eds.). *Society and health* (pp. 93–130). New York: Oxford University Press.

Kirscht, J. P. (1988). The health belief model and predictions of health actions. In D. S. Gochman (Ed.). *Health behavior: Emerging research perspectives* (pp. 27–41). New York: Plenum Press.

Koos, E. L. (1954). *The health of Regionville.* New York: Hafner Publishing Company.

Koskinen, S., Melkas, T., & Vienonen, M. (1985). Finland Country Paper: Inequalities in health and health care in Finland: A challenge for intersectoral action. In L. Kohler & J. Martin (Eds.). *Inequalities in health and health care* (pp. 69–112). Goteborg, Sweden: The Nordic School of Public Health.

Kovacs, J. (1989). Concepts of health and disease. *The Journal of Medicine and Philosophy, 14,* 3, 261–267.

Kristiansen, C. M. (1989). Gender differences in the meaning of 'Health.' *Social Behaviour, 4,* 185–188.

Kulig, J. C. (1990). A review of the health status of southeast Asian refugee women. *Health Care for Women International, 11,* 49–63.

Kumar, A. (1995). Gender and health: Theoretical versus practical accessibility of health care for women in north India. In E. B. Gallagher & J. Subedi (Eds.). *Global perspectives on health care* (pp. 16–31). Englewood Cliffs, NJ: Prentice Hall.

Kumpusalo, E., Neittaanmaki, L., Halonen, P., Pekkarinen, H., Penttila, I., & Parviainen, M. (1996). Finnish health village study: impact and outcomes of a low-cost local health promotion programme. *Health Promotion International, 11,* 2, 105–115.

Kunitz, S. J. (1983). *Disease change and the role of medicine: The Navajo experience.* Berkeley, CA: University of California Press.

Laird, R. J., & Chamberlain, K. (1990). Hassles, uplifts, and health status reports by pensioners living in a New Zealand town. *Sociology and Social Research, 75,* 1, 27–31.

Lane, S. D., & Meleis, A. I. (1991). Roles, work, health perceptions and health resources of women: A study in an Egyptian delta hamlet. *Social Science and Medicine, 33,* 10, 1197–1208.

LaVeist, T. A. (1992). The political empowerment and health status of African-Americans: Mapping a new territory. *American Journal of Sociology, 97,* 4, 1080–1095.

LaVeist, T. A. (1993). Segregation, poverty, and empowerment: Health consequences for African Americans. *The Milbank Quarterly, 71,* 1, 41–64.

Lear, D. (1996). Women and AIDS in Africa: A critical review. In J. Subedi & E. B. Gallagher (Eds.). *Society, health and disease: Transcultural perspectives* (pp. 276–301). Englewood Cliffs, NJ: Prentice-Hall.

LePranc, E. (1989). Socio-economic determinants of health status. *Social and Economic Studies, 38,* 2, 291–305.

Lewis, N. D., & Kieffer, E. (1994). The health of women: Beyond maternal and child health. In D. R. Phillips & Y. Verhasselt (Eds.). *Health and development* (pp. 122–137). New York: Routledge.

Lindbladh, E., Lyttkens, C. H., Hanson, B. S., Ostergren, P., Isacsson, S. O., & Lindgren, B. (1996). An economic and sociological interpretation of social differences in health-related behaviour: An encounter as a guide to social epidemiology. *Social Science and Medicine, 43,* 12, 1817–1827.

Mackenbach, J. P. (1992). Socio-economic health differences in the Netherlands: A review of recent empirical findings. *Social Science and Medicine, 34,* 3, 213–226.

Maeda, D., Teshima, K., Sugisawa, H., & Asakura, Y. S. (1989). Ageing and health in Japan. *Journal of Cross-Cultural Gerontology, 4,* 143–162.

Maiman, L. A., & Becker, M. H. (1974). The health belief model: Origins and correlates in psychological theory. In M. H. Becker (Ed.). *The health belief model and personal health behavior* (pp. 9–26). Thorofare, NJ: Charles B. Slack, Inc.

Mainous, A. G., & Kohrs, F. P. (1995). A comparison of health status between rural and urban adults. *Journal of Community Health, 20,* 5, 423–431.

Marmot, M., & Theorell, T. (1988). Social class and cardiovascular disease: The contribution of work. *International Journal of Health Services, 18,* 4, 659–674.

Marmot, M., Bobak, M., & Smith, G. D. (1995). Explanations for social inequalities in health. In B. C. Amick, S. Levine, A. R. Tarlov, & D. C. Walsh (Eds.). *Society and health* (pp. 172–210). New York: Oxford University Press.

Martin, L. G. (1988). The aging of Asia. *Journal of Gerontology: SOCIAL SCIENCES, 43,* 4, S99–113.

Maseide, P. (1985). Norway Country Paper: Social inequalities and inequalities related to health: The Case of Norway. In L. Kohler and J. Martin (Eds.). *Inequalities in health and health care* (pp. 143–166). Goteborg, Sweden: The Nordic School of Public Health.

McConatha, D., Tahmaseb McConatha, J., & Cinelli, B. (1991). Japan's coming crisis: Problems for the honorable elders. *The Journal of Applied Gerontology, 10,* 2, 224–235.

McCord, C., & Freeman, H. P. (1990). Excess mortality in Harlem. *New England Journal of Medicine, 322,* 173–177.

McElmurray, B. J., Norr, K. F., & Spreen Parker, R. (1993). Women's health status across the globe. *Women's health and development: A global challenge.* Boston: Jones and Bartlett.

McKinlay, J. B. (1993). The promotion of health through planned sociopolitical change: Challenges for research and policy. *Social Science and Medicine, 36,* 2, 109–117.

McKinlay, J. B. (1994). A case for refocusing upstream: The political economy of illness. In P. Conrad & R. Kern (Eds.). *The sociology of health and illness: Critical perspectives* (4th Ed.) (pp. 509–523). New York: St. Martin's Press.

Mechanic, D. (1990). Promoting health. *Society, 27,* 2, 16–22.

Mechanic, D. (1992). Health and illness behavior and patient–practitioner relationships. *Social Science and Medicine, 34,* 12, 1345–1350.

Meleis, A., & Rogers, S. (1987). Women in transition: Being versus becoming or being and becoming. *Health Care for Women International, 8,* 4, 199–217.

Mubarak, K., Shafqat, S., Malik, U., Pirzada, R., & Qureshi, A. F. (1990). Health, attitudes and beliefs of working women. *Social Science and Medicine, 31,* 9, 1029–1033.

Mullen, P. D., Hersey, J. C., & Iverson, D. C. (1987). *Social Science and Medicine, 24,* 11, 973–981.

Mutchler, J. E., & Burr, J. A. (1991). Racial differences in health and health care service utilization in later life: The effect of socioeconomic class. *Journal of Health and Social Behavior, 32,* 342–356.

Ovretveit, J. (1996). Quality in health promotion. *Health Promotion International, 11,* 1, 55–64.

Parish, R. (1995). Health promotion: Rhetoric and reality. In R. Bunton, S. Nettleton, & R. Burrows (Eds.). *The sociology of health promotion: Critical analyses of consumption, lifestyle and risk* (pp. 13–23). London: Routledge.

Poole, D. L. (1996). NAFTA, American health, and Mexican health: They tie together. *Health and Social Work, 21,* 1, 3–7.

Prins, G. (1989). But what was the disease? The present state of health and healing in African studies. *Past and Present, 124,* 159–179.

Puska, P. (1995). Health promotion challenges for countries of the former Soviet Union: results from collaboration between Estonia, Russian Karelia and Finland. *Health Promotion International, 10,* 3, 219–228.

Quah, S. A. (1993). Ethnicity, health behavior, and modernization: The case of Singapore. In P. Conrad & E. B. Gallagher (Eds.). *Health and health care in developing countries* (pp. 78–107). Philadelphia, PA: Temple University Press.

Raeburn, J. M., & Rootman, I. (1989). Towards an expanded health field concept: Conceptual and research issues in a new era of health promotion. *Health Promotion, 3,* 4, 383–392.

Raikes, A. (1989). Women's health in East Africa. *Social Science and Medicine, 28,* 5, 447–459.

Rathwell, T. (1992). Realities of health of all by the year 2000. *Social Science and Medicine, 35,* 4, 541–547.

Rosenstock, I. M. (1966). Why people use health services. *Milbank Fund Quarterly, 44,* 94–127.

Rosenstock, I. M. (1974). Historical origins of the health belief model. In M. H. Becker (Ed.). *The health belief model and personal health behavior* (pp. 1–8). Thorofare, NJ: Charles B. Slack, Inc.

Rutten, A. (1995). The implementation of health promotion: A new structural perspective. *Social Science and Medicine, 41,* 12, 1627–1637.

Seedhouse, D. (1995). "Well-being": Health promotion's red herring. *Health Promotion International, 10,* 1, 61–67.

Segall, A., & Goldstein, J. (1989). Exploring the correlates of self-provided health care behaviour. *Social Science and Medicine, 29,* 2, 153–161.

Siegrist, J. (1995). Social differentials in chronic disease: What can sociological knowledge offer to explain and possibly reduce them? *Social Science and Medicine, 41,* 12, 1603–1605.

Smaje, C. (1995). Ethnic residential concentration and health: Evidence for a positive effect? *Policy and Politics, 23,* 3, 251–269.

Stronks, K., van de Mheen, H. D., Looman, C. W. N., & Mackenbach, J. P. (1996). Behavioural and structural factors in the explanation of socio-economic inequalities in health: An empirical analysis. *Sociology of Health and Illness, 18,* 5, 653–674.

Suprasert, S., Grandjean, N., & Sittitrai, W. (1995). Two views of risky sexual practices among northern Thai males: The health belief model and the theory of reasoned action. *Journal of Health and Social Behavior, 36,* 195–212.

Taylor, R. C. R. (1989). The politics of prevention. In P. Brown (Ed). *Perspectives in medical sociology* (pp. 368–388). Belmont, CA: Wadsworth.

Thomas, L. E. (1992). Identity, ideology and medicine: Health attitudes and behavior among Hindu religious renunciates. *Social Science and Medicine, 34,* 5, 499–505.

Tout, K. (1989). *Ageing in developing countries.* London: Oxford University Press.

Townsend, P., & Davidson, N. (1992). The Black Report. *Inequalities in health.* London: Penguin.

Trumper, R., & Phillips, L. (1996). Give me discipline and give me death: Neoliberalism and health in Chile. *Race and Class, 37,* 3, 19–34.

Uitenbroek, D. G., Kerekovska, A., & Festchoeva, N. (1996). Health lifestyle behaviour and socio-demographic characteristics. A study of Varna, Glasgow and Edinburgh. *Social Science and Medicine, 43,* 3, 367–377.

Umberson, D. (1992). Gender, marital status and the social control of health behavior. *Social Science and Medicine, 34,* 8, 907–917.

Waldron, I. (1988). Gender and health-related behavior. In D. S. Gochman (Ed.): *Health behavior: Emerging research perspectives* (pp. 193–208). New York: Plenum Press.

Ware, J. E. Jr. (1986). The assessment of health status. In L. H. Aiken & D. Mechanic (Eds.). *Applications of social science to clinical medicine and health policy* (pp. 204–228). New Brunswick, NJ: Rutgers University Press.

Weaver, G. D., & Gary, L. E. (1996). Correlates of health-related behaviors in older African-American adults: Implications for health promotion. *Family & Community Health, 19,* 2, 43–57.

Weitzel, M. H., Hudak, J. L., Becker, H. A., Waller, P. R., & Stuifbergen, A. K. (1994). An exploratory analysis of health-promotion beliefs and behaviors among white, Hispanic, and black males. *Family & Community Health, 17,* 3, 23–34.

Williams, D. R. (1990). Socioeconomic differentials in health: A review and redirection. *Social Psychology Quarterly, 53,* 2, 81–99.

Williams, D. R., Wilson, L. C., & Chung, A. M. (1992). Socioeconomic status, psychological factors and health in urban Guyana. *Sociological Focus, 25,* 4, 279–294.

Williams, D. R., & Collins, C. (1995). US socioeconomic and racial differences in health: Patterns and explanations. *Annual Review of Sociology, 21,* 349–386.

Woods, N. F. (1996). Women and their health. In P. Brown (Ed.). *Perspectives in medical sociology* (2nd Ed.) (pp. 44–76). Prospect Heights, IL: Waveland Press.

World Health Organization. (1966). *Basic Documents.* (17th Ed.). Geneva, Switzerland.

World Health Organization. (1995). *The World's Women: 1995—Trends and Statistics.* Social Statistics and Indicators, Series K, No. 12. New York.

Wyke, S., & Ford, G. (1992). Competing explanations for associations between marital status and health. *Social Science and Medicine, 34,* 5, 523–532.

Young, T. K. (1994). *The health of Native Americans: Toward a bicultural epidemiology.* New York: Oxford University Press.

Zadoroznyj, M., & Svarstad, B. L. (1990). Gender, employment and medication use. *Social Science and Medicine, 31,* 9, 971–978.

CHAPTER

5

Illness Behavior—Part I

By this term (illness behavior) we refer to the ways in which given symptoms may be differentially perceived, evaluated, and acted (or not acted) upon by different kinds of persons. Whether by reason of earlier experiences with illness, differential training in respect to symptoms, or whatever, some persons will make light of symptoms, shrug them off, and avoid seeking medical care; others will respond to the slightest twinges of pain or discomfort by quickly seeking such medical care as is available. In short, the realm of illness behaviour falls logically and chronologically between two major traditional concerns of medical science: etiology and therapy. Variables affecting illness behavior come into play prior to medical scrutiny and treatment, but after etiological processes have been initiated. In this sense, illness behavior even determines whether diagnosis and treatment will begin at all.

—Mechanic, 1962, p. 189

Interpretations of Illness Behavior

Although Mechanic (1962) provides a working definition of **illness behavior** (see opening excerpt), related concepts such as *disease* and *sickness* can also be identified as distinctive qualities associated with illness behavior. For instance, **disease** is a biological explanation of a specific condition. However, "disease does not exist until we have agreed that it does, by perceiving, naming, and responding to it" (Rosenberg, 1992, p. 305). Furthermore, disease must be understood as something more than a "condition" induced by an individual who is ultimately held responsible or "blamed" for having the disease. Disease must be treated as a condition that has its origins within the political and economic realities of the social structure within which it exists (Donahue & McGuire, 1995). **Sickness,** however, "exists when people are defined by *others* as having a problem that requires a therapeutic response" (Twaddle & Hessler, 1987, p. 101). Finally, *illness* is best understood as a social response to a specific condition. Kleinman (1988, p. 3) defines **illness** as "how the sick person and the members of the family or wider social network perceive, live with, and respond to symptoms and disability" (see also Lupton, 1994). In other words, illness refers to perceptions (one's own or the perceptions of others) (Helman, 1994); or, within a structural context, Apple (1960, p. 223) points out that illness is defined by middle-class America as a disruption of "one's usual activities." Serious illnesses, however, can effect "the roles individuals assume, threatening the dreams of who individuals perceive themselves as being and becoming" (Fife, 1994, p. 312). The relationship between disease, illness, and sickness is not always direct. For example, disease can occur without the presence of illness (Eisenberg, 1977). Perhaps the clearest differentiation between these concepts is offered by Twaddle (1979, p. 18), who suggests the following classification: "disease (referring to biological capacities), illness (referring to subjective or psychological dimensions), and sickness (referring to a social dimension)."

This chapter, however, is concerned with illness experiences that result in differing behavioral outcomes (Mechanic & Volkart, 1961). Thus, to engage in illness behavior, it must first be determined that an illness, in fact, exists. The two indicators that are consistently identified relative to being ill include "(1) the duration, location, and intensity of symptoms, and (2) the social effects of the symptoms in terms of interference with either valued social activities or the fulfillment of role responsibilities" (Harwood, 1981, p. 490). Furthermore, in response to the changing complexity of symptoms, Veitch (1995) utilized illness behavior options that ranged from doing nothing to immediate care. More specific to the cultural context, Zola (1983, p. 63), states that "what the patient does about his objective clinical symptoms may well be rooted in cultural and social definitions of "health" and "sickness." In other words, how others respond to one's symptoms influences the type of illness behavior engaged in (Virtanen, 1994).

A *social constructionist* interpretation of these concepts relative to their application within developed and developing nations of the world is employed (for an analysis of the social construction of diagnosis and illness, see Brown, 1995). In addition to the social constructionist interpretation of illness, the medical model interpretation is also used, a model that is the predominant approach within the health-care community. The medical model is constructed on the belief that illness represents a departure from acceptable biological standards, "that illness is (1) deviation from normal, (2) specific and universal, (3) caused by unique biological forces, (4) analogous to the breakdown of a machine, and (5) defined and treated through a neutral, scientific process" (Weitz, 1996, p. 129). Although "medicine's monopoly includes the right to create illness as an official social role" (Dimond & Jones, 1983, p. 22), Fox (1989, p. 7) suggests that:

> Sociocultural factors influence what is defined as an illness in a given society, what it is called, how it is interpreted and experienced, and how and whether it is detected and diagnosed. Social and cultural factors also affect decisions about to whom an illness is confided; what kinds of help, if any, are sought for dealing with it and from what sorts of persons in which statuses and roles.

The influence of these sociocultural factors on illness behavior is addressed later in the chapter.

Theoretical Explanations of Illness Behavior

As societies struggle to understand concepts such as illness behavior, theoretical explanations generally offer the reader a framework from which comparisons can be made and analyses drawn. As suggested earlier, illness behavior can be understood within a medical as well as sociological context. Thus, illness behavior can be understood as "begin(ing) prior to the use of services and shapes decisions about whether to seek care and what type of help to solicit" (Mechanic, 1992, p. 1346).

This section examines the efficacy of a number of frameworks associated with illness behavior. This is best illustrated by Scambler (1991, p. 38), who states that "to begin to answer the more complex question of why people seek or decline to seek professional help is to begin to theorize about *illness behaviour*" (italics in original). Although various illness behavior models have been developed, Suchman (1965) and Mechanic (1978) developed the most salient.

Suchman's Stages of Illness Experience

One of the more significant models of illness behavior was developed by Suchman (1965) and is presented here. Sociologically, the importance of the model is its relationship between "social structure and medical orientation" (Suchman, 1965, p. 14). In other words, Suchman's model addresses the impact of variables such as social class on one's perspective to medical treatment. Within this explanation, an individual experiencing an illness encounters five distinct stages ranging from symptom-experience to recovery or rehabilitation. Table 5.1 outlines not only the individual stages, but also the transition process from initial recognition of symptoms to eventual recuperation and the assumption of normal life activities.

Stage One—Symptom-Experience. Initially, the individual may recognize that a medical problem appears to exist. However, as Suchman (1965, p. 115) states, "these

TABLE 5.1 Suchman's Stages of Illness Experience

	Stage I— Symptom Experience	Stage II— Assumption of the Sick Role	Stage III— Medical Care Contact	Stage IV— Dependent- Patient Role	Stage V— Recovery and Rehabilitation
Decision	Something is wrong	Relinquish normal role	Seek professional advice	Accept professional treatment	Relinquish sick role
Behaviors	Application of folk medicine Self-medication	Request provisional validation for sick role from members of lay-referral system— continue lay medications	Seek authoritative legitimation for sick role— negotiate treatment procedures	Undergo treatment procedure for illness— follow regimen procedures	Resume normal roles
Outcomes	← Denial (flight into health) ↓ Delay ↓ Acceptance →	← Denial ↓ ↓ Acceptance →	← Denial ↓ Shopping ↓ Confirmation →	← Rejection ↓ Secondary gain ↓ Acceptance →	← Refusal (chronic sick role) ↓ Malingerer ↓ Acceptance →

Source: Figure 4.1. The Stages of Illness Experience, p. 116 in *Sociology of Medicine,* (2nd Ed). Rodney Col. New York: McGraw-Hill. Used with permission.

symptoms . . . will be recognized and defined . . . in terms of their interference with normal social functioning." As a consequence, the individual may engage in the use of home remedies or various over-the-counter applications to correct the problem. Depending on the outcome of their efforts, the individual does one of three things: denies the existence of a health problem, postpones its acknowledgment, or accepts its existence.

Stage Two—Assumption of the Sick Role.   As the individual enters this stage there is an acknowledgment of a health-related problem, but medical advice is sought from friends and family rather than the professional community. In consultation with the lay-referral system, the person is expected to seek release from some normal role obligations. The outcome may result in the person either again denying the problem or accepting guidance from his or her lay consultants.

Stage Three—Medical Care Contact. This stage is pivotal because the person requests a "professional" rather than a lay interpretation of the medical problem. In so doing, the person is expecting either legitimation of the condition and removal from normal role obligations or a return to normal role activities. The importance of this stage is demonstrated in the statement by Suchman (1965, p. 115) that "the initial medical diagnosis and treatment will set the stage for subsequent medical care and play a crucial role in the sick individual's future medical behavior and progress towards health." Again, the person can either deny the problem, thus prolonging the period in this stage, or accept the advice of the medical profession. A third outcome for the sick person is to "shop around" for a diagnosis and the legitimation that satisfies their interpretation and needs.

Stage Four—Dependent-Patient Role. This stage represents another transition for the sick person. When the recommendation of the medical professional is accepted, the sick person assumes the role of "patient," which requires adjustment not only to a new physical environment but also a new set of social relationships, particularly with one's physician. As a result, patient dependence increases as his or her decision-making responsibilities are transferred to the medical community. Possible patient outcomes include rejection of the patient role or acceptance and movement into the fifth and final stage of illness behavior.

Stage Five—Recovery or Rehabilitation. In the final stage, the patient receives the requisite medical treatment and, on recovery from the illness, is expected to give up the patient role and resume normal role obligations. Accepting previous role obligations allows the person to withdraw from the medical community and resume the role of a healthy individual. Suchman notes that this transition is most appropriate for persons experiencing acute rather than chronic illnesses. Thus, the patient is again provided with options regarding outcomes. The patient can accept improved health outcomes, relinquish the patient role, and return to a state of health. However, if the condition is chronic, the person may experience greater difficulty relinquishing the patient role. The nature of a chronic condition may necessitate an on-going relationship with medical personnel and continued identification with the patient role. As the population of the United States continues to grow older, the implications of this final stage may become increasingly more significant.

Mechanic's General Theory of Help Seeking

The second model is a general theory of help seeking developed by Mechanic (1978). Fundamentally, the general theory of help seeking utilizes an attributional explanation constructed around two questions. The first question is, what do we know about the person or their environment that would result in illness? The second question "involves the assumption that a certain degree of aberrance is given" (Mechanic, 1978, p. 270). Thus, illness, its assessment, and implementation of help-seeking behavior are dependent on the context within which it occurs. Mechanic (1978, p. 274) also differentiates between who defines the condition (self or other) by suggesting "that in the latter the person tends to resist the definition that others are attempting to impose upon him."

The help-seeking behavior model consists of 10 determinants that characterize responses to illness. These determinants include:

1. Visibility, recognizability, or perceptual salience of deviant signs and symptoms.
2. The extent to which the symptoms are perceived as serious (that is, the person's estimate of the present and future probabilities of danger).
3. The extent to which symptoms disrupt family, work, and other social activities.
4. The frequency of the appearance of the deviant signs or symptoms, their persistence, or their frequency of recurrence.
5. The tolerance threshold of those who are exposed to and evaluate the deviate signs and symptoms.
6. Available information, knowledge, and cultural assumptions and understandings of the evaluator.
7. Basic needs that lead to denial.
8. Needs competing with illness responses.
9. Competing possible interpretations that can be assigned to the symptoms once they are recognized.
10. Availability of treatment resources, physical proximity, and psychological and monetary costs of taking action (included are not only physical distance and costs of time, money, and effort, but also such costs as stigma, social distance, and feelings of humiliation). (Mechanic, 1978, pp. 268–269).

These determinants address the theme "that *illness behavior is a culturally and socially learned response pattern*" (Wolinsky, 1988, p. 119; italics in original). Fundamental to both models (Suchman & Mechanic) is an emphasis on individual ability to determine an appropriate "response to health and illness situations" (Wolinsky, 1988, p. 122). The two models differ, however, regarding the extent of individual involvement. Whereas Mechanic emphasizes the initial decision-making process leading to care, Suchman, in the stages of illness model, argues that the individual is involved not only in the initial decision-making process, but also throughout the remaining stages. Thus, recovery and rehabilitation are, to some extent, dependent on the willingness of the individual to participate and eventually relinquish the sick role (Wolinsky, 1988).

Additional Theories of Illness Behavior

At approximately the same time as Mechanic's help-seeking model, Dingwall (1977, p. 99) offered what he referred to as an illness action model, which "proposes a general equilibrium between events in the biological sphere and events in the cognitive sphere." The illness action model suggests that:

> we may explore our experience of the body to reconcile it with our changed knowledge. . . . Alternatively, we may explore our knowledge of the body in an attempt to identify the typical nature of the biological disturbances we are experiencing. We may define them as a hangover, influenza, muscular strain or as something that we do not recognise and that requires further identification by someone with

more specialised knowledge. Such interpretation is then followed by some action to restore a sense of familiarity whose effects are themselves monitored and evaluated. Unsuccessful action may lead to a repeat of the cycle. (Dingwall, 1977, pp. 101–102).

Another theoretical perspective is offered by Spector (1985, p. 15), who broadens the examination of illness by identifying four stages of illness "that are sufficiently general to apply to any society or culture." These stages include:

Onset. This stage can be immediate or prolonged. That is, the problem can be severe and debilitating, or progress slowly. In either situation, this stage establishes the authenticity of the illness.

Diagnosis. In the diagnosis stage, health-care providers attempt to determine the nature of the illness. Identifying the illness legitimates the claim of the ill person. Although the diagnosis stage is important for the health-care provider, it can be traumatic for the person experiencing the illness. For instance, the ill person is exposed to a myriad of health professionals and their technology.

Patient Status. During this stage the person is expected to take on and conform to the role of patient. Situated within a hospital setting, the "patient" is expected to discard previous behaviors and assume a dependent, passive role in the treatment of the illness.

Recovery. The final stage represents (at least in theory) a return to biological normality. That is, whatever the problem experienced by the patient has now been removed, replaced, or rendered harmless. For example, a malignant tumor is removed or a weak heart valve is replaced, increasing blood flow. In the process, however, the patient may experience significant psychological as well as physical change. Ultimately, the goal of this stage is to return the person to the larger society. However, as Spector (1985) points out, differences regarding the meaning of health and illness may persist between the health community and the patient, thus reducing the overall effectiveness of the recovery process.

Finally, Zola (1973, p. 683) argues that because some people endure a particular condition for a protracted period of time, it is important to understand individual and social conditions that influenced their decision to seek professional advice. He suggests that the following types of "triggers" are likely to prompt a person to seek medical assistance.

1. The occurrence of an interpersonal crisis (e.g., a death in the family);
2. Perceived interference with social or personal relations;
3. "Sanctioning" (pressure from others to consult);
4. Perceived interference with vocational or physical activity; and
5. A kind of "temporalizing of symptomatology" (the setting of a deadline, e.g., "If I feel the same way on Monday . . . ")

These models (and others) offer the reader a plethora of frameworks associated with illness behavior.

The following section examines a number of sociodemographic characteristics associated with illness behavior not only in the United States, but throughout the world as well.

Illness Behavior in the Global Community

The previous section identified a number of models of illness behavior. Although instructive, these models do not necessarily address the relationship between various sociodemographic characteristics and illness behavior. This section begins with an examination of health service utilization differences on the basis of age, sex, race and ethnicity, and social class.

The significance of the data in Table 5.2 is the obvious relationship between the number of physician contacts per person and the various sociodemographic characteristics identified. Looking at the data for 1994, except for children under the age of 5, there is a direct relationship between age and the number of physician contacts. That is, as age increases, so do the number of physician contacts. Furthermore, this relationship holds for males and females. The number of physician contacts per person is also higher for females at all age categories. Physician contacts per person also differ on the basis of race. Compared to African Americans, Caucasian Americans in all age categories except 45–64 and 75 and older experience more physician contacts per person. Interestingly, family income is not related to the number of physician contacts. Whereas those with family incomes below $14,000 had the highest number of physician contacts per person, those with family income between $25,000 and $34,999 had the lowest. Although not perfect, the data would suggest a U shape, with higher physician contacts among the lower class and among those earning $35,000 or more. Finally, physician contact is highest in the west and lowest in the south and within rather than outside metropolitan statistical areas (MSAs) (National Center for Health Statistics, 1996).

The remainder of this section addresses the influence of age, sex, race and ethnicity, and social class on illness behavior. Although much of the research is specific to the United States, transcultural research is also presented.

Age

Aging is a social as well as biological process. One of the consequences of growing older is the increased probability of experiencing a chronic illness. Being vulnerable to the vicissitudes of the aging process, elderly persons are more likely than are other age groups "to have tried various ways of preventing illness" (Prohaska et al., 1985, p. 577). At the same time, one outcome of postponing the inevitable (death) is a longer period of illness and incapacity (U.S. Bureau of the Census, 1992).

At the other end of the age spectrum, Mechanic (1979) points out that relationships between various illness (and health) behaviors among young adults indi-

TABLE 5.2 Physician Contacts, According to Selected Patient Characteristics: United States, 1987–1994[1]

Characteristic	Physician contacts per person			
	1987	*1990*	*1992*	*1994*
Total[2,3]	5.4	5.5	5.9	6.0
Age				
Under 15 years	4.5	4.5	4.6	4.6
Under 5 years	6.7	6.9	6.9	6.8
5–14 years	3.3	3.2	3.4	3.4
15–44 years	4.6	4.8	5.0	5.0
45–64 years	6.4	6.4	7.2	7.3
65 years and over	8.9	9.2	10.6	11.3
65–74 years	8.4	8.5	9.7	10.3
75 years and over	9.7	10.1	12.1	12.7
Sex and Age				
Male[2]	4.6	4.7	5.1	5.2
Under 5 years	6.7	7.2	7.1	7.0
5–14 years	3.4	3.3	3.5	3.5
15–44 years	3.3	3.4	3.7	3.7
45–64 years	5.5	5.6	6.1	6.3
65–74 years	8.1	8.0	9.2	10.1
75- years and over	9.2	10.0	12.2	11.6
Female[2]	6.0	6.1	6.6	6.7
Under 5 years	6.7	6.5	6.7	6.5
5–14 years	3.1	3.2	3.3	3.3
15–44 years	5.8	6.0	6.2	6.2
45–64 years	7.2	7.1	8.2	8.3
65–74 years	8.6	9.0	10.1	10.5
75 years and over	10.0	10.2	12.1	13.4
Race and Age				
White[2]	5.5	5.6	6.0	6.1
Under 5 years	7.1	7.1	7.3	7.1
5–14 years	3.5	3.5	3.7	3.7
15–44 years	4.7	4.9	5.0	5.1
45–64 years	6.4	6.4	7.2	7.4
65–74 years	8.4	8.5	9.6	10.5
75 years and over	9.7	10.1	12.0	12.4
Black[2]	5.1	5.1	5.9	5.7
Under 5 years	5.1	5.6	5.6	5.2
5–14 years	2.3	2.2	2.3	2.5
15–44 years	4.2	4.2	5.3	4.8
45–64 years	7.3	7.1	7.8	7.7
65–74 years	8.6	9.2	10.9	9.3
75 years and over	10.8	10.4	13.7	16.3

(*continued*)

TABLE 5.2   Continued

Characteristic	Physician contacts per person			
	1987	*1990*	*1992*	*1994*
Family Income[2,4]				
Less than $14,000	6.8	6.3	7.3	7.6
$14,000–$24,999	5.6	5.6	6.0	5.9
$25,000–$34,999	5.2	5.2	5.7	5.8
$35,000–$49,999	5.2	5.7	5.9	6.2
$50,000 or more	5.4	6.0	5.8	6.0
Geographic Region[2]				
Northeast	5.2	5.2	5.9	5.9
Midwest	5.6	5.3	5.9	6.0
South	5.1	5.6	5.8	5.6
West	5.5	5.6	6.1	6.4
Location of residence[2]				
Within MSA	5.5	5.6	6.0	6.0
Outside MSA	4.8	4.9	5.6	5.7

MSA, metropolitan statistical area.

[1] Data based on household interviews of a sample of the civilian noninstitutionalized population.

[2] Age adjusted.

[3] Includes all other races not shown separately and unknown family income.

[4] Family income categories for 1989–94. Income categories for 1987 are: less than $10,000; $10,000–$14,999; $15,000–$19,999; $20,000–$34,999; and $35,000 or more. Income categories for 1986 are: less the $13,000; $13,000–$18,999; $19,000–$24,999; $25,000–$49,999; and $45,000 or more.

Source: Data compiled from Centers for Disease Control and Prevention, National Center for Health Statistics, Division of Health Interview Statistics, Division of Health Interview Statistics. Data from the National Health Interview Survey; and National Center for Health Statistics. *Health, United States, 1995.* Table 74. Hyattsville, MD: Public Health Service. 1996.

cates only a modest correlation. Whenever an illness is experienced, however, it has an impact not only on the patient, but also on family members. Consider, for example, the comments by Papadopoulos (1995, p. 29), who argues that intergenerational relationships might be effected by feelings of "indifference on the part of the parent to help the child comply with treatments, or through feelings of unwantedness or depression on the part of the child, which might have exacerbated the illness."

Research also supports the argument that elderly persons report more illnesses, and that their physician utilization rates are dependent on the severity of the illness (see, for example, Alonzo, 1979, 1980). The data in Table 5.2 also chronicle generally increasing physician contacts by age. However, as Haug (1981, p. 110) points out, elderly persons are "more likely to *over*-utilize the health care system for minor complaints . . . but are little different from the younger in *under*-utilization for conditions which should receive a doctor's attention" (italics in original). One plausible explanation is the tendency of elderly persons to equate some of their physical conditions with the aging process rather than as symptomatic of a serious illness (Brody & Kleban, 1983). However, Segall and Chappell (1991) report that only 2% of a sample of elderly persons in Winnipeg, Canada, identified their illnesses as the result of aging.

Building on the issue of age-related illness behaviors, Levkoff et al. (1988) outline the process that eventually leads to medical treatment for elderly persons. This process [which is similar to the initial stages of Suchman's (1965) Stages of Illness Experience] involves (1) disease and symptom experience, (2) symptom appraisal, (3) decision to seek care, (4) medical care contact, and (5) reporting symptoms. The authors recommend not only ongoing testing of cognitive function, but also routine assessments by the physician to detect physiological or psychological changes. Throughout this process, Levkoff et al. (1988) identify the patient–physician relationship as a significant component in the management of illness behavior among elderly persons. In a similar vein, Strain (1989, p. 337) argues that "there are identifiable pathways from symptom recognition through to resolution." These pathways range from not doing anything to professional care.

Although limited, transcultural research examining the effect of age on illness behavior does exist. One of the best cross-cultural readers in the area of aging is by Sokolovsky (1990). Although the articles address a myriad of conditions associated with aging in a number of developing as well as developed nations, many invariably touch on illness behavior by or toward the aging population. Consider, for example, the following: Glascock (1990) compares death-hastening methods of decrepit elderly persons in developing cultures to methods applied in the United States. In particular, Glascock notes the involvement of family members in the performance of the death-hastening methods. Barker (1990) examines the treatment of elderly persons in a Polynesian society and the sociocultural conditions that influence the labeling of the elderly as either frail or intact. Finally, Henderson (1990) addresses the sociocultural aspects of Alzheimer's disease within the Hispanic community. Because Alzheimer's Disease reduces the ability of the patient to remain in control, others, primarily female family members, assume responsibility regarding assessment of appropriate illness behavior. Others address issues of illness, disability, and aging in a cross-cultural context. For example, Tout (1989, p. 137) points out that physician contact is available not only to elderly persons in Malaysia (where some 40% of elderly persons had seen a doctor in the past month) but in many other Asian societies as well.

Throughout this section, it has been argued that age is related to illness behavior. Although true, there are additional demographic characteristics that also have an impact on this process. The following sections explore the influence of sex, race and ethnic heritage, and social class on illness behavior. Couched within all of these relationships are two basic points. The first is that age, sex, race, and social class do not function independent of one another. The second is that, at the same time, it is also true that an integrative explanation of illness behavior is not based solely on these four characteristics. Indeed, the cultural and social context within which the illness behavior occurs is also highly significant.

Sex

As with age, illness behavior is clearly differentiated on the basis of sex. Studying the meaning of adaptation to illness among men and women, Fife (1994, p. 312) identifies three "changes in self meaning that are related to serious illness and its treatment." These include the personal loss of control, the challenge of one's self-esteem, and changes in body image (Fife, 1994). Unfortunately, differences between men and women regarding these changes in the meaning of illness are not discussed. Although lifestyle differences between men and women have been identified as a cause of differences in illness behavior, Macintyre (1993) suggests that such explanations may not be sufficient. Instead, "different thresholds for perceiving and reporting symptoms may produce underestimates of gender differences in morbidity" (Macintyre, 1993, p. 19). Although not addressing sex differences, Calnan (1986) examined differences in attitudes and beliefs regarding the prevention of illness among working and middle-class women in England. In addition to class-based differences regarding illness prevention, Calnan (1986) identified differing interpretations of etiology. For example, working-class women were more likely to rely on personal experiences regarding the relationship between smoking and lung cancer, whereas middle-class women were more likely to rely on statistical probability.

Illness behavior of men and women is also culturally specific (Beckerleg et al., 1994). For instance, women in Thailand are more likely to utilize health professionals and engage in restricted activity (Fuller et al., 1993). Similar illness behavior differences between males and females were found in Winnipeg, Canada. Kandrack et al. (1991) report that women were more likely to use health services and to spend a greater amount of time away from normal activities. This is consistent with findings from the 1987 *General Household Survey* conducted in Great Britain. According to Scambler, (1991, p. 35, citing OPCS, 1989) "12% of men and 14% of women reported episodes of acute sickness leading to restricted activity in a 14-day reference period." Anson et al. (1993) report that symptom experience is greater among women than among men. In Gambia, however, researchers note sex-based similarities in illness symptoms. The only exception was the experience of headache and body pain (Beckerleg et al., 1994). Similarly, in Great Britain, Macintyre (1993, p. 18) reports that "men were significantly more likely than women to 'over-rate' their signs and symptoms [of a cold] compared to the clinical observer." Finally, because women utilize health services more than do men, any change in the provision of these services have an even greater impact on them. This is precisely what is happening in Latin American and Caribbean nations. As health systems in this area are being privatized, access (particularly for women) is limited through the use of copayments (Markides, 1992).

Interwoven throughout the discussion of illness behavior is the influence of political and economic factors (see, for example, the work of Turton & Chalmers, 1990, in South Africa). In Mexico, Castro (1995) examined health, illness, and subsequent experiences among residents of Ocuituco. One of the more salient features of this work is how patterned sex-based interactions influence one's perspective on health and illness. For example, women utilize pain as a tool to understand their body. In other words, if women "do not know something about the body [they say] they have not felt any pain related to it" (Castro, 1995, p. 1019). Also in southern Mexico, Whiteford (1991) studied intracultural differences of illness in the urban community of Oaxaca. There were pronounced sex-based differences regarding illness because females were primarily responsible for addressing such concerns within the family. Although poverty was recognized as the most important cause of disease in Ocuituco, factors ranging from anger to witchcraft were also identified. However, among a seemingly culturally homogeneous population, Whiteford (1991) discovered that the cause of illness differed on the basis of various criteria. For example, the respondent's world view (traditional vs. social change); their interpretation of family relationships and their responsibilities; their level of education; their economic position; and their age were all related to beliefs regarding the cause of illness.

It is apparent that illness has a different impact on males and females, regardless of the economic position of the society. Unfortunately, because women historically have utilized health services more than have men, any change within the broader health-care system will have a more negative impact on women than on men.

Race and Ethnicity

As the United States progresses into the 21st century, racial and ethnic populations will continue to increase as a percentage of the population. As a result, the cultural context of minority populations and their connection with the health-care system must be better understood. The following statement by Zola (1966, p. 630) articulates the importance of this need: "While it is obvious that not all people react similarly to the same disease process, it is striking that the pattern of response can vary with the ethnic background of the patient."

This section begins with African Americans, who currently represent the largest minority population in the United States. It is impossible to discuss illness behavior within the African American community without acknowledging their unique historical experience. This experience involved individual and institutional discrimination prescribed by a political and economic system that benefited from their subservient status. Throughout their history, many African Americans have maintained many of their traditional cultural experiences in the treatment of illnesses. The following is a sample of some home remedies:

1. Cuts and wounds can be treated with sour or spoiled milk that is placed on stale bread, wrapped in a cloth, and placed on the wound.
2. An expectorant for colds consists of chopped raw garlic, chopped onion, fresh parsley, and a little water, all mixed in a blender.
3. Garlic can be placed on the ill person or in the room to remove the "evil spirits" that have caused the illness. (Spector, 1985, p. 148)

These remedies indicate that illness is a process that involves not only biological, but also social, spiritual, and cultural factors (Bailey, 1992). In addition, these remedies indicate the importance of the household rather than the larger medical community in extracting a cure. Household members (as well as friends) are particularly important as a social support mechanism (Belgrave & Lewis, 1994). Because of the importance of family and friends, the framework of the traditional medical model may offer little for many African Americans.

A perusal of Table 5.2 indicates that depending on age, African Americans have higher rates of physician utilization than do Caucasian Americans. The higher rates of physician utilization are related to the use of multiple physicians when care is received rather than having access to a primary care physician. African Americans also experience longer hospital stays than Caucasian Americans. This would suggest that "coupled with less frequent hospital discharges, usually mean that the population is diagnosed at a later stage of the disease—that they are sicker, and therefore need more hospital care" (Reed et al., 1993, p. 101). The utilization behaviors of African Americans can be understood as the result of three basic factors: institutional racism, economic inequality, and access barriers (Jones & Rene, 1994). The consequences of these factors relative to subsequent illness behaviors continue to plague the African American community. All of this is compounded for African American males, who are at increased risk for illness compared to Caucasian American males. For example, "black men suffer higher rates of diabetes, strokes, and a variety of chronic illnesses" (Staples, 1995, p. 123).

In addition to differences in rates of illness, African Americans (as well as other minority populations) are more likely to seek out and utilize nontraditional forms of treatment. These "nontraditional" or alternative measures of health and illness are examined in greater detail in Chapter 10.

Another minority population that has suffered cultural indignities throughout American history is the Native American or indigenous population. Because Native Americans represent a multiplicity of cultural identities (Young, 1994), an overview of illness behavior would be impossible. In addition, *where* a Native American lives (for example, urban America or on a reservation) may influence their illness behavior. For example, Native Americans located in urban areas are more likely to submerge their tribal identity into an Indian identity (Flanagan, 1995). The focus in this section is on one tribe, the Navajo.

Located in northwest Arizona, the Navajo constitute the largest Native American tribe. Culturally, the Navajo value "the importance of living a balanced and harmonious life" (Quintero, 1995, p. 74). Applying this value to health and illness, the traditional Navajo belief is that illness represents an imbalance between the person who is ill and nature. It is believed that illness is the result of:

1. Natural phenomena, such as lightning, winds, thunder, and sometimes the earth, sun, or moon.
2. Some species of animal, including bear, deer, coyote, snakes, eagles, and fish.
3. Ghosts, witches, aliens (including White persons).
4. Ceremonial paraphernalia or activities that are contacted at inappropriate times. (Wyman & Kluckhohn, 1938, cited in Fox, 1987, p. 40)

Thus, health is achieved through the restoration of equilibrium. The process involves the use of various ceremonial methodologies that recreate the development of the world for the patient. The purpose of these ceremonies is to connect the person with the spiritual world. Unlike Western medicine, these ceremonies involve family as well as members of the larger community (Fox, 1992). Thus, illness behavior involves utilizing a shaman, or medicine man, to eradicate the illness through such treatment modalities as song, massage, sweatbaths, or the use of roots (Spector, 1985).

Although traditional practices continue, many Navajo have integrated Anglo or Western health care into the curative process. This medical pluralism is practiced by patients and, according to Fox (1987), staff at a non-Indian health facility on the reservation.

Exploring populations outside the United States, illness behavior demonstrates the variability of cultural beliefs and practices (Mechanic, 1985). However, one of the most consistent themes throughout the developing (and in some cases, developed) world is that of medical pluralism. That is, various therapeutic techniques coexisting within a single cultural setting (Christakis et al., 1994). Examples of medical pluralism in developed nations include Chinese medical students in Hong Kong (Cheng & Lee, 1988) and Ethiopian immigrants in Israel (Nudelman, 1993).

It is evident that beliefs and practices of traditional and Western medicine are integrative. For example, consider the work of Hunt (1993). Studying patients in two southern cities in Mexico who were receiving cancer treatment, Hunt (1993) reports that in addition to the application of biomedical interventions, families also rely on traditional interpretations of the disease. Hunt (1993) notes how one family discussed their son's cancer within a biomedical context (i.e., treatment and prognosis). When asked, however, "What did the doctor tell you was the matter with your son?" the respondent replied, "Witchcraft" (Hunt, 1993, p. 251). Thus, rather than being contradictory, these models are "compatible elements of an evolving illness understanding" (Hunt, 1993, p. 254).

As in other developing nations, medical pluralism provides a framework for an understanding of illness behavior in Iran. Consider, for example, heart distress. Heart distress is a physiological experience precipitated by situations such as "childbirth, pregnancy or contraception, or by a variety of disease" (Good, 1977, pp. 33–34). Although heart distress is more likely to occur among specific populations, it is the experience, the language, and symptoms that "give it meaning to the sufferer" (Good, 1977, p. 39). In Nepal, medical pluralism differentiates between the doctor who treats "bodily illnesses" and the shaman who treats "the extrahuman beings that cause people so much sorrow and suffering" (Pigg, 1995, p. 30). Thus, although Nepalis understand the distinction between doctors and shamans, they nevertheless engage in discriminating practices regarding treatment depending on the type of illness.

The distinction between traditional and scientific medicine, consequent disease classification, and health-service utilization is clear. The younger the respondent, the more likely they were to identify natural agents as the cause of disease (Fosu, 1981). Furthermore, females, respondents who were married or single, and increasing levels of education were also linked to belief in natural agents as the cause of disease. The significance of this research is its connection to health-service utilization "because what is done about a disease usually bears a systematic relationship to the way in which it is classified" (Fosu, 1981, p. 479). Among the Anufo of northern Ghana, illness management may involve medical pluralism. However, the use of Western medicine is generally limited, as the Anufo have color-coded illness and illness behavior. Thus, the "white zone" represents a normal state of health. When afflicted with an illness (which is indicated by its location on the body, i.e., headache), the individual engages in self-help with folk remedies. If the illness becomes progressively worse or chronic, it is referred to as the "red zone." Illness management is no longer an individual responsibility, but one that involves the larger community, particularly kin members. If the illness progresses to near death, it has entered the "black zone." At this point, illness management ends and the fate of the person is put in the hands of God (Kirby, 1997).

Examining the relationship between ethnicity, social class, and self-reported illness among different refugees and labor migrants in Sweden, Sundquist (1995) found that ethnicity of immigrants influenced utilization of medical services such as consultation rates. In addition to ethnicity, Sundquist (1995) suggests that other factors such as social class and lifestyle are also interrelated.

Social Class

Although dated, the following excerpt from *The Other America* by Michael Harrington (1971, p. 16) poignantly illustrates the relationship between being poor and sickness.

> The poor get sick more than anyone else in the society. That is because they live in slums, jammed together under unhygienic conditions; they have inadequate diets, and cannot get decent medical care. When they become sick, they are sick longer than any other group in the society. Because they are sick more often and longer than anyone else, they lose wages and work, and find it difficult to hold a steady job. And because of this, they cannot pay for good housing, for a nutritious diet, for doctors. At any given point in the circle, particularly when there is a major illness, their prospect is to move to an even lower level and to begin the cycle, round and round, toward even more suffering.

Some changes have occurred since Harrington wrote this passage. For example, in Table 5.2 the average number of physician contacts by family income level have increased, particularly among those with the lowest income. In fact, in 1994, those with family income below $14,000 had the highest average number of physician contacts, followed by those with incomes of $35,000 and above. However, the number of physician contacts does not necessarily result in improved health outcomes. If a person, because of income, waits to see a physician because of illness, they will be sicker when they make contact. Thus, they will also see more physicians, who will treat the advanced medical condition. Dutton (1986, p. 34) points out that the poor "may be less likely than the more affluent to seek care for a given illness because of limited income, and also less likely to forego wage-earning opportunities."

In a classic study, Koos (1954) examined the relationship between social-class position and response to illness in a small community in upstate New York. According to Koos, responses to specific symptoms differed by social-class position. In other words, the poor were less likely to identify symptoms as needing medical care.

More recently, Dutton (1986) constructed the cycle of poverty and pathology. Although her argument is centered primarily on illness, the cycle does recognize some aspects of illness behavior that are worth noting. She begins by identifying environmental conditions within the home and work as related to one's economic position. In other words, lower-class people are more likely to experience illness and injury in their home or place of employment than are persons in the middle class. The ever-present environmental degradation eventually leads to psychological stress and social isolation. Being poor because of unemployment or lack of sufficient wages when employed means placement at the bottom of the social hierarchy. At the same time, the lower class has fewer social contacts than do the middle or upper classes. The lack of social contact and psychological stress associated with a low social status is related negatively to health outcomes. In other words, the poor are less likely to survive a serious illness. As a result, the poor are more likely to develop lifestyles and engage in coping mechanisms that are deleterious to their health. For example, alcohol consumption and cigarette smoking are generally higher (particularly among males) among the poor. The economically disadvantaged are less likely to participate in exercise regimens and, at the same time, eat less nutritiously than do the middle and upper classes. A consequence of these coping mechanisms is that the poor experience poorer health status. The cycle is linked to the health-care system through the inadequate care received by the poor. Although the poor may have access to medical care, it is generally fragmented and inconsistent (Dutton, 1978). As a result, the poor are more likely to suffer more severe illnesses and have longer hospital stays. Because of the length of illness and hospitalization, they are likely to either lose their job or have a more difficult time finding one. With a diminished or erratic access to the job market, the poor remain economically disadvantaged, and the cycle of poverty and pathology continues (Dutton, 1986).

Examining the interactive effects of race, education, and income on utilization rates, Sharp et al. (1983) argue that African Americans and the poor have increased their use of the health-care system. In particular, African Americans and the poor have more positive attitudes towards physician utilization. However, as Sharp et al. (1983, p. 261) note: "neither attitudes nor symptoms alone affect utilization; a person must have the symptom *and* evaluate the symptom as one that is serious enough to require a doctor's care."

Within a sociological context, this chapter explores the intersection of illness behavior with variables such as age, sex, race, and social class. However, the experience of illness behavior also represents another dimension: pain. This chapter concludes with a brief examination of this concept within a cultural context.

A Sociological Analysis of Pain

Although the concept of **pain** can be traced from the Greeks to the present day (see, for example, Rey, 1995), it is not relevant here to detail these various historical periods. Rather, a sociological examination focuses on how "responses to pain are predictable on the basis of group membership and that the social meanings ascribed to pain are shared by members of groups" (Freidson, 1970, p. 280).

The classic works within sociology are by Zborowski (1952) and Zola (1966), who provide us with cultural responses to pain. Briefly, Zborowski (1952) examined responses to pain among 81 Jewish, Irish, and "Old American" patients in a Veterans Hospital in New York City (Irish patients are included in a later publication; Zborowski, 1969). The "Old American" patients can be characterized as third-generation whites, who are generally Protestant and who do not identify with any ethnic group. Zborowski reported that although Italian and Jewish patients were similar in their response, they exhibited differences toward the pain-relieving drugs. For example, an Italian is "concerned with the analgesic effects of the drugs which are administered to him" whereas "the Jewish patient . . . often is reluctant to accept the drug [because] of concern about the effects of the drug upon his health in general" (Zborowski, 1952, p. 22). However, the "Old American" approaches pain in a more stoic fashion. There is little emotion, as the "Old American" patient places considerable confidence in technology and the professionals who are treating him. Zborowski also noted that the attitudes toward pain are acquired through socialization within the family. Again, cultural differences were identified. For example, Jews and Italians were overprotected, particularly by the mother. In Jewish families, pain (and illness) was considered anything that deviated from the norm. Italian families are expressive and tend to respond to illness and pain by exhibiting considerable sympathy for the victim. Within "Old American" families, boys are encouraged to participate in activities that may result in injury and pain. However, they are also told not to exhibit emotions when in pain but rather to "act like a man" (Zborowski, 1952).

Research findings by Zola (1966) of Italian Americans are comparable to Zborowski (1952). However, as Bendelow and Williams (1995a, p. 97) point out, these studies "have been criticized for crudely reinforcing ethnic stereotypes." Although the work of Zborowski and Zola provide a historical framework for the study of pain, we must recognize the limitations associated with their findings. In addition to ethnic stereotyping, the research depicted respondents as passively accepting their sociocultural environment.

Nonetheless, although pain may be the body's response to a traumatic experience, part of the interpretation of what constitutes pain is couched within the cultural context of the recipient. Addressing the influence of culture, Helman (1994, p. 181) points out that our response to pain "is influenced by social, cultural and psychological factors." Thus, not only how we respond to pain but also whether we allow our private responses to become public are rooted in cultural traditions (Helman, 1994). In addition, there are group-level characteristics such as one's position in the class structure or one's sex or ethnicity that may influence one's interpretation of pain. As a result, "these factors all affect how pain is perceived, experienced, reacted to, and expressed physically, mentally, and emotionally" (Bendelow & Williams, 1995a, p. 98). For example, after examining the role of sex in response to pain, Bendelow (1993) reported differences in interpretation and coping with pain.

Furthermore, at the individual level, Bendelow & Williams (1995a, p. 97) suggest the need for an interpretative argument that gives "a far more active, critical and reflective role to the individual who draws upon their own lay knowledge and beliefs in shaping both their interpretation and response to pain" (see also Bendelow & Williams, 1995b).

Thus, although pain (or any aspect of illness) can be defined medically, how a person responds to a disease, acknowledges that they are ill, or interprets pain are dependent on the culture in which they live and the group-level characteristics that define them. Illich (1976) argues that within traditional cultures, pain is a manifestation of one's existence. Within medicalized civilizations, however, pain becomes "managed." That is, through the application of drug therapies, the health-care community attempts to control not only the amount but also the existence of pain within patients. Given the demographic changes toward increasingly aged societies and the greater likelihood of chronic illness among elderly persons, questions regarding pain management throughout end-of-life decisions will increase. Questions such as, "Why is pain a necessary part of the human condition? Is there an obligation to relieve pain, and if so, who is obliged to relieve it? Also, who is and who is not allowed to feel or express pain openly?" (Encandela, 1993, p. 784).

In Chapter 6, illness behavior is examined within the specific context of the sick role. Undoubtedly one of the most important concepts within medical sociology, the sick role is examined, as are complementary areas such as chronic illness and physical disability.

Summary

This chapter covers considerable theoretical and applied territory. It begins by clarifying the differences between such concepts as disease, illness, illness behavior, sickness, and pain. The second section of the chapter covers various theoretical explanations of illness behavior. Beginning with the stages of illness behavior by Suchman (1965), it specifies each stage and its connection to the larger model. The chapter then addresses the general theory of help seeking by Mechanic (1970). Again, the major points are cited as well as potential problems with the model. Other explanations of illness behavior are introduced as counterpoints to these more known models. Moving from the general to the specific, the chapter addresses the sociological variables of age, sex, race and ethnicity, and social class relative to illness behavior. It is noted that alone or combined, these factors do not completely address illness behavior. Rather, the importance of the cultural context within which the illness behavior occurs is of particular importance. These four factors do, however, combine to provide a sociological interpretation of medical conditions. Finally, the chapter addresses the meaning of pain and, in the process, examines research that connects pain response to its cultural context. The chapter concludes with a brief introduction to the relationship between pain management and end-of-life issues.

Sociologically, this chapter is important because it links medical conditions and responses to group-level characteristics of the patient. Chapter 6 continues this perspective by focusing on the sick role as a specific example of illness behavior.

CHAPTER   REVIEW

As with previous chapters, the chapter review is meant to inform the reader of significant concepts, pose questions, and create an on-going knowledge base of medical sociology.

1. Define the following concepts:
   illness
   disease
   illness behavior
   sickness
   pain
   How are these concepts related? Construct a scenario in which all five concepts are utilized to explain a particular medical condition.

2. Diagram the five stages of illness behavior. Construct an argument in support of the explanation. Construct a second argument that is critical of the explanation.

3. Consider the point of Dingwall (that the theory of help-seeking lacks sufficient depth). Do you agree or disagree? Explain your answer. In response, Dingwall offers what he refers to as an illness action model. Is his representation superior to the theory of help-seeking? Explain.

4. Compare those most at risk for health conditions in the United States with those from other countries. Are there similarities? Differences?

5. Pick the one sociodemographic variable that you consider the most important as an explanation of illness behavior. Explain your answer. Is this variable important transculturally as well? Explain.

6. Explain the relationship between illness behavior and health behavior.

7. Explain the relationship between the four sociodemographic variables associated with illness behavior and their role in epidemiology.

8. From a transcultural perspective, construct a model of illness behavior. Identify the components within the model and explain why they were included.

GLOSSARY

disease   is a biological explanation of a medical condition (the biological dimension).

illness   is a social response to a specific medical condition (the social and psychological dimension).

illness behavior   involves differential symptom outcomes depending on sociodemographic characteristics of the patient.

pain   is a natural reaction to any traumatic bodily experience. Although biological, response to pain is grounded in the culture of the recipient.

sickness   is a state or condition that, when defined by others, requires treatment (the social dimension).

SUGGESTED READINGS

Although there are any number of quality readings on illness behavior available, this author would recommend beginning with the classics. This material provides a solid foundation from which future knowledge can be built. The following is by no means a complete listing; rather, it is intended as an introduction.

Mechanic, D. (1961). Stress, illness behavior, and the sick role. *American Sociological Review, 26,* 51–58.

> Perhaps more appropriate in Chapter 6, this is an earlier article by Mechanic in which he examines the relationship between illness behavior and the sick role. Nonetheless, a good article that connects sociology to medical concepts.

Mechanic, D. (1962). The concept of illness behavior. *Journal of Chronic Disorders, 15,* 189–194.

> An early work in which the concept of illness behavior is defined. Mechanic also provides support for the earlier work of Zborowski.

Nathanson, C. A. (1977). Sex, illness, and medical care: A review of data, theory, and method. *Social Science and Medicine, 11,* 13–25.

> This article offers a solid comparative analysis of the United States with many of its Western industrialized partners. The author examines four explanations of sex differences regarding illness and health status.

Suchman, E. A. (1965). Stages of illness and medical care. *Journal of Health and Human Behavior, 6, 3,* 114–128.

> A classic in which Suchman outlines his five stages of illness behavior. This article established the framework for the study of illness behavior. Necessary reading for anyone seriously interested in medical sociology.

Zborowski, M. (1952). Cultural components in responses to pain. *Journal of Social Issues, 8, 4,* 16–30.

> Although criticized for its stereotyping of ethnic populations, this article (as the title implies) examines cultural patterns in response to pain. The author looks beyond the patient and also addresses the influence of socialization on the interpretation of pain.

Zola, I. K. (1966). Culture and symptoms—An analysis of patients' presenting complaints. *American Sociological Review, 31,* 515–630.

> Also criticized for ethnic stereotyping, this article also examines the influence of culture in response to illness and pain. Must reading for anyone seriously interested in medical sociology.

REFERENCES

Alonzo, A. A. (1979). Everyday illness behavior: A situational approach to health status deviations. *Social Science and Medicine, 13,* 397–404.

Alonzo, A. A. (1980). Acute illness behavior: A conceptual exploration and specification. *Social Science and Medicine, 14,* 515–526.

Anson, O., Paran, E., Neumann, L., & Chernichovsky, D. (1993). Gender differences in health perceptions and their predictors. *Social Science and Medicine, 36, 4,* 419–427.

Apple, D. (1960). How laymen define illness. *Journal of Health and Social Behavior, 1,* 219–225.

Bailey, E. J. (1991). *Urban African American health care.* Lanham, MD: University Press of America.

Barker, J. C. (1990). Between humans and ghosts: The decrepit elderly in a Polynesian society. In J. Sokolovsky (Ed.). *The cultural context of aging: Worldwide perspectives* (pp. 295–313). New York: Bergin & Garvey.

Beckerleg, S., Austin, S., & Weaver, L. (1994). Gender, work and illness: The influence of a research unit on an agricultural community in the Gambia. *Health Policy and Planning, 9,* 4, 419–428.

Belgrave, F. Z., & Lewis, D. M. (1994). The role of social support in compliance and other health behaviors for African Americans with chronic illnesses. *Journal of Health and Social Policy, 5,* 3–4, 55–68.

Bendelow, G. (1993). Pain perceptions, emotions and gender. *Sociology of Health and Illness, 15,* 3, 273–294.

Bendelow, G., & Williams, S. (1995a). Pain and the mind–body dualism: A sociological approach. *Body & Society, 1,* 2, 83–103.

Bendelow, G., & Williams, S. (1995b). Transcending the dualisms: Towards a sociology of pain. *Sociology of Health and Illness, 17,* 2, 139–165.

Brody, E. M., & Kleban, M. H. (1983). Day-to-day mental and physical health symptoms of older people: A report on health logs. *The Gerontologist, 23,* 1, 75–85.

Brown, P. (1995). Naming and framing: The social construction of diagnosis and illness. *Journal of Health and Social Behavior* (Extra Issue), 34–52.

Calnan, M. (1986). Maintaining health and preventing illness: A comparison of the perceptions of women from different social classes. *Health Promotion, 1,* 2, 167–177.

Castro, R. (1995). The subjective experience of health and illness in Ocuituco: A case study. *Social Science and Medicine, 41,* 7, 1005–1021.

Cheng, Y. H., & Lee, W. H. (1988). Illness behaviour in Chinese medical students. *Psychologia, 31,* 4, 207–216.

Christakis, N. A., Ware, N. C., & Kleinman, A. (1994). Illness behavior and the health transition in the developing world. In L. C. Chen, A. Kleinman, & N. C. Ware (Eds.). *Health and social change in international perspective* (pp. 275–302). Harvard: Harvard University Press.

Dimond, M., & Jones, S. L. (1983). *Chronic illness across the life span.* Norwalk, CT: Appleton-Century-Crofts.

Dingwall, R. (1977). *Aspects of illness.* New York: St. Martin's Press.

Donahue, J. M., & McGuire, M. B. (1995). The political economy of responsibility in health and illness. *Social Science and Medicine, 40,* 1, 47–53.

Dutton, D. B. (1978). Explaining the low use of health services by the poor: Costs, attitudes, or delivery systems? *American Sociological Review, 43,* 348–368.

Dutton, D. B. (1986). Social class, health, and illness. In L. H. Aiken & D. Mechanic (Eds.). *Applications of social science to clinical medicine and health policy* (pp. 31–62). New Brunswick, NJ: Rutgers University Press.

Eisenberg, L. (1977). Disease and illness. *Culture, Medicine and Psychiatry, 1,* 9–23.

Encandela, J. A. (1993). Social science and the study of pain since Zborowski: A need for a new agenda. *Social Science and Medicine, 36,* 6, 783–791.

Fife, B. L. (1994). The conceptualization of meaning in illness. *Social Science and Medicine, 38,* 2, 309–316.

Flanagan, W. G. (1995). *Urban sociology: Images and structure.* (2nd Ed.). Boston: Allyn & Bacon.

Fosu, G. B. (1981). Disease classification in rural Ghana: Framework and implications for health behavior. *Social Science and Medicine, 15B,* 471–482.

Fox, E. (1987). Hedging bets: Pluralistic practice in a Navajo hospital. *Sociological Viewpoints, 3,* 1, 39–50.

Fox, E. (1992). Crossing the bridge: Adaptive strategies among Navajo health care workers. *Free Inquiry in Creative Sociology, 20,* 1, 25–34.

Fox, R. C. (1989). *The sociology of medicine: A participant observer's view.* Englewood Cliffs, NJ: Prentice-Hall.

Freidson, E. (1970). *Profession of medicine: A study of the sociology of applied knowledge.* New York: Dodd, Mead and Company.

Fuller, T. D., Edwards, J. N., Sermsri, S., & Vorakitphokatorn, S. (1993). Gender and health: Some Asian evidence. *Journal of Health and Social Behavior, 34,* 252–271.

Glascock, A. P. (1990). By any other name, it is still killing: A comparison of the treatment of the elderly in America and other societies. In J. Sokolovsky (Ed.). *The cultural context of aging: Worldwide perspectives* (pp. 43–56). New York: Bergin & Garvey.

Good, B. J. (1977). The heart of what's the matter: The semantics of illness in Iran. *Culture, Medicine and Psychiatry, 1,* 25–58.

Harrington, M. (1971). *The other America* (Rev. Ed.). Baltimore, MD: Penguin.

Harwood, A. (1981). Guidelines for culturally appropriate health care. In A. Harwood (Ed.). *Ethnicity and medical care* (pp.482–507). Cambridge, MA: Harvard University Press.

Haug, M. R. (1981). Age and medical care utilization patterns. *Journal of Gerontology, 36,* 1, 103–111.

Helman, C. G. (1994). *Culture, health and illness.* (3rd Ed.). Oxford: Butterworth–Heinemann.

Henderson, J. N. (1990). Alzheimer's disease in cultural context. In J. Sokolovsky (Ed.). *The cultural context of aging: Worldwide perspectives* (pp. 315–330). New York: Bergin & Garvey.

Hunt, L. M. (1993). The metastasis of witchcraft: The interrelationship between traditional and biomedical concepts of cancer in southern Mexico. *Colloquim Anthropology, 17,* 2, 249–256.

Jones, W. Jr., & Rene, A. A. (1994). Barriers to health services utilization and African Americans. In I. L. Livingston (Ed.). *Handbook of Black American health: The mosaic of conditions, issues, policies, and prospects* (pp. 378–386). Westport, CT: Greenwood Press.

Illich, I. (1976). *Medical nemesis.* New York: Pantheon Books.

Kandrack, M. A. (1991). Gender differences in health related behaviour: Some unanswered questions. *Social Science and Medicine, 32,* 5, 579–590.

Kirby, J. P. (1997). White, red and black: Colour classification and illness management in northern Ghana. *Social Science and Medicine, 44,* 2, 215–230.

Kleinman, A. (1988). *The illness narratives: Suffering, healing, and the human condition.* New York: Basic.

Koos, E. L. (1954). *The health of Regionville.* New York: Columbia University Press.

Levkoff, S. E., Cleary, P. D., Wetle, T., & Besdine, R. W. (1988). Illness behavior in the aged: Implications for clinicians. *Journal of the American Geriatric Society, 36,* 622–629.

Lupton, D. (1994). *Medicine as culture: Illness, disease and the body in Western societies.* London: SAGE.

Macintyre, S. (1993). Gender differences in the perceptions of common cold symptoms. *Social Science and Medicine, 36,* 1, 15–20.

Markides, C. P. (1992). Women and access to health care. *Social Science and Medicine, 35,* 4, 619–626.

Mechanic, D. (1962). The concept of illness behavior. *Journal of Chronic Diseases, 15,* 189–194.

Mechanic, D. (1978). *Medical sociology* (2nd Ed.). New York: The Free Press.

Mechanic, D. (1979). The stability of health and illness behavior: Results from a 16-year follow-up. *American Journal of Public Health, 69,* 11, 1142–1145.

Mechanic, D. (1985). Illness behavior: An overview. In S. McHugh & T. M. Vallis (Eds.). *Illness behavior: A multidisciplinary model* (pp. 101–109). New York: Plenum.

Mechanic, D., (1992). Health and illness behavior and patient–practitioner relationships. *Social Science and Medicine, 34,* 12, 1345–1350.

Mechanic, D., & Volkart, E. H. (1961). Stress, illness behavior, and the sick role. *American Sociological Review, 26,* 51–58.

Nudelman, A. (1993). The importance of traditional healing for Ethiopian immigrants in Israel. *Colloquium Anthropological, 17,* 2, 233–239.

OPCS (Office of Population Censuses and Surveys). (1989). *General household survey, 1987.* London: HMSO.

Papadopoulos, L. (1995). The impact of illness on the family and the family's impact on illness. *Counseling Psychology Quarterly, 8,* 1, 27–34.

Pigg, S. L. (1995). The social symbolism of healing in Nepal. *Ethnology, 34,* 1, 17–36.

Prohaska, T. R., Leventhal, E. A., Leventhal, H., & Keller, M. L. (1985). Health practices and illness cognition in young, middle aged, and elderly adults. *Journal of Gerontology, 40,* 5, 569–578.

Quintero, G. A. (1995). Gender, discord, and illness: Navajo philosophy and healing in the Native American Church. *Journal of Anthropological Research, 51,* 1, 69–89.

Reed, W. L., Darity, W. Sr., & Roberson, N. L. (1993). *Health and medical care of African-Americans.* Westport, CT: Auburn House.

Rey, R. (1995). *The history of pain.* Translated by L. E. Wallace, J. A. Cadden, & S. W. Cadden. Cambridge, MA: Harvard University Press.

Rosenberg, C. E. (1992). *Explaining epidemics and other studies in the history of medicine.* New York: Oxford University Press.

Scambler, G. (1991). Health and illness behaviour. In G. Scambler (Ed.). *Sociology as applied to medicine* (3rd Ed.). (pp. 33–46). London: Bailliere Tindall.

Segall, A., & Chappel, N. L. (1991). Making sense out of sickness: Lay explanations of chronic illness among older adults. *Advances in Medical Sociology, 2,* 115–133.

Sharp, K., Ross, C. E., & Cockerham, W. C. (1983). Symptoms, beliefs, and the use of physician services among the disadvantaged. *Journal of Health and Social Behavior, 24,* 255–263.

Sokolovsky, J. (Ed). (1990). *The cultural context of aging: Worldwide perspectives.* New York: Bergin & Garvey.

Spector, R. E. (1985). *Cultural diversity in health and illness* (2nd Ed.). East Norwalk, CT: Appleton-Century-Crofts.

Staples, R. (1995). Health among Afro-American males. In D. Sabo & D. F. Gordon (Eds.). *Men's health and illness: Gender, power, and the body* (pp. 121–138). Thousand Oaks, CA: SAGE.

Strain, L. A. (1989). Illness behavior in old age: From symptom awareness to resolution. *Journal of Aging Studies, 3,* 4, 325–340.

Suchman, E. A. (1965). Stages of illness and medical care. *Journal of Health and Human Behavior, 6,* 3, 114–128.

Sundquist, J. (1995). Ethnicity, social class and health. A population-based study on the influence of social factors on self-reported illness in 223 Latin American refugees, 333 Finnish and 126 South European labour migrants and 841 Swedish controls. *Social Science and Medicine, 40,* 6, 777–787.

Tout, K. (1989). *Aging in developing countries.* New York: Oxford University Press.

Turton, R. W., & Chalmers, B. E. (1990). Apartheid, stress and illness: The demographic context of distress reported by South African Africans. *Social Science and Medicine, 31,* 11, 1191–1200.

Twaddle, A. C. (1979). *Sickness behavior and the sick role.* Cambridge, MA: Schenkman Publishing.

Twaddle, A. C., & Hessler, R. M. (1987). *A sociology of health* (2nd Ed.). New York: Macmillan.

U.S. Bureau of the Census. (1992). International Population Reports, P25, 92–3, *An Aging World II.* Washington DC: U.S. Government Printing Office.

Veitch, P. C. (1995). The development of a method for measuring anticipated illness behaviour in three common injuries. *Social Science and Medicine, 41,* 5, 747–751.

Virtanen, P. (1994). 'An epidemic of good health' at the workplace. *Sociology of Health & Illness, 16,* 3, 394–401.

Weitz, R. (1996). *The sociology of health, illness, and health care: A critical approach.* Belmont, CA: Wadsworth.

Whiteford, M. B. (1991). The patient as diagnostician: Intracultural differences in illness etiology in a Mexican neighborhood. *Journal of Developing Societies, 7,* 2, 256–268.

Wolinsky, F. D. (1988). *The sociology of health: Principles, practitioners, and issues* (2nd Ed.). Belmont, CA: Wadsworth.

Wyman, L., & Kluckhohn, C. (1938). *Navajo classification of their song ceremonials.* Menasha, Wisconsin: Memoirs of the American Anthropological Association, #50.

Young, T. K. (1994). *The health of Native Americans: Toward a biocultural epidemiology.* New York: Oxford University Press.

Zborowski, M. (1952). Cultural components in response to pain. *Journal of Social Issues, 8,* 4, 16–30.

Zborowski, M. (1969). *People in pain.* San Francisco: Jossey-Bass.

Zola, I. K. (1966). Culture and symptoms—An analysis of patients' presenting complaints. *American Sociological Review, 31,* 615–630.

Zola, I. K. (1973). Pathways to the doctor: From person to patient. *Social Science and Medicine, 7,* 677–689.

Zola, I. K. (1983). *Socio-medical inquiries: Recollections, reflections, and reconsiderations.* Philadelphia: Temple University Press.

6

Illness Behavior—Part II

The Sick Role and Beyond

. . . the role of being sick as an institutionalized role may be said to constitute a set of conditions necessary to enable the physician to bring his competence to bear on the situation. It is not only that the patient has a need to be helped, but that this need is institutionally categorized, that the nature and implications of this need are socially recognized, and the kind of help, the appropriate general pattern of action in relation to the source of help, are defined. It is not only the sick person's own condition and personal reactions to what should be done about it which are involved, but he is placed in an institutionally defined framework which mobilizes others in his situation in support of the same patterns which are imputed to him, which is such an important feature of his role. The fact that others than the patient himself often define that he is sick, or sick enough for certain measures to be taken, is significant.

—Parsons, 1970, p. 475

The Importance of the Sick Role

The statement at the beginning of this chapter not only places the concept of the sick role within an institutional setting, but also defines the relationship between patient and physician. Although dated, this relationship persists. It is built on a hierarchical status arrangement in which the physician, by virtue of occupation, is accorded social control over the patient. Acknowledging this control, Parsons (1970) argues that, in fact, the physician may engage in actions toward the body that one's sexual partner would not even consider. Although the physician may exert control over the patient, Parsons (1975) does not mean to imply that the relationship is asymmetric, whereby the patient remains completely passive.

The sick role remains important today because it represents the first significant effort to create a role specifically framed within the health-care community from the intersection of societal-level responses and expectations and illness-related behaviors. Thus, it is important to understand not only the composition of the sick role, but also the consequences of its construction. At the same time, attempts to "move beyond" the sick role have not provided an adequate alternative. As a result, the sick role remains as a central, yet flawed, concept within medical sociology.

Throughout this chapter it is important to remember the historical context of the sick role. In other words, the sick role is representative of a particular period in which disease episodes were primarily acute and therefore amenable to short-term solutions. Although the sick role may not be particularly applicable today, it did perform a valuable function when it was initially introduced.

The Sick Role: An Introduction to Illness as Deviance

What is the **sick role?** Twaddle (1979, p. 46) states that "the sick role can be seen as a limited and conditional set of privileges and obligations relative to a deviant identity." Furthermore, the sick role is available to all and is considered temporary (Parsons, 1951). More specifically, if we consider the state of health to be good or "normal," then illness is a state of deviance located in the social system (Herzlich, 1973), not in the individual. Thus, the significance of the dysfunctional nature of deviance (or illness) is that "it threatens to interfere with the stability of the social system" (Dimond & Jones, 1983, p. 21). If a person is ill, he or she is unable to perform their normal social obligations. The sick role is an acknowledgment of the "deviance" experienced by the individual. In order to return to a state of health, the individual is allowed access to the sick role that has clearly defined rights and obligations. The sick role can be conceptualized as a cycle in which participants can be observed as they "become involved in a series of social systems dealing with the problems of illness and health" (Goldstein & Dommermuth, 1961, p. 45). In other words, the sick role is acquired when others define the normative expectations associated with the incapacity (Nuttbrock, 1986). However, it is this defining of illness by others (primarily those in positions of power) that concerns Lagerwey and

Markle (1994). Analyzing the literary work of Wharton (*Ethan Frome*), they argue that illness is a social construct, allowing social characteristics of the actors to define the outcome. Thus, admission to the sick role is based on two criteria: "the extent of impairment and who initiates the definition of sickness" (Williams, 1971, p. 220).

The Sick Role: A Comparative Analysis

Removal from normal social roles because of illness is not unique to the United States or to Western industrialized nations. Most cultures provide members such an opportunity and define this departure from social roles as deviant. The following transcultural examples provide a range of sociocultural interpretations regarding the sick role.

   Turner (1995, p. 52) discusses the word "berserk" and its sociolinguistic meaning. Culturally, "berserk" is a Norse word that "refers to institutionalized deviant behavior. The berserk was somebody who occupied a special role in the tribe and was expected to put fear into tribal enemies." Among the Tzintzuntzan in Michocan, Mexico, one does not "catch" a cold (or any other illness). Rather, illnesses "strike" the patient. Because of this linguistic explanation of how one acquires the illness, Tzintzuntzans are not held responsible for their illness (Foster, 1982). Research by Parsons (1984) found that among the peoples of Tonga, illness was considered the result of family conflict. Illnesses were resolved by reestablishing kinship harmony. By comparison, illness among the Andeans was built on the concepts of balance, reciprocity, and universal harmony. Therefore, any disruption (illness) was not solely the responsibility of the individual. Rather, "the Andes notions of illness not only defined an individual state but were applicable to the conditions of society as a whole" (Silverblatt, 1983, p. 418). Thus, rather than the individual assuming total responsible for the breakdown of social norms because of illness, the larger society was also held accountable for the disruption.

   Although brief, these transcultural examples provide a range of interpretations associated with sickness and the sick role. It is interesting to note who is held responsible when an illness is contracted (or even the interpretation of *how* it is contracted). Based on these examples as well as our knowledge of illness within a Western context, individual responsibility for illness appears to increase with the level of societal modernization.

The Sociohistorical Context of the Sick Role

The sick role has been identified (by some) as the most significant contribution in the development of medical sociology (Wolinsky, 1988; Fox, 1989). However, since its original publication (Parsons, 1951), the concept has become the focus of intense interest and, consequently, criticism (Gordon, 1966, offers perhaps the most detailed criticism of the sick role). As an example of the extensive research interest in the sick role, a 1978 article by Levin and Kozloff has more than 100 citations that address the sick role. By comparison, a perusal of *Sociological Abstracts* between 1980 and 1996 identified fewer than three dozen articles under the heading of "sickness" or "sick role." This precipitous decline in interest in sick role research is explained by Glik and Kronenfeld (1989, p. 293). They argue that although the sick role is an important concept, it is "not relevant for informing current research." Earlier, Segall (1976a, p. 168) had questioned whether the sick role adequately addressed "the way in which the sick person actually thinks, feels and behaves." A categorization of criticisms is offered by Gordon (1966), Berkanovic (1972), and Twaddle and Hessler (1987). Perhaps, as Levin and Kozloff (1978, p. 339) suggest, it is time "to leave the Parsonian formulation in the background, to free ourselves of the limits of the paradigm, and to learn much more about the social behavior of the sick person." Rather than debating the merits and criticisms of the sick role, it is more important to consider the sociohistorical context within which it emerged. Initially developed in the latter 1940s by Parsons (Fox, 1989), the sick role emerged as a continuation of the dominant functionalist theoretical framework associated with that time period (refer to Chapter 1 for a historical accounting of theory development in the United States). Utilizing the functionalist argument, Waitzkin (1971) examined the latent functions of the sick role within social institutions such as the family, the military, the penal system, the mental hospital, and the state. Waitzkin (1971, p. 68) concluded that, "the sick role appears to support the institutional *status quo*" (italics in original). The status quo is maintained because, as Waitzkin (1994, p. 65) points out, "the sick role provides a convenient mechanism of social control by which institutions can allow deviant behavior within carefully controlled limits." For example, the reader is encouraged to peruse the work of McKinlay (1972) for an excellent overview of the four stages of the sick role and an insightful analysis of whether pregnancy is considered a normal state or an illness.

The Four Components of the Sick Role

Parsons (1970, p. 436) referred to the rights and obligations of the sick role as components associated with "the institutionalized expectation system relative to the sick role." The first and second components consist of rights for the patient.

The first component states that the person (patient) is exempt from responsibilities associated with normal social roles. Although others may grant provisional validation (Wolinsky & Wolinsky, 1981), it is the physician who has the final decision-making powers to legitimate the condition. However, some may be ill but resist the sick role. Depending on the illness, others may insist that the person remove him/herself from normal social roles (i.e., "What are you doing at work? You should be home in bed!"). However, once well, the patient is expected to return to the performance of those roles consistent with their normal lifestyle.

The second component of the sick role is that the person is not held responsible for his/her condition. It is incumbent upon medical professionals to treat the condition and to make the patient well. This author's recent surgery is an example of this component. The reason for the surgery was a sudden, unexplained, and continued decline of my platelet count. Was the decline in platelet count my fault? No. In fact, the condition itself is referred to as idiopathic (unexplained) thrombocytopenia purpura (ITP). I was not held responsible for the drop in platelets because the medical profession itself cannot fully explain the change (after all the tests had been conducted that would rule out extraneous explanations).

The third and fourth conditions of the sick role represent obligations of the patient. According to the third condition, the patient is not held responsible for their condition but does have an obligation to get well. This means that the patient is expected to follow institutionally constructed treatment regimens. For example, after spending some time in the hospital, this author was released to recover at home. Doing so meant following a treatment regimen of sleep, no straining or lifting, and so forth. Once removed from normal role obligations, the patient has a responsibility to follow "doctor's orders" and get well within a reasonable period of time. For example, although my condition is chronic, I am expected to recover from surgery and, within a defined period of time, assume my normal role responsibilities.

Finally, the last condition associated with the sick role is to seek technically competent help. This obligation ensures that the sick person will develop a professional relationship with a physician to treat the problem. In addition to establishing a relationship with a physician, the patient is expected to *cooperate* with the physician (Parsons, 1970).

Conceptually, the sick role is central to the development of medical sociology. Nonetheless, others have identified a number of methodological problems with the sick role. For instance, one potential problem is that the sick role may consist of multiple configurations (Twaddle, 1969). In other words, the Parsonian explanation is identified as one of some seven possible sick role variations. As a result, Twaddle (1969) argues that the Parsonian argument applies to a limited range of respondents. Another problem with the sick role is that its four components are not statistically interconnected, thus not providing a unified set of expectations (Arluke et al., 1979; Myers & Grasmick, 1990). Furthermore, "there is, then, substantially more agreement about sick-role behavioral expectations among different sectors of society than there is in actual sickness behavior" (Arluke et al., 1979, p. 33).

The Influence of Sex, Age, Race and Ethnicity, and Social Class on the Sick Role

Examining various sociocultural characteristics, researchers report a number of outcomes. For example, Britt (1975, p. 179) argues that a "reciprocal relationship between income and self-reported illness" exits. Examining characteristics such as family size, social class, and preferred right to the sick role, Petroni (1971, p. 652) found that "even in the lower class, there was an inverse relationship between family size and preferred right to the sick role." More specific to social class, Ossenberg, (1962) discovered an inverse relationship between social class and deviance among those in the hospital patient role. Beginning with the work of Parsons and expanding the sick role interpretations to the work of others (Twaddle, Mechanic, & Freidson), Reisine (1981) argues that behavior regarding oral dental care associated with the sick role is dependent on social class position. Contrary to the work of others, however, Petroni (1969a) reported an inverse relationship between sick role legitimacy and social class position. In other words, there was increased sick role legitimacy among those in the lower class. Petroni (1969b) also reported that legitimacy to assume the sick role increased with age. However, Fisher et al. (1984–1985) did not find a relationship between age and presumed role exemption. In contrast with others, Petroni also reported increased sick role legitimacy for chronic rather than acute illnesses. The sex of the respondent was not related to sick role legitimacy. Brown and Rawlinson (1975, 1977) reported differences between males and females (in addition to other characteristics) regarding the adoption and retention of the sick role following heart surgery. Meile (1978), however, has challenged these findings on the grounds of conceptual misinterpretation. Further support for differentiation of sick role behavior on the basis of sex is presented by Campbell (1978, p. 46), who found that "children's reports of how they act when ill are closely tied to their own age and sex roles and are clearly associated with status characteristics of their parents as well." Returning to the relationship between age and the sick role, Lipman and Sterne (1969) argue that society uses the sick role to create physical as well as economic dependence of elderly persons on society. Finally, Phillips (1965) examined the relationship between self-reliance and the sick role and found that as respondent self-reliance increased, the likelihood of assuming the sick role decreased.

Examining distinctions between religious belief systems, Segall (1976b) found no significant differences regarding adoption of the sick role. Although differences were not statistically significant, Segall does identify response trends associated with religious belief systems. For example, Protestant patients were less willing to succumb to the sick role, whereas Jewish patients more willingly adopted the sick role. Also, Protestant patients exhibited greater problems with the increased dependency associated with the sick role. Cross-culturally, Neutra et al. (1977) found no appreciable difference in frequency of hysteria and epilepsy on a Navajo reservation and Western culture. This is important because beyond the disease implications, epilepsy and hysteria carry additional meaning within the Navajo culture. Whereas hysteria was interpreted as either a neutral or positive condition, epilepsy carried a negative connotation. Neutra et al. (1977, p. 272) found that social rewards associated with hysteria "did not abolish a sick role . . . [whereas] social stigmatization . . . [aggravated] a sick role." Epileptics, however, "were raped, beaten, and in turn participated in violence more than was expected" (Neutra et al., 1977, p. 272). The final example is a transcultural study involving England, Yugoslavia, and the United States. Butler (1970, p. 248) found three patterns among respondents. They include the following:

1. Persons who were defined as ill on criteria that relate to deviance in action terms generally constituted a minor proportion of all persons who were classified as ill on two alternative criteria: (I) seeking professional care for perceived illness, and (II) reporting that a number of complaints had caused a high degree of bother.

2. Between one-third and one-half of the respondents in each area whose activities in the previous 2 weeks had been limited because of illness failed to seek professional care; there were no variations in this respect between chronic and acute conditions.

3. Complaints that were perceived as causing "a great deal of bother" were taken for professional care with significantly greater frequency than complaints ranked lower on the subjective severity rating; the modal reported reason for *not* seeking care was, for almost all of the complaints, that they were "not serious enough."

Perhaps the most important point however, is that the components of the sick role are grounded in the American cultural system. It cannot, however, be assumed that other cultures emulate the United States. Thus, the components of the sick role may not be applicable (Butler, 1970).

The preceding research indicates that the development of the sick role has engendered considerable analysis within medical sociology. Empirically, the evidence is generally less supportive of the sick role in the aggregate. More recent research (Bellaby, 1990), however, indicates some support for the Parsonian interpretation. Bellaby (1990) examined the relationship between the sex, age, and social class position of workers in an English pottery factory and the acceptance of sickness. In addition to finding that sex, age, and social class provide the "pretexts on which absence through sickness is acceptable," Bellaby (1990, p. 63) notes that the similarity and complementary relationship between the sick role and an employment contract. In other words, the sick role is used to regulate "temporary deviations in performance at work." The following section addresses the work of Twaddle (1979), who earlier (1969) attempted to *empirically assess* the viability of the sick role.

Criticisms of the Sick Role

In part because of its popularity, the sick role has come under intense scrutiny (for a different interpretation, see Rayner, 1981). Although research efforts have addressed the application of the sick role to various disease and illness patterns, the following material instead discusses the criticisms put forth by Freidson (1962, 1970) and further articulated by Twaddle (1979).

Maintaining organizational consistency, Twaddle (1979, pp. 47–50) frames Freidson's (1962, 1970) criticisms around the four expectations of the sick role (italics in original).

1. *The theoretical domain of the sick role is limited and Parson's formulation fails to account for much that is of interest to sociological study of sickness.* Essentially, the sick role (and thus the doctor–patient relationship) as created by Parsons is conceptually limited to modern industrialized cultures. There are also questions regarding the sick role and illness behavior. In other words, how relevant is the sick role as an explanation of illness behavior? The work of McCormack (1981) is particularly useful here. Analyzing the literature, McCormack notes that sick role research has focused primarily on the professional role of the physician with little emphasis on the patient. McCormack also questions the viability of the patient role in the sick role, as well as the physician–patient relationship constructed by the sick role. Furthermore, McCormack (1981, pp. 44–45) argues "for restructuring the notion of the sick role in a way that links sickness and health in a continuum, and considers patient behaviour, citizen behaviour, and the policy of individuals and society." In other words, locating the patient in a role "cuts the patient off from the larger socio-political context" (McCormack, 1981, p. 40).

2. *The sick role applies to a limited range of illnesses.* The sick role is applicable to acute illnesses; more specifically, serious acute illness. Based on the four stages, other types of illnesses would not apply. For instance, a trivial illness is not serious enough to warrant release from normal social roles. Other forms of illness also question the viability of the sick role. Persons with an incurable illness have little motivation to get well, whereas persons with a stigmatized illness experience ongoing social reproachment even after they have been cured. On a personal level, chronic ITP can be a lifetime problem. Knowing that, should I not worry about "getting well"?

3. *The sick role formulation suffers from a "management bias," giving undue weight to professional definitions of the situation.* Here, the criticism is built around the fact that verification and application of the sick role is limited to one person: the physician (see Honig-Parnass, 1981, for an example of lay legitimacy). However, not all illnesses are reported to the physician. As a result, when the sick role is applied it is to a relatively limited segment of the ill population. Questions could be raised regarding the willingness of those seeking the sick role versus those who do not (see, for example, Bell & Phillips, 1966; Moyer, 1966). One measure of its application would be sociodemographic and cultural differences.

4. *Parson's formulation of the sick role fails to account for known variability within modern societies.* Given a particular illness within a specific society, variability of sickness behavior remains. The problem is that the sick role does not adequately explain such variation; for example, why some people do not seek treatment (or seek alternative forms of treatment). Depending on the illness and its circumstances, society may consider the person responsible for their condition. The seriousness of the illness may determine the extent that a person may be exempt from normal social roles.

Although the purpose of this section was to draw attention to problems inherent within the conceptualization of the sick role, it is also understood that any explanation of illness behavior is a process. Thus, the sick role, as originally conceptualized, provided an appropriate explanation given the historical time period. The purpose of the criticisms presented here is to identify research outcomes associated with the sick role. For instance, the following paragraphs focus more specifically on the conceptual inability of the sick role to deal effectively with chronic illness.

Chronic Illness: A Problem for the Sick Role

As suggested earlier, chronic illnesses exemplify a problematic condition within the current context of the sick role. Compared with an acute situation in which the illness is identified, and a treatment regimen of antibiotics and time is prescribed, **chronic illness** generally results in a regimen of illness maintenance. Although some of the conditions associated with the sick role may be applicable, the obligation that one has to "get well" cannot be achieved when someone has a chronic illness. In other words, a patient may not be held responsible for having a chronic condition. Similarly, a patient with a chronic condition is expected to follow treatment regimens even if they do not result in the elimination of the disease. Kasselbaum and Baumann (1965, p. 18) identify a number of differences between chronic illness and the sick role model. The most obvious difference is that chronic illness is permanent. Thus, "role-expectations predicated on the assumption of the temporary nature of illness . . . are clearly inapplicable without respecification." Second, they point out that in the model, the sick role is the primary role performed by the patient. However, many with a chronic illness remain connected to other roles (work, family, and so forth). Thus, rather than giving up other roles for a short period of time, persons with a chronic illness adapt the new role into their broader set of expectations. Finally, chronic illness is age based. Reexamining the tables in Chapter 3, the incidence rate of chronic illness increases with age, particularly among persons older than 65. Considering these differences, Kasselbaum and Bauman (1965, p. 26) suggest that patients with a chronic illness interpret the sick role as "The impossibility of resuming full role-participation at pre-illness capacity, the necessity for adjusting to a permanent condition rather than overcoming a temporary one, and the emphasis on retaining an optimal level of role-performance and autonomy."

Furthermore, there are different subtypes of chronic illness. This section draws on the work of Conrad (1987) as it identifies and characterizes three subtypes of chronic illness. The first subtype is referred to as "lived-with illnesses." These are chronic illnesses that a person must learn to adjust to and "live with" but are not life-threatening (e.g., asthma, epilepsy). The second subtype is labeled "mortal illness." Here, the illness is life-threatening. Because of the illness, the person is forced to alter normal role performance. With this type of chronic illness the patient constructs role performances depending on whether they are in or out of remission. The obvious example of a mortal illness would be cancer. The final subtype of chronic illness is referred to as "at-risk illness." As the name implies, the emphasis is less on the illness and more on the potential risk involved. Conrad identifies these risks as predisposing, exposure, or heredity.

As a result, chronic conditions require a reconceptualization of the sick role. In particular, Stewart and Sullivan (1982) suggest a theoretical shift from the structural functionalism associated with the Parsonian sick role to negotiated order theory, which emphasizes the dynamic and fluid qualities associated with the actors and the organizations within which they function. Similarly, Charmaz (1990, p. 1165) argues for the application of a social constructionist grounded theory to explain chronic illness. This perspective advocates "the process of categorization as dialectical and active, rather than as given in the reality and passively observed by any trained observer." The reconceptualization of the sick role on different theoretical levels has considerable merit (for example, grounded theory). Grounded theory refers to "the researcher construct[ing] theory from the data" (Charmaz, 1990, p. 1162; see also Glaser & Strauss, 1967, for further explanation).

Earlier, Haber and Smith (1971) constructed an alternative sick role paradigm they considered more appropriate for understanding chronic illness. They referred to the process as the "normative adaptation to incapacity." This process involved the following three stages; recognition of inadequacy, attribution of responsibility, and legitimacy of performance behavior (Haber & Smith, 1971, p. 91). Although theoretical frameworks provide us with an explanation, it is also necessary to understand their practical application—in this case, the policy implications associated with chronic illness. Here, Strauss (1987, p. 34) provides us with the most complete listing of not only what constitutes chronic illness but also the consequences. According to Strauss,

> the prominent characteristics of chronic illness are that they (1) are long-term; (2) are uncertain; (3) require proportionately large efforts at palliation; (4) tend to be multiple diseases; (5) are disproportionately intrusive upon the lives of the ill and their families; (6) require a wide variety of ancillary services if they are to be properly cared for; (7) often imply conflicts of interpretation and authority among patients, family members, health workers, and funding agents; (8) mainly require primary care; and (9) are expensive to treat and manage.

The National Commission on Chronic Illness had previously identified a number of criteria that would satisfy the meaning of chronic illness (see McKinlay, 1972). In addition to knowing what constitutes a chronic illness, it is also important to understand the experience of the illness and its inherent consequences. First, how does a person adapt after the initial recognition that they have a chronic condition? Our choices are to either attempt to control the illness or to let it control us (Radley, 1989). This process requires active involvement as well as an adjustment to the illness itself. Barnard (1990) argues that the healing process for those with a chronic illness consists of three dimensions. These dimensions include empowerment, affirming continuity in the midst of change, and attentiveness to individuality. Briefly, empowerment can be attained through a number of sources (e.g., medication, surgery). The purpose of medication is to provide a sense of independence among the chronically ill. Secondly, the affirmation of continuity in the midst of change involves maintaining connections with the past and incorporating aspects of the previous self into the patient. The third dimension, attentiveness to individuality, requires continued effort by the chronically ill to establish the importance of their problem to the medical community. In other words, to individualize the condition rather than allow it to be trivialized by its routine nature. More specifically, Charmaz (1994, p. 283) examined the impact of chronic illness on male identity. She concludes that "an uneasy tension exists between valued identities and disparaged, that is, denigrated or shameful ones." Charmaz concludes that for the sake of increasing our knowledge of chronic illness experience it is important to engage in more comparative analyses of men and women relative to social indicators such as marital status and social class. Albeit brief, a good example is an analysis of diabetic patients in Poland (Lignowska, 1989). For example, Lignowska (1989, p. 681) found that the impact of diabetes on patients is influenced by characteristics such as level of education, sex of the patient, and the extent to which the patient was responsible for "everyday" activities.

This section expands on two chronic illnesses. Throughout this analysis, the impact of these chronic illnesses on the behavior of the patient as well as significant others is examined. We begin with multiple sclerosis (MS).

One of the more difficult problems with MS is the length of time involved in providing a diagnosis. Research by Stewart and Sullivan (1982) found that it took 5½ years for a correct diagnosis of MS among 60 patients studied. Although the length of time has improved, Lechtenberg (1995, p. 39) states that "it is much more routine for a diagnosis of multiple sclerosis to be established only after a year or two following the first symptom." Stewart and Sullivan (1982) report that patients go through various phases relative to the illness and its diagnosis. The initial or nonserious phase is self-explanatory. Symptoms were considered as minor and related to other problems. In the serious phase, the symptoms were considered representative of an acute illness. It was during this period that "patients spent an average of almost 2½ years before receiving an accurate diagnosis. During this time, they consulted 227 different physicians for a total of 407 diagnostic appointments" (Stewart & Sullivan, 1982, p. 1400). The final, or diagnosis, phase occurred during testing that lead to the conclusion that the patient had MS. Throughout the earlier phases (particularly the serious phase), the patient learned to "live with" the ambiguity of the condition and the inability of the medical community to diagnose their condition accurately. This process can have a deleterious impact on the patient, not only over the length of time to receive an accurate diagnosis but also the self-doubt regarding the legitimacy of the symptoms.

In a similar fashion, patients diagnosed with Parkinson's disease experience increased feelings of shame and reported self-imposed isolation as a result of the disease. The feeling of shame is the result of societal rule-breaking by those with Parkinson's disease. Such rule-breaking consists of involuntary or jerky muscle movements that make it difficult to engage in such basic activity as eating or walking. Rather than embarrass themselves or others, patients "retreat from the public into the private. Parkinson's Disease, in this pattern of interpretation, is the illness of a shameful withdrawal from public life" (Nijhof, 1995, p. 202).

Additional examples of the different subtypes of chronic illness include the work of Williams (1984) on rheumatoid arthritis (RA); the work of Stone (1983) on repetitive strain injury (RSI); the work of Good et al. (1993) on oncology; and the work of Kutner and Brogan (1994) on dialysis.

The effects of a chronic illness are also experienced by the patient's significant others. Utilizing the concept of a trajectory, Corbin and Strauss (1994) outline the impact of chronic illness on the non-ill spouse. The authors detail the physical and emotional difficulties experienced as well as conflicting feelings regarding the ill spouse as his or her health deteriorates. The response of significant others is also influenced by the social and cultural environment within which the illness occurs. For example, consider the following comparative analysis of native-born Canadians and immigrant Chinese families to Canada. Anderton et al. (1989) found that although language difficulties were problematic, the Chinese families experienced economic hardships more often than native-born Canadians did. These differential outcomes were related to parental responses regarding a family member's chronic illness and the ideology of normalization. As a consequence, chronic illness experiences differ depending on one's meaning of normality and its degree of congruence with health professionals.

Thus, "chronic illness forces an awareness of a permanent defect, however slight and the need to learn how to live with something less than the accustomed, previously taken for granted level of functioning" (Royer, 1995, p. 25). Unfortunately, chronic illness may also force the person, or others, to not only question expected role performance, but also to "see" only the impairment, rather than the person (Royer, 1995). Society must move from attempting to rehabilitate persons with disabilities and reexamine those attitudes and social environments that limit persons with disabilities (Weitz, 1996). It is within this broader context that this chapter turns to a brief analysis of physical disability.

Physical Disability

Most of us will, at some point in our life, experience a chronic illness or a disability. Will others then respond toward us as "damaged goods"? (Phillips, 1990). What do we expect from others? How does the illness or disability change our lives? What is the responsibility of society toward persons with disabilities? What are the consequences associated with the disproportionate utilization of health-care resources by persons with disabilities (see, for example, Turner et al., 1991; Albrecht, 1992). These questions are most important because they frame the debate (positively or negatively) regarding disability. For example, Charmaz (1995) suggests that adaptation is the best response to chronic illness or impairment. Here, adapting "means altering life and self to accommodate to physical losses and to reunify body and self accordingly. Adapting implies that the individual acknowledges impairment and alters life and self in socially and personally acceptable ways" (Charmaz, 1995, p. 657). Although true, the problem with this approach is that it appears to focus responsibility on the individual with no corresponding responsibility attributed to the broader social system or specific social institutions (e.g., health care).

Perhaps the most insightful analysis of physical disability was offered by Zola (1991, p. 2). After a brief explanation of his physical disabilities, he continues:

> I want at the very least to bring these personal bodily experiences closer to my center—not to claim that they constitute all of who I am, but that they are a central part of my identity; not that they explain all I have accomplished, but that they are essential to understanding what I have done.

The following also illustrate a lack of agreement regarding the meaning attached to terms such as *disability, impairment,* or *handicap.* Efforts to define these terms are generally grounded in theoretical or political ideologies. For example, Bickenbach (1993, p. 10), utilizing the 1980 World Health Organization's *International Classification of Impairments, Disabilities and Handicaps,* defines impairment as "any abnormality of physiological or anatomical structure or function." Disability "is any limitation (resulting from an impairment) in the ability to perform any activity considered normal for a human being or required for some recognized social role or occupation." Finally, a handicap "is any resulting disadvantage for an individual that limits the fulfillment of a normal role or occupation." Others, however, disagree with definitions they consider sterile and sexist. For instance, Wendell (1996, p. 22) argues that being non-disabled or unimpaired will "depend to some extent on the physical, social, and cultural environment in which a person is living, and is influenced by such factors as what activities are necessary to survive in an environment and what abilities a culture considers most essential to a participant." More specifically, Oliver (1990, p. 11) citing UPIAS (1976, pp. 3–4) defines "*impairment* [as] lacking part of or all of a limb, or having a defective limb, organism or mechanism of the body; [whereas] *Disability* [is] the disadvantage or restriction of activity caused by a contemporary social organisation which takes no or little account of people who have physical impairments and thus excludes them from the mainstream of social activities."

The definitions cited by Oliver move the cause of the disability out of the individual and into the social structure of society. This argument also addresses the impoverishment of the impaired as a result of the social and political structure of society. In other words, when the physically impaired are not allowed access to the same educational opportunities, transportation, housing, and employment, they are more likely to be economically disadvantaged (Oliver, 1995).

The emergence of physical disability as an area of inquiry within medical sociology has been promoted by a broadening of its meaning. As Hahn (1988) points out, the sociopolitical approach to disability adds a new dimension for analysis (see also Barton, 1996). Similar to problems associated with mental disorders (attitudinal, discrimination, labeling), disabled persons have experienced exploitation, oppression (Hahn, 1988), and stigma (Cahill & Eggleston, 1995). Thus, Hahn (1994, p. 21) argues that the minority rights model is the most appropriate format for disability research because it emphasizes "the environment as the primary source of disablement" (see also Bickenbach, 1993, for an analysis of the minority rights perspective). Even the Americans with Disability Act (ADA) of 1990 assumes that "personal impairments are the principal cause of discrimination against disabled people" (Hahn, 1994, p. 9). Outlining a special issue of the *Journal of Social Issues,* Fine and Asch (1988, pp. 8–12) identify five common assumptions about disability. They include: (italics in original)

1. *It is often assumed that disability is located solely in biology, and thus disability is accepted uncritically as an independent variable.*
2. *When a disabled person faces problems, it is assumed that the impairment causes them.*
3. *It is assumed that the disabled person is a "victim."*
4. *It is assumed that disability is central to the disabled person's self-concept, self-definition, social comparisons, and reference groups.*
5. *It is assumed that having a disability is synonymous with needing help and social support.*

These assumptions provide a framework within which continued research and analysis of disability can develop. Identifying these assumptions also helps in the construction of a more humane environment and appropriate public policy.

Examining current physical and social realities, a plethora of impediments that aid in the social–political and medical construction of disability within the larger society are encountered. The 1994 edition of *Research in the Sociology of Health Care* provides coverage of articles on social policy and the experience of and caring for persons with disability. These impediments impose limitations on everything from physical disability to chronic illness.

Historically, persons with disabilities were considered a "hidden" minority (Percy, 1989). At the same time, persons with disabilities have been used (along with many others) as economic and political pawns as funding for all programs continues to diminish (see Scotch, 1989, for a history of the disability rights movement). The result has been a politicizing of persons with disabilities relative to other persons rather than recognizing the inadequacies of the social system in general and the health-care system in particular. Zola (1989) offers an alternative policy approach. Rather than focusing on the inadequacies of persons with disabilities, society instead must understand the near universal nature of disability within the larger society. This is put into perspective by Davis (1995, p. 8), who reminds us that "those who are regarded as having a limitation or interference with daily life activities such as hearing, speaking, seeing, walking, moving, thinking, breathing, and learning" are considered disabled. Numerically, some 35 to 43 million Americans, or approximately 1 out of every 7, are disabled, and one-third of the disabled are aged 65 and older.

The presence and experiences of persons with disabilities are not limited to the United States. All societies have had members who were impaired. According to Davis (1995), some 500 million of the world's population are disabled. However, efforts to investigate impairment in traditional societies have resulted in some difficulties. For example, Scheer and Groce (1988, p. 26) point to conceptual problems such as:

> First, at any point in time, there may be only one or a few individuals with disabilities in a particular small-scale, traditional community, and they may thus appear unique to the researcher. Second, social scientists too often assume that disability automatically causes an individual to become marginal to his or her social group.

However, as Scheer and Groce (1988) point out, the assumption that because we in the United States marginalize the disabled does not mean that such behavior occurs within all societies. Rather, they suggest that there is societal variation in response to disabled members. Cross-cultural examples abound that illustrate variations in societal responses. For example, some societies engage in infanticide toward all infants. Others engage in the practice only toward disabled infants. Other societies treasure their disabled young. Similar variations in practice exist regarding societal behavior towards the elderly (Scheer & Grose, 1988). Cross-culturally, then, it is difficult to generalize the degree of marginality experienced by the disabled. Research by Ingstad (1988) offers one example of this problem. Comparing coping behavior of parents with a disabled child in Norway and Botswana, Ingstad (1988) reports substantial differences. For example, Norwegian parents were more likely to respond to the birth of a disabled infant as a "tragedy," whereas parents in Botswana are likely to attribute the event to witchcraft; in other words, the result of others (i.e., enemies). The social policy implications associated with disability also vary cross-culturally. For instance, in Sweden, there is a concerted effort by the national government to provide rehabilitative services to persons with disabilities. The purpose is to provide all members of society with an opportunity to ensure their self-worth by working. Although similar, Germany does not provide the extensive government-sponsored employment found in Sweden. However, rehabilitation and incorporation of the disabled into the workforce are considered primary goals. At the same time, American efforts in the 1980s to incorporate persons with disabilities into the workforce via training programs were decreasing (Burkhauser & Hirvonen, 1988). American efforts to implement public policy for the disabled culminated with the passage and signing into law of the ADA. The purpose of the ADA was "(1) to codify many regulatory concepts and guidelines . . . and (2) to extend the section 504 prohibition against discrimination to the private sector" (West, 1991, p. 21). More specifically, the ADA considers "a person with a disability as meeting one or more of the following criteria: (a) A physical or mental impairment that substantially limits one or more of the major life activities of such individual; (b) A record of such an impairment; and (c) Being regarded as having such impairment" (LaPlante, 1991, p. 56).

Although the ADA improves the opportunities of many, the definitions cited previously are quite distinct from those suggested by Oliver (1990). The ADA definitions are based on individuals with disabilities and do not recognize the impact of social impediments in people's lives. However, passage of the ADA provides protection to many persons that do not fit the "traditional" view of disabilities. For example, "the ADA covers a wide range of individuals—from people who use wheelchairs, to people who have vision or hearing impairments, to people with epilepsy or cerebral palsy or HIV disease or lung cancer or manic depression" (Feldman, 1991, p. 84).

It is evident that disability as an area of research will continue to expand. One reason is that the United States and other industrialized nations are experiencing a shift in the age of their populations, and, as one ages, the likelihood of experiencing a chronic disease increases. Thus, society will continue to witness, as Zola suggested earlier, a universalism of disability that should engender greater recognition, understanding, and better public policy associated with disability.

Although conceptually significant, it is understood that the sick role does not adequately address the range of available medical conditions and experiences. The following section, however, provides us with an alternative explanation based on Freidson's (1970) social construction of illness.

The Social Construction of Illness

In response to the sick role and the issue of illness as deviance, Freidson (1970) developed a classification scheme incorporating the seriousness of the deviance and the degree of legitimacy associated with the illness. With regard to **deviance,** Freidson's concerns are with the importance of the meanings attached to individuals or their actions. These meanings are also relative within the context of time, place, and perspective. Freidson's (1970, p. 230) argument is based on two variables: "the imputation of responsibility to the person being labeled (with all that responsibility implies for imputed motivation) and (2) the degree of seriousness imputed to his offense (with all that it implies for adopting a new role)."

Utilizing the criminal justice system as a model to perceive differences in illness, Freidson classified deviance as being either minor or serious and either holding or not holding the individual responsible. The outcomes of this model are presented in Table 6.1.

Freidson argues that relative to the health-care community and whether the person is held responsible, the granting of a special role is dependent on the level of deviation experienced. Given the outcomes described in Table 6.1, there is a limited range of options available. As a result, Freidson (1970, p. 234) considered the trial scheme (Table 6.1) too simplistic "to differentiate empirically significant variations in the form that socially organized illness behavior may take." Expanding beyond the original trial scheme, Freidson reasoned that the concept of *legitimacy* aided in the classification of illness. Thus, imputed legitimacy can be conditional or unconditional. When an illness is not imputed, it is considered *illegitimate*. The expanded interpretation of the relationship between imputed seriousness and legitimacy is presented in Table 6.2.

As Freidson notes, there are various meanings attached to the concept of legitimacy. For example, **conditional legitimacy** entails a brief hiatus from some role

TABLE 6.1 Types of Deviance, by Quality and Quantity of the Societal Reaction (Contemporary American Middle-Class Societal Reaction)

Imputation of Seriousness	Imputation of Responsibility	
	Individual Held Responsible	*Individual Not Held Responsible*
Minor deviation	**Parking violation** Slight addition to normal obligations; minor suspension of a few ordinary privileges.	**A cold** Partial suspension of a few ordinary obligations; slight enhancement of ordinary privileges. Obligation to get well.
Serious deviation	**Murder** Replacement of ordinary obligations by new ones; loss of ordinary privileges.	**Heart attack** Release from most ordinary obligations; Addition to ordinary privileges. Obligation to seek help and cooperate with treatment.

Source: Reprinted with permission. University of Chicago Press. *Profession of medicine: A study of the sociology of applied knowledge.* E. Freidson. 1970. Copyright © 1970 by Dodd, Mead & Company, Inc.

expectations and some extra privileges. In return, the deviant is expected to pursue appropriate medical care that will eliminate the deviance. **Unconditional legitimacy** releases the deviant from basic role expectations for life. In addition, the deviant is accorded additional privileges because of the nature of the deviance. Finally, with **illegitimacy** the deviant is not held responsible for the deviance. However, although illegitimacy releases the deviant from some role expectations it also adds new obligations and generally does not allow the addition of any new privileges.

Each cell in Table 6.2 is self-explanatory. Freidson (1970) differentiates between cells by noting that the Parsonian sick role only applies to cell 5, whereas cell 4 contains stigmatized roles and cell 6 contains chronic sick or dying roles. Freidson also articulates that any interpretation of this table is limited by social structural and cultural characteristics. Nonetheless, Wolinsky (1988) identifies three criticisms of Freidson. The first problem is that the work is theoretically based and does not have any empirical support. Secondly, as with Parsons, the model is grounded in middle-class American values. Third, the model "does not explain why people define themselves as being ill or well, nor why they decide to seek or not to seek help" (Wolinsky, 1988, p. 115).

Throughout this chapter, the Parsonian sick role and the work of Freidson explaining imputed seriousness and legitimacy associated with illness argue that illness is deviant. The final section examines how and why some seemingly normal (nondeviant) conditions of life have become medicalized. Theoretically, much of the research surrounding the medicalization of society comes out of the social constructionist argument. This section also addresses why much of this "medicalization of life" appears to occur primarily among female rather than male behavior.

TABLE 6.2   Types of Deviance for Which the Individual Is Not Held Responsible, by Imputed Legitimacy and Seriousness (Contemporary American Middle-Class Societal Reaction)

Imputed Seriousness	Illegitimate (Stigmatized)	Conditionally Legitimate	Unconditionally Legitimate
Minor deviation	**Cell 1** *Stammer* Partial suspension of some ordinary obligations; few or no new privileges; adoption of a few new obligations.	**Cell 2** *A Cold* Temporary suspension of few ordinary obligations; temporary enhancement of ordinary privileges. Obligation to get well.	**Cell 3** *Pockmarks* No special change in obligations or privileges.
Serious deviation	**Cell 4** *Epilepsy* Suspension of some ordinary obligations; adoption of new obligations; few or no new privileges.	**Cell 5** *Pneumonia* Temporary release from ordinary obligations; addition to ordinary privileges. Obligation to cooperate and seek help in treatment.	**Cell 6** *Cancer* Permanent suspension of many ordinary obligations; marked addition to privileges.

Source: Reprinted with permission. University of Chicago Press. *Profession of medicine: A study of the sociology of applied knowledge.* E. Freidson. 1970. Copyright © 1970 by Dodd, Mead & Company, Inc.

The Medicalization of Society

Although the "medicalization of society" has increased in the recent past, it is not a new phenomenon. In fact, the historical basis of this concept is important to understand its emergence within contemporary American society. At the present time there are two main issues associated with this concept. First is the question of why much of the medicalization has focused on the behavior of women. The second issue is the fundamental question of whether medicalization or demedicalization of society is occurring. As to the first question, what is "the medicalization of society"? Conrad (1992, p. 209) defines medicalization as "a process by which nonmedical problems become defined and treated as medical problems, usually in terms of illnesses or disorders." These medical problems can be categorized into either deviant behaviors (for example, alcoholism, eating disorders, compulsive gambling) or normal life conditions such as menopause, childbirth, aging, or death (see, for instance, Conrad & Schneider, 1992, for a thorough analysis of deviance and medicalization). This section focuses on what are. considered normal life conditions. We also know that medicalization occurs on three levels (Conrad, 1992). The first, or *conceptual level,* involves the use of medical language and models to identify the problem. The second, or *institutional level,* applies the medical model to those organizations that provide treatment services for those problems that have been so defined. Finally, the third, or *interactional* level, involves physicians directly. For instance, when a physician defines or treats a problem within a medical rather than in another context (i.e., the current debate over attention deficit disorder, or ADD). As these levels suggest, the medicalization of society is multifaceted. Virtually all within the health-care industry utilize and benefit from the increased application of the medicalization of society. However, the health-care community has not been alone in the push for the medicalization of some behaviors. Consider, for example, Zola's (1972, p. 500) statement that the "medicalizing of society is as much a result of medicine's potential as it is of society's wish for medicine to use that potential."

The Medicalization of Women's Life Events

The medicalization of society is not a recent phenomenon. Beginning with colonial America, childbirth was transformed from an event that involved the expectant mother (in her home) and midwives to an institutionalized process involving the mother, doctors, ancillary personnel, and an organizational structure within which the birthing process is expected to occur. Bogdan (1992) points out that as early as the mid-1700s, the expertise of women in the birthing process was being questioned and an increasing number of births were being performed by male physicians. The transition to male (medical) attendants present at birth was class-based. That is, this movement occurred within the middle and upper classes of America. Historically, the 20th century has resulted in an even greater medicalization of childbirth (Bogdan, 1992). The increased reliance on the medical profession rather than midwives occurred because of the rise of obstetrics as a specialty area within medicine in the early 1900s. In addition, medicalization occurred because (1) women wanted relief and release from the physical and emotional experiences associated with childbirth and (2) middle- and upper-class women were having fewer children. Reduced fertility rates placed greater emphasis on the health and well-being of those children being born (Riessman, 1983).

Significant changes have occurred over the 20th century with regard to the childbirthing process. Nonetheless, it remains medicalized. Consider, for example, the increased reliance on cesarean births. Although physicians are able to control when cesarean sections occur, Table 6.3 illustrates that even vaginal childbirth appears convenient for the medical staff.

It is interesting to note that fewer births occur over the weekend and that most take place during the week. Planned or not, the data suggest continued medicalization of childbirth. Another factor involved in the medicalization of childbirth is the continued attempt to "humanize" the birthing experience. For example, even as the medical community attempts to improve the quality of the birthing process, it remains within an institutional setting and controlled by medical specialists. This sanitized process is also sexist as it encourages "bonding" primarily between mother and child and generally excludes the father (Riessman, 1983).

Continuing with the female-centered medicalization processes, Riessman (1983) examines the issue of abortion. Again, within a historical context, societal and medical attitudes toward abortion have changed considerably. According to Riessman (1983), abortion became medicalized as physicians redefined its significance to the general public. As a result, since the late 19th century, a shift not only

TABLE 6.3 Live Births by Day of Week and Index of Occurrence by Method of Delivery, Day of Week, and Race of Mother: United States, 1994

Day of Week	Race of Mother	Average Number of Births	Index of Occurrence[1]				
				Method of Delivery		Cesarean	
			Total[2]	Vaginal	Total	Primary	Repeat
	All races[3]	10,829	100.0	100.0	100.0	100.0	100.0
Sunday		8,245	76.1	81.6	55.9	66.2	38.6
Monday		10,936	101.0	99.9	105.0	97.5	117.7
Tuesday		12,131	112.0	109.7	120.3	116.4	126.8
Wednesday		11,908	110.0	108.1	116.8	113.9	121.7
Thursday		11,845	109.4	107.6	116.1	113.0	121.2
Friday		11,820	109.1	105.9	120.8	115.4	129.8
Saturday		8,957	82.7	87.4	65.8	78.0	45.2
	White	8,551	100.0	100.0	100.0	100.0	100.0
Sunday		6,340	74.1	79.8	53.5	64.3	35.8
Monday		8,675	101.5	100.3	105.8	98.0	118.6
Tuesday		9,661	113.0	110.6	121.6	117.5	128.3

Wednesday	9,475	110.8	109.0	117.7	114.7	122.6
Thursday	9,424	110.2	108.4	116.8	113.8	121.7
Friday	9,395	109.9	106.4	122.3	116.3	132.0
Saturday	6,916	80.9	85.8	63.1	75.9	42.1
Black	1,744	100.0	100.0	100.0	100.0	100.0
Sunday	1,475	83.6	88.6	65.7	73.9	50.9
Monday	1,724	98.9	98.0	102.0	95.7	113.4
Tuesday	1,894	108.6	106.8	115.0	111.9	120.5
Wednesday	1,862	106.8	104.9	113.8	111.3	118.2
Thursday	1,853	106.3	104.6	112.6	109.2	118.7
Friday	1,856	106.5	103.9	115.4	112.5	120.7
Saturday	1,562	89.6	93.4	76.0	85.8	58.6

[1] Index is the ratio of the average number of births by a specified method of delivery on a given day of the week to the average daily number of births by a specified method of delivery for the year, multiplied by 100.

[2] Includes method of delivery not stated.

[3] Includes races other than white and black.

Source: Data from Ventura, S. J., Mathews, J. A., & Clarke, S. C. (1996). Advance report of final natality statistics, 1994. *Monthly Vital Statistics Report, Vol. 44, No. 11,* Supp. Table 13. Hyattsville, MD: National Center for Health Statistics.

in the public perception of abortion, but also who should perform them has been noted. For example, abortion had become illegal, particularly if not performed by a physician. Throughout this period of time, the role of the physician relative to women, increased considerably. The medicalization of abortion was also influenced to some extent by its use among middle- and upper-class women. On the one hand, middle- and upper-class use of abortion in the latter 19th century had reduced their birth rates, leading some to consider this a social problem. At the same time, middle- and upper-class women were supporting the use of abstinence rather than contraception as a form of birth control (Riessman, 1983). Even with its legality established in 1973, the Supreme Court (*Roe v. Wade,* with physician support) increased medical control over the procedure (Riessman, 1983). Thus, for many women, the problem with abortion is that historically it has been "a story of access—medically, legally, and economically" (Poirier, 1992, p. 234). Similarly, the Abortion Act of 1967 in the United Kingdom reflects the historical changes in Parliament toward the right of women. In the process, the Act continued the medicalization of the procedure by defining who can perform an abortion and where they can be performed (Grubb, 1990).

A third behavior also specific to women that is becoming increasingly medicalized is that of menopause. This normal experience is particularly important as the baby-boom generation wends its way through the life cycle. The leading edge of the baby boomers is now in its early 50s, the average age of menopause. Historically, the medicalization of menopause in the United States is grounded in the work of a small number of physicians during the 1930s and 1940s. Their work, however, has had a significant impact on the treatment of women during menopause. For example, three models of menopause emerged during the 1930s and 1940s. The *biological model* "described menopause as a physiological process caused by cessation of ovarian function" (Bell, 1987, p. 538). This model is particularly influential today with the application of estrogen replacement therapy (ERT). The biological model provides a comfortable "fit" into the medicalization of menopause because of the emphasis on the individual as the cause and, ultimately, the basis for a solution. The *psychological model* also addressed menopause on the individual level. Rather than emphasize hormone therapy, the psychological model focused on the personality of the woman. The belief was that psychotherapy would alleviate the physiological symptoms experienced by women. The third (*environmental*) model does acknowledge the existence and importance of cultural phenomenon relative to menopause. Thus, rather than addressing hormonal or personality issues, the environmental model examined changes in the social circumstances of women. Nonetheless, solutions were located in individual behavior (Bell, 1987).

These models represent a reinforcement of role and power relationships between women and physicians. Through the medicalization of menopause, aging women are expected to conform to normative behavior that has been constructed and defined by others as "appropriate" for their new role (Bell, 1987).

The medicalization of society is not limited to life-event behaviors specific to women. In addition to behaviors associated with the medicalization of deviance (e.g., alcoholism, drug abuse, mental illness), Conrad and Schneider (1992, p. 287) identify a plethora of topics (for example, aging, suicide, eating disorders) that have been researched. Although the medicalization of society has enjoyed considerable investigation in the United States, there has been limited cross-cultural research.

Some cross-cultural citations (located in Conrad, 1992) include the work of Lock (1984, 1986, 1987) in Japan; Maccoby (1974) and Kleinman (1988) in China, and Van Esterik (1989) in the Third World.

Medicalization and Demedicalization: An Analysis

Although it is evident from the range of topics that the medicalization of society is pervasive, others (Fox, 1977) argue that demedicalization is also occurring in American society. By definition, "demedicalization refers to a problem that no longer retains its medical definition" (Conrad, 1992, p. 224). One effect of medicalization has been an increase in the number of people eligible for the sick role. On the one hand, Fox (1989, p. 29) points out that medicalization "has created a less stigmatizing and punitive outlook on certain forms of deviance." On the other hand, the demedicalization movement has had considerable impetus from changes in American attitudes and behavior since the 1960s. Some examples of demedicalization include the declassification of homosexuality as a psychiatric disorder, attempts by physicians to alter their perceptions regarding women as patients, and a democratization of the patient–physician relationship (Fox, 1977). Furthermore, it is believed that the demedicalization of society is tied to societal changes such as "a less fatalistic and individualistic attitude toward illness, increased personal and communal espousal of health, and a spreading conviction that health is as much a consequence of the good life and the good society as it is of professional medical care" (Fox, 1977, p. 21). Unfortunately, many of these shifts have not occurred because economic and political changes in the larger society may potentially result in outcomes antithetical to the expected demedicalization. For instance, there has been a movement towards greater individual responsibility for one's health (see, for example, Zola, 1983, for an explanation regarding individual versus societal level analysis). However, this has come in response to for-profit managed care companies trying to increase their return to stockholders. At the same time, physicians, as employees of managed care companies, are experiencing decreasing levels of autonomy and authority. Thus, the medicalization or demedicalization of any behavior increasingly depends on the economic outcomes associated with the condition and whether such outcomes are in the interest of the corporation providing the medical services.

Summary

This chapter addressed one of the most important concepts in medical sociology: the sick role. Although there is some research support for individual components of the sick role, when taken as a whole, research efforts have not proved supportive of the concept. The sick role represents an important but dated period in the development of medical sociology. In other words, medicine in the 1950s was more likely to understand disease as a short-term, acute condition rather than long-term and chronic. The transformation of our knowledge of illness behavior will eventually lead to a reconstruction of role performance by patient and physician. Nonetheless, the Parsonian framework has been criticized for its inability to explain nonacute disease patterns.

Essentially, the sick role argues that if we consider healthy as normal, then sickness is a deviant state. The four components of the sick role include the patient's two rights to be exempt from normal social roles and to not be held responsible for their condition. At the same time, the patient has an obligation to get well and to seek technically competent help. After its introduction, the sick role engendered considerable research (primarily in the United States, but some work abroad as well). Since the latter 1970s, however, the extent of research on the sick role has declined. One of the more obvious difficulties with the sick role is its inability to address chronic illness. The reason is that chronic illness creates the need for a different type of role over an extended period of time. Again, one of the more significant differences between the sick role and acute or chronic illness are the interactive consequences relative to others in one's life. This issue is examined within the framework of physical disability.

In addition to the sick role, this chapter also examines the social construction of illness. Here, the focus was on the work of Freidson and the development of a classification scheme to explain the intersection of deviance and legitimacy. Legitimacy was considered conditional, unconditional, or illegitimate, whereas deviance was imputed to be either minor or serious. As with the sick role, criticisms of the model have emerged.

The final section of the chapter examines the medicalization of society. Medicalization is a process that defines nonmedical problems within a medical context. Examining medicalization on the conceptual, institutional, and interactional levels provides the reader with a better understanding of how this concept has been constructed to label individual rather than institutional-level behavior (particularly among women). Examples of the medicalization of society include childbirth, abortion, and menopause. The chapter concludes with an analysis of the medicalization–demedicalization debate. The conclusion drawn was that given the current climate of for-profit managed care in the United States, the expectations of those supporting demedicalization have not been achieved.

The material in this chapter provides a connection to earlier chapters and constructs a meaningful basis for the next chapter and beyond—for example, the discussion on the doctor–patient relationship as well as the relationship between individual behaviors and the larger health-care system. It is the intention of this book to establish such connections rather than construct 14 distinct chapters that appear to have little in common. Chapter 7 builds on previous knowledge of illness and health behaviors as it investigates mental illness.

CHAPTER REVIEW

There are a number of concepts in this chapter that are particularly important. As you answer the following questions, consider the level at which the analysis is directed. Some of the material in this chapter is also dated. What are the implications? Is the material relevant to today's society?

1. What is the sick role? Identify and describe the four components associated with the sick role.

2. Is the criticism of the sick role valid? Are there other criticisms that would be more appropriate given the changes in the health care community since the latter 1970s?

3. Examine Freidson's model of imputed deviance and legitimacy. Does this model explain a broader range of illness than does the sick role? In addition to the criticisms in the book, can you identify any more that are particularly relevant to contemporary society?

4. Why has there been so little research on the sick role and Freidson's model in contemporary medical sociology?

5. Given what you know of demographic changes and the relationship between age and chronic illness, is it true that chronic illness will be a significant problem for the American health-care system in the near future? How would theory influence our interpretation of this relationship?

6. Identify one condition that has been medicalized. What are the implications of medicalization? Could this condition be demedicalized? Again, what are the implications?

7. Consider the five common assumptions regarding disability. Are these assumptions consistent with the reality of how persons with disability are treated?

GLOSSARY

chronic illness   an on-going illness in which the afflicted person and the medical community attempt to maintain the condition rather than eradicate it.

conditional legitimacy   according to Freidson, a person is granted a respite from some role obligations and accorded some extra privileges.

deviance   one definition states that deviance occurs when social norms are violated. Another definition suggests that deviance is relative to factors such as time, place, and society. In addition, the social audience aids in defining whether a behavior is classified as deviant.

illegitimacy   according to Freidson, the person is not held accountable for their deviance, they are given additional role obligation and provided no new privileges.

medicalization   a process whereby nonmedical conditions are legitimated by the medical community.

sick role   a social role in which there are specific rights and obligations associated with its use.

unconditional legitimacy   here, the person is removed from normal role obligations for life and, because of the illness, is provided additional privileges.

SUGGESTED READINGS

The following books represent the classic works in the material covered in this chapter. The reader is encouraged to peruse these works to locate relevant material. Although the works listed here are dated, they represent the foundation for our understanding of some of the most important concepts in medical sociology. A secondary list of significant works would include Zola, 1972; Fox, 1977; Levine and Kozloff, 1978; and Conrad, 1992.

Albrecht, G. (1992). *The disability business: Rehabilitation in America.* Newbury Park, CA: SAGE.
Conrad, P., & Schneider, J. W. (1992). *Deviance and medicalization: From badness to sickness* (Expanded Edition). Philadelphia: Temple University Press.
Freidson, E. (1970). *Profession of medicine: A study of the sociology of applied knowledge.* New York: Dodd, Mead & Company.
   Note: Chapter 10 is most relevant to the material in this chapter.
Parsons, T. (1970). *The social system.* London: Routledgte & Kegan Paul Ltd.
   Note: Chapter 11 is most relevant to the material in this chapter.
Twaddle, A. C. (1979). *Sickness behavior and the sick role.* Cambridge, MA: Schenkman Publishing Company.

REFERENCES

Anderton, J. M., Elfert, H., & Lai, M. (1989). Ideology in the clinical context: Chronic illness, ethnicity and the discourse on normalisation. *Sociology of Health and Illness, 11,* 3, 253–278.

Arluke, A., Kennedy, L., & Kessler, R. C. (1979). Reexamining the sick-role concept: An empirical assessment. *Journal of Health and Social Behavior, 20,* 30–36.

Barnard, D. (1990). Healing the damaged self: Identity, intimacy, and meaning in the lives of the chronically ill. *Perspectives in Biology and Medicine, 33,* 4, 535–546.

Barton, L. (Ed). (1996). *Disability & society: Emerging issues and insights.* London: Longman.

Bell, G. D., & Phillips, D. L. (1966). Playing the sick role and avoidance of responsibility. *Research Previews, 13,* 1, 41–49.

Bell, S. (1987). Changing ideas: The medicalization of menopause. *Social Science and Medicine, 24,* 6, 535–542.

Bellaby, P. (1990). What is genuine sickness? The relation between work-discipline and the sick role in a pottery factory. *Sociology of Health and Illness, 12,* 1, 47–68.

Berkanovic, E. (1972). Lay conceptions of the sick role. *Social Forces, 51,* 53–64.

Bickenbach, J. E. (1993). *Physical disability and social policy.* Toronto: University of Toronto Press.

Bogdan, J. C. (1992). Childbirth in America: 1650 to 1990. In R. D. Apple (Ed.). *Women, health & medicine: A historical handbook* (pp. 101–120). New Brunswick, NJ: Rutgers University Press.

Britt, D. W. (1975). Social class and the sick role: Examining the issue of mutual influence. *Journal of Health and Social Behavior, 16,* 2, 178–182.

Brown, J. S., & Rawlinson, M. E. (1975). Relinquishing the sick role following open-heart surgery. *Journal of Health and Social Behavior, 16,* 1, 12–27.

Brown, J. S., & Rawlinson, M. E. (1977). Sex differences in sick role rejection and in work performance following cardiac surgery. *Journal of Health and Social Behavior, 18,* 3, 276–292.

Burkhauser, R. V., & Hirvonen, P. (1989). United States disability policy in a time of economic crisis: A comparison with Sweden and the Federal Republic of Germany. *The Milbank Quarterly, 67,* Supplement 2, Part 1, 166–194.

Butler, J. R. (1970). Illness and the sick role: An evaluation in three communities. *The British Journal of Sociology, 21,* 3, 241–262.

Cahill, S. E., & Eggleston, R. (1995). Reconsidering the stigma of physical disability: Wheelchair use and public kindness. *The Sociological Quarterly, 36,* 4, 681–698.

Campbell, J. D. (1978). The child in the sick role: Contributions of age, sex, parental status, and parental values. *Journal of Health and Social Behavior, 19,* 33–51.

Charmaz, K. (1990). 'Discovering' chronic illness: Using grounded theory. *Social Science and Medicine, 30,* 11, 1161–1172.

Charmaz, K. (1994). Identity dilemmas of chronically ill men. *The Sociological Quarterly, 35,* 2, 269–288.

Charmaz, K. (1995). The body, identity, and self: Adapting to impairment. *The Sociological Quarterly, 36,* 4, 657–680.

Conrad, P. (1987). The experience of illness: Recent and new directions. In J. A. Roth & P. Conrad (Eds.). *Research in the sociology of health care. Vol. 6* (pp. 1–31). Greenwich, CT: JAI Press.

Conrad, P. (1992). Medicalization and social control. *Annual Review of Sociology, 18,* 209–232.

Conrad, P., & Schneider, J. W. (1992). *Deviance and medicalization: From badness to sickness* (Expanded Edition). Philadelphia: Temple University Press.

Corbin, J. M., & Strauss, A. (1994). The trajectory perspective: Spousal work in the context of chronic illness. In H. D. Schwartz (Ed.). *Dominant issues in medical sociology* (3rd Ed.) (pp. 51–63). New York: McGraw Hill.

Davis, L. J. (1995). *Enforcing normalcy: Disability, deafness, and the body.* London: Verso.

Dimond, M., & Jones, S. L. (1983). *Chronic illness across the life span.* Norwalk, CT: Appleton-Century-Crofts.

Feldman, C. R. (1991). Employment protections. In J. West (Ed). *The Americans with Disability Act: From policy to practice* (pp. 81–110). New York: Milbank Memorial Fund.

Fine, M., & Asch, A. (1988). Disability beyond stigma: Social interaction, discrimination, and activism. *Journal of Social Issues, 44,* 1, 3–21.

Fisher, W., Arluke, A., & Levin, J. (1984–1985). The elderly sick role: An experimental analysis. *International Journal of Aging and Human Development, 20,* 3, 161–165.

Foster, G. M. (1982). Responsibility for illness in Trintzuntzan: A cognitive-linguistic anomaly. *Medical Anthropology, 6,* 2, 81–90.

Fox, R. C. (1977). The medicalization and demedicalization of American society. *Daedalus, 106,* 1, 9–22.

Fox, R. C. (1989). *The sociology of medicine: A participant observer's view.* Englewood Cliffs, NJ: Prentice-Hall.

Freidson, E. (1962). Medical sociology [Special Issue]. *Current Sociology, 10/11,* 123.

Freidson, E. (1970). *Profession of medicine: A study of the sociology of applied knowledge.* New York: Dodd, Mead & Company.

Glaser, B. G., & Strauss, A. L. (1967). *The discovery of grounded theory: Strategies for qualitative research.* Chicago: Aldine Publishing.

Glik, D. H., & Kronenfeld, J. J. (1989). Well roles: An approach to reincorporate role theory into medical sociology. In D. C. Wertz (Ed.). *Research in the sociology of health care, Vol. 8* (pp. 289–309). Greenwich, CT: JAI Press Inc.

Goldstein, B., & Dommermuth, P. (1961). The sick role cycle: An approach to medical sociology. *Sociology and Social Research, 46,* 35–47.

Good, M.-J. D., Hunt, L., Munakata, T., & Kobayashi, Y. (1993). A comparative analysis of the culture of biomedicine: Disclosure and consequences for treatment in the practice of oncology. In P. Conrad & E. B. Gallagher (Eds.). *Health and health care in developing countries: Sociological perspectives* (pp. 180–210). Philadelphia: Temple University Press.

Gordon, G. (1966). *Role theory and illness.* New Haven, CT: College and University Press.

Grubb, A. (1990). Abortion law in England: The medicalization of a crime. *Law, Medicine and Health Care, 18,* 1–2, 146–161.

Haber, L., & Smith, R. T. (1971). Disability and deviance: Normative adaptations of role behavior. *American Sociological Review, 36,* 87–97.

Hahn, H. (1988). The politics of physical differences: Disability and discrimination. *Journal of Social Issues, 44,* 1, 39–47.

Hahn, H. (1994). The minority group model of disability: Implications for medical sociology. *Research in the Sociology of Health Care, 11,* 3–24.

Herzlich, C. (1973). *Health and illness: A social psychological analysis.* Translated by D. Graham. London: Academic Press.

Honig-Parnass, T. (1981). Lay concepts of the sick role: An examination of the professionalist bias in Parsons' model. *Social Science and Medicine, 15A,* 5, 615–623.

Ingstad, B. (1988). Coping behaviour of disabled persons and their families: Cross-cultural perspectives from Norway and Botswana. *International Journal of Rehabilitation Research, 11,* 4, 351–359.

Kasselbaum, G. G., & Baumann, B. O. (1965). Dimensions of the sick role in chronic illness. *Journal of Health and Human Behavior, 6,* 1, 16–27.

Kleinman, A. (1988). *The illness narratives: Suffering, healing, and the human condition.* New York: Basic.

Kutner, N. G., & Brogan, D. (1994). Life quality as a function of aging with a chronic illness: Differential assessment by older blacks and older whites. In R. Weitz & J. J. Kronenfeld (Eds.). *Research in the Sociology of Health Care, Vol. 11* (pp. 127–150). Greenwich, CT: JAI Press.

Lagerwey, M. D., & Markle, G. E. (1994). Edith Wharton's sick role. *The Sociological Quarterly, 35,* 1, 121–134.

LaPlante, M. P. (1991). The demographics of disability. In J. West (Ed.). *The Americans with Disability Act: From policy to practice* (pp. 55–77). New York: Milbank Memorial Fund.

Lechtenberg, R. (1995). *Multiple sclerosis fact book: Second edition.* Philadelphia: F.A. Davis Company.

Levine, S., & Kozloff, M. A. (1978). The sick role: Assessment and overview. *Annual Review of Sociology, 4,* 317–343.

Lignowska, I. (1989). Beyond the Anglophone world: The impact of environmental factors upon patient attitudes and behaviour. A sociological study from Poland. *Social Science and Medicine, 29,* 5, 681.

Lipman, A., & Sterne, R. S. (1969). Aging in the United State: Ascription of a terminal sick role. *Sociology and Social Research, 53,* 2, 194–203.

Lock, M. (1984). Licorice in leviathan: The medicalization of the care of the Japanese elderly. *Culture, Medicine and Psychiatry, 8,* 121–139.

Lock, M. (1986b). Ambiguities of aging: Japanese experience and acceptance of menopause. *Culture, Medicine and Psychiatry, 10,* 23–46.

Lock, M. (1987). Protests of a good wife and wise mother: The medicalization of distress in Japan. In E. Norbeck & M. Lock (Eds.). *Health, illness and medical care in Japan* (pp. 130–157). Honolulu: University of Hawaii Press.

Maccoby, E. E. (1974). Impressions of China. *Social Research in Child Development Newsletter* (Fall), 5.

McCormack, T. (1981). The new criticism and the sick role. *The Canadian Review of Sociology and Anthropology, 18,* 1, 30–47.

McKinlay, J. B. (1972). The sick role—illness and pregnancy. *Social Science and Medicine, 6,* 561–572.

Meile, R. L. (1978). Comment on Brown and Rawlinson's sick role rejection (*JHSB* September 1977). *Journal of Health and Social Behavior, 19,* 1, 121–122.

Moyer, L. N. (1966). Status inconsistency and sick role legitimacy. *Indian Sociological Bulletin, 4,* 1, 17–21.

Myers, S. T., & Grasmick, H. G. (1990). The social rights and responsibilities of pregnant women: An application of Parson's sick role model. *The Journal of Applied Behavioral Science, 26,* 2, 157–172.

Neutra, R., Levy, J. E., & Parker, D. (1977). Cultural expectations versus reality in Navajo seizure patterns and sick roles. *Culture, Medicine and Psychiatry, 1,* 3, 255–275.

Nijhof, G. (1995). Parkinson's disease as a problem of shame in public appearance. *Sociology of Health and Illness, 17,* 2, 193–205.

Nuttbrock, L. (1986). Socialization to the chronic sick role in later life. *Research on Aging, 8,* 3, 368–387.

Oliver, M. (1990). *The politics of disablement.* Houndsmills, Great Britain: Macmillan.

Oliver, M. (1995). *Understanding disability: From theory to practice.* Houndsmills, Great Britain: Macmillan.

Ossenberg, R. J. (1962). The experience of deviance in the patient-role: A study of class differences. *Journal of Health and Human Behavior, 3,* 1, 277–282.

Parsons, C. D. F. (1984). Idioms of distress: Kinship and sickness among the people of the kingdom of Tonga. *Culture, Medicine, and Psychiatry, 8,* 1, 71–93.

Parsons, T. (1970). *The social system.* London: Routledge & Kegan Paul Ltd.

Parsons, T. (1975). The sick role and the role of the physician reconsidered. *Milbank Memorial Fund Quarterly* (Summer), 257–278.

Percy, S. L. (1989). *Disability, civil rights, and public policy: The politics of implementation.* Tuscaloosa, AL: The University of Alabama Press.

Petroni, F. A. (1969a). Social class, family size, and the sick role. *Journal of Marriage and the Family, 31,* 3, 728–735.

Petroni, F. A. (1969b). The influence of age, sex, and chronicity in perceived legitimacy to the sick role. *Sociology and Social Research, 53,* 2, 180–193.

Petroni, F. A. (1971). Preferred right to the sick role and illness behavior. *Social Science and Medicine, 5,* 645–653.

Phillips, D. L. (1965). Self-reliance and the inclination to adopt the sick role. *Social Forces, 43,* 4, 555–563.

Phillips, M. J. (1990). Damaged goods: Oral narratives of the experience of disability in American culture. *Social Science and Medicine, 30,* 8, 849–857.

Poirier, S. (1992). Women's reproductive health. In R. D. Apple (Ed.). *Women, health & medicine in America: A historical handbook* (pp. 217–245). New Brunswick, NJ: Rutgers University Press.

Radley, A. (1989). Style, discourse and constraint in adjustment to chronic illness. *Sociology of Health and Illness, 11,* 3, 230–252.

Rayner, G. (1981). Medical errors and the 'sick role': A speculative enquiry. *Sociology of Health and Illness, 3,* 3, 296–316.

Reisine, S. T. (1981). Theoretical considerations in formulating sociodental indicators. *Social Science and Medicine, 15A,* 745–750.

Riesman, C. K. (1983). Women and medicalization: A new perspective. *Social Policy, 14,* 3–18.

Royer, A. (1995). Living with chronic illness, *Research in the Sociology of Health Care, 12,* 25–48.

Scheer, J., & Groce, N. (1988). Impairment as a human constant: Cross-cultural and historical perspectives on variation. *Journal of Social Issues, 44,* 1, 23–37.

Scotch, R. K. (1989). Politics and policy in the history of the disability rights movement. *The Milbank Quarterly, 67,* Supplement 2, Part 2, 380–400.

Segall, A. (1976a). The sick role concept: Understanding illness behavior. *Journal of Health and Social Behavior, 17,* 2, 162–169.

Segall, A. (1976b). Sociocultural variation in sick role behavioural expectations. *Social Science and Medicine, 10,* 47–51.

Silverblatt, I. (1983). The evolution of witchcraft and the meaning of healing in colonial Andean society. *Culture, Medicine, and Psychiatry, 7,* 4, 413–427.

Stewart, D. C., & Sullivan, T. J. (1982). Illness behavior and the sick role in chronic disease: The case of multiple sclerosis. *Social Science and Medicine, 16,* 1397–1404.

Stone, W. (1983). Repetitive strain injury. *Medical Journal of Australia, 24,* 616–618.

Strauss, A. (1987). Health policy and chronic illness. *Society, 25,* 1, 33–39.

Turner, B. S. (1995). *Medical power and social knowledge* (2nd Ed.). London: SAGE.

Turner, R. J., Frankish, J., & Phillips, N. (1991). Physical disability and health service utilization. *Advances in Medical Sociology, 2,* 269–298.

Twaddle, A. C. (1969). Health decisions and sick role variations: An exploration. *Journal of Health and Social Behavior, 10,* 2, 105–114.

Twaddle, A. C. (1979). *Sickness behavior and the sick role.* Cambridge, MA: Schenkman Publishing Company.

Twaddle, A. C., & Hessler, R. M. (1987). *A sociology of health* (2nd Ed.). New York: Macmillan.

Van Esterik, P. (1989). *Beyond the breast–bottle controversy.* New Brunswick, NJ: Rutgers University Press.

Waitzkin, H. (1971). Latent functions of the sick role in various institutional settings. *Social Science and Medicine, 5,* 45–75.

Waitzkin, H. (1974). *The exploitation of illness in capitalist society.* Indianapolis: Bobbs-Merrill.

Weist, R. (1996). *The sociology of health, illness, and health care: A critical approach.* Belmont, CA: Wadsworth.

Wendell, S. (1996). *The rejected body: Feminist philosophical reflections on disability.* New York: Routledge.

West, J. (1991). The social and policy context of the act. In J. West (Ed.). *The Americans with Disability Act: From policy to practice* (pp. 3–24). New York: Milbank Memorial Fund.

Williams, G. (1984). The genesis of chronic illness: Narrative re-construction. *Sociology of Health and Illness, 6, 2,* 176–200.

Williams, J. I. (1971). Disease as deviance. *Social Science and Medicine, 5,* 219–226.

Wolinsky, F. D., & Wolinsky, S. R. (1981). Expecting sick-role legitimation and getting it. *Journal of Health and Social Behavior, 22,* 229–242.

Wolinsky, F. D. (1988). *The sociology of health: Principles, practitioners, and issues* (2nd Ed.). Belmont, CA: Wadsworth.

Zola, I. K. (1972). Medicine as an institution of social control. *The Sociological Review, 20, 4,* 487–504.

Zola, I. K. (1983). *Socio-medical inquiries: Recollections, reflections, and reconsiderations.* Philadelphia: Temple University Press.

Zola, I. K. (1991). Bringing our bodies and ourselves back in: Reflections on a past, present, and future "Medical Sociology." *Journal of Health and Social Behavior, 32,* 1–16.

7 Mental Illness

Although seemingly obvious, it is important to state that what may be viewed as deviant in one social group may be tolerated in another, and rewarded in still other groups. How group members view a particular behavior is likely to influence both the frequency with which it occurs and the extent to which it is exhibited. In other words, all groups exercise considerable control over their members.

"Mental illness" and other forms of deviancy become visible when persons in the participant's group recognize his inability and reluctance to make the proper responses in his network of interpersonal relations. How a particular deviant behavior is to be evaluated depends largely on the frame of reference the evaluators assume.

—Mechanic, 1976, p. 25

Mental Illness and Social Stigma

Reread the chapters' opening statement. The purpose of this statement is to demonstrate the continuity from the previous chapter. Concepts such as the sick role, chronic illness, physical disability, and deviance were discussed in Chapter 6. Here, the concept of deviance is discussed, but within the context of mental illness and the continued social stigma attached to these labels.

It is not the purpose of this chapter to provide a complete historical background regarding mental illness. Rather, this chapter constructs a framework within which the ongoing construction of (primarily negative) labels and meanings associated with mental illness can be understood. Mental illness is particularly important because once the label is attached, it becomes extremely difficult to remove.

A History of Mental Illness

Before examining the history of mental illness, three concepts must be defined. **Mental health** represents "the so-called normal state of mind of a person," whereas **mental illness** consists of "a condition in which a person manifests behaviors, feelings, ideas, and/or thought processes that are . . . serious enough to cause personal anxiety, discomfort, and problems in functioning." Finally, a **mental disorder** is "a state of personal distress or discomfort leading to impairment that threatens interpersonal relationships and individual well-being" (Gupta, pp. 3–6). More specifically, Cockerham (1996, p. 2) states that a mental disorder "is seen as a significant deviation from standards of behavior generally regarded as normal by a majority of people in a society." Thus, within a sociological framework, the relationship between the social environment, sociodemographic characteristics, and specific mental conditions is addressed. Szasz (1970) offers a poignant example of mental disorder in the epilogue of his book, *The Manufacture of Madness*. The epilogue is entitled "The Painted Bird" (from a similarly titled book by Jerzy Kosinski). In the story, a bird is painted in a rainbow of colors and, when others of its species were in close proximity, it was freed. The painted bird would fly toward the others, but because of the paint, would not be recognized. The others would attack the painted bird in the air and on the ground until it was dead. Szasz (1970, p. 292) sees the painted bird as symbolic of those with mental illness, psychiatrists as the painters, and society as the other birds, when he argues that

> the physician ought to be a protector of the individual, even when the individual comes in conflict with society, it is especially dismaying that, in our day, the painting of birds has become an accepted medical activity, and that, among the colors used, psychiatric diagnoses are most in fashion.

Cross-culturally, an overview of various mental disorders is offered by Gupta (1993) and Gallagher (1995).

Historically, the concepts of mental illness and mental disorder have undergone a number of significant transformations (this section draws heavily on the work of Gupta, 1993; Gallagher, 1995; and Cockerham, 1996, and their presentations of the historical dimension of mental illness–mental disorder). It is important to note the historical benchmarks that have influenced contemporary thought regarding mental illness and mental disorder are similar to those identified as relevant in the emergence of medicine (see Chapter 2).

During ancient times, it was believed that aberrant behavior was the result of demonic spirits that inhabited the body. The literature is rife with descriptions of the upper-class engaging in bizarre behavior. The evil spirits were removed via a belief system that utilized incantations, spells, or, if necessary, trepannation, or the boring of a hole through the skull to allow the evil spirits to escape (Gallagher, 1995).

Beliefs regarding mental illness changed considerably during the Greek and Roman periods. Hippocrates separated medicine (and mental illness) from religion and instead instilled rational thought. He believed that illness (and mental illness) was related to the four humors. Thus, like any other disorder, mental illness could be expunged from the body. Others, such as Aristotle, engaged in an analysis of the senses, which provides the foundation for the work of "hedonistic psychology, much of Freudian psychology, and a great deal of behavioral psychology" (Gupta, 1993, p. 36). Meanwhile, the Romans' contribution to our understanding of mental illness is couched in the development of three areas: "the philosophy of Cicero, the humane attitude toward mental patients furthered by the physician Soranus, and the consideration of mental illness as a concept in Roman Law" (Cockerham, 1996, p. 10). At the same time, those classified as mentally ill found their freedoms limited within the larger society.

Moving forward, Western civilizations encountered the Middle (or more appropriately the Dark) Ages and, eventually, the Renaissance. Any advances made during the previous Greek and Roman periods were lost to the Middle Ages. Returning to a religious interpretation of behavior, mental illness (as well as illness in general) degenerated into beliefs of the supernatural (i.e., the devil). If one was not considered mad, then you must be a witch and were put to death. Szasz (1970, p. 121) points out the reciprocal nature of witchcraft within society when he states that "the myth of witchcraft was thus used to account for the extraordinary privileges and duties of the inquisitor." This process was also sexist, as the majority of people killed were women. The number of women killed is unknown, but Ussher (1992, p. 43) argues that

> The trials have been seen as the embodiment of a hatred of women, organized and ritualized through patriarchal dictate, resulting in the torture and death of millions of women under the catch-all term 'witch': the ultimate in misogynistic annihilation. Or they are seen as the persecution of the insane, or of those who were evil.

By the 18th century, the mentally ill were no longer being killed. Instead, they were institutionalized along with criminals and the poor. This "period of confinement," as it was known, had multiple purposes. For example, they were used "to instill religious and moral virtue, to absorb the labour of the unemployed and finally . . . as the temple of medical science" (Turner, 1995, p. 57). In essence, the mentally ill along with other societal deviants were considered social problems and treated accordingly.

By the close of the 18th century, a therapeutic revolution in the treatment of the mentally ill had begun. In France, Pinel unchained the mentally ill while noninstitutional, rural settings were constructed in England and the United States. Physical punishment was replaced with a Victorian emphasis on morality and guilt. By the middle of the 19th century, legislation in Great Britain effectively medicalized mental illness. The result was a significant increase between the middle of the 19th century and the early 20th century in the number of people defined as mentally ill. A similar increase in the number of those considered mentally ill occurred in the United States (Turner, 1995). Not surprising, as the number of "mentally ill" increased, so did the number of institutions necessary to house them. One explanation for the increase in mental hospitals throughout the 19th century is the urbanization of America. As people moved from rural communities, where the mentally ill were cared for by family, and into cities, the burden of care was placed on the larger community (Starr, 1982). In addition, the 19th century witnessed the emergence of scientific medicine and ultimately, the medical model of treatment.

The 20th century experienced continued emphasis on the application of the medical model to mental illness. Unfortunately, the 20th century also witnessed the emergence of the eugenics movement. Essentially an attempt to engage in Social Darwinism, supporters of eugenics argued in defense of allowing only those "fit" to procreate, and limit offspring of those considered less fit. Such movements targeted ethnic and racial groups as well as the mentally ill (Turner, 1995). It is apparent that being "mentally ill" has economic and political consequences within society.

Institutionalization and Deinstitutionalization of the Mentally Ill

Although the medical model flourished throughout the 20th century, multiples of other therapeutic techniques were constructed and implemented. Not surprisingly, the number of individuals defined as mentally ill continued to increase and fill the institutions that had been constructed. As Rothstein (1995) points out, the number of mentally ill who were institutionalized increased from 20 per 10,000 population in 1903 to 34 per 10,000 in 1940. Some of this increase can be attributed to the known inverse relationship between the economy and the rates of mental hospitalization (Brenner, 1973). The warehousing of the mentally ill in the 20th century is reminiscent of a similar movement in the early 1800s. By the middle of the 20th century, the process of **deinstitutionalization** had begun in the United States (see, for example, Johnson, 1990; Grob, 1995). Because of advancements in drug therapy, it was believed many patients could be better cared for in the community rather than in a large, impersonal mental institution. The transition from large state mental hospital to supposedly community-based care was premised on three assumptions. First, that this was in the best interest of the resident; second, that the move would save money, and third, that there would be a sufficient number of community-based treatment centers to provide services to those removed from the hospitals.

All three assumptions have been challenged. Was deinstitutionalization in the best interest of the residents? There are certainly some patients who have benefited after removal from state facilities. Many other former residents, however, have not been so fortunate. For example, Wagenaar and Lewis (1989) analyze deinstitutionalization on the basis of social class. Did the move save money? It de-

TABLE 7.1 Number, Percent Distribution, and Rate[1] of Patient Residential Treatment Beds, by Type of Mental Health Organization: United States, Selected Years, 1970–1990[2]

Type of Organization	1970	1980	1990
Number of Inpatient Beds			
All Organizations	524,878	274,713	272,253
State and county mental hospitals	413,066	156,482	98,789
Private psychiatric hospitals	4,295	17,157	44,871
Nonfederal general hospitals with separate psychiatric services	22,394	29,384	53,479
VA medical centers[3]	50,688	33,796	21,712
Federally funded community mental health centers	8,108	16,264	—
Residential treatment centers for emotionally disturbed children	15,129	20,197	29,756
All other organizations[4]	1,198	1,433	23,646
Percent Distribution of Inpatient Beds			
All Organizations	100.0	100.0	100.0
State and county mental hospitals	78.7	57.0	36.3
Private psychiatric hospitals	2.7	6.6	16.5
Nonfederal general hospitals with separate psychiatric services	4.3	10.7	19.6
VA medical centers[3]	9.7	12.3	8.0
Federally funded community mental health centers	1.5	5.5	—
Residential treatment centers for emotionally disturbed children	2.9	7.4	10.9
All other organizations[4]	0.2	0.5	8.7
Inpatient Beds per 100,000 Civilian Population[1]			
All Organizations	263.6	124.3	111.6
State and county mental hospitals	207.4	70.2	40.5
Private psychiatric hospitals	7.2	7.7	18.4
Nonfederal general hospitals with separate psychiatric services	11.2	13.7	21.9
VA medical centers[3]	25.5	15.7	8.9
Federally funded community mental health centers	4.1	7.3	—
Residential treatment centers for emotionally disturbed children	7.6	9.1	12.2
All other organizations[4]	0.6	0.6	9.7

Published and unpublished inventory data from the Survey and Analysis Branch of State and Community Systems Development, Center for Mental Health Services.

[1] The population used in the calculation of these rates is the January 1 civilian population of the United States for the respective years.

[2] Some organizations were reclassified as a result of changes in reporting procedures and definitions. For the years 1979–1980, comparable data were not available for certain organization types and data for either an earlier or a later period were substituted. These factors influence the comparability of 1980, 1986, 1988, and 1990 data from those of earlier years. For details, see text and Appendix A.

[3] Includes Department of Veterans Affairs (formerly Veterans Administration, VA) neuropsychiatric hospitals, VA general hospital psychiatric services, and VA psychiatric outpatient clinics.

[4] Includes freestanding psychiatric partial care organizations and multiservice mental health organizations. Multiservice mental health organizations were redefined in 1984. For details, see text and appendix.

Source: Center for Mental Health Services. *Mental health, United States, 1994.* Table 6.2. Manderscheid, R. W. & Sonnenschein, M. A. (Eds.). DHHS Pub. No. (SMA)94-3000. Washington DC: Supt. of Docs., U.S. Govt. Print. Off., 1994.

pends on how this question is interpreted. Finally, were there a sufficient number of community-based centers to provide for the former residents? No. In fact, some have suggested that deinstitutionalization has created a new form of institutionalization in facilities where former patients now live (see, for example, Kiesler & Sibulkin, 1987). Even less fortunate were those former patients who found themselves living on the streets, thus being added to the homeless population (Johnson, 1990). Deinstitutionalization is better understood as an economic shell game.

Impact of Public Policy on Mental Health Facilities and Staffing

Tables 7.1–7.3 reflect the impact of public policy on mental health facilities and staffing. Table 7.1 identifies changes in residential beds by type of facility. There are two basic shifts that have occurred between 1970 and 1990. The first is the significant decline in the number of state and county hospital beds. The second is that there has been a corresponding increase in the number of beds in private facilities, general hospitals, and residential facilities for children.

A potential consequence of inpatient beds being moved to general hospitals and specialty facilities is the loss of options for those with limited funding sources. This is a particularly difficult problem given the changes in governmental attitudes regarding responsibility for care of the mentally ill. According to the Center for Mental Health Services (1994), the number of beds in psychiatric hospitals is expected to decline as local and state governments utilize less expensive community-care services. However, the type of patient most likely committed to a mental hospital (particularly a state hospital), according to Gallagher (1995, p. 344) is *"a lower class, single, black male, who has no relatives, no previous hospitalization record, and is referred by a physician"* (italics in original).

The depopulation of state mental facilities has meant a decrease in their function as a therapeutic treatment center. However, other organizations (public and private) have increased their role in the provision of care to the mentally ill. In fact, as Table 7.2 illustrates, the total number of inpatient additions between 1969 and 1990 has increased.

As in Table 7.1, it is particularly important to recognize that with the decline in public facilities, private psychiatric hospitals, general hospitals and residential treatment facilities for children all enjoyed substantial growth between 1969 and 1990. Thus, the decline in the total number of inpatient additions between 1969 and 1990 does not address the shift in *where* patients are provided care. The institutional structure remains, but in smaller sizes and increasingly within the for-profit sector of the economy. According to the Center for Mental Health Services (1994, p. 91):

> It could be argued, however, that if the state and county mental hospitals were restructured to provide more short-term care and rehabilitative services, they could potentially provide comparable services more cheaply than private psychiatric or general hospitals.

Thus, the policy implications associated with the status of state and county mental hospitals relative to the for-profit facilities are significant.

TABLE 7.2   Number, Percent Distribution, and Rate[1] of Inpatient and Residential Additions, by Type of Mental Health Organization: United States, Selected Years, 1969–1990[2]

Type of Organization	1969	1975	1979	1990
Number of Inpatient Additions				
All Organizations	1,282,698	1,556,978	1,541,659	2,035,245
State and county mental hospitals	486,661	433,529	383,323	276,231
Private psychiatric hospitals	92,056	125,529	140,831	406,522
Nonfederal general hospitals with psychiatric services	478,000	543,731	551,190	959,893
VA medical centers[3]	135,217	180,701	180,416	198,111
Federally funded community mental health centers	59,730	236,226	246,409	—
Residential treatment centers for emotionally disturbed children	7,596	12,022	15,453	41,588
All other organizations[4]	23,438	25,240	24,037	152,900
Percent Distribution of Inpatient Additions				
All Organizations	100.0	100.0	100.0	100.0
State and county mental hospitals	37.9	27.8	24.8	13.6
Private psychiatric hospitals	7.2	8.1	9.1	20.0
Nonfederal general hospitals with psychiatric services	37.3	34.9	35.8	47.2
VA medical centers[3]	10.5	11.6	11.7	9.7
Federally funded community mental health centers	4.7	15.2	16.0	—
Residential treatment centers for emotionally disturbed children	0.6	0.8	1.0	2.0
All other institutions[4]	1.8	1.6	1.6	7.5
Inpatient Additions per 100,000 Civilian Population[1]				
All Organizations	644.2	736.5	704.2	833.7
State and county mental hospitals	244.4	205.1	172.0	113.2
Private psychiatric hospitals	46.2	59.4	63.2	166.5
Nonfederal general hospitals with separate psychiatric services	240.1	257.2	256.7	393.2
VA medical centers[3]	67.9	85.5	84.0	81.2
Federally funded community mental health centers	30.0	111.7	110.6	—
Residential treatment centers for emotionally disturbed children	3.8	5.7	6.9	17.0
All other organizations[4]	11.8	11.9	10.8	62.6

Published and unpublished inventory data from the Survey and Analysis Branch, Division of State and Community Systems Development, Center for Mental Health Services.

[1] The population used in the calculation of these rates is the January 1 civilian population of the United States for the respective years.

(*continued*)

TABLE 7.2   Continued

[2] Some organizations were reclassified as a result of changes in reporting procedures and definitions. For the years 1979–1980, comparable data were not available for certain organization types and data for either an earlier or a later period were substituted. These factors influence the comparability of 1980, 1986, 1988, and 1990 data from those of earlier years. For details, see text and Appendix A.

[3] Includes Department of Veterans Affairs (formerly Veterans Administration, VA) neuropsychiatric hospitals, VA general hospital psychiatric services, and VA psychiatric outpatient clinics.

[4] Includes freestanding psychiatric partial care organizations and multiservice mental health organizations. Multiservice mental health organizations were redefined in 1984. For details, see text and appendix.

Source: Center for Mental Health Services. *Mental health, United States, 1994.* Table 6.3. Manderscheid, R. W. & Sonnenschein, M. A. (Eds.). DHHS Pub. No.(SMA)94-3000. Washington DC: Supt. of Docs., U.S. Govt. Print. Off., 1994.

Finally, Table 7.3 provides data regarding the growth of personnel in mental health organizations. While the number of full-time employees (FTEs) has been increasing, their growth has not been consistent across the mental health occupational spectrum. For example, psychiatrists and other physicians as a percent of the FTE staff continues to decrease, while psychologists, social workers, and other mental health professionals with a BA or higher degree has increased substantially. This shift in occupational hiring suggests two broad explanations. First, treatment modalities within the institutions have been changing, and second, the staffing of mental health organizations is a reflection of the broader culture. In other words, facilities are utilizing greater numbers of lower-paid staff to provide care and treatment to residents. The distribution of FTEs for selected years is presented in Table 7.3.

All of the data presented in these three tables reflects the changing nature of governmental and private funding sources of mental health organizations (Marmor & Gill, 1989). The future of the funding sources and concomitantly, the future of mental health organizations continues to evolve. Although predictions are difficult and certainly imprecise, it would be accurate to point to a continued reduction of inpatient institutional care in any type of mental health organization. Also, the occupational structure associated with mental health organizations will evolve as the structure and nature of the system changes.

The institutionalization–deinstitutionalization process is not limited to the United States. Other industrialized nations have experienced similar trends in the past (see, for example, Lassey et al., 1997). For instance, in Italy, a 1978 law required the closing of all mental hospitals in favor of community hospitals (Roemer, 1993). Another approach to the care of those with mental disorders can be found in the Belgium community of Geel. Here, residents of the community take mental patients into their homes and provide care (Roemer, 1991). Although unique among developed nations, in-home care of persons with mental disorders is relatively normal (Roemer, 1993).

This section has illustrated the extensive transformation associated with the organization of mental health in the United States. These organizational changes and the impact of social characteristics such as age, sex, race and ethnicity, or social class on persons defined as mentally ill are, to an extent, grounded in theoretical ex-

TABLE 7.3 Number and Percent Distribution of Full-Time Equivalent (FTE) Staff[1] in All Mental Health Organizations, by Staff Discipline: United States, Selected Years, 1972–1990[2]

Staff Discipline	1972	1978[2]	1986[2,3]	1990
Number of FTE Staff[1]				
All Staff	375,984	430,051	494,515	563,619
Patient care staff	241,265	292,699	346,630	415,719
Professional patient care staff	100,886	153,598	232,481	273,374
Psychiatrists	12,938	14,492	17,874	18,818
Other physicians	3,991	3,034	3,868	3,865
Psychologists[4]	9,443	16,501	20,210	22,825
Social workers	17,687	28,125	40,951	53,375
Registered nurses	31,110	42,399	66,180	77,635
Other mental health professionals (B.A. and above)	17,514	39,363	56,245	84,071
Physical health professionals and assistants	8,203	9,684	27,153	12,785
Other mental health workers (less than B.A.)	140,379	139,101	114,149	142,345
Administrative, clerical, and maintenance staff	134,719	137,352	147,885	147,900
Percent Distribution of FTE Staff				
All Staff	100.0	100.0	100.0	100.0
Patient care staff	64.2	68.1	70.1	73.8
Professional patient care staff	26.9	35.8	47.0	48.5
Psychiatrists	3.4	3.4	3.5	3.3
Other physicians	1.1	0.7	0.8	0.7
Psychologists[4]	2.5	3.8	4.1	4.0
Social workers	4.7	6.5	8.3	9.5
Registered nurses	8.3	9.9	13.4	13.8
Other mental health professionals (B.A. and above)	4.7	9.2	11.4	14.9
Physical health professionals and assistants	2.2	2.3	5.5	2.3
Other mental health workers (less than B.A.)	37.3	32.3	23.1	25.3
Administrative, clerical, and maintenance staff	35.8	31.9	29.9	26.2

Published and unpublished inventory data from the Survey and Analysis Branch, Division of State and Community Systems Development, Center for Mental Health Services.

[1] The computation of full-time equivalent (FTE) staff is based on a 40-hour workweek.

[2] For 1986, some organizations had been reclassified as a result of changes in reporting procedures and definitions. For details, see text and technical appendix.

[3] Includes data for community mental health clinics (CMHCs) in 1978. In 1986, 1988, and 1990, these staff are subsumed under other organization types. Data for CMHCs are not shown separately.

[4] For 1972–1978, this category included all psychologists with a B.A. degree and above; for 1986–1990, it included only psychologists with an M.A. degree and above.

Source: Center for Mental Health Services. *Mental health, United States, 1994.* Table 6.8. Manderscheid, R. W. & Sonnenschein, M. A. (Eds.). DHHS Pub. No. (SMA)94-3000. Washington DC: Supt. of Docs., U.S. Govt. Print. Off., 1994.

planations. In the following section, some of these changes are understood relative to the theoretical arguments associated with mental illness and mental disorder.

Theoretical Models of Mental Disorders

A perusal of any sociology of mental disorder textbook reveals a plethora of theoretical explanations regarding the cause of such behavior. The models include the following: medical, the antipsychiatric, social learning, social stress, and psychoanalytic (Cockerham, 1996). Addressing mental disorder as deviant behavior, Cockerham also explains conflict theory, functionalism, symbolic interaction, labeling, and social learning theory. Gupta (1993) identifies the medical–biological (psychiatric) model, symbolic interactionism, social deviance, labeling, attributional theory, social learning theory, cognitive theory, role theory, social reaction, social stress, and social selection perspectives, structural functional, conflict, social exchange, the problem of living approach, the psychodynamic perspective, and the humanistic perspective. Gallagher (1995) discusses the medical model, psychoanalytic theory, the behaviorist model, social learning theory, social stress, family systems theory, and labeling. Finally, Pilgram and Rogers (1993) address five non–sociological perspectives (the lay view, psychiatry, psychoanalysis, psychology, and the legal framework). Within sociology, they discuss three perspectives: social causation, labeling, and social constructivism.

It is obvious from this list that there are a variety of ways to approach explanations of mental disorder. Rather than attempt a description of each, this section focuses on those theoretical models that are consistently identified. This includes the medical model, the psychoanalytic model, social learning theory, and the antipsychiatric or problems in living perspective.

The Medical Model

The medical (or psychiatric) model posits that a mental disorder has the same pathology as a physical disorder. That is, once the cause of the problem can be identified, medicine can be prescribed and a treatment regimen established that will either eradicate the problem or at least control its occurrence. The growth of the medical model is, to a great extent, related to the emergence of psychotropic drugs. Relative to mental disorders, the medical model continues to advance the argument that specific chemical imbalances in the brain provide the "trigger" for those episodic events labeled as a mental disorder. The fundamental criticism of this model lies in what it does not cover. As Pilgram and Rogers (1993, p. 5) point out: "the bulk of what psychiatrists call 'mental illness' has no proven bodily cause, despite substantial research efforts to solve the riddle of a purported or assumed biological aetiology."

Nonetheless, the availability of psychotropic drugs has had a significant impact on the treatment of mental illness. The following statement by Lickey and Gordon (1991, p. 356) illustrates what they believe to be sufficient reason to apply the medical model of mental illness:

The effectiveness of drugs for the treatment of mental illness is one of the best pieces of evidence for the unity of brain and mind . . . psychological entities such as mood (depression, mania, anxiety), perception (hallucinations), and thought (delusions, incoherent speech, obsessions) can be significantly influenced by molecules that change the efficacy of synaptic transmission.

The benchmark in the emergence of psychotropic drugs is usually given as 1949, when John Cade demonstrated the effectiveness of lithium on bipolar illness (see Keltner & Folks, 1997, for a time-line of psychotropic drug development). Since then, psychotropic drugs have experienced rapid and continued growth. For instance, in 1995, Prozac was prescribed 1 million times every month in the United States alone (Kramer, in Elfenbein, 1995). By 1997, Prozac was being prescribed more than 1.8 million times per month ("The Top 200 Drugs," 1998). As a member of a relatively new line of drugs called selective serotonin reuptake inhibitors (SSRI), Prozac is utilized as a relief to a multiplicity of problems associated with mental illness with presumably fewer side effects. In keeping with the increased medicalization of illness, Bernstein (1995, p. 30) offers "a bill of rights of drug prescribing." These rights include the right of the patient to know; right drug; right dose; right schedule of administration; and the right route of administration. Although admirable, these rights are intended to educate the patient regarding their medications rather than establishing "rights" relative to the use of medications. Bernstein (1978) argues that psychotropic drugs have contributed to the reduction of hospitalization for mental health patients as well as reduce the likelihood of its reemergence. Thus, since the late 1940s, the psychiatric community has debated the efficacy of "talking" therapies versus the increasing numbers of psychotropic drugs in the treatment of mental illness. As a result, this debate has affected how mental illness is treated. In other words, what is the primary method of treatment—psychotherapies or psychotropic drugs? Although not an either/or argument, one of the underlying issues is the length of time spent in therapy. This issue will continue to divide the mental health/medical communities as cost-effective modalities become increasingly important. The American health-care system continues to change, allowing for-profit managed care systems increased control over the medical (and mental health) communities. As a result, decisions regarding mental health therapies may be made on the basis of short-term time and cost-saving outcomes that rely increasingly on the use of psychotropic drugs.

The Psychoanalytic Model

The psychoanalytic model is grounded in the writings of Sigmund Freud. Essentially, psychoanalysis argues that the personality structure of the individual is constructed around the concepts of the id, ego, and superego. The *id* is comprised of instincts such as those associated with life and death, as well as the pleasure principle. The *ego* is the mediating concept between the id and the superego. According to Freud, the ego is built on the reality principle. Finally, the *superego* represents societal expectations. Behavior is the result of the interplay between these three concepts. In addition, Freud suggested that human development is interconnected to psychosexual development that begins shortly after birth. Becoming fixated at a particular stage of development may cause a person to engage in inappropriate behavior when they become older (Gupta, 1993). Although widely applied throughout the 20th century, psychoanalysis is not without its critics. For instance, methodological questions include the lack of sound scientific principles. Another problem is that psychoanalysis cannot predict the occurrence of abnormal behavior. Cockerham (1996) offers an extensive assessment of the psychoanalytic model.

Social Learning Theory

Grounded in the behaviorist model, social learning theory argues that particular behaviors are learned through processes referred to as classical conditioning, operant conditioning and the observation and emulation of others.

Classical conditioning is built on the premise that a specific stimulus will elicit a specific response. Using a dog, Pavlov created a stimulus (a bell) that would sound when the dog was presented with food (the unconditioned stimulus). In response, the dog would salivate (the unconditioned response). After a period of conditioning, the dog would salivate (a conditioned response) at the sound of the bell (a conditioned stimulus)(Hewitt, 1991).

Operant conditioning argues that the learning of behavior is premised on the development of new responses reinforced by the environment. In this case, reinforcements (positive or negative) are key to the learning of behavior. Applying operant conditioning to the study of mental disorders, Gallagher (1995, p. 73) suggests that "substance abuse may also be linked . . . since the initial use of drugs can bring comfort."

Finally, the work of Bandura et al. (1961) is considered a classic in social learning theory. The researchers began by dividing children into two groups. One group witnessed aggressive adult behavior toward a doll (and without any repercussions). The second group of children did not observe the aggressive adult behavior. When provided an opportunity to play with the doll, children in the first group modeled their behavior after the adult they observed. Children in the second group not exposed to the abusive behavior of the model did not engage in abusive behavior toward the doll. At issue is the influence of others, particularly authority figures, on the acquisition of behavior (see also Bandura, 1961)—for example, the influence of television actors or cartoon figures on the behavior of young viewers (an early example is the work of Bandura et al., 1963). Such modeling would apply to the learning of any abnormal or deviant behavior.

The Antipsychiatric or Problems in Living Perspective

Easily the most controversial theory, the antipsychiatric model does not accept mental disorder as a disease (Cockerham, 1996). One of the leading proponents of the antipsychiatric movement is Thomas Szasz, who argues that there is a difference between a person suffering from a physical disease, which is manifested in clearly defined symptoms, and a mental disease, which cannot be clearly articulated as to its location within the body or possible avenues of treatment. In addition, when the patient seeks professional advice, the psychiatrist brings into the relationship a set of values from which he or she evaluates the patient (Szasz, 1960). According to this model, many of the difficulties experienced by patients can be referred to as *problems in living.* That is, how a person exhibits a particular behavior or communicates a thought or feeling is influenced not only by their ability but also by the method of communication. Sociologically, conflict theorists (see Sedgwick, 1982, for a history of the antipsychiatric model) hold many of these views.

The antipsychiatric model is roundly criticized for its lack of empirical evidence and its inability to address causation. The model is also criticized for its lack of alternative explanations of mental disorders.

Sociological Explanations of Mental Disorders

In addition to the biological and psychological theories presented previously, sociological explanations also assist in understanding mental disorders. Consider, for example, labeling theory (and more broadly, symbolic interactionism) and its emphasis on the audience in the determination of deviant behavior (for a classic example, see Goffman, 1961). If the audience considers the deviant behavior to be symptomatic of a mental disorder, the person is placed in a deviant role (see Gove, 1982, for an analysis of labeling theory and its current status). A classic example is the work of Rosenhan (1973).

Briefly, Rosenhan and a number of pseudo-patients gained admission to a number of mental institutions by claiming to hear words such as "dull" or "thud." Once admitted (in all but one instance, they were admitted as being schizophrenic), the pseudo-patients acted normal. Whereas many of the patients on the wards recognized the pseudo-patients for what they were, the staff did not. In fact, normal activities such as note taking by some pseudo-patients resulted in a notation in their charts characterizing the writing as yet further "proof" of their "illness." Pseudo-patients were released only when they adhered to the expectations of the staff. When released, they were labeled as being schizophrenic "in remission." As with the other theoretical explanations, there are a number of criticisms associated with labeling theory (see Pilgrim & Rogers, 1993).

The most famous sociological example relative to mental illness is that of Durkheim and his work on suicide. A summary statement by Simpson in the editor's Introduction (Durkheim, 1951, pp. 13–14 [1897]) provides us with a core statement regarding the work of Durkheim:

> all theses which require resort to individual or other extra-social causes for suicide are dispatched, leaving only social causes to be considered. This is used as a foundation for reaffirming his thesis stated in his introduction that the suicide-rate is a phenomenon *sui generis;* that is, the *totality* of suicides in a society is a fact separate, distinct, and capable of study in its own terms. Since, according to Durkheim, suicide cannot be explained by its individual forms, and since the suicide-rate is for him a distinct phenomenon in its own right, he proceeds to relate currents of suicide to social concomitants. It is these social concomitants of suicide which for Durkheim will serve to place any individual suicide in its proper aetiological setting.

Furthermore, Durkheim (1951, p. 299 [1897]) provides the connection between group level characteristics and the likelihood of suicide as follows:

> It is not mere metaphor to say of each human society that it has a greater or lesser aptitude for suicide; the expression is based on the nature of things. Each social group really has a collective inclination for the act, quite its own, and the source of all individual inclination, rather than their result.

Thus, reasoning that the rate of suicide within a society is related to social phenomena (i.e., its social institutions), Durkheim identified how social forces influence differing types of suicide. Thus, **egoistic suicide** "results from lack of integration of the individual into society" (Durkheim, 1951, p. 14). Here, Durkheim reasons that the structure of one's religious belief system influences the extent of individual integration into the group. Thus, Catholics, when compared with Protestants, experience lower rates of suicide because of greater religious emphasis on the collective rather than individual life. Similar arguments are made regarding the role of family life and political changes. For example, during a national crisis, suicide rates decline because of greater social integration.

The second type of suicide is referred to as **altruistic suicide.** In this case, suicide occurs because "the individual's life is rigorously governed by custom and habit . . . [and that the person takes] . . . his own life because of higher commandments, either those of religious sacrifice or unthinking political allegiance" (Durkheim, 1951, p. 15). An example is the military person who throws him- or herself on a live hand grenade to save the lives of fellow soldiers.

Finally, **anomic suicide** refers to a loss of "common beliefs and practices he has learned" (Durkheim, 1951, p. 15). In other words, the social norms that had provided the basis for integration are no longer applicable (i.e., becoming a millionaire because of winning the lottery). As a result, the "individual is unable to cope with the new opportunities afforded him" (Durkheim, 1951, p. 15).

Durkheim's analysis of suicide continues to withstand the test of time. Although more recent analysis has demonstrated a need to reexamine some of his points, the basic argument remains intact.

Finally, Levine and Scotch (1970, p. 2) point out there is considerable evidence to "support the notion that stress is related to and even contributes to psychological dysfunction, disease, mental disorder, and socially pathological behavior." In the process of constructing a definition of social stress and its antecedent variables, it is beneficial to pause and appreciate the significance of the following interpretation:

> Instead of beginning analyses of stress and health by looking at coping responses, cognitive–emotional appraisal, or individual forms of coping, why not begin by examining social conditions of inequality or structured arrangements, such as those that force a person to work under pressure or do not allow time to relax? (Freund & McGuire, 1995, p. 86)

As an area of research interest within medical sociology, **social stress** has resulted in literally thousands of articles (for a cogent article, see Aneshensel,

1992). Using FirstSearch, this author found 5,115 references to "social stress" in *Sociological Abstracts* (as of 3/97). Numerous explanations exist regarding the popularity of research interest in stress. One explanation is the interconnection between stress and other sociological variables. For instance, Aneshensel (1992, p. 18) states "the structural perspective on social causation understands stress both as a consequence of location in the social system and as a determinant of some outcome, most typically psychological distress." An example of stress as an independent variable is offered by Pearlin (1989, p. 244), who states that "as sociologists, we are interested in stress as it reveals patterned differences among groups and collectivities differentiated by their social and economic circumstances." First, however, what is social stress? Many definitions exist, but they provide little substance to our understanding of stress within a social science context. For example, Kessler and Wortman (1989, pp. 69–70) define stress "as a feature of the environment that, under certain circumstances, can affect the health of people exposed to it." More broadly, Spring (1989, p. 334) defines stress as "a disruption or alteration in biological, physiological, emotional, or behavioral homeostatic functioning." Hinkle (1987, p. 562) argues that a person experiences stress when "faced with a situation that implies for him two or more different kinds of behavior, based on two or more different sets of guidelines and values, which are in conflict and are not readily reconcilable." Perhaps one of the more specific definitions of stress comes from Aneshensel (1992, p. 16), who states that "stress is not an inherent attribute of external conditions, but emanates from discrepancies between those conditions and characteristics of the individual—his or her needs, values, perceptions, resources, and skills." Moving beyond a definition to an explanation of stress as an independent variable, Pearlin (1989, p. 244) points out that "as sociologists, we are interested in stress as it reveals patterned differences among groups and collectivities differentiated by their social and economic circumstances."

It is evident from these definitions that the study of stress is multidisciplinary. For instance, within medical sociology, the work of Antonovsky (1979, 1987) addresses stress relative to issues of health, whereas others such as Aneshensel et al. (1991) and Turner et al. (1995) examine stress relative to mental health. Stress occurs as a result of life events, chronic strains, or daily hassles (Thoits, 1995) and the source of stress has been identified as either the eruption of problematic events such as economic inequality or problems associated with social roles (Pearlin & Aneshensel, 1986). There are also a number of components associated with stress. For instance, Levine and Scotch (1970, p. 13) identify "the nature of the stressor, its perception or meaning for the individual, his mode of coping with the stressor, and the resultant strain or deformation produced by the stress experience." Stressors, therefore, can be understood as "experiential circumstances that give rise to stress" (Pearlin, 1989, p. 243). Research efforts have categorized stressors into *life events* and *chronic strains*. Life events as stressors have their history in the work of Holmes and Rahe (1967), Selye (1982), and others. However, chronic strains as stressors are understood as "conflicts, and threats that many people face in their daily lives" (Pearlin, 1989, p. 245), such as the multiplicity of role strains that are experienced by many throughout their daily routine. As Pearlin (1989) points out, life events and chronic strains should not be considered as incompatible experiences, but rather as interactive factors that influence one another and their creation of stress. Stressors also provide the connection between stress and mental illness.

The significance of social stress research is affirmed by the extensive literature that has been amassed since the late 1950s. Rather than attempt an exhaustive appraisal of the research, two of the more significant contributions in the analysis of social stress are examined.

Historically, the recognition of stress-related research generally begins with the development of the general adaptation syndrome (GAS) in the 1930s and its three stages of alarm reaction, resistance, and exhaustion (Seyle, 1956). Throughout these stages, the body undergoes physiological changes in response to stress (such as disease).

In the latter 1960s, the seminal Social Readjustment Rating Scale (Table 7.4; Holmes & Rahe, 1967) attempted to explicate the relationship between illness, stress, and a series of life events. Although flawed (Pearlin, 1989), the scale remains an important historical component in the research literature. Homles and Rahe (1967) developed the scale by asking approximately 400 subjects to assume that marriage was given a score of 500 and then rating each item relative to that event. It is believed that a person scoring 200 or more within a given year is at increased risk of illness. Outcomes associated with these responses are not particularly surprising, considering the homogeneity of the subjects. Later research by Masuda and Holmes (1967), however, indicates a strong correlation between minority populations and Caucasians as well as between first- and third-generational responses. The authors point out that the "degree of consensus indicated a universal agreement on the part of the subjects about the significance of the life events . . . that transcended differences in age, sex, marital status, education, social class, generation American, religion, and race" (Masuda & Holmes, 1967, p. 228).

Next, the relationship between stress and mental disorder can be understood from two perspectives. First, as the dependent variable, stress (or even the likelihood of stress) is related to one's location in society. Thus, particular populations would be considered more at risk than would others. For example, the social disadvantages associated with being poor would lead to increased stress among this population than, say, the upper-middle class (see, for example, Ferman & Gardner, 1978). The second perspective considers stress as the independent variable. In this case, stress leads to some form of psychological dysfunction (Aneshensel, 1992). Focusing on the first perspective, there is compelling evidence to support this position. Consider the work of Turner et al. (1995), who report that social stress is inversely related to social status and age, although the authors did not apply their research to persons older than age of 55. More specifically, examining the relationship between the sociological variables of age, sex, race and ethnicity, and social class with mental illness, Turner et al. (1995, p. 119) state "that differences in mental health arise, at least in part, from systematic differences in the quality and/or nature of stress experienced by individuals differentially situated in the social system." Furthermore, women identify and experience more stress than do men, and married persons experience fewer stressful events than do nonmarried persons (for a cross-cultural example, see Frankenhaeuser et al., 1989). These findings

TABLE 7.4   The Social Readjustment Rating Scale

Rank	Life Event	Mean Value
1.	Death of spouse	100
2.	Divorce	73
3.	Marital separation	65
4.	Jail term	63
5.	Death of a close family member	63
6.	Personal injury or illness	53
7.	Marriage	50
8.	Fired at work	47
9.	Marital reconciliation	45
10.	Retirement	45
11.	Change in health of family member	44
12.	Pregnancy	39
13.	Sex difficulties	39
14.	Gain of a new family member	39
15.	Business readjustment	39
16.	Change in financial state	38
17.	Death of a close friend	37
18.	Change to a different line of work	36
19.	Change in number of arguments with spouse	35
20.	Mortgage over $100,000	31
21.	Foreclosure of mortgage or loan	30
22.	Change in responsibility at work	29
23.	Son or daughter leaving home	29
24.	Trouble with in-laws	29
25.	Outstanding personal achievement	28
26.	Spouse begin or stop work	26
27.	Begin or end school	26
28.	Change in living conditions	25
29.	Revision of personal habits	24
30.	Trouble with boss	23
31.	Change in work hours or conditions	20
32.	Change in residence	20
33.	Change in schools	20
34.	Change in recreation	19
35.	Change in church activities	18
36.	Change in social activities	19
37.	Mortgage or loan less than $10,000	17
38.	Change in sleeping habits	16
39.	Change in number of family get-togethers	15
40.	Change in eating habits	15
41.	Vacation	13
42.	Christmas	12
43.	Minor violations of the law	11

Reprinted with permission from *Journal of Psychosomatic Research,* Vol. 11, T. Holmes and R. Rahe, The Social Readjustment Rating Scale, 213–218, 1967, Elsevier Science Inc.

reinforce the argument that stress is directly related to conditions of social life (see also Pearlin, 1989). It is precisely these points that are addressed in the following section.

Sociological Indicators of Mental Disorders

This section addresses the relationship between the sociodemographic variables of age, sex, race and ethnicity, and social class as they relate to rates of mental disorders. Expanding on this argument, Dohrenwend and Dohrenwend (1969), Pearlin (1989), and others have demonstrated that the rate of mental disorder is directly related to the location of particular populations in the social system. A more thorough presentation of these factors can be found in Gupta (1993), Gallagher (1995), and Cockerham (1996).

Age

The population aged 65 and older currently represents some 12.5% of the total population. That percentage is expected to increase to at least 22–23% by the middle of the 21st century. The baby boom generation will play a significant role in the increased number of elderly persons. Beginning in 2011, the baby boom generation officially turns age 65. As a result of this demographic shift, the rate of mental disorder on the basis of age is of particular importance. It is important to note that this demographic shift is occurring not only in the United States, but also throughout the industrialized world. Relative to most European nations, the United States has a young population.

In an earlier section it was noted that there was an inverse relationship between age and social stress. However, the researchers acknowledged that their subjects did not exceed age 55. This is important because research efforts regarding the relationship between increasing age and the likelihood of mental disorders are inconsistent. Although the overall rate of mental disorders declines with old age, there are particular disorders that show marked increases with age. This is particularly true of cognitive disorders such as Alzheimer's disease. The most prevalent mental disorder among elderly persons, however, is depression (Wykle & Musil, 1993), as it is among the general population. The increasing rate of Alzheimer's disease and depression among elderly persons is also true in Great Britain (Pilgrim & Rogers, 1993).

Furthermore, there are significant differences among the four sociological indicators. For example, elderly women are more likely to experience a mental disorder than are elderly men. However, if suicide is considered a mental disorder, then elderly White males older than age 85 have the highest incidence rate. Although the suicide rate among White males continues to fluctuate, the rate is not decreasing over time. Table 7.5 presents suicide rates on the basis of race, sex, and age between 1950 and 1993.

The data in Table 7.5 indicate that Caucasian American males, regardless of age, are more likely to commit suicide than anyone else. Although African American males have relatively similar rates (compared to Caucasian American males) during adolescence and early adulthood, their rates begin to decline with age. The rate of suicide for Caucasian American females peaks between 45–54 then begins to decline, whereas African American females peak between 15–44 and continue to decline as they age. Finally, rates for Hispanic Americans and persons of Asian or Pacific Island descent (across the age spectrum) continue to fluctuate, making any statement regarding historical trends difficult.

Elderly persons who are poor are more likely to experience mental disorders. In addition, the racial and ethnic background of elderly persons are related to the likelihood of mental disorders. This interconnection of variables suggests that, as stated earlier, the location of the person in the larger social system is directly related to their likelihood of being diagnosed with a mental disorder.

Race and Ethnicity

The composition of the minority group population is varied. Minority group populations range from the currently largest racial minority (African Americans) to rapidly increasing ethnic populations (Asian Americans). Shortly after the turn of the century, Hispanic Americans will become the largest minority population. By the middle of the 21st century, the minority population will constitute a majority of the total population.

There are substantial differences on the basis of race and ethnicity regarding rates of mental disorders. As with age, there is considerable interaction between the sociological indicators addressed in this section. For example, there is an ongoing debate regarding the rate of mental disorders among minority populations relative to Caucasian Americans. Although rates of mental disorder among minority groups may be higher than among Caucasian Americans, the reason is grounded in social class differences (Mirowsky & Ross, 1989; Cockerham, 1996). Analyzing changes in mental health outcomes among African Americans between 1979 and 1992, Jackson and Neighbors (1996, p. 209) state that "overall, the findings reveal increased reports of problems and major deterioration in both physical and psychological health status for the population in general." Meanwhile, in England, Pilgrim and Rogers (1993) note that Afro-Caribbean people are more likely to come into contact with the psychiatric community through the criminal justice system than are members of the Caucasian community.

Analyzing the interactive effect of minority status, sex, and aging on mental health outcomes, Jackson et al. (1995, p. 33) state that minority elderly persons are at greater risk for mental illness. More specifically, Ruiz (1995) argues that physical and psychological changes that accompany the aging process may have greater impact on minority elderly persons because of past experiences with racist attitudes and behaviors from the majority population as well as the greater likelihood of poverty experienced by minorities.

TABLE 7.5   Death Rates for Suicide, According to Sex, Detailed Race, Hispanic Origin, and Age: United States, Selected Years, 1950–1993

Sex, Race, Hispanic Origin, and Age	Deaths per 100,000 Resident Population					
	1950[1]	*1960[1]*	*1970*	*1980*	*1990*	*1993*
All Races						
All Ages, Age Adjusted	11.0	10.6	11.8	11.4	11.5	11.3
All Ages, Crude	11.4	10.6	11.6	11.9	12.4	12.1
Under 1 year	—	—	—	—	—	—
1–4 years	—	—	—	—	—	—
5–14 years	0.2	0.3	0.3	0.4	0.8	0.9
15–24 years	4.5	5.2	8.8	12.3	13.2	13.5
25–44 years	—	—	—	15.6	15.2	15.1
25–34 years	9.1	10.0	14.1	16.0	15.2	15.1
35–44 years	14.3	14.2	16.9	15.4	15.3	15.1
45–64 years	—	—	—	15.9	15.3	14.6
45–54 years	20.9	20.7	20.0	15.9	14.8	14.5
55–64 years	27.0	23.7	21.4	15.9	16.0	14.6
65 years and over	—	—	—	17.6	20.5	18.9
65–74 years	29.3	23.0	20.8	16.9	17.9	16.3
75–84 years	31.1	27.9	21.2	19.1	24.9	22.3
85 years and over	28.8	26.0	19.0	19.2	22.2	22.8
White Male						
All Ages, Age Adjusted	18.1	17.5	18.2	18.9	20.1	19.7
All Ages, Crude	19.0	17.6	18.0	19.9	22.0	21.4
Under 1 year	—	—	—	—	—	—
1–4 years	—	—	—	—	—	—
5–14 years	0.3	0.5	0.5	0.7	1.1	1.2
15–24 years	6.6	8.6	13.9	21.4	23.2	23.1
25–44 years	—	—	—	24.6	25.4	25.7
25–34 years	13.8	14.9	19.9	25.6	25.6	25.9
35–44 years	22.4	21.9	23.3	23.5	25.3	25.5
45–64 years	—	—	—	25.0	26.0	24.6
45–54 years	34.1	33.7	29.5	24.2	24.8	23.9
55–64 years	45.9	40.2	35.0	25.8	27.5	25.7
65 years and over	—	—	—	37.2	44.2	40.9
65–74 years	53.2	42.0	38.7	32.5	34.2	31.4
75–84 years	61.9	55.7	45.5	45.5	60.2	52.1
85 years and over	61.9	61.3	45.8	52.8	70.3	73.6
Black Male						
All Ages, Age Adjusted	7.0	7.8	9.9	11.1	12.4	12.9
All Ages, Crude	6.3	6.4	8.0	10.3	12.0	12.5
Under 1 year	—	—	—	—	—	—
1–4 years	—	—	—	—	—	—
5–14 years	[2]	[2]	[2]	[2]	0.8	1.1
15–24 years	4.9	4.1	10.5	12.3	15.1	20.1
25–44 years	—	—	—	19.2	19.6	19.0
25–34 years	9.3	12.4	19.2	21.8	21.9	21.5

212

TABLE 7.5 Continued

Sex, Race, Hispanic Origin, and Age	Deaths per 100,000 Resident Population					
	1950[1]	1960[1]	1970	1980	1990	1993
35–44 years	10.4	12.8	12.6	15.6	16.9	16.2
45–64 years	—	—	—	11.8	13.1	12.3
45–54 years	10.4	10.8	13.8	12.0	14.8	14.1
55–64 years	16.5	16.2	10.6	11.7	10.8	9.7
65 years and older	—	—	—	11.4	14.9	13.2
65–74 years	10.0	11.3	8.7	11.1	14.7	11.7
75–84 years	—	6.6	8.9	10.5	14.4	16.3
85 years and over	—	6.9	[2]	[2]	[2]	[2]
American Indian or Alaskan Native Male[3]						
All Ages, Age Adjusted	—	—	—	20.8	21.0	18.7
All Ages, Crude	—	—	—	20.9	20.9	18.4
15–24 years	—	—	—	45.3	49.1	31.6
25–44 years	—	—	—	31.2	27.8	30.9
45–64 years	—	—	—	[2]	[2]	12.8
65 years and over	—	—	—	[2]	[2]	[2]
Asian or Pacific Islander Male[4]						
All Ages, Age Adjusted	—	—	—	9.0	8.8	9.2
All Ages, Crude	—	—	—	8.8	8.7	9.1
15–24 years	—	—	—	10.8	13.5	12.7
25–44 years	—	—	—	11.0	10.6	11.3
45–64 years	—	—	—	13.0	9.7	10.3
65 years and over	—	—	—	18.6	16.8	19.1
Hispanic American Male[5]						
All Ages, Age Adjusted	—	—	—	—	12.4	12.6
All Ages, Crude	—	—	—	—	11.4	11.9
15–24 years	—	—	—	—	14.7	18.2
25–44 years	—	—	—	—	16.2	16.6
45–64 years	—	—	—	—	16.1	13.8
65 years and over	—	—	—	—	23.4	22.3
White, Non-Hispanic American Male[5]						
All Ages, Age Adjusted	—	—	—	—	20.8	20.0
All Ages, Crude	—	—	—	—	23.1	22.2
15–24 years	—	—	—	—	24.4	23.5
25–44 years	—	—	—	—	26.4	26.3
45–64 years	—	—	—	—	26.8	25.0
65 years and over	—	—	—	—	45.4	41.1
White Female						
All Ages, Age Adjusted	5.3	5.3	7.2	5.7	4.8	4.6
All Ages, Crude	5.5	5.3	7.1	5.9	5.3	5.0
Under 1 year	—	—	—	—	—	—
1–4 years	—	—	—	—	—	—

(*continued*)

TABLE 7.5 Continued

Sex, Race, Hispanic Origin, and Age	Deaths per 100,000 Resident Population					
	1950[1]	1960[1]	1970	1980	1990	1993
5–14 years	[2]	[2]	0.1	0.2	0.4	0.5
15–24 years	2.7	2.3	4.2	4.6	4.2	4.3
25–44 years	—	—	—	8.1	6.6	6.3
25–34 years	5.2	5.8	9.0	7.5	6.0	5.5
35–44 years	8.2	8.1	13.0	9.1	7.4	7.1
45–64 years	—	—	—	9.6	7.7	7.4
45–54 years	10.5	10.9	13.5	10.2	7.5	7.8
55–64 years	10.7	10.9	12.3	9.1	8.0	6.8
65 years and over	—	—	—	6.4	6.8	6.1
65–74 years	10.6	8.8	9.6	7.0	7.2	6.2
75–84 years	8.4	9.2	7.2	5.7	6.7	6.1
85 years and over	8.9	6.1	5.8	5.8	5.4	5.4
Black Female						
All Ages, Age Adjusted	1.7	[2]	2.9	2.4	2.4	2.1
All Ages, Crude	1.5	1.6	2.6	2.2	2.3	2.1
Under 1 year	—	—	—	—	—	—
1–4 years	—	—	—	—	—	—
5–14 years	[2]	[2]	0.2	[2]	[2]	[2]
15–24 years	[2]	[2]	3.8	2.3	2.3	2.7
25–44 years	—	—	—	4.3	3.8	3.1
25–34 years	2.6	3.0	5.7	4.1	3.7	3.1
35–44 years	2.0	3.0	3.7	4.6	4.0	3.0
45–64 years	—	—	—	2.5	2.9	2.4
45–54 years	3.5	3.1	3.7	2.8	3.2	2.2
55–64 years	[2]	3.0	[2]	2.3	2.6	2.6
65 years and over	—	—	—	[2]	1.9	2.3
65–74 years	[2]	[2]	[2]	[2]	2.6	2.2
75–84 years	—	[2]	[2]	[2]	[2]	[2]
85 years and over	—	[2]	[2]	[2]	[2]	[2]
American Indian or Alaskan Native Female[3]						
All Ages, Age Adjusted	—	—	—	5.0	3.8	5.5
All Ages, Crude	—	—	—	4.7	3.7	5.3
15–24 years	—	—	—	[2]	[2]	10.9
25–44 years	—	—	—	10.7	[2]	7.0
45–64 years	—	—	—	[2]	[2]	[2]
65 years and over	—	—	—	[2]	[2]	[2]
Asian or Pacific Islander Female[4]						
All Ages, Age Adjusted	—	—	—	4.7	3.4	3.8
All Ages, Crude	—	—	—	4.7	3.4	3.9
15–24 years	—	—	—	[2]	3.9	5.0
25–44 years	—	—	—	5.4	3.8	4.5
45–64 years	—	—	—	7.9	5.0	4.6
65 years and over	—	—	—	[2]	8.5	8.9

TABLE 7.5 Continued

Sex, Race, Hispanic Origin, and Age	Deaths per 100,000 Resident Population					
	1950[1]	1960[1]	1970	1980	1990	1993
Hispanic American Female[5]						
All Ages, Age Adjusted	—	—	—	—	2.3	2.1
All Ages, Crude	—	—	—	—	2.2	2.0
15–24 years	—	—	—	—	3.1	2.9
25–44 years	—	—	—	—	3.1	2.6
45–64 years	—	—	—	—	2.5	2.2
65 years and over	—	—	—	—	[2]	[2]
White, Non-Hispanic American Female[5]						
All Ages, Age Adjusted	—	—	—	—	5.0	4.8
All Ages, Crude	—	—	—	—	5.6	5.3
15–24 years	—	—	—	—	4.3	4.4
25–44 years	—	—	—	—	7.0	6.6
45–64 years	—	—	—	—	8.0	7.6
65 years and over	—	—	—	—	7.0	6.2

Data are based on the National Vital Statistics System.

[1] Includes deaths of persons who were not residents of the 50 states and the District of Columbia.

[2] Age-specific death rate based on fewer than 20 deaths.

[3] Interpretation of trends should take into account that population estimates for American Indians increased by 45% between 1980 and 1990, partly due to better enumeration techniques in the 1990 decennial census and to the increased tendency for people to identify themselves as American Indian in 1990.

[4] Interpretation of trends should take into account that the Asian population in the United States more than doubled between 1980 and 1990, primarily due to immigration.

[5] Excludes data from states lacking an Hispanic-origin item on their death certificate. See Appendix I.

Notes: For data years shown, the code numbers for cause of death are based on the then current International Classification of Diseases, which are described in Appendix II, tables IV and V. Data for the 1980s are based on intercensal population estimates. See Appendix I, Department of Commerce. Age groups chosen to show data for American Indians, Asian Americans, Hispanic Americans, and non-Hispanic whites were selected to minimize the presentation of unstable age-specific death rates based on small numbers of deaths and for consistency among comparison groups. The race groups (white, black, Asian or Pacific Islander, and American Indian or Alaskan Native) include persons of Hispanic and non-Hispanic origin. Conversely, persons of Hispanic origin may be of any race. Consistency of race and Hispanic origin identification between the death certificate (source of data for numerator of death rates) and data from the Census Bureau (denominator) is high for individual white, black, and Hispanic American persons; however, persons identified as American Indian or Asian American in data from the Census Bureau are sometimes misreported as white on the death certificate, causing death rates to be underestimated by 22–30% for American Indians and by about 12% for Asian Americans (Sorlie P. D., E. Rogot, and N. J. Johnson. Validity of demographic characteristics on the death certificate. *Epidemiology 3* (2):181–184, 1992). *Sources:* Centers for Disease Control and Prevention, National Center for Health Statistics. *Vital statistics of the United States,* Vol. II, Mortality, Part A, for data years 1950–1993. Washington DC: Public Health Service. Data computed by the Division of Health and Utilization Analysis from data compiled by the Division of Vital Statistics and from national population estimates for race groups from Table 1 and state or U.S. aggregate population estimates for Hispanics provided by the Census Bureau.

Source: National Center for Health Statistics. *Health, United States, 1995.* Table 143. Hyattsville, MD: Public Health Service. 1996.

Sex

As with age and minority status, the relationship between sex and mental illness is not clearly defined. For example, women are more likely to experience mental disorders than are men (Rosenfield, 1980; Dennerstein, 1995). However, admissions to public mental health facilities are greater among men than women (Cockerham, 1996). Rosenfield (1982, p. 22) offers an explanation for the differential in hospitalization rates between men and women. She suggests that it is the nature of the deviance relative to normative sex role behavior. In other words, "males are more often hospitalized for 'feminine' types of disorders than are females. Females are more often hospitalized for 'masculine' types of disorders than are males." For example, disorders associated with increased risk of hospitalization of men include neurosis and depression. Among women, disorders associated with increased risk of hospitalization included personality disorder and substance abuse (Rosenfield, 1982).

Why are women more likely to experience mental disorders? Gove and Tudor (1973, p. 814) provide a number of explanations. Although significant changes have occurred since the early 1970s, many of these explanations remain relevant. First, role opportunities for women are more restrictive than for men. Whereas the primary role for women has historically been that of housewife, role opportunities for men include work outside the home as well as within. Second, the primary role of housewife is not particularly rewarding. The activity is repetitive and boring, with little intellectual stimulation. Third, the housewife role occurs primarily inside the home. As a result, her work is virtually invisible to others within society. Fourth, married women who do work are more likely to find themselves in devalued occupations. Fifth, roles performed by women are generally considered to be in service to others. As a result, women are less satisfied and more frustrated with their position in society, thus experiencing higher rates of mental disorders (see Warren, 1991, for an insightful analysis of women and schizophrenia in the 1950s). Shehan et al. (1986, p. 414), however, report that "housewives who are most satisfied with their work role and with their family lives are significantly less depressed than are those who are less satisfied."

Since the 1970s, however, women have moved out of the home and into the workplace. In fact, more than 50% of married women with children under the age of 1 year are in the workforce. How has this changed women's experiences with mental disorders? For one thing, working women experience less distress than housewives do. Also, women who work experience increased levels of role overload because of continued societal expectations associated with family responsibility. As Kessler and McRae (1982, p. 225) report, the positive influence of work is related to the "conditions of the job and demands of family life." This argument is supported by Lennon and Rosenfield (1992), who argue that distress among women is contingent on the amount of control they have over their job. Nevertheless, sex differences regarding distress persist when family and work roles are combined. Simon (1995) found that women who combined family and work roles felt that their employment interfered with family roles. Men, however, considered their employment as supporting, rather than interfering with, their family role.

In addition to role expectations, the mental health of men and women is viewed differently by those defining and evaluating mental disorders. In a classic study of clinicians and sex-role stereotypes, Broverman et al. (1970, p. 5) examined the relationship between socially desirable behavior and stereotypic sex-based behavior. They report that "clinicians' concepts of a healthy, mature man do not differ significantly from their concepts of a healthy adult. However, the clinicians' concepts of a mature healthy woman do differ significantly from their adult health concepts." Thus, if women experience higher rates of some mental disorders, it may not be particularly surprising given the willingness of the audience to consider her behavior as less mentally healthy.

Social Class

The United States is a highly stratified society. Although this fact may run counter to our beliefs regarding equality and individuality, it is, nonetheless, true. A second fact is that there is an inverse relationship between social class position and the prevalence of certain mental disorders (for example, schizophrenia). This section details some of the classic research that has addressed this relationship.

Faris and Dunham (1939) conducted the initial research outlining the distinction between social class position and rate of mental illness. The authors examined rates of hospitalization in public and private psychiatric facilities in the city of Chicago during the 1930s. They reported that rates of admission decreased as distance from the central city increased. They also point out that within the central city, rates of hospitalization for schizophrenia were not related to racial or ethnic origin, although women were somewhat more likely to be hospitalized. The central point of their research, however, was the explicit relationship between a person's location in the social system and their likelihood of being hospitalized for a mental disorder. Although there are methodological and conceptual problems with their research, the significance of their findings cannot be diminished.

Hollingshead and Redlick (1958) in New Haven, Connecticut, conducted a second significant research project linking social class and rates of mental disorder. The authors expanded the population studied to include not only patients who had been hospitalized, but also patients receiving treatment through clinics and private practitioners (thus, including outpatient as well as inpatient populations). Utilizing the Index of Social Position, the authors divided respondents into five distinct classes. Class I was defined as the upper class, class II was upper-middle class, class III was defined as lower-middle class, class IV was the working class, and class V the lower class. In response to their hypothesis, which asked if class status was related to the rate of treatment of mental illness, the authors report that it was. Examining social class position and the type of mental disorder, Hollingshead and Redlick (1958) reported that as social class position increased, so did the likelihood of being diagnosed as neurotic. Concomitantly, as social class position decreased, the likelihood of being diagnosed as psychotic increased. Finally, Hollingshead and Redlick (1958) reported a relationship between social class and the location of treatment. They found that higher social class patients were treated in private hospitals, or under individual treatment modalities, whereas lower-class patients were more likely to be treated in public clinics or hospitals.

Two additional studies that, among other things, examined the relationship between social class and rates of mental disorder, include the Midtown Manhattan Study (Srole et al., 1962) and the Stirling County research (Leighton et al., 1963). Researchers in the Midtown Manhattan Study were interested in determining the extent of untreated cases of mental disorder. After questioning, responses from the sample were submitted to a number of psychiatrists for evaluation. One of the results clearly indicated that mental disorders increased as social class position decreased. The Stirling County study in Canada revealed a similar relationship between social class and the likelihood of mental disorder.

In addition to American research regarding the relationship between social class and mental disorder, Cockerham (1996) identifies a number of studies conducted in a variety of industrialized nations. The results of these studies indicate similar outcomes; lower-class respondents experienced greater rates of mental disorders. Unfortunately, access to such data in many countries is not available.

Throughout this section, the relationship between the four sociological indicators of age, race, sex, and social class and mental disorders has been examined. And, as discovered in previous chapters, they are interrelated. The interrelationship of these factors indicates the significance of the social environment, and particularly the location of the person in the larger social system relative to the prevalence of mental disorders.

Summary

This chapter begins with an examination of some basic terminology, a brief history of mental disorders, and an argument in which reasons for, and consequences of, deinstitutionalization are addressed. Furthermore, questions regarding the efficacy of moving patients out of large state-run facilities without providing sufficient community-level care facilities are raised. Questions are also raised regarding the concomitant growth of for-profit hospitals and increased personnel at the same time that public facilities were being closed. Throughout this process, the image and care of persons with mental disorders has undergone significant transformation. There has also been a transformation in the explanation of mental disorders.

Numerous theoretical explanations of mental disorders were identified and discussed. These explanations include the medical model (with an emphasis on the rise of psychotropic drugs), the psychoanalytic model, social learning theory, and the antipsychiatric model. Sociological explanations include labeling theory, Durkheim's seminal work on suicide, and social stress.

The relationship between mental disorder and the four sociological indicators of age, race, sex, and social class is also examined. Throughout the discussion, two points are quite clear. First, these variables provide an interrelated explanation of mental disorders. Second, social class appears to have the greatest impact relative to the other three variables.

Throughout the chapter, effort is made to provide as broad a cross-cultural perspective as possible. At the same time, the material addressed in this chapter may not be readily available from many nations. Because mental disorders and physical disability are culturally constructed, definitions and interpretation of behavior may differ between societies, thus making comparative research difficult.

CHAPTER REVIEW

The following questions address factual information as well as their consequences for the individual and society. The questions are also intended to sensitize the reader to the on-going discrimination, prejudice, and stigma attached to mental disorders.

1. Summarize the history of mental disorders. Provide a justification for the various treatments utilized throughout the ages.

2. Provide a justification for the reintroduction of large public psychiatric facilities.

3. Outline the transition from public institutionalization to deinstitutionalization. Who gained from this transition? Who lost?

4. Why is the medical model of mental disorder so popular in American society?

5. Labeling theory has lost considerable support in the recent past. Why do you think that has happened? Does labeling theory provide us with a useable explanation of mental disorder?

6. Utilizing the definitions provided, construct your own definition of stress.

7. Assess the relevance of the Social Readjustment Rating Scale.

GLOSSARY

altruistic suicide   is the taking of one's life for the good of some cause.

anomic suicide   occurs when learned social norms are lost or no longer serve an integrative function.

deinstitutionalization   is the process of transferring patients with mental disorders from large, impersonal public institutions to community care facilities or community hospital locations.

egoistic suicide   occurs when the individual is not connected to the larger society via social groups.

mental disorders   indicates a state of personal discomfort that interferes with an individual's well-being and threatens their ability to maintain interpersonal relations.

mental health   refers to a normal state of being.

mental illness   is the manifestation of behaviors or ideas that may cause harm to the individual or others.

social stress   refers to that which causes biological, social, or psychological change in an individual.

SUGGESTED READINGS

Durkheim, E. (1951). *Suicide*. New York: Free Press.
> A classic study in which empirical support for social explanations of suicide are provided.

Faris, R. E., & Dunham, H. W. (1939). *Mental disorders in urban areas*. Chicago: The University of Chicago Press.
> The first major research effort in which social class position and rate of mental disorder is established.

Goffman, E. (1961). *Asylums*. Garden City, NY: Anchor Books.
> A classic that establishes the concept of a total institution and examines the social life of mental patients.

Hollingshead, A. B., & Redlick, F. C. (1958). *Social class and mental illness*. New York: John Wiley & Sons.
> Another classic study of the relationship between social class and mental disorder.

Neighbors, H. W., & Jackson, J. S. (Eds). (1996). *Mental health in black America*. Thousand Oaks, CA: SAGE.
> An excellent resource guide. The editors bring together the best and most recent empirical evidence as they examine this issue.

Padgett, D. K. (Ed). (1995). *Handbook on ethnicity, aging, and mental health*. Westport, CT: Greenwood Press.
> Another solid resource guide. Expanding beyond research on African Americans, the editor brings together a solid knowledge base addressing minorities and the elderly regarding mental health.

REFERENCES

Aneshensel, C. S. (1992). Social stress: Theory and research. *Annual Review of Sociology, 18,* 15–38.

Aneshensel, C. S., Rutter, C. M., & Lachenbruch, P. A. (1991). Social structure, stress, and mental health: Competing conceptual and analytic models. *American Sociological Review, 56,* 166–178.

Antonovsky, A. (1979). *Health, stress, and coping*. San Francisco: Jossey-Bass.

Antonovsky, A. (1987). *Unraveling the mystery of health: How people manage stress and stay well*. San Francisco: Jossey-Bass.

Bandura, A., & Huston, A. C. (1961). Identification as a process of incidental learning. *Journal of Abnormal and Social Psychology, 63,* 2, 311–318.

Bandura, A., Ross, D., & Ross, S. A. (1961). Transmission of aggression through imitation of aggressive models. *Journal of Abnormal and Social Psychology, 63,* 3, 575–582.

Bandura, A., Ross, D., & Ross, S. A. (1963). Imitation of film-mediated aggressive models. *Journal of Abnormal and Social Psychology, 66,* 1, 3–11.

Bernstein, J. G. (1978). *Clinical psychopharmacology*. Littleton, MA: PSG Publishing Company, Inc.

Bernstein, J. G. (1995). *Handbook of drug therapy in psychiatry* (3rd Ed.). St. Louis: Mosby.

Brenner, M. H. (1973). *Mental illness and the economy*. Cambridge, MA: Harvard University Press.

Broverman, I. K., Broverman, D. M., Clarkson, F. E., Rosenkrantz, P. S., & Vogel, S. R. (1970). Sex-role stereotypes and clinical judgememts of mental health. *Journal of Consulting and Clinical Psychology, 34,* 1, 1–7.

Center for Mental Health Services. *Mental health, United States, 1994*. Mandershceid, R. W., & Sonnenschein, M. A. (Eds.). DHHS Pub. No. (SMA)94-3000. Washington DC: Supt. of Docs., U.S. Govt. Print. Off., 1994.

Charmaz, K. (1995). The body, identity, and self: Adapting to impairment. *The Sociological Quarterly, 36,* 4, 657–680.

Cockerham, W. C. *Sociology of mental disorder* (4th Ed.). Upper Saddle River, NJ: Prentice-Hall.

Dennerstein, L. (1995). Mental health, work, and gender. *International Journal of Health Services, 25,* 3, 503–509.

Dohrenwend, B. P., & Dohrenwend, B. S. (1969). *Social status and psychological disorder: A causal inquiry.* New York: Wiley-Interscience.

Durkheim, E. (1951). *Suicide.* Translated by J. A. Spaulding & G. Simpson. New York: Free Press.

Elfenbein, D. (1995). *Living with Prozac and other selective serotonin-reuptake inhibitors.* San Francisco: Harper.

Faris, R. E. L., & Dunham, H. W. (1939). *Mental disorders in urban life.* Chicago: The University of Chicago Press.

Ferman, L. A., & Gardner, J. (1978). Economic deprivation, social mobility, and mental health. In L. A. Ferman & J. P. Gordus (Eds.). *Mental health and the economy* (pp. 193–224). Kalamazoo, MI: W.E. Upjohn Institute for Employment Research.

Frankenhaeuser, M., Lundberg, U., Fredrikson, M., Melin, B., Tuomisto, M., Myrsten, A. L., Hedman, M., Bergman-Losman, B., & Wallin, L. (1989). Stress on and off the job as related to sex and occupational status in white-collar workers. *Journal of Organizational Behavior, 10,* 321–346.

Freund, P. E. S. & Mcguire, M. B. (1995). *Health, illness, and the social body: A critical sociology* (2nd Ed.). Englewood Cliffs, NJ: Prentice-Hall.

Gallagher, B. J. (1995). *The sociology of mental illness* (3rd Ed.). Englewood Cliffs, NJ: Prentice-Hall.

Goffman, E. (1961). *Asylums.* Garden City, NY: Anchor Books.

Gove, W. R. (1982). The current status of the labeling theory of mental illness. In W. R. Gove (Ed.). *Deviance and mental illness* (pp. 273–300). Beverly Hills: SAGE.

Gove, W. R., & Tudor, J. F. (1973). Adult sex roles and mental illness. *American Journal of Sociology, 78,* 4, 812–833.

Grob, G. N. (1995). Mental health policy in America: Myths and realities. In W. G. Rothstein (Ed.). *Readings in American health care: Current issues in socio-historical perspective* (pp. 295–304). Madison, WI: University of Wisconsin Press.

Gupta, G. R. (1993). *Sociology of mental health.* Boston: Allyn & Bacon.

Hewitt, J. P. (1991). *Self and society: A symbolic interactionist social psychology* (5th Ed.). Boston: Allyn & Bacon.

Hinkle, L. E. (1987). Stress and disease: The concept after 50 years. *Social Science and Medicine, 25,* 6, 561–566.

Hollingshead, A. B., & Redlick, F. C. (1958). *Social class and mental illness.* New York: John Wiley & Sons, Inc.

Holmes, T. H., & Rahe, R. H. (1967). The social readjustment rating scale. *Journal of Psychosomatic Research, 11,* 213–218.

Jackson, J. S., Antonucci, T. C., & Gibson, R. C. (1995). Ethnic and cultural factors in research on aging and mental health: A life-course perspective. In D. K. Padgett (Ed.). *Handbook on ethnicity, aging, and mental health* (pp. 22–46). Westport, CT: Greenwood Press.

Jackson, J. S., & Neighbors, H. W. (1996). Changes in African American resources and mental health: 1979–1992. In H. W. Neighbors & J. S. Jackson (Eds.). *Mental health in black America* (pp. 189–212). Thousand Oaks, CA: SAGE.

Johnson, A. B. (1990). *Out of bedlam: The truth about deinstitutionalization.* New York: Basic Books.

Keltner, N. L., & Folks, D. G. (1997). *Psychotropic drugs* (2nd Ed.). St. Louis: Mosby.

Kessler, R. C., & McRae, J. A., Jr. (1982). The effect of wives' employment on the mental health of married men and women. *American Sociological Review, 47,* 216–227.

Kessler, R. C., & Wortman, C. B. (1989). Social and psychologic factors in health and illness. In H. E. Freeman & S. Levine (Eds.). *Handbook of medical sociology* (4th Ed.) (pp. 69–86). Englewood Cliffs, NJ: Prentice-Hall.

Kiesler, C. A., & Sibulkin, A. E. (1987). *Mental hospitalization: Myths and facts about a national crisis.* Newbury Park, CA: SAGE.

Lassey, M. L., Lassey, W. R., & Jinks, M. J. (1997). *Health care systems around the world: Characteristics, issues, reforms.* Upper Saddle River, NJ: Prentice-Hall.

Leighton, D. C., Harding, J. S., Macklin, D. B., Macmillan, A. M., & Leighton, A. H. (1963). *The character of danger: Psychiatric symptoms in selected communities.* New York: Basic Books.

Lennon, M. C., & Rosenfield, S. (1992). Women and mental health: The interaction of job and family conditions. *Journal of Health and Social Behavior, 33,* 316–327.

Levine, S., & Scotch, N. A. (1970). *Social stress.* Chicago: Aldine Publishing.

Lickey, M. E., & Gordon, B. (1991). *Medicine and mental illness: The use of drugs in psychiatry.* New York: W. H. Freeman & Company.

Marmor, T. R., & Gill, K. C. (1989). The political and economic context of mental health care in the United States. *Journal of Health Politics, Policy and Law, 14,* 3, 459–475.

Masuda, M., & Holmes, T. H. (1967). The social readjustment rating scale: A cross-cultural study of Japanese and Americans. *Journal of Psychosomatic Research, 11,* 227–237.

Mechanic, D. (1976). Some factors in identifying and defining mental illness. In T. J. Scheff (Ed.). *Mental illness and social processes* (pp. 23–32). New York: Harper & Row.

Mirowsky, J., & Ross, C. E. (1989). *Social causes of psychological distress.* New York: Aldine de Gruyter.

Pearlin, L. I. (1989). The sociological study of stress. *Journal of Health and Social Behavior, 39,* 241–256.

Pearlin, L. I., & Aneshensel, C. S. (1986). Stress, coping and social supports: Their functions and applications. In L. H. Aiken & D. Mechanic (Eds.). *Applications of social science to clinical medicine and health policy* (pp. 417–437). Rutgers, NJ: Rutgers University Press.

Pilgrim, D., & Rogers, A. (1993). *A sociology of mental health and illness.* Buckingham, England: Open University Press.

Roemer, M. I. (1991). *National health systems of the world: Volume I—The Countries.* New York: Oxford University Press.

Roemer, M. I. (1993). *National health systems of the world: Volume II—The Issues.* New York: Oxford University Press.

Rosenfield, S. (1980). Sex differences in depression: Do women always have higher rates? *Journal of Health and Social Behavior, 21,* 33–42.

Rosenfield, S. (1982). Sex roles and societal reactions to mental illness: The labeling of "deviant" deviance. *Journal of Health and Social Behavior, 23,* 18–24.

Rosenhan, D. L. (1973). On being sane in insane places. *Science, 179,* 250–258.

Rothstein, W. G. (1995). A historical analysis of the treatment of the mentally ill. In W. G. Rothstein (Ed.). *Readings in American health care: Current issues in socio-historical perspective* (pp. 281–294). Madison, WI: University of Wisconsin Press.

Ruiz, D. S. (1995). A demographic and epidemiologic profile of the ethnic elderly. In D. K. Padgett (Ed.). *Handbook on ethnicity, aging, and mental health* (pp. 2–21). Westport, CT: Greenwood Press.

Sedgwick, P. (1982). Anti-psychiatry from the sixties to the eighties. In W. R. Gove (Ed.). *Deviance and mental illness* (pp. 199–223). Beverly Hills, SAGE.

Seyle, H. (1956). *The stress of life.* New York: McGraw-Hill.

Shehan, C. L., Burg, M. A., & Rexroat, C. A. (1986). Depression and the social dimensions of the full-time housewife role. *The Sociological Quarterly, 27,* 3, 403–421.

Simon, R. W. (1995). Gender, multiple roles, role meaning, and mental health. *Journal of Health and Social Behavior, 36,* 2, 182–194.

Spring, B. (1989). Stress and schizophrenia: Some definitional issues. In T. W. Miller (Ed.). *Stressful life events* (pp. 329–349). Madison, CT: International Universities Press.

Srole, L., Langer, T. S., Michael, S. T., Opler, M. K., & Rennie, T. A. C. (1962). In L. Srole & A. Fischer (Eds.). *Mental health in the metropolis: The midtown Manhattan study* (Books 1 and 2. Rev. and Enlarged Ed). New York: McGraw-Hill.

Starr, P. (1982). *The social transformation of American medicine.* New York: Basic Books.

Szasz, T. S. (1960). The myth of mental illness. *The American psychologist, 15,* 113–118.

Szasz, T. S. (1970). *The manufacture of madness: A comparative study of the inquisition and the mental health movement.* New York: Harper and Row.

The Top 200 Drugs. (1998). *American Druggist,* February, 48–49.

Thoits, P. A. (1995). Stress, coping, and social support processes: Where are we? What next? *Journal of Health and Social Behavior* (Extra Issue), 53–79.

Turner, B. S. (1995). *Medical power and social knowledge* (2nd Ed.). London: SAGE.

Turner, R. J., Frankish, J., & Phillips, N. (1991). Physical disability and health service utilization. *Advances in Medical Sociology, 2,* 269–298.

Turner, R. J., Wheaton, B., & Lloyd, D. A. (1995). The epidemiology of social stress. *American Sociological Review, 60,* 104–125.

Ussher, J. (1992). *Women's madness: Misogyny or mental illness.* Amherst, MA: University of Massachusetts Press.

Wagenaar, H. & Lewis, D. A. (1989). Ironies of inclusion: Social class and deinstitutionalization. *Journal of Health Politics, Policy and Law, 14,* 3, 503–522.

Warren, C. A. B. (1991). *Madwives: Schizophrenic women in the 1950s.* New Brunswick, NJ: Rutgers University Press.

Weitz, R. & Kronenfeld, J. J. (Eds.) (1994). *Research in the Sociology of Health Care* (p. 11). Greenwich, CT: JAI Press.

Weitz, R. (1996). *The sociology of health, illness, and health care: A critical approach.* Belmont, CA: Wadsworth.

Wykel, M. L., & Musil, C. M. (1993). Mental health of older persons: Social and cultural factors. In M. A. Smyer (Ed.). *Mental health and aging* (pp. 3–17). New York: Springer.

Zola, I. K. (1989). Toward the necessary universalizing of a disability policy. *The Milbank Quarterly, 67,* Supplement 2, Part 2, 401–428.

PART THREE

Service Providers

8 Physicians

Much of the social sciences literature on the professions has treated medicine as the exemplary expression of professional autonomy. Recent theoretical elaborations and empirical findings, however, suggest that the notion of a medical profession vested with the authority and autonomy to control every dimension of its work is no longer operative in many settings. Instead, the realities of employment by complex organizations, growing intervention by third parties, cleavages among different professional segments, and imbalanced labor markets seem to be defining the conditions of medical practice beyond the preferences of physicians or the ideology of professionalism.

—Frenk and Duran-Arenas, 1993, p. 26

The Realities of Becoming a Physician

Approximately 40% of the students in my medical sociology class are biology majors. On graduation, these students expect to enter medical school and become doctors. For some, this is a realistic expectation. For others, it is a dream that is eventually shattered. What is it about becoming a doctor that has such appeal? According to many of these students, it is not the money (although they recognize the need for a "decent" living to pay off their student loans). Is it the image of helping another person? Perhaps. When asked what area of medicine they want to practice, the overwhelming response is primary care.

It is important to recognize the importance of this chapter and its interrelationship with future material. Acknowledging that the future of physicians is tied to changes in the larger medical institution, subsequent chapters examine a variety of changes within the medical community. For instance, future chapters address changes within other health professions, the role of alternative treatments, the institutional structure of medicine, the cost and payment of health care, and the intrigue associated with other, apparently more efficient health-care systems. Thus, what happens to medicine as a profession is not an isolated consequence of a single incident. Rather, the changes that occur are the result of planned social changes constructed by the politically and economically powerful of the country.

Are these students ignorant of the realities associated with the profession of medicine in the late 1990s, or do they represent a new generation of idealists who sincerely expect to "do medicine" as they believe it should be practiced? Although they acknowledge the transformation of the profession, they generally do not see these changes as having a profound effect on their specific practice.

The History of the Physician in the United States

Medicine as a profession (and with social status) is a relatively recent phenomenon. As Starr (1982, p. 22) points out, the emergence of medicine as a profession was assisted by "standardization of training and licensing [which] became the means for realizing both the search for authority and control of the market." Prior to these changes, most physicians in the United States did not enjoy the prestige and power currently associated with the profession. This section examines the transformation of the American physician from the colonial period to the present.

During the colonial period, the term *doctor* applied not only to the legitimate doctor who had been trained in a university setting (about 5% of the total), but everyone else who "practiced" medicine (Bullough & Bullough, 1972). Throughout this period, physicians could do little for those patients whose problem involved more than setting a broken bone, pulling teeth, or treating minor illnesses. In fact, the most significant medical advancement during this period came about over the objections of physicians. The problem developed as a result of a smallpox epidemic in Boston. As a result of earlier reports regarding the success of inoculations in Europe, the Reverend Cotton Mather supported the use of inoculation against smallpox. However, many in the Boston medical community were not initially convinced. Their minds were not changed until Zabdiel Boylston, a Boston physician, provided the necessary evidence by inoculating hundreds of residents (Cassedy, 1991).

Throughout the 18th century various efforts were undertaken to improve the status of physicians. For example, an increasing number of physicians traveled to Europe for training. Because of an increasing number of university-trained doctors, efforts were made in a few states (Massachusetts, New York, and New Jersey) to require licensure. Still other physicians attempted to improve the profession by developing state-level medical societies. The public, however, was not supportive of many of these ideas because they wanted access to as wide a range of "doctors" as possible (Cassedy, 1991).

Generally speaking, the image of doctors during this period of time was extremely negative. The more qualified doctors attacked the less qualified and all doctors were attacked by the public. Nevertheless, the more qualified doctors were able to develop a comfortable lifestyle based on their earnings from patients (Duffy, 1993).

The first medical school in the United States opened in Philadelphia in 1765. Within 50 years, there were more than 40 medical schools. By comparison, France had just three (Starr, 1992). Unfortunately, the rapid expansion of medical education in the early 19th century did not mean that quality followed quantity. For example, in an effort to maximize profit and ensure student enrollment, previously low standards at many medical schools were reduced even further. By the time of the Civil War, only one-fourth of physicians who were tested for admission to the medical corps could pass the exam. Furthermore, original research was virtually nonexistent in all medical schools (Ludmerer, 1996). There was also a clear distinction in medicine between the regulars and the irregulars. The regulars were mainstream (orthodox) physicians (see Starr, 1982, for an analysis of class, status, and power among physicians during this time period), whereas the irregulars consisted of practitioners extolling a variety of beliefs and treatments (Cassedy, 1991).

Throughout the second half of the 19th century, the process of medical education began to change. In addition to developing research skills and an expanded knowledge base, medical students returning to the United States supported the German organization of medical schools. The German model is characterized in the following quote:

> No matter how the teaching hospitals were owned and operated, however, they had one characteristic in common. All were organized on the basis of *Kliniken,* while the basic medical sciences were organized as *Institute.* Each *Institute* or *Kliniken* was headed by a professor, who was not only the academic head of the department but also the director of the *Institut* or *Klinik.* Each *Institut* had its own lecture rooms, preparation rooms, library, museum, and research laboratories, so that it was essentially an autonomous unit within the university. Similarly, each *Klinik* had its own laboratories, teaching amphitheater, library, and record room . . . and there was little or no relationship among the various *Kliniken* or *Institute.* The teaching of medical students was largely by lecture and lecture demonstration; the German medical student received little direct instruction in the care of the patient. (Ebert, 1977, p. 176)

Although the German model influenced American medical education in the early 20th century, it was modified to fit the American experience.

In the United States, the model of medical education was Johns Hopkins, where the University Hospital was incorporated with the medical school. In addition, Johns Hopkins provided a model of medical education based on greater academic requirements and clinical experience. Medical education was beginning to change in other institutions as well. Following in the Hopkins model, other medical schools were increasingly connected and run by universities. Curriculums were improved, standards enhanced, and exams became compulsory. The curriculum and clinical teaching were expanded and organized. The study of medicine also required the student to become involved in the subject matter rather than observe passively (Ludmerer, 1996).

These reforms, however, were not applied to all medical schools. On the one hand, medical schools such as Johns Hopkins, Harvard, Pennsylvania, and Michigan stood out as examples of reform and progressive education. On the other hand, proprietary institutions continued to offer an inferior education to primarily under qualified students. It was within this context that a 1906 survey by the American Medical Association (AMA) brought about not only fundamental change in medical education, but also provided the basis for the professionalization of medicine.

The Flexner Report and Its Consequences

The Council on Medical Education was formed within the AMA in 1904. Two years later the council surveyed the 162 medical schools in the United States. Extremely critical of medical education in the United States, the findings were never published. Among the schools surveyed, the council "fully approved of only 82, which it rated Class A. Class B consisted of 46 imperfect, but redeemable, institutions, while 32, beyond salvage, fell into Class C" (Starr, 1982, p. 118). Instead, the council turned to the Carnegie Foundation for the Advancement of Teaching to conduct a similar study. For reasons still unknown, the Carnegie Foundation contacted Abraham Flexner, who had received his A.B. from Johns Hopkins and had recently published a book on *The American College* (Ludmerer, 1996). After visiting all of the medical schools in the United States (and a few in Canada), Flexner presented his findings in the now-famous **Flexner Report.** Flexner found many of the proprietary institutions to be understaffed, underfunded, and grossly unprepared to train physicians. The recommendations put forth by Flexner in 1910 suggested that "the first-class schools had to be strengthened on the model of Johns Hopkins, and few from the middle ranks had to be raised to that high standard; the remainder, the great majority of schools, ought to be extinguished" (Starr, 1982, p. 120). According to Flexner, only 31 of the medical schools should remain open.

Although many of the poorly run (primarily proprietary) institutions had already experienced a decline in overall enrollment prior to the report (Rothstein, 1987), the report had an impact. By the early 1920s, the number of medical schools had declined to 81, half of what had existed only 15 years earlier. As medical schools closed, the total number of students attending also declined. Although the overall number of physicians in the United States continued to increase, the rate of increase did not keep up with growth in the overall population. For example, in 1900 there were 157 physicians for every 100,000 population. By 1920, the rate had declined to 136 physicians per 100,000 population and by 1930 even further to 125 per 100,000 population. Although the total number of physicians almost doubled between 1900 and 1950, the rate per 100,000 population stood at 133, a 15% decline (Somers & Somers, 1961). By 1994 there were 653,851 active physicians (including Doctors of Osteopathy), or 252 per 100,000 population (National Center for Health Statistics, 1996). This ratio is similar to other industrialized nations. For example, member nations of the Organisation for Economic Co-Operation and Development (OECD) reported a range from 80 physicians per 100,000 in Turkey to 320 per 100,000 population in Greece. Rates for most member nations were in the 190–220 per 100,000 population range (OECD, 1994). The rate of physicians to population in less-developed nations, however, is extremely low. For example, during the period 1989–1991, there were 4 physicians for every 100,000 persons in Ghana; 2 per 100,000 in Niger; 4 per 100,000 in Uganda; 2 per 100,000 in Malawi; and 3 per 100,000 in Chad (World Health Organization, 1995).

According to Flexner, medical schools should have the following three characteristics: first, that the institutions have modern laboratory facilities; second, that the students admitted to medical schools meet a defined set of criteria; and third, that the institution encourage and expect original research from their faculty (Ludmerer, 1996). The report had its intended impact. However, the decline in the number of medical schools also had the unintended effect of shifting physicians away from private practice and into research. There is some disagreement regarding the intention of Flexner on this point. Starr (1982) argues that too many physicians became trained in the Johns Hopkins model. Ludmerer (1996), however, emphasizes Flexner's belief in the role of scientific medicine, even for those physicians not engaged in research.

Professionalization of the Physician

Although the Flexner Report had an immediate impact on medical education in the United States, it also had a long-term impact on the professionalization of medicine. As the number of medical schools declined along with available openings, competition increased. The result was an increase in the status of those accepted. In addition, stricter standards regarding licensure by states also improved the overall status of physicians. Furthermore, the increased emphasis on research within university-linked medical schools provided an opportunity not only to make significant technological changes, but also to demonstrate the importance of these advances. Within a relatively short period of time, medical education had been completely restructured (Duffy, 1993). One consequence of these changes was the increased professionalization of the profession. Consider the following features associated with the professionalization of an occupation (Goode, 1960, p. 903) and their relevance to the medical community.

1. The profession determines its own standards of education and training.
2. The student professional goes through a more far-reaching adult socialization experience than does the learner in other occupations.
3. Professional practice is often legally recognized by some form of licensure.
4. Licensing and admission boards are manned by members of the profession.

5. Most legislation concerned with the profession is shaped by the profession.
6. The occupation gains in income, power, and prestige ranking, and can demand higher caliber students.
7. The practitioner is relatively free of lay evaluation and control.
8. The norms of practice enforced by the profession are more stringent than are the legal controls.
9. Members are more strongly identified and affiliated with the profession than are members of other occupations with theirs.
10. The profession is more likely to be terminal occupation. Members do not care to leave it, and a higher proportion assert that if they had it to do over again, they would choose that type of work.

Physicians have enjoyed a continued increase in their social standing throughout the 20th century. In part, this improving status is the result of "the emergence of a more autonomous state . . . [and] the continued evolution of a capitalistically based, corporate-industrial presence" (Hafferty & Light, 1995, p. 132). More recently, however, there are indications that the professional status of physicians may be waning. For instance, McKinlay and Stoeckle (1988) address the process whereby physicians are becoming increasingly proletarianized. In other words, they are losing control of the profession to corporate interests (McKinlay & Stoeckle, 1988).

Nonetheless, as an occupation, physicians enjoy one of the highest average salaries as well as prestige and power. The average net income for all physicians in the United States in 1993 was $189,300. Physicians in general–family practice averaged $116,800, whereas the average net income of surgeons was $262,700 (U.S. Census Bureau, 1996). However, current research examining the financial return on education found that "attorneys and specialist physicians had the highest net present value of their investment. Primary care physicians had the poorest financial results of the five groups studied" (Weeks et al., 1994, p. 1284). The groups studied include the areas of "law, business, dentistry, primary care medicine, and procedure-based specialty medicine" (Weeks et al., 1994, p. 1280). On another dimension of social stratification, physicians consistently rank near the top of the occupational prestige rankings. According to the General Social Survey Cumulative Codebook (Davis & Smith, 1996), physicians were ranked at the top of the occupational listing with a prestige score of 86. In addition to prestige, this score also represents the level of education, training, and income associated with becoming a physician, relative to other occupations in the United States. Thus, being a physician provides numerous tangible and intangible rewards. However, the process of becoming a physician is long, difficult, and increasingly very expensive. For instance, in 1990 the average debt for medical students was $46,224 (Hughes et al., 1991). More recently, the Association of American Medical Colleges (1997) reports that among the 1996 graduates of public medical schools, the median debt was $65,000. Among graduates of private medical schools, median debt was $92,000. In addition to the 4-year undergraduate degree, students will spend 4 more years in medical school and additional years (depending on the specialty area) in residency.

Becoming a Doctor: The Socialization Process

In their seminal work, Becker et al. (1961) chronicle the medical socialization process experienced by medical students in the latter 1950s. Initially, first-year students approach the study of medicine from an idealistic perspective. They identify medicine as "the best of all professions" and believe that the balance between helping people and earning a living is compatible. More recently, Good and Good (1989, p. 309) concluded that: "the problem of overcoming the 'disabling' qualities of medical education is often restated as the problem of how to maintain caring attitudes while developing the knowledge and skills of the competent physician." Returning to Becker et al. (1961), first-year students soon realized that they would not be involved in patient care. Instead, they were relegated to classroom activities where the focus was on rote memorization of basic facts where students soon realize they could not read/study/memorize everything they need to know. As a result, students experience a degree of uncertainty in their advancement throughout their medical training. This includes not only what to study, but even how to prepare for exams. Among students at Cornell University Medical College in the 1950s, Fox (1957, pp. 239–241) describes uncertainty as "limitations in the current state of medical knowledge . . . imperfect mastery of what is currently known in the various fields of medicine . . . [and] the uncertainties of medicine."

The second year is similar to the first. Students, however, were less anxious because they were able to integrate the perspective of knowing and studying what the professor wanted, thus focusing on a more limited range of information.

According to Becker et al. (1961), the third and fourth years are referred to as the *clinical years*. The third year was divided into three rotation areas: medicine, surgery, and pediatrics. At this point, students receive exposure to a variety of cases by participation in workups of patients and through daily rounds. Rather than formal classroom experiences, the third-year student attends lectures on specialty areas. The student also learns through informal conversations with residents and physicians.

Similarly, the fourth year was divided into medicine and psychiatry, obstetrics and gynecology, surgical specialties, and a preceptorship. Students were assigned to new cases or a continuation of an older case that they had treated earlier. The preceptorship involved working with a general practitioner for 1 week in a small community in Kansas (the research was conducted at the University of Kansas).

Becker et al. (1961) and others (for example, Merton et al., 1957) have described in exquisite detail the experiences associated with the socialization process to medical school in the 1950s. Fortunately, sociological research of medical education has continued (for example, Conrad, 1988; Hafferty, 1988; Light, 1988; Richman & Flaherty, 1990; Hafferty, 1991), but not at the pace of earlier years. Colombotos (1988) offers a clear summation of research on medical education throughout the 1960s and early 1970s. Also, Fox (1989) provides historical continuity by addressing changes and similarities with medical students in the 1960s through the 1980s (see also Fox, 1988, Part I for brief excerpts of some of these classics). For example, the 1960s represented a "scientific" era as well as a period of government involvement in health-care responsibility for the poor and elderly (Medicaid and Medicare, respectively). The latter 1960s and early 1970s also represented a period in which medical students began to challenge the authority of the institution, question medical practices, and attempt to democratize the physician–patient relationship (Bloom, 1988; Fox, 1989). Medical schools continued to undergo change throughout the 1970s and 1980s (see, for example, Kendall & Reader, 1988, for an example of innovations in medical education in the 1970s and 1980s).

Becoming a Doctor: Current Realities

The recent history of applications to medical school indicates an increase in the number of applicants beginning in the 1960s and lasting until the mid-1970s (Fox, 1989). Since then, however, the number of applicants to medical school generally decreased until the 1989–1990 academic year. Throughout the 1990s the numbers of applications to medical school continues to increase yearly. Consider, for example, that there were 42,303 applicants for the 1975–1976 academic year. At that time, the 114 medical schools accepted 15,365 applicants for an applicant acceptance ratio of 2.8 and an actual first-year enrollment of 15,351 students. The decline in applications reached its low point in the 1988–1989 academic year, when 26,721 applicants applied for admission. At that time, the 127 medical schools enrolled 16,781 first-year students. The actual number of accepted applicants was 17,108, resulting in an acceptance ratio of 1.6. By 1995–1996, however, there were 46,591 applicants. The 125 medical schools accepted 17,357 applicants (an acceptance ratio of 2.7) and enrolled 17,024 first-year medical students. One final note: the current mean undergraduate grade point average (GPA) of admitted students was 3.4 (out of a possible 4.0) (Barzansky et al., 1996). This current interest in medicine has exacerbated two fundamental issues that have persisted for some time: the oversupply of physicians and the appropriate balance of generalists to specialists. Although the following paragraphs address these issues, their resolution does not appear imminent.

The number of practicing physicians is expected to increase. Examining physician supply in New York State, Salsberg et al. (1996, p. 688) conclude that "even allowing for higher need, however, it would appear that New York is likely to have future surpluses of physicians in many specialties." Although their findings are not generalizable to the nation as a whole, the issue raises some basic questions regarding the national affordability of excess physicians. Hafferty (1988) reminds us, however, that the emergence of recent beliefs regarding a physician surplus was grounded in political and economic motivations to reduce governmental involvement in social programs in general and medical education in particular.

Earlier, the ratio of physicians to the general population indicated that the United States currently ranks in the middle when compared with other industrialized nations. Nonetheless, the question of oversupply must be raised, not necessarily within the context of total numbers, but rather in terms of specialty area and geographic location of practice. Evidence from the Canadian system suggests that national and provincial policy initiatives can effectively control physician oversupply problems as well as the balance between primary care and specialists (Sullivan et al., 1996), although not all would agree (see the section on Canada in this chapter).

As mentioned earlier, there are currently 230 active non-Federal physicians per 100,000 population in the United States. However, physicians are not distributed uniformly throughout the country. For example, areas with the highest ratios of physicians per 100,000 population include the District of Columbia (641), Massachusetts (373), and New York State (343). States with the lowest ratios of physicians per 100,000 population include Alaska (143), Wyoming (141), and Mississippi (132) (U.S. Bureau of the Census, 1996). Within-state distribution of physicians is also not uniform. For example, in Minnesota, the 1982 population to physician ratio ranged from 253.25 in the southeast section of the state to 1,385.47 in the northwestern section (Hafferty, 1988). These geographic differences in Minnesota and throughout the United States are the result of a number of factors. For instance, larger metropolitan areas have the technologies many physicians became accustomed to in medical school. These areas also have the clientele base necessary to ensure a particular standard of living. It is also known that almost 50% of physicians leave the state in which they received their graduate medical education (Seifer et al., 1995). As a result, some areas of the United States are beginning to experience a saturation of particular specialty areas. Examining marketplace demand for primary care and specialty areas, Seifer et al. (1996) report significant declines for specialists as well as some areas within primary care. They report that family medicine was the only area within primary care to witness continuing employment opportunities (Table 8.1).

Interconnected with the issues of location and oversupply of physicians is the appropriate balance between primary care and specialization. Throughout the first 60 years of the 20th century, primary care physicians were the norm. However, beginning shortly after World War II, the ratio of generalists to specialists began to shift. Today, almost 70% of physicians are specialists. According to data from the National Center for Health Statistics (1996), primary care generalists made up 59.1% of active doctors in 1949. By 1994, however, they accounted for only 33.0% of active doctors. More specifically, general–family practice physicians declined from 50.1% of active doctors in 1949 to 12.1% in 1994, whereas other areas of primary care (internal medicine and pediatrics) increased as a percentage of total physicians. Pol and Thomas (1992) provide a breakdown of specialty and subspecialty areas as well as the medical categories associated with primary versus specialty care. There have been concerted efforts to increase not only the total number of generalists, but to also increase their percentage of the total physician population (see, for example, research by Kindig & Libby, 1994). The problem, however, has been to convince medical students to bypass the more lucrative specialties and remain in primary care. Unfortunately, Martini et al., (1994, p. 667) report that the number of students interested in primary care medicine will increase when "the appropriate selection of students and a supportive medical school environment are among the most important factors under the control of the medical school related to the production of generalist physicians." Noting that attitudes and actions of others can influence career choices, Block et al. (1996) examined the support and encouragement provided by medical school faculty toward primary care. Their findings suggest that much of the academic community is "poorly aligned with the goals of enhancing the education and environment for primary care" (Block et al., 1996, p. 681). Surveying fourth-year medical students, Rosenthal et al., (1994) were interested in those factors that would influence their decision to seek a career in primary care. The two primary inducements were (1) if the student had a debt of at least

TABLE 8.1   Active Health Personnel and Number per 100,000 Population, According to Occupation and Geographic Region: United States, 1970, 1980, and 1993

Year and Occupation	Number of Active Health Personnel	United States	Geographic Region[1]			
			Northeast	Midwest	South	West
1970						
Physicians	—	—	—	—	—	—
Federal	—	—	—	—	—	—
Nonfederal	290,862	142.7	185.0	127.5	114.8	158.2
Doctors of medicine[2]	279,212	137.0	178.7	118.2	111.5	154.8
1980						
Physicians	427,122	189.8	—	—	—	—
Federal	17,642	7.8	—	—	—	—
Doctors of medicine[2]	16,585	7.4	—	—	—	—
Nonfederal	409,480	182.0	224.5	165.2	157.0	200.0
Doctors of medicine[2]	393,407	174.9	216.1	153.3	152.8	195.8
1993						
Physicians	629,815	242.9	—	—	—	—
Federal	22,661	8.7	—	—	—	—
Doctors of medicine[2,3]	21,311	8.2	—	—	—	—
Nonfederal	607,154	234.2	314.3	222.3	207.1	223.3
Doctors of medicine[2,3]	576,073	222.2	297.6	203.2	199.3	216.3

[1] Number per 100,000 population. Ratios for physicians and dentists are based on civilian population; ratios for all other health occupations are based on resident population.

[2] Excludes physicians not classified according to activity status from the number of active health personnel.

[3] Data for doctors of medicine are as of January 1, 1994.

Source: Physician Marketplace Statistics, American Medical Association, Copyright 1994. Physician Marketplace Statistics, American Medical Association, Copyright 1981.

$50,000 and (2) if the income for a primary care physician was at least $180,000. The following quote best explains the relationship between these variables: "as debt levels increased, the percentage of NPC [non-primary care] students who would change for loan repayment increased while the income and hours worked factors decreased in relative importance" (Rosenthal et al., 1994, p. 916). However, even with these incentives, only 45% of the students surveyed were interested in becoming a primary care physician (this percentage included those who were already committed to primary care). Others (for example, Cooper, 1994; Whitcomb, 1995) question the need for percentage parity between primary care physicians and specialists. Instead, Cooper (1994) argues for a 33–67 split between primary care and specialists. The debate over numbers and percentages of physicians in primary care versus specialty areas will continue. Many medical schools have begun training increased numbers of physicians in primary care areas. However, it is too early to tell if this movement will have the desired effects of decreasing the maldistribution of physicians in the United States as well as the overall cost of medical care. Although an increasing number of medical students are identifying primary care as their career choice (family medicine, internal medicine, and pediatrics), Block et al. (1996) point out that, given current trends, "the actual proportion of 1996 US medical graduates who enter primary care practice will be 35%" (Block et al., 1996, p. 677). Furthermore, efforts to increase the numbers and percentage of primary care physicians will take a considerable length of time given the time-line between entering medical school and practicing medicine. A particularly disturbing trend in medical education is the declining enrollment of minorities. According to the Association of American Medical Colleges (1996), underrepresented minorities as a percentage of medical school enrollments peaked (8.1%) in 1975. Application and matriculation trends of underrepresented minorities indicate that "minority underrepresentation in U.S. medical schools [is more severe] in 1990 than existed 15 years earlier" (Association of American Medical Colleges, 1996, p. 3).

A Comparative Analysis of Physicians

Many of the issues regarding the medical profession are not unique to the United States. For example, questions such as numbers of physicians, their cost, or the most efficient primary–specialist ratio apply to virtually all societies. The following section outlines some of the concerns expressed in developed as well as developing nations regarding the medical profession.

The term *physician* evokes particular images and definable criteria associated with its attainment among most Americans. These images and expectations are, to some extent, culturally specific. Hafferty (1995) suggests that it is important to capture the multiplicity of cultural implications associated with the meaning and application of medicine as a profession.

The World Health Organization (WHO) broadly defined "physician" in 1972. Essentially, this definition stated that "a physician was . . . anyone trained to be a physician for the 'independent' promotion of health, according to the legal standards of each country" (Roemer, 1991, p. 34). Although the definition provides flexibility in describing the variety of culturally specific characteristics associated with being a physician, it is vague. More specifically, a "physician" is someone trained to provide culturally approved health-care services to members of a given population. Organizationally, the occupation of physician is located within the resource production component of the broader health system model (Roemer, 1991). The other components of Roemer's health system model include the organization of programs, economic support mechanisms, management methods, and the delivery of services. All of these components are discussed in subsequent chapters and as a model in Chapter 13. In a rather different categorization, Field (1980) places the position of the physician and the role of professional associations within a broad schema in which health systems range from anomic to socialized. This classification is instructive as it offers a comparative analysis of the role of physicians vis-à-vis the state. Examining professional dominance within various countries, Hafferty and McKinlay (1993a, p. 225) conclude that "professionalism is neither inevitable nor irreversible."

Canada

Medical education in Canada is different from the United States because of its emphasis on training practitioners in general medicine. As a result, 50% of physicians are now either general or family practitioners (Lassey et al., 1997). As in the United States, however, there are significant provincial differences regarding the ratio of physicians to the population. These ratios range from a high of 10.5 general practitioners and family physicians per 10,000 population in the Yukon to a low of 5.74 per 10,000 population in New Brunswick. The ratio of specialists to population ranges from a high of 9.17 per 10,000 population in Québec to a low of 1.26 in the Yukon (Krishnan, 1992). Organizationally, a significant difference between American and Canadian medical education is the ability of the central government to define health policy (see Coburn, 1993a,b, for an analysis of the relationship between the state and medicine). One of the ongoing myths of the Canadian health-care system [or National Health Insurance (NHI), or simply Medicare] is that it interferes with the physician–patient relationship. In reality, all patients in Canada are free to select the physician of their choice (Marmor & Mashaw, 1990).

Nonetheless, government efforts to control the numbers of medical students and the total number of physicians will still result in a surplus number of physicians in general practice and medical specialties and a shortage in surgical and laboratory specialists by the year 2000 (Taylor, 1990). At the same time, there are questions as to whether family practitioners are, in fact, reaching those members of the population most in need of care (Eyles et al., 1995). These findings raise serious questions regarding not only the distribution of physicians, but also of the ability of the Canadian health-care system to provide effectively for its citizens.

Financially, Canada has the second highest percentage of gross domestic product (GDP) spent on health care (the United States is first). However, physician expenditure per capita is 60% of the United States (Schieber et al., 1991). Although some changes in Canada address the broad health-care system, others have a direct impact on the physicians. For instance, there is discussion of imposing a user fee in an effort to reduce the number of visits to physicians (Graig, 1993). Thus, regardless of country, the role of physicians and the physician–patient relationship within the larger health-care system is being changed.

Great Britain

Physicians in Great Britain provide a contrasting view of the relationship between the state and the medical profession. Here, most physicians are employees of the national government and work within the National Health System (NHS). There are significantly fewer physicians per 1,000 population in Great Britain than the United States (1.4 versus 2.3). Great Britain also spends considerably less as a percentage of GDP on health care (approximately one-half of the amount spent by the U.S.) (Schieber et al., 1991). Most physicians are general practitioners and provide care on a capitation (per head) basis. Medical education is developed around (1) the hospital consultant, (2) the general practitioner, and (3) the public health doctor in community medicine. Medical school for all consists of a 5-year program with a 1-year internship. After receiving their license, they choose an area of medicine in which they spend their residency. Compared to the United States, areas of medicine are not as open. Many specialized areas are already full, making residency difficult, whereas other areas, such as geriatrics, provide considerable opportunities (Lassey et al., 1997, p. 23).

Historically, medicine as a profession in Great Britain has enjoyed a tenuous relationship with the national government. Most recently, efforts by the conservative governments of Margaret Thatcher and John Major have attempted to increase the surveillance and management of physicians (Larkin, 1993). Concomitantly, the 1980s witnessed an increasing percentage of patients who begin within the NHS but eventually become private-pay patients. These patients have the available funds to enjoy the security of the NHS and the speed associated with the ability to pay. Nationally, private-pay patients occupy less than 10% of all hospital beds (Organisation for Economic Co-Operation and Development, 1992). Efforts incorporating a free-market philosophy have been met with considerable skepticism (Lee & Etheridge, 1989).

Although there are a number of fundamental changes occurring, the future of medicine as a profession in Great Britain is secure. Nonetheless, the 1989 White Paper outlined changes between practitioners and patients. The changes allow large group practices to purchase those services (including hospital) necessary for their patients (OECD, 1992; Lassey et al., 1997). Increasing the competition for patients between general practitioners "is expected to make them more efficient health care providers and establish linkage between the primary and secondary sectors, as GPs coordinate the services provided to patients" (Graig, 1993, p. 162). The outcomes of these changes has yet to be understood.

Czech Republic

The role of the physician is next examined in the emerging free-market state of the Czech Republic. Physicians in the Czech Republic are rapidly making the transition from state employees to private practitioners. Physicians are also experiencing the effects of market forces on their skills. In other words, while the need for general practitioners continues, there is an oversupply in some specialty areas (partly because of their connection to the university system). Financially, however, the market economy has dramatically improved the salary of physicians who are in private practice (Lassey et al., 1997). This transition remains difficult for others without the requisite capital to establish a private practice (Heitlinger, 1993). Although short-term economic gains appear impressive for physicians, Massaro et al. (1994) suggest that the Czech Republic will need to examine a number of basic issues such as certification and licensure of their physician population.

Poland

Another country experiencing a rapid change to a free-market economy is Poland. On the one hand, Poland is similar to other former communist nations with a high percentage of physicians who are female. Poland is also quite unique in that one-half of the nations' physicians were killed during World War II, creating a continued shortage of practicing physicians. As a result, the current status of the physician in Poland is generally considered quite high (Lubicz & Wlodarczyk, 1988). Their status and limited numbers allow some of them to maintain two separate practice: a full-time day job as an employee of the state and a part-time private practice in the evening. Retired physicians are also allowed to work part-time in private practice (Roemer, 1991). In addition to a physician shortage, Poland is also experiencing a maldistribution of physicians (Wnuk-Lipinski, 1990), even though financial incentives were offered to those willing to practice in rural areas (Roemer, 1985). As the medical profession in Poland emerges from its post-communist structure and orientation, continued change would be expected.

Developing Nations

In addition to the previously mentioned nations, the emergence and role of the medical profession has been documented in developed as well as many developing nations. For example, Rosenthal and Frederick (1987), Roemer (1991), Hafferty and McKinlay (1993), and Lassey et al. (1997) analyze the emergence of physicians primarily in developed as well as a limited number of developing nations. For research within developing countries, see, for example, the classic works by Field (1957) in the erstwhile Soviet Union, or Sidel and Sidel (1973) in China. More recent works include that of Subedi and Subedi (1993), who address the role of physicians within the larger context of medicine in Nepal, or Akhtar and Azhar (1994), who document changes (and provide explanations) in the numbers of physicians in India and Zambia. Also, Schwabe (1995), in a comparative analysis of Cuba and the Dominican Republic, addresses the role of the physician within the context of each country. A particular problem within many developing nations is the continued "brain drain" of qualified health practitioners to developed nations such as the United States.

A Comparative Analysis Revisited

Based on material presented here, it is evident that regardless of the country investigated, "there is no *one* medical profession undergoing some universal and unidirectional process of professional ascension, maintenance, or decline" (Hafferty, 1995, p. 233). Within a comparative context, "the process of professionalization is influenced by the historical interplay of professional/state/market/cultural/

etiological/epidemiologic factors" (Hafferty, 1995, p. 233). At the same time, variables such as the role, education, and training create a degree of homogeneity among physicians, regardless of geographic location. For instance, Gallagher (1993) points out that (Western) medical school curriculum, goals, and attributes of medical education are relatively consistent throughout the world. Recognizing the significance of the physician, it is instructive to remember the context within which 20th century medicine (and the professionalization of physicians) emerged. For example, although McKinlay and McKinlay (1977) attribute only 3.5% of the gains made in infant mortality in the twentieth century to the role of medicine, they argue in support of earlier findings that suggest improvements in areas such as public health issues were of far greater importance. Thus, the increasing status of the physician throughout the 20th century must be understood within the framework of the larger medical community and its impact on the general public.

Perhaps one of the most consistent aspects of medicine has been the generally exclusive nature of who practiced medicine. In the following section, we examine the history of women in medicine, in the United States.

Women as Physicians

Historically, males have dominated the practice of medicine. Today, women constitute an increasing percentage of medical students. Women are also improving as a percentage of the total physician population. According to the data in Table 8.2, women made up 42% of first-year medical students in 1993–1994 and 40% of the total enrollment in medical school. Twenty-two years earlier, the percentages were 13.7 and 10.9, respectively. These numbers represent significant strides for women. As recently as the late 1950s, 5% of the physicians were women. More recently (1995–1996), Barzansky et al. (1996) identify the percentage of women entering the first-year class at 43.2 and the total percentage of women enrolled in medical school at 41.8%.

The History of Women as Physicians

The history of women as physicians in the United States begins with Elizabeth Blackwell, the first female to receive a medical degree, and Harriot Hunt, who is generally identified as the first female physician. Blackwell was admitted to the Geneva Medical School in upstate New York in 1847 and graduated in 1849 at the head of her class. Blackwell then moved to Paris to study obstetrics and gynecology because no American hospital would accept her. In 1857, Blackwell, her sister Emily, and Maria Zakrewska (a German physician) founded the New York Infirmary for Women and Children. Eight years later, the same three women founded the Women's Medical College of the New York Infirmary (Lopate, 1968). Encouraged by the admission of Blackwell, Hunt applied to the Harvard Medical School (1847) but was denied. Later (1850), she requested and was granted the right to attend

TABLE 8.2   First-Year and Total Enrollment of Women in Schools for Selected Health Occupations, According to Detailed Race and Hispanic Origin: United States, Academic Years 1971–1972, 1980–1981, 1990–1991, and 1993–1994

Enrollment, Occupation, Detailed Race, and Hispanic Origin	Women			
	1971–1972[1]	*1980–1981*	*1990–1991*	*1993–1994[2,3]*
First-year Enrollment		Percent of Students		
Allopathic Medicine[4]	13.7	28.9	38.8	42.2
White, non-Hispanic	—	27.4	37.7	40.0
Black, non-Hispanic	22.7	45.5	55.3	60.2
Hispanic	—	31.5	42.0	45.2
Mexican American	8.5	30.6	39.3	44.3
Mainland Puerto Rican	15.0	43.2	43.3	51.6
Other Hispanic[5]	—	29.7	43.3	44.5
American Indian	34.8	35.8	40.8	43.4
Asian	19.4	31.5	40.3	41.2
Total Enrollment				
Allopathic Medicine[3]	10.9	26.5	37.3	40.3
White, non-Hispanic	—	25.0	35.4	38.3
Black, non-Hispanic	20.4	44.3	55.8	58.2
Hispanic	—	30.1	39.0	42.6
Mexican American	9.5	26.4	38.5	39.9
Mainland Puerto Rican	17.1	35.9	43.1	43.2
Other Hispanic[5]	—	31.1	38.4	41.2
American Indian	23.8	28.5	42.6	45.3
Asian	17.9	30.4	37.7	40.2

Data are based on reporting by health professions associations.

[1] Total enrollments for registered nurse students are for 1972–1973.

[2] First-year enrollments for optometry and nursing students are for 1992–1993. Total enrollments for optometry are for 1992–1993.

[3] Data for pharmacy and allopathic medicine for the three Hispanic subgroups are for 1992–1993.

[4] Includes race and ethnicity unspecified.

[5] Includes Puerto Rican Commonwealth students.

Notes: Data not available on total enrollment of women in schools of pharmacy. Total enrollment data are collected at the beginning of the academic year, whereas first-year enrollment data are collected at the end of the academic year.

Source: AAMC Data Book: Statistical Information Related to Medical Education. Eds. Paul Jolly, PhD, and Dorothy M. Hudley. Association of American Medical Colleges, 1995. Reprinted with permission.

lectures without being admitted to the college (Walsh, 1977). The admission of Blackwell did, however, have an impact on medical school opportunities for other women. Shortly after the acceptance of Blackwell, the Central Medical College in Syracuse admitted three women. The Women's Medical College of Pennsylvania was founded in 1850 and the New England Female Medical College was chartered in Boston in 1856 (Morantz-Sanchez, 1985). The emergence of separate medical schools for women was in response to a lack of available medical training within preexisting institutions. Nonetheless, women continued to make advances throughout the final decades of the 19th century as hospitals began to open their doors to women physicians. Women were also increasingly accepted at many of the top medical schools across the country. For instance, women were accepted to the University of Michigan in 1870, Johns Hopkins in 1893, and Cornell in 1899 (Drachman, 1985). In addition to gaining access to formerly all-male institutions, 19 medical schools for women opened between 1850 and 1895 (Lopata, 1968). As a result, the total number of women as physicians continued to increase. By the end of the 19th century, women constituted some 10% of the total physician population. In Boston, 18% of the physicians were women (Morantz-Sanchez, 1992). This was a "golden age" of medicine for women (Walsh, 1977). As Morantz-Sanchez (1985, p. 161) suggests, one reason for the entrance of women into medicine involved the "broader 19th century movement toward self-determination in which all reformist women, from conservative social feminists to radical suffrage advocates, played a significant part." With the beginning of the 20th century, however, the relationship between the medical community and women began to change. By 1910, only two medical schools for women remained open. The closing of medical schools for women was not a consequence of the Flexner Report. The number of medical schools for women as well as number of students began their decline by the turn of the 20th century (Walsh, 1977). Furthermore, as increasing numbers of formerly all-male medical schools opened their doors, fewer women accepted their offer. The result was a continuing decline in the number of women entering medical school and as a percentage of all physicians. Eventually, women constituted only 5% of the total number of physicians in the United States. This percentage remained relatively constant (except for a large increase in the latter 1940s) until the early to mid-1960s, when enrollment of women in medical school began to increase and has continued to do so for some 30 years.

Explanations for the decrease in women as physicians at the beginning of the 20th century are varied. For example, in an overview of the literature, Morantz-Sanchez (1992) discusses explanations ranging from sexism as an institutional barrier (see Walsh, 1977) to a conflict between emerging professional values espousing "individualism, scientific objectivity, careerism, and rationality and their separate experience as women" (Morantz-Sanchez, 1992, p. 478). Lopata (1968) offers a rather different interpretation of the emergence of women physicians into the 20th century. Constructing two broad categories, Lopata (1968) locates a small but militant group of women that focused on addressing issues such as equal opportunity. Meanwhile, a larger group of women physicians were interested in maintaining the status quo by working within the system. The strain between women physicians in these two categories is illustrated by Lopata (1968, p. 20), who states that:

> those few women physicians in the twentieth century who have fought for equal rights or special arrangements for their sex have been an embarrassing minority to the larger group. Often the tone of protest has put them off more than the causes themselves, which they might readily agree.

As a result, there have been limited opportunities for women physicians in the United States. Throughout the 20th century the medical profession has been slow to accept and accommodate women physicians, and, when they have been accepted into the profession, women physicians continue to experience discrimination (Lopata, 1968).

Continued Gender-Based Differences

Although the number and percentage of women in medical school and the profession continues to increase today, gender differences regarding such issues as professional status continue to persist. For example, women are more likely to be found in specialty areas "with lower prestige and lower income, and those that involve shorter periods of training" (Bowman & Gross, 1995, p. 192). These areas include "anesthesiology and the five "P" specialties . . . pediatrics, psychiatry, pathology, preventive medicine (public health), and physical medicine and rehabilitation" (Bowman & Gross, 1995, p. 192; see also Martin et al., 1989). Although some differences exist today, a review of resident physicians by sex reveals general consistency (except for anesthesiology) with earlier observations (Graduate Medical Education, 1996).

In addition to the emergence (and eventual decline) of women as physicians, women "health-care providers" faced similar restraints regarding their role within the health-care community. This was especially evident among women engaged in the birthing process as midwives. Historically, midwives in the United States can be traced back to the colonial period. However, by the early 1800s, midwifery was increasingly becoming a male profession. In addition, upper-middle class women were turning to physicians during the birthing process (Starr, 1982). Nonetheless, midwives attended to one-half of all births through the early 1900s.

Additional transformations of physicians continue to occur. The changing role of the physician relative to demographics characteristics such as sex, race, and social class are examined in the following section.

The Changing Role of the Physician

Consider the image of a typical physician in America (or any) society today. What images have been constructed? In the late 1960s, "Marcus Welby, MD" gave us an image of a white male treating all of his adoring patients with fatherly care. Is that the image today? Consider the popular television series "ER" or "Chicago Hope." These programs depict physicians quite differently (although some stereotypes remain). Here, physicians are female as well as male, African American as well as Caucasian American. Many exhibit concern for patients while others appear less caring. In other words, our image of a physician today is less homogenized. Instead, our image represents the diversity that is increasingly evident within the medical profession as well as society. The data in Table 8.3 reflect one of the changing characteristics of physicians.

TABLE 8.3 Total Enrollment of Minorities in Schools for Selected Health Occupations, According to Detailed Race and Hispanic Origin: United States, Academic Years 1970–1971, 1980–1981, 1990–1991, and 1993–1994

Occupation, Detailed Race, and Hispanic Origin	Total Enrollment (%)			
	1970–1971[1]	1980–1981	1990–1991	1993–1994[2]
Allopathic Medicine				
All Races[3]	100.0	100.0	100.0	100.0
White, non-Hispanic	94.3	85.0	73.5	68.7
Black, non-Hispanic	3.8	5.7	6.5	7.4
Hispanic	0.5	4.2	5.4	6.0
Mexican American	—	1.5	1.7	2.2
Mainland Puerto Rican	—	0.5	0.7	0.7
Other Hispanic[4]	—	2.3	3.0	3.1
American Indian	0.0	0.3	0.4	0.5
Asian	1.4	3.0	12.9	16.1

Data are based on reporting by health professions associations.

[1] Data for osteopathic medicine, podiatry, and optometry are for 1971–1972. Data for pharmacy and registered nurses are for 1972–1973.

[2] Data for optometry are for 1992–1993. Data for podiatry excludes New York College of Podiatric Medicine.

[3] Includes race and ethnicity unspecified.

[4] Includes Puerto Rican Commonwealth students.

Note: Total enrollment data are collected at the beginning of the academic year.

Source: AAMC Data Book: Statistical Information Related to Medical Education. Eds. Paul Jolly, PhD, and Dorothy M. Hudley. Association of American Medical Colleges, 1995. Reprinted with permission.

Although data in Tables 8.1 and 8.2 indicate improvement for women and minorities within the medical profession, differential occupational opportunities based on sex or race continue to persist. Martin et al. (1989) point not only to gender differences in socialization to the medical profession, but also to economic and professional outcomes as well. For example, women physicians are more likely to choose lower status and pay specialty areas. Women physicians are also more likely to remain in academic medicine. However, women medical faculty are less likely to be promoted and receive tenure (Martin et al., 1989). More recent research indicates continued gender differentiation (DeAngeis & Johns, 1995; Tesch et al., 1995). Among practicing physicians, women earn less than their male counterparts. One explanation for the earnings differential is the number of hours worked per week. For instance, women physicians worked 9.2 hours less per week than did male physicians (Grant et al., 1990). However, this differential exists primarily among mothers with young children relative to other physicians. These findings also support the traditional gender-role socialization patterns that identify women as responsible for childrearing activities. Examining incomes of young physicians, Baker (1996) reports that young female physicians earned 14% less per hour than did men. Average income for young male physicians in 1990 was $155,400, whereas young female physicians earned, on average, $109,900. According to Baker, the income differences are attributable to "differences in hours worked, specialty, practice setting, and other characteristics" (1996, p. 963). Furthermore, Baker reports that income differences between young male and female physicians surveyed in 1986 had not changed after 4 years. These numbers reflect the impact of gender socialization as well as institutional discrimination.

Internationally, gender differences within the medical profession are similar to the United States. For example, 31% of French physicians were women, as were 55% of Czech physicians, 45% of Hungarian physicians, and 70% of Chinese physicians. In other countries, such as Mexico and Japan, women continue to increase their presence in medical schools. In the Netherlands and Sweden, women constitute more than 50% of the entering medical student body. Gender differences also exist in other countries regarding areas of specialization. Similar to the United States, women physicians in other countries are more likely to be found in primary care areas (Lassey et al., 1997). In the former Soviet Union, the majority of medical students and physicians are women (Roemer, 1993).

The increasing numbers of women in the medical profession and the persistent income and prestige gaps reflect not only continued gender-based power differentials, but also the influence of the state in maintaining such inequality. The continued divergence of specialty area and concomitant economic reward by sex further legitimates a two-tiered occupational model. One area within which such gender-based occupational differentiation can be understood is the relationship between the physician and his or her patients.

Physician–Patient Relationships

This may be hard to believe, but this author actually enjoys going to see his doctor. He has a bedside manner that evokes a genuine concern for me not only as a patient, but also as a human being. He believes that it is important to talk to his patients and to learn about *them,* not just their diseases. He is forever asking about my interests and the progression of my work. When he has completed his examination, we discuss the current status of the American and European health-care systems. Have I found the perfect doctor? No. Does it matter that I have a Ph.D. with a specialization in medical sociology? Does he spend more time with me because we are more alike than the next patient who is poor and on Medicaid? Consider the following statement by Little (1995, p. 18):

> Medical professionals are taught at school and university that precise language is a virtue, and they tend to admire those who can express themselves clearly and concisely. They also tend to like those patients who express themselves well and give a 'good history,' that is, a history which fits the pattern of a 'classical' story of a disease.

Although Little (1995) presents the "ideal patient," Glass (1996, p. 147) questions why the physician–patient relationship is experiencing adversity in the face of fundamental change. The problems with the relationship are grounded in (1) the difficult balance between rising technology and the practice of medicine, and (2) the changing organizational structure within which the relationship is carried out—in other words, the economics of medicine. One result is a continued strain between an increasingly technically competent physician and an increasingly active patient/consumer. The increase in "patient-centered medicine" (Laine & Davidoff, 1996) requires physicians to listen to and involve the patient in the decision-making process. Unfortunately, not all patients are accorded the same treatment and respect. Consider the following assessment of physician–patient relationships made by Brewster (1993, p. 1972): "When faced with people who differ from ourselves, or with 'difficult' patients, an easy way out is to seek a medical label for behavior that we cannot understand or control. How often do we base differential diagnoses on stereotypes?"

Although there are a number of characteristics that may distinguish the physician from his or her patient, one obvious difference is social class. Research by Barney et al. (1993) indicates that physicians respond to patient behavior depending on the social class of the physician and the particular circumstances involved. Analyzing data from the National Health Survey in Australia, Scott et al. (1996) report some treatment differences by physicians depending on the social class of the patient [more diagnostic tests and fewer prescriptions given to higher socioeconomic status (SES) patients].

In addition to social class, the sex of the physician and/or patient is also important. For example, Lurie et al., (1993) examined whether women related the sex of the physician to the utilization of preventive services. Their findings support the argument for same-sex relationships between physicians and patients. The authors also question the influence of SES in the eventual relationship. Scott et al. (1996) suggest that the sex of the patient may produce the same impact as low SES on the physician–patient relationship. Perhaps the most disturbing consequence of the physician–patient relationship is patient-initiated sexual harassment of female physicians. Research by Phillips and Schneider (1993) of family physicians in Ontario, Canada, found that three-fourths of the physicians experienced sexual harassment at least once in their career. Although much of the abuse occurred in emergency rooms, Phillips and Schneider found that more than one-half of the female physicians had been sexually abused by their own patients (who they continued to treat). Such interaction defies the intuitive belief of the presumed relationship between physician and patient.

In addition to characteristics such as sex and social class of the physician and patient, what other variables are related to this potentially difficult relationship? Perhaps the most basic element is that of communication. Mintz (1992) illustrates how medical terminology distances the physician from the patient—for example, the use of euphemisms, objectifying the patient by treating the disease rather than the patient ("the stomach cancer patient" instead of "John Smith, who has stomach cancer"). Although communication between physician and patient is considered central to the relationship, research by Wyatt (1991, p. 159) located only "168 articles on physician–patient relationships" between the years 1983 and 1989. Articles on physician–patient relationships constituted less that 1% of all articles published in any of the medical specialties. Conducting a content analysis of the 168 articles addressing the physician–patient relationship, Wyatt was able to classify them into 11 categories that ranged from 'recognition of a problem' to 'giving bad news' to 'cross-cultural communication.' The work of Wyatt reflects the unimportance attached to the communication process within the medical community. Concomitantly, Rowland-Morin and Carroll (1990) point to a growing literature indicating patient discontent with physician communication. As suggested earlier, the extent of communication between physician and patient is dependent on various criteria. One characteristic is the sex of the patient. Utilizing a feminist perspective of physician–patient relationships in the United States and Great Britain, Foster (1989, p. 340) identifies a number of problems for women. In particular, the medical profession attempts to "protect itself not only from unreasonable patient demands but even from reasonable patients who simply wish to play an active rather than a purely passive role in their own health care." The transition from passive to active participant is discussed further when models of the physician–patient relationship are examined. Developing a more active role requires change not only among physicians, but also among women. Todd (1989) suggests that when women are in a physician–patient relationship, they must learn to ask the right questions. A second characteristic associated with differential communication patterns is that of age. In particular, aging individuals experience communication difficulties with physicians. For example, Garrity and Lawson (1989) suggest that, relative to older patients, "subculture differences" interfere with the likelihood of patient compliance. Waitzkin (1991, p. 175) points out that communication between physician and aging patients "focuses on technical adjustments to psychotropic medications."

The physician–patient relationship is not limited to the United States or Great Britain. Research by Herselman (1996) indicates that barriers to communication in South Africa are similar those in the United States (e.g., social class, roles, status). As a result of sociodemographic differences, communication difficulties between patients in Third-World countries and their doctors are extensive (Homedes & Ugalde, 1993). Examining the physician–patient relationship in Mexico, Finkler and Correa (1996) discuss the importance of physician as educator.

In addition to the previously mentioned characteristics associated with the physician–patient relationship, numerous efforts to explain the associations have been made. For example, identifying the "ideal" physician–patient relationship, Veatch (1991, p. 34) refers to it as a friendship that "involves knowledge and even responsibility across a wide range of issues and many spheres of the individual's life." In reality, however, the stranger–physician relationship is what most patients encounter. This relationship is not endemic to the late 20th century. According to Katz (1984, p. 28), the history of medicine is replete with silence between doctor and patient that "bears testimony to physicians' inattention to their patients' right and need to make their own decisions."

Models of the Physician–Patient Relationship

In addition, a number of models have been constructed that attempt to explain the relationship between physician and patient. Three that are relatively similar are examined here. The first is by Szasz and Hollender (1956) and consists of three different forms of interaction between the physician and patient (see Table 8.4 for an outline).

The first type of interaction is referred to as the *activity–passivity model*. In this model, interaction is limited or nonexistent. The physician does something *to* or *for* the patient. An unconscious accident victim brought to an emergency room best exemplifies this model. The physicians are actively involved in saving the person's life. The patient is completely passive in this situation.

The second type of interaction is the *guidance-cooperation model*. This model is best exemplified by the onset of acute illness. The person becomes ill and in need of expert advice and analysis (the physician). The patient is expected to comply with the treatment regimen (cooperation). This is a learning situation, with the analogy of a parent teaching an adolescent child most appropriate.

Finally, the *mutual participation model*. This model requires equality between the actors. Szasz and Hollender (1956, p. 587) point out that this model requires "that participants (1) have approximately equal power, (2) be mutually interdependent (i.e., need each other), and (3) engage in activity that will be in some ways satisfying to both." This model is best applied to those patients capable of caring for themselves through knowledge of symptoms and appropriate lay responses. For example, this author is aware of the symptomology associated with diminished platelet counts (unexplained bruising, bleeding from the gums, and so forth). Szasz and Hollender (1956) also point out that this model is most appropriate when the physician and patient experience educational and intellectual similarities.

Veatch (1991) offers another broad model of physician–patient relationships. This model is designed around four basic themes that include the engineering model, the priestly model, the collegial model, and the contractual model.

TABLE 8.4 Three Basic Forms of the Physician–Patient Relationship

	Activity–Passivity	**Guidance–Cooperation**	**Mutual Participation**
Physician's Role	Does something to patient	Tells patient what to do	Helps patient to help self
Patient's Role	Recipient (unable to respond or inert)	Cooperator (obeys)	Participant in partnership (uses expert help)
Clinical Application	Anesthesia, acute trauma, coma, delirium, etc.	Acute infectious processes, etc.	Most chronic illnesses, psychoanalysis, etc.
Prototype of Model	Parent–infant	Parent–child (adolescent)	Adult–Adult

Source: T. S. Szasz and M. H. Hollender. (1956). The basic models of the doctor–patient relationship. *Archives in Internal Medicine, 97,* 585–592. Copyright © 1956, American Medical Association.

The Engineering Model.   This model presents the physician as an "engineer" who provides the patient with all the relevant information and options regarding the relationship. The physician is also described as a plumber; in other words, someone who fixes broken pipes or makes repairs without enquiring why the problem exists. The patient is allowed to make their own medical decisions and pick those values consistent with their actions.

The Priestly Model.   This model is similar to the paternalistic model established by Szasz and Hollender. Here, the physician is considered a "priest" who offers advice based on his status "as a physician." This model bestows all decision-making to the physician (as father figure) and removes the patient from the process.

The Collegial Model.   This model assumes that the physician–patient relationship is built on a common set of goals (the elimination of the disease) and equality between the participants. Although a worthy endeavor, social class, sex, race, ethnicity, and age differences between participants does not create an environment conducive to mutual respect grounded in similar needs.

The Contractual Model.   This model is based on an agreement between the physician and patient regarding the rights and obligations associated with each status. This model assures the integration of values and the proper balancing of decision-making between physician, patient, and the larger society.

Similarly, Emanuel and Emanuel (1992) offer another model of the physician–patient relationship. Again, four themes are identified: the paternalistic model, the informative model, the interpretative model, and the deliberative model.

The Paternalistic Model.   This model is similar to the priestly model developed by Veatch. The physician utilizes his or her skills and knowledge to assist the patient and alleviate the medical condition. Essentially, for the good of the patient, the physician acts on the patient and the medical condition (although the patient is given involvement in the process).

The Informative Model.   This model is similar to the "engineering" model developed by Veatch. In this model, the physician elucidates all available options and the patient picks the one he or she prefers (a cafeteria style). Here, physicians provide technical information without injecting their values into the possible options.

The Interpretive Model.   This model considers the physician as a cabinet advisor. That is, the physician offers advice to the patient regarding the medical condition. The physician also provides advice and direction relative to the patient's values. In this style, the patient maintains autonomy by learning who they are and what they want through the facilitation of the physician.

The Deliberative Model.   This model envisions the physician as teacher or friend of the patient. The physician assists the patient in understanding through a dialogue not only medical options, but also the value imperatives associated with each decision.

The Szasz–Hollender model attempts to address physician–patient changes vis-à-vis the medical care system. However, the Veatch model and the Emanuel and Emanuel model infuse a contractual and values-based orientation within any decision-making process between physician and patient. The implications of this shift are yet to be understood. Furthermore, efforts to illustrate the physician–patient relationship do not consider the broader implications associated with significant changes in the organizational structure of health-care delivery.

Future Trends

Because this material is examined in greater detail in later chapters, this section only begins to address the changes occurring within the American health-care system. Relative to this chapter, the physician–patient relationship is undergoing a fundamental economics-driven alteration. For instance, although research supports continuity of care as central to patient satisfaction (Weiss & Ramsey, 1989; Ward, 1991), Ben-Sira (1990) reminds us that the physician–patient relationship also includes an organizational structure with its own self-interests.

Issues Associated with Managed Care

Increasingly, the self-interests of **managed care** organizations have come to dominate the health-care industry in the United States. Beginning in the 1980s, managed care has also been exported to various European nations, resulting in increasingly two-tiered health-care systems.

Very broadly, managed care refers to a "widely diverse set of organizational and financial arrangements" (Schroeder, 1994, p. 239). More specifically, managed care consists of

> several institutional arrangements whereby all (or nearly all) services are coordinated under one administrative roof. The 'arrangements' can vary from owning everything to cobbling all the services together through a series of contrasts between distinct entities. The 'one roof' is typically a corporation, usually for-profit. That corporation can be an insurance company, a hospital, or hospital chain, or a large group of doctors. (Light, 1994, p. 344)

Under managed care, the physician loses some professional autonomy regarding the physician–patient relationship as well as power. For example, the length of the visit is blocked in time increments of 10 or 15 minutes. As a result, physicians are increasingly placed in an organizational gatekeeping function for their patients (Budrys, 1993), which alter the physician–patient interaction models addressed previously.

The training of physicians within a managed care environment creates unique challenges not only for the physician, but also for the medical school and its curriculum. One challenge is financial, as subsidies for medical education may be less available. The second challenge concerns the education necessary to work within a managed care (primarily for-profit) environment (Blumenthal & Thier, 1996). Veloski et al. (1996) point out that medical students gain experience in staff or group model health maintenance organizations (HMOs) instead of the more rapidly expanding for-profit managed care facilities. Regardless, the domination of American medicine by for-profit companies providing health care is a concern for physicians as well as for patients. Through a series of questions related to cost and quality, Brook et al. (1996) examine changes occurring within the American health-care system. One of their "solutions" is the implementation of questionnaires assessing the quality of care provided within managed care organizations. Although such an approach may benefit patients, the more fundamental issue is providing access to care. Because managed care is primarily a for-profit industry, the owners are interested in providing services to the most healthy and least expensive members of society. The interface between the "bottom line" and quality care will, perhaps, become increasingly clear as the managed care industry increases its domination of physicians and their patients.

Summary

Throughout this chapter, the historical emergence of medicine (among men and women) as a profession within the United States is detailed. In the process, a number of historical markers such as the Flexner Report are identified as the impetus for the increased level of professionalization. As a result, physicians have experienced changes regarding an improved social status, power, and income. Today, however, physicians in the United States are experiencing a diminished sense of control, autonomy, and income as a result of for-profit managed care. A cross-cultural overview of physician education and status is also presented.

In addition to the professionalization of medicine, this chapter also addresses the relationship between physician and patient. Ideally, the association between doctor and patient should be one of partnership and agreement. In reality, a number of models describe not only the functional relationship, but also the moral qualities associated with the decision-making process. This relationship is also dependent on socio-demographic characteristics such as the sex of the patient (and physician), age, and social class. As a result, any one of these qualities may enhance or diminish the overall effectiveness of the physician–patient relationship.

CHAPTER REVIEW

The following questions address material primarily from this chapter. However, it is important to understand how diverse topic areas are related. Therefore, some questions will force the reader to revisit material in previous chapters.

1. Outline the development of medicine in the United States.

2. Outline the development of women as physicians in the United States. What is the future for women in medicine?

3. How do other countries differ from the United States relative to the education and status of physicians? What do all of these countries have in common?

4. Health-care expenditures as a percentage of GDP rank Canada second only to the United States. However, Canadian per capita expenditures are 60% of the American total. Discuss the implications of these numbers relative to the medical profession.

5. Compare and contrast the three models of physician–patient interaction discussed in this chapter.

6. What impact will for-profit managed care have on the future of American physicians?

7. Consider concepts such as the sick role or Suchman's stages of illness behavior. How does the physician–patient relationship influence health outcomes? Explain the impact of sociodemographic variables relative to these outcomes.

8. Explain the interface between health behavior and the physician–patient relationship.

9. Why is there continued disparity between the sex of the physician and the area of specialization? What impact will managed care have on this inconsistency?

GLOSSARY

Flexner Report   authored by Abraham Flexner in the early 1900s, this report helped shape the medical profession by improving the overall quality and professional status of the physician.

managed care   an American effort to control the cost of health care by allowing (primarily) for-profit companies to provide health-care services to those clients who pay a monthly fee for health-care coverage.

SUGGESTED READINGS

Becker, H. S., Geer, B., Hughes, E. C., & Strauss, A. L. (1961). *Boys in white: Student culture in medical school.* Chicago: The University of Chicago Press.
   A classic that examines, as the title indicates, the changes medical students encounter as they progress through their 4 years of medical school.
Hafferty, F. W., and McKinlay, J. B. (Eds.). (1993b). *The changing medical profession: An international perspective.* New York: Oxford University Press.
   The editors provide an excellent theoretical and conceptual overview in the first four chapters before presenting case studies that address the ongoing struggles between the medical profession and the state.
Merton, R. K., Reader, G. G., & Kendall, P. L. (1957). *The student physician: Introductory studies in the sociology of medical education.* Cambridge, MA: Harvard University Press.
   Another classic that examines the expectations and outcomes associated with medical school training.
Rosenthal, M. M., & Frederick, D. (1987). Physician maldistribution in cross-cultural perspective: United States, United Kingdom, Sweden, and the People's Republic of China. *Research in the Sociology of Health Care, 5,* 101–136.
   This article offers the reader an opportunity to consider the physician within the broader context of the health-care system and cross-culturally.

Starr, P. (1982). *The social transformation of American medicine.* New York: Basic Books.
Perhaps the best sociohistorical analysis of medicine as a profession.

Walsh, M. R. (1977). *Doctors wanted: No women need apply.* New Haven, CT: Yale University Press.
Here is an excellent examination of the sexual–political constraints imposed on women who were interested in the medical profession.

REFERENCES

Akhtar, R., & Izhar, N. (1994). Spatial inequalities and historical evolution in health provision: Indian and Zambian examples. In D. R. Phillips & Y. Verhasselt (Eds.). *Health and development* (pp. 216–233). London: Routledge.

American Association of Medical Colleges. (1996). "Project 3000 X 2000 Year Four Progress Report." [April, 1996, pp. 1–15] [www.aamc.org] (2/18/98).

Baker, L. C. (1996). Differences in earnings between male and female physicians. *The New England Journal of Medicine, 334,* 15, 960–964.

Barney, J. A., Fredericks, J., Fredericks, M., & Robinson, P. (1993). Social class of physicians: Attitudes toward health care. *Education, 113,* 3, 497–502.

Barrett-Litoff, J. (1992). Midwives and history. In R. M. Apple (Ed.). *Women, health & medicine in America: A historical handbook* (pp. 435–450). New Brunswick, NJ: Rutgers University Press.

Barzansky, B., Jonas, H. S., & Etzel, S. I. (1996). Educational programs in US medical schools, 1995–1996. *Journal of the American Medical Association, 276,* 9, 714–719.

Becker, H. S., Geer, B., Hughes, E. C., & Strauss, A. L. (1961). *Boys in white: Student culture in medical school.* New Brunswick, NJ: Transaction Books.

Ben-Sira, Z. (1990). Universal entitlement for health care and its implications on the doctor–patient relationship: A new perspective on medical care. *Advances in Medical Sociology, 1,* 99–128.

Block, S. D., Clark-Chiarelli, N., Peters, A. S., & Singer, J. D. (1996). Academia's chilly climate for primary care. *Journal of the American Medical Association, 276,* 9, 677–682.

Bloom, S. W. (1988). Structure and ideology in medical education: An analysis of resistance to change. *Journal of Health and Social Behavior, 29,* 294–306.

Blumenthal, D., & Thier, S. O. (1996). Managed care and medical education: The new fundamentals. *Journal of the American Medical Association, 276,* 9, 725–727.

Bowman, M., & Gross, M. L. (1995). Overview of research on women in medicine: Issues for public policymakers. In W. G. Rothstein (Ed.). *Readings in American health care: Current issues in socio-historical perspective* (pp. 190–198). Madison, WI: The University of Wisconsin Press.

Brewster, A. (1993). Occasional notes: A student's view of a medical teaching exercise. *The New England Journal of Medicine, 329,* 26, 1971–1972.

Brook, R. H., Kamberg, C. J., & McGlynn, E. A. (1996). Health system reform and quality. *Journal of the American Medical Association, 276,* 6, 476–480.

Budrys, G. (1993). Coping with change: Physicians in prepaid practice. *Sociology of Health and Illness, 15,* 3, 355–374.

Bullough, B., & Bullough, V. (1972). A brief history of medical practice. In E. Freidson & J. Lorber (Eds.). *Medical men and their work* (pp. 86–102). Chicago: Aldine.

Cassedy, J. H. (1991). *Medicine in America: A short history.* Baltimore: The Johns Hopkins University Press.

Coburn, D. (1993a). State authority, medical dominance, and trends in the regulation of the health professions: The Ontario case. *Social Science and Medicine, 37,* 2, 129–138.

Coburn, D. (1993b). Professional powers in decline: Medicine in a changing Canada. In F. W. Hafferty & J. B. McKinlay (Eds.). *The changing medical profession: An international perspective* (pp. 92–103). New York: Oxford.

Colombotos, J. (1988). Continuities in the sociology of medical education: An introduction. *Journal of Health and Social Behavior, 29,* 271–278.

Conrad, P. (1988). Learning to doctor: Reflections on recent accounts of the medical school years. *Journal of Health and Social Behavior, 29,* 323–332.

Cooper, R. A. (1994). Seeking a balanced physician workforce for the 21st century. *Journal of the American Medical Association, 272,* 9, 680–687.

Davis, J. A., & Smith, T. W. *General social surveys, 1972–1996* [machine-readable data file]. Principal Investigator, James A. Davis; Director and Co-Principal Investigator, Tom W. Smith. NORC Ed. Chicago: National Opinion Research Center, producer, 1996; Storrs, CT: The Roper Center for Public Opinion Research, University of Connecticut, distributor. 1 data file (35,284 logical records) and 1 codebook (1295 pp).

DeAngelis, C. D. (1995). Promotion of women in academic medicine: Shatter the ceilings, polish the floors. *Journal of the American Medical Association, 273,* 13, 1056–1057.

Drachman, V. G. (1985). Female solidarity and professional success: The dilemma of women doctors in late 19th-century America. In J. W. Leavitt & R. L. Numbers (Eds). *Sickness and health in America: Readings in the history of medicine and public health* (pp. 173–182). Madison, WI: The University of Wisconsin Press.

Duffy, J. (1993). *From humors to medical science: A history of American medicine* (2nd Ed.). Urbana, IL: University of Illinois Press.

Ebert, R. H. (1977). Medical education in the United States. In J. H. Knowles (Ed.). *Doing better and feeling worse: Health in the United States* (pp. 171–184). New York: W.W. Norton.

Emanuel, E. J., & Emanuel, L. L. (1992). Four models of the physician–patient relationship. *Journal of the American Medical Association, 267,* 16, 2221–2226.

Eyles, J., Birch, S., & Newbold, K. B. (1995). Delivering the goods? Access to family physician services in Canada: A comparison of 1985 and 1991. *Journal of Health and Social Behavior, 36,* 4, 322–332.

Field, M. G. (1957). *Doctor and patient in Soviet Russia.* Cambridge, MA: Harvard University Press.

Field, M.G. (1980). The health system and the polity: A contemporary American dialectic. *Social Science and Medicine, 14A,* 397–413.

Finkler, K., & Correa, M. (1996). Factors influencing patient perceived recovery in Mexico. *Social Science and Medicine, 42,* 2, 199–207.

Foster, P. (1989). Improving the doctor/patient relationship: A feminist perspective. *Journal of Social Policy, 18,* 3, 337–361.

Fox, R. C. (1957). Training for uncertainty. In R. K. Merton, G. G. Reader, & P. L. Kendall (Eds). *The student physician: Introductory studies in the sociology of medical education* (pp. 207–241). Cambridge, MA: Harvard University Press.

Fox, R. C. (1988). *Essays in medical sociology: Journeys into the field* (2nd Ed.) (Enlarged). New Brunswick, NJ: Transaction Books.

Fox, R. C. (1989). *The sociology of medicine: A participant observer's view.* Englewood Cliffs, NJ: Prentice-Hall.

Frenk, J., & Duran-Arenas, L. (1993). The medical profession and the state. In F. W. Hafferty & J. B. McKinlay (Eds.). *The changing medical profession: An international perspective* (pp. 25–42). New York: Oxford University Press.

Gallagher, E. B. (1993). Goals and aspirations in a new Arab medical college. In P. Conrad & E. B. Gallagher (Eds.). *Health and health care in developing countries: Sociological perspectives* (pp. 135–153). Philadelphia: Temple University Press.

Garrity, T. F., & Lawson, E. J. (1989). Patient–physician communication as a determinant of medication misuse in older, minority women. *The Journal of Drug Issues, 19,* 2, 245–259.

Glass, R. M. (1996). Editorial: The patient–physician relationship: *JAMA* focuses on the center of medicine. *Journal of the American Medical Association, 275,* 2, 147–148.

Good, M. D., & Good, B. J. (1989). Disabling practitioners: Hazards of learning to be a doctor in American medical education. *American Journal of Orthopsychiatry, 59,* 2, 303–309.

Goode, W. J. (1960). The profession: Reports and opinion. *American Sociological Review, 25,* 6, 902–914.

Graduate Medical Education. (1996). *Journal of the American Medical Association,* Appendix II, Table 1, 276, 9, 739–748.

Graig, L. A. (1993). *Health of nations: An international perspective on U.S. health care reform* (2nd Ed.). Washington, DC: Congressional Quarterly Inc.

Grant, L., Simpson, L. A., Rong, X. L., & Peters-Golden, H. (1990). Gender, parenthood, and work hours of physicians. *Journal of Marriage and the Family, 52,* 39–49.

Hafferty, F. W. (1988). Physician oversupply as a socially constructed reality. *Journal of Health and Social Behavior, 27,* 4, 358–369.

Hafferty, F. W. (1991). *Into the valley: Death and the socialization of medical students.* New Haven, CT: Yale Universtity Press.

Hafferty, F. W. (1995). Medicine as a profession: Lessons from some cross-national case studies. In E. B. Gallagher & J. Subedi (Eds.). *Global perspectives on health care* (pp. 231–243). Englewood Cliffs, NJ: Prentice-Hall.

Hafferty, F. W., & Light, D. W. (1995). Professional dynamics and the changing nature of medical work. *Journal of Health and Social Behavior* (Extra Issue), 132–153.

Hafferty, F. W., & McKinlay, J. B. (Eds). (1993b). *The changing medical profession: An international perspective.* New York: Oxford.

Hafferty, F. W., & McKinlay, J. B. (1993a). Conclusion: Cross-cultural perspectives on the dynamics of medicine as a profession. In F. W. Hafferty & J. B. McKinlay (Eds.). *The changing medical profession: An international perspective.* New York: Oxford.

Heitlinger, A. (1993). The medical profession in Czechoslovakia: Legacies of state socialism, prospects for the capitalist future. In F. W. Hafferty & J. B. McKinlay (Eds.). *The changing medical profession: An international perspective* (pp. 172–183). New York: Oxford.

Herselman, S. (1996). Some problems in health communication in a multicultural clinical setting: A South African experience. *Health Communication, 8,* 2, 153–170.

Homedes, N., & Ugalde, A. (1993). Patients' compliance with medical treatments in the Third World. What do we know? *Health Policy and Planning, 8,* 4, 291–314.

Hughes, R. G., Barker, D. C., & Reynolds, R. C. (1991). Are we mortgaging the medical profession? *The New England Journal of Medicine, 325,* 6, 404–407.

Katz, J. (1984). *The silent world of doctor and patient.* New York: The Free Press.

Kendall, P. L., & Reader, G. R. (1988). Innovations in medical education of the 1950s contrasted with those of the 1970s and 1980s. *Journal of Health and Social Behavior, 29,* 279–293.

Kindig, D. A., & Libby, D. (1994). How will graduate medical education reform affect specialties and geographic areas? *Journal of the American Medical Education, 272,* 1, 37–42.

Krishnan, V. (1992). A macro model of change in specialty and spatial distribution of physicians in Canada, 1971–1981. *Social Science and Medicine, 26,* 2, 111–127.

Laine, C., & Davidoff, F. (1996). Patient-centered medicine: A professional evolution. *Journal of the American Medical Association, 275,* 2, 152–156.

Larkin, G. V. (1993). Continuity in change: Medical dominance in the United Kingdom. In F. W. Hafferty & J. B. McKinlay (Eds.). *The changing medical profession: An international perspective* (pp. 81–91). New York: Oxford.

Lassey, M. L., Lassey, W. R., & Jinks, M. J. (1997). *Health care systems around the world: Characteristics, issues, reforms.* Upper Saddle River, NJ: Prentice-Hall.

Lee, P. R., & Etheridge, L. (1989). Clinical freedom: Two lessons for the UK from US experience with privatisation of health care. *The Lancet,* February 4, 263–265.

Light, D. W. (1988). Toward a new sociology of medical education. *Journal of Health and Social Behavior, 29,* 307–322.

Light, D. W. (1994). Managed care: False and real solutions. *The Lancet, 344,* 1197–1199.

Little, M. (1995). *Humane medicine.* Cambridge, UK: Cambridge University Press.

Lopate, C. (1968). *Women in medicine.* Baltimore: The Johns Hopkins Press.

Lubicz, M., & Wlodarczyk, W. C. (1988). Poland. In R. B. Saltman (Ed.). *The international handbook of health-care systems.* New York: Greenwood Press.

Ludmerer, K. M. (1985). *Learning to heal: The development of American medical education.* Baltimore: The Johns Hopkins University Press.

Lurie, N., Slater, J., McGovern, P., Ekstrum, J., Quam, L., & Margolis, K. (1993). Preventive care for women: Does the sex of the physician matter? *The New England Journal of Medicine, 329,* 7, 478–482.

Marmor, T. R., & Mashaw, J. L. (1992). Canada's health insurance and ours: The real lessons, the big choices. *The American Prospect,* Fall, 3, 18–29.

Martin, S. C., Arnold, R. M., & Parker, R. M. (1989). Gender and socialization. *Journal of Health and Social Behavior, 29,* 333–343.

Martini, C. J. M., Veloski, J. J., Barzansky, B., Xu, G., & Fields, S. K. (1994). Medical schools and student characteristics that influence choosing a generalist career. *Journal of the American Medical Association, 272,* 9, 661–668.

Massaro, T. A., Nemec, J., & Kalman, I. (1994). Health system reform in the Czech Republic: Policy lessons from the initial experience of the general health insurance company. *Journal of the American Medical Association, 271,* 23, 1870–1874.

McKinlay, J. B., & McKinlay, S. M. (1977). The questionable contribution of medical measures to the decline of the mortality in the United States in the twentieth century. *Milbank Memorial Fund Quarterly, 55,* Summer, 405–428.

McKinlay, J. B., & Stoeckle, J. D. (1988). Corporatization and the social transformation of doctoring. *International Journal of Health Services, 18,* 2, 191–205.

Merton, R. K., Reader, G. G., & Kendall, P. L. (1957). *The student physician: Introductory studies in the sociology of medical education.* Cambridge, MA: Harvard University Press.

Mintz, D. (1992). What's in a word: The distancing function of language in medicine. *The Journal of Medical Humanities, 13,* 4, 223–233.

Morantz-Sanchez, R. M. (1985). The "connecting link": The case for the woman doctor in 19th-century America. In J. W. Leavitt & R. L. Numbers (Eds). *Sickness and health in America: Readings in the history of medicine and public health* (pp. 161–172). Madison, WI: University of Wisconsin Press.

Morantz-Sanchez, R. M. (1992). Physicians. In R. D. Apple (Ed). *Women, health, and medicine in America: A historical handbook* (pp. 469–487). New Brunswick, NJ: Rutgers University Press.

National Center for Health Statistics. (1996). *Health, United States, 1995.* Hyattsville, MD: Public Health Service.

Organisation for Economic Co-Operation and Development. (1992). *The reform of health care: A comparative analysis of seven OECD countries.* Paris: OECD.

Organisation for Economic Co-Operation and Development. (1994). *The reform of health care systems: A review of seventeen OECD countries.* Paris: OECD.

Phillips, S. P., & Schneider, M. S. (1993). Sexual harassment of female doctors by patients. *The New England Journal of Medicine, 329,* 26, 1936–1939.

Pol, L. G., & Thomas, R. K. (1992). *The demography of health and health care.* New York: Plenum Press.

Richman, J. A., & Flaherty, J. A. (1990). Gender differences in medical student distress: Contributions of prior socialization and current role-related stress. *Social Science and Medicine, 30,* 7, 777–787.

Roemer, M. I. (1991). *National health systems of the world: Volume 1—The countries.* New York: Oxford.

Roemer, M. I. (1993). *National health systems of the world: Volume II—The issues.* New York: Oxford.

Rosenthal, M. M., & Frederick, D. (1987). Physician maldistribution in cross-cultural perspective: United States, United Kingdom, Sweden and the People's Republic of China. *Research in the Sociology of Health Care, 5,* 101–136.

Rosenthal, M. P., Diamond, J. J., Rabinowitz, H. K., Bauer, L. C., Jones, R. L., Kearl, G. W., Kelly, R. B., Sheets, K. J., Jaffe, A., Jonas, A. P., & Ruffin, M. T. (1994). Influence of income, hours worked, and loan repayment on medical students' decision to pursue a primary care career. *Journal of the American Medical Association, 271,* 12, 914–917.

Rothstein, W. G. (1987). *American medical schools and the practice of medicine: A history.* New York: Oxford University Press.

Rowland-Morin, P. A., & Carroll, J. G. (1990). Verbal communication skills and patient satisfaction: A study of doctor–patient interviews. *Evaluation and the Health Professions, 13,* 2, 168–185.

Salsberg, E. S., Wing, P., Dionne, M. G., & Jeriolo, D. J. (1996). Graduate medical education and physician supply in New York State. *Journal of the American Medical Association, 276,* 9, 683–688.

Schieber, G. J., Poullier, J.-P., & Greenwald, L. M. (1991). Health care systems in twenty-four countries. *Health Affairs,* Fall, 22–38.

Schroeder, S. A. (1994). The latest forecast: Managed care collides with physician supply. *Journal of the American Medical Association, 272,* 3, 239–240.

Schwabe, A. M. (1995). International dependency and health: A comparative case study of Cuba and the Dominican Republic. In E. B. Gallagher & J. Subedi (Eds.). *Global perspectives on health care* (pp. 292–310). Englewood Cliffs, NJ: Prentice-Hall.

Scott, A., Shiell, A., & King, M. (1996). Is general practitioner decision making associated with patient socio-economic status? *Social Science and Medicine, 42,* 1, 35–46.

Seifer, S. D., Vranizan, K., & Grumbach, K. (1995). Graduate medical education and physician practice location. *Journal of the American Medical Association, 274,* 9, 685–691.

Seifer, S. D., Troupin, B., & Rubenfeld, G. D. (1996). Changes in marketplace demand for physicians. *Journal of the American Medical Association, 276,* 9, 695–699.

Sidel, V. W., & Sidel, R. (1973). *Serve the people: observations on medicine in the People's Republic of China.* New York: Josiah Macy Jr. Foundation.

Somers, H. M., & Somers, A. R. (1961). *Doctors, patients, and health insurance: The organization and financing of medical care.* Washington, DC: The Brookings Institute.

Starr, P. (1982). *The social transformation of American medicine.* New York: Basic Books.

Subedi, J., & Subedi, S. (1993). The contribution of modern medicine in a traditional system: The case of Nepal. In P. Conrad & E. B. Gallagher (Eds.). *Health and health care in developing countries: Sociological perspectives* (pp. 109–121). Philadelphia: Temple University Press.

Sullivan, R. B., Watanabe, M., Whitcomb, M. E., & Kindig, D. A. (1996). The evolution of divergences in physician supply policy in Canada and the United States. *Journal of the American Medical Association, 276,* 9, 704–709.

Szasz, T. S., & Hollender, M. H. (1956). The basic models of the doctor–patient relationship. *Archives in Internal Medicine, 97,* 585–592.

Taylor, M. G. (1990). *Insuring national health care: The Canadian experience.* Chapel Hill, NC: The University of North Carolina Press.

Tesch, B. J., Wood, H. M., Helwig, A. L., & Nattinger, A. B. (1995). Promotion of women physicians in academic medicine: Glass ceiling or sticky floor? *Journal of the American Medical Association, 273,* 13, 1022–1025.

Todd, A. D. (1989). *Intimate adversaries: Cultural conflict between doctors & women patients.* Philadelphia: University of Pennsylvania Press.

U.S. Bureau of the Census. (1996). *Statistical Abstract of the United States: 1996* (116th Ed.). Washington, DC.

Veatch, R. M. (1991). *The patient–physician relation: The patient as partner, part 2.* Bloomington, IN: Indiana University Press.

Veloski, J., Barzansky, B., Nash, D. B., Bastacky, S., & Stevens, D. P. (1996). Medical student education in managed care settings: Beyond HMOs. *Journal of the American Medical Association, 276,* 9, 667–671.

Waitzkin, H. (1991). *The politics of medical encounters: How patients and doctors deal with social problems.* New Haven, CT: Yale University Press.

Walsh, M. R. (1977). *Doctor's wanted: No women need apply.* New Haven, CT: Yale University Press.

Ward, R. A. (1991). Patient/provider ties and satisfaction with health care. *Research in the Sociology of Health Care, 9,* 169–190.

Weeks, W. B., Wallace, A. E., Wallace, M. M., & Welch, H. G. (1994). A comparison of the educational costs and incomes of physicians and other professionals. *New England Journal of Medicine, 330,* 18, 1280–1286.

Weiss, G. L., & Ramsey, C. A. (1989). Regular source of primary medical care and patient satisfaction. *Quality Review Bulletin, 15,* 6, 180–184.

Whitcomb, M. E. (1995). A cross-national comparison of generalist physician workforce data: Evidence for US supply adequacy. *Journal of the American Medical Association, 274,* 9, 692–695.

Wnuk-Lipinski, E. (1990). The Polish country profile: Economic crisis and inequalities in health. *Social Science and Medicine, 31,* 8, 859–866.

World Health Organization. (1995). *The World Health Report: Bridging the gaps.* Geneva, Switzerland.

Wyatt, N. (1991). Physician–patient relationships: What do doctors say? *Health Communications, 3,* 3, 157–174.

Within the context of gender-divided America, nursing provided a place in medicine for women and women's work, needed but not honored. Segregated as nurses, women did their traditional tasks—caretaking, managing, coordinating disparate parts, attempting to meet everyone's needs no matter how much they conflicted with one another, and never quite achieving their impossible goals. Now American society moves further and further away from honoring women's roles. As our most talented women strive to approximate more and more the life patterns of men, the women's traditions inherent to nursing are in danger of extinction or of being relegated to the interpretation and practice of less gifted people.

—Baer, 1992, p. 466

The Realities of Nursing

This chapter examines what is perhaps one of the least respected medical professions: nursing. Not surprisingly, nursing historically has been an occupation for women, whereas males dominate primarily all other medical professions. The importance of this chapter is located in the ongoing differentiation of opportunities based on gender. Regardless of the historical period, women have been relegated to perceived secondary occupations, with commensurate salaries and status. In particular, nursing, as a predominantly female occupation, has fit this description. The consequences of gender-specific occupational stratification are understood in the ongoing difficulties associated with efforts to professionalize nursing. Furthermore, nursing (as well as Chapter 8 on physicians) is connected to the final section of the book. For example, as a labor-intensive occupation within an increasingly expensive health-care industry, there have been efforts to undermine the professionalization movement by hiring less-qualified staff to perform nursing duties.

The History of Nursing

There is no historical benchmark that signifies "This is when nursing began." Instead, as Baer (1992) suggests, nursing has been a gender-specific occupation grounded in particular behavioral patterns consistent with societal expectations of women. For example, Roemer (1993, p. 19) states that "from the earliest times, however, in a family's home, the women took care of sick relatives." Thus, "nursing" is presented as an extension of traditionally defined women's roles and is one of many problems for the profession today. In fact, the word "nurse" has its roots in middle English and Old French, but ultimately the Latin word *nutricius,* or nurturing (Kalish & Kalish, 1978).

The history of nursing is consistent with the history of medicine. Kalish and Kalish (1978) outline, in broad detail, the history of nursing using virtually the same historical periods found earlier in Chapter 2. Although unnecessary to revisit these historical periods, it is interesting to note that Benedictine monks provided nursing services during the Crusades (11th to 13th centuries). Known as the Knights Hospitalers of St. John of Jerusalem, they provided care not only to pilgrims, but also to the poor. Founded in 1050 in Jerusalem, the Knights of St. John represented one of three military orders of men providing nursing services. Nursing consisted of providing services that were "mainly custodial and palliative (aimed at reducing the severity of the symptoms) rather than treatment-oriented" (Mitchell & Grippando, 1993, p. 7). Over time however, Hospitalers began to assume a new role: that of fighting nurses that became legendary during the Crusades as they defended their hospitals and patients. According to Ellis and Hartley (1992, p. 26), the Knights "wore a suit of armor under their habits" as they defended the Holy Land. On their habits was a Maltese cross that eventually became the current nursing pin (Ellis & Hartley, 1992). Enlisting women into the order of Hospitaler Dames, a large number of additional hospitals were eventually founded to serve the order (Kalish & Kalish, 1978). Finally, because medicine was "out of favor" with the Catholic Church, many hospitals of this time had limited physician services available (Mitchell & Grippando,1993).

Moving forward to the 19th century, modern nursing emerged in the mid-1830s, primarily through the efforts of Theodor Fleidner, a pastor in Kaiserwerth, Germany. In need of "nurses for his new infirmary" (Kalish & Kalish, 1978, p. 32), Fleidner revived the deaconess movement as he and his wife began educating women as nurses at the Deaconess Institute at Kaiserwerth. Briefly, the Deaconess movement has its origins in the early years of the Eastern Church. Composed of women who were either widowed or unmarried, the Deaconess movement involved performing "works of mercy" toward those most in need of assistance. In their efforts to assist those most in need of food, shelter, and clothing, these deaconesses are considered "early counterparts to the community health nurses of today" (Ellis & Hartley, 1992, p. 24). The most famous student to train at Kaiserwerth was **Florence Nightingale,** who was born in 1820 into a wealthy English family. Because of her social position, Florence was not only well traveled, but also well educated. At an early age, Florence expressed an interest in becoming a nurse. Early training at an English hospital was followed by further training in Alexandria, Egypt, and eventually in 1850, Florence went to Kaiserwerth for a short period of time. She returned the following year and remained for 3 years of training (Kalish & Kalish, 1978). Initially unimpressed with the process and content of Kaiserwerth, Florence used the experience to shape what would eventually become her approach to nursing (Smith, 1982).

Returning to England, Nightingale became the supervisor of the Establishment for Gentlewomen that became a hospital for women. A year later, Nightingale was asked by the Secretary of War to visit the Crimea and reform the care of sick and wounded soldiers. With the aid of some three dozen nurses, Nightingale was able to reduce the death rate in one hospital from 42.7% to 2.2% within a 6-month period of time (Hamilton, 1992). Interestingly, Mary Grant Seacole, a black nurse practicing in Jamaica, requested permission from the British government to join Nightingale as a nurse in the Crimea. Although Nightingale refused to accept her as one of her nurses, Seacole traveled to the Crimea and worked evenings as a volunteer with Nightingale (Carnegie, 1995). Returning to England, Nightingale was considered a hero by many. Through the Nightingale Fund, sufficient resources were raised to pay for a residence hall for students enrolled in the Nightingale School of Nursing at St. Thomas Hospital. The school is credited as the first "modern" school of nursing (Mitchell & Grippando, 1993). Nightingale continued her efforts to reform the military system of nursing. Analyzing mortality rates of British troops stationed in India, Nightingale concluded that many of the problems experienced by the military medical system in the Crimean War remained problematic in India. For example, she identified environmental problems associated with the hospital itself as well as behavioral characteristics of the patients such as "diet, exercise, [and] alcohol consumption" (Hays, 1989, p. 152). Her efforts, however, were met with considerable opposition within the army. Again, over time, she was successful in the implementation of new rules and regulations regarding the care of military patients (Smith, 1982; Hays, 1989).

What did Florence Nightingale prescribe? Not an ardent supporter of the germ theory, Nightingale instead believed that illnesses developed without warning. Relative to nurses and their role within the medical community, Nightingale believed that "nurses should spend their time caring for patients, not doing menial jobs, that they should be educated, use their knowledge to improve patient care, have social standing, and continue to learn throughout life" (Hamilton, 1992, p. 22). Nightingale also distinguished between the roles of females and nurses when she declared that "it has been said and written scores of times, that every woman makes a good nurse. I believe, on the contrary, that the very elements of nursing are all but unknown" (Nightingale, 1960, p. 455 [1859]). Furthermore, Nightingale believed in the use of fresh air, light, and warmth for the patient as treatment modalities for illness (Baly, 1986). Nightingale also "emphasized character training and strict discipline . . . and a female hierarchy with deference and loyalty to physician authority" (Reverby, 1987, p. 43).

Following the success of Nightingale, nursing (and nursing programs) increased and improved in status. The Nightingale School of Nursing was exported throughout the world. In addition to the development of the Nightingale System throughout England and the European continent in the latter 19th and early 20th centuries, Abu-Saad (1979) also outlines the emergence of modern nursing and nursing education in eastern European countries, Latin America, and the Near and Far East (see also Dock, 1912 for an early 20th century assessment of nursing programs throughout Europe and the Far East). The role and impact of blacks on nursing in various African nations, the Caribbean, as well as the United States is examined by Carnegie (1995). This transcontinental overview provides a glimpse into the broader changes occurring within the medical profession of most countries during this period of time.

Nursing in the United States

Nightingale nursing arrived in the United States in 1873 with the opening of "Bellevue Hospital Training School in New York, Massachusetts Hospital Training School in Boston, and the Connecticut Training School in New Haven" (Mitchell & Grippando, 1993, p. 25). During these early years of nursing, students attending these early schools were, like Nightingale, drawn from upper-class families and college educated. With the rise of the feminist movement, nursing was viewed as an appropriate career among these women (Mitchell & Grippando, 1993). Although an earlier school had been established in 1861 at the Women's Hospital in Philadelphia, it was not initially successful (Abu-Saad, 1979). Similar to the Crimean War and the rise of Florence Nightingale, the American Civil War highlighted the important contributions made by female nurses (for a biography of the more significant nurses in the United States during the latter 1800s and early 1900s, see Yost, 1947).

Nursing and Minorities

Beginning in the latter half of the 19th and throughout the 20th century, African American women have made a particular contribution to the world of nursing. Although many African American women worked as nurses for years, Mary Eliza Mahoney was the first African American women to earn a professional nursing diploma from the New England Hospital for Women and Children in 1879. Almost 100 years earlier, James Derham of New Orleans worked as a nurse, and with his earnings bought his freedom, and became the first African American physician in the United States (Carnegie, 1995). Others followed, as some 200 African American hospitals and nursing schools were established by the 1920s. As with all public policy at the time, racial quotas and discrimination were part of everyday life for African Americans. For example, the reorganization of the American Nurse's Association in 1916 accepted members through state organizations. However, 16 states and the District of Columbia would not admit African American nurses to their state organizations. In addition, the program that graduated Mary Mahoney in 1879 had a strict policy of admitting only one African American and one Jewish student each year (Hine, 1989). Although nursing generally provided women with an economic opportunity to establish legitimate career potentials, one's race and religion remained a constant reminder of the social and political realities.

Early Growth of Nursing

Throughout the latter 1800s and early 1900s, nursing schools experienced considerable growth. For example, in 1880 there were 15 professional nursing schools in the United States. By 1900 there were 432, and by 1910, more than 1,100 (Hine, 1989). A benchmark in the professionalization of nursing occurred in 1900 with the founding of the *American Journal of Nursing,* considered to be the official journal of nurses. Also, at the time, the majority of nurses were employed as private duty nurses (Roberts, 1964). The employment location for nurses (primarily to hospitals) did not change until the 1930s (Reverby, 1996). Throughout the 20th century, the nursing community has enjoyed dramatic numerical growth, but questions regarding its professional status remain (Lindeman & McAthie, 1990). In addition to the professional status is the social class position of women entering nursing. Initially, nursing at the elite schools (e.g., Johns Hopkins, Massachusetts General) attracted women from the upper class. Other nursing institutions, however, accepted women primarily from the middle and working classes (Reverby, 1987). Throughout the 20th century, nursing has attracted women primarily from working and lower-middle class families (Fox, 1989), whereas doctors have primarily been drawn from upper-middle class backgrounds.

Educational Requirements and Nursing

Perhaps the greatest impediment to improved professional status is the educational process involved in becoming a nurse. Historically, the distinction has been between hospital-trained and academically based nurses (Duffy, 1993). Unlike physicians who have a standard medical school program regardless of their desired specialty, there are multiples of nursing programs with varying educational requirements. The continuum of nursing education programs ranges from practical nursing, diploma programs, associate degree, baccalaureate degree, to graduate programs. (The following material is drawn primarily from the work of Hamilton, 1992, and Mitchell & Grippando, 1993).

Licensed Practical Nurse Training

Licensed practical nursing (LPN) involves some 12–18 months of training and the receipt of a certificate on completion. Training occurs either at a junior college, adult or vocational program, or through a hospital. Although programs may vary between states, an increasing percentage of practical nurses see this as an initial step in a nursing career path. Practical nursing experienced considerable growth in the number of graduates and schools between 1950 and 1980. Since the 1980s, however, the number of students has fluctuated while the number of graduates and schools continues to decline.

Diploma-Based Programs

Over the past several decades there has been a fundamental shift away from diploma programs that generally require 27–36 months of study. **Diploma nurse programs,** which have been offered since 1873, are affiliated with hospitals, although some now have programs associated with colleges or universities (for an analysis of the relationship between hospitals and diploma-based programs, see Reverby, 1985). Perhaps the most significant difference between diploma-based nursing education and the other formats is the amount of direct patient care. Diploma-based nursing students receive extensive training on all floors within the hospital. The demise of the diploma nurse has been because of the increasing educational costs for many hospitals. Examining the numbers of diploma-based students, graduates, and schools, it is evident that there has been a significant shift away from the practical or skilled training toward an academic orientation of nursing. Between 1960 and projected numbers for the year 2000, graduates of diploma schools will decline from more than 25,000 to less than 5,000, whereas the number of schools will decrease from more than 900 to 152 (National Center for Health Statistics, 1996).

Associate Degree Programs

Although diploma-based nursing has declined significantly, **associate degree nurse programs** have increased dramatically. An associate degree takes between 18–24 months of study to complete and is generally offered through junior or community colleges. Begun through the nursing program in the Teachers College at Columbia University in 1952, the program has enjoyed phenomenal growth. For example, in 1960 there were fewer than 800 graduates. By 1994, there were almost 59,000 (National Center for Health Statistics, 1996). Although the numbers are expected to decrease in the near future, associate degree nursing programs enroll some two-thirds of all nursing students.

Associate degree programs are attractive because of lower costs and less time commitment compared to diploma schools. In addition, students in the associate degree program can live at home rather than in residence at the diploma school. This has been particularly important because of the type of student attracted to the associate degree program. The associate degree program has opened nursing to a wider student population that includes "older individuals, minorities, men, and married women" (Zerwekh & Claborn, 1994). The location of the training also changed the focus of nursing from service to education. These nurses "were to be prepared to function as bedside nurses in staff level positions, under supervision" (Mitchell & Grippando, 1993, p. 77). Associate degree nurses were also eligible to take the licensing examination for **registered nurses.**

Baccalaureate Degree Programs

Baccalaureate nurse programs (or BSN) programs were first developed in the early 1900s. Although the popularity of the BSN program has grown, there has been considerable fluctuation in numbers in the past. Historically, nursing has not been considered an appropriate area of study within the university setting because of its lack of a theoretical framework and its emphasis on skill acquisition. In fact, it was not until 1919 that the University of Minnesota became the first school to institute an undergraduate program in nursing. Once adopted, the BSN program generally represented an integration of the 3-year diploma program and 2 years of liberal arts courses. In fact, many BSN programs required 5 years of study until the 1950s, when the length of time was reduced to 4 years. Today, many BSN programs require students to take courses across the college curriculum. The BSN is becoming the normal route for future advancement into administrative or managerial positions within the health-care industry (Mitchell & Grippando, 1993).

Graduate Nursing Programs

Graduate level nursing programs have a considerable history that dates to the latter 1800s (well before the implementation of BSN programs). Graduate level (master's degree) training allows students access to a variety of areas within nursing. As in other departments, graduate level nursing faculties have developed a (clinical) specialization that allows them to provide instruction to students. A more limited graduate level program is the Doctor of Science in Nursing (DSc) or the PhD in nursing. The value of a doctoral program for nursing has generated considerable controversy. Although the degree may be a valuable educational asset under some circumstances, its overall value has not been clarified (Mitchell & Grippando, 1993).

Clinical Nurse Specialists and Nurse Practitioners

In addition, there are a number of specialty areas within nursing. Two areas that deserve mention here include the clinical nurse specialist and the nurse practitioner. The clinical nurse specialist is a relatively new role within nursing. Trained at the graduate level, the clinical nurse specialist is in a rather unique situation. Because their roles may vary, they experience considerable occupational autonomy. For example, clinical nurse specialists may see patients who have been referred by physicians or other nurses. Clinical nurse specialists may also engage in or evaluate clinical practice, teach, engage in research, or coordinate the delivery of health care from a multiplicity of areas within the medical community (Mitchell & Grippando, 1993).

The development of nurse practitioners continues to spark heated debate. For instance, differences of opinion continue regarding whether nurse practitioners are in nursing or medicine (there is even debate over who should teach students in nurse practitioner programs: nurses or physicians). As with traditional nursing, the educational training of nurse practitioners varies from short-term awarding of a certificate to long-term programs leading to advanced degrees. The distinction between nurse practitioners and traditional nursing is "in the autonomy of her practice patterns, in her status in the delivery of health care, and in her relationship to patients, physicians, and health care agencies" (Kalisch & Kalisch, 1978, p. 661). Beyond these differences of professional location, the purpose of the nurse practitioner is to provide a holistic approach to the treatment of patients. Nurse practitioners are found in community clinics, physician offices, and in managed care organizations. Wherever they are located, nurse practitioners "provide nursing services to a healthy client rather than being hired by an employing health care facility to provide nursing services" (Mitchell & Grippando, 1993, p. 238).

The Status of Nurses

The preceding discussion illustrates the range of educational options available in nursing. As a result, the professional status of nurses continues to be an area of debate that may result in occupational anomie (Schwartz et al., 1994). In other words, nursing as a career is moving in two broad directions: in one direction, nurses are increasing their level of education and influence (professionalization) within the larger medical community. The second direction is that of nurse practitioners who take on the more routine activities of physicians. As a result, role ambiguity (thus anomie) remains a constant problem within the nursing profession (see also Levi, 1995). Furthermore, nursing, within the context of the bureaucratic framework of the hospital where most nurses are now employed, suffers from its subordinate position to physicians (Turner, 1995). Testing this argument in primary health clinics in Israel during a physician's strike, Shoham-Yakubovich et al. (1989) discovered that the primary care nurses in the clinics experienced increased job satisfaction during the strike. These nurses not only had more work, but also were able to control their professional lives. As a result, their self-image and sense of professional autonomy improved. Current changes within the health-care industry today may influence the education of nurses in the future.

The Socialization of Nursing Students

Nursing education involves the incorporation of two interrelated socialization processes. On the one hand is the socialization to the student role. On the other hand, students are also socialized into the nursing role. Consider the findings from a Canadian study of nursing students in a 4-year baccalaureate program (Reutter et al., 1997). In the first year, students internalize two central values: caring and a scientific perspective. Throughout this initial year, students place a premium on learning to communicate with patients. They value floor experience over the classroom because "the internalization of knowledge takes place when the skills are practiced in the clinical setting" (Reutter et al., 1997, p. 151). With the second year comes a need to "confront reality" and discriminate between ideal and real situations. As with medical students, nursing students feel pressured regarding the amount of information available and the time frame within which to learn it. Because of the time constraints, students are also learning that nursing involves classroom knowledge, expertise on the hospital floor, and organizational skills so they can effectively arrange their work and study schedule. Students also learn the reality that nursing is not a homogeneous set of behaviors, but rather an amalgamation of knowledge and skills culled through practice and observation.

By the third year, students are better able to understand and cope with the reality of nursing. With increased independence from nursing faculty, students begin to make decisions on their own or in consultation with other students. At the same time, students are identifying role models and are increasingly viewing themselves as "nurses" rather than "students." The major problem for some students is the continual 6-week rotation between units. As a result, students are continually being exposed to new (and potentially different) sets of expectations as they move from one unit to the next. Students are also forced to negotiate with a new set of nurses and other personnel at each unit. Although some students relish the diversity of training, others see this "new reality" as potentially stressful.

Accepting their role as student, fourth-year students recognize the significant occupational shift that occurs when they complete their nursing program. Students also understand how their current status insulates them from total responsibility for their actions. At the same time, fourth-year students want greater exposure to experiences that will broaden their knowledge base. This interplay between increased independence as a professional and the security of the student role that plagues the fourth-year student. These students also see their role as nurses expand beyond the health-care community within which they work. With a vested interest in politics and public policy issues that effect the health-care system in general and nursing in particular, fourth-year students are likely to take an interest in current issues and their outcomes (Reutter et al., 1997) (see also, Smith, 1976, for a brief but similar description of student nurse socialization in England). Examining differences in values between nursing students and faculty, Eddy et al. (1994) provide support for the socialization process discussed previously. Eddy et al. (1994) report those students and faculty identified different values within nursing as being important. For instance, whereas faculty valued greater freedom and rights for the patient, students valued work environments that foster the provision of care. In South Africa, socialization of the nurse role is intertwined with that of mother. According to Walker (1995, p. 821), "the professional socialization of nurses reinforces them [traditional burdens] by ascribing to women the role of the total care-giver and home-provider."

As Reutter et al. (1997, p. 155) point out, "socialization to the professional nursing role [is related to] professional values, norms, and behaviors." Here, nursing students begin to develop an understanding of the relationship between nurse and physician. They also encounter a new phenomenon, the **doctor–nurse game.** In his original research, Stein (1967) argued that the relationship between doctor and nurse was hierarchical. In other words, any recommendation by a nurse to a doctor would have to be stated so that the doctor could take credit for the initiative. At the same time, a physician seeking a recommendation from a nurse must not appear to ask for it. Remember that in 1967 nurses were primarily the products of diploma-based programs in which they understood rather early the status relationship that exists on the hospital floor, or in any health-care arrangement, between doctor and nurse (see also Johnson & Martin, 1958; Muyskens, 1982). Today, doctors are no longer characterized by the white male image of the past. Instead, they are increasingly female and represent a broader cross-section of American society. That does not mean, however, that the doctor–nurse game has become more equal or that gender-based stereotyping does not exist (Campbell-Heider & Pollock, 1987; Porter, 1992). Rather, the relocation of nurse training to an academic setting instead of a hospital has minimized the contact that students have with physicians, thus reducing the paternalistic attitudes perpetuated earlier. The following is an extended excerpt from Stein et al. (1990) in which they explain the doctor–nurse game in 1990.

The scene is a surgical ward in which each patient is assigned to a specific nurse who has the primary responsibility for the patient's nursing care. The patient is Ms. Brown, a woman who has had a mastectomy and has confided in her nurse, Ms. Smith, that she is worried that her husband will no longer find her sexually desirable. The nurse has scheduled a meeting with Ms. Brown and her husband for the following afternoon. Dr. Jones, unaware of the problem and the scheduled session, has written a discharge order for Ms. Brown. The dialogue is as follows:

MS. SMITH: Dr. Jones, I understand you are planning to discharge Ms. Brown today.

DR. JONES: Yes, she has done remarkably well since her surgery, and she is ready to go.

MS. SMITH: I agree. Her incision looks good, and her stamina has returned; but what about her concern about her husband?

DR. JONES: What concern are you talking about?

MS. SMITH: I have written detailed nursing notes about her concern that her husband will be sexually uninterested in her because of her mastectomy. I also noted that I have arranged a joint meeting with her and her husband tomorrow to discuss the problem. [This statement is made without a hint of apology for taking independent action.]

DR. JONES: I was not aware of that, and I have already decided she is ready to be discharged. I can refer her to someone later if it becomes a problem.

MS. SMITH: Dr. Jones, it is already a problem for her, and I strongly recommend that you delay the discharge until after tomorrow's meeting with her husband. In addition, it would help our collaborative effort if you read my notes as carefully as I read yours. [Note the undisguised recommendation and the assertion of the equal importance of diagnosis and documentation by nurses.]

This exchange illustrates the changing nature not only of the doctor–nurse relationship, but more broadly, the role of the nurse within the medical community. In addition, the nurse–patient relationship has also undergone a paradigmatic shift.

In the same context that physicians have begun to understand the patient as a *person* rather than a *disease,* nurses have attempted a more egalitarian relationship with patients. A consequence of such a shift does not mean an improved nurse–patient relationship (see, for example, the work of Bottorff & Varcoe, 1995, regarding the dynamic interactive qualities between nurse and patient). In fact, May (1992) suggests that patients may, in fact, wield greater power than previously thought over nurses by not responding to their questions, thus calling into question their legitimacy. The next section addresses some of the changes within the world of nursing and examines some of the consequences.

Nursing Today

In concert with the larger health-care industry, nursing continues to adapt to the changing social and economic forces within society. This adaptation may have negative as well as positive outcomes for the nursing profession. A perusal of recent nursing texts demonstrates the range of nonmedical topics considered important for today's nurse. Beyond the standard topics of the history of nursing, levels of nursing education, and credentialling, consider the following topics: ethical concerns, legal issues, health-care systems, change, power, politics, and collective bargaining (Hamilton, 1992; Mitchell & Grippando, 1993). A reader by Lindeman and McAthie (1990) offers articles ranging from the relationship between theory and research to the sociopolitical environment and nursing practice.

In addition to the range of topics presented, nurses are also providing care to an increasingly diverse population. Patients no longer represent cultures representative of Western or northern European descent. Rather, growing minority groups such as African Americans, Hispanic Americans, and Asian Americans represent the broader population. As a result, the education of nurses requires a transcultural perspective. For example, Giger and Davidhizar (1991) examine assessment and intervention techniques within various cultural groups (for example, African Americans, Appalachians, Italian Americans, and Chinese Americans). An analysis of each cultural group extends beyond the biological and includes an assessment of the social organization, concepts of time and communication, and environmental control. Not limited to the United States, nurses throughout the world provide care to patients from diverse cultural backgrounds. In an effort to ensure that patients receive care consistent with their cultural values, Leininger (1991, p. 7) developed the theory of Culture Care, which focuses "on cultural care factors and ways people expect nursing care that is meaningful to them." The theory has been applied by Wenger (1991) on the Amish; Stasiak (1991) on Mexican Americans; and by Bohay (1991) on Ukrainian Americans. Others that have applied the theory include Spangler (1991) to work in the Philippines; Leininger (1991) in New Guinea; and Rosenbaum (1991) in Canada.

Demographic Changes within Nursing

Current occupational projections identify nursing as a growth industry in the United States (U.S. Bureau of the Census, 1996). One of the reasons for this growth is the aging of the population, which will require continued health-care supportive services for larger numbers of patients who will live for longer periods of time. In addition to this demographic shift, social policy initiatives such as Medicare and Medicaid, new technologies, and the delivery of nursing care itself have led to an increasing shortage of nurses in the early 1990s (McKibbin, 1990). The shortage of registered nurses identified in the early 1990s is being offset somewhat by changes in the organization and delivery of health-care services within an increasingly for-profit industry. Before addressing that issue, however, how do nurses today compare to their earlier counterparts?

A 1992 survey of recent nursing graduates indicates that the average age at graduation continues to increase and also differs depending on the degree program. For example, in 1992 the average age of BSN nursing degree recipients was 29.2. Among diploma and associate degree graduates, the average ages were 31.3 and 35.7, respectively. In 1988, the average age at graduation by degree program was 25.4, 25.9, and 31.6, respectively (Rosenfeld, 1994). In addition to an increasing average age, nursing students are more likely to be married, have at least one child, and to be male. The numbers of minority graduates was slightly lower in 1992 compared with 1990 (Rosenfeld, 1994). According to the National Center for Health Statistics (1996), current minority student populations when compared with 1990–1991 are generally flat. In fact, the percentage of Caucasian American nursing students increased from 82.8 to 84.4 between 1990–1991 and 1993–1994. African American student enrollment decreased from 10.4% to 8.7%. Hispanic American student enrollment remained the same at 3.0%, whereas Native American enrollment decreased from 0.8% to 0.7%. Asian Americans were the only minority population to register an increase in enrollment (from 3.0% to 3.3%). Efforts to increase the number of minority nursing students is not an easy task, in part because improving cultural diversity and sensitivity in nursing schools or in the curriculum is not always warmly endorsed (Hyche-Johnson, 1994). In fact, Gerrish et al. (1996, p. 129) suggest that in England, "hostility to minority ethnic persons, and to investing in meeting their needs, must therefore be acknowledged as a factor to be faced in the development of professional development." At the turn of the 20th century the majority of nurses were employed as private duty nurses. Today, some 90% of newly employed nurses were working in hospital settings (Rosenfeld, 1994).

Data in Table 9.1 illustrates the distribution of nurses by type of education per 100,000 persons by region of the country. Comparing 1993 to 1980, there has been significant growth in the number of nurses within the American population. However, examining the data by level of education by area of country suggests a geographic shift within the health-care delivery system. Although the northeast continues to report more nurses (at all educational levels) per 100,000 population, the Midwest and south substantially increased the ratio of nurses to total population, whereas growth in the west was more moderate. This is particularly true among

TABLE 9.1   Active Health Personnel and Number per 100,000 Population, According to Occupation and Geographic Region: United States, 1970, 1980, and 1993

| Year | Number of Active Health Personnel | Geographic Region[1] | | | | |
		United States	Northeast	Midwest	South	West
1970						
Registered nurses	750,000	368.9	491.2	367.5	281.8	355.9
1980						
Registered nurses	1,272,900	560.0	736.0	583.6	443.4	533.7
Associate and diploma	908,300	399.9	536.0	429.2	316.5	351.1
Baccalaureate	297,300	130.9	161.0	127.8	103.8	148.1
Masters and doctorate	67,300	29.6	39.0	26.7	23.0	34.6
1993						
Registered nurses	1,946,300	754.6	930.2	821.4	678.0	643.2
Associate and diploma	1,180,200	457.6	552.5	516.1	423.1	362.2
Baccalaureate	606,400	235.1	289.7	248.2	198.7	229.0
Masters and doctorate	159,700	61.9	88.1	57.2	56.3	52.1

Data are compiled by the Bureau of Health Professions.

[1] Number per 100,000 population. Division of Health Professions Analysis, Bureau of Health Professions: Supply and Characteristics of Selected Health Personnel. DHHS Pub. No. (HRA) 81–20. Health Resources Administration. Hyattsville, MD, June 1981.

Source: National Center for Health Statistics. *Health, United States, 1995.* Table 101. Hyattsville, MD: Public Health Service. 1996.

nurses with a masters or doctorate degree. In 1980, the west had the second highest ratio of graduate-level nurses per 100,000 population. By 1993, the west had the lowest ratio in the country. These changes reflect in part the broader changes within the health-care system that have increased the demand for nurses, but not necessarily the compensation necessary to hire and retain their skills (see, for example, Friedman, 1990). Although the eastern region continues to maintain its number one position, the Midwest and the south have increased their levels significantly. Another statistic that illustrates the dilemma associated with the professionalization of nursing is that of salary. Although overall average salaries have increased considerably throughout the early 1990s, there is little difference between income and degree program. According to Rosenfeld (1994), new baccalaureate and diploma nursing graduates averages just over $29,000 compared with an average of $28,000 for associate degree graduates. Such similarity does little to quell the criticism of those who question the professionalization of nursing. Such numbers also question the need for additional years of nursing education when 45.3% of the new graduates identified income as the motivating factor for their current position (Rosenfeld, 1994).

The preceding data reflect an ongoing shift among those entering the nursing profession. Although expectations of others toward nurses and nursing have changed, so have the opportunities for nurses. Yet age-old problems persist. Consider the following quote:

> It is more in demand than ever, but its leaders question the appropriateness of much of that demand. It seeks to end the shortages that have occurred through much of this century, but also wants to raise minimum standards for entry into the profession. (Friedman, 1990, p. 2977)

Problems for the Nursing Profession: A Cross-Cultural View

The problems for the nursing profession are multifaceted. On the one hand, professionalization continues to be a problem, despite the increasing leverage of nurses in the early 1990s. On the other hand, educational standards are a problem as the occupation diversifies to meet the complex needs of their patients. The nursing profession in many European countries is facing similar problems (Keyzer, 1994). Lassey et al. (1997) report that nursing shortages exist throughout the industrialized world and in many former eastern European nations as well as Russia. Nurses in all of these countries are experiencing similar problems of low wages and status relative to physicians. An additional problem is that the educational standards for becoming a nurse are quite low. In Turkey, students can begin a 4-year training to become a nurse at the age of 14 with no licensure laws requiring students to demonstrate competency once they finish (Solomon, 1990). A more structured nursing education program has been developed in the United Arab Emirate (UAE). Similar to the United States, the program consists of three levels of nursing education; secondary school, associate degree, and bachelor degree program. Nurses within each level can be categorized as either basic nurse, nurse technician, or nurse manager (Kronfol & Athique, 1986). Similarly, the Jordanian educational system for nursing is built around a baccalaureate program. As is the case in many countries, the nursing role lacks clarity and there are few role models for young women (AbuGharbieh & Suliman, 1992). However, the Ministry of Health (rather than Education) now controls nursing in Iraq. The significance of this shift is that nursing is no longer within the university system, but rather, the hospital. As a consequence, nurses are paraprofessionals whose numbers can be strictly controlled. Such a relationship is in keeping with a traditional context of gender roles (Boyle, 1989). Finally, in the Mideast, nursing in Kuwait is particularly difficult. The majority of nurses are imported and are either Indian or Egyptian. The Kuwaiti government attempted to attract young Kuwaiti women into nursing, but because of its status and paternalistic doctor–nurse games, most women have not been interested (Dalayon, 1990). In the Far East, nursing in Pakistan is considered a menial occupation that does not attract women from the middle class. In addition, there are age, residence, and educational requirements that reduce the pool of eligible women for nursing. As a result, there are more physicians than nurses in Pakistan, where the ratio is four physicians for every one nurse (Harnar et al., 1992). A similar situation exists in India. In addition to more doctors than nurses, there are also more registered pharmacists than registered nurses. Mehra (1989, p. 122) characterizes the extent of the problem by stating that "we will surely regress back to the 19th century when medical students, orderlies, *ayahs* and relatives provided most of the nursing care."

Thus, the social organization of the profession as well as expected role performance remain areas of concern. The following pages explore some of these issues to better understand the future of nursing.

The Changing Health-Care System and Nursing

Since the demise of the Clinton National Health Plan, the United States' health-care system has experienced a dramatic shift in the delivery of health services. Within the last 5 years, for-profit health-care companies are beginning to dominate not only local communities and states, but also entire regions of the country. The increase in managed care (for-profit and not-for-profit) has limited the freedom of patients and the employment opportunities of physicians and nurses. In fact, research by Stevenson et al. (1995) on the rationing of medical resources found American nurses more supportive of such procedures when compared with their British counterparts. Predictions of serious nursing shortages in the early 1990s are now overshadowed by the layoff of RNs in favor of less-qualified personnel, the closing of hospitals, and, according to Bloor et al. (1997), the continued examination of hospital staffing patterns. The relevance of nursing education is again being questioned with suggestions for broadening the base of knowledge (i.e., socially relevant material), greater utilization of health-care facilities beyond the hospital, and developing in nurses a greater awareness of cultural diversity, political skills, and health economics (Redmond, 1997). Again, these issues are important because they improve the employment opportunities of nurses, but devalue their legitimacy as a profession (i.e., loss of autonomy and decision making).

As the health-care system continues to move patients away from hospitals and into outpatient clinics and managed care facilities, the role of the nurse will evolve as well. For example, there are predictions that fewer than 50% of nurses will be employed in hospital settings at the turn of the 21st century. Nurses remaining in the hospital face increased pressure to do more with less, and the problem is increasing (Lippman Collins, 1990). Professionally, it is the transience of the nursing role and its continual need to reevaluate its educational role and requirements relative to changes in the larger system that are particularly vexing. Although nurses will find employment within the changing health-care system, the continuing fragmentation of the profession into specialty and subspecialty areas decreases occupational cohesion.

Future Trends in Nursing

The future of nursing is secure. What is uncertain is the organizational structure of the nursing profession relative to the health-care system. Zerwekh and Claborn (1994, p. 219) identify 10 trends they believe will influence nursing in the future.

1. Nursing will assume an undisputed dominant role in the healthcare delivery system, resulting in positions of high esteem with better salaries, incentives, responsibilities, and authority.
2. Care of the geriatric population will become a prominent and respected nursing specialty.
3. Nurses will play a major leadership role in determining and implementing healthcare policies.
4. Nurses will provide the expertise to integrate the multiple facets of healthcare—pharmacology, nutrition, preventive medicine, rehabilitation, etc.—in order to provide holistic care for an individual client.
5. Technological advances will assist the nurse in providing high-quality care that is cost effective.
6. Specific outcome criteria will be important in determining the quality of care and will become healthcare facilities' overriding concern in the future.
7. Case managed care will replace the traditional sick care approach, as prevention will be the key to reducing healthcare costs.
8. Increased numbers of women and nurses will be making policy and governmental decisions affecting healthcare.
9. Education will become more user friendly as the trend moves to a service economy in which knowledge is utilized.
10. Nursing will begin sharing healthcare beliefs, cultural practices, resources, and the expanding body of nursing knowledge as globalization occurs.

These trends represent an optimistic view of nursing. Furthermore, many of the problems identified earlier are not addressed. Instead, education, for example, is stressed as being user friendly rather than a means of division between graduate levels. Another problem is the inconsistency between the for-profit nature of the American health-care system and the use of high-paid nurses to provide care to an increasingly geriatric population. These issues (and others) will continue to fragment the nursing profession.

Nonetheless, nursing, as an occupation, will experience continued growth. The need for someone trained to provide care and services to patients within a health-care setting preserves nursing as a viable occupation. In addition, nurses will continue their involvement in various health-related decision-making processes. However, questions remain regarding the organization and structure of the profession.

Summary

This chapter addresses a range of topics associated with nursing. The chapter begins with a global history of nursing culminating in the work of Florence Nightingale.

Expanding on the framework constructed by Nightingale, nursing emerged in the latter half of the 19th century as a profession for women, regardless of social class position (although the Nightingale nursing programs attracted predominantly middle-class women). With the advent of the 20th century, nursing began to broaden its appeal to the larger health-care system (and to other social classes of women).

Throughout the 20th century, however, nursing has experienced an identity problem. Attempting to market itself as a professional occupation, nursing has built its argument on such topics as licensure and autonomy regarding health-care decision making. At the same time, nursing has experienced external control over various facets of its existence, thus leading to questions regarding its viability as a legitimate professional occupation.

Throughout this process, the education of nurses in the United States has experienced a paradigmatic shift. Originally structured within the hospital, nursing education was grounded in the diploma program. Today, the associate degree (or 2-year) program is the overwhelming favorite of most nursing students. In addition to changing the structure of nursing education, the associate degree program has also changed the type of students enrolled in a nursing program. The democratization of nursing has not meant an improved image. Perhaps to the contrary, the image of nursing continues to wither because of an inability to state unequivocally what it means, educationally, to be a nurse. Similarly, the socialization process associated with nursing education (at least among 4-year programs) identifies two different yet overlapping role performances: that of the student and that of the nurse.

Throughout this chapter nursing has been examined not only within the United States but also cross-culturally. The result has been a relatively consistent image of an occupation at the mercy of the political and economic forces of the society. This cross-cultural view is disconcerting in that the legitimacy of nursing is generally lost within the framework of changes associated with the larger health-care system.

Addressing the future of nursing, a number of social and health-related trends are examined. Although these trends address some of the concerns facing the nursing profession, they are also an optimistic forecast of the future. It is concluded that nursing, as an occupation, continues to experience problems legitimating its professionalization, and future trends may portend increasing difficulty.

CHAPTER REVIEW

The purpose of this review, as with others, is to encourage the reader to reexamine the information presented throughout the chapter. This review also provides the reader an opportunity to integrate and critically examine all of the information presented in the book.

1. Chronicle the work of Florence Nightingale. Why did nursing become an occupation for the more wealthy women in society?

2. Consider the role of African American women in the emergence and development of nursing (19th and 20th centuries).

3. Compare the socialization processes for becoming a physician and a nurse. What are the similarities and differences?

4. Outline the differences between the various educational methods available for a nursing degree.

5. Should nursing be considered a profession, as is medicine? Explain your response.

6. Is the image of nursing a problem only for the United States?

7. Construct a scenario in which nursing would be considered a profession (similar to physicians). What changes would be required within nursing? Is this scenario possible?

GLOSSARY

associate degree nurse   the fastest growing nursing program that takes between 18–24 months to complete. Generally offered at junior or community colleges, this program is attractive to older and nontraditional students.

baccalaureate nurse program   the preferred nursing program to ensure professional status. This program is housed in colleges or universities and requires 4 years to complete. Similar to the associate degree program with additional liberal arts courses required.

diploma nurse program   the original nursing program housed within hospitals. This is generally a 2½ to 3-year program that is currently training a decreasing number of nursing students.

Doctor–Nurse Game   a status-based relationship between doctors and nurses that required each to verbally and nonverbally negotiate needs and expectations without infringing on the rights of the other and, at the same time, not exceed the boundaries of one's position.

Florence Nightingale   an Englishwoman who founded the "modern" school of nursing.

licensed practical nursing (LPN)   a 1- to 1½-year nursing program offered in community or junior colleges, vocational training programs, or high schools. The student receives a certificate on completion of the program.

registered nurse (RN)   a degreed nurse who has passed the exam for her or his nursing license.

SUGGESTED READINGS

Abu-Saad, H. (1979). *Nursing: A world view.* St. Louis: C.V. Mosby Company.
Although dated, the author provides a comparative overview of nursing and nursing education.
Carnegie, M. E. (1995). *The path we tread: Blacks in nursing worldwide, 1854–1994.* New York: National League for Nursing Press.
Expanding on the work of Hine (1989), the material in this book is not confined to the United States. Instead, the author treats the reader to a worldwide examination of Blacks in the nursing profession.

Hine, D. C. (1989). *Black women in white: Racial conflict and cooperation in the nursing profession, 1890–1950*. Bloomington, IN: Indiana University Press.
This book chronicles the changes and difficulties experienced by women of color in the United States as they pursued social and occupational parity within the nursing profession.
Reverby, S. M. (1987). *Ordered to care: The dilemma of American nursing, 1850–1945*. Cambridge: Cambridge University Press.
This is perhaps the best description and analysis of early American nursing.

REFERENCES

AbuGharbieh, P., & Suliman, W. (1992). Changing the image of nursing in Jordan through effective role negotiation. *International Nursing Review, 39,* 5, 149–152.

Abu-Saad, H. (1979). *Nursing: A world view.* St. Louis: C.V. Mosby Company.

Baer, E. D. (1992). Nurses. In R. D. Apple (Ed.). *Women, health & medicine in America: A historical handbook* (pp. 451–467). New Brunswick, NJ: Rutgers University Press.

Baly, M. E. (1986). *Florence Nightingale and the nursing legacy.* London: Croom Helm.

Bloom, J. R., Alexander, J. A., & Nuchols, B. A. (1997). Nurse staffing patterns and hospital efficiency in the United States. *Social Science and Medicine, 44,* 2, 147–155.

Bohay, I. Z. (1991). Culture care meanings and experiences of pregnancy and childbirth of Ukrainians. In M. M. Leininger (Ed.). *Culture care diversity & universality: A theory of nursing* (pp. 203–230). New York: National League of Nursing Press.

Bottorff, J. L., & Varcoe, C. (1995). Transitions in nurse–patient interactions: A qualitative ethology. *Qualitative Health Research, 5,* 3, 315–331.

Boyle, J. S. (1989). Professional nursing in Iraq. *IMAGE: Journal of Nursing Scholarship, 21,* 3, 168–171.

Campbell-Heider, N., & Pollock, D. (1987). Barriers to physician–nurse collegiality: An anthropological perspective. *Social Science and Medicine, 25,* 5, 421–425.

Carnegie, M. E. (1995). *The path we tread: Blacks in nursing worldwide, 1854–1994.* New York: National League for Nursing Press.

Dalayon, A. (1990). Nursing in Kuwait: Problems and prospects. *Nursing Management, 21,* 9, 129–134.

Dock, L. L. (1912). *A history of nursing: From the earliest times to the present day with special reference to the work of the past thirty years. Volume IV.* New York: G.P. Putnam's Sons.

Duffy, J. (1993). *From humors to medical science: A history of American medicine.* Urbana, IL: University of Illinois Press.

Eddy, D. M., Elfrink, V., Weis, D., & Schank, M. J. (1994). Importance of professional nursing values: A national study of baccalaureate programs. *Journal of Nursing Education, 33,* 6, 257–262.

Ellis, J. R., & Hartley, C. L. (1992). *Nursing in today's world: Challenges, issues, and trends* (4th Ed.). Philadelphia: J.B. Lippincott Company.

Fox, R. C. (1989). *The sociology of medicine: A participant observer's view.* Englewood Cliffs, NJ: Prentice-Hall.

Friedman, E. (1990). Nursing: New power, old problems. *Journal of the American Medical Association, 264,* 23, 2977–2982.

Gerrish, K., Husband, C., & Mackenzie, J. (1996). *Nursing for a multi-ethnic society.* Buckingham: Open University Press.

Giger, J. N., & Davidhizar, R. E. (1991). *Transcultural nursing: Assessment and intervention.* St. Louis: Mosby-Year Book.

Hamilton, P. M. (1992). *Realities of contemporary nursing.* New York: Addison-Wesley.

Harnar, R., Amarsi, Y., Herberg, P., & Miller, G. (1992). Health and nursing services in Pakistan: Problems and challenges for nurse leaders. *Nursing Administration Quarterly, 16,* 2, 52–59.

Hays, J. C. (1989). Florence Nightingale and the India sanitary reforms. *Public Health Nursing, 6,* 3, 152–154.

Hine, D. C. (1989). *Black women in white: Racial conflict and cooperation in the nursing profession, 1890–1950.* Bloomington, IN: Indiana University Press.

Hyche-Johnson, M. (1994). Nursing care in a culturally diverse nation. In B. Bullough & V. Bullough (Eds.). *Nursing issues for the nineties and beyond* (pp. 187–198). New York: Springfield Publishing Company.

Johnson, M. M., & Martin, H. W. (1958). A sociological analysis of the nurse role. *American Journal of Nursing, 58,* 373–377.

Kalish, P. A., & Kalish, B. J. (1978). *The advance of American nursing.* Boston: Little, Brown & Company.

Keyzer, D. (1994). European aspects of the nursing role. In G. Hunt & P. Wainwright (Eds.). *Expanding the role of the nurse: The scope of professional practice* (pp. 86–98). Oxford: Blackwell Scientific Publications.

Kronfol, N. M., & Athique, M. M. (1986). Nursing education in the United Arab Emirates. *International Journal of Nursing Studies, 23,* 1, 1–10.

Lassey, M. L., Lassey, W. R., & Jinks, M. J. (1997). *Health care systems around the world: Characteristics, issues, reforms.* Upper Saddle River, NJ: Prentice-Hall.

Leininger, M. M. (Ed). (1991a). *Culture care diversity & universality: A theory of nursing.* New York: National League for Nursing Press.

Leininger, M. M. (1991b). Culture care of the Gadsup Akruna of the Eastern highlands of New Guinea. In M. M. Leininger (Ed.). *Culture care diversity & universality: A theory of nursing* (pp. 231–280). New York: National League for Nursing Press.

Levi, M. (1995). Functional redundancy and the process of professionalization: The case of registered nurses in the United States. In W. G. Rothstein. (Ed.). *Readings in American health care: Current issues in socio-historical perspective* (pp. 199–212). Madison, WI: University of Wisconsin Press.

Lindeman, C. A., & McAthie, M. (1990). Nursing at the cross roads: Learning from the past, growing toward the future. In C. A. Lindeman & M. McAthie (Eds.). *Readings in nursing trends and issues* (pp. 1–10). Springhouse, PA: Springhouse Corporation.

Lippman Collins, H. (1990). When the profit motive threatens patient care. In C. A. Lindeman & M. McAthie (Eds.). *Readings: Nursing trends and issues* (pp. 432–440). Springhouse, PA: Springhouse Corporation.

May, C. (1992). Nursing work, nurses' knowledge, and the subjectification of the patient. *Sociology of Health and Illness, 14,* 4, 472–487.

McKibbin, R. C. (1990). *The nursing shortage and the 1990s: Realities and remedies.* Kansas City, MO: American Nurses Association.

Mehra, P. (1989). Outlook for nursing in India. *International Nursing Review, 36,* 4, 121–122.

Mitchell, P. R., & Grippando, G. M. (1993). *Nursing perspectives* (5th Ed.). Albany, NY: Delmar Publishing.

Muyskens, J. L. (1982). *Moral problems in nursing: A philosophical investigation.* Totawa, NJ: Rowman and Littlefield.

National Center for Health Statistics. (1996). *Health, United States, 1995.* Hyattsville, MD: Public Health Service.

Nightingale, F. (1960). From *Notes on Nursing.* L. Clendening. *Source book on medical history* (pp. 454–463). New York: Dover Publications.

Porter, S. (1992). Women in a women's job: The gendered experience of nurses. *Sociology of Health and Illness, 14,* 4, 510–527.

Redmond, G. M. (1997). LPN–BSN: Education for a reformed health care system. *Journal of Nursing Education, 36,* 3, 121–127.

Reutter, L., Field, P. A., Campbell, I. E., & Day, R. (1997). Socialization into nursing: Nursing students as learners. *Journal of Nursing Education, 36,* 4, 149–155.

Reverby, S. M. (1985). The search for the hospital yardstick: Nursing and the rationalization of hospital work. In J. W. Leavitt & R. L. Numbers (Eds.). *Sickness & health in America: Readings in the history of medicine and public health.* (2nd Ed., Revised) (pp. 206–216). Madison, WI: University of Wisconsin Press.

Reverby, S. M. (1987). *Ordered to care: The dilemma of American nursing, 1850–1945.* Cambridge: Cambridge University Press.

Reverby, S. M. (1996). A caring dilemma: Womanhood and nursing in historical perspective. In P. Brown (Ed.). *Medical sociology* (2nd Ed.) (pp. 667–683). Prospect Heights, IL: Waveland Press.

Roberts, M. M. (1964). *American nursing: History and interpretation.* New York: The Macmillan Company.

Roemer, M. I. (1993). *National health systems of the world: Volume II–The issues.* New York: Oxford University Press.

Rosenbaum, J. (1991). Culture care theory and Greek Canadian patients. In M. M. Leininger (Ed.). *Culture care diversity & universality: A theory of nursing* (pp. 305–344). New York: National League for Nursing Press.

Rosenfeld, P. (1994). *Profiles of the newly licensed nurse* (2nd Ed.). New York: National League for Nursing Press.

Schwartz, H. D., deWolf, P. L., & Skipper, J. K. Jr. (1994). Gender, professionalization, and occupational anomie: The case of nursing. In H. D. Schwartz (Ed.). *Dominant issues in medical sociology* (3rd Ed.) (pp. 266–276). New York: McGraw-Hill.

Shoham-Yakubovich, I., Carmel, S., Zwanger, L., & Zaltcman, T. (1989). Autonomy, job satisfaction and professional self-image among nurses in the context of a physicians' strike. *Social Science and Medicine, 28,* 12, 1315–1320.

Smith, F. B. (1982). *Florence Nightingale: Reputation and power.* New York: St. Martin's Press.

Smith, J. P. (1976). *Sociology and nursing.* Edinburgh: Churchill Livingstone.

Solomon, J. (1992). From Florence Nightingale to critical care nursing: A visit to Istanbul. *Focus on Critical Care, 17,* 5, 370–373.

Spangler, Z. (1991). Culture care of Philippine and Anglo-American nurses in a hospital context. In M. M. Leininger (Ed.). *Culture care diversity & universality: A theory of nursing* (pp. 119–146). New York: National League for Nursing Press.

Stasiak, D. B. (1991). Culture care theory with Mexican-Americans in an urban context. In M. M. Leininger (Ed.). *Culture care diversity & universality: A theory of nursing* (pp. 179–202). New York: National League of Nursing Press.

Stein, L. I. (1967). The doctor–nurse game. *Archives of General Psychiatry, 16,* 699–703.

Stein, L. I., Watts, D. T., & Howell, T. (1990). The doctor–nurse game revisited. *The New England Journal of Medicine, 322,* 8, 546–549.

Stevenson, D. V., Levinson, R. M., & Thompson, N. J. (1995). Rationing medical resources: From advocacy to allocation in British and American nurses. In E. B. Gallagher & J. Subedi (Eds.). *Global perspectives on health care* (pp. 244–254). Englewood Cliffs, NJ: Prentice-Hall.

Turner, B. S. (1995). *Medical power and social knowledge* (2nd Ed.). London: SAGE.

U.S. Bureau of the Census. (1996). *Statistical Abstract of the United States: 1996* (116th Ed.). Washington, DC.

Walker, L. (1995). The practice of primary health care: A case study. *Social Science and Medicine, 40,* 6, 815–824.

Wenger, A. F. (1991). The culture care theory and the old older Amish. In M. M. Leininger (Ed.). *Culture care diversity & universality: A theory of nursing* (pp. 147–178). New York: National League for Nursing Press.

Yost, E. (1947). *American women of nursing.* Philadelphia: J.B. Lippincott.

Zerwekh, J., & Claborn, J. C. (1994). *Nursing today: Transition and trends.* Philadelphia: W.B. Saunders Company.

10 Traditional and Alternative Medicines/Practitioners

Traditional medicine varies in the different countries from the classical systems such as the traditional Chinese and Ayurvedic systems of medicine to faith healing and other practices based on the supernatural and to simple folk remedies propagated by oral traditions. It has often been regarded by professional health personnel as a second-class medicine of no importance. This was a fallacy. Cultures of which traditional medicine was an integral part was neither static nor dead. Even in cultural changes, traditional medicine has survived and preserved its role of providing health care in all countries.

—Velten-Schuberth, 1993, p. 210

Alternative Medicines and Their Practitioners: An Overview

One of the few television series this author has watched and enjoyed was "Northern Exposure." Set in Alaska, the program featured a New York City physician fresh out of medical school (which was paid for by the State of Alaska.) On his arrival in Alaska, the good doctor is informed that his services are not needed in metropolitan Anchorage, but rather, in the small, rural community of Cicely. Although each episode featured multiple story lines involving the central cast of characters, the subtext often addressed differences between Western medicine and traditional Indian medicine. Throughout the series the young doctor (who had been trained in the "best" medical facilities in the United States) was often faced with medical situations beyond his explanation and interpretation. Rather than rely on the folk wisdom of the local Indian population, he would search, unrelentingly, for an answer built around the medical model. With the passage of time and continuing exposure to the beneficial effects of local folk medicine, the doctor begins to acknowledge its value within a pluralistic medical context. In fact, prior to his return to New York City, the doctor gave up the trappings of Western medicine and moved to a remote fishing village where he practiced pluralistic medicine.

Although a television series offers us a socially constructed glimpse of the distinctions between Western and **traditional medicine,** the reality is often quite different. Beginning with some definitions, Bodeker (1996, p. 279) says that "*traditional medicine or traditional systems of health,* refer to the long-standing indigenous systems of health care found in developing countries and among the indigenous populations of industrialized countries." Such a definition provides the flexibility necessary to address a very large and culturally specific concept. **Alternative medicine** (also referred to as complementary, unconventional or unorthodox medicine) has a number of definitions. For example, Dyer (1996, p. 578) states that alternative medicine refers to "those treatments and practices that have not gained wide acceptance or have not yet had adequate scientific research to be considered standard medical treatment." Examples of alternative or unorthodox medicine include chiropractic, botanical, and osteopathic medicine.

Are these practitioners of traditional (or alternative) medicine marginal to the health-care system or the larger society today? The answer, surprisingly, is "No." Rather, these practitioners are central to the lives of many in their community and are an integral component of the health-care system. Often, patients utilize traditional and modern medicine in tandem (Hedley, 1992). As a result of the growth in alternative medicine, the number of alternative practitioners in England is expanding at a rate 5 to 6 times that of regular physicians (Cant & Calnan, 1991). And England is not unique. Research by Eisenberg et al. (1993) found that one-fourth of respondents in the United States utilized alternative or unconventional therapy in 1990. Further, Eisenberg et al. (1993) report that patients spent almost $14 billion on such therapies. The reason for the rise in popularity of alternative forms of medicine is the "failure of modern medicine weighed with the attractiveness of alternative care" (Cant & Calnan, 1991, p. 55). In Denmark and Sweden, one-fifth of all adults utilize alternative therapies (Launso, 1989). Vincent and Furnham (1996) point out that consultation with practitioners of alternative medicine accounted for 6½% of the total number of consultations in the United Kingdom. They also note that "in Europe, studies suggest that between a third and a half of the adult population have used complementary medicine at some time" (1996, p. 38; see also Furnham & Kirkcaldy, 1996). Although research indicates extensive utilization of alternative medicine within the industrialized world, there are segments of the medical community that continue to oppose government coverage. For example, the national medical association in Australia "is proposing to use new accreditation rules to refuse Medicare rebates to users of alternative practitioners" (Easthope, 1993, p. 289).

Although there are a multiplicity of alternative therapies, Collinge (1996) identifies three basic categories, including *somatic therapies,* or some form of direct physical contact with the body; *herbal and nutritional therapies,* which involve replenishing the body with herbs or nutrients; and *energetic* therapies, which utilize energy systems within the body. Collinge (1996) provides a categorization of these approaches within the framework of various alternative medical formats.

What are the characteristics of alternative practitioners that make them different? Research from Sweden suggests that alternative therapists embody an occupational philosophy that differs from most. Utilizing an earlier construct by Mars (1983), Sellerberg (1991; see also Sellerberg, 1989) believes that the use of animal metaphors provides an accurate description of alternative therapists.

How does this relate to alternative medicine? According to Sellerberg (1991), the Swedish medical system creates an environment within which health care becomes centralized, as well as highly specialized. Alternative medicine (and therapists) provides patients with an approach that contradicts much of the behavior and expectations associated with Western medicine.

Explanation and Assessment of Alternative Medicine

For many, however, alternative medicine continues to be viewed as suspect. Consider the following three explanations of alternative medicine offered by Gevitz (1988). Beginning with the *dominant perspective,* offered by the medical community, alternative or unorthodox medicine is viewed as deviant. Historically, the medical community has publicly and professionally condemned those who utilized alternative forms of medicine. A second perspective of alternative medicine is referred to as the *unorthodox.* From this perspective, those practicing alternative medicine condemned the "regulars" of the medical community for the intrusive regimens that were often fatal, that is, "massive bloodletting, dangerous emetics and purgatives" (Gevitz, 1988, p. 17). In other words, the orthodox approach created more problems through its solutions than it solved; that is, iatrogenesis (see Illich, 1976). From these polar opposites developed a third perspective built on the research of both orthodox and unorthodox medicine. Utilizing the scientific process and an assumed unbiased approach, the scientific perspective offers positive and negative assessments of regular and alternative medicine. In its supposed ability to maintain neutrality, the scientific perspective "allows for a broader understanding of the phenomenon of alternative healing and its relationship to regular medicine and the larger society" (Gevitz, 1988, p. 28). Similarly, this perspective contains as much dogma and ethnocentrism as the others. Rather than debate the relevance or irrelevance of traditional or alternative medicine, it is more important to examine *why* alternative forms of medicine developed and continue to exist in social systems in which Western medicine has been firmly entrenched for extended periods of time. It is also important to understand why alternative medicine continues to flourish in developing nations after the introduction of Western-style medicine (see, for example, the work of Finkler, 1981).

Beginning in the 19th century, alternative medicine was, and still is, in some measure, a response to a growing public dissatisfaction with regular or allopathic medicine (see, for example, Deierlein, 1995, as well as earlier material in Chapter 8). In addition, Starr (1982) argues that the growth of medical sectarianism in the 19th century coincided with an increase in religious sectarianism, and in some cases overlapped. In the latter portion of the 20th century, alternative medicine emerged as a result of a broader conceptualization of such terms as health as well as the potential for structural reform of the larger health-care system (Salmon, 1984). Beginning with chiropractic medicine, the following section addresses various types of alternative medicine.

Chiropractic Medicine

The largest alternative form of health care in the United States is provided by chiropractors, who are the "third largest independent health profession in the Western world, following allopathic medicine and dentistry" (Redwood, 1996, p. 91). The following material outlines the historical framework and future of chiropractic medicine.

Historically, **chiropractic medicine** has been practiced for two millennia. In the United States, Daniel David Palmer in Davenport, Iowa, administered the first application of chiropractic medicine in 1895. Working as a "magnetic healer," Palmer provided significant relief and hearing to a janitor who had been deaf for 17 years by manipulating the vertebrae (Redwood, 1996). By 1897, Palmer opened the Palmer School and Cure, which became the Palmer Infirmary and Chiropractic Institute in 1902 (Wardell, 1988). The theoretical basis of the relationship between the vertebrae and disease was formally published in 1910 and became the foundation of chiropractic medicine (Caplan, 1984). Essentially, chiropractic argues that

> a vertebra can move so as to impinge upon a nerve. This vertebral misalignment, called a 'subluxation,' causes the transmission of impaired impulses and can result in a wide variety of bodily disorders such as peptic ulcers, high blood pressure, diabetes,

epilepsy, and even cancer. Chiropractic therapy involves the detection and correction of these subluxations. The latter is accomplished without the use of drugs or surgery through a series of manual manipulations of the spine called 'adjustments.' These adjustments are designed to restore the proper functioning of the nervous system, thereby allowing the body to heal itself. (Caplan, 1984, p. 83)

Within 3 years, Kansas became the first state to officially license chiropractic. Paradoxically, Palmer also died that year. Throughout the next 50 years, chiropractic was licensed in most states. His son, B. J. Palmer, not only practiced chiropractic but also was perhaps a better businessperson. In 1907, B. J. Palmer purchased the Palmer Infirmary and Chiropractic Institute from his father and renamed it the Palmer School and Infirmary of Chiropractic (PSC). B. J. Palmer not only turned PSC into a profitable venture, but through his marketing skills and use of radio, was able to turn PSC into one of the largest health-related training institutions in the country (Wardwell, 1988). As with other alternative health programs, chiropractic soon experienced a division among its practitioners. The two basic subgroups consist of the "straights" on the one hand, who believe and adhere to the original theoretical formulations established by D. D. Palmer. On the other hand, the "mixers," who represent the largest of the two factions, have expanded beyond the spine to other parts of the body and employ various nutritional and electric-based techniques in tandem with chiropractic therapy (Caplan, 1984).

The future of chiropractic is optimistic. As the number of patients seeking chiropractic therapy either alone or in conjunction with modern medicine continues to increase, the role of the chiropractor will become increasingly solidified within the broader health-care system (see Coulter et al., 1996). Unlike osteopaths, however, chiropractors are not interested in merging their particular style and knowledge of medicine with allopathic medicine. Chiropractors are interested in collaboration and bilateral referrals with allopaths. As Redwood (1997, p. 108) suggests: "each side must learn to recognize its own strengths and weaknesses, as well as those of the other. No one has all the answers."

Osteopathy

The second largest alternative to allopathic or Western medicine in the United States (and most industrialized nations) is **osteopathic medicine.** According to the data in Table 10.1, osteopathic medicine continues to grow. Although osteopathy is considerable smaller than allopathic medicine, there are currently more than 31,000 nonfederal osteopathic practitioners in the United States (National Center for Health Statistics, 1996). Although osteopathic practitioners in the United States are similar to their allopathic counterparts, this is not true in Great Britain (Forsyth & Thayer-Doyle, 1990).

Andrew Taylor Still founded osteopathy. A veteran of the Civil War, Still practiced "regular" medicine until 1874. Initially, Still practiced magnetic therapy or a "laying on of hands" in an effort to cure patients. Quickly ostracized, Still left his family behind in Kirksville, Missouri, and began a career as an itinerant throughout

TABLE 10.1 Active Health Personnel and Number per 100,000 Population, According to Occupation and Geographic Region: United States, 1970–1980, and 1993

Year and Occupation	Number of Active Health Personnel	United States	Northeast	Midwest	South	West
			Geographic Region			
1970						
Nonfederal Doctors of Osteopathy	11,650	5.7	6.3	9.3	3.3	3.4
1980						
Federal Doctors of Osteopathy	1,057	0.5	—	—	—	—
Nonfederal Doctors of Osteopathy	16,073	7.1	8.4	11.9	4.2	4.2
1993						
Federal Doctors of Osteopathy	1,350	0.5	—	—	—	—
Nonfederal Doctors of Osteopathy	31,081	12.0	16.7	19.1	7.8	7.0

Data are compiled by the Bureau of Human Professions.

Source: American Osteopathic Association Yearbook and Directory of Osteopathic Physicians (various years), Chicago. Reprinted with permission.

Missouri (Gevitz, 1982). Engaging in skeletal manipulation, Still eventually developed a theoretical explanation of osteopathy "which emphasizes the integration of the body's communication and regulatory mechanisms, the inherent defenses and healing powers of the body" (Collinge, 1996, p. 206). Essentially, Still was developing what is referred to today as *holistic medicine.*

With the eventual acceptance of his work in Kirksville, Missouri (where his family lived), Still established an infirmary and eventually a 4-year school of osteopathy in 1892. With the assistance of Dr. William Smith, a Scottish physician, students received a grounding in anatomy as well as the manipulation of the skeletal system. In addition to the American School of Osteopathy (ASO), the *Journal of Osteopathy* was soon publishing results of Still and his students. Within a relatively short period of time, a number of schools were providing instruction in osteopathic medicine. However, the Flexner Report recommended closing all osteopathic schools. Although disagreeing with closure of schools, the American Osteopathic Association (AOA) Committee on Education recommendation did agree with Flexner that an increase in educational standards was necessary (Gevitz, 1982). Within two decades, schools of osteopathy had developed a curriculum similar to allopathic medicine. With time, Doctors of Osteopathy have become assimilated into mainstream medicine.

As with homeopathy, the success of osteopathy was not initially accepted within the medical community. The American Medical Association (AMA) attempted to stop its practitioners by branding them as "cultists" (Collinge, 1996). However, osteopathic practitioners legitimated their presence by gaining the right to practice in all states. The culmination of legitimacy occurred in 1961 with the merger of the California Medical Association and the California Osteopathic Association. As a result, the majority of DOs became MDs (Baer, 1987). Today, there are 17 schools of osteopathic medicine and some 200 teaching hospitals approved by the AOA. Relative to their allopathic counterparts, osteopathic physicians consider themselves equal but offering a distinct perspective with regard to the provision of medicine (Collinge, 1996). This distinctive perspective involves "manipulation of the bones, muscles, and joints" as therapeutic techniques (Spector, 1985, p. 53).

Finally, internal disagreement within osteopathy has resulted in a split between those practitioners dedicated to the initial beliefs of Still and those who employed a greater involvement (the "broads") of osteopaths within the medical profession (Gevitz, 1988). These schools of thought can also be understood as the pragmatic and the classical. Consider the following distinction:

> The "pragmatic school . . . believes that its system of manipulation of the back (and attached limbs) is the best method of improving back pain and some joint pains. The . . . "classical" school . . . believes that *all* diseases manifest themselves by an imbalance in the spine and that correct manipulation of the appropriate part of the spine will improve the disease, no matter where in the body that disease might be." (Buckman & Sabbagh, 1995, p. 58)

Examining the more recent numbers of Doctors of Osteopathy in the United States (see Table 10.1), it is evident that significant professional growth has occurred since the early 1980s. To a certain extent, this growth is the result of a shift toward holistic medicine in the United States. A second explanation is that the Doctor of Osteopathy has become an acceptable substitute for the increasing numbers of students attempting admission to medical school.

Homeopathic Medicine

The emergence of **homeopathic medicine** is associated with the work of Samuel Hahnemann, who first used the term "to refer to the pharmacological principle, the law of similars, that is its basis" (Ullman, 1988, p. 33). Applying "natural" drugs, the law of similars proposes that "substances which produced a given symptom in a well person would cure similar symptoms in the sick" (Pernick, 1985, p. 104). Although Hahnemann is generally credited as the founder, the principles of homeopathy can be traced to the work of Hippocrates and the development of modern medicine. The law of similars emerged from a process referred to as "proving," in which Hahnemann tested the effects of small doses of various drugs either on himself, family, or friends. In addition to its utilization of a scientific approach, homeopathy was also built on the knowledge of folk medicine found throughout the world. An example from the laws of similars is that "mercurical preparations, used to treat syphilis since the late fifteenth century, have been found to yield the typical symptoms of syphilis . . . explaining mercury's efficacy in this traditional application" (Coulter, 1984, p. 60). Weis (1983) contends that homeopathy has been successful for three basic reasons. First, the health of the patient would have improved regardless of the intervention. Second, homeopathic treatments elicit a placebo effect. Finally, the treatments do, in fact, work. Weis (1983, p. 38) suggests that "none of these hypotheses is satisfactory, and there is no way to decide among them. Maybe all of them contribute to the right answer, if there is an answer." Perhaps the best known critic of homeopathy was Dr. Oliver Wendell Holmes, who concluded that apparent positive medical outcomes would occur with the use of any remedy.

Begun in Europe, homeopathy found its way to the United States in 1825. Homeopathy became popular among the more affluent and educated within society. Within a relatively short period of time, homeopathic medicine in the United States had developed not only its own delivery system (from clinics to hospitals), but also its own journals and medical societies (Cassedy, 1991). In part, the popularity of homeopathic medicine was in its less intrusive approach when compared with allopathic medicine of the mid-18th century (e.g., the use of bloodletting). Although grounded in Western medical thought and generally practiced by former "regular" physicians, the allopathic community of physicians did not accept homeopathic medicine. Nonetheless, homeopathic medicine continued to grow throughout the mid- to latter 1800s. In fact, homeopathy established the first national medical organization 3 years before the AMA (1844 and 1847, respectively) (Duffy, 1993). However, the effect of the Flexner Report on homeopathic medical schools was significant. After the recommendations of Flexner, only four homeopathic schools remained. Within a relatively short period of time even they were converted to "regular" or allopathic medicine. In addition, professional differences existed between various factions of homeopathic physicians. As a result, homeopathic medicine was almost nonexistent by the 1960s (Kaufmann, 1988; Ludmerer, 1996). However, by the 1980s, the number of practicing homeopathic physicians had increased dramatically. In addition, utilization of homeopathic principles by other health professionals continues to increase.

The United States is not the only nation experiencing a resurgence of homeopathic medicine. According to Ullman (1988), homeopathic medicine is growing in Great Britain, throughout Europe, and South America, but is most popular in the Asian nations of India, Pakistan, and Sri Lanka. As a result, the future of homeopathic medicine worldwide appears optimistic. Ullman (1988), who outlines the role of homeopathic medicine in the 21st century, offers the most extensive future-based presentation of homeopathy. Some patients are attracted to alternative therapies such as homeopathic medicine because of its emphasis on concepts such as "energy" and "life force" relative to health and illness. As Pietroni (1996, p. 391) suggests, this focus allows patients to "understand this language and respond to it. It is the language of the spirit."

Acupuncture

Moving from a primarily American focus on alternative medicine and practitioners, the next two forms of traditional medicine have their origins in China (acupuncture) and India (Ayurveda) respectively. The history of **acupuncture** is the history of China itself (see Ergil, 1997). Medically, acupuncture involves the insertion of various-sized needles into the body. The purpose of acupuncture is "to redirect and normalize the flow of chi" (Chow, 1984, p. 123). *Chi* or *qi* is the vital energy found within the body. When *qi* is out of balance, illness exists. The use of acupuncture is to locate *qi* and reestablish a balance within the body (*yin* and *yang*). Consider the following quote from Ergil (1997, p. 205) regarding the use of acupuncture and the location of *qi*.

> The sensation of the arrival of qi often is felt by the practitioner as a gentle grasping of the needle at the site, as if one is fishing, and one's line has suddenly been seized by the fish. The patient senses the arrival of qi as a sensation of itching, numbness, soreness, or a swollen feeling. The patient might experience local temperature changes or a distinct 'electrical' sensation.

According to Chow (1984), there are 722 known points on the body, although only 40 or 50 are generally utilized. Croizier (1976) argues that political and ideological emphasis on barefoot doctors at the expense of modern facilities and medical training is partially responsible for the limited utilization of known acupuncture needle points. Although similar to chiropractic (Hufford, 1988), acupuncture offers a distinctive explanation of health care within the larger social context. Initially discredited within the United States (Buckman & Sabbagh, 1995), acupuncture continues to gain adherents and practitioners. There are currently more than 6,000 acupuncturists accredited in the United States (Todd, 1996). As a result of extensive research, acupuncture has gained considerable support and adherents not only in the United States but also throughout the world. Extensive research supports the basic premise of acupuncture, thus lending credence to its application not only as a complementary form of medicine but also, for example, as a legitimate anesthesia (Buckman & Sabbagh, 1995). Although acupuncture may not offer a painless surgery, for many it is a bridge between Western and Eastern medicine and philosophy (Chow, 1984).

Ayurveda

Grounded in the history of India, the basic principles of traditional Ayurveda include the elements of "earth, air, fire, water, and space . . . the three *doshas,* forces that, along with the seven *dhatus* (tissues) and three *malas* (waste products), make up the human body" (Zysk, 1997, pp. 233–234). Disturbances within these elements lead to disease. Traditional Ayurveda believes that health and illness outcomes within the body are interwoven with the larger world environment within which the person exists. As such, "it is a holistic approach that has as its goal a long, healthy, and happy life" (Patel, 1986, p. 42).

As with previous forms of alternative medicine, Ayurveda can be differentiated between traditional (explained previously) and Maharishi Ayurveda. Although acknowledging the same origin, the theoretical basis of health care differs. According to Sharma (1997, p. 244), "Maharishi Ayurveda is based on the body's *non*material substrate, which is conceived as a field of pure intelligence." Transcendental meditation (TM) is the method by which one regains control of one's inner being. Similar to traditional Ayurveda, it is through the principles of *doshas* that the body maintains its equilibrium.

While under British rule, efforts were made to reduce the importance of Ayurveda and increase the relevance of Western medicine. Although differences existed between Indian officials, Ayurveda remains a significant component of the larger health-care system. In fact, efforts were put forth in 1975 to integrate traditional and Western medicine within the broader frame of Indian health care, particularly within rural areas of India (Akhtar & Izhar, 1994).

The extent to which traditional Ayurveda is engrained within Indian health culture is evident by the number of colleges offering training (at least 5 years) for potential practitioners. As of 1975, there were 91 colleges in India offering training in traditional Ayurveda medicine. At the same time, there were some 200,000 registered practitioners and another 200,000 who were practicing without being properly registered. In addition, there were almost 200 Ayurveda hospitals in operation (Roemer, 1993). However, Leslie (1976) has criticized the apparent willingness of the state to allow schools providing instruction in Ayurveda medicine to become inferior to "cosmopolitan medical schools." Leslie (1976) also points out that Ayurveda schools were the recipients of students denied admission in other medical schools. Although Ayurveda medicine is generally available within rural as well as urban areas and "generally cuts across lines of social and economic status as never before," the Ayurveda physician, or *vaid,* remains primarily a male occupation (Dunn, 1976).

Sachs and Tomson (1992, p. 309) offer an example of how Ayurveda is integrated into defining symptoms within a cultural context: "Excess phlegm is thought to cause common colds, as well as many other symptoms. Colds are treated with a careful balance of food, drink and therapy, such as medicines and bathing. The cultural preoccupation with the head and colds, together with the Ayurveda theory that neglect of the head causes phlegm diseases, may make people especially vulnerable to specific diseases."

In addition to India, Ayurveda medicine is practiced in a number of Asian countries. Although considered a developing nation, Sri Lanka has achieved remarkable success with regard to overall health status for its population. Although the health-care system is generally given credit for the current health of the population, it is also important to recognize the role Ayurveda medicine has played in the formation of the current pluralistic system (Sachs & Tomson, 1992).

Throughout this chapter there is an interface between traditional and alternative medicine and their practitioners. The following sections return us to relatively modern practitioners of traditional and modern medicine within China and Russia, respectively.

Modern Practitioners of Traditional Medicine

Barefoot Doctors

The history of **barefoot doctors** is relatively young. Originating in Shanghai in the latter 1950s, the training of barefoot doctors throughout China did not begin until the latter 1960s. The term itself is somewhat of a misnomer with much lost in translation. In reality, they are not doctors and they are not barefoot. Rather, they are peasant health workers who receive modest training in health care. Their initial training may range from 1 month to 2 years, with additional training on a regular basis. As practitioners, their primary role is to provide health education within the rural communities of China (Lassey et al., 1997). More specifically, their duties include local sanitation and primary care, such as immunizations and first aid (Sidel & Sidel, 1973). According to a manual prepared for instruction in barefoot medicine, the major headings include: "understanding the human body, hygiene, introduction to diagnostic techniques, therapeutic techniques, birth control planning, diagnosis and treatment of common diseases, and Chinese medicinal plants" (Roemer, 1991, p. 588; see also Sidel & Sidel, 1973, Appendices G and H for a detailed description of the contents of the medical bag and cabinet, as well as a more detailed outline of the barefoot doctor's handbook). As Sidel and Sidel (1973, p. 80) point out: "the barefoot doctor is considered by his community, and apparently thinks of himself, as a peasant who performs some medical duties rather than as a health worker who does some agricultural work." Although a relatively recent practitioner, more than 1 million peasants have been trained as barefoot doctors. Although the magnitude of this effort and the outcome of their work has impressed others in the developing world (Roemer, 1993), their numbers have been declining in the recent past.

Feldshers

Although there are similarities with the barefoot doctors of China, the **feldshers** of Russia represent yet another distinct example of health-care practitioners providing care for rural residents. A feldsher, or assistant doctor, provides primary care and emergency treatment at the local level (Lassey et al., 1997). The difference between barefoot doctors and feldshers is quite clear. In China, barefoot doctors consider themselves as one with the community in which they serve. In Russia, feldshers consider themselves as members of the medical community (Sidel & Sidel, 1973). Historically, feldshers were trained as medical assistants during the reign of Peter the Great in the 17th century. By 1900, there were 32 schools throughout Russia that provided training to feldshers and feldsher-midwives. Although feldshers outnumbered physicians at the turn of the 20th century, their presence has declined as the number of physicians increased. The role of the feldsher was, to some extent, dependent on the location and availability of regular medical personnel. For example, Field (1957, p. 98) points out that health departments could provide feldshers "who have worked three or more years in a medical institution . . . [with] the permission to perform simple operations, prepare prescriptions when no pharmacists are available, and perform other similar medical tasks." Educationally, feldshers receive considerable academic and clinical training that includes three broad areas: general studies, general medicine, and clinical studies (Pickard, 1987). Although feldshers remain a vital component of the health-care system, they are more likely to be found in specialized areas such as environmental sanitation or school health (Roemer, 1993).

The final section of this chapter is an amalgamation of belief systems found throughout the world. However, the material concentrates primarily on subsets of the American population relative to these belief systems.

Folk Medicine

This section begins with an overview of what folk medicine is and the extent of its application. The section concludes with a brief examination of a number of specific applications of folk medicine within the United States.

What is folk medicine? Broadly speaking, folk medicine is any medical activity that is outside of Western medicine (see, for example, Hufford, 1988; Greenberg, 1995; Murphy & Kelleher, 1995). Consider, for example, the criteria applied by Bakx regarding the meaning of folk medicine (1991, p. 21): "it combines two distinct but essentially connected elements: the first is that of culture; the second is that of choice." Similarly, Hyma and Ramesh (1994) overlap the use of the terms "folk medicine" and "traditional medicine." More specifically, Subedi and Subedi (1993, p. 111) clearly distinguish between folk and other forms of medicine. They point out, for example, that in Nepal, folk medicine "is practiced by witch doctors, religious healers, or curers, who attribute particular diseases to either natural or supernatural causes" (see also Helman, 1994). With reference to Zuni Indian medicine, Camazine (1986, pp. 27–28) states that "folk remedies are certainly based upon primitive beliefs of the cause of disease, principles such as the doctrine of signatures, and a variety of folklore and superstitions" (for a medical anthropological explanation, see Romanucci-Ross et al., 1991). Located within all of these definitions is the utilization of botanical or pharmacological remedies that are applied to the afflicted person (for an extensive cross-cultural examination, see Steiner, 1986).

Regardless of definition, Hufford (1988, pp. 237–241) identifies a number of common features associated with folk medicine. Some of these features include: an emphasis on "underlying causes of disease . . . as well as immediate causes; an emphasis on various kinds of 'energy' . . . and is crucial in mediating the concepts of harmony, balance, and integration . . . [and] the meaning of disease and suffering within the system that speaks to cause and cure."

Black Folk Medicine

Folk medicine among African Americans in the United States is grounded in a historical and political context of the African American community relative to the larger society. In particular, Snow (1977a,b; 1978) offers insight into the dynamics associated with the medical and concomitant religious belief system of African Americans in the American southwest and African American folk healers and their work in urban America in the early 1970s.

Historically, African Americans have had lower rates of physician contact than have Caucasian Americans. These differences can be understood as a consequence of greater economic deprivation among African Americans relative to Caucasian Americans as well as institutional racism inherent within the medical care system. African Americans are also more likely to use folk medicine as an available alternative to Western medicine than are Caucasian Americans. Furthermore, utilization of folk medicine at an early age appears to have a cumulative effect. In other words, experiences with folk medicine at an early age create a shared socialization, thus increasing the legitimacy of such health practices in older age (Semmes, 1990).

According to **black folk medicine,** the cause of the problem is much more important than whatever symptoms the patient may be manifesting. Also, illness can be understood as either 'natural' or 'unnatural." A natural illness, which occurs within the context of environmental causes or divine punishment, is always in accordance with the will of God. For example, not wearing proper clothing if it is cold outside will result in an upper respiratory infection. Divine punishment is reflected in paralysis associated with a stroke, thus giving the patient time to contemplate transgressions associated with their earlier life. Unnatural illnesses lie beyond the will of God and the ability of others such as relatives, friends, or the medical profession to treat the victim. The healing of such an illness is left to those with special connections with God or who possess powers beyond those of the general population. It is believed that sorcery or the use of magic can bring about an unnatural illness. The following is an example of how magic is employed in defining the cause of the illness.

> A middle-aged man develops a rash "only where it shows," that is, on his hands, face, and neck. He goes to a physician who . . . gives him a prescription for some ointment. Two weeks later the rash has not gone away—the failure of the doctor's medicine plus the fact that the symptom was seen as being highly unusual results in a root doctor . . . [who] makes a diagnosis of witchcraft and blames the victim's girl friend for putting something in his food. A fee of $250 is charged and a bottle of "jinx-removing" lotion is provided. (Snow, 1979, p. 182)

As the example illustrates, victims of unnatural illnesses oftentimes consult a healer who is usually picked on the basis of their ability to treat a particular problem. And, as Bailey (1991) points out, there are a number of healers from which to choose. According to Watson (1984a), the outcome of folk medicine practitioners "are largely grounded in the patient's (1) faith that the doctor has the ability to heal, and (2) trust that the doctor has holistically understood the patient's disorder and prescribed the correct treatment." Furthermore, medical outcomes are predicated on the ability of the folk doctor to perform a variety of social roles relative to the patient and his or her community (Watson, 1984a). Thus, as a member of the generally lower social class community, healers provide an alternative to the high cost of allopathic medicine. In addition, healers employ greater flexibility in their schedule, and provide much quicker results than do regular health practitioners. Healers also provide a connection between the illness and the larger social and physical environment within which the client lives (Snow, 1978).

Healers are also classified according to the process by which they became healers: "(1) learning, (2) ability conferred during an altered state of consciousness, or (3) ability conferred at birth" (Snow, 1978, pp. 87–88). This is important because the status of the healer is dependent on the method by which they became a healer. Thus, those learning to become a healer have the lowest status, whereas those born with the ability have the highest. Although some healers are well known, others utilize local newspapers as an avenue for exposure within the larger community. For example, Snow (1978) discusses an attempt to continue research by offering healers a small reimbursement for their time and effort. The one healer who responded instead wanted $190 to "straighten out" her (Snow's) love life and help her keep her man. The healer claimed she could tell Snow was having problems with men by the sound of her voice.

Others report similar findings regarding black folk medicine. For example, Blake (1984) chronicles the beliefs of primarily aged African Americans living in the Sea Islands off of Georgia and South Carolina. Here, health and illness are intricately tied to the religious connotations of good and evil. As a result, when faced with an illness, the inhabitants of the island turn first to folk medicine. Blake (1984) describes how a midwife uses the tide as an indicator of birth (only during flood tide).

In a slightly different view of folk medicine, Primm (1984) and Watson (1984b) provide cogent arguments regarding the use of self-medication among African Americans and the potential interactive effects with Western pharmaceuticals. In essence, they argue that modern health practitioners need to become more like folk healers by interacting with and knowing their patients rather than writing prescriptions (see also Holmes & Holmes, 1995).

Black folk medicine requires more than an act of faith by the patient. It requires the healer to know and understand the broad social environment within which the patient lives, as well as the personal environment in which the patient functions. The intricacy of the patient–healer relationship creates a set of norms not generally found in traditional Western-based physician–patient relationships. In addition, the healer connects the illness to the problems and difficulties inherent within the social and physical environments. More specifically, the practice of black folk medicine is intimately connected to religion as the healer is "called by God" to perform such acts. Snow (1981, p. 95) provides the following example of a healing:

> One informant who is such a "blood doctor" told me how she stopped the bleeding from a deep cut by reciting a passage from Ezekiel while also applying an ice pack. When I inquired as to whether the ice pack might have had something to do with the cessation bleeding, I was reprimanded gently with, "God sewed it with His needle darlin'."

Curanderismo

Similar to black folk medicine (Watson, 1984a), Mexican Americans have created a practice of folk healing referred to as **Curanderismo,** which is essentially folk psychiatry with *curanderos* (curer) in the role of therapist (Rose, 1978).

The historical context of curanderismo is that of European medicine in the 15th and 16th centuries and the religious and ethnic traditions associated with Catholicism and the Spanish in Mexico (Watson, 1984a). Others (for example, Trotter, 1997) identify seven historical bases that provide the foundation for curanderismo. These include the Greeks, Christianity and Judeo–Christian writings, the defeat of Southern Europe by the Moors, homeopathic remedies, Native American influences, parapsychology and new age spirituality, and Eastern influences such as acupuncture. As a result of this amalgamation of sociocultural influences, Mexican Americans place considerable emphasis on two primary social institutions: family and religion. In addition, Mexican Americans live in a present-time orientation that is the result of an "acceptance and appreciation of things as they are" (Williams, 1977, p. 112) rather than the future orientation of the dominant Caucasian American culture.

As with black folk medicine, curanderismo also considers health and illness an expression of a dichotomy involving 'natural' and 'supernatural' illnesses. Natural illness fits generally into a biomedical model and is treatable, whereas supernatural illnesses are the result of evil spirits and are treatable only by a curandero. One becomes a curandero either through "the blessings of God" or as a result of experiences that include visions, dreams, and so forth (Rose, 1978). The learning process also involves an apprenticeship with an older curandero. There is also considerable status associated with being a healer. At the same time, as Kiev (1968) points out, there are few negative consequences. Consider, for example, the following statement by Kiev (1968, p. 31) regarding failure: "while his reputation depends upon his successes, he is not blamed for his failures because the group accepts the role of God's will in all matters of health." The role of religion is central to the work of the curandero and is tied to the illness as well as the treatment. In addition, Kiev (1968) identifies the American or Anglo social system as creating the life and lifestyle that brings about illness. This is particularly true for urban Mexican Americans. Urban living is considered antithetical to the beliefs of God. For example, if women work outside the home (as many do in American society), they are unable to come home and provide the care and nurturance necessary for the family. Similarly, increased rates of extramarital affairs, which are the result of changing social roles, and increased dissatisfaction within the family lead to breakdown within the family, all of which increase the risk of illness (Kiev, 1968).

One reason for the success of the curandero is his incorporation of Mexican American culture in the interpretation of physical and mental illness behavior within patients. For example, Kiev (1968, pp. 154–155) argues that the sick role "is a necessary antecedent to a re-examination of patterns of living gone awry and a preliminary step toward reintegration of the individual into the community and re-establishment of a previous harmony."

Curanderismo is practiced on three levels; the material, the spiritual, and the mental. At the material level, the curandero manipulates physical objects to provide relief to the patient. At the spiritual level, the curandero engages in healing practices similar to shaman rituals. Finally, at the mental level, the curandero utilizes thought processes to treat mental and physical conditions experienced by the patient. An example of how a curandero treats a patient at the material level follows.

> Curanderos use several types of rituals for supernatural cures. The *barrida* is one of the most frequent rituals. These cleansings are designed to remove the negative forces that are harming the patient, while simultaneously giving the patient the spiritual strength necessary to enhance recovery. Patients are always "swept" from head to toe, with the curandero making sweeping or brushing motions with an egg, lemon, herb, or whatever object is deemed spiritually appropriate. Special emphasis is given to areas in pain. While sweeping the patient, the curandero recites specific prayers or invocations that appeal to God, saints, or other supernatural beings to restore health to the patient. (Trotter, 1996, p. 264)

Acceptance of the curandero is not universal within the Mexican American community. Research by Kay (1977) found considerable disagreement among her female informants regarding the value of the curandero in eradicating disease. Some young women were, in fact, ignorant of the role performed by the curandero (see also Sanchez Mayers, 1989, for a more recent analysis of generational differences).

Native American Healers

Because of the heterogeneity of the Native American population, it is impossible to suggest a singular interpretation or knowledge base associated with indigenous healers. Instead, this section can only begin to address the multiplicity of tribal folklore associated with health and illness. Consider the following comment by Maddox (1923, p. 24) regarding terminology.

> The name of the mediator between gods and men differs among different people. He is variously called the shaman, the angakok, the voudoo-man, the obi-man, the conjurer, the magician, the wizard, and the sorcerer, to mention only a few of his many titles. For the sake of simplicity and clearness, however, he is here called "the medicine man."

Similarly, in Alaska, the folk healer is referred to as a *diviner* (Subedi et al., 1995). Although the name is different, the methodology is consistent (i.e., use of the supernatural and the spiritual world) with native populations within the lower 48 states.

Although Maddox (1923) suggests that the term "medicine man" is perhaps the best representation available for Native Americans, he also points out that a male did not always hold the position. The history of some Native American tribes indicates that women were considered equally qualified, and often performed as medicine men—for example, the work of Jones (1972) and his portrayal of Sanapia, a Comanche medicine woman. Jones (1972) relates the ability of Sanapia to cure primarily adult patients of "ghost sickness," more commonly referred to in Western medicine as Bell's Palsy, a paralysis of the seventh cranial nerve. The most common term associated with indigenous healers (**shaman**) is not specific to the United States. Originating in Asia, and eventually arriving in the Americas, shamans are found throughout the world (Weil, 1983). For examples of shamanism in various Asian societies, see Blacker, 1975 (Japan), and Kendall, 1988 (Korea).

In general, some Native Americans' concept of health and illness is similar to the curanderismo and black folk medicine. That is, health refers to a state of "balance," whereas illness represents an "unbalanced" state. Furthermore, concepts such as health and illness are understood not only within a physical (i.e., the body), but also within a spiritual and psychological context (Campbell, 1989). Jewell (1979) illustrates the significance of culture definition of behavior relative to accepted psychological well-being. Jewell (1979) also details the apparent psychotic behavior of a Navaho Indian male who had spent some 18 months in a mental hospital in California classified as a catatonic schizophrenic. Although his behavior was consistent with Navaho beliefs, it was interpreted within an Anglo context as suggesting psychosis. Once institutionalized, behavioral expectations associated with the psychotic label were reinforced. Concomitantly, the concepts of health and illness for many urban Native Americans are addressed through the use of traditional Western medicine. Research by Taylor (1989) supports earlier findings regarding sociodemographic characteristics of urban Native Americans utilizing health clinics. Other research is also critical of traditional medicine and the medicine man. Weibel-Orlando (1989, p. 151) argues that "a regimen of teas, chants and blessings" was not particularly effective in the treatment of alcoholism. Among those residing on reservations, health differences between men and women relative to the level of acculturation with Anglo culture were noted. Han et al. (1994) found that the healthiest Lakota women were the least acculturated, whereas the healthiest Lakota men were the most acculturated to Caucasian American culture.

Although it is difficult to categorize Native American medicine, it is important to recognize the extensive range of botanical knowledge they held. Their botanical efforts were intended to relieve symptoms rather than cure (Rothstein, 1988). Compared to the efforts of Anglos, Native American efforts were considerably more extensive. Moerman (1991) points out that the American Medical Ethnobotany has identified some 4,869 species, whereas medicinal plants of Native Americans number some 15,843. Medicine men, or shamans, utilize not only botanical aids, but also various techniques that are manifested in the traditions and customs of the local tribal community. For example, among the Navaho, "treatments used by the singer [medicine man] include massage and heat treatment, the sweatbath, and the use of the yucca root" (Spector, 1985, p. 185). The shaman also learns to differentiate himself from the larger community that he serves. Through the use of drugs, sleeplessness, and acute concentration, the medicine man may experience a vision, a calling, or a connection with the spirit world. It is through these demonstrations of his power that the local members of the community respect him. And, as Maddox (1923) notes, knowing the potential for failure may be death, the shaman has become quite shrewd. For example, rather than establishing a time frame within which an outcome can be expected, those engaged in rainmaking continue to perform those rituals expected to bring rain until it does and then take credit for its success.

The medicine man provides the Native American cultures with a similar connection between the worlds of the known and of the unknown. As such, the medicine man performs a number of functions within the tribal community. He is not only a healer, but also a sorcerer, a rainmaker, educator, and prophet (Maddox, 1923); in essence, the most powerful person in the community.

Summary

This chapter addresses, in rather broad terms, the concept of traditional–alternative and folk medicine. The symbiotic relationship between modern and traditional–alternative or folk medicine allows patients to utilize respective interpretive and treatment modalities exclusively or in combination.

Beginning with alternative medicines, chiropractic medicine involves working the vertebrae that can impinge on nerves, causing various disorders. Osteopathic medicine is built on the belief that under normal circumstances the human body is capable of maintaining its defenses against disease. When necessary, manipulation thereapy is utilized to return the body to a normal state. Osteopathic medicine treats the body as a whole, rather than focusing on one component. Homeopathy involves the use of natural drugs and substances that, if given to a person who is not sick, elicit a specific symptom. Ergo, the natural substances eliminate similar symptoms in a sick person.

Traditional medicines include acupuncture, which is the redirection of the vital energy within the body. This is accomplished by inserting needles along meridians in the body that rebalance the energy flow. Located primarily in India, Ayurveda believes that the larger environment is intimately involved in health and illness. As with previous forms of medicine, a number of elements interact to bring about the outcomes of either health or illness.

Two practitioners that have had relative success within their respective countries include barefoot doctors (China) and feldshers (Russia). Barefoot doctors are peasants who have been trained in basic health care and health education. They "practice" in rural areas of China, where doctors are not available. Although their presence offers villagers access to a modicum of medicine, the barefoot doctor movement has been criticized for lessening the focus on basic medical education and training within academic and institutionalized settings. However, feldshers have provided care to peasants in rural Russia for centuries. Because feldshers were trained as medical assistants, they have had a connection with the larger medical community.

In the final section of the chapter a number of different folk or traditional medicines are examined. First, black folk medicine is grounded in the historical context of African Americans. As with other forms of folk medicine, black folk medicine is based on the belief within the patient that the healer has the power to cure because he knows the cause of the particular problem. Similarly, curanderismo is a folk psychiatry practiced primarily among Mexican Americans living in the southwest. As with black folk medicine, curanderismo is based on natural and supernatural illness. Supernatural illness is treated by a curandero, who has been trained to extricate the evil spirits that have created the illness. Finally, a shaman or medicine man utilizes Native American medicine. Considerable similarities exist between concepts of health and illness and the role of the healer relative to the patient in black folk medicine, curanderismo, and Native American folk medicine.

CHAPTER REVIEW

As with all chapters, the purpose of this review is to provide the reader with the opportunity to reexamine the information in the chapter and appreciate its relevance within the broader context of medical sociology.

1. How is alternative medicine portrayed in the media today? Identify a network program in which alternative medicine is applied. How is the practitioner portrayed? Are these portrayals consistent with information in this chapter?

2. Compare and contrast homeopathy, osteopathy, and chiropractic medicines.

3. Discuss the similarities and differences between barefoot doctors and feldshers.

4. Compare and contrast black folk medicine, curanderismo, and native American folk medicines.

5. As we prepare to enter the 21st century, what is the appeal of alternative medicine? (Not only in the United States, but throughout the world.)

6. Discuss differences and similarities between practitioners of traditional and alternative medicine with modern medicine.

GLOSSARY

acupuncture   involves the insertion of needles along meridians in the body. The purpose of acupuncture is to redirect the flow of energy within the body (i.e., cure illness).

alternative medicine   refers to medical treatments that are not taught or offered in Western medical practice.

Ayurveda   consists of various elements that when disturbed result in illness. As a form of medicine, Ayurveda incorporates the impact of the broader environment in determining health and illness.

barefoot doctors   peasants who have been trained to provide some basic health care and health education to rural farm workers in China.

black folk medicine   involves unnatural illness that occurs as a result of the environment or divine punishment, but is always the will of God. Healers who have the power and connection with the supernatural are summoned to remove the illness.

chiropractic medicine   a form of medicine that involves a hands-on mastery of vertebrae in order to relieve pressure on nerves. The purpose is to eliminate the disorders caused by the misalignment of the vertebrae on the nerves.

curanderismo   is folk psychiatry. Associated with the dichotomy between natural and supernatural disorders among Mexican Americans.

feldshers   in existence for centuries, have been trained as medical assistants to provide primary care to the rural populations of Russia.

homeopathic medicine   involves the use of natural drugs to cure patients. This form of medicine is built around the belief that if a small amount of a natural substance will precipitate symptoms in a healthy person, then a similar amount in a sick person will aid in his or her recovery.

osteopathic medicine   involves the manipulation of the spine to reduce the presence of disease and pain.

shaman   originated in Asia and eventually spread throughout the world. Among Native Americans, the *shaman* (medicine man or woman) is the contact between the natural and supernatural worlds. The shaman is also a healer of disease caused by supernatural events or beings.

traditional medicine   includes those remedies and practitioners that are indigenous to a particular culture.

SUGGESTED READINGS

There are a number of excellent books that address each one of the forms of medicine discussed throughout this chapter. The following represent only a beginning for the serious reader.

Gevitz, N. (Ed.). (1988). *Other healers: Unorthodox medicine in America.* Baltimore: The Johns Hopkins University Press.
A solid coverage of many forms of alternative medicines practiced in the United States. The editor has selected a number of well-written articles addressing the emergence of these various forms of alternative medicines.
Jones, D. E. (1972). *Sanapia: Comanche medicine woman.* New York: Holt, Rinehart and Winston.
The author provides an account not only of the role of the medicine man (woman), but also an in-depth analysis of "ghost sickness."
Micozzi, M. S. (Ed.). (1997). *Fundamentals of complementary and alternative medicine.* New York: Churchill Livingstone.
This is an excellent (and relatively recent) resource guide. Although the author is not a sociologist, he has edited an excellent text on traditional medicines throughout the world.
Watson, W. H. (1984). (Ed.). *Black folk medicine: The therapeutic significance of faith and trust.* New Brunswick, CT: Transaction Books.
A short but useful edited volume that addresses black folk medicine in the United States, Jamaica, and Ghana.

REFERENCES

Akhtar, R., & Izhar, N. (1994). Spatial inequalities and historical evolution in health provision: Indian and Zambian examples. In D. R. Phillips & Y. Verhasselt (Eds.). *Health and development* (pp. 216–233). London: Routledge.
Baer, H. A. (1987). The divergent evolution of osteopathy in America and Britain. *Research in the Sociology of Health Care, 5,* 63–99.

Bailey, E. J. (1991). *Urban African American health care.* Lanham, MD: University Press of America.

Bakx, K. (1991). The 'eclipse' of folk medicine in Western society. *Sociology of Health and Illness, 13,* 1, 20–38.

Blacker, C. (1975). *The catalpa bow: A study of shamanistic practices in Japan.* London: George Allen & Unwin Ltd.

Blake, J. H. (1984). "Doctor can't do me no good": Social concomitants of health care attitudes and practices among elderly blacks in isolated rural populations. In W. H. Watson (Ed.). *Black folk medicine: The therapeutic significance of faith and trust* (pp. 33–40). New Brunswick, CT: Transaction Books.

Bodeker, G. C. (1996). Global health traditions. In M. S. Micozzi (Ed.). *Fundamentals of complementary and alternative medicine* (pp. 279–290). New York: Churchill Livingstone.

Buckman, R., & Sabbagh, K. (1995). *Magic or medicine? An investigation of healing & healers.* Amherst, NY: Prometheus Books.

Camazine, S. (1986). Zuni Indian medicine: Folklore or pharmacology, science or sorcery? In R. P. Steiner (Ed.). *Folk medicine: The art and the science* (pp. 23–39). Washington, DC: American Chemical Society.

Campbell, G. R. (1989). The changing dimension of native American health: A critical understanding of contemporary native American health issues. *American Indian Culture and Research Journal, 13,* 3 & 4, 1–20.

Cant, S. L., & Calnan, M. (1991). On the margins of the medical marketplace? An exploratory study of alternative practitioners' perceptions. *Sociology of Health and Illness, 13,* 1, 39–57.

Caplan, R. L. (1984). Chiropractic. In J. W. Salmon (Ed.). *Alternative medicines: Popular and policy perspectives* (pp. 80–113). New York: Tavistock Publications.

Cassedy, J. H. (1991). *Medicine in America: A short history.* Baltimore: The Johns Hopkins University Press.

Chow, E. P. Y. (1984). Traditional Chinese medicine: A holistic system. In J. W. Salmon (Ed.). *Alternative medicines: Popular and policy perspectives* (pp. 114–137). New York: Tavistock Publications.

Collinge, W. (1996). *The American Holistic Health Association complete guide to alternative medicine.* New York: Warner Books.

Coulter, H. L. (1984). Homeopathy. In J. W. Salmon (Ed.). *Alternative medicines: Popular and policy perspectives* (pp. 57–79). New York: Tavistock Publications.

Coulter, I. D., Hays, R. D., & Danielson, C. D. (1996). The role of the chiropractor in the changing health care system: From marginal to mainstream. *Research in the Sociology of Health Care, 13A,* 95–117.

Croizier, R. C. (1976). The ideologies of medical revivalism in modern China. In C. Leslie (Ed.). *Asian medical systems: A comparative study* (pp. 341–355). Berkeley, CA: University of California Press.

Deierlein, K. (1995). Predictors of alternative medical help seeking behavior: Dissatisfaction and desensitization. Paper Presentation at the Eastern Sociological Society.

Duffy, J. (1993). *From humors to medical science: A history of American medicine* (2nd Ed). Urbana, IL: University of Illinois Press.

Dunn, F. L. (1976). Traditional Asian medicine and cosmopolitan medicine as adaptive systems. In C. Leslie (Ed.). *Asian medical systems: A comparative study* (pp. 133–158). Berkeley, CA: University of California Press.

Dyer, K. A. (1996). Recognizing the potential of alternative medical treatments. *Journal of the American Medical Association, 275,* 8, 578.

Easthope, G. (1993). The response of orthodox medicine to the challenge of alternative medicine in Australia. *The Australian and New Zealand Journal of Sociology, 29,* 3, 289–301.

Eisenberg, D. M., Kessler, R. C., Foster, C., Norlock, F. E., Calkins, D. R., & Delbanco, T. L. (1993). Unconventional medicine in the United States: Prevalence, costs, and patterns of use. *The New England Journal of Medicine, 328,* 4, 246–252.

Ergil, K. V. (1997). China's traditional medicine. In M. S. Micozzi (Ed.). *Fundamentals of complementary and alternative medicine* (pp. 185–223). New York: Churchill Livingstone.

Field, M. G. (1957). *Doctor and patient in Soviet Russia.* Cambridge, MA: Harvard University Press.

Finkler, K. (1981). A comparative study of health seekers: Or, why do some people go to doctors rather than to spiritualist healers? *Medical Anthropology, 5,* 3, 383–424.

Forsyth, C. J., & Thayer-Doyle, C. (1990). Divergent paths of development: A sociological analysis of osteopathy in Britain and the United States. *Free Inquiry in Creative Sociology, 18,* 1, 87–92.

Furnham, A., & Kirkcaldy, B. (1996). The health beliefs and behaviours of orthodox and complementary medicine clients. *British Journal of Clinical Psychology, 35,* 1, 49–61.

Gevitz, N. (1982). *The D.O.'s: Osteopathic medicine in America.* Baltimore: The Johns Hopkins University Press.

Gevitz, N. (Ed.). (1988a). *Other healers: Unorthodox medicine in America.* Baltimore: The Johns Hopkins University Press.

Gevitz, N. (1988b). Osteopathic medicine: From deviance to difference. In N. Gevitz (Ed.). *Other healers: Unorthodox medicine in America* (pp. 124–156). Baltimore: The Johns Hopkins University Press.

Greenberg, O. (1995). The case of Hannah Azulai, illustrating the confluence of Western and folk medicine in an Israeli immigrant community. In E. B. Gallagher & J. Subedi (Eds.). *Global perspectives on health care* (pp. 95–108). Englewood Cliffs, NJ: Prentice Hall.

Han, P. K. J., Hagel, J., Welty, T. K., Ross, R., Leonardson, G., & Keckler, A. (1994). Cultural factors associated with health-risk behavior among the Cheyenne River Sioux. *American Indian and Alaska Native Mental Health Research Journal, 5,* 3, 15-29.

Hedley, R. A. (1992). Industrialization and the practice of Medicine: Movement and countermovement. *International Journal of Comparative Sociology, 33,* 3–4, 208–214.

Helman, C. G. (1994). *Culture, health and illness* (3rd Ed.). Oxford: Butterworth-Heinemann Ltd.

Hendrick, G. (1987). Washington Irving and homeopathy. In A. Wrobel (Ed.). *Pseudo-science and society in nineteenth-century America* (pp. 166–179). Lexington, KY: University Press of Kentucky.

Holmes, E. R., & Holmes, L. D. (1995). *Other cultures, elder years* (2nd Ed.). Thousand Oaks, CA: SAGE.

Hufford, D. J. (1988). Contemporary folk medicine. In N. Gevitz (Ed.). *Other healers: Unorthodox medicine in America* (pp. 228–264). Baltimore: The Johns Hopkins University Press.

Hyma, B., & Ramesh, A. (1994). Traditional medicine: Its extent and potential for incorporation into modern national health systems. In D. R. Phillips & Y. Verhasselt (Eds.). *Health and development* (pp. 65–82). London: Routledge.

Illich, I. (1976). *Medical nemesis.* New York: Pantheon Books.

Jewell, D. P. (1979). A case of a "psychotic" Navaho Indian male. In N. Klein (Ed.). *Culture, curers & contagion* (pp. 155–165). Novato, CA: Chandler & Sharp Publishers, Inc.

Jones, D. E. (1972). *Sanapia: Comanche medicine woman.* New York: Holt, Rinehart & Winston.

Kaufman, M. (1988). Homeopathy in America: The rise and fall and persistence of a medical heresy. In N. Gevitz (Ed.). *Other healers: Unorthodox medicine in America* (pp. 99–123). Baltimore: The Johns Hopkins University Press.

Kay, M. A. (1977). Health and illness in a Mexican American Barrio. In E. H. Spicer (Ed.). *Ethnic medicine in the south west* (pp. 99–166). Tucson: The University of Arizona Press.

Kendall, L. (1988). *The life and hard times of a Korean shaman: Of tales and the telling of tales.* Honolulu: University of Hawaii Press.

Kiev, A. (1968). *Curanderismo: Mexican-American folk psychiatry.* New York: The Free Press.

Lassey, M. L., Lassey, W. R., & Jinks, M. J. (1997). *Health care systems around the world: Characteristics, issues, reforms.* Upper Saddle River, NJ: Prentice-Hall.

Launso, L. (1989). Integrated medicine—A challenge to the health care system. *Acta Sociologica, 32,* 3, 237-251.

Leslie, C. (1976). The ambiguities of medical revivalism in modern India. In C. Leslie (Ed.). *Asian medical systems: A comparative study* (pp. 356–367). Berkeley, CA: University of California Press.

Ludmerer, K. M. (1996). *Learning to heal: The development of American medical education.* Baltimore: Johns Hopkins University Press.

Maddox, J. L. (1923). *The medicine man: A sociological study of the character and evolution of shamanism.* New York: The Macmillan Company.

Mars, G. (1982). *Cheats at work. An anthropology of workplace crime.* Winchester, MA: Allen & Urwin.

Moerman, D. E. (1991). Poisoned apples and honeysuckles: The medicinal plants of native America. In L. Romanucci-Ross, D. E. Moerman, & L. R. Tancredi (Eds.). *The anthropology of medicine: From culture to method* (2nd Ed.). (pp. 147–157). New York: Bergin & Garvey.

Murphy, A., & Kelleher, C. (1995). Contemporary health practices in the Burren. *The Irish Journal of Psychology, 16,* 1, 38–51.

National Center for Health Statistics. 1996. *Health, United States: 1995.* Hyattsville, MD: Public Health Service.

Patel, N. G. (1986). Ayurveda: The traditional medicine of India. In R. P. Steiner (Ed.). *Folk medicine: The art and the science* (pp. 41–65). Washington, DC: American Chemical Society.

Pernick, M. S. (1985). The calculus of suffering in 19th-century surgery. In J. W. Leavitt & R. L. Numbers (Eds.). *Sickness & health in America: Readings in the history of medicine and public health* (2nd Ed., revised) (pp. 98–112). Madison, WI: University of Wisconsin Press.

Pickard, R. B. (1987). Divided medical labor: Physician assistants assessed in light of the Soviet feldsher experience. *Research in the Sociology of Health Care, 5,* 137–199.

Pietroni, P. C. (1996). The greening of medicine. In B. Davey, A. Gray, & C. Seale (Eds). *Health and disease: A reader* (pp. 388–392). Buckingham: Open University Press.

Primm, B. J. (1984). Poverty, folk remedies, and drug misuse among the black elderly. In W. H. Watson (Ed.). *Black folk medicine: The therapeutic significance of faith and trust* (pp. 67–70). New Brunswick, CT: Transaction Books.

Redwood, D. (1996). Chiropractic. In M. S. Micozzi (Ed.). *Fundamentals of complementary and alternative medicine* (pp. 91–110). New York: Churchill Livingstone.

Roemer, M. I. (1991). *National health systems of the world: Volume I—The Countries.* New York: Oxford University Press.

Roemer, M. I. (1993). *National health systems of the world: Volume II—The Issues.* New York: Oxford University Press.

Romanucci-Ross, L., Moerman, D. E., & Tancredi, L. R. (1991). *The anthropology of medicine: From culture to method.* New York: Bergin & Garvey.

Rose, L. C. (1978). *Disease beliefs in Mexican-American communities.* San Francisco: R & E Research Associates, Inc.

Rothstein, W. G. (1988). The botanical movements and orthodox medicine. In N. Gevitz (Ed.). *Other healers: Unorthodox medicine in America* (pp. 29–51). Baltimore: The Johns Hopkins University Press.

Sachs, L., & Tomson, G. (1992). Medicines and culture—A double perspective on drug utilization in a developing country. *Social Science and Medicine, 34,* 3, 307–315.

Salmon, J. W. (Ed.). (1984). *Alternative medicines: Popular and policy perspectives.* New York: Tavistock Publications.

Sanchez Mayers, R. (1989). Use of folk medicine by elderly Mexican-American women. *The Journal of Drug Issues, 19,* 2, 283–295.

Sellerberg, A. M. (1989). Alternative care practitioners: Creating commitment in an unstructured occupation. *International Review of Modern Sociology, 19,* 55–68.

Sellerberg, A. M. (1991). "Hawks" in Swedish medical care: A study of alternative therapists. *Research in the Sociology of Health Care, 9,* 191–205.

Semmes, C. E. (1990). When medicine fails: Making the decision to seek natural health care. *National Journal of Sociology, 4,* 2, 175–178.

Sharma, H. M. (1997). Maharishi Ayurveda. In M. S. Micozzi (Ed.). *Fundamentals of complementary and alternative medicine* (pp. 243–257). New York: Churchill Livingstone.

Sidel, V. W., & Sidel, R. (1973). *Serve the people: Observations on medicine in the People's Republic of China.* New York: Josiah Macy Jr. Foundation.

Snow, L. F. (1977a). Popular medicine in a black neighborhood. In E. H. Spicer (Ed.). *Ethnic medicine in the southwest* (pp. 19–95). Tucson: The University of Arizona Press.

Snow, L. F. (1977b). The religious component in southern folk medicine. In P. Singer (Ed.). *Traditional healing: New science or new colonialism? (Essays in critique of medical anthropology)* (pp. 26–51). Owerri: Conch Magazine Limited.

Snow, L. F. (1978). Sorcerers, saints and charlatans: Black folk healers in urban America. *Culture, Medicine and Psychiatry, 2,* 69–106.

Snow, L. F. (1979). Voodoo illness in the black population. In N. Klein (Ed.). *Culture, curers & contagion: Readings for medical social science* (pp. 179–184). Novato, CA: Chandler & Sharp Publishers, Inc.

Snow, L. F. (1981). Folk medical beliefs and their implications for the care of patients: A review based on studies among Black Americans. In G. Henderson & M. Primeaux (Eds). *Transcultural health care* (pp. 78–101). Menlo Park, CA: Addison-Wesley.

Spector, R. E. (1985). *Cultural diversity in health and illness* (2nd Ed). Norwalk, CT: Appleton-Century-Crofts.

Steiner, R. P. (1986). *Folk medicine: The art and the science.* Washington, DC: American Chemical Society.

Subedi, J., & Subedi, S. (1993). The contribution of modern medicine in a traditional system: The case of Nepal. In P. Conrad & E. B. Gallagher (Eds.). *Health and health care in developing countries* (pp. 109–121). Philadelphia: Temple University Press.

Subedi, J., Andes, N., & Subedi, S. (1995). Society and indigenous health care: The cases of Nepal and Alaska. In E. B. Gallagher & J. Subedi (Eds.). *Global perspectives on health care* (pp. 268–276). Englewood Cliffs, NJ: Prentice Hall.

Taylor, T. L. (1989). Determinants of primary medical care use among urban American Indians. *American Indian Culture and Research Journal, 13,* 3, 215–232.

Todd, A. D. (1996). Western reflections on Eastern medicine. In P. Brown (Ed.). *Medical sociology* (2nd. Ed) (pp. 353–382). Prospect Heights, IL: Waveland Press, Inc.

Trotter, R. T. (1997). Curanderismo. In M. S. Micozzi (Ed.). *Fundamentals of complementary and alternative medicine* (pp. 259–277). New York: Churchill Livingstone.

Ullman, D. (1988). *Homeopathy: Medicine for the 21st century.* Berkeley, CA: North Atlantic Books.

Velten-Schuberth, E. (1993). Traditional and modern medicine in developing countries—Coexistence or integration? *Collegium Antropologicum, 17,* 2, 209–217.

Vincent, C., & Furnham, A. (1996). Why do patients turn to complementary medicine? An empirical study. *British Journal of Clinical Psychology, 35,* 1, 37–48.

Wardwell, W. I. (1988). Chiropractors: Evolution to acceptance. In N. Gevitz (Ed.). *Other healers: Unorthodox medicine in America* (pp. 157–191). Baltimore: The Johns Hopkins University Press.

Watson, W. H. (1984a). Introduction. In W. H. Watson (Ed.). *Black folk medicine: The therapeutic significance of faith and trust* (pp. 1–15). New Brunswick, CT: Transaction Books.

Watson, W. H. (1984b). Folk medicine and older blacks in southern United States. In W. H. Watson (Ed.). *Black folk medicine: The therapeutic significance of faith and trust* (pp. 53–66). New Brunswick, CT: Transaction Books.

Weil, A. (1993). *Health and healing: Understanding conventional and alternative medicine.* Boston: Houghton Mifflin Company.

Wiebel-Orlando, J. (1989). Hooked on healing: Anthropologists, alcohol and intervention. *Human Organization, 48,* 2, 148–155.

Williams, C. H. (1977). Utilization of persisting cultural values of Mexican-Americans by Western practitioners. In P. Singer (Ed.). *Traditional healing: New science or new colonialism? (Essays in critique of medical anthropology)* (pp. 108–122). Owerri: Conch Magazine Limited.

Zysk, K. G. (1997). Traditional Ayurveda. In M. S. Micozzi (Ed.). *Fundamentals of complementary and alternative medicine* (pp. 233–242). New York: Churchill Livingstone.

PART FOUR

The Organization of Health Care in Society

CHAPTER

11 Hospitals

The hospital is in some ways peculiarly characteristic of our society. Within the walls of a single building, high technology, bureaucracy, and professionalism are juxtaposed with the most fundamental and unchanging of human experiences—birth, death, pain. It is no accident that both black comedy and soap opera should have found the hospital a natural setting. It is an institution clothed with an almost mystical power, yet suffused with a relentless impersonality and a forbidding aura of technical complexity. Like the ship of fools that symbolized man's ineradicable frailties in early modern Europe, the hospital can be seen as a late twentieth century symbol of the gap between human aspirations and necessary human failings—displayed not in the confines of a ship adrift at sea, but in an institution that reproduces values and social relationships of the wider world yet manages at the same time to remain isolated in its particular way from the society that created and supports it.

—Rosenburg, 1987, pp. 3–4

The Symbolic Nature of the Hospital

This chapter begins the final section of the book. Chapters 12, 13, and 14 examine the institutional structure within which the medical community operates. Chapter 11 examines the evolutionary role of the hospital in the United States and other countries. Chapter 12 addresses the financial considerations associated with health and illness, and Chapter 13 offers a comparison of health-care systems within industrialized and industrializing nations. Finally, Chapter 14 provides an overview of the future of medical sociology.

Rosenberg's (1987) statement provides a framework within which the history and the future of the hospital can be understood. Thus, on the one hand, hospitals represent all that a society does in an effort to save the lives of its citizens. On the other hand, hospitals represent the social and economic inequalities inherent within American society as well as its abandonment of psychological freedoms and philosophical rights for the patients (see, for example, Helman, 1994). In the end, hospitals are, as Strauss et al. (1989, p. 342), suggest, "variegated workshops—places where different kinds of work are going on, where very different resources . . . are required to carry out that work . . . in the direct or indirect service of managing patients' illness."

The Development of the Hospital

From a systems perspective, the health-care community is made up of a number of interrelated components that include (1) management, (2) resource production, (3) organization of programs, (4) economic support, and (5) delivery of services (Roemer, 1991). This chapter examines the role of the hospital as an integral element within the production of resources component. Functionally, the hospital provides a physical location for physicians and other health-related personnel (also related to the production of resources component) to work. In essence, then, the evolution of the hospital is interconnected with the emergence of medicine (Bullough & Bullough, 1972), and has evolved from an almshouse to a state of the art center of biotechnology (Mechanic, 1976). Simultaneously, the profession of medicine has grown from one of ridicule by the public to one of the most respected occupations in society. Unfortunately, in the latter years of the 20th century, a consequence of the relationship between physicians and the hospital is the devolving of medicine as a profession and the changing nature of hospitals, particularly within the American for-profit health-care system. However, before projecting the future of hospitals, the chapter begins some two-millenium ago to discuss the beginnings of hospitals as they are known today.

The Emergence of the Premodern Hospital

The Western concept of a hospital as a location for the caring of the sick can be traced back to the 6th century BC in Greece. Similarly, hospitals began to appear in

Buddhist temples in India (Roemer, 1993). Others (Ackerknecht, 1982), however, argue that hospitals in India predate their emergence in Western civilizations. In Egypt, hospitals have been traced back to the time of Imhotep, some 5,000 years ago. Understanding the importance of cleanliness in these hospitals, "physician–priests wore spotless white linen while performing their duties, and their drinking water was always boiled or filtered" (Risley, 1961, p. 49). Another example of hospital advancement in non-Western cultures is in the city of Jundisapur (in Persia), which was founded in the 3rd century. Three hundred years later a medical school was established in Jundisapur and efforts were made to encourage physicians from various religious and ethnic backgrounds to establish a hospital. By the 10th century, the hospital and medical school at Jundisapur represented not only the best medicine in the Arab world, but also "held a place of leadership in the world" (Risley, 1961, p. 85).

Returning to the development of hospitals in Western culture, Greek hospital wards "were places for inpatient nursing, including bed rest, treatments, medication, baths, diet, and exercise" (Thompson & Goldin, 1975, p. 3). Expanding on the viability of hospitals, the Romans constructed military field hospitals over small creeks, thus providing running water within the facility (Walker, 1955; Krause, 1977). Roman hospitals served more than a military function. According to Bryant (1995), nurses established hospitals in the early medieval period. Three of these hospitals, the Hotel Dieu in Lyons (founded in 542), the Hotel Dieu in Paris (founded in 650), and the Santo Spirito Hospital in Rome (founded in 717) still exist today.

More broadly, the development of the hospital can be divided into three historical periods of time (the last two historical periods are constructed around significant health system events in Great Britain). Although the earliest period incorporates the Roman involvement, it does not recognize the contributions of previous civilizations such as the Greeks. The first historical period began in 335 and lasted until 1550—in other words, from the efforts of Constantine "to close pagan temples and erect Christian hospitals . . . [to] the collapse of monastic hospitals in the sixteenth century" (Turner, 1995, p. 158). Throughout this period, hospitals were interconnected with religious orders. The second historical period in the development of hospitals begins in 1719 (the establishment of charity hospitals in London) and ends with the National Insurance Act of 1913. The third historical period began in 1913 and ends in 1948, with the development of the National Health Service in Great Britain (Turner, 1995).

However, it was not until the 14th century in Italy (and later in other parts of Europe) that hospitals began to provide medical services to their patients. It is also important to understand that throughout this historical development, hospitals were a repository for the poor and the homeless. Hospital patients were not a reflection of the social class structure within a given society. Those with the economic means received medical treatment at home (Roemer, 1993). For example, Thompson and Goldin (1975, p. 3) point out that among the Greeks, some hospital "patients" were substitutes for the real patient who remained at home because they were "too ill to undertake the pilgrimage." As a result, the hospital provided a refuge within the larger societal framework for those unable to afford the medical care and attention necessary. This dualistic role of the hospital is best summarized by Enos and Sultan (1977, p. 189), who state that "this mixture of poverty and altruism set the stage for the evolution of the modern hospital, as an institution where the very best of scientific care could be expected."

The Hospital since the Industrial Revolution

With the advent of the Industrial Revolution, the structure and function of the hospital began to change dramatically. England witnessed considerable growth in the number of hospitals in the 17th century (Roemer, 1993). Although many were still connected to the almshouse, they were increasingly a medical facility. In fact, Guy's Hospital in London began admitting paying patients in 1724 (Roemer, 1993). A century later, a new type of hospital began to emerge in Europe: a voluntary nonsectarian facility—in other words, a hospital owned and operated by members of the community not connected with either the church or the state. Generally speaking, the owners consisted of a very small number of relatively wealthy residents who donated money for the creation of the facility (Roemer, 1993). This was the beginning, however, of a new relationship between the hospital and the community. The progressive movement away from a religious or political affiliation required concomitant support for the hospital from other sectors of the economy. This process transformed the evolution of hospitals throughout Europe and the United States. However, the emergence of voluntary hospitals funded by a small number of benefactors created additional problems. For example, hospitals could impose restrictions on those admitted to the facility. Admission to many of the voluntary hospitals in London required a "letter" from a subscriber (Cartwright, 1977). Turner (1995), however, presents the charitable hospitals as repositories for the destitute and homeless. At the same time, the Industrial Revolution was depopulating rural areas and transforming urban communities. Throughout the 19th century, the population of England and Wales increased significantly, particularly urban communities (Flanagan, 1995). However, it was not until the end of the 19th century that England had established adequate public health laws (Stubbs & Bligh, 1931).

The system of charitable hospitals was unable to keep up with the extent of poverty and worker dislocation associated with the Industrial Revolution. Turner (1995) also argues that large-scale warfare beginning with the Crimean War (and the rise to fame of Florence Nightingale) in the 1850s to World War I demonstrated the inadequacies of the charitable hospital system in England.

The French Revolution and the Development of the Hospital in France

The emergence of the modern hospital, however, is credited to the French Revolution of 1789. With a heightened sense of social responsibility by the state, citizens were entitled to an increasing amount of public support that included health care. During the early 1800s, Paris became the medical center of the world. French hospitals, when compared with their English counterparts, were unique. Rather than rely on the beneficence of the wealthy to build hospitals, "French hospitals were part of a government-owned hospital *system* which was integrated, metropolis-wide, and centrally administered, with specialized hospitals for certain age groups (children, old people) or diseases (kidney, mental illness)" (Krause, 1977, p. 18). Furthermore, the French changed the profession of medicine by making surgeons specialized physicians and by locating their practice in the hospital. The French hospital also provided medical faculty with a subject pool of patients for their students who included some of the best-known American doctors of their time.

Although begun in France, the concept of the modern hospital spread throughout Europe. Hospitals gained considerable importance within European societies for a number of reasons. First, the status and prestige of the medical profession was improving because of increased professionalization. Furthermore, nurses were being trained and available to provide patient care within a hospital setting. Second, the use of antiseptics improved the overall quality of hospitals leading to a significant reduction in mortality rates. Third, a growing middle class and insurance system made the cost of hospitalization affordable to an increasingly larger segment of the population (Turner, 1995).

Throughout the 20th century, hospitals across Europe have experienced not only the ravages of two World Wars but also the lack of public funding for new construction. Nonetheless, hospital beds in European nations are primarily in the public sector.

In France, hospitals are now classified as local, second level, hospital centers, or regional teaching hospitals. Although the majority of hospitals are now in the private sector, the majority of beds are in the public sector (65%), although that percentage has been decreasing. The differentiation between private and public hospitals reflects differences in the size of the facility. Generally, public hospitals are much larger in size than their private counterparts (Lassey et al., 1997). The private hospital sector consists of two types of hospitals; the not-for-profit and the for-profit facilities that make up 15% and 20%, respectively, of the hospital beds in France (Berger et al., 1990). As with other industrialized nations, French hospitals are experiencing the continued need for new technologies (particularly in private hospitals) while controlling the overall cost of health care. Although funding for public sector hospitals increased, they are mandated to provide a defined set of services while sharing more specialized services as well as personnel. Because of salary differences with private hospitals, public hospitals have had difficulty keeping qualified surgeons (Lassey et al., 1997).

The Hospital in England

In England, public hospitals are arranged into a number of regional hospital boards. Public hospitals consist of community hospitals, district hospitals, and tertiary level health centers. Although the percentage of gross domestic product (GDP) spent on health care in England is considerably lower than in other industrialized nations, more than half of their overall health-care costs are spent on hospitalization (Lassey et al., 1997). Although labor costs (staff) are generally identified as a major contributor, Pascall and Robinson (1993) suggest otherwise. Citing Moores (1997), Pascall and Robinson report that between 1962 and 1984 the workload for nursing staff increased by 32%. Nonetheless, English hospitals [and the larger National Health System (NHS)] have been used as an example of system-based rationing (see, for example, Aaron & Schwartz, 1984). Access to the hospital and its services requires a referral, and with limited space and technology, patients are often forced to queue, or wait their turn. This can be understood within the broader system context of physician differentiation. Primary care physicians provide patient services at the point of entry into the health-care system. If the general practitioner (GP) determines that a patient is in need of a specialist, a referral is made. Specialists are located in hospitals and provide services to patients on entrance to the facility (Kaufmann, 1994). Specialists also have considerable power within the hospital, although the government has attempted to impose limits (McCarthy & St. George, 1990). Nonetheless, Cooper and Worden (1990, p. 96) report that hospital experiences in Great Britain provide a "more stimulating, informal social environment than the atomistic U.S." In other words, the hospital experience in the United States tends to isolate patients, whereas hospitalization in Great Britain requires considerable patient involvement in the provision of care.

Efforts have been made to reduce the cost of hospitalization by allowing large hospitals to develop what are referred to as *self-governing trusts*. The purpose of the trust is to allow the hospital to engage in activity it normally would not. For example, hospitals with a self-governing trust would have the freedom to raise their own capital, control their finances, determine salaries for staff, and establish contractual relations for the delivery of services (Graig, 1993).

Finally, England continues to experience a growing private sector health-care system (including hospitals). This movement is drawing the more wealthy (and healthy) individuals out of the larger pool of recipients, creating a two-tiered system of health care at all levels.

Characteristics of Hospitals in Other Industrialized Nations

Other industrialized nations are experiencing similar problems with their hospital systems. In Italy, the number of hospitals has been declining since the early 1960s, while the number of beds has actually increased slightly. Between the latter 1950s and the latter 1980s, the number of cases increased from less than 4 million to more than 9 million, yet patient days decreased. All of this indicates the changing nature of the hospital. Although more patients are provided care, it is on an outpatient basis, further reducing the need for inpatient care (Venanzoni, 1993). Extensive reform of the public hospital system is not possible, however, given the problems with inflation throughout the 1980s and continued political instability of the central government (Roemer, 1991). In Norway, there are too many hospital beds. Efforts to trim the number of hospital beds from 5.5 per 1000 population to 4.5 have met with opposition because the Norwegian health-care system ensures that all citizens receive the same treatment and care when hospitalized (Album, 1989). Although privatization of hospitals has not occurred, the present system does encourage overutilization of facilities. Any attempt to close hospitals or reduce services is inconsistent with accepted cultural values ensuring equality among citizens (Stevens, 1989).

Overutilization of hospital beds is not limited to Norway (see Kohlmann & Siegrist, 1989). Although most Organization for Economic Co-operation and Development (OECD) nations have instituted hospital reforms and have reduced average length of stay, there is little incentive for further efforts at efficiency. However, the OECD (1994a) reports that the average length of stay in acute-hospitals decreased in all reporting countries. For example, the average length of stay declined from 14.5 to 9.6 days in Austria (1980 and 1992, respectively). In Denmark, the decline was from 9.1 to 6.3 days, whereas the United States experienced a decline from 7.6 to 7.2 days. However, efforts to control hospital-based costs vary widely throughout OECD nations. As Culyer (1990, p. 37) points out, hospital cost reduction is related to "relatively short lengths of stay and short turnover intervals . . . [and] a low rate of hospitalization." Thus, countries that utilize a per-diem method of payment for hospital stays encourage longer treatment periods. In addition, the number of beds and acute hospitalization rates also influence the cost of hospital care. For comparative purposes, there were 7.6 acute hospital beds per 1,000 population in Germany in 1989 and 3.2 acute hospital beds per 1,000 population in the United Kingdom. Other European nation studies also fell within that range. However, acute hospital admissions per 1,000 population in 1989 ranged from 9.0 in Spain to 20.6 in France. According to the OECD (1992), the relationship between admissions and the number of beds is relatively weak because of the broad differences in the average length of hospital stay within each country (OECD, 1992). An example of the mean length of stay in eight OECD countries in 1988 by procedure offers an opportunity to engage in a comparative analysis of similar patient types. The findings indicate rather significant differences between member OECD nations. The mean length of stay for tonsillectomy–adenoidectomy ranged from 1.2 days in the United States to 6.1 days in Ireland. Other countries averaged between 1.8 and 3.1 days. Interestingly, the United States had the lowest mean number of inpatient days for all identified diseases or procedures (OECD, 1994b). The United States also has the most expensive health-care system in the world.

Characteristics of Hospitals in Developing Nations

The hospital sector of the health-care system is not only a problem in industrialized nations. Many of the industrializing nations continue to experience problems of cost and access within their hospital systems. Mills (1990a,b) undertook an extensive investigation of hospital systems in developing countries. Although there are considerable problems with the availability of data, Mills (1990a) offers some broad observations regarding the allocation of resources to the hospital sector in developing countries. For instance, one-third to one-half of health-care resources is spent on hospitals. Furthermore, the larger general hospitals receive a disproportionate share of these resources. Examining how the hospital resources are spent, Mills (1990b) concludes that in developed nations, wages consume a smaller percentage of the total cost of care than in developing nations. In addition, the larger the hospital, the more expensive it is to operate. Finally, within most developing nations, hospitals are located in the public sector. Addressing the question of public–private hospital differences, Mills (1990b) concludes that the paucity of information does not allow for a definitive answer. Although private hospitals do exist in some developing nations, they constitute a small percentage of the overall number of available hospitals. In addition, these private hospitals generally represent and provide for the needs of the upper class rather than a cross-section of the population.

Hospitals in developing nations are often a hybrid of distinctive cultural influences (see, for example, the work of Colfer & Gallagher, 1993, in Oman). Structurally, hospitals may assume the characteristics of any Western facility and, at the same time, maintain their cultural identity. For instance, most Chinese hospitals represent a mixture of Western and distinctive Chinese culture. Perhaps the one distinguishing feature of Chinese hospitals is that they are always overcrowded (Hu, 1984). As a result, the overall quality of Chinese hospitals is inconsistent. For instance, the average length of stay is at least 30 days. In addition, the cost of hospitalization in China is expensive relative to the overall cost of living (Anderson, 1992). Furthermore, family members are a source of considerable physical labor in hospitals. Schneider (1993) recounts observations of immediate kin members cleaning and washing floors, bringing in food, and taking the patient to labs or x-ray. This behavior is not unrecognized by the state. According to Schneider (1993), a son or daughter can receive time off from work (with pay) to provide such support to a family member. In Russia, the changing political and economic structure is not lost on the health care system. Before the collapse of the Soviet Union, hospitals were managed by the state. The system was centralized and highly bureaucratized. The transformation of the former Soviet Union into independent states is beginning to create changes in the hospital sector of the health-care system. Although hierarchical arrangements remain (i.e., with polyclinics), some hospitals are beginning to experiment with private sector initiatives that will raise needed capital (Curtis et al., 1995). For example, hospitals have begun to restructure their facilities to accommodate patients that have private insurance coverage that will cover the cost of hospitalization.

Throughout the world, the nature of the hospital continues to evolve as nations struggle with economic and political change. This is particularly true in the United States. The remainder of this chapter is devoted to the emergence, development, and future of the hospital in America.

Hospital Development in the United States

There is some disagreement regarding the location of the first hospital in the United States. According to Ackerknecht (1982), the first hospital was the Pennsylvania Hospital founded in 1752 in Philadelphia. However, Duffy (1993) points out that Charity Hospital of New Orleans was actually founded some 16 years earlier. The problem is one of semantics. Was Charity Hospital an almshouse prior to becoming a hospital? If so, does that disqualify it as the first hospital? Ackerknecht (1982) qualifies his statement regarding the Pennsylvania Hospital by noting it was the first in the United States, conceding that French and Spanish colonies were founded earlier (see Rosenberg, 1992, for a lengthy examination of the Philadelphia Hospital).

The principles on which American hospitals were founded reflected the political and economic attitudes of colonial America. Many of those same attitudes remain characteristic of American values today. Rosenberg (1987) points out that initially, these hospitals clearly distinguished between the deserving and undeserving poor and needy within society. In fact, the Pennsylvania Hospital required a reference from a "respectable" member of society who would vouch for the moral integrity of the person requesting admission to the hospital. Similarly today, governmental programs intended to provide health-care coverage to those in need continue to classify recipients as being worthy or unworthy of assistance. For instance, Medicare is a federal program that provides limited health care to the elderly. Because Medicare applies primarily to the middle and working class, recipients are considered "worthy" of medical assistance. However, Medicaid is a federal–state program that provides health care to the poor, regardless of age. Given the American attitude toward work as a prerequisite to assistance, Medicaid recipients are generally considered "less worthy" because of misguided American beliefs regarding the causes of poverty. These misguided beliefs involve a plethora of stereotypes regarding the poor. For example, the poor are not poor because they are not willing to work like middle-class Americans. In reality, many people in poverty work every day, but because of the low pay are unable to purchase health insurance. Also, because employers are increasingly passing the cost of health care to workers, low-income workers are less likely to afford the rising cost of health-care co-payments.

Initial Period of Development: 1750–1870

Throughout this initial period of development that began in 1750 and ended in 1870, hospitals (and physicians) eventually began redefining their roles relative to the patients being served (the identification of historical periods is drawn from the work of Burns, 1990). The provision of medical support to the less fortunate served as an example of community responsibility (Burns, 1990). Regardless of the intention, hospitals in the early 19th century provided care, rather than a cure. As Starr (1982, p. 72) points out, "when sick, people were safer at home."

The Expansion Period: 1870–1919

The second major historical period is relatively short. Beginning in 1870 and ending in 1919, the second historical period is noted for the expansion of the hospital across the United States. During this period of time, the total number of hospitals and hospital beds increased dramatically, as did the level of technology (see Bernheim, 1948, for a history of Johns Hopkins, the most famous hospital to emerge during this period). In addition, the type of patient also began to change the image of the hospital. Increasingly, the hospital was the location of choice for the wealthy as well as the poor (Rosenberg, 1987). The middle class either could not afford hospital care or desired not to be admitted. Throughout this period, three forces helped shape the development of these new hospitals include the germ theory of disease, medical technology, and urbanization (Temin, 1988). The impact of these forces on the American hospital in the early 20th century can be understood in the following quote: "By World War I diagnosis had replaced dependency as the key to hospital admission" (Rosenberg, 1989, p. 11).

Throughout this period of growth, hospitals maintained the religious and ethnic heritage of their founders (as well as control over the provision of care to constituents). It was the continued development of non-governmental, nonprofit hospitals built around religious or ethnic communities that eventually led to the construction of public hospitals in those communities with a multiplicity of ethnic or religious traditions. Perhaps less known is the fact that many of these hospitals were either founded or managed by women (Lynaugh, 1992). A third type of hospital also emerged during the early years of the 20th century. These were generally smaller and specialized for-profit or proprietary hospitals funded by physicians who utilized the facility for their patients (Hollingsworth & Hollingsworth, 1987). Throughout this period, however, the control of hospitals was primarily through the lay community (Burns, 1990).

The Period of Historical Influence: 1930–1965

The third historical period began in 1930 and ended in 1965. There were two significant changes during this period of time (Burns, 1990). First was the emergence of private insurance, and second, the increased levels of government involvement and regulation of the industry. By 1935, the three types of hospitals (public, nonprofit, and proprietary) were serving relatively different patient populations in distinct locations. For example, public hospitals were, on average, the largest (in terms of number of beds). The size of the community was also related to the type of hospital, with smaller, for-profit facilities more likely located in small communities. Concomitantly, public and nonprofits were more likely located in larger communities (Hollingsworth & Hollingsworth, 1987).

Hospital development during this period was shaped by a number of broad historical changes. The first significant historical event was the Great Depression. During the height of the Depression, one-fourth of the adult workforce was unemployed. On the surface, the Depression did not appear to have a negative impact the hospital as a social institution. Looking only at overall admission rates, there was a slight drop in the early 1930s, but a gradual rise thereafter. However, admission rates were dependent on the type of hospital. For instance, occupancy rates were as low as 35% in private nonprofit hospitals in New York City, whereas public hospitals were experiencing occupancy rates greater than 100% (Stevens, 1989b).

Perhaps the most important impact on hospitals during this period occurred when Dr. Justin Ford Kimball, an executive vice president at Baylor University in Dallas, Texas, organized a prepayment plan for teachers that would guarantee hospitalization for 3 weeks at the Baylor University Hospital. Although not the first such pre-payment program developed, this plan became the impetus for Blue Cross (Law, 1994). Initially covering a relatively small segment of the overall population, the "third-party payment" system quickly spread throughout the United States in the decades ahead. Following the initial success of Blue Cross, for-profit insurance companies began offering group coverage for hospital expenses (Starr, 1982). Beginning with one plan in 1929, there were more than 70 by 1943. The relationship between hospitals, Blue Cross, and the state is summarized by Fein (1986, p. 16):

> The plans were exempt from state insurance legislation and, as charitable organizations, from state and federal taxation. Furthermore, since, without reserves, the hospitals were "at risk," control of these nonprofit hospital corporations was vested in representatives (administrators and trustees) of hospitals and physicians rather than in the lay public. In return for these benefits, the corporations were expected to serve the entire community and to assure the availability of insurance to persons of moderate and low income.

Beginning in the 1940s, the availability of Blue Cross and for-profit insurance carriers led to health insurance as a fringe benefit in labor negotiations. As a result, demand for health services and utilization rates increased, thereby increasing the cost of health care (Burns, 1990). For example, the average daily cost for care in a New York City hospital in the early 1940s was $6.70 (Ginzburg, 1977). Also in the 1940s, the passage of the Hill–Burton Act encouraged (through federal funding) the construction of voluntary and public hospitals throughout the United States. The result was an unprecedented expansion in the number of community hospitals and beds. Although the act initially brought hospitals to primarily rural communities across the nation (Temin, 1988), the long-term effect of the act has been to exacerbate the structural problems associated with the health-care system by creating an over-supply of facilities that are underutilized. Research by the American Hospital Association listed occupancy rates in small (less than 50 beds) rural hospitals at 40% (Kiel, 1993). Because of underutilization among many rural hospitals, closures have increased throughout the 1980s. However, as Alexander et al. (1996) report, some rural hospitals have successfully converted to other health-related activities. Thus, the Hill–Burton Act had a tremendous impact not only on the construction of hospitals, but also on the organization of a regional planning network of hospitals across the United states (Stevens, 1989b; see also Ludtke et al., 1990).

Another change during this period was the introduction and eventual passage in 1965 of Medicare and Medicaid. These two federal health programs ensured coverage for two impoverished segments of the population: the poor and the elderly. However, passage of these programs came with a cost: increased governmental regulation of the health-care community. Although government financing of health care increased as a result of these programs, the production of medical care by the government decreased. One consequence was the eventual increase in the number of for-profit hospitals (Starr, 1982).

The Period of Change, Cost Control, and Contraction: 1965–1990

The final historical period in the development of the hospital in America begins in 1965 and ends in 1990. During this period of time, hospitals experienced considerable change, particularly in terms of hospital costs and patient utilization.

Throughout the 1960s and 1970s, health-care costs were increasing at a double-digit rate, with hospital costs the most expensive component of the American health-care system. Before examining the data, however, there are three interrelated characteristics associated with hospitals that must be identified. The first is the owner-ship of the facility. Hospitals can be categorized into three basic types: nongovernmental nonprofit (voluntary), for-profit (proprietary), and governmental (local, county, state, or federal). Second is the type of hospital. The majority of hospitals are referred to as *community hospitals* and are owned by the government, voluntary, or for-profit organizations. There are also hospitals that provide specialized treatment (e.g., alcohol and drug rehabilitation). Ownership of specialized hospitals had been primarily in the public sector. Increasingly, the private sector has begun to develop hospitals designed for either specific diseases or age categories. The third characteristic is the size of the facility. Although mentioned earlier, it is important to reiterate this point. Larger facilities are operated primarily within the public sector, whereas smaller hospitals are generally disease-specific and owned by for-profit companies. The large public hospitals (300 or more beds) also provide more services to the uninsured than any other type of hospital (Davis et al., 1990). Smaller hospitals are also more likely to be located in rural areas of the United States. Because of shifting populations, these hospitals face an uncertain future, which could include closure or conversion (Alexander et al., 1996). However, one of the most significant changes has been the rise of for-profit chain hospitals. The growth of companies such as Columbia/HCA and Humana has been substantial (Gray, 1996). This is an issue that is examined in greater detail in the remaining chapters. Another significant change is occurring among nonprofit community hospitals. These facilities are increasingly becoming business rather than service oriented (Relman, 1991). For instance, Bogdanich (1991) discusses the various techniques hospitals have implemented as they attempt to discourage the uninsured from utilizing their facility. One hospital near the border with Mexico, for example, dressed their security personnel in the same color clothing as the border patrol. The purpose was to scare illegal immigrants and keep them from using the hospital.

Although the data in Table 11.1 identify all health services, it is important to see the cost of hospital care relative to the other components within the system. Notice, however, that the amount of money spent on hospitals has been decreasing since 1980. Furthermore, the annual percent change in amount spent on hospitals has been considerably less than other components. The data reflect changes within the health-care system regarding the movement toward outpatient care and downsizing the role of hospitals.

Efforts to control the cost of health care have utilized various techniques ranging from the legal system to budgetary constraints to market remedies. These efforts

TABLE 11.1 National Health Expenditures, Percent Distribution, and Average Annual Percent Change, According to Type of Expenditure: United States, Selected years 1960–1994

Type of Expenditure	1960	1970	1980	1990	1994
Amount in billions					
Total	$26.9	73.2	247.2	697.5	949.4
Percent distribution					
All expenditures	100.0	100.0	100.0	100.0	100.0
Health services and supplies	93.7	92.7	95.3	96.5	96.8
Personal health	88.0	87.1	87.8	88.1	87.6
Hospital care	34.5	38.2	41.5	36.8	35.7
Physician services	19.7	18.5	18.3	21.0	19.9
Dentist services	7.3	6.4	5.4	4.5	4.4
Nursing home care	3.2	5.8	7.1	7.3	7.6
Other professional services	2.3	1.9	2.6	5.0	5.2
Home health care	0.2	0.3	1.0	1.9	2.8
Drugs and other medical non-durables	15.8	12.0	8.7	8.6	8.3
Vision products and other medical durables	2.4	2.2	1.5	1.5	1.4
Other personal health care	2.6	1.8	1.6	1.6	2.3
Program administration and net cost of health insurance	4.3	3.7	4.8	5.5	6.2
Government public health activities	1.4	1.8	2.7	2.8	3.0
Research and construction	6.3	7.3	4.7	3.5	3.2
Noncommercial research	2.6	2.7	2.2	1.8	1.7
Construction	3.7	4.6	2.5	1.8	1.5

Types of expenditure	1960–1965	1970–1975	1980–1985	1990–1991	1993–1994
		Average annual percent change			
All expenditures	8.9	12.3	11.6	9.1	6.4
Health services and supplies	8.4	12.5	11.8	9.4	6.5
Personal health care	8.3	12.4	11.6	10.0	5.7
Hospital care	8.6	13.4	10.4	10.1	4.4
Physician services	9.2	12.0	13.1	8.4	4.6
Dentist services	7.3	11.2	10.2	5.6	7.5
Nursing home care	1.6	15.5	11.7	12.2	7.8
Other professional services	7.4	14.2	21.2	10.4	7.1
Home health care	9.6	23.2	18.9	22.4	13.8
Drugs and other medical nondurables	6.8	8.1	11.4	9.5	4.5

(continued)

TABLE 11.1   Continued

Types of expenditure	1960–1965	1970–1975	1980–1985	1990–1991	1993–1994
		Average annual percent change			
Vision products and other medical durables	9.1	9.5	12.4	6.8	4.6
Other personal health care	3.5	13.8	8.8	21.1	22.5
Program administration and net cost of health insurance	10.6	12.5	15.0	0.2	15.2
Government public health activities	10.8	16.8	11.5	9.1	12.4
Research and construction	15.1	9.4	7.1	1.7	3.5
Noncommercial research	17.1	11.2	7.5	5.8	9.9
Construction	13.7	8.3	6.7	−2.4	−2.8

Note: Data are compiled by the Health Financing Administration. These data include revisions in health expenditures back to 1960 and differ from previous editions of *Health, United States.*

Source: Office of National Health Statistics, Office of the Actuary. National health expenditures, 1994. Health Care Financing Review vol. 17, no. 3. HCFA Pub. No. 03373. Washington: Health Care Financing Administration, Spring 1996.

Source: National Center for Health Statistics. *Health, United States, 1995.* Table 119. Hyattsville, Maryland: Public Health Service, 1996.

are discussed in Chapter 12 on the financing of the health-care system. Nonetheless, hospitals have been forced to reexamine their role within the broader context of health-care providers. As Thompson (1977) points out, hospitals have experienced pressure from four distinctively different groups. (Although significant changes have occurred since the late 1970s, these four broad points illustrate the nature of the problem for hospitals.) First, these groups consist of provider interests. That is, physicians who are members of the medical staff who expect the hospital to maintain the latest technologies so they can perform their role relative to the patient. The second group consists of the patients who generally have a choice of hospitals from which to choose. Patients (as members of the community) also want to participate in the decision-making process of the hospital. In other words, to make the hospital receptive to their needs. Third is the third-party payers (insurance companies or levels of government). Thompson (1977, p. 110) recognizes these groups as relatively powerless because they are "payers of care; they are not buyers of care." In other words, third-party payers pay the bills, but do not dictate where patients should or will go for treatment. This point has changed dramatically in the recent past and is examined in greater detail in Chapter 12. The fourth group involves the requests (and demands) of the larger society (formulated by governmental bodies) toward the hospital. This is perhaps the most problematic because of inherent inconsistencies associated with competing constituencies. In response to these four competing areas, hospitals must determine the most effective and efficient allocation of available funds that will accommodate these diverse demands.

The second major change during this historical period involves patient utilization of hospitals. For instance, the average length of stay and occupancy rates has decreased within American hospitals. Furthermore, the total number of admissions to hospitals and hospital personnel per 100 patients has increased along with the average cost per patient day and per patient stay. Similarly, the number of outpatient visits has also increased. What are the implications of these changes? First, examine the data in Tables 11.2 and 11.3.

Table 11.2 provides a 33-year history of the average length of stay by type of hospital ownership and 18-year history by size of facility. The most consistent finding in this table is the decrease in the average length of stay, except for proprietary and small hospitals. Although their lengths of stay increased, they remain the lowest lengths of stay among all types and sizes. The implication of these numbers is reflected in the average cost per patient stay. According to the U.S. Census Bureau (1996), for-profit hospitals represent the lowest average per patient cost ($5,529) when compared to public and nongovernmental nonprofit facilities ($6,513 and

TABLE 11.2   Average Length of Stay According to Type of Ownership and Size of Hospital: United States, Selected Years 1960–1993

Type of Ownership and Size of Hospital	Number of Days				
	1960	*1975*	*1980*	*1990*	*1993*
Average length of stay					
All ownerships	8.4	8.0	7.8	7.5	7.3
Federal	21.4	14.4	12.9	12.3	12.5
Nonfederal	7.6	7.7	7.6	7.3	7.0
Nonprofit	7.4	7.8	7.7	7.3	6.9
Proprietary	5.7	6.6	6.5	6.4	6.3
State–local government	8.8	7.6	7.4	7.8	7.9
Size of hospital					
6–99 beds	—	6.5	6.3	6.7	6.7
100–199 beds	—	7.2	7.1	7.1	6.9
200–299 beds	—	7.6	7.5	7.0	6.8
300–499 beds	—	8.2	8.0	7.3	7.0
500 or more beds	—	10.2	9.6	8.9	8.7

Note: Data are based on reporting by a census of hospitals. Excludes psychiatric and tuberculosis and other respiratory disease hospitals.

Source: Reprinted with permission of Healthcare InfoSource, Inc., a subsidiary of the American Hospital Association, copyright 1981, 1986–95.

TABLE 11.3   Hospitals—Summary Characteristics: 1972–1994

Item	1972	1980	1990	1994
Number				
All hospitals	7,061	6,965	6,649	6,374
Hospitals with 100 beds or more	2,710	3,755	3,620	3,492
Nonfederal[1]	6,660	6,606	6,312	6,067
Community hospitals[2]	5,746	5,830	5,384	5,229
Nongovernmental nonprofit	3,301	3,322	3,191	3,139
For-profit	738	730	749	719
State and local government	1,707	1,778	1,444	1,371
Long-term general and special	216	157	131	110
Psychiatric	529	534	757	696
Tuberculosis	72	11	4	5
Federal	401	359	337	307
Beds (1,000)				
All Hospitals[3]	1,550	1,365	1,211	1,128
Rate per 1,0000 population[4]	7.4	6.0	4.9	4.3
Beds per hospital	220	196	182	177
Nonfederal[1]	1,407	1,248	1,113	1,044
Community hospitals[2]	879	988	928	902
Rate per 1,000 population[4]	4.2	4.3	3.7	3.6
Nongovernmental nonprofit	617	692	657	637
For-profit	57	87	102	101
State and local government	205	209	169	164
Long-term general and special	54	39	25	19
Psychiatric	457	215	158	121
Tuberculosis	13	2	(Z)	1
Federal	143	117	98	84
Occupancy rate[5]				
All Hospitals	78.0	77.7	69.7	66.1
Nonfederal[1]	78.0	77.4	69.4	65.4
Community hospitals[2]	75.4	75.6	66.7	62.9
Nongovernmental nonprofit	77.5	78.2	69.3	64.8
For-profit	68.7	65.2	52.6	50.1
State and local government	71.0	71.1	65.3	63.5
Long-term general and special	83.0	85.9	85.9	82.9
Psychiatric	82.8	85.2	82.5	80.3
Tuberculosis	61.2	67.0	66.4	80.7
Federal	80.0	80.1	73.3	74.9
Expenses ($ Billion)[6]				
All Hospitals	32.7	91.9	234.9	310.8

TABLE 11.3   **Continued**

Item	1972	1980	1990	1994
Nonfederal[1]	30.0	84.0	219.6	290.8
Community hospitals[2]	25.5	76.9	203.7	275.8
Nongovernmental nonprofit	18.4	55.8	150.7	204.2
For-profit	1.4	5.8	18.8	23.4
State and local government	5.7	15.2	34.2	48.1
Long-term general and special	0.7	1.2	2.7	2.3
Psychiatric	3.1	5.8	12.9	12.3
Tuberculosis	0.1	0.1	0.1	0.1
Federal	3.1	7.9	15.2	20.0
Personnel (1,000)[7]				
All Hospitals	2,671	3,492	4,063	4,270
Nonfederal[1]	2,439	3,213	3,760	3,969
Community hospitals[2]	2,051	2,873	3,420	3,692
Nongovernmental nonprofit	1,473	2,086	2,533	2,719
For-profit	105	189	273	302
State and local government	473	598	614	672
Long-term general and special	63	56	55	38
Psychiatric	307	275	280	233
Tuberculosis	12	3	1	1
Federal	232	279	303	301
Personnel per 100 Patients[7]	221	329	482	573
Outpatient Visits (mil)	219.2	263.0	368.2	453.6
Emergency	60.1	82.0	92.8	96.0
Closures	(NA)	73	63	40

Covers hospitals accepted for registration by the American Hospital Association; see text, section 3. Short-term hospitals have an average patient stay of less than 30 days; long-term, an average stay of longer duration. Special hospitals include obstetrics and gynecology; eye, ear, nose, and throat; rehabilitation; orthopedic; and chronic and other special hospitals except psychiatric, tuberculosis, alcoholism, and chemical dependency hospitals. See also *Historical Statistics, Colonial Times to 1970,* Series B 305-318, B 331-344, and B 413-422.

NA, Not available. Z, less than 500 beds, $50 million, or 0.5%.

[1] Short-term (average length of stay less than 30 days) general and special (e.g., obstetrics and gynecology; eye, ear, nose, and throat; rehabilitation, etc., except psychiatric, tuberculosis, alcoholism, and chemical dependency). Includes hospital units of institutions.

[2] Excludes hospital units of institutions.

[3] Beginning 1989, number of beds at end of reporting period; prior years, average number in 12-month period.

[4] Based on Bureau of the Census estimated resident population as of July 1. Estimates reflect revisions based on the 1990 Census of Population.

[5] Ratio of average daily census to every 100 beds.

[6] Excludes new construction.

[7] Includes full-time equivalents of part-time personnel.

Source: 1995/96 *Hospital Statistics,* Healthcare InfoSource, Inc., A Subsidiary of the American Hospital Association, copyright 1995.

$6,257, respectively). The implications of these findings is addressed later in the chapter.

The data in Table 11.3 support the argument that there has been increased growth in the numbers of personnel and expenses incurred by hospitals. Furthermore, the data also indicate a continued decrease in the size and occupancy rates of hospitals. More specifically, the rate of growth in expenses is greatest among for-profit hospitals. At the same time, for-profit hospitals have the lowest occupancy rates and the greatest increase in the number of personnel. (Previous data also indicates for-profit hospitals had the lowest overall cost per patient stay and the shortest length of stay.) Thus, consider the following equation (Wolinsky, 1988) as a representation of those characteristics necessary in determining hospital costs.

$$\text{Total Hospital Costs} = \text{Admissions} \times \text{Length of Stay} \times \text{Cost per Patient Day}$$

Based on this equation, it is known that admission rates have increased (primarily among larger hospitals) while length of stay has decreased and cost per patient day has increased. Table 11.4 provides data from 1970 to 1994 regarding the average cost per day and per stay by type of hospital. Relative to the equation presented here, hospital costs will continue to rise unless limitations are applied to hospital admissions or to services and personnel within the facility. In relation to

TABLE 11.4   Average Cost to Community Hospitals per Patient: 1970–1994

Type of Hospital	1970	1980	1990	1994
Average Cost per Day, Total	74	245	687	931
Annual Percent Change[1]	12.7	12.9	7.8	5.7
Nongovernmental nonprofit	75	246	692	950
For-profit	71	257	752	924
State and local government	71	239	634	859
Average Cost per Stay, Total	605	1,851	4,947	6,230
Nongovernmental nonprofit	615	1,902	5,001	6,257
For-profit	486	1,676	4,727	5,529
State and local government	614	1,750	4,838	6,513

In dollars, except percent. Covers nonfederal short-term general or special hospitals (excluding psychiatric or tuberculosis hospitals and, beginning 1975, hospital units of institutions). Total cost per patient based on total hospital expenses (payroll, employee benefits, professional fees, supplies, etc.). Data have been adjusted for outpatient visits.

[1] Change from immediate prior year, except 1970, average annual change from 1965. For explanation of average annual change, see Guide to Tabular Presentation.

Source: 1995/96 *Hospital Statistics,* Healthcare InfoSource, Inc., a subsidiary of the American Hospital Association, copyright 1995.

other nations, these characteristics are somewhat unique. According to Iglehart (1993, p. 372), "in almost every instance, the United States has fewer beds per 1000 population, a lower average admission rate, and a shorter length of stay, but more employees per bed and a lower occupancy rate than other major industrialized countries."

As stated earlier, hospitals today are undergoing rapid change. As with all industries, hospitals are being decentralized and downsized. As a result, former allegiances and lines of authority are changing within the hospital structure. Perhaps the most noticeable change is in the dual line of authority that has permeated hospital bureaucracy for some time.

Lines of Authority and the Modern Hospital

Regardless of the form of ownership, size, or type of facility, hospitals are bureaucracies, "characterized by a highly developed horizontal division of labor, a hierarchical authority system, and an elaborate structure of roles and rules for controlling behavior" (Flood & Scott, 1987, p. 14). Similarly, Mechanic (1978, p. 365) points out that hospitals are "characterized by many lines of authority, various sources of power, and complicated lines of communication." Although the broad-scale governing of hospitals is maintained by a board of directors, the daily functioning has been shared between two competing lines of authority: the hospital administrators and the physicians (Fox, 1989). That is, until recently. In the past, hospital administrators controlled the daily financial aspects of the hospital while physicians performed their tasks of caring for and curing patients. As Poirier-Bures and Bures (1987, p. 367) point out, "under the dual-authority system, clashes between 'money' and 'services' were usually resolved in favor of service—doctors held the edge of power." Historically, the unique position of physicians within the hospital has been as guest. In that capacity, physicians have controlled not only their organizational autonomy, but they also have a direct impact on the work experiences of others within the organization. For example, nurses are employees of the hospital, yet carry out the orders of the physicians (Coe, 1978). It is this effort to maintain professional autonomy within an increasingly bureaucratized organization that has resulted in ongoing goal conflict between physicians and hospital administrators. As Coe (1978, p. 306) points out, as hospitals increase in size, so too will the bureaucratization of the organization, which "impinges directly on the functional autonomy of the medical staff." Figure 11.1 illustrates the organizational outline of the dual line of authority within a general hospital. Notice the various hospital services directly under the control of the hospital director, who also is responsive to the medical staff, thus creating a "dual line of authority" within the organization.

Today, however, the relationship between physicians and hospital administrators is changing and creating a more integrated authority-based relationship (see, for example, the findings of Leicht et al., 1995, regarding the impact of organiza-

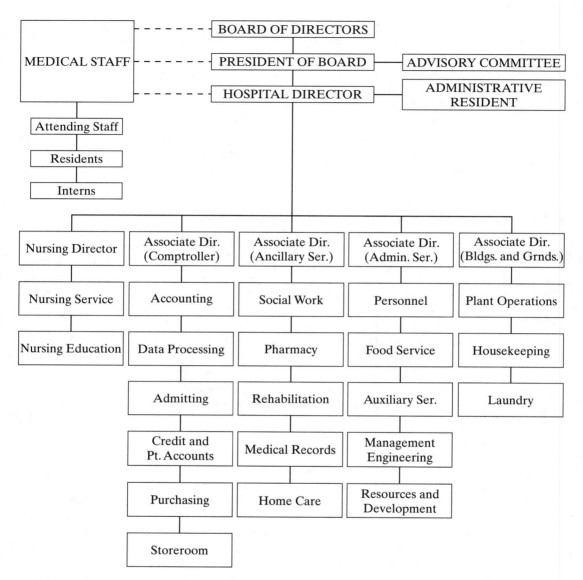

FIGURE 11.1   Administrative organization of a general hospital.

Source: R. M. Coe (1978). *Sociology of medicine* (2nd Ed), p. 299. New York: McGraw Hill. Reprinted with permission.

tional change on physicians and hospital administrators). This changing relationship can be understood as a result of the following:

1. The boundaries between medical and business decisions are blurring because of changes in the mechanisms through which hospitals are paid.

2. Physicians are entering a more competitive environment . . . [in which] physicians may be more willing to trade off complete autonomy in their practices to gain the security of an income and/or institutional affiliation.
3. The changing organizational structure of health care delivery has exerted severe strain on traditional hospital-physician relationships. (Alexander et al., 1986, p. 221)

As hospitals continue to downsize and restructure, the dual line of authority is being revisited on a regular basis. Young and Saltman (1985) point to increased inter-occupational differences between physicians and other hospital staff as an indication of a diminishing social position for physicians. From a management perspective, Wirth and Allcorn (1993) address the networking relationship of group practices to hospital needs. What these diverse responses indicate is a dramatic shift in the distribution of power between the previous two lines of authority within the hospital bureaucracy.

Perhaps more disturbing however, is the assessment by Lindorff (1992) of for-profit hospital chains that neither physicians nor hospital administrators are really in charge. Instead, power is concentrated in the "top management in the central corporate office" (Lindorff, 1992, p. 96). Thus, as the bureaucratic structure of the hospital undergoes change, the statuses and roles of its participants will also change.

The Future of Hospitals: Will They Survive?

Consider the implications of the following statement: "It should be hardly surprising then, that many believe the days of the stand-alone hospital, like those of the solo practitioner, are numbered" (Zelman, 1996, p. 97). The hospital will survive, as it has for centuries. However, the functions it performs and its role within the community and the larger society will continue to undergo significant change. For example, currently 55% of total expenses within community hospitals is attributed to wages and benefits (AHA Hospital Statistics, 1993). Thus, the number of personnel necessary for a hospital to function will continually be examined. Furthermore, Ginzberg, (1996, p. 143) suggests that "the acute-care hospital . . . may be relegated to a secondary role in the health care system by the early part of the next century." Voluntary hospitals are also shifting away from "altruistic motives" and toward a business philosophy (Relman, 1994). Some of the changes, such as the increased availability of medical technology, not only improve the lives of many patients, but also add to the rising overall cost of health care. Interrelated with the application of medical technology are an aging population and a belief system that encourages the perpetuation of life at all costs. Before addressing the impact of technology and demographic changes, Ginzberg (1996) identified three scenarios for the hospital in the 21st century. Briefly, these scenarios address the following issues: (1) "managing better in difficult times" (p. 62), (2) "hospital–physician realignments" (p. 77), and (3) "from freestanding hospital to an integrated health plan" (p. 95). At the same time, it is known that elderly persons are more likely to develop chronic diseases than any other age group. It is also known that elderly persons spend longer periods of time in the hospital than do any other age group. Finally, the majority of deaths occur among those age 65 and over (McMillan et al., 1990). Therefore, it is not surprising that some locate the problem of an increasing cost of health care within the aging (and particularly among the old-old) population (Schneider & Guralnik, 1990; Campion, 1994). For instance, it is generally stated that one-third of all health-care costs are spent on the last year of life (Fuchs, 1984; Jecker, 1995). More specifically, Scitovsky (1994, p. 578) points out that relative to medical care costs, elderly Medicare decedents account for "27 to 30 percent of the total budget." However, not all elderly persons utilize extensive medical technology in their last year. Instead, extensive medical technology (thus, higher medical costs) applies to a relatively small percentage of those who are dying (see Levinsky, 1990; Getzen, 1992; Lubitz & Riley, 1993). In a review of the research, Scitovsky (1994, p. 580) argues that it is not "high-cost, high technology treatment of patients who die that has driven up medical care costs. The use of new, more expensive technologies and greater intensity of care appear to have affected the costs of care of both decedents and survivors."

The dying process has also become increasingly institutionalized (see, for example, Zusman & Tschetter, 1984; Matcha & Hutchinson, 1997), thereby creating an artificial (technologically and culturally) environment within which the patient lives (and dies). As a result, technology has been identified as responsible for "33 to 75 percent of health care cost increases, depending on the mode of cost calculation" (Lassey et al., 1997, p. 46).

Finally, women are more likely to be hospitalized than are men. However, males experience greater lengths of stay than women, except among the very young (under the age of 4) and among elderly persons (65 and older) (U.S. Bureau of the Census, 1996). In addition, some 60% of elderly persons are women, and elderly women are more likely to experience poverty than are elderly men. Thus, as the population ages, hospitals can potentially expect greater utilization of their services by a population less economically capable of paying for such care.

The Influence of Technology

Throughout the centuries, the cultural context of medical technology has shaped the direction and impact of medicine. As a result, it is important to understand that the influence of technology is culturally and historically relative. For example, Hewa and Hetherington (1993) and Hewa (1994) provide an analysis of technology vis-à-vis the work of Weber and rationalization. Cross-culturally, considerable differences occur regarding the use of technology. For example, technology such as magnetic resonance imaging (MRI) is utilized some eight times more in the United States than in Canada (Lassey et al., 1997). According to Howell (1995), the

> imbedding of technology within a larger set of values is of more than merely theoretical interest. To conceptualize technology as autonomous is to deny the contingent

> and cultural nature of the choice that people made, and continue to make, about what technology means, what it does, and how it should fit into our larger systems of action and belief. (p. 229)

Technology influences the provision of patient care from the hospital to the home. For example, the availability of technology attracts patients in need of those services (Patel & Rushefsky, 1995). At the system level, the consequences of technology are attributed to a number of factors that apply cross-culturally (Field, 1989, pp. 18–19). First is the increased cost of technology because it "is both labor and capital intensive." Second, after proved effective, the technology effectively argues for its continued use regardless of its costs. Third is the increasing maldistribution of physicians because of the location of technology appropriate to their area of specialization. Fourth, the extent of technology in the health-care system is dependent on the willingness of the political leadership to allow its introduction. Finally, technology can create a sense of alienation because it "depersonalizes treatment."

In addition to questions of cost and efficacy, the role of technology within the larger economic structure has also been questioned. From a Marxist perspective, private industry should not profit from the benefits of medical technology outcomes. Rather, the state should retain control over the industry, thus ensuring public access to the benefits of technology (Waitzkin & Waterman, 1974; Bell, 1989; Waitzkin, 1994).

At present, access to medical technology is determined primarily by the ability to pay for its privilege. Thus, health inequalities are reinforced by economic determinism that benefits the privileged of society at the expense of the disadvantaged. For instance, Kutner (1987) argues that the less wealthy are less likely to receive organ transplants. Although wealth is an initial factor in determining who shall receive a transplant, additional financial costs involving travel and preparation are also important. Thus, the questions raised by Fagerhaugh et al. (1987, p. 379) are most salient: "Who is worthy to receive costly medical care? And perhaps most important of all: Who shall decide?"

Juxtaposing the increasing cost of medical technology against the corporatization of American hospitals does not bode well for the future democratization of applied medical knowledge and skills. Sociologically, Stevens (1989, p. 363) asks perhaps the most basic question regarding the future of the hospital: "What [will] hospitals actually treat—the social individual, the patient's body (the physiological machine), or the cell?" In other words, as the hospital evolves, will it emerge as a high-technology treatment center dedicated to the eradication of disease at the expense of the patient, or as a facility that treats human beings with medical problems. Thus, the role of the hospital is pivotal to an understanding of the interaction between role relationships and structural characteristics of the medical system (see, for example, Rutten & Bonsel, 1992). Chapter 12 expands beyond the hospital and examines how health care is financed. There, various financing methods currently employed and the consequences of limited economic growth within the health-care community are explored.

Summary

This chapter not only addresses the history and future of hospitals, but also offers an integration of earlier material that examined the role of physicians and nurses. This chapter begins by acknowledging the emergence of the hospital with the development of medicine. Nonetheless, the function of the hospital in contemporary society is being questioned.

Historically, the hospital in Western medicine dates to the 6th century BC in Greece. Furthermore, hospital development that either predates or coincides with Western development has been found in a number of cultures that include Egypt, Persia, and India. Thus, as medicine developed (see Chapter 2), so did the hospital. Rather than reiterate the basic overview of medicine presented earlier, this chapter focuses on hospital development from the Industrial Revolution (primarily in France and England) to the present. Hospital development in other industrialized nations as well as the industrializing world is also briefly addressed.

The hospital dates to the mid-1700s in the United States. As with its European counterparts, hospital development has been experienced in a number of stages in the United States. Similarly, hospitals in the United States and in Europe represent a range of ownership types as well as function and size. In the United States, for instance, there are three basic ownership types: voluntary (nongovernmental and nonprofit), proprietary, and public. In addition to type, hospitals in the United States vary on the bases of size and purpose. Data are presented illustrating recent historical changes within American hospitals and differentiating between the three types of facilities.

Perhaps one of the most recognizable changes within community hospitals has been the diminution of the dual lines of authority. The organizational changes that have caused this shift in organizational power have had an impact on the entire hospital industry. In particular, the development of medical technology continues to change the role of the hospital vis-à-vis the patient and employees (including the physician). The impact of technology on the function of the bureaucratic functions of the hospital is unknown.

CHAPTER REVIEW

This chapter integrates much of what this author has addressed in earlier chapters of the book. Although the hospital is, in fact, a bureaucratic organization, it incorporates an occupational mix that includes physicians and nurses, who respond to such sociological constructs as health and illness behavior and the sick role. These responses are couched by the sociodemographic characteristics of the patient as well as the provider.

1. Compare the historical development of medicine with the hospital.

2. Explain the influence of France in the emergence of the hospital after the Industrial Revolution.

3. Compare and contrast the development of the hospital in England and France with the United States.

4. Discuss the relationship between the professionalization of physicians and the development of the dual lines of authority in hospitals.

5. Discuss the emergence and impact of Blue Cross on hospitals in particular and the health-care system in general.

6. Reexamine the equation on page 324. Explain how the cost of hospital care can be contained and the potential consequences of your response.

7. Continued development of medical technology is a given. However, there are questions regarding who should retain ownership and control the profits. Discuss the implications of private sector and public sector ownership.

GLOSSARY

community hospitals   are the backbone of the American hospital system. Generally nonprofit, these hospitals provide a range of services to their patients.

dual line of authority   involved the medical director and the hospital administrator of community hospitals. Because of their status, each influenced a different aspect of the hospital. These dual lines have begun to diminish as community hospitals are converted to proprietary institutions.

nonproprietary or voluntary hospitals   are owned by a nonprofit organization and overseen by a local board of trustees.

proprietary hospitals   are for-profit institutions either owned or operated by a group of physicians or, more recently, by a national chain.

public hospitals   are owned and operated by a governmental body at the state or local level.

SUGGESTED READINGS

Rosenberg, C. E. (1987). *The care of strangers: The rise of America's hospital system.* Baltimore: The Johns Hopkins University Press.
   Although the title indicates the content of the book, Rosenberg offers effective insight into the early development of the hospital.
Starr, P. (1982). *The social transformation of American medicine.* New York: Basic Books.
   Starr addresses the historical changes within the American hospital relative to the larger health-care industry. Although more recent events are not covered, the book offers an extensive historical overview.
Thompson, J. D., & Goldin, G. (1975). *The hospital: A social and architectural history.* New Haven, CT: Yale University Press.
   In addition to the historical development of hospitals throughout Europe and the United States, the authors provide an explanation and visual overlays. This book is particularly effective as a reference tool, as well as a guide to the changing structure of hospitals.

REFERENCES

Aaron, H. J., & Schwartz, W. B. (1984). *The painful prescription: Rationing hospital care.* Washington, DC: The Brookings Institution.

Ackerknecht, E. H. (1982). *A short history of Medicine* (Revised Edition). Baltimore: The Johns Hopkins University Press.

Album, D. (1989). Patient's knowledge and patient's work. Patient–patient interaction in general hospitals. *Acta Sociologica, 32,* 3, 295–306.

Alexander, J. A., Morrisey, M. A., & Shortell, S. M. (1986). Effects of competition, regulation, and corporatization on hospital–physician relationships. *Journal of Health and Social Behavior, 27,* 220–235.

Alexander, J. A., D'aunno, T. A., & Succi, M. J. (1996). Determinants of profound organizational change: Choice of conversion or closure among rural hospitals. *Journal of Health and Social Behavior, 37,* 3, 238–251.

American Hospital Association. (1993). Hospital Statistics, 1993–94. Chicago: American Hospital Association.

Anderson, J. G. (1992). Health care in the People's Republic of China: A blend of traditional and modern. *Central Issues in Anthropology: A Journal of the Central States Anthropological Society, 10,* 67–75.

Bell, S. E. (1989). Technology in medicine: Development, diffusion, and health policy. In H. E. Freeman & S. Levine (Eds.). *Handbook of medical sociology* (4th Ed) (pp. 185–204). Englewood Cliffs, NJ: Prentice-Hall.

Berger, P., Carrere, M. O., Duru, G., Geffroy, L., Pelc, A., Rochaix, L., & Roche, L. (1990). Market forces in health care in France. In A. F. Casparie, H. E. G. M. Hermans, & J. H. P. Paelinek (Eds.). *Competitive health care in Europe* (pp. 121–146). Aldershot, England: Dartmouth Publishing Company.

Bernheim, B. M. (1948). *The story of Johns Hopkins: Four great doctors and the medical school they created.* New York: McGraw Hill.

Bogdanich, W. (1991). *The great white way.* New York: Simon & Schuster.

Bryant, N. H. (1995). Progress and constraints of nursing and nursing education in Islamic societies. In E. B. Gallagher & J. Subedi (Eds.). *Global perspectives on health care* (pp. 45–72). Englewood Cliffs, NJ: Prentice-Hall.

Bullough, B., & Bullough, V. (1972). A brief history of medical practice. In E. Freidson & J. Lorber (Eds.). *Medical men and their work* (pp. 86–102). Chicago: Aldine.

Burns, L. R. (1990). The transformation of the American hospital: From community institution toward business enterprise. *Comparative Social Research, 12,* 77–112.

Campion, E. W. (1994). The oldest old. *The New England Journal of Medicine, 330,* 25, 1819–1820.

Cartwright, F. F. (1977). *A social history of medicine.* London: Longman.

Coe, R. M. (1978). *Sociology of medicine* (2nd Ed.). New York: McGraw Hill.

Colfer, C. J., & Gallagher, E. B. (1993). Home and hospital birthing in Oman: An observational study with recommendations for hospital practice. In P. Conrad & E. B. Gallagher (Eds.). *Health and health care in developing countries: Sociological perspectives* (pp. 247–264). Philadelphia: Temple University Press.

Cooper, D., & Worden, S. (1990). Social control in medical settings: A comparison of U.S. and U.K. institutions. *Free Inquiry in Creative Sociology, 18,* 1, 93–96.

Culyer, A. J. (1990). Cost containment in Europe. In *Health care systems in transition: The search for efficiency.* Social Policy Studies No. 7. (pp. 29–40). Paris: Organisation for Economic Co-Operation and Development.

Curtis, S., Petukhova, N., & Taket, A. (1995). Health care reforms in Russia: The example of St. Petersburg. *Social Science and Medicine, 40,* 6, 755–765.

Davis, K., Anderson, G. F., Rowland, D., & Steinberg, E. P. (1990). *Health care cost containment.* Baltimore: Johns Hopkins University Press.

Duffy, J. (1993). *From humors to medical science: A history of American Medicine* (2nd Ed.). Urbana, IL: The University of Illinois Press.

Enos, D. D., & Sultan, P. (1977). *The sociology of health care: Social, economic, and political perspectives.* New York: Praeger Publishers.

Fagerhaugh, S., Strauss, A., Suczek, B., & Weiner, C. (1987). The impact of technology on patients, providers, and care patterns: An overview. In H. D. Schwartz (Ed.). *Dominant issues in medical sociology* (2nd Ed.) (pp. 375–380). New York: Random House.

Fein, R. (1986). *Medical care, medical costs: The search for a health insurance policy.* Cambridge, MA: Harvard University Press.

Field, M. G. (Ed.). (1989). *Success and crisis in national health systems: A comparative approach.* New York: Routledge.

Flanagan, W. G. (1995). *Urban sociology: Images and structure.* Boston: Allyn & Bacon.

Flood, A. B., & Scott, W. R. (1987). *Hospital structure and performance.* Baltimore: The Johns Hopkins University Press.

Fox, R. C. (1989). *The sociology of medicine: A participant observer's view.* Englewood Cliffs, NJ: Prentice-Hall.

Fuchs, V. R. (1984). Though much is taken: Reflections on aging, health, and medical care. *Milbank Memorial Fund Quarterly, 62,* 2, 143–166.

Getzen, T. E. (1992). Population aging and the growth of health expenditures. *Journal of Gerontology, 47,* 3, S98–104.

Ginzberg, E. (1977). Health services, power centers, and decision-making mechanisms. In J. H. Knowles (Ed.). *Doing better and feeling worse: Health in the United States* (pp. 203–213). New York: W. W. Norton.

Ginzberg, E. (1996). *Tomorrow's hospital: A look to the twenty-first century.* New Haven, CT: Yale University Press.

Graig, L. A. (1993). *Health of nations: An international perspective on U.S. health care reform.* Washington, DC: Congressional Quarterly.

Gray, B. H. (1996). The evolution of investor-owned hospital companies. In P. Brown (Ed.). *Perspectives in medical sociology* (2nd Ed.) (pp. 477–490). Prospect Heights, IL: Waveland Press.

Helman, C. G. (1994). *Culture, health and illness: An introduction for health professionals.* Oxford, England: Butterworth Heinemann.

Hewa, S. (1994). Medical technology: A Pandora's box? *The Journal of Medical Humanities, 15,* 3, 171–184.

Hewa, S., & Hetherington, R. W. (1993). The rationalization of illness and the illness of rationalization. *International Journal of Contemporary Sociology, 30,* 2, 143–153.

Hollingsworth, J. R., & Hollingsworth, E. J. (1987). *Controversy about American hospitals: Funding, ownership, and performance.* Washington DC: American Enterprise Institute.

Howell, J. D. (1995). Technology in the hospital: Transforming patient care in the early twentieth century. Baltimore: The Johns Hopkins University Press.

Hu, T. W. (1984). Health services in the People's Republic of China. In M. W. Raffel (Ed.). *Comparative health systems: Descriptive analysis of fourteen national health systems* (pp. 133–152). University Park, PA: The Pennsylvania State University Press.

Iglehart, J. K. (1993). The American health care system: Community hospitals. *The New England Journal of Medicine, 329,* 5, July 29, 372–376.

Jecker, N. S. (1995). Societal aging. In W. T. Reich (Ed.). *Aging and the Aged. Encyclopedia of bioethics* (Revised Edition). New York: Simon & Schuster.

Kaufmann, C. (1994). Rights and the provision of health care: A comparison of Canada, Great Britain, and the United states. In H. D. Schwartz (Ed.). *Dominant issues in medical sociology* (3rd Ed.) (pp. 376–396). New York: McGraw Hill.

Kiel, J. M. (1993). How state policy affects rural hospital consortia: The rural health care delivery system. *The Milbank Quarterly, 71,* 4, 625–643.

Kohlmann, T., & Siegrist, J. (1989). Sociology of hospitals and of patient–physician interactions in West Germany. *Social Science and Medicine, 29,* 1, 107–108.

Krause, E. A. (1977). *Power and illness: The political sociology of health and medical care.* New York: Elsevier.

Kutner, N. G. (1987). Issues in the application of high-cost medical technology: The case of organ transplantation. *Journal of Health and Social Behavior, 28,* 23–36.

Lassey, M. L., Lassey, W. R., & Jinks, M. J. (1997). *Health care systems around the world: Character- istics, issues, reforms.* Upper Saddle River, NJ: Prentice-Hall.

Law, S. A. (1994). Blue Cross—What went wrong? In P. Conrad & R. Kern (Eds.). *The sociology of health and illness: Critical perspectives* (4th Ed.) (pp. 261–269). New York: St. Martin's Press.

Leicht, K. T., Fennell, M. L., & Witkowski, K. M. (1995). The effects of hospital characteristics and radical organizational change on the relative standing of health care professionals. *Journal of Health and Social Behavior, 36,* 151–167.

Levinsky, N. G. (1990). Age as a criterion for rationing health care. *The New England Journal of Medicine, 322,* 25, 1813–1816.

Lindorff, D. (1992). *Marketplace medicine: The rise of the for-profit hospital chains.* New York: Ban- tam Books.

Lubitz, J. D., & Riley, G. F. (1993). Trends in Medicare payments in the last year of life. *The New England Journal of Medicine, 328,* 15, 1092–1096.

Ludtke, R. L., Ahmed, K., & Geller, J. M. (1990). Affordable rural coalitions for health (ARCH): An application of sociology. *The Great Plains Sociologist, 3,* 1, 27–44.

Lynaugh, J. E. (1992). Institutionalizing women's health care in nineteenth- and twentieth-century America. In R. D. Apple (Ed.). *Women, health & medicine in America: A historical handbook* (pp. 247–269). New Brunswick, NJ: Rutgers University Press.

Matcha, D. A., & Hutchinson, J. (1997). Location and timing of death among the elderly: An analy- sis of obituary notices. *OMEGA: The Journal of Death and Dying, 35,* 4, 393–403.

McCarthy, M., & St. George, D. (1990). Prospects in health care for the United Kingdom. In A. F. Casparie, H. E. G. M. Hermans, & J. H. P. Paelinck (Eds.). *Competitive health care in Europe: Future prospects* (pp. 379–392). Aldershot, England: Dartmouth Publishing Company.

McMillan, A., R. Mentnech, M., Lubitz, J., McBean, A. M., & Russell, D. (1990). Trends and patterns in place of death for Medicare enrollees. *Health Care Financing Review, 12,* 1, 1–7.

Mechanic, D. (1976). *The growth of bureaucratic medicine: An inquiry into the dynamics of patient behavior and the organization of medical care.* New York: John Wiley & Sons.

Mechanic, D. (1978). *Medical sociology.* (2nd Ed.). New York: The Free Press.

Mills, A. (1990a). The economics of hospitals in developing countries. Part I: Expenditure patterns. *Health Policy and Planning, 5,* 2, 107–117.

Mills, A. (1990b). The economics of hospitals in developing countries. Part II: Costs and sources of income. *Health Policy and Planning, 5,* 3, 203–218.

Moores, B. (1987). The changing composition of the British hospital nursing workforce, 1962–1984. *Journal of Advanced Nursing, 12,* 499–504.

O'Cleireacain, C. (1989). Hospital workers and the health care crisis. *Journal of Public Health Pol- icy, 10,* 2, 178–186.

Organisation for Economic Co-operation and Development. (1992). *The reform of health care: A comparative analysis of seven OECD countries.* Health Policy Studies No. 2. Paris.

Organisation for Economic Co-Operation and Development. (1994a). *The reform of health care systems: A review of seventeen OECD countries.* Paris.

Organisation for Economic Co-Operation and Development. (1994b). *Health: Quality and choice.* Health Policy Studies No. 4. Paris.

Pascall, G., & Robinson, K. (1993). Health work: Divisions in health-care labour. In B. Davey & J. Popay (Eds.). *Dilemmas in health care* (pp. 81–102). Norwich, England: Open University Press.

Patel, K., & Rushefsky, M. E. (1995). *Health care politics and policy in America.* Armonk, NY: M. E. Sharpe.

Poirier-Bures, S., & Bures, A. L. (1987). Doctor–hospital relations: An old partnership reconsid- ered. In H. D. Schwartz (Ed.). *Dominant issues in medical sociology* (2nd Ed.) (pp. 366–374). New York: Random House.

Relman, A. S. (1994). The health care industry: Where is it taking us? In P. Conrad & R. Kern (Eds.). *The sociology of health and illness: Critical perspectives* (4th Ed.) (pp. 236–242). New York: St. Martin's Press.

Risley, M. (1961). *House of healing: The story of the hospital.* Garden City, NY: Doubleday & Company.

Roemer, M. I. (1991). *National health systems of the world: Volume I—The countries.* New York: Oxford University Press.

Roemer, M. I. (1993). *National health systems of the world: Volume II—The issues.* New York: Oxford University Press.

Rosenberg, C. E. (1987). *The care of strangers: The rise of America's hospital system.* Baltimore: The Johns Hopkins University Press.

Rosenberg, C. E. (1989). Community and communities: The Evolution of the American hospital. In D. E. Long & J. Golden (Eds.). *The American general hospital: Communities and social contexts* (pp. 3–17). Ithaca, NY: Cornell University Press.

Rosenberg, C. E. (1992). *Explaining epidemics and other studies in the history of medicine.* Cambridge: Cambridge University Press.

Rutten, F. F. H., & Bonsel, G. J. (1992). High cost technology in health care: A benefit or a burden? *Social Science and Medicine, 35,* 4, 567–577.

Schneider, E. L., & Guralnik, J. M. (1990). The aging of America: Impact on health care costs. *Journal of the American Medical Association, 263,* 17, 2335–2340.

Schneider, J. W. (1993). Family care work and duty in a "modern" Chinese hospital. In P. Conrad & E. B. Gallagher (Eds.). *Health and health care in developing countries: Sociological perspectives* (pp. 154–179). Philadelphia: Temple University Press.

Scitovsky, A. A. (1994). "The high cost of dying" revisited. *The Milbank Quarterly, 72,* 4, 561–591.

Starr, P. (1982). *The social transformation of American medicine.* New York: Basic Books.

Stevens, R. (1989a). Cultural values and Norwegian health services: Dominant themes and recurring dilemmas. *Scandinavian Studies, 61,* 199–212.

Stevens, R. (1989b). *In sickness and in wealth: American hospitals in the twentieth century.* New York: Basic Books.

Strauss, A., Fagerhaugh, S., Sucjek, B., & Wiener, C. L. (1989). The hospital as multiple work sites. In P. Brown (Ed.) *Perspectives in medical sociology* (pp. 341–343). Belmont, CA: Wadsworth.

Stubbs, S. G., & Bligh, E. W. (1931). *Sixty centuries of health and physick: The progress of ideas from primitive magic to modern medicine.* London: Sampson Low, Marston & Co., Ltd.

Temin, P. (1988). An economic history of American hospitals. In H. E. Frech III (Ed.). *Health care in America: The political economy of hospitals and health insurance* (pp. 75–102). San Francisco: Pacific Research Institute for Public Policy.

Thompson, J. D. (1977). The hospital—its role and limitation in the health care system. In L. Corey, M. F. Epstein & S. E. Saltman (Eds.). *Medicine in a changing society* (2nd Ed.) (pp. 107–130). St. Louis: The C.V. Mosby Company.

Thompson, J. D., & Goldin, G. (1975). *The hospital: A social and architectural history.* New Haven, CT: Yale University Press.

Turner, B. S. (1995). *Medical power and social knowledge* (2nd Ed.). London: SAGE.

U.S. Bureau of the Census. (1996) *Statistical Abstract of the United States: 1996* (116th Edition). Washington, DC.

Waitzkin, H. B., & Waterman, B. (1974). *The exploitation of illness in capitalist society.* Indianapolis: Bobbs-Merrill.

Waitzkin, H. B. (1994). A Marxian interpretation of the growth and development of coronary care technology. In P. Conrad & R. Kern (Eds.). *The sociology of health & illness: Critical perspectives* (pp. 243–255). New York: St. Martin's Press.

Walker, K. (1955). *The story of medicine.* New York: Oxford University Press.

Wirth, T. S., & Allcorn, S. (1993). *Creating new hospital–physician collaboration.* Ann Arbor, MI: Health Administration Press.

Wolinsky, F. D. (1988). *The sociology of health: Principles, practitioners, and issues* (2nd Ed.). Belmont, CA: Wadsworth.

Venanzoni, G. (1993). The evolution and prospects of the national health service. *Revue Internationale de Sociologie, 3,* 65–106.

Young, D. W., & Saltman, R. B. (1985). *The hospital power equilibrium: Physician behavior and cost control.* Baltimore: The Johns Hopkins University Press.

Zelman, W. A. (1996). *The changing health care marketplace: Private ventures, public interests.* San Francisco: Jossey-Bass Publishers.

Zusman, M. E., & Tschetter, P. (1984). Selecting whether to die at home or in a hospital setting. *Death Education, 8,* 365–381.

12 Financing the Health-Care System

Foreign experience had clearly shown that in order to control costs of health care and to expand health benefits to the whole population, the government had to control far more than the prices of the services provided by the hospital per diagnostic. It had to intervene actively in the planning, organization, regionalization, and delivery of health services, making sure that people's needs, and not business and professional profits, were the primary determinants of the funding and organization of health care.

—Navarro, 1994, p. 38

The Sociology of Health-Care Financing

This chapter addresses a basic component of health care—the relationship between the provision of health services and subsequent payment. Although the economic subtext is generally understood as a transaction between two rational actors, a sociological explanation offers a potentially different interpretation. For instance, what are the economic implications of health-care costs on the general population relative to the social indicators such as social class, age, sex, and race and ethnic origin? Health-care financing is also understood as one component within the larger context of the health-care system. Also, economic resources within the health-care system consist of various forms of taxes, as well as contributions from individuals, corporations, and various governmental agencies (Roemer, 1991). The distribution of health-care funds from these sources has changed since the late 1960s. In 1960, almost one-half of the health-care dollar came from out-of-pocket expenses, one-fourth from the government, and 22% from private health insurance. By 1990, out-of-pocket expenses declined to 20%, whereas government programs increased to 42% of the health-care dollar. A similar increase in private health insurance and other private monies accounted for 38% of the health-care dollar (Kronenfeld, 1993).

Before examining the specifics presented in this chapter, consider the overall cost of the American health-care system. The most recent numbers available put the cost of health care at $1 trillion annually. In other words, approximately 14%, or one-seventh of the gross domestic product (GDP) is spent on health care (Graig, 1993). Currently the most expensive in the world, future predictions indicate American health-care costs could reach 18% of GDP shortly after the turn of the 21st century (Canham-Clyne et al., 1995). Placing health-care cost in a global context, 41% of all the money spent in the world on health care in 1990 was spent in the United States. Furthermore, almost 90% of all money spent on health care in 1990 was spent in the industrialized nations. Finally, per capita spending on health in 1990 ranged from $4 in Tanzania to more than $2,700 in the United States (World Development Report, 1993).

Although per capita spending or percent of GDP is important, it is difficult to assume a strong correlation between health spending and health outcomes. Data in the following section illustrate the problem with this relationship. For example, Chapter 3 demonstrated that crude health indicators such as life expectancy and infant mortality are poorer in the United States than in other industrialized nations. Furthermore, as data in earlier chapters indicated, the distribution of health outcomes vary on the basis of social characteristics such as income level, race, age, and sex.

Health-Care Costs: A Comparative Perspective

This section examines the cost of health care not only in the United States but also in other industrialized nations as well. Table 12.1 presents health expenditures as a

TABLE 12.1 Total Health Expenditures as a Percentage of Gross Domestic Product and Per Capita Health Expenditures in Dollars: Selected Countries and Years 1960–1993

Country	1960	1970	1980	1990	1993[1]
Health Expenditures as a Percent of Gross Domestic Product					
Australia	4.9	5.7	7.3	8.2	8.5
Austria	4.4	5.4	7.9	8.4	9.3
Belgium	3.4	4.1	6.6	7.6	8.3
Canada	5.5	7.1	7.4	9.4	10.2
Denmark	3.6	6.1	6.8	6.5	6.7
Finland	3.9	5.7	6.5	8.0	8.8
France	4.2	5.8	7.6	8.9	9.8
Germany	4.8	5.9	8.4	8.3	8.6
Greece	2.9	4.0	4.3	5.3	5.7
Iceland	3.3	5.0	6.2	7.9	8.3
Ireland	3.8	5.3	8.7	6.7	6.7
Italy	3.6	5.2	6.9	8.1	8.5
Japan	3.0	4.6	6.6	6.8	7.3
Luxembourg	—	3.8	6.3	6.5	6.9
Netherlands	3.8	5.9	7.9	8.0	8.7
New Zealand	4.3	5.2	7.2	7.4	7.7
Norway	3.3	5.0	6.6	7.5	8.2
Portugal	—	2.8	5.8	6.6	7.3
Spain	1.5	3.7	5.7	6.9	7.3
Sweden	4.7	7.1	9.4	8.6	7.5
Switzerland	3.3	5.2	7.3	8.4	9.9
Turkey	—	2.5	3.4	2.9	2.7
United Kingdom	3.9	4.5	5.6	6.0	7.1
United States	5.1	7.1	8.9	12.1	13.6
Per Capita Health Expenditures[2]					
Australia	$97	$213	$671	$1,315	$1,493
Austria	67	166	697	1,395	1,777
Belgium	53	130	586	1,247	1,601
Canada	105	255	739	1,716	1,971
Denmark	67	215	595	1,068	1,296
Finland	55	164	521	1,291	1,363
France	72	206	711	1,538	1,835
Germany	93	216	819	1,520	1,815
Greece	16	59	187	395	500
Iceland	51	139	588	1,372	1,564
Ireland	35	97	451	749	922
Italy	49	155	581	1,317	1,523
Japan	26	129	526	1,188	1,495
Luxembourg	—	168	693	1,532	1,993
Netherlands	69	207	702	1,279	1,531
New Zealand	92	178	556	996	1,179

(*continued*)

TABLE 12.1   Continued

Country	1960	1970	1980	1990	1993[1]
Norway	48	136	558	1,202	1,592
Portugal	—	45	263	616	866
Spain	14	83	332	813	972
Sweden	90	274	867	1,464	1,266
Switzerland	92	270	851	1,761	2,283
Turkey	—	23	76	133	146
United Kingdom	76	147	452	955	1,213
United States	141	341	1,052	2,688	3,331

Note: Data compiled by the Organisation for Economic Co-Operation and Development. Some numbers in this table have been revised and differ from previous editions of *Health, United States.*

[1] Preliminary figures.

[2] Per capita health expenditures for each country have been adjusted to U.S. dollars using gross domestic product purchasing power parities for each year.

Source: © OECD. (1995). Total health expenditures as a percent of gross domestic product and per capita health expenditures in dollars: Selected countries and years 1960–93. Reproduced by permission of the OECD.

percentage of GDP from 1960 to 1993, as well as per capita expenditures. Examining the data, there are a number of trends that are quite obvious. First is the fact that the United States spends more as a percent of GDP as well as per capita than any other industrialized nation. Second, look at the numbers for 1960 and 1970. At that time, expenditures in the United States were not significantly different from other countries. In fact, spending in Sweden at that time matched and eventually, exceeded the United States by 1980. After 1980, whereas other industrialized nations were slowing the rate of increase, health-care costs in the United States exploded. Finally, look at health expenditures as a percent of GDP for the United States and Canada in 1970. Compare health expenditures as a percent of GDP for these two countries in 1993. What happened? This question is answered in Chapter 13. For now, think of the time since the late 1970s as an experiment in health-care costs that the United States lost and Canada won (Evans et al., 1991). Finally, consider the following statement by Schieber et al. (1991, p. 23): "In comparison with other major industrialized countries, health care in the United States costs more per person and per unit of services, is less accessible to a large portion of its citizens, is provided at a more intensive level, and offers comparatively poor gross outcomes."

The data in Table 12.1 indicate that health-care costs are higher in the United States than anywhere else in the world. One explanation for these differences is the financing of the health-care system. The United States, for example, finances health care primarily through the private sector of the economy, such as insurance premiums and out-of-pocket expenditures. Davis et al. (1990) report that the lack of a unified financing system in the United States has resulted in higher health-care costs. Other industrialized countries finance health care primarily through the public sector of the economy (there are a number of good books that cover, to some extent, cross-cultural health-system financing; see, for example, Lynch & Raphael, 1963; OECD, 1990, 1992, 1994; Roemer, 1991; Chollett, 1993; Graig, 1993; Lassey, Lassey, & Jinks, 1997). Briefly, European nations can be categorized into three types of health-care financing:

1. Financed by a mixture of social and private insurance with mainly private providers (The Netherlands).
2. Financed mainly by social insurance with mixed public and private providers (Belgium, France, Germany, Luxembourg).
3. Financed mainly by taxation, with mainly public providers (Denmark, Spain, Greece, Ireland, Italy, Portugal, United Kingdom). (Abel-Smith et al., 1995, p. 24)

In addition, there is a growing body of literature addressing the financing of health care within industrializing nations. For example, Yoder (1989) examined the effect of user fees on patient utilization of services in Swaziland. Similarly, Moen (1990) explored sociodemographic and utilization differences between members and nonmembers of a prepaid plan in Zaire. Xingyuan et al. (1993) highlight the various financing methods within China, whereas Weiss and Theno (1991) examine the financing of the health-care system in the former Soviet Union.

Although system differences between the United States and other industrialized nations are be examined in greater detail in Chapter 13, Pfaff (1990, p. 22) argues that relative to health status, nations with centralized control of health-care spending are "more cost-effective than the latter" (decentralized systems). Angell (1993, p. 1778) distills the reasons for excessive health-care cost in the United States into the following three points: "The United States treats health care as a market commodity, not as a social good . . . Second, is that it is not really a system at all . . . third, the United States does not attempt to limit the total amount spent on health care by establishing a global cap."

American Health-Care Costs: An Analysis

Moving from an international comparison of total health-care costs, this section focuses on health-care costs in the United States. The data in Table 12.2 elucidate expenditure changes within the American system.

The data in Table 12.2 illustrate a number of policy changes in the American health-care system since 1960. First, notice the change from 1965 to 1970. In 1965, Medicare and Medicaid were signed into law. These programs have had a significant impact on the American health-care system. As a health insurance program primarily for Americans aged 65 and older, Medicare provides coverage for a range of physician and hospital services (U.S. Department of Health and Human Services, 1995). Unfortunately, Medicare coverage is extremely limited. As a result, many elderly persons purchase additional "Medi-gap" insurance coverage to ensure protec-

TABLE 12.2 National Health Expenditures: 1960–1994[1]

		Private				Public	Medical Payments	
	Total ($ Billion)							
Year	Total[2]	Total[3]	Out-of-Pocket Payments	Percent of Total Private	Insurance Premiums[4]	Total	Medicare	Public Assistance
1960	26.9	19.5	13.1	67.2	5.9	5.7	(X)	0.5
1965	41.1	29.4	18.5	62.9	10.0	8.3	(X)	1.7
1970	73.2	43.0	24.9	57.9	16.3	24.9	7.7	6.3
1975	130.7	72.3	38.1	52.7	31.3	50.1	16.4	14.5
1980	247.2	138.0	60.3	43.7	69.7	97.6	37.5	28.0
1985	428.2	247.4	100.6	40.7	132.2	164.4	72.2	44.4
1990	697.5	402.9	148.4	36.8	232.4	270.0	112.1	80.4
1994	949.4	517.1	174.9	33.8	313.3	402.2	169.2	134.8

Data includes Puerto Rico and outlying areas. X, Not applicable.

[1] Health services and supplies.

[2] Includes medical research and medical facilities construction.

[3] Includes other sources of funds not shown separately.

[4] See footnote 2, Table 155.

Source: Data compiled from U.S. Health Care Financing Administration, *Health Care Financing Review*, Spring, 1996; and, U.S. Bureau of the Census. *Statistical Abstract of the United States: 1996* (116th Edition.) Table 154. Washington, DC.

tion against large medical bills (O'Keefe, 1994). Although Medicare is financed and administered at the federal level, Medicaid is a federal health insurance program administered by individual states. Unfortunately, in 1991 the Medicaid program covered only 57.5% of the poor who did not have any other form of public or private insurance (Medicaid Source Book: Background Data and Analysis, 1993). According to the data in Table 12.2, Medicare and Medicaid costs have increased significantly since they were signed into law. However, Medicare and Medicaid have been credited with improving the health status of the poor and aging populations they serve. Although some of the increase can be attributed to greater usage of the health-care system, a more important explanation is structural, particularly with Medicare (Ginsburg, 1988). For example, one reason for rapidly increasing costs within Medicare is price inflation within the medical community. Price inflation refers to "the price of hospital and medical services that benefit providers and suppliers but not the patient" (Navarro, 1994, p. 40). As a consequence, significant price increases associated with medical technology are directly attributable to the overall rise in health-care costs (National Center for Health Statistics, 1993). More specifically, Littrell (1989) argues that one outcome of the relationship between physicians and hospital managers relative to the purchase and application of medical technology is increased medical cost. Littrell (1989, p. 266) suggests greater sociological investigation into the interconnection of these variables and the extent to which they are "embedded in the social organization of medical practice." For example, 50% to 80% of the total cost of health care is the result of decisions made by physicians (Grace, 1988). Thus, rather than blaming the recipients of these programs, consider the following. In 1987 there were 30.5 million Americans covered by Medicare and 20.2 million covered by Medicaid. In 1994, those numbers increased to 33.9 million and 31.6 million, respectively. In other words, the number of Medicare recipients increased 11.1% while Medicaid recipients increased 56.4%. However, during the same time period, program costs rose 104.8% and 149.6%, respectively (U.S. Bureau of the Census, 1996). Thus, efforts to blame elderly or poor persons for rising health-care costs are inaccurate and misleading. Furthermore, the percentage of Americans aged 65 and older is comparable to or less than most European nations. Population projections indicate that the United States will remain "younger" than its European counterparts well into the 21st century (U.S. Bureau of the Census, 1992). The result will be strained health-care systems throughout the industrialized world as they attempt to provide medical services to an increasingly aged population (Hurd, 1997).

Moving beyond intergenerational issues, Jencks and Schieber (1991) locate a number of factors within the structure of the health-care industry that are related to increased medical costs. These factors include:

1. Insurance coverage and premium subsidies
2. Nonprice competition among providers
3. Open-ended payment systems
4. Developments in technology
5. Malpractice litigation

6. Self-referral
7. Costs of cost-containment and competition
8. Increasing physician supply
9. Upcoding (the reporting of more costly codes when reporting services provided to patients)

Thus, rather than attempting to locate the blame for rising health-care costs on a particular age category, these factors focus on the changing strategies and players within the heath-care system. These factors also reflect the interdependence of health-care components.

Who Pays for Health Care?

In addition to being the most expensive health-care system in the world, the United States' method of health-care financing can only be described as a shell game (Califano, 1986). In other words, the pea represents the cost of health care and the shells represent the vendors (federal government, insurance companies, and so forth) who provide funding for health care. Thus, "Congress puts a cap on Medicare payments to hospitals, and the hospitals move the cost to the states and other customers" (Califano, 1986, p. 160). In another example, Zelman (1996, p. 269) points out that "Medicare and Medicaid public insurance programs have indirectly subsidized the care of the uninsured and most vulnerable populations." What happens is called **cost-shifting,** or "charging different prices to different groups" (Morrisey, 1994, p. 2). In 1984, the "uncompensated care" to those who could not afford to pay represented 5% of hospital costs. In addition, some hospitals (for example, general, public, and teaching) were more likely to provide uncompensated care (Kronenfeld, 1991). Cost-shifting has even been tied to the migration of the population and corporations from the northeast and midwest to the southern and western states. Birenbaum (1993) points out that although Sun Belt states offered economic advantages such as lower taxes and wages, corporations that relocated to these states soon realized that health-care benefits were more expensive. An explanation offered by Birenbaum (1993) points out that providers were making up loses incurred by Medicare and Medicaid by charging those with better coverage more for the same services. Thus, in reality we all pay for health care either directly or indirectly. Later in this chapter, the role of various payment methods is examined, as is the issue of the uninsured within the health-care system.

Before turning to these issues, however, there are two major points regarding who pays for health care that must be addressed. First is the growing generational chasm regarding responsibility for health care and, concomitantly, economic viability (generational cost-shifting). For example, if I am a healthy 25-year old, should my health insurance company or health maintenance organization (HMO) charge me more (in premiums) to cover the cost of taking care of someone who is 75 and has a chronic condition that requires weekly medical intervention? In other words, should health-care costs be determined by characteristics such as age (or perhaps sex, race, social class, or health status)? Menzel (1983, p. 9) raises an intriguing but disturbing line of thinking by suggesting that the well should be consulted to determine "what care it is costworthy to insure for, to encourage, and to use." The ramifications of such logic are far-reaching. Consider the possible implications of an aging society. Should persons who are well be able to decide that certain treatments for elderly persons be curtailed because of the expense? Should this be a community decision? Would this apply to genetic disorders that afflict specific ethnic or racial groups? Would the social status of the patient(s) influence the viability of providing care? On a personal level, this author faces the potential of being on drug therapy whenever his platelet count drops below a minimum level. Should persons who are well in society or in my community decide whether I receive the drug therapy I need? Could other characteristics about me influence the decision reached by the well? The potential is a return to the eugenics movement. Although not confined to the United States, such divisive arguments are more likely to occur as a result of the American health-care system, which is discussed in detail in Chapter 13. This argument is examined on a slightly different level when health-care rationing is discussed later in this chapter.

The image of elderly persons as "greedy geezers" who live the good life at the expense of younger generations is a socially constructed argument (see Binstock & Post, 1991, for a rebuttal of the argument). This chasm will potentially widen as baby boomers begin retiring in 2011. As the number of elderly persons increase, the dependency ratio (the number of workers per population younger than age 18 and older than age 65) will shrink. The result will be increased pressure on the workforce to pay a larger proportion of their income to support the health-care needs of those elderly persons. (The reader is referred to the work of the International Labor Organisation, 1989, for a non-American analysis of health and maintenance costs for aging populations in European nations). This leads to the second issue: that employment legitimates health care as a benefit.

The results of a 1994 Gallop poll indicate the legitimacy of work relative to health care for many Americans. In essence, respondents reported that:

> guaranteed coverage is more important than universal coverage by 54% to 31%; it is more important to provide guaranteed coverage to those who have it now than to cover those who presently cannot afford insurance . . . controlling costs is also more important than universal coverage by 57% to 32%; respondents say that it is more important to control cost than it is to cover those who cannot afford insurance. (Gallop, 1995, p. 112)

The irony is that these images, like the images of elderly persons, are also socially constructed. In other words, the words that we use define our image of reality. Thus, attaching "greedy geezer" to elderly persons creates in our mind an image of elderly persons. The data from the Gallop poll also identify the extent to which Americans are fearful of losing access to their own health care. Although the workplace has legitimated the right to health care in the past, changes in the economics of society (part-time work, fewer benefits) are beginning to challenge that argument

(Freidman, 1991). Government research indicates that slightly more than one-half of the workers (51.9%) "had employer-provided health insurance policies in their own name" (U.S. Bureau of the Census, 1994, pp. 2–3). Even the ill-fated health reform effort put forth by President Clinton located responsibility for health-care coverage in the workplace (The White House Domestic Policy Council, 1993). The problem with employer-based health-care funding is the fear of losing one's employment or experiencing a reduction in health benefits. As a result, employees (and their dependents) are dependent on the employer for continuation of whatever health benefits are provided, even when health benefit packages are reduced (Fein, 1992).

The Insured and the Uninsured

The cost of health care represents the provision of medical services to two basic groups of recipients: those who have the means (primarily through some insurance plan) to pay for services and those who cannot afford to pay. Table 12.3 presents a breakdown of health coverage by type of provider.

Among those insured in 1993, 70.2% had private insurance, 12.2% were receiving Medicaid, 12.7% were on Medicare, and 3.7% were covered through mili-

TABLE 12.3   Type of Health Insurance Coverage, 1993

	All Persons (%)	Poor Persons (%)
Private Insurance		
Any private plan	70.2	22.1
Group health	57.1	11.2
Government Insurance		
Medicaid	12.2	47.9
Medicare	12.7	11.6
Military		
Health care[1]	3.7	2.2
No Insurance	15.3	29.3

Note: The percentages by type of coverage are not mutually exclusive; in other words, persons can be covered by more than one type of health insurance during the year.

[1] Military health care includes CHAMPUS (Comprehensive Health and Medical Plan for Uniformed Services) CHAMPVA (Civilian Health and Medical Program of the Department of Veteran's Affairs), veteran's and military health care.

Source: U.S. Bureau of the Census. (1994). Statistical Brief. *Health Insurance Coverage—1993*. SB/94-28. U.S. Department of Commerce. Economics and Statistical Administration.

tary health. Although the majority of Americans have some form of health-care coverage, an increasing number and percentage of the total are uninsured. Swartz (1994, p. 65) states that "close to a quarter of the nonelderly population [are] without health insurance sometime during a year." Add to that the underinsured and the percentage increases to approximately one-third of all Americans (Canham-Clyne et al., 1995). More recent figures place the percentage of uninsured at 17% of the American population during the first half of 1996 (Vistnes & Monheit, 1997).

According to the data in Table 12.3, 15.3% of all persons and 29.3% of poor persons were without health care for some or all of 1993. Interestingly, among the uninsured, only 28.9% were poor. Finally, less than one-half of the poor (47.9%) were on Medicaid at some point during 1993 (U.S. Bureau of the Census, 1994). The data indicate the level of fragmentation within the financing of the American health-care system. Designed to provide assistance to the poor, Medicaid is an inadequate response to a seriously flawed health-care system. Stated differently, 51.3% of the uninsured are under the age of 65 *and are employed.* More than one-fourth (27.5%) of the uninsured are children, whereas less than 17% (16.8%) are adults who are unemployed (Birenbaum, 1993). More specifically, who are the uninsured? Table 12.4 offers a categorization of the uninsured by age, race, education level, and work experience (see also Bennefield, 1994; Summer, 1994; Hellander et al., 1995; Vistnes & Monheit, 1997).

The data require some explanation. First, why are males more likely to be uninsured than are females? Remember that single-parent households are more likely to be headed by women than by men, and programs such as Medicaid provide some of the poor with access to health-care services (see, for example, Miles & Parker, 1997). Among all persons, men are more likely to be employed and to have health-care benefits. Thus, if married, their spouse would be less likely to be uninsured. The reverse is less likely to occur as women are more likely to occupy positions in the secondary labor market, where health benefits are less available.

Further analysis of the data in Table 12.4 indicates that age differences exist relative to the likelihood of being uninsured. Understandably, poor young adults and middle-aged poor persons in the labor market will find few economic opportunities that provide work benefits such as health care. Additional research by Himmelstein et al. (1992, p. 383) reports that between 1989 and 1991, "the entire increase in the number of uninsured was among working-age adults." The improvement among elderly persons is primarily the result of Medicare. There is an interesting (and disturbing) trend between level of education and the lack of insurance coverage. According to the data, as one's level of education rises, the likelihood of being uninsured decreases. However, among poor persons, the relationship is not as clearly defined. In fact, as level of education improves among the poor, the probability of not being insured does not necessarily increase. One explanation is that the types of employment opportunities available are less likely to provide health-care benefits to persons who are poor.

The data presented in Table 12.4 also indicate that many of the poor who work are uninsured. In fact, the poor who work full-time were more likely to be uninsured than were the poor who worked part-time or did not work. This can be understood

TABLE 12.4   Percent of All Persons [and Poor Persons] Not Covered by Health Insurance at Any Time during the Year, by Selected Characteristics, 1993

	All Persons (%)	Poor Persons (%)
Total	15.3	29.3
Male	17.1	34.2
Female	13.6	25.5
Age		
Under 18	13.7	20.1
18–24	26.8	43.0
25–34	21.6	39.3
35–44	16.8	44.5
45–64	13.7	39.5
65	1.2	3.6
Race and Hispanic Origin		
White	14.2	31.3
Black	20.5	23.5
Hispanic origin	31.6	40.8
Education (Persons Aged 25 and Older)		
No high school diploma	21.7	31.1
High school graduate only	15.3	34.6
Some college, no degree	13.2	33.3
Associate degree	11.9	42.2
Bachelor's degree or higher	7.3	38.0
Work Experience (Persons Aged 15 and Over)		
Worked during the year	17.0	48.2
Worked full-time	16.2	50.1
Worked part-time	20.0	45.6
Did not work	13.9	26.7

Note: Persons of Hispanic origin may be of any race.

Source: U.S. Bureau of the Census. 1994. Statistical Brief. *Health Insurance Coverage—1993.* SB/94-28. U.S. Department of Commerce. Economics and Statistics Administration.

within the context of the current welfare system, in which full-time work potentially removes the client from public benefits.

Finally, consider the impact of the uninsured on the health-care system. According to research by the U.S. Bureau of the Census (1995), providing persons who were uninsured or underinsured between 1990 and 1992 with private insurance would have had a minimal impact on the demand side of the system. However, improving the health status of persons between the ages of 16 and 64 and decreasing the prevalence of disability would have a dramatic impact on the demand for physician and hospital services. Thorpe (1997) outlines current proposals to provide insurance coverage to the uninsured. These proposals include Medicaid expansion for children and their parents as well as health-care assistance to persons who are unemployed. Even with implementation of the proposal to cover some of the uninsured children, the result is a continued increase in the number of uninsured in the United States. Whatever effort is made to improve access to the health system for the poor will not alter the two-tiered system that currently exists (see, for example, the work of Weismann & Epstein, 1993). A two-tiered health system refers to differences between segments of the population regarding access to and the provision of health care. In other words, although the poor may have access to health care (Medicaid), the provision of health care may occur in an emergency room of a hospital. As a result, there is a lack of continuity of care and follow-up by the same health-care provider, resulting in less effective care. Two-tiered medical care options relative to overall costs and the location of the poor within the system offer some understanding as to why the United States remains committed to its current system (Fuchs, 1993). Furthermore, this two-tiered system is a reflection of social class differences and their impact on access to health services as well as health outcomes such as perceived health status (Rice, 1991; Krieger & Fee, 1994). As Himmelstein and Woolhandler (1986) suggest, the reason the United States does not have a universal health-care system is the result of political rather than economic obstacles.

Financing the Health-Care System

All health-care systems are financed either directly or indirectly through the general population. This section briefly examines the multiple financing routes that exist within the American health-care system. The fragmentation of funding sources has been implicated as one of the more serious impediments to a more cost-efficient health-care system.

Government Financial Support

A reexamination of earlier tables indicates that government-sponsored health care has experienced considerable growth since the late 1960s. The passage of Medicare and Medicaid in the mid-1960s represented an economic boon for the medical community. Although reimbursement levels were not consistent with the private sector, these programs offered a new and growing pool of medically needy persons to the medical community. As a result, Medicare and Medicaid soon established the government as the nation's largest insurer (OECD, 1994). However, these programs have also had their problems. Enos and Sultan (1977) identify the following: (1) the size and cost of the programs relative to the financial cost of the system, (2) payment mechanisms, (3) services offered, and (4) their quality. Regardless of the problems associated with these programs, Enos and Sultan (1977, p. 165) argue that these programs established "the principle of government responsibility for providing medical services to large population groups." Nonetheless, Medicare and Medicaid have experienced significant changes within the recent past. The implementation of diagnostic related groups (DRGs) and the enrollment of Medicare beneficiaries in HMOs in the 1980s and 1990s are only two of the efforts to curb costs within the system.

Insurance Companies

The significant role of private health insurance is one of the defining characteristics of the American method of health-care financing (Somers & Somers, 1977). Throughout this section, the term *private* (or *commercial*) *health insurance* excludes insurance programs such as Blue Cross and Blue Shield as well as prepayment programs. (An extensive analysis of private insurance can be found in Starr, 1982.)

Private health insurance programs have been in existence throughout most of this century. However, it was not until the latter 1940s that companies began offering health benefit packages to their employees (Davis et al., 1990). A fundamental difference between commercial insurers and Blue Cross involves who is covered. Commercial insurers employ *risk rating,* also known as *experience rating.* In other words, they limit insurance coverage to those groups that historically underutilize the health-care system (the young, the healthy). However, *community rating* refers to insurance rates based on a cross-section of the community (Somers & Somers, 1977).

The result is a "skimming" of the healthiest members of the population paying relatively low insurance premiums and increasing profits for the commercial carriers. This is also related to the "wellness" concept addressed in Chapter 4. There is an increasing expectation by employers that employees will change their behavior patterns (increase the amount of exercise, quit smoking, eat healthier foods, and so forth) in an effort to improve their health. In turn, this keeps health-care costs down for the employer and maintains commercial insurance profits. Unfortunately, this cost-shifting means increased cost for taxpayers who are left covering the cost of persons who are poor, unhealthy, or elderly (Light, 1996).

The percentage of Americans covered by private health insurance peaked in 1980 at 81.1%. By 1992, 70.5% of the population were covered by private health insurance (Hall, 1994). In part, this decline is the result of self-ensuring by larger corporations. Also, the decline in insurance coverage has been experienced mostly among the working poor. Conversely, the percentage of upper-income Americans covered by health insurance has increased slightly (Seccombe, 1996). Regardless of the changes, private health insurance remains a vital component of the American health-care system and is generally identified as a vehicle through which universal coverage could be implemented (Davis et al., 1990). Private health insurance has also been identified as an impediment to a national health insurance program.

The "Blues"

Blue Cross and Blue Shield emerged during the Great Depression in response to decreasing hospital utilization rates. In essence, these programs were developed to ensure the viability of hospitals and physicians (Navarro, 1994). Blue Cross was created in 1929 in Dallas, Texas, at Baylor University. At the time, less than 2% of the population were enrolled in any insurance program. Within 50 years that figure would increase to more than 80% (Miller, 1996). Blue Shield emerged after a 1939 effort in California to ensure payment for physician services. The emergence of Blue Cross was also regional. In other words, those states with predominantly governmental or proprietary hospitals were less likely to establish prepayment programs. Northeastern and midwestern states were more likely to have nonprofit facilities, whereas hospitals in states such as Georgia, Texas, Oklahoma, and Nebraska were more likely to be proprietary (Stevens, 1989).

Initially, Blue Cross and Blue Shield differed from commercial insurance companies on two specific points. They include "payment of service benefits to hospitals rather than cash benefits to the individual insured; and community rating, that is, the provision of benefits to all members of the community at the same rate, rather than higher rates to high risk groups" (Law, 1994, p. 264). Over time, however, Blue Cross has shifted increasingly from a service agreement whereby the patient knows they are responsible for the stated deductible or copay when hospitalized to an indemnity plan. An indemnity plan means that the insurance company pays the patient "a fixed dollar amount per day or period of hospitalization" (Law, 1994, p. 264). The patient then assumes responsibility for paying the hospital bill. Secondly, Blue Cross began by offering community rating. In other words, charging everyone a similar rate. Blue Cross has been moving increasingly in the direction of commercial insurance companies and offering experience rating (charges based on the likelihood of use) (Law, 1994).

The purpose of Blue Cross was to ensure recipient access to hospital services as well as to maintain a pool of potential patients for the hospital. The growth of Blue Cross was phenomenal. Within 9 years, membership stood at almost 1.5 million. By the end of World War II, 61% of those with hospital insurance were enrolled in Blue Cross. Shortly thereafter, commercial insurance companies began to surpass Blue Cross in terms of total membership. By 1969, Blue Cross enrolled only 37% of those under the age of 65 (Law, 1994). Commercial carriers surpassed Blue Cross because they were able to provide more favorable rates to those they insured.

The evolution of the "Blues" throughout the 20th century offers insight into the changing nature of health insurance and the health-care system (see Starr, 1982). Initially offered tax-exempt status in return for community rating, the "Blues" are now similar to other commercial insurance corporations. As Mechanic (1994, p. 25) points out, the use of community rating by Blue Cross offered many an opportunity to receive health care "who otherwise might have become indigent patients if they became ill." The "Blues" no longer enjoy a tax-exempt status. Because the "Blues" engage in experience rating, they have become similar to the commercial health-care carriers with whom they compete (Navarro, 1994). Blue Cross and Blue Shield are also identified as contributing to the increasing cost of health care by supporting the concept of first-dollar coverage. According to Frech (1988, p. 311), "this type of insurance leads to high demand for health care and discourages competition."

Health Maintenance Organizations

A more recent attempt to control the cost of health care is the **health maintenance organization** (HMO). Essentially, HMOs are built on the following principles:

1. It accepts the responsibility to deliver comprehensive medical care to its members.
2. Its members enroll voluntarily and pay a fixed amount periodically, regardless of the amount of services they actually receive. (Schlenker, 1977, p. 131)

More specifically today, HMOs "assume contractual responsibility for providing a stated range of health care services to an enrolled population on a prepaid, capitation basis" (Davis et al., 1990, p. 131).

Although the birth of HMOs can be traced to the establishment of the U.S. Marine Hospital Service in 1798, HMOs did not seriously emerge unto the healthcare scene until the HMO Act of 1973 (Paley, 1993), although a number have been in existence for decades. For example, Kaiser-Permanente was founded in the late 1930s and is considered the "granddaddy" of prepaid programs. Other group plans such as the Health Insurance Plan (HIP) of Greater New York and the Group Health Cooperative of Puget Sound (Seattle) are also dated to the 1940s and 1950s (James & Nash, 1995). Since the 1970s, however, HMOs have become increasingly popular among the American public. After passage of the HMO Act of 1973, however, national interest was slow to develop. In 1980, HMOs enrolled 9.1 million Americans. By 1995, more than 46 million were enrolled in various types of HMOs (U.S. Bureau of the Census, 1996).

There are a number of organizational structures associated with HMOs. For instance, staff model HMOs "own and operate the health care delivery system . . . [whereas] the group model is usually an exclusive contract between the HMO and the providers both in a sense acting as operational partners" (Paley, 1993, p. 7). Another model is referred to as an individual practice association (IPA). In this model, physicians within the community are contracted by the HMO to provide services to members. The HMO pays physicians on a capitation, or per head, basis for their patient load of HMO members (Paley, 1993). In addition, there are group and network models of HMOs. Group model HMOs provide the facility (which may include hospitals) and necessary administrative and ancillary medical staff but contract with "one large, multispecialty medical group practice for physician services" (Davis et al., 1990, p. 131). In this model, physician profit sharing may occur. Conversely, network model HMOs utilize the facilities and staff provided by the various groups of physicians who enter into agreement with the HMO. As with the group model, the HMO pays each physician group a capitation fee to provide services to those members provided care by that group of physicians (Davis et al., 1990).

One of the most important characteristics associated with HMOs is their ability to provide quality preventive care for less money. Initially, research supported the argument that HMOs were more cost-efficient. More recent data, however, is less suggestive of significant cost savings through HMOs (see, for example, Davis et al., 1990; Light, 1995; Weiss, 1997). Research also indicates that one's social and health status at the time of enrollment is related to outcome. According to Luft

(1994, p. 47), reporting on outcomes from the RAND study (also known as RHIE or RAND Health Insurance Experiment) indicate that "low-income enrollees who were in poor health at the beginning of the experiment did less well in the HMO than in the FFS (Fee For Service) plan." The RAND study examined data between 1976 and 1981 and "compared the performance of a staff HMO plan, Group Health Cooperative in Seattle, Washington, with indemnity plans" (Miller & Luft, 1994, p. 1512). Faced with increased levels of competition between various types of HMOs and an increasing presence of for-profit HMOs, there has been greater emphasis on "marketing" services to customers in an effort to increase productivity and profitability (Higgins et al., 1991). In effect, HMOs engage in what Mechanic (1996, p. 214) refers to as "constructive rationing," whereby consumers agree to "a lower premium, more comprehensive benefits, or both, [and in return] accept the plan's judgment as to what services are necessary." This arrangement is particularly beneficial to local governments as they attempt to reduce health-care outlays by moving Medicaid recipients into less-expensive HMO settings. Unfortunately for the poor, many of these early HMOs were not strictly regulated, resulting in considerable abuse of the system by the HMOs (Roemer, 1986) and less than adequate care for beneficiaries (Weiss, 1997).

Although HMOs represent an improvement over traditional medicine, class-based medicine remains a problem. However, as Luft (1982) points out, socioeconomic differences in HMO health care appear to be the result of "market forces and government policies" rather than the organization of delivering medicine.

Research also points to additional problems for HMOs. For example, Lutz (1989, p. 29) argues that there is a relationship between HMO utilization and type of family (i.e., traditional multiple earner or sole female earner). The data indicate that "non-traditional family women had appreciably less preventive care than other women." Furthermore, Lutz (1989) points to various economic and noneconomic characteristics within the family that may influence outcome. In addition to consumer utilization and satisfaction levels, HMO research indicates less than supportive responses from physicians. For example, a comparative analysis of FFS and HMO physicians indicates "FFS physicians felt that FFS is the *better* arrangement while HMO physicians felt working conditions in HMOs are only *about equal* to that found in FFS practices" (Ferraro, 1993, p. 125). More recently, Borowsky et al. (1997) surveyed physicians in three HMO plans (two network and one staff model) in the Minneapolis–St. Paul, Minnesota area. Rating the plan in which they worked, physicians were not particularly supportive of HMOs. When respondents were asked if they would recommend the health plan they rated to their family, 37% said yes. However, there was considerable variation between the three plans. The staff model had the highest positive response (92%), whereas responses from physicians in the two network types of HMOs ranged from 24% to 64%. In fact, the staff model was rated higher than the network models consistently. Thus, it would appear that physician dissatisfaction with HMOs is highly dependent on the type of HMO.

Finally, there are increasing problems with the consolidation of the HMO marketplace. According to Woolhandler and Himmelstein (1996), 10 companies controlled 70% of the HMO marketplace in 1993. Since that time, mergers between some of these companies has further reduced the level of competition. The consolidation of services within a few corporations is of concern to the health community and further strains the physician–patient relationship as efficiency of service provision rather than patient care dictates expected outcomes. Chapter 13 examines the evolution of managed care as an outgrowth of the HMO movement.

Out-of-Pocket Expenses

Among all of the various payment methods, out-of-pocket expenses have become the primary organizational and bureaucratic tool to control the overall cost of health care. It is widely held that increasing the cost of care to the patient reduces physician visits, thereby reducing overall health-care expenditures. Out-of-pocket expenses have decreased from 49.8% of the total cost of health care in 1965 to 19.8% in 1991 (National Center for Health Statistics, 1996). However, third-party payments (private insurance and government programs) have increased as a percentage of the total cost (Roemer, 1991).

The amount of out-of-pocket expenses reflects, to a great extent, the economic reality of the patient. In addition to its socioeconomic consequences, these expenses are increasingly viewed as a "responsibility" of the individual to ensure their own well-being. Today, a more sanitized phrase is that such expenditures represent "cost-sharing" efforts between the patient and the health-care providers. The concept of "cost-sharing" is not unique to the United States. Many OECD countries require some form of cost-sharing between citizens and the health-care system. According to the Organisation for Economic Co-Operation and Development (1994, p. 17), Canada is the only country that does not charge "for services covered by federal law."

Does cost-sharing reduce health-care costs? Eden (1994, p. 12) argues that "no evidence exists that people make better choices and decisions about their health care when they bear some of the cost." Nonetheless, cost-sharing is increasingly applied as a technique to reduce health-care consumption within populations. The continued problem with increased levels of cost-sharing is that those segments of the population most in need of services will be denied access because they lack the requisite economic resources necessary.

Charities

The final category from which health-care resources are obtained include monies from charitable organizations. These organizations have raised and donated considerable sums of money to the medical community. Although the amount has increased over the years, charitable giving has remained minimal considering the large rise in the overall cost of health care (Roemer, 1991). Charitable monies represent, to some extent, an American philosophy regarding the role of philanthropy relative to medical outcomes (remember the development of hospitals?). Although not unique, Americans place an inordinate amount of faith in those with the financial means to subsidize the work of others.

Regardless of how health care is financed, the final section addresses two fundamental outcomes of spending. First, is there a limit to the percentage of the GDP the United States is willing to spend on health care? If so, can the United States reallocate spending priorities to achieve maximum outcomes for the largest percentage of the population? Second, what impact will the reallocation of monies have on the inevitable rationing of health care?

How Much Is Enough?

This section examines not only why health care costs more, but also an alternative explanation that will help in the construction of a critical framework of the American health care system. This critique is expanded in Chapter 13 as a number of health-care systems are examined that exemplify the continuum on which they exist.

Global Budgeting: The Allocation of Available Funds

One of the most significant health system–level differences between the United States and other OECD member states is the lack of a **global budget** in the United States. In other words, other nations determine how much they will spend on health care during a given period of time and then allocate those funds to the various components within the system. The process of **allocation** means "setting broad budgetary or policy priorities" (for example, deciding whether to reimburse for a certain kind of service or treatment) (Moody, 1991, p. 188). However, the American approach is to provide health care, determining its overall cost at the end of a specified time period. This does not mean that health-care allocation does not occur in the United States. Indeed, any decision-making process that determines where and how monies will be spent is engaged in allocation. Relative to health-care costs, Mariner (1995) argues that limiting the supply of services forces their rationing, thus reducing cost. Aaron and Schwartz (1984) outline what that would entail. For example, constraining hospital budgets, limiting new therapies and technology, and developing waiting lists by reducing hospital admissions. Enactment of such policies in the United States appears remote at the present time. At the individual level, Mechanic (1986, p. 49) argues that health-care costs can be controlled by limiting "the needs and desires among patients for medical care."

Within other industrialized nations, global budgets offer a systematic and institutionalized process for the allocation of limited resources. For example, consider the Canadian and British systems. Hospital budgets in the Canadian system are determined at the provincial level by taking into account staffing and other changes. Hospitals receive payment in monthly or semimonthly installments (Taylor, 1990). In addition, a "global physician expenditure budget" identifies the amount of monies available for physician reimbursement of specified services within a given time frame (Hurley et al., 1997). This process limits administrative overhead as well as available services. The Canadian system also controls health-care costs by limiting the amount of technology available. For instance, there are 15 magnetic resonance imaging (MRI) machines in Seattle, "which is equal to the number found in all of Canada" (Kaufmann, 1994, p. 381). The political controversies that arise as a result of allocation are not without conflict. In fact, "the allocation of health care resource is at the center of the health care debate in these countries" (Grogan, 1992, p. 231).

The allocation of medical services is not limited to Canada. Great Britain also utilizes an allocative process that limits health resources and services. As a result, Great Britain spends approximately one-half the amount of GDP on health care compared to the United States. Global budgeting requires that "the central government sets the health budget prospectively each year and then allocates amounts to the regional and district health authorities" (Graig, 1993, p. 154).

Considering that the United States now spends 15% of GDP on health care is not an encouraging indication of our willingness to constrain our spending. Whether the United States has reached the upper limits of spending remains debatable. What is known is that current health resource allocation is not equitable. At the same time, the American political and economic elite has not indicated a willingness to depart from a system that is financially and medically rewarding to them.

Turning from the macro-level of allocation to the micro-level analysis of health-care rationing, the following section addresses perhaps one of the most difficult aspects of health care. Because of the emotive qualities associated with this concept, it is susceptible to diversion and inaccuracy.

Health-Care Rationing

This section begins with a number of definitions of **rationing.** Consider the following:

> an action undertaken when there is (a) a recognition that resources are limited, and (b) when faced with scarcity, a method that must be devised to allocate fairly and reasonably these resources. Rationing is the effort to distribute equitably scarce resources. (Callahan, 1992, p. 3)

> it pertains to efforts to discourage the use of 'normal' health care resources, such as diagnostic tests, surgery, drugs, and hospitals. (Rosenblatt, 1981, p. 1404)

> a process of distributing resources differentially. (Blank, 1988, p. 81)

> to decide whether specific individuals will or will not be accepted for treatment. (Moody, 1991, p. 188)

Examine the similarities as well as differences within these definitions. First, all of the definitions state that health-care resources are rationed or limited. However, the definitions disagree on the issue of how the resources will be rationed. Callahan (1992) suggests there is an equitable distribution of resources, whereas Blank (1988) and Moody (1991) argue that the resources are distributed unequally. In a perfect world, equity may be possible. However, given the level of corporate involvement in the health-care system, inequalities based on the economic and social characteristics of health-care recipients will prevail.

On a comparative level, health-care rationing occurs within all health-care systems. However, system differences arise based on the type of rationing utilized. For instance, Mechanic (1994, pp. 73–74) differentiates between explicit and implicit rationing. *Explicit rationing* involves "legislative mandates and administrative decisions," whereas *implicit rationing* involves "regulatory authorities [setting] general constraints on expenditures, entitlements, and expensive technologies." Others interpret the terminology differently. Conrad and Brown (1993, p. 11) categorize three types of rationing: allocative, tacit, and explicit. *Allocative rationing* refers to "differential access to services and medical care. This is the most invisible form, in that it is a feature of social structural inequalities." *Tacit rationing* excludes (or includes) specific services to particular categories of the population. Finally, *explicit rationing* employs national budgetary caps without identifying specific limitations.

Whether health-care rationing in the United States (or any other country) is implicit or explicit is dependent on the definition applied. The reader is referred to Lassey et al. (1997) for a useful visual of the various forms of rationing by country. Thus, rather than debate what constitutes the correct definition, what follows addresses the implications of health-care rationing as a cost-controlling measure.

One of the most celebrated examples of health-care rationing is the limitation placed on older patients with end stage renal disease (ESRD) in Great Britain (Aaron & Schwartz, 1984; Halper, 1989). Although not codified, a review of those receiving kidney transplants in Great Britain indicates a dramatic decline among those aged 65 and older. As a result, the British are portrayed as "agist" in their behavior. There is disagreement, however, regarding the findings of Aaron and Schwartz. For instance, there is considerable application of home-based dialysis in Great Britain, allowing access to a broad sector of the population. Nonetheless, others question whether age-based rationing is fair (and respond that it is). Consider the following statement and its support for age-based rationing: "It is thus unfair for people in their fourth quadrant of their lives to ask younger people to forgo resources for their sake. Intergenerational fairness mandates that when resources are scarce, people in the fourth quadrant of their lives should be the first to forgo them" (Baker, 1993, p. 145). Similar statements have been made of elderly persons in America (see, for example, Thomasma, 1991, for an overview of American responses). As a result, serious debate has occurred since the mid-1980s regarding what health-care "rights" elderly persons should be accorded (whereas other researchers, such as Schroeder, 1994, argue that age-based rationing is less frequent in the United States than in other nations). Such utilitarian approaches to the aging process could have dire consequences. Uhlenberg (1992, p. 465) points out that "policies to invest fewer resources in extending life at the oldest ages could reduce the growth of the oldest-old population." Research has begun to demonstrate the impact of agist attitudes towards a "responsibility to die." In an American survey, Zweibel et al. (1993, p. 79) report that "older persons tended to be more likely than younger ones to agree with the aged-based rationing policy question." They also found a significant relationship between age and responses to the query regarding the duty to refuse care.

In addition to elderly persons, the impact of efforts to ration health care on poor persons has also been identified as being disproportionate. With the poor, questions of "social worth" are raised (Schwartz, 1994). Thus, although rationing is generally defined in terms of limited resources, the persons singled out to receive fewer of those resources are generally the disadvantaged and powerless of society (Conrad & Brown, 1993).

Health-care rationing, then, is a socially constructed economic tool used to differentiate health-care access based on defined criteria. However, regardless of how rationing is masked in the economic pretense of limited resources, it is the defining of which resources are scarce that creates the potential for rationing. Thus, the macro-level policy-oriented resource allocation process clearly establishes which segments of the population will be denied or awarded access to medical treatment. In effect, the financing of health care has a direct impact on medical encounters associated with illness and health behavior, the sick role, and the doctor–patient relationship.

Summary

This chapter begins by examining the financial implications of one's social position within society. In the process, it was discovered that health care is more affordable to some segments of society than to others. Previous chapters taught us that the lack of access to health care results in lower health status and increased risk of disease. These characteristics are implicated in potentially long-term medical problems that are then identified as causative agents in the spiral of expenses among elderly persons and persons considered less "socially worthy" of society.

The United State spends more per capita and, as a percentage of GDP, on health care than any other nation in the world. In addition, the American method of financing health care is relatively unique in comparison to other industrialized nations. The United States relies on a fragmented system consisting of governmental programs such as Medicare and Medicaid, the private insurance industry, Blue Cross and Blue Shield, HMOs, as well as patient out-of-pocket expenses, and charitable donations. Together, these diverse funding sources provide the health-care system with enough money to ensure adequate health coverage for a shrinking majority of the population.

Conversely, the uninsured population continues to grow. This is particularly true among the poor and working-class populations. The lack of affordable health insurance coverage for some segments of society also reflects a growing class disparity within American society. Overall, the financing of American health care (and the resultant consequences) is a reflection of the larger social system in general and the characteristics of the health-care system in particular.

Finally, in an effort to control the ever-rising costs, health systems allocate where and how health-care dollars are spent. Because the United States does not utilize global budgeting, it differs considerably from other industrialized nations regarding the allocation of health-care dollars. As a result, health care is rationed differently. The United States employs explicit rationing, whereas other industrialized nations engage in implicit rationing. In other words, the United States rations on the basis of ability to pay for services (cost). Other nations ration based on established social policy that limits the availability of services (need).

CHAPTER REVIEW

As with other chapters, this review integrates current material with information grounded in earlier chapters. As a result, the following questions are more cumulative in scope.

1. Examining the data on the cost of health care, explain why the United States has become more expensive than any other industrialized nations.

2. Refer to previous chapters and address how European nations are able to control the cost of health care.

3. Utilizing the data on the uninsured and previous information regarding the relative status of women, minorities, and elderly persons in the United States, discuss the future of health care for each group.

4. Given what you know of the allocation process, discuss the potential impact of global budgeting on the American health-care system.

5. Rationing is a necessary component of any health-care system. Explain the impact of rationing on health-related interpersonal relationships such as illness behavior, the sick role, and the doctor–patient relationship.

6. Address how the economics of health-care financing interface with the sociology of health care.

GLOSSARY

allocation   refers to the establishment of funding priorities within a given health-care environment.

cost-shifting   involves passing health-care costs from one group to another.

global budget   determines the total amount to be spent in a given time period within a specific health-care environment.

health maintenance organization   offers members prepaid health insurance. HMOs were intended as an alternative to the traditional fee-for-service approach to medicine.

rationing   involves the (generally unequal) distribution of health resources on the basis of patient-level characteristics such as age.

SUGGESTED READINGS

Davis, K., Anderson, G. F., Rowland, D., & Steinberg, E. P. (1990). *Health care cost containment.* Baltimore: The Johns Hopkins University Press.
The authors provide a solid description of the multiple components involved in efforts to control health-care costs in the United States.

Organisation for Economic Co-Operation and Development. (1990). *Health care systems in transition: The search for efficiency.* Social Policy Studies No. 7. Paris.
  A compilation of studies addressing health expenditures within European nations and the United States.
Organisation for Economic Co-Operation and Development. (1992). *The reform of health care: A comparative analysis of seven OECD countries.* Health Policy Studies No. 2. Paris.
  An overview of economic and service relationships between the general population and specific funding sources.

REFERENCES

Aaron, H. J., & Schwartz, W. B. (1984). *The painful prescription: Rationing hospital care.* Washington, DC: The Brookings Institution.

Abel-Smith, B., Figueras, J., Holland, W., McKee, M., & Mossialos, E. (1995). *Choices in health policy: An agenda for the European union.* Aldershot: Dartmouth Publishing Company Limited.

Angell, M. (1993). How much will health care reform cost? *The New England Journal of Medicine, 328,* 24 (June 17), 1778–1779.

Baker, R. (1993). Visibility and the just allocation of health care: A study of age rationing in the British national health service. *Health Care Analysis, 1,* 139–150.

Bennefield, R. L. (1994). *Dynamics of economic well-being: Health insurance, 1990 to 1992.* U.S. Bureau of the Census. Current Population Reports, P70–37, U.S. Government Printing Office, Washington, DC.

Binstock, R. H., & Post, S. G. (1991). Old age and the rationing of health care. In R. H. Binstock & S. G. Post (Eds.). *Too old for health care? Controversies in medicine, law, economics, and ethics* (pp. 1–12). Baltimore: The Johns Hopkins University Press.

Birenbaum, A. (1993). *Putting health care on the national agenda.* Westport, CT: Praeger.

Blank, R. H. (1988). *Rationing medicine.* New York: Columbia University Press.

Borowsky, S. J., Davis, M. K., Goertz, C., & Lurie, N. (1997). Are all health plans created equal? The physician's view. *Journal of the American Medical Association, 278,* 11, 917–921.

Califano, J. A. Jr. (1986). *America's health care revolution: Who lives? Who dies? Who pays?* New York: Random House.

Callahan, D. (1987). *Setting limits: Medical goals in an aging society.* New York: Simon & Schuster.

Callahan, D. (1992). Symbols, rationality, and justice: Rationing health care. *American Journal of Law and Medicine, 18,* 1–2, 1–13.

Canham-Clyne, J., Woolhandler, S., & Himmelstein, D. (1995). *The rational option for a national health program.* Stony Creek, CT: The Pamphleteer Press.

Caplan, R. L. (1989). The commodification of American health care. *Social Science and Medicine, 28,* 11, 1139–1148.

Chollett, D. J. (1993). Health care financing in selected industrialized nations: Comparative analysis and comment. In *Trends in health benefits* (pp. 9–25). U.S. Department of Labor. Pension and Welfare Benefits Administration. U.S. Government Printing Office, Washington, DC.

Conrad, P., & Brown, P. (1993). Rationing medical care: A sociological reflection. *Research in the Sociology of Health Care, 10,* 3–22.

Davis, K., Anderson, G. F., Rowland, D., & Steinberg, E. P. (1990). *Health care cost containment.* Baltimore: The Johns Hopkins University Press.

Eden, J. (1994). From the Congressional Office of Technological Assessment. *Journal of the American Medical Association, 272,* 1, 12.

Enos, D. D., & Sultan, P. (1977). *The sociology of health care: Social, economic, and political perspectives.* New York: Praeger Publishers.

Evans, R. G., Barer, M. L., & Hertzman, C. (1991). The 20-year experiment: Accounting for, explaining, and evaluating health care cost containment in Canada and the United States. *Annual Review of Public Health, 12,* 481–518.

Fein, R. (1986). *Medical care, medical costs: The search for a national insurance policy.* Cambridge, MA: Harvard University Press.

Fein, R. (1992). Health care reform. *Scientific American, 46,* 46–53.

Ferraro, K. F. (1993). Physician resistance to innovations: The case of contract medicine. *Sociological Focus, 26,* 2, 109–131.

Frech, H. E. III. (1988). Monopoly in health insurance: The economics of Kartell *v.* Blue Shield of Massachusetts. In H. E. Frech III (Ed.). *Health care in America: The political economy of hospitals and health insurance* (pp. 293–320). San Francisco: Pacific Research Institute for Public Policy.

Friedman, E. (1991). The uninsured: From dilemma to crisis. *Journal of the American Medical Association, 265,* 19, 2491–2495.

Fuchs, V. R. (1993). *The future of health policy.* Cambridge, MA: Harvard University Press.

Gallop, G. Jr. (1995). *The Gallop Poll: Public opinion 1994.* Wilmington, DE: Scholarly Resources Inc.

Ginsburg, P. B. (1988). Public insurance programs: Medicare and Medicaid. In H. E. Frech III (Ed.). *Health care in America: The political economy of hospitals and health insurance* (pp. 179–215). San Francisco: Pacific Research Institute for Public Policy.

Grace, H. K. (1988). Instilling cost-consciousness into the practice of health professionals. In *Stemming the rising costs of medical care: Answers and antidotes* (pp. 7–8). Battle Creek, MI: W.K. Kellogg Foundation.

Graig, L. A. (1993). *Health of nations: An international perspective on U.S. health care reform* (2nd Ed.). Washington, DC: Congressional Quarterly, Inc.

Grogan, C. M. (1992). Deciding on access and levels of care: A comparison of Canada, Britain, Germany, and the United States. *Journal of Health Politics, Policy and Law, 17,* 2, 213–232.

Hall, M. A. (1994). *Reforming private health insurance.* Washington, DC: The American Enterprise Institute.

Halper, T. (1985). Life and death in a welfare state: End-stage renal disease in the United Kingdom. *Milbank Quarterly, 63,* 1, 52–93.

Hellander, I., Moloo, J., Himmelstein, D. U., Woolhandler, S., & Wolfe, S. M. (1995). The growing epidemic of uninsurance: New data on the health insurance coverage of Americans. *International Journal of Health Services, 25,* 3, 377–392.

Higgins, L. F., Ferguson, J. M., & Winston, W. J. Understanding and assessing service quality in health maintenance organizations. *Health Marketing Quarterly, 9,* 1 & 2, 5–21.

Himmelstein, D. U., & Woolhandler, S. (1986). Socialized medicine: A solution to the cost crisis in health care in the United States. *International Journal of Health Services, 16,* 3, 339–354.

Himmelstein, D. U., Woolhandler, S., & Wolfe, S. M. (1992). The vanishing health care safety net: New data on uninsured Americans. *International Journal of Health Services, 22,* 3, 381–396.

Hurd, M. D. (1997). Adequacy and equity issues: Another view. In E. R. Kingson & J. H. Schulz (Eds.). *Social Security in the 21st century* (pp. 219–224). New York: Oxford University Press.

Hurley, J., Lomas, J., & Goldsmith, L. J. (1997). Physician responses to global physician expenditure budgets in Canada: A common property perspective. *Milbank Quarterly, 75,* 3, 343–363.

International Labour Organisation. (1989). *From pyramid to pillar: Population change and social security in Europe.* Geneva.

James, T. III, & Nash, D. B. (1995). Health maintenance organizations: A new development or the emperor's old clothes? In W. G. Rothstein (Ed.). *Readings in American health care: Current issues in socio-historical perspective* (pp. 266–277). Madison, WI: University of Wisconsin Press.

Jencks, S. F., & Schieber, G. J. (1991). Containing United States health care costs: What bullet to bite? *Health Care Financing Review, 13,* Suppl., 1–12.

Kaufmann, C. (1994). Rights and the provision of health Care: A comparison of Canada, Great Britain, and the United States. In H. D. Schwartz (Ed.). *Dominant issues in medical sociology* (3rd Ed.) (pp. 376–396). New York: McGraw Hill.

Krieger, N., & Fee, E. (1994). Social class: The missing link in U.S. health data. *International Journal of Health Services, 24,* 1, 25–44.

Kronenfeld, J. J. (1991). Access to health and proposed government changes: Impacts for business and the public. *Free Inquiry in Creative Sociology, 19,* 1, 61–69.

Kronenfeld, J. J. (1993). *Controversial issues in health care policy.* Newbury Park, CA: SAGE.

Lassey, M. L., Lassey, W. R., & Jinks, M. J. (1997). *Health care systems around the world: Characteristics, issues, reforms.* Upper Saddle River, NJ: Prentice-Hall.

Law, S. A. (1994). Blue Cross—What went wrong? In P. Conrad & R. Kern (Eds.). *The sociology of health and illness: Critical perspectives* (4th Ed.) (pp. 261–269). New York: St. Martin's Press.

Light, D. W. (1995). *Homo Economicus:* Escaping the traps of managed competition. *European Journal of Public Health, 5,* 3, 145–154.

Light, D. W. (1996). Excluding more, covering less: The health insurance industry in the U.S. In P. Brown (Ed.). *Perspectives in medical sociology* (2nd Ed.) (pp. 464–477). Prospect Heights, IL: Waveland Press.

Littrell, W. B. (1989). New technology, bureaucracy, and the social construction of medical prices. *The Journal of Applied Behavioral Science, 25,* 3, 249–269.

Luft, H. S. (1982). Health maintenance organizations and the rationing of medical care. In N. S. McKenzie (Ed.). *The crisis in health care: Ethical issues* (pp. 70–110). New York: Meridian Books.

Luft, H. S. (1994). Health maintenance organizations: Is the United States experience applicable elsewhere? In *Health: Quality and choice.* Health policy studies No. 4 (pp. 45–62). Organisation for Economic Co-Operation and Development: Paris.

Lutz, M. E. (1989). Women, work, and preventive health care: An exploratory study of the efficacy of HMO membership. *Women and Health, 15,* 1, 21–33.

Lynch, M. J., & Raphael, S. S. (1963). *Medicine and the state.* Springfield, IL: Charles C. Thomas Publishers.

Mariner, W. K. (1995). Rationing health care and the need for credible scarcity: Why Americans can't say no. *American Journal of Public Health, 85,* 10, 1439–1445.

Mechanic, D. (1986). *From advocacy to allocation: The evolving American health care system.* New York: The Free Press.

Mechanic, D. (1994). *Inescapable decisions: The imperatives of health reform.* New Brunswick, NJ: Transaction Publishers.

Medicaid Source Book: Background Data and Analysis. (1993). A report prepared by the Congressional research service for the use of the Subcommittee on Health and the Environment of the Committee on Energy and Commerce. U.S. House of Representatives. U.S. Government Printing Office, Washington, DC.

Menzel, P. T. (1983). *Medical costs, moral choices: A philosophy of health care economics in America.* New Haven, CT: Yale University Press.

Miles, S., & Parker, K. (1997). Men, women, and health insurance. *The New England Journal of Medicine, 336,* 3, 218–221.

Miller, I. (1996). *American health care blues: Blue Cross, HMOs, and pragmatic reform since 1960.* New Brunswick, NJ: Transaction Publishers.

Miller, R. H., & Luft, H. S. (1994). Managed care plan performance since 1980: A literature analysis. *Journal of the American Medical Association, 271,* 19, 1512–1519.

Moen, F. (1990). Design, implementation, and evaluation of a community financing scheme for hospital care in developing countries: A prepaid health plan in the Bwamanda health zone, Zaire. *Social Science and Medicine, 30,* 12, 1319–1327.

Moody, H. R. (1991). Allocation, yes: Age-based rationing, no. In R. H. Binstock & S. G. Post (Eds.). *Too old for health care? Controversies in medicine, law, economics and ethics* (pp. 180–203). Baltimore: The Johns Hopkins University Press.

Morrisey, M. A. (1994). *Cost shifting in health care: Separating evidence from rhetoric.* Washington, DC: The AEI Press.

National Center for Health Statistics. (1993). *Health, United States, 1992.* Hyattsville, MD: Public Health Service.

National Center for Health Statistics. (1996). *Health, United States, 1995.* Hyattsville, MD: Public Health Service.

Navarro, V. (1994). *The politics of health policy: The U.S. reforms, 1980–1994.* Cambridge, MA: Blackwell Publishers.

O'Keefe, J. (1994). The right to health care and health care reform. In A. R. Chapman (Ed.). *Health care reform: A human rights approach* (pp. 35–64). Washington, DC: Georgetown University Press.

Organisation for Economic Co-Operation and Development. (OECD). (1990). *Health care systems in transition: The search for efficiency.* Social Policy Studies No. 7: Paris.

Organisation for Economic Co-Operation and Development. (OECD). (1992). *The reform of health care: A comparative analysis of seven OECD countries.* Health Policy Studies No. 2: Paris.

Organisation for Economic Co-Operation and Development. (OECD). (1994). *The reform of health care systems: A review of seventeen OECD countries.* Paris.

Paley, W. D. (1993). Overview of the HMO movement. *Psychiatric Quarterly, 64,* 1, 5–12.

Pfaff, M. (1990). Differences in health care spending across countries: Statistical evidence. *Journal of Health Politics, Policy and Law, 15,* 1, 1–67.

Rice, D. P. (1991). Ethics and equity in U.S. health care: The data. *International Journal of Health Services, 21,* 4, 637–651.

Roemer, M. I. (1986). *An introduction to the U.S. health care system* (2nd Ed.). New York: Springer.

Roemer, M. I. (1991). *National health systems of the world: Volume 1—The countries.* New York: Oxford University press.

Rosenblatt, R. E. (1981). Rationing "normal" health care: The hidden legal issues. *Texas Law Review, 59,* 1401–1420.

Schieber, G. J., Poullier, J.-P., & Greenwald, L. M. (1991). Health care systems in twenty-four countries, *Health Affairs,* 22–38.

Schlenker, R. E. (1977). Health maintenance organizations. In L. Corey, M. F. Epstein, & S. E. Saltman (Eds.). *Medicine in a changing society* (pp. 131–140). St. Louis: The C.V. Mosby Company.

Schroeder, S. A. (1994). Rationing medical care—A comparative perspective. *The New England Journal of Medicine, 331,* 16, 1089–1091.

Schwartz, H. D. (1994). Rationing and the ideology of exclusion. In H. D. Schwartz (Ed.). *Dominant issues in medical sociology* (3rd Ed.) (pp. 416–425). New York: McGraw Hill.

Seccombe, K. (1996). Health insurance coverage among the working poor: Changes from 1977 to 1987. *Research in the Sociology of Health Care, 13A,* 199–227.

Somers, A. R., & Somers, H. M. (1977). *Health and health care: Policies in perspective.* Germantown, MD: Aspen Systems Corporation.

Starr, P. (1982). *The social transformation of American medicine.* New York: Basic Books.

Stevens, R. (1989). *In sickness and in wealth: American hospitals in the twentieth century.* New York: Basic Books.

Summer, L. (1994). The escalating number of uninsured in the United States. *International Journal of Health Services, 24,* 3, 409–413.

Swartz, K. (1994). Dynamics of people without health insurance: Don't let the numbers fool you. *Journal of the American Medical Association, 271,* 1 (January 5), 64–66.

Taylor, M. G. (1990). *Insuring national health care: The Canadian experience.* Chapel Hill, NC: The University of North Carolina Press.

The White House Domestic Policy Council. (1993). *The president's health security plan.* New York: Time Books.

Thomasma, D. C. (1991). From ageism toward autonomy. In R. H. Binstock & S. G. Post (Eds.). *Too old for health care? Controversies in medicine, law, economics, and ethics* (pp. 138–163). Baltimore, MD: The Johns Hopkins University Press.

Thorpe, K. E. (1997). Incremental strategies for providing health insurance for the uninsured: Projected federal costs and number of newly uninsured. *Journal of the American Medical Association, 278,* 4, 329–333.

Uhlenberg, P. (1992). Population aging and social policy. *Annual Review of Sociology, 18,* 449–474.

U.S. Bureau of the Census. (1992). International Population Reports, P25, 92-93, *An Aging World II.* U.S. Government Printing Office, Washington, DC.

U.S. Bureau of the Census. (1994). *Health insurance coverage—1993.* SB/94-28. U.S. Department of Commerce. Economics and Statistics Administration.

U.S. Bureau of the Census. (1995). Statistical Brief. *Just what the doctor ordered: The effect of health insurance coverage on doctor and hospital visits.* SB/95-12. U.S. Department of Commerce. Economics and Statistics Administration.

U.S. Bureau of the Census. (1996). *Statistical Abstract of the United States: 1996* (116th Edition.). Washington, DC.

U.S. Department of Health and Human Services. (1995). *Your Medicare handbook, 1995.* Health Care Financing Administration. Publication No. HCFA 10050. Baltimore, MD.

Vistnes, J. P., & Monheit, A. C. (1997). Health insurance status of the civilian noninstitutionalized population: 1996. Rockville (MD): Agency for Health Care Policy and Research: 1997. *MEPS Research Findings No. 1.* AHCPR Pub. No. 97-0030.

Weiss, L. D. (1997). *Private medicine and public health: Profit, politics, and prejudice in the American health care enterprise.* Boulder, CO: Westview Press.

Weiss, L. D., & Theno, S. A. (1991). Perestroika and health care in the USSR: Innovations in state financing. *Journal of Public Health Policy,* Summer, 229–240.

Weissman, J. S., & Epstein, A. M. (1993). The insurance gap: Does it make a difference? *Annual Review of Public Health, 14,* 243–270.

Woolhandler, S., & Himmelstein, D. U. (1996). Galloping toward oligopoly: Giant H.M.O. "A" or Giant H.M.O. "B"? In P. Brown (Ed.). *Perspectives in medical sociology* (2nd Ed.) (pp. 490–495). Prospect Heights, IL: Waveland Press, Inc.

World Development Report. (1993). *Investing in health: World Development Indicators.* New York: Oxford University Press.

Xingyuan, G., Bloom, G., Shenglan, T., Yinga, Z., Shougi, Z., & Xingbao, C. (1993). Financing health care in rural China: Preliminary report of a nationwide study. *Social Science and Medicine, 36,* 4, 385–391.

Yoder, R. A. (1989). Are people willing and able to pay for health services? *Social Science and Medicine, 29,* 1, 35–42.

Zelman, W. A. (1996). *The changing health care marketplace: Private ventures, public interests.* San Francisco: Jossey-Bass publishers.

Zweibel, N. R., Cassel, C. K., & Karrison, T. (1993). Public attitudes about the use of chronological age as a criterion for allocating health care resources. *The Gerontologist, 33,* 1, 74–80.

13

Health-Care Systems

A Comparison

Comparison is at the heart of the scientific enterprise. It permits us to examine and evaluate the features of a system by contrasting it with another one of the same general type. Comparison, therefore, adds a new perspective to an examination of the situation and the problems each society faces. And it may be instructive. If there is comparative anatomy, physiology, or religion, why not comparative health systems?

—Field, 1989, p. 5

The Importance of a Comparative Health-Care Systems Perspective

This chapter represents more than a cursory explanation of various **health-care systems** throughout the world. The material presented in this chapter provides the reader with a culmination of cross-cultural information regarding medical sociology that has been presented throughout the book, and with a macro-level examination of health-care systems in a number of industrialized, developing, and former Eastern Bloc nations. The practicality of a comparative perspective is perhaps best understood because "the distinction between domestic and international health is increasingly antiquated" (Gellert et al., 1989, p. 423).

The chapter begins by acknowledging the relevance of health system analysis to medical sociology. Consider the importance of the following trends (Roemer, 1977):

1. Increasingly, the cost of health-care services is being paid through social rather than through individual contributions.
2. The ratio of physicians to the total population continues to increase throughout the world.
3. Allied health personnel continue to increase relative to the total population. In addition, allied health personnel are involved in an increasing diversity of health-related areas.
4. There is continual growth of hospitals and hospital beds, particularly within developing nations. Many developed nations are experiencing an oversupply of facilities.
5. The delivery of services is becoming increasing systematic through the employment of health-care professionals by the state rather than in individual practice.
6. The role of preventive medicine is becoming increasingly important throughout the world.
7. Because of the increasing cost of health care, there is greater regulation of expenditures.
8. Similarly, efficiencies of administration are leading to greater state involvement as well as increased efficiency within the private sector (see also van de Ven, 1996).

The importance of this chapter is understood through its integrative structure. That is, all material applicable within previous chapters is located within one of the components associated with health-care systems. In other words, everything from the patient–physician relationship to the sick role to the financing of health care is representative of a specific configuration of norms and values associated with numerous social institutions that constitute the health-care system within each country. Given the amount of material, it is impossible to examine in depth all components within all countries in a single chapter (this would be a book in itself). Therefore, this chapter provides the reader with a general framework within which sociopolitical and economic factors operate to influence the structure and process of health care within any given society (Ertler et al., 1987; van Atteveld et al., 1987). An example of comparative research is the work on health system satisfaction by Blendon et al. (1990)

and Blendon et al. (1995). In their research, the authors examined survey outcomes across nations (10 in 1990 and 3 in 1995). Others, van Atteveld et al. (1987), argue that international health system comparisons are generally more descriptive rather than analytical. In other words, "is there a summary of facts" (descriptive) or "are the relationships between facts described and are the facts assessed by using an already prepared framework of analysis?" (van Atteveld et al., 1987, p. 106). They argue that the type of comparison depends on the extent to which external factors such as demographic, economic, and political characteristics are included in the analysis. For instance, applying the Physical Quality of Life Index (PQLI), Cereseto and Waitzkin (1986) and Lena and London (1993) assess the impact of the political system on health outcomes. In this case, the general conclusion is that "strong left regimes and democracies generate better health outcomes for their populations than do strong right-wing and less democratic nations" (Lena & London, 1993, p. 596).

System Analysis: The Application of Models

This section examines three distinct models of health systems. First, however, what is a health system? Health systems can be defined as "the combination of resources, organization, financing, and management that culminate in the delivery of health services to the population" (Roemer, 1991, p. 31; see also Elling, 1980, for a listing of similar components). Furthermore, a number of health-related trends have been identified relative to changes in the economic, political, and social structures throughout various societies (Roemer, 1993). However, health-system analysis has yet to develop a framework that incorporates all appropriate characteristics (Mechanic & Rochefort, 1996), although the work by Twaddle (1996) offers valuable insight into the possibilities of system reform analysis. The presentation of models begins with a typology by Field (1980).

Field's Typology

Initially, Field (1980) categorized health systems into an external and two distinct internal components. The external component refers to the clinical aspects of medicine (or what Field refers to as the "gross medical product"). The first internal component involves the cultural expectations and changes associated with health personnel. The second internal component addresses the broader issues of education and research relative to health personnel. Furthermore, the health system relies on resources from the following components within society in order to function:

1. legitimacy/mandate (a political resource);
2. knowledge and techniques (a cultural resource);
3. personnel (a human resource);
4. physical resources—land, building, capital (economic resources) (Field, 1980, p. 400).

Taken together, these components represent the health system, which, according to Field (1980, p. 401) is a *"societal mechanism that absorbs generalized resources (of the type just mentioned) and metabolizes them into specialized outputs of pre-sumed significance in meeting the functional problems posed by incapacitation"* (italics in original).

Finally, Field identifies five different health systems. Although these systems represent "ideal types," representative systems exist within societies. Scheme 13.1 depicts the range and content of these five types of health-care systems.

Beginning with general characteristics identified along the left side, changes between health systems can be identified as we move from the anomic to the socialized system. Moving from left to right, the most basic difference is the increasing involvement of the state. According to the general definition of health care, the anomic position places responsibility within individual consumers. At the other end of the spectrum, health care is a responsibility of the state and is provided as a public service. The position of the physician ranges from the solo practitioner to a state employee. Concomitantly, the importance of professional organizations ranges from being powerful in the anomic type to nonexistent within socialist types of health systems. Similarly, facilities begin as private entities within anomic systems, but quickly become jointly operated and eventually all public under the socialist system. Economic transfer refers to the method of payment for services. Within anomic systems, payment of medical services is direct; the patient pays the physician for the performance of services. Moving to the right, payment becomes increasingly indirect. In other words, payment for services is provided through prepayments or taxes to third-party payees, or the state. Correspondingly, the role of the state is minimal within the anomic system but becomes progressively involved until there is total state control in the socialist system. Finally, Field offers prototypes for each system.

Although limited, the representation offered by Field provides a good overview of those characteristics associated with health systems. Perhaps the most obvious problem with the proposed outline is the lack of a non-Western interpretation. For comparative purposes, it is important to locate industrializing nations within the scheme and determine if the patterns can be similarly applied.

The Sociopolitical Characteristics of Systems (Elling)

Quite differently, Elling (1980, 1989) offers an explanation of health systems based on sociopolitical characteristics and grounded in the historical underpinnings of the society. Elling (1980, p. 92) begins his argument by suggesting that the central goal of a health system is to achieve "an improved health status for all persons in a nation's population (or a subnational region's population) within expenditure limits the nation can sustain." In the process of achieving this goal, health systems establish a number of intermediate goals and experience a multiplicity of problems. The ultimate goal of improved health status is directly and indirectly influenced by the structure of the health system itself, as well as political and economic characteristics of the system. More importantly, however, is the context within which these variables develop. As Elling (1980, p. 98) argues, this includes "the cultures and physical conditions of the population, which have a direct bearing on health." The logic and flow of this argument is presented in Figure 13.1.

SCHEME 13.1 Fields' Ideal Types of Health Systems

	Type 1	Type 2	Type 3	Type 4	Type 5
Health system	Anomic	Pluralistic	Insurance/Social Security	National Health Service	Socialized
General definition	Health care as item of personal consumption	Health care as predominantly a consumer good or service	Health care as an insured/guaranteed consumer good or service	Health care as a state supported consumer good or service	Health care as state-provided public service
Position of the physician	Solo entrepreneur	Solo entrepreneur and member of variety of groups/organizations	Solo entrepreneur and member of medical organizations	Solo entrepreneur and member of medical organizations	State employee and member of medical organization
Role of professional associations	Powerful	Very strong	Strong	Fairly strong	Weak or nonexistent
Ownership of facilities	Private	Private and public	Private and public	Mostly public	Entirely public
Economic transfers	Direct	Direct and indirect	Mostly indirect	Indirect	Entirely indirect
Role of the polity	Minimal	Decentralized/indirect	Central/indirect	Central/direct	Total
Prototypes	U.S.; Western Europe in 19th century	U.S. in 20th century; South Africa	Sweden; France; Japan 20th century; Canada; Italy; Switzerland	Great Britain 20th century; Australia	Soviet Russia 20th century; Eastern Europe

Source: Reprinted from *Social Science and Medicine, 14A*, M. G. Field, The health system and the polity: A contemporary American dialectic, pp. 397–413. Copyright 1980, with kind permission from Elsevier Science Ltd, The Boulevard, Langford Lane, Kidlington OX5 1GB, UK.

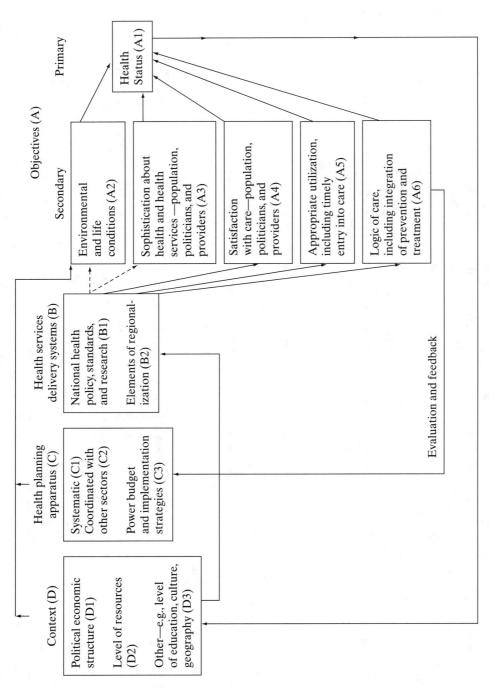

FIGURE 13.1 Major Blocks of Variables and Flow of Influence in Health Systems.

Source: Reprinted by permission of Transaction Publishers. "Organization of Authority in Societies," In *Cross National Study of Health Systems* by R. Elling, (1980). Copyright © 1980 Transaction Inc., all rights reserved.

Elling (1980) also constructed a typology of cross-national systems based on the organization of authority within centralization–decentralization and concertedness–fractionation as the dimensions. The results of this typology are evident in Table 13.1. Here, Elling (1980) locates countries on the basis of "face value" or available information because hard data were not available. Given the four possible outcomes within the typology, Elling (1980, p. 107) argues that countries in the concertedness–decentralized cell are most likely to support what he terms "idealized health and medical system." Politically, these nations represent democratic socialist systems in which "the forces and relations of production are controlled by the worker and peasant class."

Later, Elling (1989, pp. 212–213) identified a number of elements that assist in our understanding of differences between nations and their health systems. These include:

1. the labor theory of value . . .
2. an historically evolving class-based system of production . . .
3. class-struggle over the surplus of production . . .
4. a state apparatus . . .
5. a hegemony of social power exercised sometimes through raw force or military police power and the law . . .
6. an evolving world-system with core-capitalist, semi-peripheral, peripheral and semi-independent socialist-oriented nation states inter-related through international finance and production mechanisms, backed up by covert and overt military force.

TABLE 13.1   Organization of Authority in Societies

	Concertedness	
Concentration	Pluralistic-Divided, Fractionated	Concerted—"Got it Together"
Centralized	Chile Iran Franco Spain Argentina ?	? ← USSR GDR and other Eastern European
Decentralized	India → USA FRG ?	Tanzania China ? ← Sweden Cuba ? ← Angola Yugoslavia

FRG, Federal Republic of Germany.

Source: Reprinted by permission of Transaction Publishers. "Organization of Authority in Societies" in *Cross National Study of Health Systems* by R. Elling, (1980). Copyright © 1980 Transaction Inc.; all rights reserved.

On the basis of these elements, Elling (1989) constructs a "working" typology of nations. He considers this typology to be dynamic because nations can move from one category to the next depending on interpretation. The categories and accompanying explanation and appropriate countries include:

1. *Core capitalist*   In these countries there is considerable economic disparity between social classes, with wealth and power concentrated in the upper tier of individuals within the country. Conversely, workers within these nations are poorly organized and have little impact. Relative to health care characteristics such as class, race, age, and sex influence level of access. Examples include the United States, Switzerland, and the Federal Republic of Germany.

2. *Core capitalist, social welfare*   Although economic and health disparity exists, it is not as pronounced as in number 1. The worker's movement is stronger and there are elements of national health insurance or a national health system within the country. Examples include Canada, the United Kingdom, Japan, and Scandinavian countries such as Sweden and Norway.

3. *Industrialized socialist-oriented* (or state capitalist)   in which there is centralized government control over all aspects of life, including health care. Examples include the former Soviet Union, the German Democratic Republic, as well as other Eastern European countries (this was written before the breakup of the former USSR and the Eastern European Nations).

4. *Capitalist dependencies in periphery and semi-periphery*   This is the largest category with huge economic and health disparities. There are virtually no workers' movements and what does exist is usually suppressed by the national government. Examples include Brazil, India, Indonesia, Guatemala, Haiti, and the Philippines.

5. *Socialist-oriented, quasi-independent of world system*   Contrary to number 4; workers' movements are strong. Countries are organized around a democratic-centralist authority, with greater distribution and equality of resources including health care. Health indicators are generally more favorable among these nations than nations in number 4. Examples are the People's Republic of China, Cuba, Nicaragua, and Tanzania.

Elling refers to this typology as "working" and dynamic. Admittedly, the location of countries within any one of the categories is subject to change depending on economic and political circumstances. Although dated, the typology offers a perspective that incorporates not only indicators of health, but also economic and political criteria. A more recent analysis of this typology would offer further insight into the impact of workers' movements as well as changes wrought by political and economic structures on health outcomes.

Health System Components (Roemer)

Roemer (see, for example, 1977, 1985, 1991, 1993) developed the final health system model to be examined. Figure 13.2 illustrates the five basic components identified by Roemer as central to any health-care system. Beginning with the production of

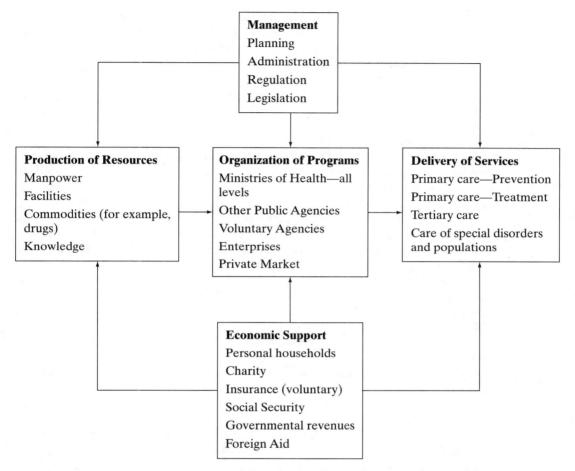

FIGURE 13.2   A Health Services System—Structure, Relationships, and Function.

Source: From *National Health Systems of the World, Volume 1: The Countries* by M. I. Roemer. Copyright © 1991 by Oxford University Press, Inc. Used by permission of Oxford University Press, Inc.

resources, it is obvious that health care is dependent on other social institutions for resources; for instance, the educational and economic systems for personnel and the cost of their training. An area of growing importance is that of commodities, such as drugs and medical equipment. The second component is the organization of programs. The level of involvement of the various sectors is dependent on the society. Roemer also points to varying programs and organizational structures within governmental and nongovernmental units (again, depending on the particular society). Third is that of economic support. Again, depending on the particular society, the mix of these financing methods varies although general taxation occurs in all societies. Variations exist on what is taxed and how much. In addition to the mix of financing measures is the impact these measures have on the health system itself. For instance, the level of private (individual-based) funding influences the level of access to the health-care system. One trend has been that the percentage of monies from the private sector continues to decline while the percentage of monies from the public sector has been increasing. Fourth is the management component, within which is located various forms of social control that can be located either in the public or private domain. For example, regulation is generally considered a governmental responsibility, but may be controlled within the private sector through the use of industry standards. Evaluation offers care providers at all levels the opportunity to assess the quality and efficacy of their work. Evaluation can also be used to control the physician–patient relationship by determining the length of time necessary for a physician to spend with a patient, depending on the condition identified. The final component is the delivery of services. Similarly, the method of delivery as well as the type of services is dependent on the country. In particular, there are considerable differences between developed and developing nations. For instance, delivery of services within developed nations may occur primarily within physician offices, whereas initial delivery of services in developing nations may occur at the local clinic level.

These components provide the reader with an excellent overview of health-care system structure. Although criticized by Elling for being ahistorical, Roemer's work provides the reader with a solid grasp of cross-cultural criteria associated within a health-care system. Roemer (1991) also developed a typology of health care systems utilizing levels of economic development and the political–economic characteristics associated with the type of health-care system. This typology is particularly effective as it locates virtually all societies within one of the possible 16 available cells.

The following sections move from the general (system level) to specific health-care systems. The purpose of this analysis is to briefly examine differences and similarities between health-care systems. It is also the purpose of these sections to demonstrate the value of macro-level analysis by identifying how many of the previous areas of analysis are interwoven within our understanding of health-system analysis.

Health-Care System Analysis of Developed Nations

This section briefly analyzes the health-care systems of various industrialized nations. Although these nations represent the health system spectrum, they are strikingly similar. For example, they are all advanced capitalist societies experiencing an aging of their population.

The United States

The health-care system of the United States is often described as a nonsystem. This description is used to illustrate the fragmentation of services and financing associated with the health-care system (see, for example, Iglehart, 1994, for a listing of various state proposals regarding health-care reform). The American system can, however, be located within the five components identified earlier by Roemer (1986, 1988). Nonetheless, the United States is the only developed nation that does not provide universal health care for its citizens.

Even South Africa (at least on paper) now ensures its citizens equal access to health care, although efforts to institutionalize primary health care throughout the provinces of South Africa have not had the desired results. The reason is that primary health care remains only one of many components within the system, rather than the central focus of the system (Coughlan, 1995). Although health care has undergone considerable change in South Africa, disparities between racial populations remain. According to Benatar (1997), health-care reform in South Africa is premised on (1) redistributing health-care monies between provinces, (2) restructuring the public sector in terms of racial and gender composition, (3) improving the image of the primary health care, and (4) addressing needed changes in health research. Essentially, the new system is based on an alliance between the central government, the provinces, and the district level (Kirsch, 1997).

Returning to the American health-care system, Roemer (1973, pp. 77–78) best summarizes the problem by pointing out that "The basic fault in American health service is the discrepancy between our assertion of health care as a basic human right and our practice of treating it as a marketplace commodity." The inability of the American system to assert that health care is a social good has had a profound impact on the structure of the system. Many of the reasons why the United States has not enacted a universal health system include "pragmatism, political imperatives, periodic health crises, the exercise of power by private interests, and a strong belief in limited government, individual freedom, and science and technology" (Iglehart, 1992, p. 963) (see also Alford, 1972).

Previous chapters outline many of the characteristics of the American health-care system. This chapter examines the more recent changes and their impact on the future of the system. Although all of these efforts have failed, the system has not remained static. Indeed, the American health-care system has undergone significant change since the mid-1920s. Consider, for example, the birth of Blue Cross and Blue Shield, Medicare, Medicaid, health maintenance organizations (HMOs), and most recently, **managed care.**

The AMA defines managed care as "The control of access to and limitation on physician and patient utilization of services by public or private payers or their agents through the use of prior and concurrent review for approval or referral to service or site of service, and financial incentives or penalties" (Iglehart, 1992, p. 965). Managed care represents an evolutionary process begun with the development of prepaid plans such as HMOs in the 1960s and 1970s (Lassey et al., 1997). Continuing throughout the 1980s, efforts were underway to enroll Medicare recipients in HMOs (Organisation for Economic Co-Operation and Development, 1994a). Although intended to contain costs and provide quality health care, the managed care movement has not met expectations. Furthermore, the managed care movement has become increasingly for-profit. As a result, the balance between offering access to care runs counter to the bottom line of corporate profits for the organization.

In a similar vein, the United States has also produced the era of **managed competition** in health care. Enthoven and Kronick (1989a,b) argue that the purpose of managed competition is to encourage prepaid programs to compete for subscribers by offering the lowest possible cost with quality care. Those individuals unable to afford health care would be "sponsored" by the government and offered coverage. Perhaps the most celebrated effort has been the Oregon Plan, in which Medicaid recipients were enrolled in one of the managed care plans in the state. The purpose of the Oregon Plan is to limit the list of medical services available to those individuals enrolled. In other words, Oregon rationed health care services to the poor (The Oregon Basic Health Services Act, 1990; Bodenheimer, 1997a,b). Similarly, the ill-fated and poorly planned Health Security Act (The White House Domestic Policy Council, 1993; Brock & Daniels, 1994) proposed by President Clinton utilized the basic framework of managed competition. The problem with managed competition is its continued reliance on the workplace as the initial point of entrance to the health-care system. Navarro (1995a) provides an analysis of the Clinton health plan, whereas Light (1995) analyzes the flaws of managed competition.

Because of American reliance on the marketplace to control cost and the workplace to provide access to health care, reform efforts are severely limited. Within a political context, Gill (1990, p. 493) suggests that health-care reform will not occur until "the country's political system can present real ideological alternatives— real choices between left and right—to the electorate." More specifically, Navarro (1992a, 1994) argues that the inability of the United States to enact health-care reform is the result of a weakened working-class and labor movement. Contrary to other industrialized nations, the United States has never experienced the growth and importance of the working class relative to the capitalist class. As a result, the capitalist class, represented by the medical industrial complex and members of congress, has a vested interest in maintaining the current structure of the health-care system (Himmelstein & Woolhandler, 1990). Thus, efforts to institute a single-payer system threaten their power and dominance within society (Navarro, 1995b).

Nonetheless, there has been a concerted effort in the United States to restructure American health care into a universal, single-payer system (McDermott, 1994) or some derivation (see, for example, Scott & Schapiro, 1992). For an overview of the various "plans" that have been put forth to "solve" the American health-care dilemma, see Huefner (1992). Others (Anderson, 1989) suggest that the United States is, in fact, moving toward universal coverage, but in an incremental and fragmented manner. This process involves coverage of various segments of the population (i.e., elderly persons, poor persons, and, most recently, some of the uninsured children). Because of this continued fragmented approach to health care, efforts to restructure the American health-care system have focused increased interest in the Canadian system (see, for example, Iglehart, 1989; Navarro et al., 1989; Evans et al., 1991; Marmor & Mashaw, 1992; Jacobs, 1993; Kaufman, 1994). Unlike the United States, most Canadians remain supportive of their health-care system, even with its current financial problems.

The future of the American health-care system is uncertain. As Roemer (1977) suggests, the United States cannot decide whether health is a social good or a commodity. An editorial in *The Lancet* (What price cost control, 1997, p. 295) best summarizes what the United States should do: "Comprehensive health-care reform, even if it means government intrusion, would assist a more equitable distribution of health-care resources, an outcome that will never be achieved by the ruthless hand of the market alone."

If health is a social good, Angell (1993) identifies three changes necessary within the American system. These changes include a global budget, a single-payer system (funding), and finally, a shift away from a market philosophy of competition. If, however, health is a commodity to be purchased and used by those with the economic means, then the United States will become increasingly polarized on the basis of access to health and health outcomes.

Canada

What is it about the Canadian health-care system that so many Americans would like to emulate (see, for example, Mizrahi et al., 1993; Neuschler, 1994; Marmor, 1996)? A historical accounting of the emergence of the current health-care system can be found in a variety of sources (Crichton, 1982; Hatcher et al., 1984; Taylor, 1990; Roemer, 1991; Graig, 1993; Organisation for Economic Co-Operation and Development, 1994a). The Canadian health-care system had its origins in the British North American Act of 1867 (Graig, 1993). However, it was not until World War I and the deplorable physical condition of recruits that promoted national action to improve the health status of the population. One significant difference between the United States and Canada is in terms of the role of the national government vis-à-vis the provincial government. Thus, for example, the British North American Act "reserves for the Government of Canada all residual powers, including a general grant of authority for the 'peace, order, and good government' of the people of Canada" (Hatcher et al., 1984, p. 87). Although the national government began discussing statutory health insurance in 1919, it was the 1944 election of a socialist government in Saskatchewan that provided the impetus for concrete action. By 1946, the Saskatchewan Hospital Service Plan (SHSP) provided a publicly funded insurance system for hospital services. Historically, the province of Saskatchewan has been at the forefront of health-system change in Canada. For example, in 1914 the town of Sarnia, Saskatchewan, hired the first municipal doctor for $1,500 a year. The province covered the cost of hiring and retaining a physician by levying taxes on members of the community (Dickenson, 1993). By the 1920s, union hospital districts were formed to raise money for hospital construction. Returning to the election of the Cooperative Commonwealth Federation (CCF) in 1946, the need to provide province-wide health-care services efficiently and cost-effectively to a large, primarily rural province resulted in a regionalization of hospital services and personnel. A similar program was instituted in British Columbia in 1949. By 1956 the national government enacted the Hospital and Diagnostic Services Act (essentially the Saskatchewan program). The program was adopted by all 10 provinces in 1961. With hospital coverage assured, the Medical Care Insurance Act of 1962 was passed in Saskatchewan. The intention of this act was to provide a government payment of a fixed fee schedule to physicians who went on strike in opposition to the act. When the strike was settled, the government retained control of the program and maintained the basic element of universal coverage. In return, physicians were given the right to charge patients beyond the official fee if the patient chose that doctor. Again, the rest of Canada followed the lead of Saskatchewan (Roemer, 1991). Later (1966), the national government passed the Medical Care Act, which provided for a 50–50 cost-sharing relationship between the national government and the provinces (which was reduced by the national government), and by 1971, the Medicare or national insurance program was established. Here, the concept of medical necessity has become significant because of its definition in the Canada Health Act. Essentially, medical necessity has had various interpretations that have accommodated "the different political interests of specific groups" (Charles et al., 1997, p. 36). Particularly important within this legislation were the five principles on which Canadian health care is based: "universal coverage, comprehensive service coverage, reasonable access, portability of coverage, and public administration of insurance plans" (Organisation of Economic Co-Operation and Development, 1994a, p. 104). More specifically, Taylor (1990, p. 214) points out those values by which the government became involved in the health care of its people:

1. That health service is available to all Canadians on equal terms and conditions.
2. That the indignities of the means test, with its accompanying harassment by municipal relief inspectors demanding reimbursement, no longer be imposed on the"medically indigent."
3. That the costs of health services for the indigent be assumed by the senior levels of government and not by municipal government, where the heaviest burdens were likely to occur in municipalities least able to pay.
4. That the costs of health services no longer be borne primarily by the sick and the minority able to obtain voluntary insurance but by all income earners, roughly in accordance with their ability to pay.
5. That the "Robin Hood" function of equalizing health care costs to patients, performed in the past by physicians through the "sliding scale of fees" principle, be accomplished through the tax system.
6. That the programs be administered by public agencies accountable to legislatures and electors.

Essentially, the Canadian health-care system provides universal health insurance but delivers care within the private sector (Brody & Lie, 1993; see also Deber, 1994). As mentioned earlier, the United States and Canada had similar levels of health-care expenditures when national health insurance was initiated. The implementation of the "Canadian experiment" has had a dramatic impact on the cost of health care. Although the cost of American health care continues to increase, the Canadian system has been effective in controlling their health-care costs. As Evans et al. (1991) point out, the reason is a "sole-source funding" method that provides greater control over expenditures. However, disparities in health outcomes remain. According to a forum on health care, one's socioeconomic status, education level, and whether one was aboriginal were directly related to life expectancy and health status (National Forum on Health, 1997).

Since its inception, the Canadian Medicare system has undergone change. For example, the government has banned extra billing by physicians. Fee schedules are negotiated between the provincial government and provincial medical associations. However, as Williams et al. (1995, p. 317) point out, Canadian physicians experience "relatively few of the intrusions into practice which have characterized the rapid expansion of corporate medicine in the United States." Similarly, hospital budgets are determined through negotiated global budgets. Nonetheless, the Canadian health insurance system is facing its greatest crisis since it was introduced. This crisis is, to some extent, the result of the current health-care system itself (its focus on the medical model of curative health) as well as the aging of the population. For example, "over half [of the health care dollar] goes to hospitals and nursing homes" (Chappell, 1993, p. 489). Furthermore, the rate of long-term care institutionalization is relatively high in Canada (6.7%) when compared with other industrialized nations (4.6% in the United States and 2.7% in England) (Chappell, 1993). Efforts to control costs have resulted in a reduction in the number of physicians in medical school. Other cost-costing measures have attempted to reduce physician and hospital costs. These efforts have resulted in issues of access to the health-care system itself, leading Lassey et al. (1997, p. 96) to suggest that a "two-tiered system may be emerging." In other words, two distinct levels of health access depending on some criteria such as ability to pay.

United Kingdom

The National Health Service (NHS) in England is quite different from the Canadian health insurance system. Although the beginnings of health care can be traced to the 10th century, the material presented here focuses on the emergence of the NHS. Beginning in the early 1800s, various workplace organizations, generally referred to as "friendly societies," provided health and sickness insurance to workers throughout England and Europe. In 1911 the British government passed the National Insurance Act of 1911, which provided sickness coverage for manual and other workers making below a specified wage. Although the act did not cover workers' dependents, it did include spousal maternity benefits. Dependents could receive free care at the voluntary hospitals (Anderson, 1972). The state, employers, and employees all contributed to the act (Allen, 1984). However, the advent of World War II raised questions regarding the efficacy of the friendly societies. As a result, Sir William Beveridge conducted a survey of existing programs. In 1942, the now famous Beveridge Report was presented. While the report covered a number of social issues, it specifically addressed the need for a national health service that would provide all citizens with access to necessary medical care (Roemer, 1991). In 1946, the Labour Party government acted on the report and by 1948, the National Health Service was established. The NHS has provided quality level health care for a fraction of the cost in the United States. The percentage of gross domestic product (GDP) spent on health care in Great Britain is currently between 6% and 7%.

Since its inception, the NHS has undergone a number of changes. However, the primary objectives of the NHS, identified in a 1976 Royal Commission, remain important. These objectives include:

- to influence individuals to remain healthy;
- to provide equality of entitlement to health services;
- to provide a broad range of services of a high standard;
- to provide equality of access to these services;
- to provide service free at the time of use;
- to satisfy the reasonable expectations of its users;
- to remain a national service responsive to local needs. (Barnard & Pendreigh, 1982, p. 310)

These points illustrate the intention of the NHS. Ideally, health-care opportunities and services are equally available to all within society. Gill (1994, p. 455) best distinguishes between an NHS and other forms of health care by stating that: "it is a delivery system accountable, through the body politic, to the population it serves."

The foundation of the NHS is built on a number of pillars that include the "general practitioners . . . a network of regional hospital boards (RHBs) . . . teaching hospitals and a . . . network of local health authorities" (Roemer, 1991, pp. 194–197). Since its inception in 1948, however, the pillars of the NHS have undergone change. Some of the more recent efforts to improve the efficiency of the NHS are discussed. First, however, it is necessary to revisit what is perhaps the most important research of the National Health Service: the **Black Report.**

Initially presented in Chapter 4, the Black Report represents the work of a working group on health inequality established in 1977. The group consisted of two medical doctors and two social scientists. The Black Report was issued in 1980 amid attempts by the Thatcher government to stop its publication. Essentially, the Black Report identified continuing health differences between social classes in Great Britain. For some, these findings indicate the failure of the NHS. Among others, however, the explanations and recommendations put forth by the working group generally locate blame for the continuing inequality within the broader context of continuing social inequality within British society (Townsend & Davidson, 1992). The reader is directed to Chapter 4, where a discussion of the explanations associated with the Black Report can be found. Here, the numerous recommendations made by the working group are outlined. According to MaCintyre (1997, pp. 729–730):

For policy within the health sector it (the Black Report) had three priorities:

1. for children to have a better start in life;
2. for disabled people bearing the brunt of cumulative ill health and deprivation; and
3. for preventive and educational action to encourage good health;

for broader social policy it had two main priorities:

    1. a comprehensive anti-poverty strategy; and
    2. improving education;

and for research it had six main priorities:

    1. surveillance of the development of children, especially in relation to accidents;
    2. better understanding of the health effects of such aspects of behaviour as smoking, diet, alcohol consumption and exercise;
    3. the development of area social conditions and health indicators for use in resource allocation;
    4. study of health hazards in relation to occupational conditions and work;
    5. better measures of the prevalence and course of disability; and
    6. study of the interaction of social factors implicated in ill health over time and within small areas.

These recommendations provide a framework for further discussion and analysis of the relationship between the broader social structural characteristics of a society and potential health outcomes among its citizenry. Since its release, the Black Report has generated considerable discussion and increased research. For instance, Turner (1995) argues for a "comparative sociology of health-care systems, which will transcend the limitations of the political economy perspective." Similarly, Scott-Samuel (1997) reports increasing class differences since the beginning of conservative rule in 1980, suggesting that health inequalities are rooted in the lack of economic opportunity (see also Wilkinson, 1996).

    Throughout the 1980s the NHS experienced a number of reforms (Day & Klein, 1989). One of the more significant efforts at reform was the 1989 White Paper, which argued for the "separation of the purchasing and provision of hospital services, mediated by contracts" (Organisation for Economic Co-Operation and Development, 1992, p. 122). These reforms were an effort to increase the level of competition between general practitioners (GPs) for patients. The reforms also gave purchasing authorities broader opportunities to "seek lowest-cost providers" (Mahon, 1996, p. 676; see also, Williams et al., 1993; Edgar, 1995). For example, consider the following options now available to hospitals:

> Hospitals were now invited to consider opting out of the existing area framework; were enabled to offer better wages and incentives to staff, to compete for staff across boundaries, to borrow funds from outside the system, and to offer services outside their administrative area, not excluding services to the private sector. (Madden, 1991, pp. 382–383)

    In effect, the reforms are an attempt to shift current power relationships within the British system. For instance, reforms increase the power of general practitioners at the expense of specialists. In addition, hospitals and hospital managers have increased power, as do patients. The White Paper is also expected to increase the emphasis on health promotion (Roberts et al., 1993). Given the findings of Wardle and Steptoe (1991), health promotion efforts are necessary. For example, the knowledge base of British men regarding testicle examination and of British women regarding breast examination appears rather limited. The potential consequences of these reforms, however, will be to increase the economic disparity between those GPs who opt for the market reforms over the GPs who do not. Similarly, income differences will increase between specialists depending on their level of supply. In other words, the distribution of health actors and services will become increasingly unequal (Scheffler, 1992).

The reforms are an outgrowth of increased privatization of the British health service. As Wiles (1993) reports, the consumerism of health care in Great Britain has become particularly important for those women who currently utilize private facilities. It is important to realize, however, that these women are not representative of the larger population. Rather, they are disproportionately from classes I and II (the economically affluent). Furthermore, the American influence on the NHS is analyzed by Light (1997), who questions the feasibility of managed competition within the NHS.

The future of the NHS is not in doubt. Although significant changes have occurred since the late 1970s, and with public satisfaction in the NHS at an all-time low, the basic framework of the NHS remains intact. Efforts to privatize the service have increased, but have not changed the overall purpose of the system to provide universal service at a reasonable price. Privatization does, however, increase the likelihood of a growing two-tiered health-care service in Great Britain. In other words, one tier for a small minority able to pay for private health-care services, and a second tier for the vast majority receiving care through the NHS.

Sweden

Although the NHS is the most centralized health system among OECD members, the Swedish health-care system receives the highest percentage of public funds as a percentage of GDP (Organisation for Economic Co-Operation and Development, 1994a). Private sector health care constitutes a small but growing segment of the overall system. Similar to Great Britain, conservatives in the Swedish system have been influenced by the American export of managed competition.

Grounded in a 300-year history of publicly sponsored health care via district physicians, Sweden has created a regionalized, universal health-care system (Lassey et al., 1997) with an emphasis on equity and preventive medicine. Throughout the 20th century, Sweden has augmented earlier health programs with increased coverage. Although the cost of health care (as a percentage of GDP) is one of the highest among OECD nations, the Swedish government has brought costs under control while maintaining high quality health care (Borgenhammar, 1984). (For a historical account of the Swedish system, see Lynch & Raphael, 1963).

Initially, the structure of the Swedish health-care system began with 23 county councils and three municipalities. Later, the country was divided into seven regions with approximately 1 million residents in each. The Swedes, in an effort to organize and rationalize the health-care process, created a four-level model of providing care.

1. At the regional level, a single regional hospital serves a population of a million or more. The superspecialties are concentrated at this level.

2. The county central hospital serves a population from 250,000 to 300,000. As a rule, this hospital has 800 to 1,000 beds, most of the usual specialties, a large outpatient department, rehabilitation facilities, family planning, welfare services, etc.
3. The local district hospital, typically serving 60,000 to 90,000, is still in process of transition. Nearly all authorities agree on the need for merging, closing, or converting many of the formerly small district hospitals into nursing homes, health centers, or a combination of the two. Local resistance is considerable, but the policy remains to eliminate all district hospitals with less than 300 beds.
4. The local health center, serving a population of 10,000 to 20,000 with ambulatory preventive and curative care, is not formally part of the hospital system. However, with 300 such centers in operation today, the goal is to integrate their activities with the nearest district hospital. (Somers & Somers, 1977, p. 371)

Against the economic climate of the 1980s, the Swedish system continues to undergo structural and financial changes. For instance, the use of diagnostic related groups (DRGs) as an analytic tool has increased. Similarly, hospitals are distinguishing between "the production and financing of services" (Organisation of Economic Co-Operation and Development, 1994b, p. 37). In other words, beyond the implementation of DRGs, hospitals in Sweden are attempting to increase revenues by selling services to local health districts. These changes reflect an economic reality that all health systems must address: an increasing number of patients expecting greater technological intervention by more health personnel that ultimately increases the overall cost of providing services. Finally, although equity remains a central tenet of the Swedish health-care system, Lahelma et al. (1994) report that women in Sweden experience greater health inequalities than do women in Norway or Finland. That is, the socioeconomic position of women in Sweden is more likely to influence their level of health and illness when compared with women in Norway and Finland. The implications of such findings relate to earlier suggestions in Great Britain that equality in health status alone is insufficient. As Lahelma et al. (1994, p. 523) argue, "both the general level of health *and* its socio-economic distribution are constituents of egalitarian health and welfare policies." Equity in health care, however, has been a constant goal not only in Sweden, but also throughout the European region of the World Health Organization (see, for example, Whitehead, 1992).

Germany

This brief tour of industrialized nations concludes with an examination of the German health-care system. More than 100 years ago, German Chancellor Otto von Bismarck introduced social health care in the form of the German Sickness Insurance Act (1883). Under the provisions of the Act, "all German artisans and industrial workers [were obliged] to join sickness insurance funds" (Stollberg, 1993, p. 270) which were established as a nonprofit organization for the purpose of providing health insurance to its members. Because the sickness funds were compulsory, there was a sense of solidarity among those belonging to the fund. Interestingly, sickness funds were developed under the auspices of a conservative government and consequent social policy (Sass, 1995). The system is also referred to as the

German Statutory Health Insurance System (SHI) (Cassel & Boroch, 1995, p. 657). Quite simply, "the sickness funds collect premiums in the form of employee and employer-paid payroll taxes and pay the providers from these revenues" (Graig, 1993, p. 84). Thus, the German model is characterized by an employer–employee relationship with little government involvement. There are more than 1100 sickness funds providing coverage to some 92% of the German population (see Roemer, 1991, for a time-line identifying major historical periods in the evolution of sickness funds). Also, as Luschen et al. (1997, p. 884) point out, "this system has one of the broadest coverages within free market societies." In terms of service delivery, hospitals are either owned by local government, religious organizations, or by doctors and run as proprietary facilities. The majority of the beds are located in the local government hospitals (Organisation of Economic Co-Operation and Development, 1992). Although there is some variation between funds, employees and employers contribute equally to cover the approximately 13% average of employees' gross earning into the sickness fund. The unemployed are covered through government and sickness fund contributions (Lassey et al., 1997). Those not covered by sickness funds purchase health care through the private sector (Luschen et al., 1997). In addition, health benefits differ depending on where one lives and one's job. As a result, Germany has a two-tiered health-care system (Navarro, 1992b). Efforts to reduce inequality have been made through the Health Care Reform Act of 1993 (Lassey et al., 1997). Light (1994) refers to the German system as a "Mutual-Aid or Community Model" of health care. In other words, this model "leads to planning and coordination of services within a consumer-controlled health care system" (Light, 1994, p. 459). Not surprisingly, the United States has become increasingly interested in the features of the German health-care system. However, as with all health-care systems in the world today, the German model has begun experiencing financial contractions. For example, some 10.6% of the population will be age 75 or older by the year 2020. Fortunately, health-care costs for elderly persons are lower in Germany than in most other European nations (Taylor-Gooby, 1996). Nonetheless, the provision of nursing home care is one area that Germany has not addressed adequately until recently (Organisation for Economic Co-Operation and Development, 1994b).

An interconnected problem with the changing demographics is the use of payroll taxes to fund the system. Although the number of elderly persons increase as a percentage of the population, the percentage of the population in the workforce is declining. As a result, changes may be necessary within the funding process (Lassey et al., 1997).

Another problem for the German health-care system has been the reunification between East Germany and West Germany. Until reunification, the East German health-care system was modeled on the principle of central planning. Although the two countries had shared medical traditions prior to their separation, East German medicine after 40 years under socialist rule became substandard when compared to West Germany. Thus, for example, life expectancy differences between East Germans and West Germans had been increasing prior to reunification (Luschen et al., 1997).

Other Industrialized Nations

Research of health-care systems throughout the industrialized world reflects similar, yet distinctive, patterns of organization, development, and financing. The limitations of space do not allow for an elaboration and explanation of additional systems. However, interested readers are referred to the work of ten Have and Keasberry (1992), ter Meulen (1995), and van der Wilt (1995) [Netherlands]; Norheim (1995) [Norway]; Holm (1995) [Denmark]; Quintana and Infante (1995) [Spain]; Pohoryles (1988) [Austria]; Shuval (1991) [Israel]; Gallagher and Searle (1985) and Berhie (1991) [Saudi Arabia]; and Chappell (1992) [Bermuda] as examples in the variation in health-care systems. In addition, works by Ertler et al. (1987), Svensson and Stephenson (1992), and Lueschen et al. (1994) address cross-national research efforts.

Health-Care System Analysis of Former Eastern European Nations

The political changes in Eastern Europe and the former Soviet Union beginning in the mid-1980s and continuing into the early 1990s have had a significant impact on existing health-care systems. Whereas some (Elling, 1980, 1989; Cereseto & Waitzkin, 1986) have argued forcefully that health care under state socialism provides improved health outcomes (see Deacon, 1984, for an analysis of health policy under state socialism and communism), more recent data would suggest otherwise. For instance, Roemer (1991) points to an increasing infant mortality rate in the 1970s and a decreasing rate of life expectancy in the latter 1980s.

Russia

Field (1995) details in stark fashion the demographic changes occurring in Russia. The nation's population is decreasing because of increased mortality rates and a falling birth rate. As Field points out, women want to avoid pregnancy because of the deepening economic crisis. However, distinguishing between the principles of the Soviet health-care system and its implementation, Field (1990, p. 144) argues that, *in principle*, "socialized medicine is one of the most popular and accepted aspects of the Soviet system. It is its execution that is faulted" (see Field, 1957, for an in-depth analysis of the Soviet health-care system). Similarly, Davidow (1996) points to the collapse of the Soviet Union and its infrastructure as undermining the health-care system. Unfortunately, solutions incorporating an American philosophy of managed care and redistributive financial measures (Davidow, 1996) may create outcomes consistent with American medicine: differential levels of access and increasing numbers of uninsured.

Health system problems are not confined to the Russian health-care system. Similar difficulties are being experienced throughout former Eastern European nations.

Czech Republic

In the Czech Republic, efforts to privatize and Westernize the health-care system have resulted in significant loss of personnel and a shifting of funds. As physician salaries continue to increase, fewer will remain in research and academic settings (Schreiber, 1993), exacerbating an already problematic area. In addition, the nation is experiencing a "brain drain" as younger people are leaving to work in the West.

Hungary

In Hungary, there has been a shift from a socialized health-care system that emphasized a highly centralized system that provided services to all citizens to a system that emphasizes primary health care and an altered health financing system. Since 1992, pensions and health care are financed from employer and employee contributions. Pension funds and local government revenues supply additional funds. However, the economic circumstances in Hungary have left many unemployed and unable to pay taxes to local governments. In turn, these governmental units are unable to contribute their share to the funding of the health-care and pension system (Roemer, 1994). Hungary, like other former Eastern European nations, is attempting to ensure health care as a fundamental right within an increasingly privatized environment built on market forces (Angelus, 1992).

Poland

In contrast, the Polish health-care system remains relatively centralized with financing under government control. As a result, a more realistic approach to health-care planning envisions a number of financing mechanisms including universal insurance, alternative insurance funds, and governmental and commercial insurance. Thus, rather than completely restructure the health-care system, Poland appears ready to improve the socialist health system instead (Roemer, 1994).

Yugoslavia

Finally, in Yugoslavia, concerns regarding the distribution of monies and services appear to be of primary importance. Efforts to privatize the health-care system are identified as resulting in increased levels of inequality between regions of the country (Mastilica, 1992). Parmelee et al. (1982), reporting on the structure and quality of the Yugoslavian health-care system, indicate that although overall indicators of health status have improved, regional differences remain. As a result of recent "ethnic cleansing," Yugoslavia, as a nation, will have considerable difficulty addressing inconsistencies in the distribution and service allocation of health care. This will remain a problem for a country that has become increasingly divided on the basis of ethnic identity.

It is apparent that former Eastern European nations face an uncertain future regarding the type of health-care system available to the larger population. Efforts to establish a "Western" style health-care system appear to be counterproductive within many of the countries. Although the desire to shed an imposed political and economic structure is understandable, privatization of the health-care system is not necessarily in the best health interests of the nation.

Health-Care System Analysis of Developing Nations

The health-care systems of developing nations again provides comparable, yet distinctive, structures and problems. Thus, locating the health-care systems of developing nations within a typology based on economic resources and political structure allows for a comparative analysis of systems. Applying Roemer's (1991) typology, there are four economic levels based on GNP per capita: affluent and industrialized, developing and transitional, very poor, and resource rich. In addition, Roemer identifies four methods of market intervention: entrepreneurial, welfare-oriented, universal and comprehensive, and socialist and centrally planned. This section briefly examines the health-care systems of a number of countries that are considered economically transitional or poor.

Cuba

This analysis begins with a country that is economically in the developing and transitional stage with a socialist health-care system. This is, of course, the Cuban health-care system. Prior to the 1959 revolution that installed Fidel Castro, health-care access and services were stratified. In the early 1960s, Castro established health care as a right. The structure of the health-care system was realigned to promote health prevention through primary health professionals. Medical education emphasized primary care training as well as technology. As a result, indicators of health status for the years 1983 through 1988 (life expectancy and infant mortality rates) suggest that the new Cuban health-care system has been successful in improving the health of its citizens. For example, the Cuban infant mortality rate for 1983–1988 was 15 per 1,000 live births and life expectancy was 76 years (Nayeri, 1995). These figures place Cuba far ahead of other Latin American and Caribbean nations for the same time period (infant mortality rate of 54 per 1,000 live births and a life expectancy of 64 years). Unfortunately, American foreign policy and Cuba's relationship with the former Soviet Bloc have had a negative impact on the economy and, subsequently, the health-care system. Cuba continues to trade with other Western industrialized nations and is increasingly turning to its people as a resource in preserving not only the economy but also an unprecedented health-care system (Nayeri, 1995).

Ghana

By contrast, Ghana is considered a poor nation with an entrepreneurial-type of health-care system. Not surprisingly, the role of the government in the health-care system is somewhat limited. However, in 1983, 88% of monies spent by the central government went for curative medicine. For many workers, individual benefits are tied directly to individual and employer contributions rather than pooled as in a social insurance program (Roemer, 1991). Furthermore, these benefits provide for wage substitution when ill; they do not provide for medical care. As a result, the private health-care market is dominant, particularly in large urban areas.

Health outcomes in Ghana are considerably lower than in Cuba. Although overall life expectancy is 54 years, it is less than 40 years in rural areas, where the majority of the population resides. Similarly, overall infant mortality is 89 deaths per 1,000 live births. Again, rural Ghana experiences a much higher infant mortality rate with the Upper Regions reporting some 234 deaths per 1,000 live births (Quaye, 1991).

The lack of available health care in rural Ghana is the result of an extreme maldistribution of health services. More than one-half of all physicians in Ghana live and work in the capital city, where less than 9% of the total population resides. Quaye (1991) also reports that available monies have been spent on constructing hospitals (with higher levels of technology) rather than promoting the development of clinics to provide primary health-care services.

As a result of an entrepreneurial approach to health-care services in Ghana, the majority of the population receives little, if any, preventive health care. With minimal government involvement in the health-care system, economic stratification translates into similar health differentials. Unfortunately, such outcomes are not limited to Ghana. Roemer (1991) illustrates similar conditions and outcomes in Kenya, another very poor African nation with an entrepreneurial health-care system (see also Dahlgren, 1994).

Mexico

The last health-care system to be examined is that of Mexico. Economically, Mexico is in a transitional state with a welfare-oriented health-care system. Mexico offers a health-care system that is unique relative to its geographic neighbors. Essentially, it is a three-tiered system involving, first, those covered by Social Security (the working class, civil servants, and professionals). The Social Security sector covers approximately 60% of the population. The second tier of health care is covered by public health institutions. This includes the urban poor, the majority of the rural population, and those in the informal economy. The public health sector insures some 35% of the Mexican population. The third tier consists of private health services covering approximately 5% of the population (Sherraden, 1995).

Historically, health-care coverage was limited to the elite prior to 1917. Although the 1917 revolution promised health care to all, it was not until the 1930s that serious discussion even began at the national level. By the 1940s, Social Security became available to a limited number of Mexicans (Stebbins, 1993). Eventually, by the early 1980s, the Mexican government declared universal coverage under a national health-care system.

Although claims of coverage have been made, considerable disparity continues to exist. For instance, access to health services among the rural population is more difficult than for their urban counterparts. The ruling elite continue to enjoy superior access and delivery of health-care services. Although life expectancy and infant mortality rates are not disaggregated between rural and urban populations, the numbers are significant when compared with that of Cuba. In 1991, infant mortality in Mexico was 36 per 1,000 live births. That represents a drop of 50% since 1970. Life expectancy in Mexico in 1991 was 70 years (World Development Report, 1993). The reader is encouraged to compare these numbers with similar outcomes in Cuba.

The future of the Mexican health-care system does not appear to be tied directly to the economic conditions of the country. Instead, some observers (for instance, Sherraden, 1995) suggest the importance of political attention to specific areas in need of reform and development (such as health care in rural Mexico).

Limitations on space prohibit further investigation of transitional and very poor nations. Readers are encouraged to examine available research from a variety of countries—for example, Laurell (1989) [Latin America]; Alubo, 1993 [Nigeria]; or Kidanermaiam (1995) [Brazil].

Summary

This chapter addresses the macro-level analysis of health systems. Throughout this chapter, a comparative perspective is applied. Although the material in this chapter did not address information included within previous chapters, it is, to an extent, a culmination of efforts to construct the health-care community within which medical sociology functions.

The chapter begins by examining three models of health systems. Beginning with the work of Field and his typology of ideal types of differences between health-care systems grounded in various political ideologies can be identified. Quite differently, the second model by Elling is based on the political and economic characteristics of a society. Building on his original work, Elling constructs a typology built around the basic properties of centralization–decentralization and concertedness–fractionation. The third model constructs health systems around five components. Roemer offers the reader insight into the application of these components via a multiple of countries ranging from advanced industrial to transitional to very poor to resource rich. Roemer also classifies these by type of health-care system.

Moving from the general to the specific, the chapter examines the American, Canadian, British, Swedish, and German systems. Although differences exist, there are also similarities between systems. A number of health-care systems in former Eastern European nations and Russia are briefly examined. The chapter does point out that the rapid movement from state-controlled to private-sector involvement is creating difficulty for many within these countries (with Poland appearing to be the exception). Finally, the health-care systems of various countries identified by the type of market intervention they employed as well as their economic position (transitional or very poor) were examined. Based on the systems examined, it appears that the type of health-care system has a direct impact on health access and outcomes such as life expectancy and infant mortality rates.

CHAPTER REVIEW

As with previous chapters, the information presented in Chapter 13 requires the reader to integrate the broad knowledge base constructed throughout previous chapters. These questions are meant to test the reader's ability to examine conceptual frameworks and articulate reasoned responses.

1. Discuss the similarities between the models presented by Field, Elling, and Roemer.
2. Drawing on the work of the one model you find best explains health-care systems, explain your choice.
3. Compare and contrast the American health-care system to the Canadian, British, Swedish, or German systems.
4. Address the importance of sociological variables such as sex, age, social class, and race and ethnicity to health-care system analysis.
5. Considering the political and economic changes that have occurred in the former Eastern European nations and the former Soviet Union (relative to their health-care systems), what will happen to such basic medical sociological concepts as doctor–patient relationship, illness behavior, or health behavior?
6. Given the current economic conditions in many poor countries, discuss the implications of the increased reliance on Western medicine and the maintenance of alternative forms of medicine relative to one's socioeconomic position.

GLOSSARY

Black Report   a 1980 publication in England that identified continued health inequalities based on social class position within society. The report also identified a number of explanations for the continued inequalities as well as areas for further investigation.

health-care system   refers to the integration of various levels of health-related information and synthesizes them into a coherent framework that explains how and why they function within a specified cultural context.

managed care   involves any (increasingly for-profit) health-service delivery that controls the availability of providers to clients, restricts client access to services or providers and charges an established fee for service.

managed competition   ideally involves numerous health providers competing against one another for patients and their services. In an ideal world, this would contain costs.

SUGGESTED READINGS

The following books represent some of the best comparative health system analysis since the early 1970s. These books address systems in the industrialized and industrializing worlds. Interested readers are encouraged to consult any or all of these authors as an initial guide to system-level analysis.

Anderson, O. W. (1972). *Health care: Can there be equity? The United States, Sweden, and England.* New York: John Wiley & Sons.

Anderson, O. W. (1989). *The health service continuum in Democratic states: An inquiry into solvable problems.* Ann Arbor, MI: Health Administration Press.

Blendon, R. J., Leitman, R., Morrison, I., & Donelan, K. (1990). Satisfaction with health systems in ten nations. *Health Affairs, 9,* 2, 185–192.

Blendon, R. J., Benson, J., Donelan, K., Leitman, R., Taylor, H., Koeck, C., & Gitterman, D. (1995). Who has the best health care system? A second look. *Health Affairs, 14,* 4, 220–230.

Conrad, P., & Gallagher, E. B. (Eds.). (1993). *Health and health care in developing countries: Sociological perspectives.* Philadelphia: Temple University Press.

Field, M. G. (Ed.). (1989). *Success and crisis in national health systems: A comparative approach.* New York: Routledge.

Gallagher, E. B., & Subedi, J. (Eds.). (1995). *Global perspectives on health care.* Englewood Cliffs, NJ: Prentice-Hall.

Graig, L. A. (1993). *Health of nations: An international perspective on U.S. health care reform* (2nd Ed.). Washington, DC: Congressional Quarterly, Inc.

Lassey, M. L., Lassey, W. R., & Jinks, M. J. (1997). *Health care systems around the world: Characteristics, issues, reforms.* Upper Saddle River, NJ: Prentice-Hall.

Organisation for Economic Co-Operation and Development. (1994). *The reform of health care systems: A review of seventeen OECD countries.* Paris.

Pannenborg, C. O., Hirsch, G. B., & Bernard, K. (Eds.). (1982). *Reorienting health services: Application of a system approach.* New York: Plenum Press.

Raffel, M. W. (1984). *Comparative health systems: Descriptive analysis of fourteen national health systems.* University Park, PA: The Pennsylvania State University Press.

Roemer, M. I. (1991). *National health systems of the world: Volume 1—The countries.* New York: Oxford University Press.

Subedi, J., & Gallagher, E. B. (Eds). (1995). *Society, health, and disease: Transcultural perspectives.* Englewood cliffs, NJ: Prentice-Hall.

REFERENCES

Alford, R. R. (1972). The political economy of health care: Dynamics without change. *Politics and Society, 2,* 127–164.

Allen, D. (1984). Health services in England. In M. W. Raffel (Ed.). *Comparative health systems: Descriptive analysis of fourteen national health systems* (pp. 197–257). University Park, PA: The Pennsylvania State University Press.

Alubo, S. O. (1993). Implementing health for all in Nigeria: Problems and constraints. In P. Conrad & E. B. Gallagher (Eds.). *Health and health care in developing countries: Sociological perspectives* (pp. 228–245). Philadelphia: Temple University Press.

Anderson, O. W. (1972). *Health care: Can there by equity? The United States, Sweden, and England.* New York: John Wiley & Sons.

Anderson, O. W. (1989). Issues in the health services of the United States. In M. G. Field (Ed.). *Success and crisis in national health systems: A comparative approach* (pp. 49–71). New York: Routledge.

Angell, M. (1993). How much will health reform cost? *The New England Journal of Medicine, 328,* 24, 1778–1779.

Angelus, T. (1992). Consensus and health policy in Hungary. *The Journal of Medicine and Philosophy, 17,* 455–562.

Barnard, K., & Pendreigh, D. (1982). The health services system of the United Kingdom. In C. O. Pannenborg, A. van der Werff, G. B. Hirsch, & K. Bernard (Eds.). *Reorienting health services: Applications of a systems approach* (pp. 309–345). New York: Plenum Press.

Benatar, S. (1997). An old health care system gives place to new. *The Lancet, 349* (May 24), 1537–1538.

Berhie, G. (1991). Emerging issues in health planning in Saudi Arabia: The effects of organization and development on the health care system. *Social Science and Medicine, 33,* 7, 815–824.

Blendon, R. J., Leitman, R., Morrison, I., & Donelan, K. (1990). Satisfaction with health systems in ten nations. *Health Affairs, 9,* 2, 185–192.

Blendon, R. J., Benson, J., Donelan, D., Leitman, R., Taylor, H., Koeck, C., & Gitterman, D. (1995). Who has the best health care system? A second look. *Health Affairs, 14,* 4, 220–230.

Bodenheimer, T. (1989a). The Oregon health plan–Lessons for the nation, Part 1. *The New England Journal of Medicine, 337,* 9, 651–655.

Bodenheimer, T (1989b). The Oregon health plan–Lessons for the nation, Part 2. *The New England Journal of Medicine, 337,* 10, 720–723.

Borgenhammer, E. (1984). Sweden. In M. W. Raffel (Ed.). *Comparative health systems: Descriptive analyses of fourteen national health systems* (pp. 470–487). University Park, PA: The Pennsylvania State University Press.

Brock, D. W., & Daniels, N. (1994). Ethical foundations of the Clinton Administration's proposed health care system. *Journal of the American Medical Association, 271,* 15, 1189–1196.

Brody, B. A., & Lie, R. K. (1993). Methodological and conceptual issues in health care system comparisons: Canada, Norway, and the United States. *The Journal of Medicine and Philosophy, 18,* 437–463.

Cassel, D., & Boroch, W. (1995). Free choice of sickness funds: Economic implications and ethical aspects of the 1992 health care reform in Germany. *The Journal of Medicine and Philosophy, 20,* 657–667.

Cereseto, S., & Waitzkin, H. (1986). Capitalism, socialism, and the physical quality of life. *International Journal of Health Services, 16,* 643–658.

Chappell, N. L. (1992). Utilization of health and social services in Bermuda. *International Journal of Health Services, 3,* 2, 91–103.

Chappell, N. L. (1993). The future of health care in Canada. *Journal of Social Policy, 22,* 4, 487–505.

Charles, C., Lomas, J., Giacomini, M., Bhatia, V., & Vincent, V. A. (1997). Medical necessity in Canadian health policy: Four meanings and a funeral. *The Milbank Quarterly, 75,* 3, 365–394.

Coughlan, F. J. (1995). Primary health care organization in South Africa: Some conceptual issues. *South African Journal of Sociology, 26,* 1, 9–14.

Crichton, A. (1982). The Canadian health services system. In C. O. Pannenborg, A. van der Werff, G. B. Hirsch, & K. Bernard (Eds.). *Reorienting health services: Application of a systems approach* (pp. 283–308). New York: Plenum Press.

Dahlgren, G. (1994). The political economy of health financing strategies in Kenya. In L. C. Chen, A. Kleinman, & N. C. Ware (Eds.). *Health and social change in international perspective* (pp. 453–470). Cambridge, MA: Harvard University Press.

Davidow, S. L. (1996). Observations on health care issues in the former Soviet Union. *Journal of Community Health, 21,* 1, 51–60.

Day, P., & Klein, R. (1989). The politics of modernization: Britain's National Health Service in the 1980s. *The Milbank Quarterly, 67,* 1, 1–34.

Deacon, B. Medical care and health under state socialism. *International Journal of Health Services, 14,* 3, 453–480.

Deber, R. B. (1994). Philosophical underpinnings of Canada's health care system. In J. Lemco (Ed.). *National health care: Lessons for the United States and Canada* (pp. 43–68). Ann Arbor, MI: The University of Michigan Press.

Dickenson, H. D. (1993). The struggle for state health insurance: Reconsidering the role of Saskatchewan farmers. *Studies in Political Economy, 41,* Summer, 133–156.

Edgar, A. (195). Enterprise association or civil association? The UK national health service. *The Journal of Medicine and Philosophy, 20,* 669–688.

Elling, R. (1980). *Cross national study of health systems.* New Brunswick, NJ: Transaction Inc.

Elling, R. (1989). The comparison of health systems in world-system perspective. *Research in the Sociology of Health Care, 8,* 207–226.

Enthoven, A., & Kronick, R. (1989a). Universal health insurance in a system designed to promote quality and economy (part 1). *The New England Journal of Medicine, 320,* 1, 29–37.

Enthoven, A., & Kronick, R. (1989b). Universal health insurance in a system designed to promote quality and economy (part 2). *The New England Journal of Medicine, 320,* 2, 94–101.

Ertler, W., Schmidl, H., Treytl, J. M., & Wintersberger, H. (1987). The social dimensions of health and health care: An international comparison. *Research in the sociology of health care, 5,* 1–62.

Evans, R. G., Barer, M. L., & Hertzman, C. (1991). The 20-year experiment: Accounting for, explaining, and evaluating health care cost containment in Canada and the United States. *Annual Review of Public Health, 12,* 481–518.

Field, M. G. (1957). *Doctor and patient in Soviet Russia.* Cambridge, MA: Harvard University Press.

Field, M. G. (1980). The health system and the polity: A contemporary American dialectic. *Social Science and Medicine, 14A,* 397–413.

Field, M. G. (Ed.). (1989). *Success and crisis in national health systems: A comparative approach.* New York: Routledge.

Field, M. G. (1990). Noble purpose, grand design, flawed execution, mixed results. Soviet socialized medicine after seventy years. *American Journal of Public Health, 80,* 2, 144–145.

Field, M. G. (1995). The health crisis in the former Soviet Union: A report from the 'post-war' zone. *Social Science and Medicine, 41,* 11, 1469–1478.

Gallagher, E. B., & Searle, C. M. (1985). Health services and the political culture of Saudi Arabia. *Social Science and Medicine, 21,* 3, 251–262.

Gellert, G. A., Neumann, A. K., & Gordon, R. S. (1989). The obsolescence of distinct domestic and international health sectors. *Journal of Public Health Policy, 10,* 1, 421–424.

Gill, D. (1994). A national health service: Principles and practice. In P. Conrad & R. Kern (Eds.). *The sociology of health and illness: Critical perspectives* (pp. 474–487). New York: St. Martin's Press.

Graig, L. A. (1993). *Health of nations: An international perspective on U.S. health care reform* (2nd Ed.). Washington, DC: Congressional Quarterly Inc.

Hatcher, G. H., Hatcher, P. R., & Hatcher, E. C. (1984). Canada. In M. W. Raffel (Ed.). *Comparative health systems: Descriptive analyses of fourteen national health systems* (pp. 86–132). University Park, PA: The Pennsylvania University Press.

Himmelstein, D. U., & Woolhandler, S. (1990). The corporate compromise: A Marxist view of health policy. *Monthly Review, 42,* 1, 14–29.

Holm, S. (1995). "Socialized medicine," resource allocation and two-tiered health care—the Danish experience. *The Journal of Medicine and Philosophy, 20,* 631–637.

Huefner, R. P. (1992). Designing a health care system: Considering the need to know. In R. P. Huefner & M. P. Battin (Eds.). *Changing to national health care: Ethical and policy issues* (pp. 251–299). Salt Lake City: University of Utah Press.

Iglehart, J. K. (1989). The United States looks at Canadian health care. *The New England Journal of Medicine, 321,* 25, 1767–1772.

Iglehart, J. K. (1992). The American health care system: Introduction. *The New England Journal of Medicine, 336,* 14, 962–967.

Iglehart, J. K. (1994). Health care reform: The states. *New England Journal of Medicine, 330,* 1, 75–79.

Jacobs, L. R. (1993). Health reform impasse: The politics of American ambivalence toward government. *Journal of Health Politics, Policy and Law, 18,* 3, 629–655.

Kaufmann, C. (1994). Rights and the provision of health care: A comparison of Canada, Great Britain, and the United States. In H. D. Schwartz (Ed.). *Dominant issues in medical sociology* (3rd Ed.) (pp. 376–396). New York: McGraw Hill.

Kidanemariam, A. (1995). Health and development in the third world: The political economy of infant mortality in Brazil. In E. B. Gallagher & J. Subedi (Eds.). *Global perspectives on health care* (pp. 141–152). Englewood Cliffs, NJ: Prentice-Hall.

Kirsch, R. (1997). The future of health care. *The Lancet, 349* (May 24), 1544–1545.

Lahelma, E., Manderbacka, K., Rahkonen, O., & Karisto, A. (1994). Comparisons of inequalities in health: Evidence from national surveys in Finland, Norway and Sweden. *Social Science and Medicine, 38,* 4, 517–524.

Lassey, M. L., Lassey, W. R., & Jinks, M. J. (1997). *Health care systems around the world: Characteristics, issues, reforms.* Upper Saddle River, NJ: Prentice-Hall.

Laurell, A. C. (1989). Social analysis of collective health in Latin America. *Social Science and Medicine, 28,* 11, 1183–1191.

Lemco, J. (Ed.). (1994). *National health care: Lessons for the United States and Canada.* Ann Arbor, MI: The University of Michigan Press.

Lena, H. F., & London, B. (1993). The political and economic determinants of health outcomes: A cross-national analysis. *International Journal of Health Services, 23,* 3, 585–602.

Light, D. W. (1994). Comparative models of "health care" systems. In P. Conrad & R. Kern (Eds.). *The sociology of health and illness: Critical perspectives* (4th Ed.) (pp. 455–470). New York: St. Martin's Press.

Light, D. W. (1995). *Homo economicus:* Escaping the traps of managed competition. *European Journal of Public Health, 5,* 3, 145–154.

Light, D. W. (1997). From managed competition to managed cooperation: Theory and lessons from the British experience. *The Milbank Quarterly, 75,* 3, 297–340.

Lueschen, G., Neimann, S., & Apelt, P. (1997). The integration of two health systems: Social stratification, work and health in East and West Germany. *Social Science and Medicine, 44,* 6, 883–899.

Lueschen, G., Stevens, F., van der Zee, J., Cockerham, W. C., Diederijks, J., d'Houtaud, A., Ferrando, M. G., Peeters, R., & Niemann, S. (1994). Health care systems and the people: A five-nation study in the European union. *International Sociology, 9,* 3, 337–362.

Lynch, M. J., & Raphael, S. S. (1963). *Medicine and the state.* Springfield, IL: Charles C. Thomas.

MacIntyre, S. (1997). The Black Report and beyond: What are the issues? *Social Science and Medicine, 44,* 6, 723–745.

Madden, T. A. (1991). The reform of the British national health service. *Journal of Public Health Policy, 12,* 3, 378–396.

Marmor, T. R. (1996). Patterns of fact and fiction in use of the Canadian experience. In P. Brown (Ed.). *Perspectives in medical sociology* (2nd Ed.) (pp. 566–582). Prospect Heights, IL: Waveland Press.

Marmor, T. R., & Mashaw, J. L. (1992). Canada's health insurance and ours: The real lessons, the big choices. *The American Prospect, 3,* 18–29.

Mastilica, M. (1992). Health inequalities and health system changes in the former Yugoslavia. *International Journal of Health Sciences, 3,* 3–4, 195–203.

McDermott, J. (1994). The case for a single-payer approach. *Journal of the American Medical Association, 271,* 10, 782–784.

Mechanic, D., & Rochefort, D. A. (1996). Comparative medical systems. *Annual Review of Sociology, 22,* 239–270.

Mizrahi, T., Fasano, R., & Dooha, S. M. (1993). Canadian and American health care: Myths and realities. *Health and Social Work, 18,* 1, 7–12.

Mohan, J. (1996). Accounts of the NHS reforms: Macro-, meso-, and micro-level perspectives. *Sociology of Health and Illness, 18,* 5, 675–698.

National Forum on Health. (1997). Final Report—Volume 1: Canada Health Action: Building on the Legacy. The Bigger Picture of Health—What really matters. http://wwwnfh.hwc.ca/whatnew.htm (15 Feb. 1997).

Navarro, V. (1992). Why some countries have national health insurance, others have national health services, and the United States has neither. In V. Navarro (Ed.). *Why the United States does not have a national health program* (pp. 131–152). Amityville, NY: Baywood Publishing Company.

Navarro, V. (1992b). The West German health care system: A critique. In V. Navarro (Ed.). *Why the United States does not have a national health program* (pp. 209–215). Amityville, NY: Baywood Publishing Company.

Navarro, V., Himmelstein, D. U., & Woolhandler, S. (1992). The Jackson national health program. In V. Navarro (Ed.). *Why the United States does not have a national health program* (pp. 173–198). Amityville, NY: Baywood Publishing Company.

Navarro, V. (1994). *The politics of health policy: The U.S. reforms, 1980–1994.* Cambridge, MA: Blackwell.

Navarro, V. (1995a). Why Congress did not enact health care reform. *Journal of Health Politics, Policy and Law, 20,* 2, 455–462.

Navarro, V. (1995b). The politics of health care reform in the United States, 1992–1994: A historical review. *International Journal of Health Services, 25,* 2, 185–201.

Nayeri, K. (1995). The Cuban health care system and factors currently undermining it. *Journal of Community Health, 20,* 4, 321–334.

Neuschler, E. (1994). Is Canadian-style government health insurance the answer for the United States' health care cost and access woes? In J. Lemco (Ed.). *National health care: Lessons for the United States and Canada* (pp. 121–146). Ann Arbor, MI: The University of Michigan Press.

Norheim, O. F. (1995). The Norwegian welfare state in transition: Rationing and plurality of values as ethical challenges for the health care system. *The Journal of Medicine and Philosophy, 20,* 639–655.

Organisation for Economic Co-Operation and Development. (1992). *The reform of health care: A comparative analysis of seven OECD countries.* Health policy studies No. 2. Paris.

Organisation for Economic Co-Operation and Development. (1994a). *The reform of health care systems: A review of seventeen OECD countries.* Paris.

Organisation for Economic Co-Operation and Development. (1994b). *Health: Quality and choice.* Health Policy Studies No. 4. Paris.

Parmelee, D. E., Henderson, G., & Cohen, M. S. (1982). Medicine under socialism: some observations on Yugoslavia and China. *Social Science and Medicine, 16,* 1389–1396.

Pohoryles, R. (1988). Current trends in health policy in the working environment. *Innovation, 1,* 2–3, 299–331.

Quaye, R. (1991). Planning the health care system in a decade of economic decline: The Ghanaian experience. *Crime, Law and Social Change, 16,* 303–311.

Quintana, O., & Infante, A. (1995). Setting priorities in the Spanish health care system. *The Journal of Medicine and Philosophy, 20,* 595–606.

Roberts, H., Smith, S., & Bryce, C. (1993). Prevention is better . . . . *Sociology of Health and Illness, 15,* 4, 447–463.

Roemer, M. I. (1973). An ideal health care system for America. In A. L. Strauss (Ed.). *Where medicine fails* (2nd Ed.) (pp. 77–93). New Brunswick, NJ: Transaction Books.

Roemer, M. I. (1977). *Comparative national policies on health care.* New York: Marcel Dekker, Inc.

Roemer, M. I. (1985). *National strategies for health care organizations: A world overview.* Ann Arbor, MI: Health Administration Press.

Roemer, M. I. (1986). *An introduction to the U.S. health care system* (2nd Ed.). New York: Springer Publishing Company.

Roemer, M. I. (1988). United States of America. In R. B. Saltman (Ed.). *The international handbook of health-care systems* (pp. 355–382). New York: Greenwood Press.

Roemer, M. I. (1991). *National health systems of the world: Volume 1—The countries.* New York: Oxford University Press.

Roemer, M. I. (1993). *National health systems of the world: Volume II—The issues.* New York: Oxford University Press.

Roemer, M. I. (1994). Recent health system development in Poland and Hungary. *Journal of Community Health, 19,* 3, 153–163.

Sass, H. M. (1995). The new triad: Responsibility, solidarity and subsidiary. *The Journal of Medicine and Philosophy, 20,* 587–594.

Scheffler, R. M. (1992). Culture versus competition: The reforms of the British national health service. *Journal of Public Health Policy, 13,* 2, 180–185.

Schreiber, V. (1993). The medical sciences in Czechoslovakia. *Technology in Society, 15,* 1, 131–136.

Scott, H. D., & Shapiro, H. B. (1992). Universal insurance for American health care: A proposal of the American College of Physicians. *Annals of Internal Medicine, 117,* 6, 511–519.

Scott-Samuel, A. (1997). Health inequalities recognised in UK. *The Lancet, 350,* September 30, 753.

Sherraden, M. S. (1995). Development of health policy and services for rural Mexico. In E. B. Gallagher & J. Subedi (Eds.). *Global perspectives on health care* (pp. 122–140). Englewood Cliffs, NJ: Prentice-Hall.

Shuval, J. T. (1991). Political processes in health care: A case study of Israel. *Research in the Sociology of Health Care, 9,* 279–304.

Somers, A. R., & Somers, H. M. (1977). *Health and health care: Policies in perspective.* Germantown, MD: Aspen Systems Corporation.

Stebbins, K. R. (1993). Constraints on successful public health programs: A view from a Mexican community. In P. Conrad & E. B. Gallagher (Eds.). *Health and health care in developing countries: Sociological perspectives* (pp. 211–227). Philadelphia: Temple University Press.

Stollberg, G. (1993). Health and illness in German workers' autobiographies from the nineteenth and early twentieth centuries. *The Society for the Social History of Medicine, 6,* 2, 261–276.

Svensson, P.-G., & Stephenson, P. (1992). Health care consequences of the European community in 1993 and beyond. *Social Science and Medicine, 35,* 4, 525–529.

Taylor, M. G. (1990). *Insuring national health care: The Canadian experience.* Chapel Hill, NC: The University of North Carolina Press.

Taylor-Gooby, P. (1996). The future of health care in six European countries: The views of policy elites. *International Journal of Health Services, 26,* 2, 203–219.

ten Have, H., & Keasberry, H. (1992). Equity and solidarity: The context of health care in the Netherlands. *The Journal of Medicine and Philosophy, 17,* 463–477.

ter Meulen, R. H. J. (1995). Limiting solidarity in the Netherlands: A two-tiered system on the way. *The Journal of Medicine and Philosophy, 20,* 607–616.

The Oregon Basic Health Services Act. (1990). John Kitzhaber, M.D. Senate President. Oregon State Senate, State Capitol, Salem, Oregon.

The White House Domestic Policy Council. (1993). *The President's health security plan.* New York: Times Books.

Townsend, P., & Davidson, N. (1992). *The Black Report: Inequalities in health.* London: Penguin.

Turner, B. S. (1995). *Medical power and social knowledge* (2nd Ed.). London: SAGE.

Twaddle, A. C. (1996). Health system reforms—Toward a framework for international comparisons. *Social Science and Medicine, 43,* 5, 637–654.

Van Atteveld, L., Broeders, C., & Lapre´, R. (1987). International comparative research in health care: A study of the literature. *Health Policy, 8,* 105–136.

Van de Ven, W. P. M. M. (1996). Market-oriented health care reforms: Trends and future options. *Social Science and Medicine, 43,* 5, 655–666.

Van der Wilt, G. J. (1995). Towards a two tier health system in the Netherlands: How to put theory into practice. *The Journal of Medicine and Philosophy, 20,* 617–630.

Wardle, J., & Steptoe, A. (1991). The European health and behaviour survey: Rationale, methods and initial results from the United Kingdom. *Social Science and Medicine, 33,* 8, 925–936.

What price cost control? (1997). *The Lancet,* 349 (Feb. 1), 295.

Whitehead, M. (1992). The concepts and principles of equity and health. *International Journal of Health Services, 22,* 3, 429–445.

Wiles, R. (1993). Women and private medicine. *Sociology of Health and Illness, 15,* 1, 68–85.

Wilkinson, R. G. (1996). *Unhealthy societies: The afflictions of inequality.* London: Routledge.

Williams, A. P., Vayda, E., Cohen, M. L., Woodward, C. A., & Ferrier, B. M. (1995). Medicine and the Canadian state: From the politics of conflict to the politics of accommodation. *Journal of Health and Social Behavior, 36,* 303–321.

Williams, S. J., Calnan, M., Cant, S. L., & Coyle, J. (1993). All change in the NHS? Implications of the NHS reforms for primary care prevention. *Sociology of Health and Illness, 15,* 1, 43–67.

World Development Report. (1993). *Investing in health: World development indicators.* New York: Oxford University Press.

14 The Future of Medical Sociology

Medical sociology as a subdiscipline has exhibited astonishing growth in the numbers of scholars engaged in it, in the topics studied, and in the range and sophistication of its theory. The field has always had strong connections to related fields, such as epidemiology, medical anthropology, health services research, and medical history. While maintaining these connections, medical sociology is fostering new ones, with fields such as bioethics, gerontology, environmental sociology, and the sociology of science. Where it intersects with bioethics, it raises questions of professional and institutional controls over health and life, patient autonomy, governmental regulation, and philosophical views on the proper extent of medical intervention. With gerontology, it studies the many health problems of an aging population, especially with regard to chronic disease. With environmental sociology, it extends our attention to the social causes of disease. And with the sociology of science, it is concerned with the social construction of knowledge and the social functions of science and ecology.

—Brown, 1991, p. 603

Medical Sociology: An Overview of Current Problems and Opportunities

Applying a cross-cultural framework, the preceding chapters examine many of the core topical areas within medical sociology. Chapters examine issues ranging from the doctor–patient relationship and health and illness behavior to the financing and organization of health-care systems. Interconnected within these topical areas is an investigation of sociological variables such as age, sex, race and ethnicity, and social class. Not surprisingly, these variables are inextricably interconnected with health processes and outcomes. However, the intent of this chapter is not to present a summary of previous material. Instead, the purpose of this chapter is to reflect on the breadth and temporal significance of medical sociology within the United States and throughout the world.

In addition to extolling the opportunities of medical sociology, this chapter also addresses some current problems. For instance, the section on medical sociology in the American Sociological Association (ASA) suffered a decline in membership and is now the third largest section rather than the largest. The most recent numbers available, however, (August 1998) reflect an increase in membership. Another problem is the fragmentation of the discipline (Levine, 1995). Although not unique to medical sociology or even to sociology in general, fragmentation is a consequence of the diversity of theoretical and methodological frameworks available. An example of this fragmentation is offered by Pearlin (1992), who categorized medical sociologists into two broad categories: "structure seekers" and "meaning seekers." Accordingly, *structure seekers* believe that "the structure of the contexts in which people lead their lives will tend to influence the structure of their experience" (Pearlin, 1992, p. 3). In other words, structure seekers attempt to understand the impact of stratified economic arrangements (such as social class) as well as various institutional arrangements (family, work, and so forth) on health outcomes. Utilizing a comparative perspective, structure seekers analyze relationships and health outcomes between components such as lower- versus middle-class respondents. Methodologically, structure seekers are quantitative. That is, they utilize large-scale surveys and analyze the data through the use of computer-assisted statistical packages. However, *meaning seekers* "endeavor to get inside the heads and hearts of society's participants as they interact with others and encounter different situations" (Pearlin, 1992, p. 4). That is, meaning seekers attempt to elicit from respondents their understanding and interpretation of those events or experiences that shape their lives. As with structure seekers, meaning seekers do not constitute a homogeneous category of medical sociologists. Methodologically, meaning seekers generally employ unstructured or semistructured interviews with their subjects. Rather than analyzing numbers, the researcher must interpret the information. It is obvious that these two approaches to medical sociology reflect significantly different perspectives of the discipline. The point, however, is not that one is right and the other wrong. Rather, the fragmentation of the discipline means that medical sociologists talk past one another based on the interpretation of the social world and how it should be studied. Medical sociology is not unique in terms of the increasing fragmentation of thought. As Pearlin (1992) notes, this is also true of sociology in general. Unfortunately, for sociology in general and medical sociology in particular, Pearlin (1992, p. 1) warns that, "as sub-fields proliferate, the centers from which they originate begin to erode and lose their clear identity."

Considering the broad interest in health and health care at all levels of society, recent fluctuations in membership is disconcerting. Although one may speculate as to the cause, there is no single explanation. At the same time, other disciplines within the health community continue to expand. For example, the number of students applying to medical school continues to increase despite continued reports of a "physician surplus." Policy issues such as the health reform efforts of President Clinton and subsequent Congressional action regarding health for uninsured children should be of particular interest to medical sociologists. Other areas of interest that intersect with medical sociology include the aging of the American population. The impact of this demographic shift continues to raise serious questions regarding the affordability of care within a profit-driven health-care system. The sociology of bioethics cuts across the age, race and ethnicity, sex, and social class spectra. Also, the globalization of issues related to health care. Finally, in an edition of the *Medical Sociology Newsletter,* the Medical Sociology Section Chairperson, Catherine Kohler Riessman, identifies "personal narratives of illness experience, and the sociology of the body" as "emerging, exciting intellectual trends in the social sciences" (*Medical Sociology Newsletter,* 1997, p. 1) (see also Turner, 1995, for a discussion on the sociology of the body).

For years, medical sociology was instrumental in identifying and defining many of the relevant issues within the health community. Today, others within the health community such as health economists, demographers, and health policy experts are as likely to define and address many of these issues (see, for example, Elinson, 1985; Fox, 1985; Freeman & Levine, 1989; Thomas & Pol, 1993; Mechanic, 1994; Gray & Phillips, 1995). This loss of status by medical sociology can be understood within the context of changing political expectations regarding health policy. The impact of this intellectual shift is important. For example, an economics perspective is likely to assume that as rational human beings, health-related behavior is based on cost–benefit outcomes. Such assumptions generally ignore the influence of social–structural characteristics on the interactive processes that emerge between the social actors as they negotiate health relationships. However, as Gray and Phillips (1995) point out, health-policy research is not particularly interested in a "social problems" approach. Thus, rather than examining the social construction of the "physician surplus," medical sociologists need to address the implications of an expanding occupation on the potential redistribution of health services and its resultant consequences.

The Future of Medical Sociology

Medical sociology will survive well into the 21st century. The disciple will evolve to meet the changing needs of a postindustrial society in which health and illness behavior will become increasingly individualized, whereas system-level characteristics will incorporate greater diversity of thought and explanation. The basis for this optimistic view is grounded in the efforts lead by Hafferty and Pescosolido (1996).

Others, for example, Wolinsky (1988), identified a number of factors associated with the future of medical sociology. Although somewhat dated, these points remain pertinent as we progress into the next century.

1. Medical sociology will remain an area of interest, not only among medical sociologists in medicine, but increasingly among those concerned with health-related issues.
2. In association with the growing interest in *health* rather than in *medicine,* there is a need for applied research efforts to address areas such as changes in health policy–financing and delivery.
3. As a result of number 2, a resulting third factor is the distancing of the medical sociologist from health professionals.
4. Consistent with the increasing "consumer" mentality sweeping the country, medical sociology will become more consumer-oriented in its perspective and interpretation of associated concepts (e.g., the sick role).
5. As a result of increasing diversification, employment opportunities within medical sociology will improve, particularly outside of the academy.
6. Health-related research (applied and basic) will become increasingly interdisciplinary.
7. Medical sociologists will enjoy greater visibility among health-policy makers.

Although raised in the mid-1980s, some of these points remain viable indicators regarding the future and direction of medical sociology. For example, see points 1 and 2, which reflect medical sociology's need to reexamine its core and its relationship with other health-related disciplines (see Hafferty & Pescosolido, 1996). However, the time since their creation has shown a need to modify some of these suggested trends. For example, point number 7 has not occurred: Medical sociologists do not enjoy greater visibility among health-policy makers. As mentioned earlier, this position is particularly problematic, as other academic disciplines assume greater professional dominance in defining the health-care agenda. Gray and Phillips (1995) suggest that one reason for the decreasing significance of medical sociology among policy makers is the style of work. For example, the tendency of sociology to examine policy issues as social problems. Concomitantly, if medical sociologists have not been in the forefront of defining the health-care agenda, then the first, second, and third trends would also appear to be in doubt. Also, the fourth trend has not been supported. Medical sociologists have been reluctant to interpret the changes in the health-care community as the result of increased "consumerism." Other trends suggested by Wolinsky (1988), such as an increased interdisciplinary research activity as well as diversity within medical sociology leading to greater employment opportunities, are becoming increasingly apparent. Thus, although medical sociology is moving slowly toward greater intellectual diversity, its efforts to incorporate a policy orientation have not been realized. In addition to Wolinsky, others (Olesen, 1989; Bloom, 1990) have identified a similar set of trends for the discipline. Earlier, Claus (1982a,b) discussed the future of medical sociology in Britain and the European continent. In general, the conclusions are positive, but reflect cultural differences on the continent and economic difficulties in England. More specifically, Rahkonen et al. (1988) discuss the problems of medical sociology as a component of Finnish medical education. As we construct a framework for the future of medical sociology, the impact of changes in age, sex, race and ethnicity, and social class structure on health care are revisited. First, however, consider the following statement as a necessary first step in the future of medical sociology: "Medical sociology must build a strong bridge between the conceptual world, the academic world (both disciplinary and multidisciplinary), and the real world. Given the potential of the moment, the contributions of sociology and medical sociology could not be more crucial" (Pescosolido & Kronenfeld, 1995, p. 27). In other words, the future of medical sociology lies in its ability to create the contextual framework within which issues associated with the health-care community are defined and analyzed. The most recent effort to examine the future of medical sociology began in 1993. With financial support from the Robert Wood Johnson Foundation, a number of prominent medical sociologists began the arduous task of assessing the current field of medical sociology as well as its future. Meeting throughout the summer of 1996, this group constructed a working document that outlines the changes necessary for medical sociology to more effectively compete within the intellectual marketplace of ideas. In an effort to strengthen medical sociology, the group identified the following core challenges:

1. Increasing the visibility and utility of Medical Sociology for those outside the field;
2. Improving intra-groups relations within the discipline of Sociology and enhancing the professional development of medical sociologists; and
3. Reshaping the training structures and content of course work in Medical Sociology. (Hafferty & Pescosolido, 1996, p. 3)

Reflecting a realistic appraisal of medical sociology, these challenges were then addressed through a series of action steps that provide a vehicle for continued investigation and assessment of the field. Throughout these meetings, the relevance of medical sociology to the current changes and challenges associated with the American health-care system was addressed. As a result, efforts to improve the visibility and legitimacy of medical sociology will require increased cross-fertilization of the field with other social sciences as well as with schools of business; in other words, the application of a multidisciplinary approach. The efforts put forth in this document reflect perhaps the most realistic appraisal of medical sociology. Recognizing its weaknesses as well as strengths, this report injects the reality of a changing health-care community on the fortunes of medical sociology. Nonetheless, those involved in the project remain optimistic regarding the future role of medical sociology.

The Changing Health-Care Community

The health-care community in the United States and around the world is undergoing massive change. The United States, for instance, continues to experience a shift in health-care delivery from fee-for-service to managed care (and increasingly, for-profit). Relative to these organizational changes, the position of the physician is also changing. For example, in what is considered to be a first, "hundreds" of physicians in private practice in New Jersey who are upset over HMO efforts to regulate them are attempting to unionize (*Times Union,* A2, October 28, 1997). These changes appear to reflect what McKinlay and Stoeckle (1988) referred to as the "proletarianization" of physicians. In other words, physicians losing control of their profession.

As the American health-care system attempts to create an ever-increasing level of technologically advanced services for an ever-diminishing number of potential patients, critics point to the social and economic disparities and suggest fundamental change. Consider the following comment by Evans and Barer (1990, p. 80): "most European countries have achieved a reasonably satisfactory system of health care funding and delivery, any one of which the United States would be wise to emulate. If only they could."

Similarly, the worldwide health-care community has not been immune from structural change. Among the industrialized nations, the most fundamental change has been the growth of the private health-care market within such countries as Great Britain and Sweden. However, overall satisfaction with health care is generally higher in European nations than in the United States. For example, Abel-Smith et al. (1995) report a 71% average within the European Union agreeing that the quality of health care people receive is good. However, public opinion polls conducted in the United States indicate considerable American dissatisfaction with the current health-care system (see Navarro, 1994). For example, Blendon et al. (1995) examined American, Canadian, and former West German attitudes regarding their respective health-care systems. Americans, when compared with Canadians and former West Germans, were far more likely to respond that the current health-care system was in need of a complete restructuring. Similarly, many of the former Eastern European nations have abandoned centralized state-operated health-care systems in favor of a mix of public and private enterprises. Within many developing nations, changing the health-care system involves a transition from, or integration of, traditional medicine with an ever-growing Western influence. More specifically, Gallagher (1989) identifies health manpower and the role of traditional health personnel in Third World countries as key issues for medical sociology.

Worldwide changes within the health-care community can be attributed to a number of sociopolitical trends that reflect the role of the governmental and economic institutions on the health-care system. Relative to medical sociology, however, "the interactions between health and social change" (Brown, 1996, p. xxi) are paramount. Roemer (1993) identifies the following trends:

1. *Urbanization and industrialization.* Regardless of level of economic development, all countries have increased the number and proportion of its citizens residing in urban areas. Similarly, most countries have also increased their level of industrialization. In other words, an increasing proportion of the workforce is engaged in occupations in the industrial or service sector rather than in the agricultural sector.

2. *Governmental structure.* Worldwide, the movement has been away from authoritarian types of systems and toward an increasing democratic state. However, the impact of this movement on the health-care community is not necessarily consistent (see, for example, the summary by Garner & Garner, 1994).
3. *International trade.* The health-care community within any nation, regardless of its economic position, needs international trade for the continued acquisition of relevant technology. Considering the cost of medical technology, at any level, this trend will continue to increase the overall cost of health care.
4. *Demographic changes.* The continued aging of the world's populations will have an impact on the availability and delivery of health-care services. The impact of this trend on medical sociology will be examined in greater detail in the following section of this chapter.
5. *Demands for privatization.* One consequence of the 1980s was an increased emphasis on moving the health-care community from the public to the private sector. Although the private sector predominates in the United States, other developed nations (except Turkey) rely more on government than private expenditures for health-care costs. Increased political conservatism worldwide and greater emphasis on defining who should pay for health services has led to increased levels of privatized health care within many developed and developing nations. This trend is not in the best interests of health equity.
6. *Public expenditure and system type.* Governmental involvement in health-care expenditures is generally dependent on the type of health-care system. Generally speaking, the increased role of government in health care will lead to increasing levels of government expenditure on health care. As Roemer (1993) demonstrates, however, this relationship does not hold for most socialist health-care systems.

These trends provide medical sociology a plethora of topical areas for continued investigation in the United States and throughout the world. Furthermore, these trends offer medical sociology an opportunity to investigate the long-term impact of social structural characteristics on individual- and system-level health behavior and outcomes. However, these national and international trends require extensive funding that may not be available.

An Emerging Area of Research and Social Policy Opportunity: Demographics, Economics, and Politics

This section outlines an emerging area of research and social policy opportunity for medical sociologists worldwide. Specifically, this refers to the aging of populations and their impact on the health-care community. This demographic reality is occurring not only within the United States, but also throughout the developed as well as the developing nations. In fact, demographic indicators suggest higher rates of growth among elderly persons in developing rather than developed countries

TABLE 14.1   Percentage Age 65 or Older by Selected Country, 1970, 1990, 2010, and 2025

	1970	1990	2010	2025
United States	**9.8**	**12.5**	**13.3**	**18.7**
Western Europe				
Austria	14.1	15.2	18.4	22.9
Belgium	13.4	15.0	18.4	24.2
Denmark	12.3	15.6	17.8	23.3
France	12.9	14.6	17.2	22.6
Germany	13.2	15.0	20.4	24.4
Greece	11.1	14.1	20.1	24.0
Italy	10.9	14.6	19.8	24.1
Luxembourg	12.4	13.6	18.4	25.5
Norway	12.9	16.4	16.4	22.4
Sweden	13.7	18.0	19.6	23.7
United Kingdom	12.9	15.7	17.1	21.5
Eastern Europe				
Bulgaria	9.6	13.0	18.0	22.5
Czechoslovakia	11.2	11.8	14.3	20.4
Hungary	11.5	13.4	16.7	22.4
Poland	8.2	10.1	13.2	20.3
North America/Oceania				
Australia	8.3	11.2	13.4	18.8
Canada	7.9	11.5	14.3	20.7
New Zealand	8.5	11.2	14.2	20.6
Africa				
Egypt	4.3	3.4	3.9	5.6
Kenya	3.9	2.2	2.7	3.8
Liberia	3.7	3.4	3.7	4.4
Malawi	2.3	2.7	2.6	2.9
Morocco	4.2	4.2	5.4	8.3
Tunisia	3.8	4.7	6.8	9.8
Zimbabwe	2.7	2.7	3.0	4.5
Asia				
Bangladesh	3.5	3.0	3.4	4.8
China	4.3	5.8	8.3	13.3
India	3.7	3.7	5.3	7.8
Indonesia	3.1	3.0	5.9	9.8
Israel	6.7	9.7	10.1	13.7
Japan	7.1	11.8	21.3	26.7
Korea, Rep. of	3.3	4.8	9.0	15.2
Malaysia	3.4	3.7	5.0	7.8
Pakistan	3.2	4.0	3.8	4.1

TABLE 14.1 Continued

	1970	1990	2010	2025
Philippines	2.7	3.6	4.9	7.7
Singapore	3.4	5.8	10.4	20.6
Sri Lanka	3.6	5.2	8.0	12.7
Thailand	3.0	4.0	7.2	12.6
Turkey	4.4	4.7	6.8	9.7
Latin America/Caribbean				
Argentina	6.9	9.0	10.3	12.7
Brazil	3.5	4.2	6.2	9.4
Columbia	3.3	3.9	6.3	11.2
Costa Rica	3.2	4.5	6.4	10.5
Cuba	6.2	8.8	12.3	16.7
Guatemala	2.9	3.3	4.4	6.2
Jamaica	5.6	6.6	6.8	10.3
Mexico	3.4	3.8	5.6	8.3
Peru	3.5	3.8	5.6	8.7
Uruguay	8.9	11.6	12.6	13.4

Source: U.S. Bureau of the Census, International Population Reports, P25, 92-3, *An aging world II.* Appendix A, Table 1. U.S. Government Printing Office, Washington, DC, 1992.

(Matcha, 1997a). The importance of aging worldwide is demonstrated in an edition of the *Journal of the American Medical Association,* which devoted an entire issue to current research on aging (see, for example, Steel, 1997; Wetle, 1997; Winker, 1997, for editorial comments).

Aging populations also require an examination of issues such as sex, race and ethnicity, and social class distinctions relative to health outcomes (see, for example, Pol & Thomas, 1992). The sex, race, and class-based differences that exist within aging populations reflect the outcomes of specific governmentally defined social policy initiatives.

Aging Populations: Current and Future Trends

Examining available data shown in Table 14.1 regarding the percentage of persons age 65 and older within selected developed and developing nations in 1970, 1990, 2010, and 2025 provides us with a context within which we can rank countries relative to current numbers and future trends.

The projected population changes reveal that throughout the industrialized world, between 20% and 25% of the population will be age 65 or older by the year 2025 (except in the United States). More specifically, growth rates will be even greater among persons age 80 or older. For instance, the percentage of the population age 80 and older will almost double between 1990 and 2025 in many developing countries (U.S. Bureau of the Census, 1992). The significance of this age category is the level of health costs associated with their care (refer to Chapter 12 for a more detailed explanation of this argument).

The demographic reality of an aging population and rising health-care costs creates an interesting conundrum not only for the United States, but also for all countries. The following analysis, however, concentrates on data for the United States.

The Relationship between Age, Sex, Race and Ethnicity, and Social Class

In addition to growing older in the United States, persons age 65 and older are primarily women, Caucasian American, not engaged in the workforce, and, with age, increasingly more likely to be widowed. Furthermore, the educational levels of elderly persons are lower than for the general population. Finally, income is inversely related to age. That is, as age (older than 65) increases, income levels decrease and the rate of poverty increases (Table 14.2). Although poverty levels decrease throughout early and middle adulthood, they begin to increase in late adulthood. Among persons those age 75 and older, poverty rates are near or above the national average for almost all race and ethnic categories.

TABLE 14.2   Persons below Poverty Level, by Selected Characteristics, 1994

	Percent below Poverty Level			
Age and Region	*All Races[1]*	*White*	*Black*	*Hispanic[2]*
Total	14.5	11.7	30.6	30.7
Under 18 years old	21.8	16.9	43.8	41.5
18–24 years old	18.0	15.7	29.0	30.2
25–34 years old	13.2	10.9	24.7	25.6
35–44 years old	10.6	8.6	21.9	23.0
45–54 years old	7.8	6.4	16.8	19.3
55–59 years old	10.4	8.9	21.2	23.2
60–64 years old	11.4	9.4	28.0	22.0
65 years old and over	11.7	10.2	27.4	22.6
65–74 years old	10.1	8.5	26.0	22.3
75 years old and over	13.9	12.5	29.4	23.2
Northeast	12.9	10.3	29.7	35.6
Midwest	13.0	10.1	35.2	24.1
South	16.1	12.2	30.1	30.2
West	15.3	14.1	25.0	30.4

Persons as of March 1995.

[1] Includes other races not shown separately.

[2] Persons of Hispanic origin may be of any race.

Source: U.S. Bureau of the Census, *Statistical Abstract of the United States: 1996* (116th Edition). Table 733. Washington, DC, 1996.

Thus, growing older is about more than chronological age. Growing older is inextricably interconnected with other marginal identities such as being female and poor. As Choudhury and Leonesio (1997, p. 33) point out, "most poor older women had low incomes in mid-life." Furthermore, elderly minority women face even greater economic hardships. According to data in Table 14.3, elderly minority women experience considerably more economic hardships than do their white or male counterparts.

The Relationship between Age and Health

It is also known that there is an inverse relationship between age and health status. However, there is a direct relationship between age and the number of physician contacts and average length of hospital stay (National Center for Health Statistics, 1996). The relationship between age and prevalence of chronic disorders as well as limitations on activity is not quite as clear. The purpose of this data is to demonstrate that, first, the United States will begin experiencing a dramatic shift in its population. Second, we already understand many of the economic and social consequences of the aging process. Third, we are cognizant of the health-related implications associated with the aging process. Given our current knowledge base, it should be of little surprise that in the near future the United States will experience an increasing number of elderly women who, as they age, will be increasingly unable to provide for their economic support. Furthermore, as this increasing number of el-

TABLE 14.3   Persons 65 Years Old and Over Below Poverty Level: 1970–1994

Characteristic	Percent below Poverty Level				
	1970	*1979*[1]	*1990*[2]	*1990*	*1994*
Total[3]	24.6	15.2	12.2	12.2	11.7
White	22.6	13.3	10.1	10.7	10.2
Black	48.0	36.2	33.8	28.0	27.4
Hispanic[4]	NA	26.8	22.5	21.4	22.6
In families	14.8	8.4	5.8	6.5	6.0
Unrelated individuals	47.2	29.4	24.7	24.1	23.1

Persons as of March of following year.

NA, Not available.

[1] Population controls based on 1980 census.

[2] Beginning 1987, data based on revised processing procedures and not directly comparable with prior years.

[3] Beginning 1979, includes members of unrelated subfamilies not shown separately. For earlier years, unrelated subfamily members are included in the "in families" category.

[4] Persons of Hispanic origin may be of any race.

Source: U.S. Bureau of the Census, *Statistical Abstract of the United States: 1996* (116th Edition.) Table 734. Washington, DC, 1996.

derly women ages, they will experience proportionally more chronic illnesses and require proportionally more health services. However, aging itself is not the primary reason for increasing health-care costs. As Cassel and Neugarten (1991, p. 80) argue, "it is only a small fraction of older persons in any one year who are responsible for the high usage of medical services." Furthermore, "most old people are not very sick until the last year of their lives." Thus, elderly persons experience more health-related problems, but these problems are generally confined to the latter years of life. However, high-cost medical intervention at the end of life occurs less frequently than believed. Nonetheless, an alternative to medical intervention is offered through the hospice movement (see, for example, Levy, 1989).

Concomitantly, the cost of health care in the United States is greater than in any other country. Health-care costs continue to escalate, now reaching the $1 trillion level. In response to the rising cost of health care, some (for example, Callahan, 1987) have suggested that elderly persons, after a determined age, should not be given life-saving technology. Although the issue of health-care rationing was discussed in Chapter 12, within this context the implication is for health-care rationing based on age. More specifically, it could be argued that given our knowledge of the demographics of aging, age-based rationing is also sex- and class-based.

The preceding example illustrates the impact of an aging population on the health-care system in general and components such as health financing in particular. In addition, the demographic changes that result from an aging population will also have an impact on physician–patient relationships, concepts such as illness behavior and the sick role, as well as values associated with end-of-life decisions.

End-of-Life Decisions and Their Implications

All of the areas identified previously offer medical sociology an opportunity to assess pertinent cross-cultural implications. Consider, for example, the issue of euthanasia. An end-of-life decision, euthanasia refers to either physician-assisted suicide (PAS) or voluntary active euthanasia (VAE). The distinction between PAS and VAE is determined by the physicians' level of involvement. *Physician-assisted suicide* means the physician provides a patient with the means necessary for that patient to commit suicide. However, *voluntary active euthanasia* refers to a physician providing and administrating the means necessary for a patient to end his or her life (Finn & Baccetta, 1995). Although VAE is illegal throughout the United States, residents in the state of Oregon voted in 1994 to allow PAS. The first "official" application of this law was recently reported (Albany *Times Union*, A13, March 26, 1998).

The implications associated with these end-of-life decisions are particularly important to medical sociology. Moving beyond the moral and religious arguments, medical sociologists could be investigating the impact of euthanasia as it relates to such fundamental issues as physician–patient relationships, the changing role of the physician, health-care costs, and the changing role of medical technology. However, as DeVries and Subedi (1998) point out, sociologists have not been particularly interested in bioethical issues. Yet sociology (and in particular, medical sociology) has a great deal to offer regarding bioethical issues. DeVries and Subedi (1998, p. xiii) argue that, "A sociological approach lifts bioethics out of its clinical setting, examining the way it defines and solves ethical problems, the modes of reasoning it employs, and its influence on medical practice."

Euthanasia is not an American phenomenon. Cross-culturally, medical sociologists should be particularly interested in comparative analyses of factors such as cultural values relative to the acceptance or rejection of euthanasia. The importance of such research points to areas of similarity or dissimilarity between comparable nations regarding attitudes toward end-of-life decisions (Matcha, 1997b). Such research also addresses the influence of health-care factors such as the organizational and financial structure of health-care systems on patient decision making; in other words, learning from the experiences of other nations such as the Netherlands. Couched within the broader context of euthanasia are those issues that address the interrelationship of societal attitudes and behaviors toward specific segments of the population (i.e., elderly or poor persons). For example, consider the following statement: "Economic factors can be expected to play a more prominent role in assisted deaths in the US than in the Netherlands. One concern is that in the US persons who are uninsured or under-insured may feel compelled to opt for an earlier death to avoid imposing a financial burden on others" (Jecker, 1994, p. 675). Addressing the issue of cost, research examined the impact of socioeconomic and sociopolitical characteristics of Americans toward euthanasia and suicide. Not surprisingly, younger, better-educated, and wealthier responders were generally more supportive of euthanasia and suicide—in other words, what Inglehart (1997) refers to as *postmodernists*. These respondents were also the least likely to discriminate between the acceptance of euthanasia and suicide. Thus, considering the economic impact of an aging population relative to the economic security necessary for postmodernism to exist, these findings provide potential support for the "slippery slope" argument (Matcha & Sessing-Matcha, 1998).

The purpose of the preceding example is to illustrate one of the future areas of investigation within medical sociology. Although some medical sociologists are currently involved in bioethical and aging-related research, a plethora of health-related issues exist that provide research and social policy opportunities. This is particularly important as cross-cultural relationships further not only a global economy, but also the potential for a global health-care system. In other words, the emergence of an organizational structure, delivery system, and financing method that would ensure basic health care throughout the world. For example, Lee (1998) outlines a number of issues associated with the global health cooperation effort coordinated by the World Health Organization (WHO). Many of these issues are particularly appropriate for study by medical sociologists. These include: "globalisation and disease; global migration and mobility of people; global information and telecommunications; global civil society and governance" (Lee, 1998, p. 900). Here, medical sociologists can offer a unique perspective on the application of global-based health-related knowledge. Thus, the future of medical sociology depends on those in the field to effectively communicate and demonstrate its contributions to society in general, and the health-care community in particular.

Summary

This chapter provides the reader with an overview of the problems and future of medical sociology. Given the national and state involvement in health policy initiatives, the contributions of medical sociology have been limited. Furthermore, there are few medical sociologists involved in social policy analysis. It is important for medical sociology to reestablish its position of leadership in health-related research and analysis.

Although numerous problems exist, the future of medical sociology is one of optimism. Throughout the chapter, factors associated with the future of medical sociology are identified. Although these factors represent a 1980s perspective, they remain temporally relevant. One of the most important reasons for optimism within medical sociology is the dynamic quality of the health-care community. Furthermore, structural, financial, and interpersonal changes within the health-care system create ongoing opportunities for medical sociologists worldwide. Many of the changes are the result of demographic shifts as well as change in governmental policy.

The chapter concludes with an overview of the worldwide phenomenon of population aging. Focusing on the United States, the chapter identifies additional characteristics such as sex, race and ethnicity, and social class and addresses their interrelationship with health care and its outcomes. Finally, the issue of age-based rationing as a consequence of escalating health-care costs and the ethical application of euthanasia is raised. The purpose of the overview on aging is to demonstrate the importance of medical sociology within the interdisciplinary context presented by Brown (1991) at the beginning of the chapter.

CHAPTER REVIEW

As an overview, all of the information presented in this chapter is interconnected with material in earlier chapters. Nonetheless, this chapter also provides the reader with additional insight into future trends and socio-political characteristics that continue to shape health-care communities throughout the world.

1. Given that other areas (medicine, economics) are enjoying continued growth and prominence, why do you think the Medical Sociology Section in the American Sociological Association has lost members recently?

2. Revisit the seven factors associated with the future of medical sociology. As we progress into the 21st century, which factor do you consider the most important? The least important?

3. How will changes in the health-care community (worldwide) have an impact on medical sociology? Hint: Consider the efforts by some physicians in New Jersey to unionize. What are the sociological implications associated with such an effort?

4. Choose one of the sociopolitical trends identified by Roemer (1993) and examine its impact on a country other than the United States.

5. Given the aging of the world's population, examine its impact on the health-care community of a country other than the United States.

6. Based on your reading of this (and previous) chapters, what is the future of medical sociology?

SUGGESTED READINGS

The following suggestions are offered not as the only material available, but rather, as a beginning for the reader who is interested in the future of medical sociology.

Brown, P. (1991). Themes in medical sociology. *Health Politics, Policy and Law, 16,* 594–604.
  The author provides a broad overview of medical sociology. In addition, he offers a brief background, current developments, and suggestions for the future of medical sociology.
Chen, L. C., Kleinman, A., & Ware, N. C. (Eds). (1994). *Health and social change in international perspective.* Boston: Harvard University Press.
  This edited volume provides excellent coverage of numerous medical sociology issues in a cross-cultural perspective.
Freeman, H. E., & Levine, S. (1989). The present status of medical sociology. In H. E. Freeman & S. Levine (Eds.). *Handbook of medical sociology* (4th Ed.) (pp. 1–13). Englewood Cliffs, NJ: Prentice-Hall.
  This is an excellent overview of the field and a logical starting point for those interested not only in the future, but also in the changing nature of medical sociology.
Journal of Health and Social Behavior, 1995 (Extra Issue). Forty years of medical sociology: The state of the art and directions for the future.
  Because the articles address the basic areas within medical sociology, this issue provides the reader with the most current overview of the discipline.
Mechanic, D. (1994). *Inescapable decisions: The imperatives of health reform.* New Brunswick, NJ: Transaction Publishers.
  The appendixes are particularly relevant to this chapter and are strongly recommended.

REFERENCES

Abel-Smith, B., Figueras, J., Holland, W., McKee, M., & Mossialos, E. (1995). *Choices in health policy: An agenda for the European union.* Aldershot, UK: Dartmouth Publishing.
Blenon, R. J., Benson, J., Donelan, K., Leitman, R., Taylor, H., Koeck, C., & Gitterman, D. (1995). Who has the best health care system? A second look. *Health Affairs, 14,* 4, 220–230.
Bloom, S. W. (1990). Episodes in the institutionalization of medical sociology: A personal view. *Journal of Health and Social Behavior, 31,* 1–10.
Brown, P. (1991). Themes in medical sociology. *Health Politics, Policy and Law, 16,* 594–604.
Brown, P. (1996). Introduction. In P. Brown (Ed.). *Perspectives in medical sociology* (2nd Ed.) (pp. xix–xxv). Prospect Heights, IL: Waveland Press, Inc.
Callahan, D. (1987). *Setting limits: Medical goals in an aging society.* New York: Simon & Schuster.
Cassel, C. K., & Neugarten, B. L. (1991). The goals of medicine in an aging society. In R. H. Binstock & S. G. Post (Eds.). *Too old for health care? Controversies in medicine, law, economics, and ethics* (pp. 75–91). Baltimore: The Johns Hopkins University Press.
Choudhury, S., & Leonesio, M. V. (1997). Life-cycle aspects of poverty among older women. *Social Security Bulletin, 60,* 2, 17–36.
Claus, L. M. (1982a). *The growth of a sociological discipline: On the development of medical sociology in Europe. Volume I: The general study.* Katholeike Universiteit Leuven, Sociological Research Institute, Leuven.

Claus, L. M. (1982b). *The growth of a sociological discipline: On the development of medical sociology in Europe. Volume II: Case studies.* Katholeike Universiteit Leuven, Sociological Research Institute, Leuven.

DeVries, R., & Subedi, J. (1998). *Bioethics and society: Constructing the ethical enterprise.* Upper, Saddle River, NJ: Prentice-Hall.

Elinson, J. (1985). The end of medicine and the end of medical sociology. *Journal of Health and Social Behavior, 26,* 4, 268–275.

Evans, R. G., & Barer, M. L. (1990). The American predicament. *Health care systems in transition: The search for efficiency.* Social Policy Studies No. 7 (pp. 80–86). Organisation for Economic Co-Operation and Development: Paris.

Finn, J. J., & Bacchetta, M. D. (1995). Framing the physician-assisted suicide and voluntary active euthanasia debate: The role of deonotolgy, consequentialism, and critical pragmatics. *Journal of the American Geriatric Society, 43,* 563–568.

Fox, R. C. (1985). Reflections and opportunities in the sociology of medicine. *Journal of Health and Social Behavior, 26,* 1, 6–14.

Freeman, H. E., & Levine, S. (1989). The present status of medical sociology. In H. E. Freeman & S. Levine (Eds.). *Handbook of medical sociology* (4th Ed.) (pp. 1–13). Englewood Cliffs, NJ: Prentice Hall.

Gallagher, E. B. (1989). Sociological studies of third world health and health care: Introduction. *Journal of Health and Social Behavior, 30,* 4, 345–352.

Garner, R., & Garner, L. (1994). Socialism, capitalism and health: A comment. *Science & Society, 58,* 1, 79–84.

Gray, B. H., & Phillips, S. R. (1995). Medical sociology and health policy: Where are the connections? *Journal of Health and Social Behavior* (Extra Issue), 170–181.

Hafferty, F. W., & Pescosolido, B. A. (1996). Charting a future course for medical sociology. Final report: Executive summary and action steps. Robert Wood Johnson Foundation.

Inglehart, R. (1997). *Modernization and postmodernization: Cultural, economic, and political change in 43 societies.* Princeton, NJ: University of Princeton Press.

Jecker, N. S. (1994). Physician–assisted death in the Netherlands and the United States: Ethical and cultural aspects of health policy development. *Journal of the American Geriatric Society, 42,* 672–678.

Lee, K. (1998). Shaping the future of global health cooperation: Where can we go from here? *The Lancet, 351,* (March 21), 899–902.

Levine, S. (1995). Time for creative integration in medical sociology. *Journal of Health and Social Behavior* (Extra Issue), 1–4.

Levy, J. A. (1989). The hospice in the context of an aging society. *Journal of Aging Studies, 3,* 4, 385–399.

Matcha, D. A. (1997a). *The sociology of aging: A social problems perspective.* Boston: Allyn & Bacon.

Matcha, D. A. (1997b). Cultural values, aging, and end-of-life decisions: A comparative analysis. Section on Aging, Roundtable on the Sociological Study of Ethics, Values and Aging. American Sociological Association Meetings, Toronto, August, 1977.

Matcha, D. A., & Sessing-Matcha, B. A. (1998). Euthanasia and suicide: The impact of socio-economic and socio-political characteristics on end-of-life decisions, 1977–1994. Paper presented at the Eastern Sociological Society Meetings, Philadelphia, PA, March, 1998.

McKinlay, J. B., & Stoeckle, J. D. (1988). Corporatization and the social transformation of doctoring. *International Journal of Health Services, 18,* 2, 191–205.

Mechanic, D. (1994). *Inescapable decisions.* New Brunswick, NJ: Transaction Publishers.

Medical Sociology Newsletter. (1997). Message from the New Section Chair. XXXIV, 1, 1–8.

National Center for Health Statistics. (1996). *Health, United States, 1995.* Hyattsville, MD: Public Health Service.

Navarro, V. (1994). *The politics of health policy: The U.S. reforms, 1980–1994.* Cambridge, MA: Blackwell.

Olesen, V. L. (1989). Caregiving, ethical and informal: Emerging challenges in the sociology of health and illness. *Journal of Health and Social Behavior, 30,* 1–10.

Pearlin, L. I. (1992). Structure and meaning in medical sociology. *Journal of Health and Social Behavior, 33,* 1–9.

Pescosolido, B. A., & Kronenfeld, J. J. (1995). Health, illness, and healing in an uncertain era: Challenges from and for medical sociology. *Journal of Health and Social Behavior* (Extra Issue), 5–33.

Pol, L. G., & Thomas, R. K. (1992). *The demography of health and health care.* New York: Plenum Press.

Rahkonen, O., Palosuo, H., & Hemminki, E. (1988). The place of medical sociology. *Scandinavian Journal of Social Medicine, 16,* 283–285.

Roemer, M. I. (1993). *National health systems of the world: Volume II—The Issues.* New York: Oxford University Press.

Steel, K. (1997). Research on aging: An agenda for all nations individually and collectively. *Journal of the American Medical Association, 278,* 16, 1374–1375.

Thomas, R. K., & Pol, L. G. (1993). Health demography comes of age. *Health Marketing Quarterly, 10,* 3–4, 67–82.

Times Union. (Albany, NY). HMO doctors try to form union. A2, October 28, 1997.

Times Union. (Albany, NY). New assisted-suicide law used. A13, March 26, 1998.

Turner, B. S. (1995). *Medical power and social knowledge* (2nd Ed.). London: SAGE.

U.S. Bureau of the Census. (1992). International Population Reports, P25, 92–3, *An aging world II.* U.S. Government Printing Office, Washington, DC.

Wetle, T. (1997). Living longer, aging better: Aging research comes of age. *Journal of the American Medical Association, 278,* 16, 1376–1377.

Winker, M. A. (1997). Aging: A global issue. *Journal of the American Medical Association, 278,* 16, 1377.

Wolinsky, F. D. (1988). *The sociology of health: Principles, practitioners, and issues* (2nd Ed.). Belmont, CA: Wadsworth.

INDEXES

Name Index

415

417

Subject Index

420